THE ROXBURY DICTIONARY

of

CRIMINAL JUSTICE

Key Terms and Major Court Cases

Dean J. Champion

Minot State University

Roxbury Publishing Company

Los Angeles, California

Library of Congress Cataloging-in-Publication Data

The Roxbury dictionary of criminal justice: key terms and major court cases/Dean J.
  Champion
  p. cm
  Includes index.
  ISBN 0-935732-84-5
1. Criminal justice, Administration of—Dictionaries. 2. Criminology—Dictionaries. 3. Criminal justice, Administration of—United States—Cases. 4. Criminal law—United States—Cases. I. Title.
HV7411.C48 1997
364'.03—dc20   96-8392
                                                                                                        CIP

THE ROXBURY DICTIONARY OF CRIMINAL JUSTICE: KEY TERMS AND MAJOR COURT CASES

Publisher and Editor: Claude Teweles
Supervising Editor: Dawn VanDercreek
Copy Editors: Susan Converse Winslow, Joyce Rappaport, C. Max-Ryan, and Sacha Howells
Editorial Assistants: Heidi Edeskuty, Erin Record, J. Scott Strayer, Colleen O'Brien, and David
  Stoops
Cover Design: Marnie Deacon
Typesetting and Design: Synergistic Data Systems

Printed on acid-free paper in the United States of America. This book meets the standards for recycling of the Environmental Protection Agency.

ISBN 0-935732-84-5

ROXBURY PUBLISHING COMPANY
P.O. Box 491044
Los Angeles, California 90049-9044
Tel.: (213) 653-1068
Fax: (213) 653-4140
Email: roxbury@crl.com

Table of Contents

Preface

The Roxbury Dictionary of Criminal Justice: Key Terms and Major Court Cases will be useful to every student of the criminal justice system. Like any good dictionary, this resource will assist students in a variety of courses—as well as in writing papers and understanding terminology in journal articles. The book was written to enable the reader to quickly identify both key terms and leading United States Supreme Court cases in a single ready reference.

The Dictionary Section

This dictionary is not intended to replace conventional legal dictionaries, such as *Black's Law Dictionary*, or to substitute for detailed expositions of how to do legal research and writing. Rather, the book attempts to pull together key terms and concepts from diverse areas, including criminology, criminal justice, corrections, probation/parole, juvenile justice, and policing. This interdisciplinary approach greatly enhances the dictionary's effectiveness as a "one stop" resource. Students will no longer need to spend precious study time seeking out definitions in numerous specialized sources. The coverage greatly enhances the information provided in most standard textbook glossaries, as do the examples drawn from the research literature accompanying many definitions.

In many cases, terms which refer to similar phenomena have been grouped under a single definition or a series of definitions, with minor variations to reflect slight differences in application. One feature of this dictionary is the inclusion of the names of researchers and criminologists who have done important work and influenced the nature and direction of criminology and criminal justice. It is beyond the scope of this book to include *every* criminologist, however. Choices were made according to which theorists are most closely associated with various key terms, issues, and theories.

The Supreme Court Cases Section

Conveniently alphabetized and indexed, the most recent and significant United States Su-preme Court cases are summarized, offering students an easy-to-read account of the events leading to each case, how the Court decided the case, the rationale used in the decision, and the case's significance for criminal justice.

The Supreme Court Cases section represents the most comprehensive and current assemblage of decisions to date. This eases instruction, eliminating the necessity of duplicating and distributing case summaries. Especially for students who do not have immediate access to a large legal library, the cases included here are critical and have wide application and relevance. Departing from other dictionaries, in which cases are grouped under particular amendment headings or subject-matter designations, these cases have been arranged alphabetically. They have also been indexed according to important categories in order to permit those doing legal research to search out relevant and related topics more easily. A particular case may have relevance for more than one legal issue. Thus, in looking up a particular topic, the reader will find the most up-to-date cases associated with it.

The case compilation in **The Roxbury Dictionary of Criminal Justice** is considerably more extensive than that found in most standard textbooks. The coverage consists primarily of United States Supreme Court cases. This does not mean that the cases of circuit courts of appeal, state supreme courts, and district courts are not important. The opinions in this volume were chosen because they represent laws applicable throughout the United States, rather than to specific geographical areas.

The reader should note that some cases have been reported which were subsequently overturned, overruled, or replaced with new or revised interpretations. For the legal scholar, it is important not only to know where we are now, but where we have been in the past regarding the application of our laws. It is important for students to understand that case law is constantly changing. The United States Supreme Court is always refining old laws and views and providing us with exceptions, increasingly specific interpretations, and modifications of previous decisions governing how the police, courts, and corrections conduct their business with arrestees, defendants, convicted offenders, and clients.

Before studying these cases, it would be useful for students to read the discussion of case referencing under "Court Cases" at the beginning of the section. This will familiarize the reader with the abbreviations and numbers following cases and how to locate them in library collections. Furthermore, the examples of protocol to follow when referencing legal citations will help students in preparing research papers.

* * *

While the author accepts full responsibility for any errors of fact or interpretations of United States Supreme Court cases, the criticisms and

suggestions of several experts in the fields of criminal justice and criminology are gratefully acknowledged. Among those who examined the original proposal and helped to shape the project's nature and direction were: Paul Cromwell, University of Miami; Chris W. Eskridge, University of Nebraska, Omaha; Frank R. Scarpitti, University of Delaware, and Richard A. Wright, University of Scranton. Also, my thanks are extended to those who read the manuscript in its entirety and offered constructive criticisms and suggestions: Mitchell B. Chamlin, University of Cincinnati; Frederic L. Faust, Florida State University; Charles B. Fields, California State University-San Bernardino, and William Geary, University of Florida.

Dean J. Champion
Minot State University

DICTIONARY
of
TERMS

A

abate. To declare null and void.

abduction. Unlawfully stealing or taking away another, with or without the use of force.

abeyance. A temporary halting of an intended or continuing action; temporary termination of action where resolution is expected. Removal is prohibited by law.

abnormal psychology. The study of behavioral disorders, including mental retardation and illness; focuses upon etiology of such disorders and examines physical and biochemical causal factors associated with such disorders.

abortion. Termination of a pregnancy by use of drugs or medical operation. Abortions are performed for a variety of reasons and are either permitted or prohibited, depending on the jurisdiction; the leading abortion case is *Roe v. Wade* (1973).

abrogate. To abolish or annul.

ABSCAM. A 1980 federal detection of political corruption whereby FBI undercover agents posed as wealthy Arab business persons to identify politicians susceptible to bribes and other forms of wrong-doing.

abscond. To flee a geographical area or jurisdiction prescribed by the conditions of one's probation or parole without authorization. To intentionally leave unlawfully to avoid prosecution.

absolute deterrent. A legal control action intended to discourage or eliminate certain criminal acts.

abuse, child, child sexual, spousal. Intentional psychological or physical injury caused by one person to another; may involve prohibited sexual relations or exploitation.

abused child. Any child who has been intentionally physically, sexually, or mentally injured. Most jurisdictions consider a child abused where forced into delinquent conduct by a parent or guardian.

Academy of Criminal Justice Sciences (ACJS). An international organization founded in 1963 that serves to further the development of the criminal justice profession and whose membership is involved in various components of the criminal justice system and universities.

accelerant. Any chemical that hastens the occurrence of an event; in forensics, for instance, a substance that speeds up a reaction. Any substance that quickens combustion, such as a fire-enhancing material or liquid employed by an arsonist.

acceptance of responsibility. A genuine admission or acknowledgment of wrong-doing. In federal presentence investigation reports, for example, convicted offenders may write an explanation and apology for the crime(s) they committed. A provision that may be considered in deciding whether leniency should be extended to offenders during the sentencing phase of their processing.

access control. Crime prevention mechanism stressing "target-hardening" security measures, including alarm systems, making it more difficult for criminals to commit their crimes.

accessory. Person who assists another to commit a crime.

accessory after the fact. One who is indirectly involved in criminal conduct, facilitating such conduct once it has occurred, by assisting, aiding or abetting the perpetrator(s) in various ways.

accessory before the fact. Anyone who is indirectly involved in criminal conduct, facilitating such conduct before it has occurred, by assisting, aiding, abetting the perpetrator(s) in various ways.

accident investigation (AI). Law enforcement protocol following any accident, including the collection of physical evidence, photographing the accident scene, and determining the cause or causes of the occurrence; often includes a determination of fault for the occurrence.

accomplice. One who helps another commit a crime.

accountability. Responsibility of either adults or children for their actions, criminal or delinquent; may involve restitution to victims, community service, other forms of compensation to manifest one's acceptance of responsibility.

accountability and control. Organizational subcomponents that greatly restrict individual discretion and lower-echelon decision making. Disciplinary mechanism whereby people can be employed to perform an exacting task.

accountability system. Any method of dealing with law enforcement, prosecution, court, or correctional corruption by making superiors responsible for the behavior of their subordinates.

accreditation. A prescribed program generally receiving the approval of a recognized group of professionals, where desired program components have been identified and are used to compare other programs in terms of their effectiveness. In law enforcement and corrections, any professional organizational approval of curriculum, training procedures, and instruction designed to train personnel to perform their jobs in a capable manner.

accusation. An allegation of wrong-doing; a complaint alleging that a crime has been committed or a tort perpetrated; may be a criminal information, grand jury presentment or indictment.

accusatory process. All phases commencing with the arrest of suspects to the filing of formal charges against them either through an indictment or information.

accusatory stage. Any event in a criminal investigation where a suspect has been identified and designated for prosecution. A suspect's rights attach at this stage and the Miranda warning must be given; the accused is entitled to an attorney and other constitutional rights and protections.

accused. Person alleged to have committed a crime; the defendant in any criminal action.

acquittal. Any judgment by the court, considering a jury verdict or a judicial determination of the factual basis for criminal charges, where the defendant is declared not guilty of the offenses alleged.

act of God. An explanation for any naturally occurring phenomenon, such as a disaster (e.g., tornado, earthquake, hurricane) where property is destroyed and/or persons are killed or injured. Used to limit personal or business liability for personal injuries or physical losses sustained.

Act to Regulate the Treatment and Control of Dependent, Neglected and Delinquent Children. Passed by Illinois legislature in 1899 creating the first juvenile court.

ACT UP (Aids Coalition to Unleash Power). An aggressive organization expressly formed to protest the lack of governmental funding for AIDS research; has used disruptive tactics and occasionally resorted to civil disobedience as a means of promoting their cause.

action, actions at law. A court proceeding; either civil, to enforce a right, or criminal, to punish an offender. Court litigation where opposing parties litigate an issue involving an alleged wrong-do-

ing; may be for the protection of a right or for the prevention of a wrong.

active intrusion sensor. Any device capable of detecting movement, usually of persons, on premises where persons should not be during particular periods.

actual enforcement. Implementation of the law at a level that reflects such factors as civil liberties, discretion, resources, and community values.

actuarial prediction. Forecast of future inmate behavior based on a class of offenders similar to those considered for parole.

actuarial records. Public records concerning the demographic characteristics of the population served by the record-keeping agency.

Actus reus. One component of a crime; any overt act which accompanies the intent to commit a crime (e.g., pulling out a pistol in front of a convenience store clerk while robbing the store is an *actus reus* or overt act); drawing plans of a bank floor layout while conspiring to rob the bank would be an overt act in furtherance of the criminal conspiracy.

Addams, Jane (circa 1860-1910). Founded Hull House in the 1890s in Chicago, a shelter for runaways and others who were in need of housing, food, and clothing.

adjudicate. To judge, decide a case, conclude a matter.

adjudication, adjudicated. Legal resolution of a dispute; when a juvenile is declared delinquent or a status offender, the matter has been resolved; when an offender has been convicted or acquitted, the matter at issue (guilt or innocence) has been concluded by either a judge or jury.

adjudication hearing, adjudication inquiry. Formal proceeding involving a prosecuting attorney and a defense attorney where evidence is presented and a juvenile's status or condition is determined by the juvenile court judge.

adjudication petition. Formal, written request or application to juvenile court to take judicial action on a certain matter, to determine whether juvenile is delinquent or not, filed by parent, school official, police officer, intake officer or any other interested party.

adjudication withheld. A cessation of court proceedings pending some alternative action, such as diversion or alternative dispute resolution; conditions are imposed and jurisdiction is maintained over person subject to compliance with conditions for a specified duration, such as one year. In some cases, persons may be released on their own recognizance unconditionally.

adjudicatory hearing. *See* adjudication hearing.

adjustment. Settlement or conclusion so that opposing parties are in agreement without official court intervention.

Adler, Freda. Wrote *Sisters in Crime: The Rise of the New Female Criminals* (1975); former president of the American Society of Criminology.

administration of justice. Covers such areas as police management, criminal procedure, pretrial services, arraignment and trial, prosecution and defense, court organization, pleadings, sentencing, appeals, probation, and parole.

administrative law. Branch of public law dealing with the powers and duties of government agencies.

administrative model. Sentencing scheme where control over sentence length is vested with correctional officials.

Administrative Office of United States Courts. Organization which hires federal probation officers to supervise federal offenders. Also supervises pretrial divertees; probation officers prepare presentence investigation reports about offenders at the request of district judge.

administrative regulations. Rules created by governmental agencies to implement specific public policies.

administrative segregation. Residential units in prison that isolate prisoners from the general population for nondisciplinary reasons.

administrative services. Unit in a police department assigned police-community relations tasks and the selection and training of police personnel.

admiralty, admiralty courts, admiralty law. Tribunals originating in England centuries ago to handle maritime cases (those involving sailors, ships, and activities on the high seas) and maritime law (dealing with ocean vessels and their regulation and commerce).

admissible. An evidentiary term designating testimony or physical evidence that may be presented to the finders of fact (juries or judges) in criminal proceedings. Restrictions and conditions are usually articulated in federal, state rules of evidence.

admission. A confession; a concession as to the truthfulness of one or more facts, usually associated with a crime which has been committed. May also apply to tort actions.

admission, corrections. The entry of an offender into the legal jurisdiction of a corrections agency and/or physical custody of a correctional facility.

admit. A plea of guilty, an acknowledgment of culpability, accuracy of the facts alleged in either an adult, juvenile proceeding.

adolescence. A diffuse age range from puberty to adulthood, generally 12 to 18 or 21 years of age.

adolescent court. Limited jurisdictional handling of juvenile delinquents by unofficial and informal means, sanctions, and characterized by an absence of record-keeping and labeling.

adult. Depending upon the jurisdiction, anyone who has reached the age of majority and is subject to criminal court laws.

Adult Inmate Management System (AIMS). System used by South Carolina prison officials classifying prisoners into three basic aggressiveness levels, the alphas, betas, and gammas.

adultery. Consensual sexual intercourse between persons, at least one of whom is married to another person.

adversary system of justice, procedure, process. Legal system involving a contest between two opposing parties under a judge who is an impartial arbiter.

advocate. A proponent of some cause or issue. In law, any attorney who acts on behalf of a client.

affiance. An agreement between parties wherein mutual expectations are articulated and observed.

affiant. Person who makes an affidavit.

affidavit. A statement in writing given under oath before someone who is authorized to administer an oath.

affirmation. In courts, an oath, declaration in place of an oath, for persons whose religious beliefs prohibit oaths, to tell the truth and nothing but the truth when giving testimony.

affirmative action. A formal program to correct previous discriminatory hiring practices through aggressive recruitment and promotion of previously disadvantaged groups.

affirmative defense. Response to a criminal charge where defendant bears the burden of proof (e.g., automatism, intoxication, coercion, duress, mistake). Goes beyond simple denial of facts and gives new facts in favor of the defendant, if facts in the original complaint are true.

affray. Any impromptu altercation or fight between two or more persons in public, where such a fight causes attention and results in disturbing the peace.

aftercare. General term to describe a wide variety of programs and services available to both adult and juvenile parolees. Includes halfway houses, psychological counseling services, community-based correctional agencies, employment assistance, and medical treatment for offenders or ex-offenders.

agar. In forensics, a material used to make plaster casts of footprints or other tangible evidence at crime scenes.

age composition of the population. The breakdown of an entire population into age-specific categories. In criminological and corrections research, an important variable in the prediction of crime rates or incarceration rates, since younger groups are at greater risk.

age-graded theory. Life course theory positing that delinquency, deviance, and/or criminality develop early in the lives of adult criminals as a part of their cognitive development. Associated with the work of Robert Sampson and John Laub in *Crime in the Making* (1993).

agent. Any individual, usually with legal expertise, who acts on behalf of another (called a principal). Any officer of various federal and state law enforcement agencies, civil or criminal, who is empowered to enforce the laws of these agencies.

agent provocateur. A spy or secret agent, usually in the employ of the government, to conduct surveillance of a group or organization; an undercover person, either a police officer or working on behalf of the police who infiltrates a group for the purpose of learning about the group's illegal activities.

age-specific arrest rate. Number of arrests per 100,000 persons in a given age category.

aggravated assault. An unlawful attack by one person on another for the purpose of inflicting severe bodily injury, or the attempt, or threat thereof.

aggravating circumstances. Events about crime that may intensify the severity of punishment, including bodily injury, death to victim, or the brutality of the act.

aggregate. Persons who are in the same place at the same time but who have no sense of common identity or close interaction or a portion of the population sharing similar characteristics and who do not necessarily have to be in a given place at the same time.

aggression. Any intentional act designed to bring harm to another.

aggressive patrol. A police patrol strategy designed to maximize the number of police interventions and observations in the community.

aggressive preventive patrol. Any police patrol technique designed to prevent crime before it occurs.

aging-out phenomenon. Notion that as offenders grow older, they commit less crime because of less energy and interest. James Q. Wilson and Richard Herrnstein have argued that an aging-out process is responsible for the decline of crime among persons as they grow older.

Agnew, Robert. Sociologist who has examined general strain theory (GST) in order to account for criminal behavior (1992); crime results from negative affective states.

aiding and abetting. Assisting in or otherwise furthering the commission of a crime.

AIDS (Acquired Immune Deficiency Syndrome). Deadly illness caused by human immunodeficiency virus (HIV), spread through exchange of some bodily fluids.

Akers, Ronald. Sociologist and criminologist who wrote *Deviant Behavior: A Social Learning Approach* (1973, 1977), among other substantial writings. Former president of the American Sociological Association. Advocate of differential reinforcement theory, a revision of Edwin Sutherland's work on differential association theory.

alarm system. Any electronic apparatus designed to alert persons that there are intruders or that an emergency exists that must be dealt with.

Alaska judicial council. Public council that evaluates judicial sentencing practices and assesses all matters pertinent to the Alaska judiciary.

Alcoholics Anonymous. Voluntary organization originating in 1935. Membership consists of people who are either addicted to alcohol or wish to avoid becoming addicted to alcohol. Group meets informally, discusses family, personal and social problems that contributed to alcohol abuse and ways of overcoming such problems. Employs a multi-step program with social support to avoid alcohol on a day-to-day basis. Occasionally used in conjunction with state sanctions for individuals convicted of driving while intoxicated.

Alford Plea. A *nolo contendere* plea whereby defendants plead "no contest" to the factual scenario as outlined in the charges; originated with the case of *North Carolina v. Alford* (1970) whereby a defendant did not wish to admit guilt, but entered a *nolo contendere* plea, admitting to certain facts as specified by the prosecution.

alias. Any name by which someone is known other than one's legal name on public documents; used to change identity for various purposes, legal or otherwise.

alibi. Defense to a criminal allegation that places an accused individual at some other place than the crime scene at the time the crime occurred.

alien conspiracy theory. The idea that organized crime was imported by Europeans and that criminal organizations limit their membership to people of their own ethnic background.

alienation. A social psychological state wherein a person feels varying levels of powerlessness, normlessness, self-estrangement, and meaninglessness; psychological detachment from society or other persons; a negative feeling toward someone, usually in authority. Some citizens may feel estranged from the police officers who patrol their neighborhoods and regulate their conduct.

alimony. Support awarded to a party in a divorce action.

allegation. Assertion or claim made by a party to a legal action.

allege. To aver, assert, claim; usually a prosecutor will allege certain facts in developing a case against a criminal defendant.

allocution. Right of convicted offenders to address the court personally prior to the imposition of sentences.

alternative care cases. Borderline cases in which judges may sentence offenders to either incarceration or probation subject to compliance with various conditions.

alternative dispute resolution (ADR). Procedure whereby a criminal case is redefined as a civil one and the case is decided by an impartial arbiter, where both parties agree to amicable settlement. Usually reserved for minor offenses.

alternative facility. Alternative place of limited confinement, such as treatment centers for drug-dependent offenders.

alternative sanctions. The group of punishments falling between probation and prison; Business "probation plus." Community-based sanctions, including house arrest and intensive supervision, serve as an alternative to incarceration.

alternative sentencing. Judge imposes sentence other than incarceration. Often involves good works such as community service, restitution to victims, and other public service activity. *See also* creative sentencing.

Alveolar Air Breath Alcohol System. Name of device to test breath of suspects stopped for driving under the influence to ascertain blood-alcohol ratio.

amenability issue. The possibility that certain kinds of offenders are amenable or suited to a particular type of treatment.

amendment. A modification, addition, deletion.

amentia. Insanity.

amercement. A fine, other monetary penalty.

American Civil Liberties Union (ACLU). An organization originating in 1920 and dedicated to guaranteeing civil rights of persons charged with crimes or persons who have been wronged, often by a government agency.

American Correctional Association. Established in 1870 to disseminate information about correctional programs and correctional training. Designed to foster professionalism throughout correctional communities.

American Dream. Term described by Steven Messner and Richard Rosenfeld (1993). Describes the goal of accumulating material wealth under conditions of open competition. "Success at all costs" ethos causes those without the means to achieve goals to adopt criminal or deviant options to acquire wealth.

American Society of Criminology. An international professional society of criminology commenced in 1941, which is devoted to enhancing the status of the discipline.

Americans with Disabilities Act (ADA). Makes it illegal to discriminate against persons with disabilities. These individuals are entitled to equal access to employment, including the processes of recruitment, hiring, promotion, and any other benefits and privileges of employment.

amicus curiae. A friend of the court. Persons may initiate petitions on behalf of others, perhaps for someone who is in prison. Such *amicus* briefs are designed to present legal arguments or facts on behalf of someone else. Person allowed to appear in court or file a brief even though the person has no right to participate in the litigation otherwise.

amphetamine. A synthetic drug consisting of benzedrine sulfate, designed to stimulate the central nervous system. Sometimes referred to as an "upper."

anamnestic prediction. Forecast of inmate behavior according to past circumstances.

anarchism. A political ideology in which overthrowing the government is advocated.

anarchist ideology of punishment. Contains the beliefs that modern society is based on structured power relationships, that deviance is a product of fitting human relationships into hierarchical rules, and that the current punishment system preserves the power system while reducing human capacity for cooperation.

Anderson, Elijah. Social critic and sociologist who has written about the siege mentality in his book, *Streetwise: Race, Class and Change in an Urban Community* (1990).

anger rape. A rape prompted by a rapist's desire to release pent-up anger and rage.

animus furundi. Intent to steal property or otherwise deprive owner of it.

anomalous plea. Court plea containing both positive and negative statements and arguments.

anomie, anomie theory. Robert Merton's theory, influenced by Emile Durkheim, alleging that persons acquire desires for culturally approved goals to strive to achieve, but they adopt innovative, sometimes deviant, means to achieve these goals (e.g., someone may desire a nice home but lack or reject the institutionalized means) to achieve this goal, instead using bank robbery, an innovative mean, to obtain money to realize the culturally approved goal. Implies normlessness.

answer. A written response in relation to a filed complaint prepared by a litigant or defendant.

Antabuse therapy. For alcohol users and addicts, a safe drug, disulfiram, designed to cause nausea and vomiting whenever alcohol is consumed.

anthropometry. Scientific study of body measurements for comparative purposes. *See also* Bertillon identification.

anthropophagy. Cannibalism.

anticipatory socialization. A reference group theory term, referring to the tendency of some individuals to internalize the values and norms of a group or category to which they do not yet belong but with which they wish to be identified or to join.

Antiracketeering Act. 1934 law making it a crime to interfere with interstate commerce. Especially aimed at organized crime in which large criminal organizations can create work stoppages and other forms of interference for extortion purposes.

antitrust actions, cases. Any cases designed to prevent large organizations from monopolizing particular industries.

apathy. A sense of uncaring, unfeeling about an issue, a person.

apparent danger. In a self-defense response to alleged criminal activity, defendant can use this type of danger to justify self-preservation; must be obvious, manifest and clear.

appeal, appeal proceedings. Any request by the defense or prosecution directed to a higher court to contest a decision or judgment by a lower court.

appeal bond. The money or surety posted by one who requests a hearing before a higher court on a lower-court decision; money or surety is provided to defray the costs of failed appeals.

appeal to higher loyalties. A technique of neutralization that justifies a violation of the law by the demands of a group that is smaller than the whole society and that requires of its members conformity to standards that may be incompatible with the law.

appearance. Act of coming into a court and submitting to the authority of that court.

appellant. Person who initiates an appeal.

appellate court, judge. A court hearing appeals emanating from lower courts. These courts typically do not try criminal cases.

appellate jurisdiction. Authority to rehear cases from lower courts and alter, uphold, or overturn lower court decisions.

appellate review. A comprehensive rehearing of a case in a court other than the one in which it was previously tried.

appellee. Party who prevailed in lower court, who argues on appeal against reversing the lower court's decision.

appose. An examination of an organization's business officer, especially when embezzlement is suspected.

apprehend. To take into custody or arrest someone suspected of a crime.

apprenticeship. Binding out children to serve time with a master craftsman either learning a trade, or in the case of involuntary apprenticeship, working as a servant or field hand.

arbitrage, argot. The unique language that influences prison culture.

arbitrator. A third party who intervenes, conducts meetings between opposing parties, and decides unresolved issues or disputes.

argot. *See* arbitrage.

Arkansas prison scandal. Notorious illegal exploitation of inmates in the Tucker, Arkansas prison farm. Prisoners were forced to work for private enterprises outside of prison, where profits would be paid to prison administrators. Prisoners were tortured with electrodes attached to their penises, nipples, or testicles and to an old crank-type telephone ("Tucker Telephone"), if they violated prison rules; these electrical shocks were sometimes fatal. Torture, malnutrition, starvation, and exploitation were eliminated with entry of new warden, Thomas O. Murton, who fired abusive officers and made living conditions at Tucker prison farm more humane. Murton himself was fired by the Governor later for uncovering the scandal and making it public.

armory. Storehouse for firearms and a place where military maneuvers are conducted.

arms, right to bear. Second Amendment providing for a well-regulated and armed militia. Controversial issue in gun control and regulation.

arraignment. Official proceeding in which defendant is formally confronted by criminal charges and enters a plea; trial date is established.

arrest. Taking persons into custody and restrain them until they can be brought before court to answer the charges against them.

arrest rate. Number of persons arrested in relation to number of crimes reported or known to police during a given period (e.g., arrest rate of .30 for 1996 would mean that of all crimes reported or known to police in 1996, arrests were made for 30 percent of these reported crimes).

arrest report. Document prepared by a law enforcement officer or other official, articulating which led to arrest. Information includes arrestee's name, address, telephone number, occupation/profession, and prior record, if any. Reasons for arrest and personal observations and interpretations of events.

arrest warrant. Document issued by a court ordering law officers to arrest a specific individual.

arrestee. Person who is arrested.

arson. Any willful, malicious burning, attempt to burn, with or without intent to defraud, a dwelling house, public building, motor vehicle, aircraft, or the personal property of another.

artificial presumption. Any presumption based on law rather than on actual physical facts or events. Persons are presumed dead if they have been missing for seven years or more in some jurisdictions, which may not be true.

Aryan Brotherhood. A white supremacist prison gang.

asportation. Carrying away of something. In kidnapping, the carrying away of the victim. In larceny, the carrying away of a victim's property.

assassin. One who kills a public figure, such as a head of state or president.

assassination. The murder of a head of state, government, other highly important public figure.

assault. Any unlawful attempt with force, violence to harm, frighten another. *See also* aggravated assault, simple assault.

assault and battery. An assault carried into effect by doing some violence to the victim.

assault with a deadly weapon. Unlawful intentional inflicting, attempted or threatened inflicting of injury, death with the use of a weapon capable of killing the victim.

assembly, lawful or unlawful. Congregating in a particular place for a lawful or unlawful purpose.

assembly-line justice. Term applied to overworked, inadequately staffed court which is unsympathetic and unfair to criminal defendants.

assessment centers. Organizations for selecting entry-level officers for correctional work. Assessment centers hire correctional officers and probation or parole officers.

asset forfeiture. The governmental seizure of personal assets obtained from or used in a criminal enterprise. For example, a yacht may be forfeited to the government if the yacht was used to facilitate a crime, such as distributing narcotics.

assignation house. A location where prostitution occurs.

assigned counsel, assigned counsel system. Program wherein indigent clients charged with crimes may have defense attorneys appointed for them; these defense attorneys may be private attorneys who agree to be rotated to perform such services for a low rate of reimbursement from the city, county, or state.

assistance, writ of. A document issued by the judge ordering the return of property held by another person (e.g., if someone occupies your land illegally and will not leave it when you ask, you seek such a writ to have your property returned to you and the person or persons occupying your land to be ejected from it).

assisting in arrests. Civilians may come to the aid of officers making arrests of criminal suspects; other officers who assist fellow officers in making arrests are credited with "assists."

assumpsit. Lawsuit alleging breach of contract.

asylum. Sanctuary; a place of refuge.

asylum state. Jurisdiction to which persons seeking to escape prosecution in other jurisdictions flee.

atavism, atavistic characteristics. Positivist school of thought arguing that a biological condition renders a person incapable of living within the social constraints of a society. According to Cesare Lombroso, the physical characteristics that distinguish born criminals from the general population and are evolutionary throwbacks to animals or primitive people.

atavistic stigmata. Physical human characteristics noted by Cesare Lombroso which distinguish born criminals from others in populations.

attachment. A bond between persons and their families, friends, and school associates; a component of Travis Hirschi's social bond theory. In law, property seizure or asset forfeiture.

attainder. The loss of civil rights because of a felony conviction.

attempt, criminal attempt. An overt action associated with a crime and done with criminal intent. The act which goes beyond preparation but does not necessarily mean a criminal act has been completed.

Attention Deficit Disorder (ADD). Characterized by impulsivity, hyperactivity, and an inappropriate lack of concentration. Condition is associated with poor school performance and lack of response to discipline.

attestation. Verbal authentication that indicates truthfulness; property documents may need authenticating, for instance, to determine whether signatures and/or factual information contained in these documents are true and authentic.

attitude. All of a person's inclinations, prejudices, ideas, fears, and convictions about a given topic. A tendency to act in a given way.

attorney general. Senior United States prosecutor in each federal district court. A cabinet member who heads the Justice Department.

attorney, lawyer, counsel. Anyone trained in the law who has received a law degree from a recognized university and who is authorized to practice law in a given jurisdiction.

Auburn State Penitentiary, Auburn System or Style. Prison constructed in Auburn, New York in 1816. Pioneered use of "tiers" where inmates were housed on different floors or levels, usually according to their offense seriousness. Introduced congregate system, in which prisoners had opportunities to mingle with one another for work, dining, and recreation, and stereotypical "striped" uniforms for prisoners. Prison system developed in New York during nineteenth century that emulated this model and depended upon mass prisons, where prisoners were held in congregate fashion. Style of imprisonment was compared with Pennsylvania system.

Augustus, John (1785-1859). Originator of probation in United States in 1841. Considered first informal probation officer, this Boston shoemaker and philanthropist, active in reforming petty offenders and alcoholics charged with crimes, assumed responsibility for them and posted their bail while attempting to reform them.

authenticity. The genuineness of private records.

authoritarian conflict pathway. The course to a criminal career commencing with early rebellious behavior and defiance of parents.

authoritarian model. Prison management style characterized by a high degree of centralization of power and decision making.

autocracy. Dictatorship.

autoerotic death, asphyxia. Terminating one's life by accident during a sexual interlude. Involves strangulation during sexual intercourse. Sexual excitement is allegedly heightened by the life-threatening experience.

automatic weapons. Firearms capable of firing multiple rounds with a single trigger pull.

automatism. A set of actions taken during a state of unconsciousness.

automobile theft. Any stealing of a motorized vehicle. *See also* vehicular theft.

autopsy. Dissection of a body to determine the cause of death.

autrefois **acquit, convict.** A plea of "formerly acquitted" or "formerly convicted" in not guilty proceedings on double jeopardy grounds.

auxiliary police. Trained and uniformed volunteer civilians who work with local police in law enforcement activities.

aversion therapy. A method to alter a person's behavior by conditioning particular actions with painful or unpleasant stimuli.

avertable recidivist. Offender who would still have been in prison serving a sentence at a time when new offense was committed.

avowtry. Adultery.

axiom, axiomatic system. A theoretical system that contains a set of concepts and definitions, a set of existence statements, a set of relational statements divided into postulates and theorems, and a logical system used to relate concepts to statements and to deduce theorems from axioms.

B

backdooring cases. Judicial practice of sentencing borderline (low risk) offenders to incarceration with strong admonishment that they be encouraged to apply for intensive probation supervision programs.

back-door solution, corrections. Answer to prison or jail overcrowding problem after inmates have been incarcerated. Court-ordered prison or jail population reductions, use of early release or parole, furloughs, work release, administrative release.

backlog. Number of impending cases that exceeds the court's capacity that cannot be acted upon because the court is occupied in acting upon other cases.

back-to-the-people movement. Community-oriented policing. Focus upon foot patrols and neighborhood beats. Proactive policing stressing community wellness.

bail. Surety provided by defendants or others to guarantee their subsequent appearance in court to face criminal charges. Available to anyone entitled to it (not everyone is entitled to bail); is denied when suspects are considered dangerous or likely to flee. *See also* preventive detention and *United States v. Salerno* in list of cases.

bail bond, bail bonding. A written guarantee, often accompanied by money or other securities, that the person charged with an offense will remain within the court's jurisdiction to face trial at a time in the future.

bail bondsperson, bail bondsman. Person who is in the business of posting bail for criminal suspects. Usually charges a percentage of whatever bail has been set.

Bail Reform Act of 1984. Act to revise bail practices and to assure that all persons, regardless of their financial status, shall not needlessly be detained to answer criminal charges. Does not mean that all persons are entitled to bail regardless of their alleged offense.

bail revocation. Judicial decision to deny a previously granted bail for a defendant.

bail system. Practice of releasing defendants after they place a financial guarantee with the court to ensure their subsequent trial appearance. Usually defendants may place the entire amount with the court or pay a premium to the bondsman.

bailiff. Court officer who maintains order in the court while it is in session. Bailiff oversees jury during a trial proceeding, sometimes has custody of prisoners while they are in the courtroom. Also known as messengers.

bailiwick. A jurisdiction or place of authority, usually in reference to a sheriff or constable or police chief.

balance of sentence suspended. Judicial sentencing option whereby convicted offenders are given credit for the time they have served and permitted to be free from jail. Often accompanied by payment of fine and court costs.

ballistics. Dealing with the motion, appearance, modification of missiles (bullets), other vehicles acted upon by propellants, wind, gravity, temperature, any other modifying substance, condition, force.

banditry. Aggravated robbery.

Bandura, Albert. Psychologist and child development expert who has investigated social learning relevant to criminology; has examined stages of development among children and has concluded that criminal conduct develops at particular stages when certain interaction stimuli are present.

banishment. Physical removal of undesirables, criminals, political and religious dissidents to remote locations.

Bank Secrecy Act. Federal statute protecting the confidentiality of banking transactions, but which makes certain information available to the government in connection with criminal proceedings.

bankruptcy fraud. A scam in which individuals falsely attempt to claim bankruptcy (and thereby erase financial debts) by taking advantage of loopholes in the laws.

bar. Aggregate denoting all attorneys admitted to practice law in every jurisdiction.

barbiturates. Any drug functioning as a depressant on the central nervous system; also known as "downers."

base penalty. Modal sentence in a structured sentencing state, which can be enhanced or diminished to reflect aggravating or mitigating circumstances.

basic car plan. Method of patrolling a particular neighborhood or geographical area of a city, whereby a police cruiser is assigned to the neighborhood as the primary patrol vehicle. All calls for service in that neighborhood are directed to that patrol cruiser unless the cruiser officers request additional assistance from other cruisers and officers nearby. Furthers community-oriented policing, because police officers get to know neighborhood residents and have their confidence and respect.

baton. "Night stick" carried by police officers. A weighted club between one to two feet in length, designed as a defensive device by law enforcement officers involved in physical confrontations.

battered child syndrome. Emotional and physical injuries to children intentionally inflicted by others, usually parents or guardians; often causes psychological problems in coping with reality.

battered woman's syndrome. Violent reactions by women who have been battered by men with whom they have had a close relationship. Has been used successfully as defense in some cases in which women have been tried for the murder of their husbands.

battery. Civil offense involving intentional touching or inflicting hurt on another.

bayonet. Knife which attaches to the barrel of a rifle. Often used by youth gangs as a weapon.

beam test. A test to determine under microscopic conditions whether a substance is marijuana (cannabis) or some other substance.

beat patrolling. Police patrol style originating in early 1900s designed to bring officers into closer physical contact with area residents. Beats are small geographical areas of neighborhoods or cities that are patrolled by individual officers, usually on foot.

Beccaria, Cesare Bonesana, Marchese di (1738-1794). Developed classical school of criminology. Wrote *Essays on Crimes and Punishments*. Believed corporal punishment unjust and ineffective, that crime could be prevented by clear legal codes specifying prohibited behaviors and punishments and promoted "just deserts" philosophy. Also endorsed a utilitarianistic approach to criminal conduct and its punishment by suggesting that useful, purposeful, and reasonable punishments ought to be formulated and applied. Viewed criminal conduct as pleasurable to criminals, believing they sought pleasure and avoided pain; thus, pain might function as a deterrent to criminal behavior. *See also* Jeremy Bentham.

Becker, Howard. Criminologist and social psychologist who has studied deviance and criminality. Wrote *Outsiders: Studies in the Sociology of Deviance* (1963). Labeling theorist, believes or considers deviance relative to a particular group in a particular time and place.

behavioral approach. Type of police discretion typified by a blend of sociology, psychology, and political science. A developmental scheme whereby police officers attempt to negotiate their way through each public encounter.

behavioral modeling. Learning how to behave by fashioning one's behavior after others.

behavior modification. A treatment program that attempts to change behavior, rather than personality, by rewarding favorable actions and punishing unfavorable ones.

behaviorism. Branch of psychology concerned with the study of observable behavior, rather than unconscious motives. Focuses on relationship between particular stimuli and persons' responses to them.

bench probation, parole. Action by court to permit convicted offenders to remain free in their communities only under the jurisdiction of the sentencing judge.

bench trial. Tribunal where guilt or innocence of defendant is determined by the judge rather than a jury.

bench warrant. Document issued by judge and not requested by the police demanding that a specified person be brought before the court without undue or unnecessary delay.

benefit of clergy. An early form of clemency in England originally intended for clergy convicted in King's Courts but transferred to church jurisdiction for punishment. Eventually extended to many non-clerics who could read or who claimed to be able to read. Primarily an escape from the death penalty.

Bentham, Jeremy (1748-1832). British hedonist. Wrote *Introduction to the Principles and Morals of Legislation*. Believed criminals could be deterred by minimizing pleasures derived from wrongdoing and punishment should be swift, certain, and painful.

bequeath. To provide in a will for the legal transfer of property or valuables to others.

Bertillon identification. Nineteenth-century identification method deriving its name from the inventor, Alphonse Bertillon, head of the Paris police. Bertillon used body measurements to compare persons and photographs to make positive identifications.

best evidence rule. In the course of presenting evidence in court, this edict states that if factual information or tangible documents are offered as proof, the original information or documents are preferred; if such original information or documents are unavailable, then a reasonable facsim-

ile is the next most preferred item (e.g., a photocopy of an unavailable automobile title would be the best evidence, in the event that the original automobile title was destroyed or missing).

bestiality. Any act involving sexual intercourse between a human being and an animal.

beyond a reasonable doubt. Standard used in criminal courts to establish guilt of criminal defendant.

bifurcated trial. Tribunal in capital cases where jury is asked to make two decisions. First decision is to determine guilt or innocence of defendant; if guilty, jury meets to decide punishment which may include the death penalty.

bigamy. Crime of being married to more than one spouse at a time.

Big Brothers. An organization loosely organized throughout communities, designed to provide delinquent children or those in need of supervision with a caring adult, who functions as a "big brother" to the child and is viewed as a possible role model. An anti-delinquency program.

bill of attainder. A legislative act imposing punishment without trial upon persons deemed guilty of treason or felonies. Currently prohibited by United States Constitution.

bill of exceptions. Written listing of the objections made by either the prosecution or defense during a trial proceeding. Such bills may be used later if the case is appealed by either side.

bill of indictment. A document submitted to a grand jury by the prosecutor asking it to take action and indict a suspect.

bill of particulars. A written statement that specifies additional facts about a charge.

Bill of Rights. First ten Amendments to the U. S. Constitution setting forth certain freedoms and guarantees to U. S. citizens.

bill of sale. Legal document transferring ownership or title of some property to another.

bind over. Following a finding of probable cause that a crime has been committed and the defendant has committed it, a court action to cause the defendant to be tried on the charges later in a criminal court.

Binet, Alfred (1857-1911). Psychologist who designed tests to measure intelligence. Suggested that a high correlation exists between criminality and IQ.

biocriminology. The subdiscipline of criminology that investigates biological and genetic factors and their relation to criminal behavior.

biographical method. A research strategy in which the experiences of a single individual are examined in detail.

bio-social criminology. *See* sociobiology.

birth cohort. An aggregate consisting of all persons born in the same year.

bisexuality. Acts of persons who have sexual relations with persons of both the same and different genders.

blacklist. To deny privileges and rights to others because of their political or social beliefs or other criteria.

blackmail. Extorting money or valuables by threatening to reveal or disclose information a person would not want generally known (e.g., if a public official has an illegitimate child and is running for political office).

blameworthiness. The amount of culpability or guilt a person maintains for participating in a particular criminal offense.

blaming the victim. The stereotypical practice of charging the socially and psychologically handicapped with the lack of motivation. An attitude or belief that the adverse conditions and negative characteristics of a group, often of minorities, are the group's own fault.

blood alcohol level (BAL). Amount of alcohol in blood as measured by various devices and by which intoxication can be inferred; can be determined by breath, blood, or urine samples; devices yield a percentage, such as .13, which means that there are 13/100ths of a part alcohol per 1,000 parts of blood; generally, .08 or .10 are conventional BALs for determining whether motorists are legally intoxicated; if a motorist registers .08 or higher in a state with a .08 standard, then legally, the motorist is intoxicated.

bludgeon. A club similar to a short baseball bat used to attack an opponent.

blue curtain. When police agencies "investigate their own." The very language used in such investigations is telling of the reluctance among police officials to punish one of their colleagues when a citizen complains.

blue laws. Any local laws or ordinances prohibiting store operations on Sunday, race-track betting, or other activities that may be morally questionable if performed on Sunday. Blue laws in most jurisdictions have been overturned by United States Supreme Court as unconstitutional.

blue-ribbon jury. A jury considered by either side, prosecution or defense, to be ideal because of its perceived likelihood of rendering a verdict favorable to that side.

board of pardons. Special appointed board in different jurisdictions that convenes to hear requests from inmates to be pardoned or to receive executive clemency from governors.

boards of review. Special boards convened to review evidence and make recommendations; may also make recommendations for citations or rewards. Law enforcement agencies have such boards in cases involving allegations of officer misconduct.

bobbies. British police. Named after Sir Robert "Bobby" Peel, the British Home Secretary, in the 1820s.

body belt. Restraining device worn by prisoners, with wrist restraints at the center of the abdomen.

body types. Early nineteenth and twentieth century theorists conjectured about association between one's physical features and criminal conduct. Typologies were invented showing patterns of association between body types and behaviors. Currently outmoded.

boiler room. Operation run by one or more stock traders and manipulators who, through deception and misleading sales techniques, seduce unsuspecting buyers into purchasing stocks in obscure and poorly financed corporations.

bomb training school. Department of Justice-initiated schools, later replicated in certain state jurisdictions, whereby persons acquire knowledge about bombs, their construction and operation, and how to defuse them.

bona fide. "In good faith." Without the attempt to defraud or deceive.

bond. Written document indicating that defendants or sureties assure the presence of these defendants at a criminal proceeding; if not, then the bond will be forfeited.

bond act. A common means of financing public construction with private funds by selling bonds to be paid back at moderate interest over a number of years. Bond financing drastically increases costs of construction, but also removes construction costs from yearly operating costs.

bonding, bonding theory. A key concept in a number of theoretical formulations. Emile Durkheim's notion that deviant behavior is controlled to the degree that group members feel morally bound to one another, are committed to common goals and share a collective conscience. In social control theory, the elements of attachment, commitment, involvement and belief; explanation of criminal behavior implying that criminality is the result of a loosening of bonds or attachments with society; builds on differential association theory. Primarily designed to account for juvenile delinquency.

Bonger, Willem Adrian (1876-1940). Dutch theorist who advocated Marxist socialist views about crime and its causes. Believed that crime is of social origin rather than biological, that crime is behavior within boundaries of normal human behavior, and that methods to control crime should include punishment of sufficient severity to deter offenders, thus off-setting the gratifying element derived from committing crime. Endorsed Marxist view of class conflict, believing that law functions to benefit the ruling (bourgeoisie) class rather than the working class (proletariat). Wrote *Criminality and Economic Conditions* (1910).

bookie. Person who engages in illegal practice of betting on, accepting bets relating to horse, dog races, athletic events, any other contest, event whose outcome is in doubt.

booking. Process of making written report of arrest, including name and address of arrested persons, the alleged crimes, arresting officers, place and time of arrest, physical description of suspect, photographs, sometimes called "mug shots," and fingerprints.

bookmaking. Illegal activity of accepting or making bets or wagers on athletic events, races, Academy Award winners, and any other event whose outcome is in doubt.

boot camp. A short-term institutional sentence, usually followed by probation, that puts the offender through a physical regimen designed to develop discipline and respect for authority. *See also* shock probation.

bootlegging. Illegally manufacturing alcohol or alcoholic beverages and/or transporting such contraband for sale.

born criminal. In Cesare Lombroso's deterministic view, one who is born with genetically transmitted criminal characteristics and thereby destined to become a criminal. Atavist.

borstal. British facilities for juveniles. The equivalent of U. S. industrial schools, where British juvenile offenders are sentenced to a term of supervision where they may receive therapy, vocational or educational training, and/or remedial help.

Boston Children's Aid Society. Privately funded philanthropic society founded by Rufus R. Cook in 1860, catering to orphans and other minors who did not have adequate adult supervision. Used volunteers to assist juvenile offenders.

Boston Offender Project (BOP). Experimental juvenile treatment program commenced in 1981 through the Massachusetts Department of Youth Services. Aimed at reducing recidivism, reintegrating youths, and increasing offender accountability.

bot. Under Anglo-Saxon law, the restitution paid for killing someone in an open fight.

bounty, bounty hunter. Monetary rewards offered for capture of persons who escape prosecution from a given jurisdiction. Often, such persons have posted a bond with a bonding company and the bonding company hires a bounty hunter (person who earns living by apprehending these persons) to track them down so that monies deposited with the courts by the bonding company can be recovered.

bourgeoisie. In Marxist theory, owners of the means of production. The capitalist ruling class.

Bow Street Runners. A small organization of paid police officers who attempted to apprehend criminals in England originating in 1754.

brain dead. Physical condition where oxygen has been deprived from the brain to the extent that brain function ceases but the body continues to survive, usually through mechanical means and artificial life-support systems. Person is presumed dead with a brain death.

Brawner rule. The legal rule that a person will be found not guilty by reason of insanity "if at the time of such conduct as a result of mental disease or mental defect, he lacks substantial capacity either to appreciate the criminality of his conduct or to conform his conduct to the requirements of the law."

breach of the peace. Any disruption of public decorum, such as loud noises, fighting, and any other interference with neighborhood equilibrium, is the basis for a complaint to the police to intercede and stop the disruption.

breach of trust. Contractual term implying a failure to comply with one or more terms of a contract or mutual agreement between parties. A criminal act involving a fiduciary, possibly embezzlement.

breaking, breaking and entering. Forceful, unlawful entry into a building or conveyance.

Breathalizer. Product or device used to test the breath of suspected motorists or pedestrians to determine whether they are legally intoxicated; measures blood-alcohol content.

bribe, bribery. Crime of offering, giving, requesting, soliciting, receiving something of value to influence a decision of a public official.

Bridewell. First correctional institution in England. Confined both children and adults considered to be idle and disorderly.

brief(s). A document filed by a party to a lawsuit to convince the court of the merits of that party's case.

British Crime Survey. Annual compilation of victimization figures for both England and Wales. Comparable to the *National Crime Survey* published in the United States.

Brockway, Zebulon (1827-1920). First superintendent of New York State Reformatory at Elmira in 1876. Arguably credited with introducing first "good time" system in United States whereby inmates could have their sentences reduced or shortened by the number of good marks earned through good behavior.

"Broken windows" approach. Form of police patrol stressing better communication with citizens. Foot patrols, team policing, and other "back to the people" programs are consistent with this patrol form. The term used to describe the role of the police as maintainers of community order and safety.

broker. Probation/parole officer work-role orientation where probation/parole officer functions as a referral service and supplies offender-client with contacts to agencies who provide needed services.

Bronner, Augusta. Together with William Healy conducted a study in 1926 of delinquent boys and reported that they were five to ten times more likely to be subnormal in intelligence compared with nondelinquents.

brothel. A house of prostitution, typically run by a madam who sets prices and handles "business."

brutalization effect, process. The belief that capital punishment creates an atmosphere of brutality that enhances, rather than deters, the level of violence in society, that the death penalty reinforces the view that violence is an appropriate response to violence.

budget. Plan for the accomplishment of programs relating to objectives and goals within a definite time period including an estimate of financial resources required together with an estimate of resources available, usually compared with past periods and showing future requirements.

bug, bugging. An electronic device enabling a listener to intercept conversations of other persons. Devices are usually secreted on premises or in a telephone device. Law enforcement officers must obtain judicial authorization to conduct such surveillance, also known as wiretapping.

buggery. *See* sodomy.

building tenders. Inmates who achieve supervisory positions to assist prison officials with maintenance of an institution and the control of other inmates.

burden of proof. The requirement to introduce evidence to prove an alleged fact or set of facts.

Bureau of Justice Assistance. Bureau created in 1984 to make grants available to researchers for the purpose of learning more about crime prevention and control.

Bureau of Justice Statistics. Bureau created in 1979 to distribute statistical information concerning crime, criminals, and crime trends.

bureaucracy. Organizational model that vests individuals with authority and spheres of competence in a predetermined hierarchy with abstract rules and selection by test.

Burger court. The United States Supreme Court under the leadership of Chief Justice Warren Burger.

Burgess, Ernest W. (1886-1966). Helped to form the Chicago School of thought, a social ecology view that related crime with various sectors or zones emanating from city centers. The concentric zone hypothesis posited that different types of behavior or criminal conduct could be found in particular well-defined zones emanating away from the center of a city. Zones undergoing urban renewal, known as interstitial areas, were believed to contain a high degree of criminality because social disorganization was a key feature of such areas, with neighborhoods in transition and families in disarray, heightening conditions for criminal conduct.

burglary. Unlawful entry of a structure to commit a felony or theft.

burnese. A form of highly concentrated cocaine used by drug abusers.

burnout. *See* Maslach burnout inventory.

Bursik, Robert. Criminologist who collaborated with Janet Heitgerd (1987) in noting phenomenon that as parts of communities undergo change, adjacent areas not undergoing change will experience a change in their crime rates.

business organization. In criminology, a reference to any permanent structure that profits from extortion and the provision of illegal goods and services; more commonly called "organized crime." Term is also applied in traditional usage to any legitimate enterprise.

C

cache. A collection of hidden contraband; often associated with an illegal storage of weaponry.

cadaver. A dead body.

cadet programs. Programs designed to bring underage, but otherwise qualified individuals, into police service.

caliber. The diameter of a cartridge; different calibers (e.g., .44, .44 special, .38, .22) are used to designate the sizes of cartridges fired by certain types of weapons.

call girls. Prostitutes who make dates via the telephone and then service customers in hotel rooms or apartments. Call girls typically have a steady clientele of repeat customers.

calumny. A spoken degradation of some person. Slander or malicious speech about someone or their qualities and personality.

camp, ranch, farm. Any of several types of similar correctional confinement facilities for adults or juveniles, usually located in rural areas.

Canadian Centre for Justice Statistics. Reports annually the amount of crime in Canada; comparable to the Bureau of Justice Statistics in the United States.

canine (K-9). Detector dog unit of police department. Use of dogs to sniff out illegal contraband, such as marijuana, from suspect vehicles, homes. Use also includes inspection of luggage at airports, ships, aircraft, and vessel cargo.

cannabis. The hemp plant which produces hashish and marijuana.

canons of police ethics. Standards and ethics adopted by the International Association of Chiefs of Police, embracing primary job responsibility, limitation of authority, duty to be familiar with the law, utilizing proper means to gain proper ends, and proper conduct toward the public.

capacitance alarm device. A crime prevention device associated with burglar alarms. Such devices are activated by one's presence in proximity to the device, wherever it may be located on one's premises. Approaching or walking near such a device activates an alarm elsewhere notifying surveillance or security personnel that an intruder is present.

capacity. Mental state of being legally responsible; having the mental acuity to know the difference between right and wrong and to realize and appreciate the nature and consequences of particular actions.

capias. "That you take." A general term for various court orders requiring that some named person be taken into custody.

capital crime, offense. Any crime punishable by death.

capital punishment. Imposition of the death penalty for the most serious crimes. May be administered by electrocution, lethal injection, gas, hanging, shooting.

capper. An old term to denote persons who solicit business for lawyers.

carabiniere. An Italian policeman.

carbofuchsin. A dye that is applied to various objects, including bands used to wrap currency; when touched by someone, the dye stains the skin or clothing. Thus, when a robber is apprehended, the presence of carbofuchsin is evidence implicating the person in the crime.

career criminals. Those offenders who make their living through crime. Usually offenses occur over the lifetime of the offender.

career integrity workshops. An in-service training program in the Los Angeles County Sheriff's

Department. In-house instructors lead small groups of deputies into creating "questionable conduct" scenarios and facilitate group discussions that delve into possible causes of actions or inactions and possible results. Participants see behaviors more clearly and are more closely in tune with reality than in "canned" situations brought into the training environment.

carjacking. A recent phenomenon emerging on a large scale in the mid-1980s in which persons stop motorists and illegally take their vehicles by force.

carnal knowledge. Sexual intercourse. Act of having sexual bodily connection or familiarity.

Carroll Doctrine. Ruling from United States Supreme Court's case of *Carroll v. United States* (1925) in which it was held that warrantless searches of vehicles are permissible where reasonable suspicion of illegal actions exists.

cartography, cartographic school. An approach to the study of crime that uses official data to map or chart patterns of crime.

case. Incident investigated by law enforcement officers. A single charging document under the jurisdiction of a court. A single defendant.

case law. Legal opinions having the status of law as enunciated by the courts (e.g., United States Supreme Court decisions become case law and governing cases when identical or very similar cases are subsequently heard in lower courts).

case-level sentencing. The sentencing of specific offenders.

caseload, case load. The number of clients a probation or parole officer is assigned according to some standard such as per week, month, year.

case study. An analysis of any pertinent aspects of one unit of study, such as a person, a group, or an organization. An in-depth analysis of a small number of persons.

casework, case work. A treatment program designed to help offenders cope with specific problems they face.

cash bailbond. Cash payment for situations in which charges are not serious and the scheduled bail is low. Defendants obtain release by paying in cash the full amount, which is recoverable after the required court appearances are made.

cast. A plaster mold made of some impression, such as a tire track or footprint.

castle doctrine. "A man's home is his castle." In common law, the right to use whatever force is necessary to protect one's dwelling and its inhabitants from an unlawful entry or attack.

cause *celebre*. Major case receiving widespread attention by media.

cause, challenges for. In jury selection, the method used by either the prosecution or defense attorneys to strike or remove prospective jurors from the available jury pool because of prejudices they might have, either toward the defendant or prosecution. Prospective jurors may also be excused from jury duty because of being law enforcement officers, relatives of law enforcement officers, court officers, or relatives of court officers. Any obvious bias for or against a defendant may result in the exclusion of the biased prospective juror.

caveat. Notice served to a judge to refrain from engaging in certain actions.

CCH. An abbreviation for computerized criminal history.

cease-and-desist, cease-and-desist order. An injunction to discontinue a practice or refrain from continuing a particular action until a court can settle the pending issue.

celerity. The speed with which a suspect is apprehended by police. Also the speed with which punishment is applied for offending.

cellblock. A group of individual or multiple-inmate cells in a locked enclosure, such as a prison or jail.

cellular telephone device. Electronic monitoring device worn by probationers or parolees that emits radio signal received by local area monitor.

censorship. A practice of forbidding the distribution of particular materials, books, movies. Censorship may seek to limit speech so that certain issues are not raised.

censure. The practice of punishing someone because of particular acts they have committed. If a judge has acted improperly, for instance, a higher judicial body may censure such conduct by issuing the judge an informal or formal reprimand. Differs from formal punishment for a criminal offense, such as a fine and/or term of confinement in a jail or prison.

Center for the Administration of Justice. Organization seeking to combine law and social science skills to develop demonstration programs and research activities to improve criminal justice agency operation.

Central Intelligence Agency (CIA). Under the National Security Act of 1947, an organization created to investigate matters of national security.

central station alarm system. Any alarm system whose installation is connected with other alarm systems and is monitored by a central headquarters.

centurions. In early Roman times, from about 100 B.C. to 200 A.D., centurions were soldiers used for policing purposes. Usually commanded units of 100 men each.

certification (juvenile). *See* waiver.

certification, offender. The social verification by the criminal justice system or by conventional persons that an offender is rehabilitated.

certified copy. Any document which has been notarized by a notary. Authentication of the veracity of one signing a document and attesting to its truthfulness or accuracy.

certiorari, **writ of.** A writ issued by a higher court directing a lower court to prepare the record of a case and send it to the higher court for review; a means of accessing the United States Supreme Court in order for a case to be heard.

chain of custody. In evidence gathering, the sequence of possession and transmission of evidence from one department or unit or person to another. If the chain of custody of evidence is broken for any reason, the value of the evidence is tainted or devalued.

challenge. *See* peremptory challenge.

challenges of jurors. Questions raised of jurors by the judge, prosecutor, and/or defense attorney relating to their qualifications as impartial finders of fact; a determination of juror bias one way or another for or against the defendant.

chambers. Usually a judge's office in a courthouse.

Chamblis, William. Criminological theorist who has written extensively about conflict theory and radical criminology, including *Law, Order and Power*; this treatise extends conflict theory and explains more precisely how rich and powerful interests are able to control less powerful interests; political and economic factors are considered as significant determinants of societal conflict.

chancellors. King's agents used to settle disputes between neighbors in his behalf, such as property boundary issues, trespass allegations, and child misconduct. Early equivalent of the chancellor

with similar duties and responsibilities was the justice of the peace, dating back to about 1200 A.D.

chancery court. Tribunal of equity rooted in early English common law where civil disputes are resolved. Also responsible for juvenile matters and adjudicating family matters such as divorce. Has jurisdiction over contract disputes, property boundary claims, and exchanges of goods disputes.

change of venue. A change in the place of trial, usually from one county or district to another. Changes of venue are often conducted to avoid prejudicial trial proceedings, where it is believed that a fair trial cannot be obtained in the specific jurisdiction where the crime was alleged to have been committed.

charge. A formal allegation filed against some defendant in which one or more crimes are alleged.

charge bargaining, charge reduction bargaining. Negotiation process between prosecutors and defense attorneys involving dismissal of one or more charges against defendants in exchange for guilty plea to remaining charges, or in which prosecutor downgrades the charges in return for a plea of guilty.

charisma, charismatic authority. Phenomenon meaning "gift of grace." Attributed to persons who have strong personal qualities and who are able to attract others to do what they want, thus exercising charismatic authority.

chattel. Property of a landowner or another, including an inventory of farm animals and other stock. Personal, tangible property, assets.

chattel mortgage. Any lien on property in exchange for money.

cheating. Fraudulent act to obtain something of value from a victim.

check forging or fraud. Criminal offense of making or altering a negotiable instrument, such as a check, in order to obtain money by fraud.

Chesney-Lind, Meda. Feminist criminologist who believes that criminology is largely male-focused. Examines relation between crime and treatment of females in society. Attempts to balance coverage of both males and females in criminological research.

Chicago Area Project. Delinquency prevention program commenced in 1934 by Clifford Shaw and Henry McKay, designed to establish recreational centers and counseling programs for high-risk youths.

Chicago Crime Commission. A citizen action group set up in Chicago to investigate problems in the criminal justice system and explore avenues for positive change.

Chicago school. Name given to sociologists at the University of Chicago during the 1920s; founded by Albion Small in 1892.

Chicago Seven. Notorious group of persons who were tried in federal court in 1970 in Chicago because of their attempt to disrupt the Democratic National Convention in 1968. Group consisted of Abbie Hoffman, Tom Hayden, Jerry Rubin, Lee Weiner, John Eroines, David Dellinger, and Renard Davis. Originally known as "Chicago Eight" with the inclusion of Bobby Seales, who was subsequently ejected from court because of his disruptive and outrageous conduct.

chicanery. Trickery.

chief justice. The presiding or principal judge of a court, possessing nominal authority over the other judges (e.g., the Chief Justice of the United States Supreme Court).

chief of police. A local law enforcement officer who is the appointed or elected head of a police department.

child. Any person under the age of legal majority. Age varies among states, but is 18 in most jurisdictions.

child abuse. Any form of cruelty to the physical, moral, mental well-being of a child. The sexual abuse, exploitation, negligent treatment, maltreatment of a child by a person who is responsible for the child's welfare.

child molestation, child molester. Any one of several forms of handling, fondling or other contacts of a sexual nature with a child; may include photographing children in lewd poses. "Molester" is one who commits these acts.

child neglect. Any deliberate act by the parents or legal guardians of minors which deprives minors of life's necessities, including protection, adequate sustenance, and behavioral regulation.

child savers. Groups who promoted rights of minors during the nineteenth century and helped create a separate juvenile court. Their motives have been questioned by modern writers who see their efforts as a form of social control and class conflict.

child sexual abuser. *See* child molester.

child support. Court-ordered monetary payments to maintain dependent children.

child welfare agency. An agency licensed by the state to provide care and supervision for children. An agency that provides service to the juvenile court and which may accept legal custody. May also be licensed to accept guardianship, accept children for adoption, and license foster homes.

Children in need of supervision (CHINS). Typically unruly or incorrigible children who cannot be supervised well by their parents. Also includes children from homes where parents are seldom present. State agencies exist to find housing for such children.

Children's Aid Society. Early child-saving organization which attempted to place homeless city youths with farm families.

Children's Bureau. United States agency operated during 1912-1940 and charged with compiling statistical information about children and methods whereby delinquency could be prevented and treated.

children's courts, hearings, tribunals. Judicial mechanisms to deal with errant and unruly children during nineteenth century. Replaced with juvenile courts commencing in Illinois in 1899.

children's rights. A term with various referents, such as natural rights (those that are inalienable because they belong to all persons as human beings), civil rights (those conferred by legal enactment), nurturance rights (those things that nourish or sustain the person or promote human development), and self-determined rights (opportunities for children that allow them considerable self-control and autonomy).

chilling effect. Law or policy that discourages persons from exercising their rights.

CHINS. *See* children in need of supervision.

Chiricos, Theodore. Criminologist who has examined the relation between class and race bias and punishment in the criminal justice system (1970); also the relation between unemployment and crime.

chivalry hypothesis. Explanation for judicial leniency toward female offenders. Posits that much of the criminality among females is hidden because of the generally protective and benevolent attitudes toward them by police, prosecutors, juries and judges.

choke hold. A defensive maneuver performed by police when subduing suspects. Often, a baton is used, being placed around the neck of a suspect, temporarily disabling the suspect by cutting off air. A controversial defensive action because sometimes death to a suspect results.

Christopher Commission. An investigatory body led by Warren Christopher that investigated the Los Angeles Police Department in the wake of the Rodney King beating.

chromatograph. In forensics, device which measures and evaluates gaseous substances.

chromosomes. Basic cellular structures containing genes.

chronic 6 percent. Result of birth cohort study by Marvin Wolfgang, Thorsten Sellin, and Robert Figlio, in which male birth cohorts from Philadelphia were studied over time, between 1945 and 1963. Revealed that 6 percent of these males accounted for over 50 percent of all criminality and delinquency in the entire cohort.

churning. Broker trading in which a client's shares of stock are used for the sole purpose of generating large commissions.

chuzaishos. "Live-in" units in Japan, providing accommodations for an officer's entire family. Staffed on a 24-hour basis, both kobans and chuzaishos are strategically located to ensure close contacts between police officers and community residents.

Circuit, Circuit Courts. Originally, courts that were held by judges who followed a circular path, hearing cases periodically in various communities. Now refers to courts with several counties or districts within their jurisdiction.

circumstantial evidence. Material provided by a witness from which a jury must infer a fact.

citation, citation to appear. Any document issued by a law enforcement or court officer directing one to present oneself in court on a specific date and time.

cite, citation. Any legal reference in which a point of law is made. In law enforcement, a summons.

citizen complaints. Grievances filed by citizens against police officers for alleged misconduct.

citizen dispute settlement. *See* alternative dispute resolution.

citizen value system. Parole board decision-making model appealing to public interests in seeing that community expectations are met by making appropriate early release decisions.

citizen's arrest. Apprehension of a criminal suspect by a private citizen unaffiliated with any law enforcement agency.

city courts. Lower courts of special original jurisdiction. Rural counterparts are the justice of the peace courts.

civil action. Any lawsuit brought to enforce private rights and to remedy violations thereof.

civil commitment. Legal confinement to a hospital or other treatment facility for a period of time, usually to undergo an examination or receive some type of therapy.

civil commotion. *See* disturbing the peace.

civil courts. Tribunals that handle civil cases, as opposed to criminal cases. Objectives of civil cases are to recover damages (money), whereas object of criminal courts is to seek punishment of imprisonment and/or fines and victim restitution.

civil death. The custom of terminating all civil rights of convicted felons (e.g., forbidding them the right to vote or to marry). No state uses civil death today.

civil disabilities. Rights forfeited as the result of a criminal conviction (e.g., in some states, convicted offenders lose the right to vote).

civil disobedience. Any public action, which violates the law, involving political demonstrations or picketing, in order to protest a government action, law, proclamation.

civil disturbances. Riots; collective, aggravated public demonstrations resulting in physical injury and loss of property.

civil forfeiture. The relinquishing of assets to the state as the consequence of crime.

civil law. All state and federal law pertaining to noncriminal activities, also referred to as municipal law. Laws pertain to private rights and remedies. A body of formal rules established by any society for its self-regulation.

civil liability. In tort law, the basis for a cause of action to recover damages.

civil liberties. Rights guaranteed by the United States Constitution and Bill of Rights.

Civil Rights Act. Title 42, Section 1983 of the U. S. Code permitting inmates of prisons and jails as well as probationers and parolees the right to sue their administrators and/or supervisors under the "due process" and "equal protection" clauses of the Fourteenth Amendment; may also pertain to civil suits filed by employees against their employers where discrimination is alleged.

Civil Rights Division. That part of the United States Justice Department that handles cases involving violations of civil rights guaranteed by the Constitution and federal law.

civil rights movement. Multi-racial movement commenced in 1960s to combat racial injustice and inequality.

civil service. Employment by a local, state, federal government; public employees are civil service employees.

civilian complaint review boards. Panels of citizens that judge acts of misconduct committed by police officers and recommend appropriate sanctions.

civilianization. Incorporating into police departments private citizens to perform particular law enforcement functions, such as directing traffic, office duties.

Clark, Benjamin C. Philanthropist and "volunteer" probation officer who assisted courts with limited probation work during 1860s, carrying on John Augustus's work.

Clarke, Ronald. Criminologist who wrote *Situational Crime Prevention*, describing three crime prevention tactics, including increasing the effort required to commit crime, increasing the risk of committing crime, and reducing the rewards of committing crime. Advocate of target-hardening and caller-ID. Together with David Weisburd, Clarke has argued that crime displacement may occur through extinction, diffusion of benefits, and discouragement. Extinction occurs when burglar-proof neighborhoods cause potential burglars to cease burglary and move to other forms of crime in other areas; diffusion of benefits occurs whenever crime prevention measures calculated to prevent one type of crime may actually deter other types of crime in the same area; discouragement occurs when criminals give up particular types of crime because they no longer pay.

class action, class action suit. Any lawsuit on behalf of a segment of the population with specific characteristics, namely that they are victims of whatever wrongs are alleged. The class of persons may persist over time and change, but the action is for all current and future members of the class.

classic research design. An experimental design format, usually associated with research in the biological and social sciences, that consists of two comparable groups, an experimental and a control group. These two groups are equivalent except that the experimental group is exposed to the independent variable and the control group is not.

classical school of criminology, classical criminology, classical philosophy of criminal law. A criminological perspective indicating that people have free will to choose either criminal or conventional behavior. People choose to commit crime for reasons of greed or personal need. Crime can be controlled by criminal sanctions, which should be proportionate to the guilt of the perpetrator.

classification. Inmate security designation based on psychological, social and sociodemographic criteria relating to one's potential dangerousness or risk posed to the public in order to categorize offenders according to the level of custody they require while incarcerated. Measures potential disruptiveness of prisoners and early release potential of inmates for parole consideration.

classification of crimes. Categories of misdemeanors and felonies facilitating the compilation of statistical information relating to such crimes.

classification system. Means used by prisons and probation/parole agencies to separate offenders according to offense seriousness, type of offense, and other criteria. No classification system has been demonstrably successful at effective prisoner or client placements.

clearance. The event in which a known occurrence of a crime may be followed by an arrest or other decision which indicates a solved crime at the police level of reporting.

clearance rate. Percentage of crimes known to the police that they believe have been solved by arrest. Statistic used as a measure of a police department's productivity.

clear and present danger doctrine. In constitutional law, doctrine that First Amendment does not protect those forms of expression that pose an obvious and immediate danger of bringing about some substantive evil that government has a right to prevent.

cleared by arrest. Term used by FBI in *Uniform Crime Reports* to indicate that someone has been arrested for a reported crime. Does not necessarily mean that the crime has been solved or that the actual criminals who committed the crime have been apprehended or convicted.

clemency. A grant of mercy by an executive official commuting a sentence or pardoning a criminal.

clerk of the court. A court official who handles much of the routine paperwork associated with the administration of the court.

client specific plan(ning). One alternative sentencing program involving selective tailoring of sentence (other than imprisonment for each individual offender), depending upon offense committed. Requires judicial approval.

clinical prediction. Forecast of inmate behavior based upon professional's expert training and direct work with offenders.

closed-ended question. A question that offers respondents a set of answers from which they are asked to choose the one that most closely fits their views.

Cloward, Richard. Sociologist who collaborated with Lloyd Ohlin in describing the theory of opportunity in *Delinquency and Opportunity* (1960), positing that delinquent subcultures exist independent of but within mainstream society. Youth gangs emerge because there is a lack of opportunity for many youths to achieve socially approved and desirable goals; slum children, therefore, may wish to conform to institutionalized or socially approved means to achieve culturally approved goals, but lack the means to do so. This is a prelude to deviance, delinquency, and criminality. Influenced President Lyndon B. Johnson's War on Poverty program by highlighting disruptive effects of slum areas and poverty conditions in relation to delinquency and crime.

cocaine. A stimulant manufactured from the coca plant (an "upper" in the drug community). Used as a pain reliever in certain forms.

co-corrections, co-ed prisons. Penal facilities where male and female prisoners live, supervised by female and male staff, and prisoners participate in all activities together. Sharing same quarters is prohibited.

code. A systematic collection of laws.

code of ethics. Regulations formulated by major professional societies that outline the specific problems and issues that are frequently encountered in the types of research carried out within a particular profession. Serves as a guide to ethical research practices.

Code of *Hammurabi*. The first written criminal code developed in Babylonia about 2000 B.C.

code of silence. Tacit agreement among police officers that discourages "whistle blowing" regarding misconduct of fellow officers as negative and potentially self-destructive.

codefendants. Two or more defendants charged with the same crime and tried in the same judicial proceeding.

coeducational prison. *See* co-corrections.

coercive intervention. In juvenile law, out-of-home placement of juveniles, detainment, or mandated therapy or counseling. For adults, may include similarly court-ordered interventions for individual family members or entire family units.

coercive power. Form of influence by which a superior elicits compliance by subordinates through threats of punishment.

cognitive development theory. Also called "developmental theory," stresses stages of learning process whereby persons acquire abilities to think and express themselves, respect the property and rights of others, and cultivate a set of moral values.

cognitive theory. The study of the perception of reality; the mental processes required to understand the world in which we live.

Cohen, Albert K. Criminologist who developed notion of delinquent subculture as a culture existing within the larger mainstream conventional culture. Delinquents develop their own value system, complete with rewards and punishments, which becomes inculcated in others seeking to become a part of the delinquent subculture. Strain arises because of inability of persons to gain status and acceptance. Applied to juveniles, strain would be generated by not doing well in school or not being accepted into social groups. Thus poor scholastic ability and interpersonal relations would lead persons toward deviant conduct as an alternative means to achieve goals.

Cohen, Lawrence. Developed routine activities theory, with Marcus Felson. Theory suggests that motivation to commit crime and numbers of offenders are rather constant; thus, it is inevitable that in every society there will be someone willing to commit crime for diverse reasons. Predatory crime, a vital component of their theory, rests upon the existence of suitable targets (victims), capable guardians (police), and motivated offenders (criminals). "Routine activities" refer to the activities of the normal American lifestyle.

cohort. *See* birth cohort.

cohort effects. The effect of belonging to a given generation (e.g., the 60s generation). Sometimes people mistakenly assume that a difference between people of different age groups is the result of biological aging when the difference is really due to the two groups having different backgrounds because they grew up in different eras.

cohort study. Any examination over time of a segment of persons born in a given year for varied purposes. Criminologists seek to show that a certain percentage of persons born in a particular year will commit disproportionately larger numbers of crimes compared with others in the same cohort.

cold blood. A term denoting premeditation and aggravation, usually in association with a homicide.

collateral attack. The attempt to defeat the outcome of a judicial proceeding by challenging it in a different proceeding or court.

collateral facts. Any material fact not directly connected with the case in question.

collective child abuse. Attitudes held as a group in society that impede the psychological and physical development of children.

collective incapacitation. A policy of giving the same prison sentence to everyone convicted of a particular offense, in order to reduce the crime rate.

collusion. A conspiracy or compact between two or more persons to commit a crime or perpetrate a fraud.

colony, penal. Any aggregate of prisoners kept in a secluded geographical area.

color of authority. Acting in one's official capacity, usually as a law enforcement officer or judicial official.

Colquhoun, Patrick (1745-1820). Proponent of organized police agencies to combat crime. Created early training programs for police officers and stressed particular recruitment standards. Wrote *A Treatise on the Police of the Metropolis* (1795).

combination sentence. *See* split sentencing.

combined designs. The merging of two or more research designs into a single study to increase the inferential powers of that study.

comes stabuli. Non-uniformed mounted early law enforcement officers in medieval England.

Early police forces were small and relatively unorganized, but made effective use of local resources in the formation of posses for the pursuit of offenders.

comity. Interjurisdictional judicial courtesy, whereby one state recognizes the laws of another jurisdiction.

commercial crime. Any crime committed against a company or business, as opposed to crime against particular individuals.

commercial law. Pertaining to businesses and interstate commerce.

commissary. Refers both to the prison store and to the incidental items sold to inmates. May also be an inmate's account, which is debited when an item is purchased.

commitment to conformity. Theoretical ingredient of social control positing that real, present, and logical reasons exist to obey the rules of society.

common law. Authority based on court decrees and judgments which recognize, affirm, and enforce certain usages and customs of the people. Laws determined by judges in accordance with their rulings.

common-law marriage. After a man and a woman reside together in a common residence for a certain amount of time, sometimes seven years, the parties become married without an official ceremony but with all legal rights of married persons.

common pleas courts. Used in the United States, courts with this title are usually courts of general and original jurisdiction.

communal consensus model. *See* consensus model.

community-based corrections (correctional) programs. Locally operated services offering minimum security, limited release, work release alternatives to prisoners about to be paroled. May also serve probationers.

community-based policing. An umbrella term encompassing any law enforcement agency or community citizen or group-initiated plan or program to enable police officers and community residents to work cooperatively in creative ways that will reduce or control crime, fear of crime, and the incidence of victimizations; promote mutual understanding for the purpose of enhancing police officer/citizen coproduction of community safety and security; and establish a police-citizen communications network through which mutual problems may be discussed and resolved.

community-based supervision. Reintegrative programs operated publicly or privately to assist offenders by providing therapeutic, support, and supervision programs for criminals. May include furloughs, probation, parole, community service, and restitution.

community control. *See* home confinement.

community correctional center. An institution, usually located within an urban area, that houses inmates soon to be released. Such centers are designed to help inmates establish community ties and thus to promote their reintegration with society. Also called community pre-release center.

Community Corrections Act. Statewide mechanism included in legislation whereby funds are granted to local units of government and community agencies to develop and deliver "front end" alternative sanctions in lieu of state incarceration.

Community Diversion Incentive (CDI). Virginia diversion program established in 1981 for prison-bound offenders. Participants were required to perform specified unpaid community services and make financial restitution to victims. Clients were also subject to intensive supervised probation.

community facility. *See* community correctional center.

Community Patrol Officer Program (CPOP). A problem-oriented community policing effort involving other community agencies, commenced as a pilot project in 1984 in New York City. Officers were assigned to foot patrols for 16 to 60-block beats. Most important function of CPOP was the prevention of street-level drug problems. Seventy-five precincts used the CPOP by 1989.

Community-Police Educational Program. Implemented by the Philadelphia Police Department in 1980. Designed to educate citizens by explaining the necessity for certain police actions and to reduce their criticism of police performance.

community policing. A philosophy rather than a specific tactic. A proactive, decentralized approach designed to reduce crime, disorder and fear of crime by intensely involving the same officer in a community for a long term so that personal links are formed with residents.

Community Projects for Restoration. Federal law enforcement and social welfare program begun under the Bush Administration. In 1992, $18 million in federal funds were targeted for community policing, public housing assistance and gang prevention efforts under the "weed and seed" program.

Community Protection Program. New York State county-based program as an alternative to prison where prison-bound offenders are diverted to intensive supervision and treatment.

community reintegration. Process whereby offender who has been incarcerated is able to live in community under some supervision and gradually adjust to life outside of prison or jail.

community service, restitution. An alternative sanction requiring offenders to work in the community at such tasks as cleaning public parks or working with handicapped children in lieu of an incarcerative sentence. Restitution involves paying back a victim through money received from one's work.

community service officer. Any police officer assigned the duty of handling non-crime related matters for a police department.

Community Treatment Project. Famous California Youth Authority program that released selected juveniles to aftercare immediately after reception. The project included classification by interpersonal maturity levels and attempted differential treatments based upon classification.

community wellness. A proactive collaborative effort between police departments and community residents to initiate watch and alert programs to inform police about possible criminal activities. As residents take a more active role in preventing crime, there are substantial decreases in crime observed in their neighborhoods over time.

commutation, commutation of sentence. Reduction of one's sentence to a less severe one; usually by administrative authority.

comparative corrections. Study of similarities and differences in the correctional systems of other cultures, societies, and institutions.

comparative criminal/juvenile justice. Analyses of criminal justice systems of other countries, studying their similarities and differences.

comparative research. A research strategy that looks at crime, policing, corrections, or any other common phenomena in societies with different cultures and different social structures.

comparison microscope. Any magnification device capable of viewing two objects simultaneously for purposes of comparison.

compelling interest. A legal concept that provides the basis for suspicionless searches when public safety is at issue (e.g., urinalysis tests of train engineers).

compensation. Money awarded to victims of crime to repay them in part for their losses and injuries. In research, subjects in the control group attempt to make up for being deprived of a desired treatment.

competence, competent, competency. State of being fit to give testimony or stand trial.

complaint. Written statement of essential facts constituting the offense alleged, made under oath before a magistrate or other qualified judicial officer.

complaint denied, granted. Decision by prosecutor to decline or grant a request that he or she seek an indictment, file an information, complaint against a specified person for a specific offense.

complete count census. The census of population and housing taken every ten years intended to reach every household in the country. Includes only basic demographic information on each member of the household plus a few questions about the housing unit.

compliance-involvement scheme. System devised by Amitai Etzioni in which relation is drawn between type of power used by superior to elicit compliance from subordinates, and the type of involvement resulting from power used. "Congruent" types would be reward-calculative, coercive-alienative, or normative-moral.

complicity. Conspiratorial conduct whereby two or more persons plan a crime and attempt to commit it. Any effort by one person to assist or aid another who is about to commit or has committed a crime.

compounding a crime. The crime of receiving something of value in exchange for an agreement not to file a criminal complaint.

comprehension. An important element of informed consent that refers to the confidence that the participant has provided knowing consent when the research procedure is associated with complex or subtle risks.

Comprehensive Crime Control Act of 1984. Significant Act which authorized establishment of U. S. Sentencing Commission, instituted sentencing guidelines, provided for abolition of federal parole and devised new guidelines and goals of federal corrections.

compulsion. Irresistible impulse. Inability to control behavior which may be criminal.

Compulsory School Act. Legislation passed in Colorado in 1899 directed to prevent truancy among juveniles; Act included juveniles who were habitually absent from school, who wandered the streets, and had no obvious business or occupation.

compurgation. Method of trial used before the thirteenth century in which a person charged with a crime could be absolved by swearing to innocence and producing a number of other persons willing to swear that they believed the accused's declaration of innocence.

computer-aided dispatch (CAD). Computer-driven program capable of performing routine clerical tasks in dispatch offices, including filing and sorting information.

computer-assisted telephone interviewing (CATI). Type of telephone survey in which the interviewer sits at a computer terminal and, as a question flashes on the screen, asks it over the telephone. Respondent's answers are typed and coded directly on a disk.

computer crime. Any form of crime in which a computer is used (e.g., transferring funds from one account into another illegally by means of a computer or stealing software programs by means of computer copying).

computer fraud. Falsification of stored data or deception in legitimate transactions by manipulation of data or programming, including the unlawful acquisition of data or programs for purposes of financial gain.

computer hacking. In criminology, activities that include the gaining of unauthorized access to data banks for malicious though not necessarily destructive purposes, and for neither financial gain nor purposes of espionage.

Comte, Auguste (1798-1857). French positivist considered to be the "father of sociology." Believed that social forces dominate individual behaviors and that the strict use of scientific methods ought to be used in order to understand the nature and implications of these forces upon individual behavior. Wrote *A System of Positive Reality* (1851).

concept. An abstraction representing an object, a property of an object, or a certain phenomenon that scientists use to describe the empirical world. A term that has a direct empirical referent.

conceptual framework. A level of theory in which descriptive categories are systematically placed within a broad logical structure of explicit and assumed propositions.

conceptual replication. An attempt to demonstrate an experimental phenomenon with an entirely new paradigm, set of measures, manipulations.

conclusive evidence. Any compelling evidence that is so strong that it cannot be disputed or discounted. Proof establishing guilt beyond a reasonable doubt.

concurrent jurisdiction. Situation in which offender may be held accountable in several different jurisdictions simultaneously. Courts in the same jurisdiction.

concurrent sentence, sentencing. Prison sentences for two or more criminal acts that are served simultaneously, or run together. More than one sentence handed out on the same occasion to a convicted offender and to be served during a common time period while incarcerated or on probation or parole.

concurring opinion. A judge's written opinion agreeing with the result in the case, but disagreeing with the reasoning of the majority opinion.

condemn. To find guilt or sentence a convicted offender to a particular punishment. In civil terminology, to find a dwelling unsuitable for habitation.

condemnation of the condemners. A technique of neutralization that asserts that it is the motives and behaviors of the people who are condemning offenders, rather than offender motives and behaviors, that should be criticized.

conditional disposition. Decision by juvenile court judge authorizing payment of fines, community service, restitution, or some other penalty after an adjudication of delinquency has been made.

conditional diversion. Suspension of prosecution in pretrial stage, while specific conditions are met; if conditions are satisfied, prosecution may be dismissed or charges reduced in seriousness.

conditional pardon. Any pardon action by a governor or pardon board in which program requirements are articulated.

conditional release. Freedom of defendant who agrees to meet specific conditions in addition to appearing in court later (e.g., remaining in the jurisdiction, maintaining steady employment, avoiding contact with victims or other known criminals).

conditional variable. A contingency necessary for the occurrence of the relationship between the independent and dependent variables.

conditions of probation and parole. The general (state-ordered) and special (court-ordered or board-ordered) limits imposed on offenders who are released either on probation or parole. General conditions tend to be fixed by statute; special conditions are mandated by the sentencing authority and take into consideration the background of the offender and circumstances surrounding the offense.

conduct norms. Behaviors expected of social group members. If group norms conflict with those of general culture, members of the group may find themselves described as outcasts or criminals.

confabulation. A fictitious rendering of events by someone who is mentally disturbed.

confession. An admission to a crime by a suspect.

confidence games. Obtaining of money by means of deception through the trust a victim places in the offender.

confidentiality, confidential communication. Protection of the identity of research participants. Any privileged communication between a client and an attorney.

confinement, congregate or solitary. Placement in a secure facility or area where an individual's movements are restricted or controlled.

confinement facility. A correctional facility, usually a jail or prison, where inmates are not permitted to depart unaccompanied.

conflict, class. Karl Marx's concept of clashes between bourgeoisie and proletariat classes over their different vested interests. Proletariat works for the bourgeoisie, who own the means of production.

conflict criminology. *See* radical criminology.

conflict gangs. Type of gangs described by Richard Cloward and Lloyd Ohlin in their work, *De-*

linquency and Opportunity (1960), characterized by engagement in violence with other gangs or community residents; also known as "fighting gangs." Primary interest is not criminal activity. *See also* criminal gangs and retreatist gangs for goal comparisons.

conflict model, approach, perspective. Legal model that asserts that the political power of interest groups and elites influences the content of the criminal law.

conflict resolution. Interpersonal strategy whereby persons in a group resolve their differences through discussion and compromise.

conflict, social. Any dispute between groups of people, often of different classes or cultures. May include physical confrontation.

confrontation. In court, any direct meeting between an accused person and the accuser. The Fifth Amendment assures every citizen the right to confront and cross-examine one's accuser.

congregate system. Introduced at Auburn State Penitentiary in New York where prisoners could work and eat together in common work and recreational areas; prisoners segregated at night.

conjugal visits, visitation. Programs, usually in jails or prisons, permitting inmates to have contact with their spouses or significant others to maintain positive relationships. Permitted sexual contact between inmates and their spouses.

"connects." In prison slang, inmates whose prison assignments allow them to acquire scarce information and resources that can be used for personal gain.

connivance. Conspiracy to commit a crime. Involvement in a crime or an attempted crime.

conscientious objector. Person who refuses military service on moral grounds.

consecutive sentences, sentencing. More than one sentence imposed on the same occasion to a convicted offender requiring that the sentences be served one after another and not concurrently.

consensual transaction, exchange. Mutually agreeable action between two or more parties. Prostitution is a consensual transaction in which sex is exchanged for money.

consensus model, approach, perspective, view of crime. Model of criminal lawmaking that assumes that societal members agree on which conduct is right or wrong and such law is codified to reflect agreed-upon societal values.

consent. Voluntarily yielding to the will or desire of another person.

consent decree. A formal agreement involving the child, parents, and the juvenile court in which the youth is placed under the court's supervision without an official finding of delinquency.

consent, implied. Inferred consent based upon an agreement between parties. There is implied consent between a probation officer and a probationer to permit routine home or apartment searches and inspections whenever the probation officer believes the probationer may be secreting contraband or using drugs.

consent of the victim. Any voluntary yielding of the will of the victim, accompanied by his or her deliberation, agreeing to the act of the offending party.

consent search. Any search of a dwelling, person, or vehicle in which the owner has given permission to search.

consenting adult, consenting adult laws. Right of two or more adults to engage in acts that otherwise might be regulated. Often refers to sexual acts between members of the same gender.

conspiracy. The crime of two or more persons agreeing or planning to commit a crime. The overt act itself is a tangible indication of the furtherance of the conspiratorial act. *See also* complicity.

constables. Favored noblemen of the King who commanded neighborhood groups. Forerunners of modern-day police officers.

Constitution Act of 1867. Bestowed the Canadian Parliament with the legislative authority to define all criminal law throughout the provinces (has undergone extensive revision).

constitutional law. An area of study in law schools involving the United States Constitution and its Amendments. An investigation and discussion of the principles articulated by the United States Supreme Court and its interpretations of the law in different legal contexts.

constitutional officer. Any law enforcement officer specifically and expressly provided for in either the United States Constitution or a state constitution. The sheriff, constable, and coroner are constitutional officers in several states.

constitutional rights. Rights guaranteed to all United States citizens by the United States Constitution and its Amendments.

constitutionalism. Philosophy that articulated principles of an organization or jurisdiction should be strictly interpreted and enforced as a regulatory medium for social action.

constructive contempt. An out-of-court contempt on the part of either the prosecution or defense whereby one or more ground rules or conditions are violated during a trial proceeding.

construction. Interpretation.

constructive breaking. Where the law implies breaking into a dwelling or business (e.g., persons who pose as city termite inspectors may enter dwelling in order to commit theft, even though residents have invited them in. They are guilty of constructive breaking).

constructive intent. The finding of criminal liability for an unintentional act that is the result of negligence or recklessness.

constructive possession. In the crime of larceny, willingly giving up temporary physical possession of property but retaining legal ownership.

contact patrols. A project funded by the British Home Office, promoted greater police officer contact with community residents through more continuous police presence in "beat" areas.

contact surveillance. Any application of trace substances which attach to clothing or body parts when one comes into contact with these substances. Useful in identifying persons who may have been at crime scenes and thus are considered suspects.

containment theory. Explanation elaborated by Walter Reckless and others that positive self-image enables persons otherwise disposed toward criminal behavior to avoid criminal conduct and conform to societal values. Every person is a part of an external structure and has a protective internal structure providing defense, protection, and/or insulation against one's peers, such as delinquents.

contemnor. Person found to be in contempt of court.

contempt of court. Disobeying orders from judges in their courtrooms. Failing to observe the proper decorum of legal proceedings. Crossing the line of proper conduct, either as a defense attorney or prosecutor (e.g., failing to give testimony when compelled to do so).

context of justification. Activities of scientists as they attempt logically and empirically to verify claims for knowledge.

contingency. A factor that determines movement from one criminal role to another, and from one crime to another.

contingency question. A question that applies only to a subgroup of respondents because it is relevant only to certain people.

continuance. An adjournment of a scheduled case until a future date.

continuity of crime. Idea or theory that crime begins early in life and continues throughout the life course, and the best predictor of future criminality is past criminality.

continuous crime. Any criminal act that extends over a prolonged period, such as possessing and driving a stolen car for several days.

continuous signalling devices. Electronic monitoring devices that broadcast an encoded signal that is received by a receiver-dialer in the offender's home. *See also* electronic monitoring.

contraband. Any item, including weapons, drugs, alcohol, the possession of which is illegal.

contract. Enforceable agreement between two or more parties.

contract system, attorney. Providing counsel to indigent offenders by having an attorney under contract to the county to handle some or all of these types of cases.

contract system, prison. System used in the early twentieth century in which inmates were leased out to private industry to work.

contraventions. French crime designation denoting petty offenses or violations. Comparable with misdemeanors in United States jurisdictions.

contributing to the delinquency of a minor. Any act by an adult that induces a juvenile to engage in a criminal act.

contributory negligence. Indicates share of responsibility of victim in any negligent act for which the victim's own lack of care is partially at fault.

Controlled Substances Act, controlled substances. Comprehensive Drug Abuse and Control Act of 1970 seeking to control drugs in the United States by classification and specification of penalties for possession or distribution. Replaced by the Comprehensive Crime Control Act of 1984. Any drug designated by law as contraband is a controlled substance.

controller value system. Parole board decision-making a system that emphasizes the functions of parole supervision and management.

control theories. Any explanations of a person's conduct which rely upon the cohesiveness of social ties and interpersonal obligations.

conventional model, conventional model with geographic considerations. Caseload assignment model in which probation or parole officers are assigned clients randomly. When geography is considered, assignments are based upon the travel time required for probation officers to meet with offender-clients regularly.

conversion. The unlawful assumption of the rights of ownership to someone else's property without their permission.

conveyance, legal. Any written document authorizing the transfer of property from one person to another.

convict. Adult who has been found guilty of a crime. An inmate of a jail or prison.

convict labor. Use of inmates to perform menial labor either inside or outside of prison.

convict subculture. The separate culture that exists in the prison, which has its own set of rewards and behaviors. The traditional culture is now being replaced by a violent gang culture.

conviction. State of being judged guilty of a crime in a court, either by the judge or jury.

Cook, Rufus R. Social reformer associated with Temperance Movement in mid-1800s, dedicated to reforming alcoholics charged with crimes.

Cooley, Charles Horton (circa 1875-1940). Sociologist who developed concept of primary and secondary groups. Primary groups are face-to-face groups with whom we have close interaction. Secondary groups might be football teams or college fraternities or sororities. Developed concept of the "looking-glass self," consisting of (1) our impressions of how others view us, (2) our interpretations of these impressions as either good or bad, and (3) our persistence or change in the behaviors eliciting the approval or disapproval of others.

"cools." Term used to describe female inmates by other inmates. "Cools" are those females with prior records who attempt to violate prison rules and remain undetected.

"copping out." Entering a plea of guilty, normally following plea bargaining. Copping-out ceremony consists of a series of questions that the judge asks defendants as to the voluntariness of their plea. Rule 11 of the Federal Rules of Criminal Procedure in the United States Code governs plea agreement hearings and the litany judges must pronounce in order for guilty pleas and "copping-out" to be accepted.

coroner. Physician who performs autopsies or examines corpses to determine the manner and time of death.

corporal punishment. The infliction of pain on the body by any device or method as a form of punishment.

corporate crime. Crime committed by wealthy or powerful persons in the course of their professions or occupations, but in which liability is distributed throughout organizational leadership. Includes price-fixing, fraudulent stock manipulation or insider trading, and establishment of illegal trusts. *See also* white collar crime.

corporate gangs. Coalitions of juveniles formed to emulate organized crime.

corpus delicti. The body of the crime made up of the *actus reus* and *mens rea.* The fact which proves that a crime has been committed.

correctional agencies. Any publicly or privately operated organization or facility responsible for the supervision of convicted offenders; may include prisons, penitentiaries, jails, community agencies, day programs, probation, and parole departments.

correctional client. Any person, usually a convicted offender, who is assigned to a community correctional facility for treatment and/or supervision.

correctional day program. Any publicly or privately operated supervision plan for convicted offenders; encompasses all community corrections agencies, including halfway houses, work release/study release plans, counseling centers, and probation/parole department activities.

Correctional facility, institution. Building or set of buildings designed to house convicted offenders or adjudicated delinquents.

correctional interest group. A group that interacts with a correctional organization to protect its investment in correctional activities.

correctionalism. Belief by Marxists and radical criminologists that most of the mainstream research conducted by criminologists is calculated to unmask the weak and powerless members of society so that they may be more effectively dealt with by the legal system.

correctional network. That collection of agencies and decision-makers which funds, manages, and regulates the correctional process.

correctional process. The sequence of decisions and activities through which convicted offenders are processed until the completion of sentence.

corrections. The aggregate of programs, services, facilities, and organizations responsible for the management of people who have been accused or convicted of criminal offenses.

corrections (correctional) officer. Guard in a prison who supervises or manages inmates.

corrections (correctional) officer task inventory. Cataloging of skills and tasks administered to correctional officers to determine which tasks are considered most important or vital to operation of institution or which skills have been transmitted during officer training.

corrective prevention. Focuses upon eliminating conditions that lead to or cause criminal behavior. Also called "primary prevention."

corrective works. Productive labor in Soviet corrective-labor colonies.

corroboration. Evidence that strengthens the evidence already given.

corruption. Behavior of public officials who accept money or other bribe for doing something they are under a duty to do anyway, to exercise a legitimate discretion for improper reasons.

cortical arousal. Activation of cerebral cortex, a structure of the brain responsible for higher intellectual functioning, information processing, and decision making.

cottage system. The design of many prisons built with a series of cottage-like living facilities that surround the administration and other general-use buildings. Design developed at the turn of the century to provide inmates with a homelike atmosphere that would preserve or create a family orientation.

Council of Europe. Formed in 1949, discusses issues including definitions of crime among different countries and extradition matters. Although Council activities have been largely informal, much international cooperation has been achieved to combat certain types of crime effectively.

counsel. A lawyer who represents a party in either a civil or criminal matter.

count. The general name given to each separate offense of which a person is accused in an indictment or an information.

counterculture. Associated with "hippie movement" of the 1960s, a complex of ideas and behavior patterns running counter to, or in opposition of the prevailing, traditional society.

counterfeiting. Any unauthorized manufacture of currency or any item of value, such as art work, precious coins, or artifacts.

county court. A court whose jurisdiction is limited to the boundaries of a county. May be either a court of special original jurisdiction or a court of general jurisdiction.

coup d'etat. An overthrow of a government or political entity by another political force or body.

court. Public judiciary body that applies the law to controversies and oversees the administration of justice.

court administrator. Any individual who controls the operations of the court in a particular jurisdiction. May be in charge of scheduling, juries, judicial assignment.

court, adolescent. A New York City-based type of juvenile court based upon informality and informal dispositions of delinquent conduct practiced during the 1960s and 1970s. Juveniles would often meet in judge's home, not in courtroom, to determine what is best for the juvenile. Often judge would prescribe victim restitution or community service in some form to promote juvenile offender accountability.

court calendar. Docket; the schedule of events for any judicial official.

court clerk. Court officer who may file pleadings, motions, or judgments, issue process, and may keep general records of court proceedings.

Court Delay Reduction Program. Commenced in Oregon, a program designed to facilitate the processing of criminal cases. A streamlined version of a speedy trial.

court disposition. The final outcome of a judicial proceeding, referring to the punishment imposed, such as probation, confinement to a jail or prison, community service, restitution, fines, or electronic monitoring and house arrest.

court, inferior. Any lower-level court with misdemeanor jurisdiction or limited jurisdiction such as a municipal court.

court, juvenile. *See* juvenile court.

court master. An official appointed by a judge to oversee the implementation of an institutional order.

court-martial, courts-martial. A military court convened by senior commanders under authority of the Uniform Code of Military Justice for the purpose of trying members of the armed forces accused of violations of the Code.

court of appellate jurisdiction. *See* appellate court.

court of common pleas. Any early court designed to try minor cases under prevailing common law.

court of equity. *See* chancery court.

court of general jurisdiction. *See* trial court of general jurisdiction.

court of general sessions. Similar to municipal courts, jurisdiction includes traffic violations and low-grade misdemeanor cases.

court of last resort. The last court that may hear a case. In the United States the Supreme Court is the court of last resort for many kinds of cases.

court of limited jurisdiction. *See* trial court of limited jurisdiction.

court of nonrecord. Any court that does not make a written record of a trial. Many juvenile courts are courts of nonrecord.

court of primary jurisdiction. Any court with originating jurisdiction to hear special types of cases.

court of record. Any court where a written record is kept of court proceedings.

court order. Any judicial proclamation or directive authorizing an officer to act on behalf of the court.

court packing. Any attempt by a United States President to influence the composition or political climate of the United States Supreme Court by nominating persons with political and policy views similar to the president.

court probation. A criminal court requirement that defendants fulfill specified conditions of behavior in lieu of a sentence of confinement, but without assignment to a probation agency's supervisory caseload.

court report, pre-trial or presentence. A document submitted by a person designated by the court before the disposition of cases. Contains a social history of a child and a plan of rehabilitation, treatment, and/or care.

court reporter. Court official who keeps a written word-for-word and/or tape-recorded record of court proceedings. *See also* transcript.

court, superior. Any court with the jurisdiction to try any felony case as well as any misdemeanor case.

court-ordered prison population reductions. Judicially mandated reductions in inmate populations of prisons and/or jails to comply with health and safety standards.

courtroom workgroup. The phrase denoting all parties in the adversary process who work together cooperatively to settle cases with the least amount of effort and conflict.

courtyard design. A recent prison design adaptable to a number of security settings; buildings are arranged around the perimeter of an internal open space.

covenant. Any legally binding document whereby two or more parties agree to abide by one or more conditions and fulfill particular obligations.

covert. Describes any activity which is undertaken in secret.

covert pathway. A path to a criminal career that begins with minor underhanded behavior and progresses to theft.

crack. A smokable form of purified cocaine that provides an immediate and powerful high.

crackdown. Concentrating police resources on a particular problem area, such as street-level drug dealing, in order to eradicate or displace criminal activity.

craft organization. A small and relatively permanent group of two or three thieves or confidence tricksters, each of whom plays a well-defined role in a specific type of crime that the group commits.

"creaming." Term to denote taking only the most qualified offenders for succeeding in a rehabilitative program. These offenders are low-risk, unlikely to reoffend.

creative sentencing. A broad class of punishments as alternatives to incarceration that are designed to fit the particular crimes. May involve community service, restitution, fines, becoming involved in educational or vocational training programs, or becoming affiliated with other "good works" activity.

credit card fraud. Use or attempted use of a credit card in order to obtain goods or services with intent to avoid payment.

Cressey, Donald. Criminologist who has advocated the consensus modes of crime, suggesting that the public generally defines what is criminal behavior, then reacts to such behavior as repugnant. The law is applicable to all persons, regardless of their status, and through enforcement and adherence of the law, the society persists over time.

crime. Act or omission prohibited by law, by one who is held accountable by that law. Consists of legality, *actus reus, mens rea*, consensus, harm, causation, and prescribed punishment.

crime analysis. Any systematic effort to track crimes in various jurisdictions over time, according to specified criteria, such as age, race/ethnicity.

Crime Classification System (CCS). System for collecting data on the severity of crimes and the effect those crimes have on victims.

Crime Clock. Graph used in *Uniform Crime Reports* to show number of specific types of crime committed according to some time standard such as minutes or seconds. Calculated by dividing number of crimes reported annually by number of minutes or seconds in a year.

crime construction. A process whereby the police and prosecutor interpret information concerning the accused's behavior in order to determine whether a crime has been committed and to ascertain whether the legal elements necessary to prosecute are present.

crime control, crime control model. A model of criminal justice that emphasizes containment of dangerous offenders and societal protection. Method of criminal justice system that assumes that freedom is so important that every effort must be made to repress crime. Emphasizes efficiency and the capacity to apprehend, try, convict, and dispose of a high proportion of offenders.

crime displacement. An effect of crime prevention efforts in which efforts to control crime in one area shift illegal activities to another.

crime fighter. The proactive police style stressing dealing with violent crimes and arresting dangerous criminals.

Crime Index. Eight serious crimes identified by the FBI in the *Uniform Crime Reports* to chart crime trends; includes arson, murder and nonnegligent manslaughter, motor vehicle theft, theft/larceny, robbery, aggravated assault, forcible rape, and burglary.

crime of passion. A spontaneous crime prompted by intense anger and emotion, often arising between spouses or lovers (e.g., during a heated argument, a wife may grab a nearby pistol and shoot her husband).

crime of violence. *See* violent crime.

crime prevention. Any overt activity conducted by individuals or groups to deter persons from committing crimes. May include "target hardening" by making businesses and residences more difficult to burglarize; neighborhood watch programs, in which neighborhood residents monitor streets during evening hours for suspicious persons or automobiles and equipping homes and businesses with devices to detect crime.

crime rate. The number of reported crimes divided by the number of persons in an area, often expressed as a rate of crimes per 100,000 persons.

Crime Stoppers. Organization commenced in Albuquerque, NM in 1976 offering rewards for information leading to the arrest and conviction of crime perpetrators.

Crime Watch, crime watch programs. A crime reduction and control program facilitated through greater police presence in neighborhoods and use of neighborhood observers. Any program utilizing a cooperative alliance between police and citizens to prevent and/or control crime.

crimen fals. Indicates the class of offenses that involve the perpetration of a falsehood (e.g., forgery, perjury, counterfeiting).

crime(s) against property. Nonviolent or passive crimes, where no physical harm is inflicted upon victims (includes vehicular theft, burglary, and larceny).

crime(s) against the person. Violent crimes, including all crimes committed in the victim's presence (includes murder, rape, robbery, and aggravated assault).

crimes known to the police. All criminal offenses that have been reported to police for which the police have sufficient evidence to believe that the crimes were actually committed.

crimes without victims. *See* victimless crime(s).

criminal. Any person found guilty of either a misdemeanor or a felony.

criminal action. Any action at law involving prosecution of someone for a crime.

Criminal attempt. Any act or omission constituting a substantial step in a course of conduct planned to culminate in the commission of a crime.

criminal bankruptcy. *See* bankruptcy fraud.

criminal behavior. Any conduct involving committing a crime. If a person has the *mens rea* and *actus reus* involved in a criminal act, then criminal behavior is suspected. Person is not a criminal until adjudicated or convicted.

criminal career incapacitation. An approach that would reduce crime by identifying and incarcerating classes of offenders who seem to be especially likely to remain active in crime.

criminal careers. A concept describing the onset of criminal behavior, the types and amount of crime committed, and the termination of such activity.

criminal charge. *See* charge.

criminal courts. Tribunals handling criminal cases. May also handle civil cases, and are then called criminal courts only in reference to the criminal cases that they handle.

criminal culture. A generalized set of values and standards followed by persons considering themselves to be criminals. A subcultural phenomenon, in which a group of criminals follow particular behavior patterns and support those patterns which happen to be criminal.

Criminal Division. The branch of the United States Justice Department that prosecutes federal criminal violations.

criminal gangs. One form of gang described by Richard Cloward and Lloyd Ohlin in their book, *Delinquency and Opportunity* (1960). Such gangs recruit members to engage in illegal activity, which is primary reason for existence. Members go through apprenticeship and learn how to commit crimes. Compare to conflict gangs and retreatist gangs for other gang goals.

criminal history information. Any background details of a person charged with a crime; refers to any legal actions, such as prior convictions, indictments, and arrests.

criminal homicide. The name the *Uniform Crime Reports* gives to all offenses causing the death of another person without justification or excuse.

criminal incident. In *National Crime Survey* terminology, a criminal event involving one or more victims and one or more offenders.

criminal intent. A necessary element of a crime. The evil intent, the *mens rea* associated with the commission of a crime.

Criminal Investigation Division (CID). Internal Revenue Service agency charged with responsibility of investigating violations of federal tax laws. Recommends prosecution against income tax law violators. Has arrest powers.

criminal justice. Interdisciplinary field studying nature and operations of organizations providing justice services to society.

Criminal Justice Act of 1948. Act that authorizes the compilation, maintenance, and distribution of information about crime in England and Wales for both adults and juveniles.

criminal justice agency. Any one of numerous organizations which comprise the processing of defendants charged with crimes; conventionally includes law enforcement, prosecution, the courts, and corrections.

criminal justice standards. Models, commentaries, recommendations for the revision of criminal justice procedures and practices.

criminal justice system or process. An interrelated set of agencies and organizations designed to control criminal behavior, to detect crime, and to apprehend, process, prosecute, punish, and/or rehabilitate criminal offenders. The processual aspect suggests that the interrelatedness implied by "system" may not be strong (e.g., judges might not contact jail or prison officials to inquire whether there is sufficient space whenever offenders are sentenced to jail or prison terms).

criminal justice wedding cake. A model of the criminal justice process in which criminal cases form a four-tiered hierarchy with a few celebrated cases at the top, and each succeeding layer increasing in size as its importance in the eyes of officials and the public diminishes.

criminal law. Body of law that defines criminal offenses and prescribes punishments (substantive law) and that delineates criminal procedure (procedural law).

criminal mischief, malicious mischief. *See* vandalism.

criminal negligence. A failure to exercise the degree of caution necessary to avoid being charged with a crime.

criminal nuisance. Any conduct that is unreasonable and endangers the health and safety of others.

criminal organization. *See* organized crime.

criminal procedure(s), proceedings. Rules of law governing the procedures by which crimes are investigated, prosecuted, adjudicated, and punished. Activities in a court of law undertaken to determine the guilt or innocence of an adult accused of a crime.

criminal punishment. *See* criminal sanctions.

criminal responsibility. Any liability incurred as the result of committing a crime.

criminal sanctions. The right of state to punish persons if they violate the rules set down in criminal codes. The punishment connected to the commission of specific offenses.

criminal subculture. A pattern of behaviors shared by persons engaged in illegal activity. Special jargon and gestures are used to convey meanings unknown to noncriminals. A standard of conduct and ideas within the mainstream culture that are adhered to by persons engaged in illegal activity.

criminal syndicalism. The crime of advocating violence as a means to accomplish political change.

criminal trespass. Crimes that are generally misdemeanors or violations, and are differentiated from burglary when breaking with criminal intent is absent or when the trespass involves property that has been fenced in a manner designated to exclude intruders.

criminal trial. An adversarial proceeding within a particular jurisdiction, in which a judicial determination of issues can be made, and in which a defendant's guilt or innocence can be decided impartially.

criminal typologies. Any categories devised by criminologists whereby offenders are classified. Once typologies have been generated, then theories can be fashioned to explain particular "types" of crime.

criminalistics. Use of scientific techniques derived from physics, chemistry, and biology to solve crimes. Also known as forensic science.

criminally insane. State of mind of being mentally incompetent, impaired to the extent that such an impairment may either induce or accompany violent and criminal conduct.

criminate. To make an accusation against another person that has committed a crime.

criminogenic, criminogenic factors. Variables thought to bring about criminal behavior in persons (e.g., imprisonment with other criminals is believed to be a criminogenic atmosphere).

criminologist. Professional or scholar who studies crime, criminal law, criminals and criminal behavior, examining the etiology of crime and criminal behavior and crime trends.

criminology. The study of crime, the science of crime and criminal behavior, the forms of criminal behavior, the causes of crime, the definition of criminality, and the societal reaction to crime. An empirical social-behavioral science which investigates crime, criminals, and criminal justice.

crisis intervention, crisis intervention center. Action or agency established to enable others to cope appropriately with stressful life situations.

critical criminology. A school of criminology that holds that criminal law and the criminal justice system have been created to control the poor and have-nots of society. Crimes are defined depending upon how much power is wielded in society by those defining crime.

critical ideologies, critical theory. Philosophies that challenge the dominant ideology, typically by analyzing social control systems as behaviors emerging from particular political and economic structures. *See also* radical criminology.

critical phase. Stage of investigation by law enforcement officers where case moves from investigatory to accusatory against specific suspects.

critical stage. Any decision or processing point made by criminal justice agencies or personnel that is so important that the United States Supreme Court has attached to it specific due process rights.

Crofton, Sir Walter (1815-1897). Director of Ireland's prison system during 1850s, considered "father of parole" in various European countries. Established system of early release for prisoners, issuing "tickets of leave" as an early version of parole.

cross-cultural corrections. *See* comparative corrections.

cross-examination. Questioning of one side's witnesses by the other side's attorney, either the prosecution or defense.

cross-projection. Sketch of a crime scene enabling investigators to determine the location of physical evidence on ceilings and walls in relation to floors. A forensics device to understand how and where the crime occurred.

cruel and unusual punishment. Prohibited by Eighth Amendment of United States Constitution. Vague and unspecified by United States Supreme Court, subjectively interpreted on case-by-case basis. The electric chair has been determined to be "cruel and unusual" punishment for purposes of administering the death penalty, whereas lethal injection has not been determined to be cruel and unusual.

culpable, culpability. State of mind of persons who have committed an act that makes them liable for prosecution for that act.

culprit. Perpetrator of a crime who has not been convicted.

cult. Small, closely-knit group loosely organized around some obscure religious dogma. Engages in ritualistic behavior, possibly murder and torture or sacrifice of animals.

cult killings. Murders that occur whenever members of religious sects or cults are ordered to kill by their leaders. Some cults engage in devil worship and human sacrifice whenever such types of killings occur.

cultural deviance theories. Explanations that posit that crime results from cultural values that permit, even demand, behavior in violation of the law.

cultural transmission theory, cultural transmission. Explanation emphasizing transmission of criminal behavior through socialization. Views delinquency as socially learned behavior transmitted from one generation to the next in disorganized urban areas.

culture. Shared norms and values of a society. Material and nonmaterial artifacts and language shared by members of a society.

culture conflict, culture conflict theory. View that two groups may clash when their conduct norms differ, resulting in criminal activity.

culture of poverty. Culture characterized by helplessness, cynicism, and mistrust of authority as represented by schools and police. Described by sociologist Oscar Lewis in 1966.

curative statute. A legal remedy to correct an earlier deficiency or defect in a previously enacted law.

curfew violation. A status offense for juveniles. The act of being a juvenile and in a public place after an hour where such a presence is prohibited by statute or ordinance.

curtilage. The fields attached to a house.

custodial care. Any caregiver. Care provider services associated with agencies that accommodate physically or mentally impaired persons.

custodial convenience. The principle of giving jailed inmates the minimum comforts required by law in order to contain the costs of incarceration.

custodial disposition. Outcome by juvenile judge following adjudication of juvenile as delinquent. Includes nonsecure custody (in a foster home, community agency, farm, camp), secure custody (in a detention center, industrial, reform school).

custodial model. Suggested ideal type of arrangement for housing female offenders, where main interest is confinement, containment, discipline, and uniformity.

custodian. A person to whom legal custody of a child has been transferred by the court, but not a person who has only physical custody. A person other than a parent or legal guardian who stands in *loco parentis* to the child or a person to whom legal custody of the child has been given by order of a court.

custody. Restraint of a person held on suspicion of committing or charged with a criminal offense; may include the use of handcuffs or leg irons or simple placement in a cell or locked room.

custody, close. Method of supervising inmates by continuous monitoring.

custody, discharge from. Legal release from custody. State statutes provide that a child shall be released to a parent, guardian, legal custodian unless it is impractical, undesirable, otherwise ordered by the court. The legal custodian serves as a guarantor that the child will appear in court and may be asked to sign a promise to that effect (this takes the place of bail in adult court).

custody, protective. Any effort by a law enforcement agency to protect someone who may be harmed by a defendant, a defendant's friends or associates. Witnesses may be placed in protective custody so that they cannot be silenced by death.

custody, taking into. The term used instead of "arrest" when a child is taken by a law enforcement officer. State codes and laws prescribe that a child may be taken into custody only under the following conditions: (1) whenever ordered by the judge for failure to obey a summons (petition); (2) whenever a law enforcement officer observes or has reasonable grounds to believe that the child has broken a federal, state, or local law and deems it in the public interest; (3) whenever the officer removes children from conditions that threaten their welfare; (4) when the child is believed to be a runaway from parents or legal custody; or (5) whenever the child has violated the conditions of probation.

customs. Social conventions, mores, and folkways. Common ways of behaving which are not ordinarily subject to legal sanctions. Also slang for United States Customs Service.

D

dactyloscopy. Use or study of fingerprints as means of identification.

Dahrendorf, Ralf. Conflict theorist who believed that society is organized into imperatively coordinated associations—two groups, one who possesses authority and uses it for social domination and the other who lacks authority and is dominated. Wrote *Class and Conflict in Industrial Society* (1959). Believed that social conflict is pervasive and persistent, that coercion is the controlling element in social organization, that every person is an element potentially possessing the power to change society, and that every society is changeable.

Dalton, Katharina. Wrote *The Premenstrual Syndrome* (1971) and pioneered explanation of female antisocial, aggressive behavior attributable to PMS (premenstrual syndrome).

Daly, Katherine. Feminist criminologist who regards criminology as mostly male-focused. Researches the relation between crime and the treatment of females in society. Attempts to balance the coverage of men and women in criminology.

damages. Monetary sums awarded to prevailing litigants in civil actions.

dangerous classes. Described by Terance Miethe and Charles Moore (1987) as young, single, poor urban males who are discriminated against by judges, prosecutors and others in the criminal justice system because of the belief that these persons pose a greater risk to society than those with different social characteristics.

dangerousness. Defined differently in several jurisdictions. Prior record of serious offenses. Potential to commit future crimes if released. Predicted risk of convicted offender or prison or jail inmate. Likelihood of inflicting harm upon others.

dangerous-tendency test. Any subjective method of determining whether particular kinds of speeches are contrary to the public good.

DARE. An acronym for Drug Abuse Resistance Education, a school-based anti-drug program initiated by the Los Angeles Police Department and now adopted throughout the United States

dark figure (of) crime. A metaphor that emphasizes the dangerous dimensions of crime that are never reported to the police (e.g., if someone steals a tire out of my pickup truck, the police won't recover it, so why report it? If my uncle rapes his daughter and no one knows about it, who will ever know? This is the dark figure of crime).

Darwin, Charles (1809-1882). Wrote *The Origin of Species* (1859), describing evolution. Several criminologists have used Darwin's theory to explain particular kinds of criminals who have particular sets of genetic attributes.

date rape. Sexual intercourse without the consent of the victim, perpetrated by a person the victim has selected for a social occasion. Victim may have engaged voluntarily in some form of intimate interaction but did not agree to sexual intercourse.

day fines. Monetary sanctions geared to the average daily income of convicted offenders in an effort to bring equity to the sentencing process, or to compensate victims or the state (for court costs and supervisory fees).

day parole or day pass. *See* work release.

day programs. Any of a variety of programs entailing daily but nonresidential supervision of juvenile offenders.

day reporting center. A community correctional center where offenders report daily to comply with conditions of their sentence, probation, parole program.

day watch. In the 1500s, citizens were obligated to perform day or night watch duties in their villages on a rotating basis, comparable to modern-day shiftwork. Watchmen would be expected to yell out a hue and cry in the event they detected crimes in progress or any other community disturbance.

de facto. "In fact," as a matter of fact.

de jure. "In law," as a matter of law.

de minimus. Minimal.

de novo. Anew, afresh, as if there had been no earlier decision.

deadly force. Any force used by law enforcement officers or any other person (as in citizen's arrests) to apprehend those suspected of or engaging in unlawful acts which may result in death or great bodily harm. *See also* fleeing felon rule.

deadly weapon. Any instrument designed to inflict serious bodily injury or death, or capable of being used for such a purpose.

death penalty. *See* capital punishment.

death-qualified jury. Term applied to a jury which has been selected on the basis of their willingness to impose the death penalty in a capital case if the situation warrants such a decision. Implies exclusion of persons from possible jury duty who could not vote for a death penalty even if defendant were guilty of capital crime.

death row. Arrangement of prison cells where inmates who have been sentenced to death are housed.

death squads. Politically sponsored groups or troops who are ordered to destroy political opponents or commit acts of terrorism against others for a variety of reasons.

death warrant. A written document authorizing a time and place for the execution of a convicted offender sentenced to death for a capital offense.

debtor's prisons. Incarcerative facilities established in Middle Ages in England where people owing money were held until they or their friends paid their debts.

decarceration. Prohibition of detention for juveniles. Removal of inmates from prisons or jails.

decedent. Person who has died recently.

deception, police. *See* entrapment.

decision. A court decree or resolution of an issue.

declaration. An utterance, statement.

declaratory judgment. A judicial resolution of a dispute, wherein the facts have been decided and a conclusion has been reached concerning the matter.

deconstructionism. The theory that terms used in everyday language are value-laden, as are rules and regulations. They reflect the inequities of the social structure, which is influenced directly by capitalism; thus, this phenomenon is a type of radical criminology.

decoy. Person, sometimes an undercover officer, who is in a position to be a crime victim, when in fact, the "victim" is under surveillance by other officers who will move in and make an arrest once a crime is attempted against the decoy.

decree. A judicial proclamation, decision, judgment.

decriminalization, decriminalize. Legislative action whereby an act or omission, formerly criminal, is made non-criminal and without punitive sanctions.

deface. To mar or damage the surface of property.

defame. To commit slander against another. To speak falsely or unduly critically about another.

default. To fail to make good on an agreement. A failure to appear (in court).

defeminization. Process whereby policewomen become enculturated into the police profession at the expense of their feminine identity.

defendant. Person against whom a criminal proceeding is pending.

defendant dispositions. Any one of several adjudication and dispositional options available to a judge at various places during a criminal proceeding, ranging from dismissal of the case to long-term imprisonment.

defendant's sentencing memorandum. Version of events leading to conviction offense in the words of the convicted offender. Memorandum may be submitted together with victim impact statement.

defense. A response by defendants in criminal law or civil cases. May consist only of a denial of the factual allegations of the prosecution (in a criminal case) or of the plaintiff (in a civil case). If defense offers new factual allegations in an effort to negate the charges, this is called an affirmative defense.

defense attorney, counsel. A lawyer who represents a client accused of a crime.

defense-of-life standard. Criteria by which law enforcement officers decide whether to use deadly force in effecting arrest of criminal suspects. Involves discretion whether officer's life or the lives of others are in jeopardy as the result of suspect's actions. Standard established in leading case of *Tennessee v. Garner* (1985).

defenses to criminal charges. Includes claims based upon personal, special and procedural considerations that defendants should not be held accountable for their actions, even though they may have acted in violation of the criminal laws.

defensible space. The principle that crime prevention can be achieved through modifying the physical environment to reduce the opportunity criminals have to commit crime. Opportunities for surveillance that the physical environment offers. *See also* target-hardening.

deferred sentencing. A mechanism whereby a judge postpones sentencing an offender until other actions have occurred. Sometimes, offenders are placed on various types of probation and if their behavior is acceptable over a given time period, then any incarcerative penalties are waived.

defounding. Artificially, through statistical means, reducing felonies to misdemeanors in cases where the crimes have remained unsolved.

defraud. To falsely deal with another; to cheat someone out of property or something of value by deviousness.

degenerate anomalies. According to Cesare Lombroso, the primitive physical characteristics that make criminals animalistic and savage.

deinstitutionalization. Providing programs in community-based settings instead of institutional ones.

deinsitutionalization of status offenses (DSO). Movement to remove non-delinquent juveniles from secure facilities by eliminating status offenses from the delinquency category and removing juveniles from or precluding their confinement in juvenile correction facilities. Process of removing status offenses from jurisdiction of juvenile court.

delegated sentencing policy. The practice by the legislature of permitting or authorizing the construction of sentencing policy by a group other than itself.

deliberation. *See* premeditation.

delicts. Serious offenses, comparable to property crimes, felonies in United States jurisdictions. Used by French government as a crime category.

delinquent, delinquent act, delinquent child, delinquency. Child who has committed an offense that would be a crime if committed by an adult. In some states, status offenses are considered delinquent conduct and subject to identical punishments, including incarceration. Offense itself is the delinquent act. Child of not more than a specified age who has violated criminal laws or engages in disobedient, indecent or immoral conduct, and is in need of treatment, rehabilitation, or supervision. Delinquency is status acquired through an adjudicatory proceeding by juvenile court.

delirium tremens. A reaction among chronic alcoholics when deprived of alcohol; reaction lasts several days and is manifested by vomiting, nausea, and violent cramping.

delit. A particular grade or classification of crime (e.g., Class A, B, and C misdemeanors or felonies).

delusion. A psychological malady characterized by irrational beliefs about the real world.

demeanor. Way in which persons outwardly manifest themselves to others.

dementia. Mental impairment.

demonstration, public. A public gathering of varying size, dedicated to promoting a particular view or ideology by various means, such as parading or carrying placards.

demonstrative evidence. Material related to a crime that is apparent to the senses, in contrast to material presented by the testimony of other persons.

demur, demurrer. Document challenging the legal sufficiency of a complaint or an indictment. Taking exception, making an objection.

demystify. Process whereby Marxists unmask the true purpose of the capitalist system's rules and laws.

denial of injury. Technique of neutralization that claims no one is hurt by an offender's crime, even if it technically violates the law.

denial of responsibility. Technique of neutralization involving the denial of personal responsibility for actions that violate criminal laws.

denial of the victim. Technique of neutralization that claims that a crime is justified as a rightful retaliation against the victim.

density. Number of persons per square mile in a given geographical area.

deny. A plea of "not guilty" in juvenile proceedings.

Department of Justice, United States. Organization responsible for prosecuting federal law violators, headed by attorney general of United States. Oversees Federal Bureau of Investigation and the Drug Enforcement Administration.

dependency. Legal status of juveniles over whom juvenile court has assumed jurisdiction because the court has found their care by parents or guardians to be short of the standard of reasonable and proper care.

dependent, dependent child. A child adjudged by the juvenile court to be without parent, guardian, or custodian. Child needs special care and treatment because the parent, guardian, or custodian is unable to provide for his or her physical or mental condition. The parents, guardian, or custodian desire to be relieved of legal custody for good cause. The child is without necessary care or support through no fault of the parents, guardian, or custodian.

deponent. Person who gives testimony through a deposition. If someone cannot physically attend a trial and give testimony under oath, then a deposition is taken and read into the court record.

deport, deportation. Banishment from a country. Aliens who commit crimes in the United States may be deported.

deposition. A sworn written record of oral testimony.

depraved mind. A serious moral deficiency. The highest level of malice.

deprived child. One who is without proper parental care or control, subsistence, education as required by law, or other care or control necessary for his or her physical, mental, or emotional health or morals, whose deprivation is not due primarily to the lack of financial means of the parents, guardians, or other custodians.

deprivation model. Suggested method of prisonization based on the idea that the prisoner's subculture stems from the way other inmates adapt to the severe psychological and physical losses imposed by imprisonment.

deputy, deputy sheriff. A subordinate to the sheriff, usually of a county. A law enforcement officer at the county level.

derivative evidence. Information obtained as the result of previously discovered evidence (e.g., residue from an automobile tire may suggest that a crime was committed in a part of the city where such residue is found and police discover subsequent "derivative" evidence by investigating that area).

descriptive guidelines. Sentencing guidelines in which the sentence values are determined by studying the normal patterns for certain offenses and offender types. The sentence values in this case describe past practice.

desert-based sentences. Sentences where the length is based upon the seriousness of the criminal act and not the personal characteristics of the defendant or the deterrent impact of the law.

desert model. *See* justice model.

desertion. Abandonment.

design capacity. Optimum number of inmates that architects originally intended to be housed or accommodated by jail or prison.

desistance. *See* aging-out phenomenon.

detainee. Person held in local or very short-term confinement while awaiting consideration for pretrial release or an initial appearance for arraignment.

detainer. A hold order against persons incarcerated in another jurisdiction, which seeks, upon their release from current confinement, to take them into custody to answer other criminal charges.

detainer warrants. Notices of criminal charges or unserved sentences pending against prisoners, usually authorized by one jurisdiction to be served on prisoners held in other jurisdictions. After prisoners serve their sentences in one jurisdiction, they are usually transferred under detainer warrants to other jurisdictions where charges are pending against them.

detective. Police agency assigned to investigate crimes after they have been reported. A special police officer who has been trained to gather evidence and identify perpetrators.

detector. Probation/parole officer work-role orientation in which probation/parole officer attempts to identify troublesome clients or those who are most likely to pose high community risk.

detention. Period of temporary custody of juveniles before their case dispositions.

detention center. Any publicly or privately operated confinement facility for either adults or juveniles; usually a secure facility designed to hold individuals for short periods, such as awaiting trial on criminal charges.

detention hearing. Judicial or quasi-judicial proceeding held to determine whether or not it is appropriate to continue to hold a juvenile in a shelter facility.

deter. To discourage criminals from committing crimes.

determinate sentencing. Sanctioning scheme in which court sentences offender to incarceration for fixed period, and which must be served in full and without parole intervention, less any good time earned in prison.

determinism. Concept holding that persons do not have a free will but rather are subject to the influence of various forces over which they have little or no control.

deterrence, general or specific. Actions that are designed to prevent crime before it occurs by threatening severe criminal penalties or sanctions. May include safety measures to discourage potential lawbreakers such as elaborate security systems, electronic monitoring, and greater police officer visibility. Andenaes (1975) defines deterrence as influencing by fear, where fear is of apprehension and punishment.

deterrence model. Model of crime control based upon the philosophy that stronger penalties imposed on criminals will cause potential offenders to refrain from crime. Three requirements must exist before any deterrence is successful: (1) severity of punishment, (2) certainty of punishment, and (3) swiftness of punishment.

detoxification, detoxification center. Process whereby persons can be cured of alcoholism or drug abuse. Place where persons are treated for alcohol or drug dependency.

developmental theory. *See* cognitive development theory.

deviance. Conduct which departs from accepted codes expected by society or a particular group. Also includes illegal behavior prohibited by statute.

diagnosis or classification center. Functional unit within a correctional institution, or a separate facility, that holds persons kept in custody in order to determine to which correctional facility or program they should be committed.

dialed number recorders. Devices that can be used to identify numbers dialed on a telephone by printing out the numbers associated with sounds produced when someone dials a particular number.

dicta. Written portions of a judicial opinion that are not part of the actual ruling or holding of the court, and which therefore are not legally binding precedents for future court decisions.

Diderot, Denis (1713-1784). Anarchist, French novelist, penal reformer. Wrote about cruel and inhuman punishments in French prisons.

differential association-reinforcement. Theory of criminality based upon the incorporation of psychological learning theory and differential association with social learning theory. Criminal behavior is learned through associations and is contained or discontinued as a result of positive or negative reinforcements.

differential association theory. Edwin Sutherland's theory of deviance and criminality through associations with others who are deviant or criminal. Theory includes dimensions of frequency, duration, priority, and intensity; persons become criminal or delinquent because of a preponderance of learned definitions that are favorable to violating the law over learned definitions unfavorable to it.

differential identification theory. A theory that people engage in criminal or delinquent behavior because they identify with real or imaginary persons from whose perspective their crime or delinquency seems acceptable.

differential involvement hypothesis. The hypothesis that racially different incarceration rates are caused by different levels of involvement of different racial groups in specific types of crime.

differential opportunity theory. Explanation of criminality linking concepts of anomie and differential association by analyzing both the legitimate and illegitimate means of attaining goals (e.g., theft or hard work) available to persons. Suggests that these means are unequally distributed.

differential response. A police patrol strategy that prioritizes calls for service and assigns various response options.

diffusion of benefits. An effect that occurs when an effort to control one type of crime has the unexpected benefit of reducing the incidence of another.

diffusion of responsibility. The situation that exists among groups of witnesses to an emergency or a crime, when people believe that someone should act but that it need not be themselves because other potential helpers are present.

diffusion of treatment. Whenever the treatment given to the experimental group is spread to the control group by treatment group subjects (e.g., a professor hands out sample tests to one section of a class but not to the other; students who get the sample test make copies and give them to their friends in the control group). May result in a failure to observe any differences between groups and thus falsely conclude that the treatment has no effect.

diplomatic immunity. Protection from prosecution enjoyed by various envoys or diplomats from foreign countries.

dipsomania. Urge toward intoxication. Alcoholism.

direct control. External controls that depend on rules, restrictions and punishments.

direct costs. Operating expenses such as salary, fringe benefits, program services, equipment and contractual costs, plus expenses and capital costs.

direct evidence. Evidence offered by an eyewitness who testifies to what was seen or heard.

direct examination. Questioning by attorney of one's own (prosecution or defense) witness during a trial.

direct loss. The result of a crime in which a stock of useful things is reduced, as in arson or vandalism.

direct sentencing policy. The construction of sentencing policy directly by the legislature.

direct supervision jails. Temporary confinement facilities that eliminate many of the traditional barriers between inmates and correctional staff, allowing staff members the opportunity for greater interaction within, and control over, residents.

directed patrol. A police patrol strategy designed to direct resources proactively in high-crime areas.

directed verdict. Order by court declaring that the prosecution has failed to produce sufficient evidence to show defendant guilt beyond a reasonable doubt.

disability. Any physical or mental impairment.

discharge. To release a convicted offender from supervision and/or confinement.

disciplinary punishment. Any punishment imposed on an inmate for violating institutional

rules. May include solitary confinement for a prolonged period, a withdrawal of privileges for a specified time.

disclaimer. Any denial or statement attempting to absolve oneself of responsibility for the operation or performance of a product.

disclosure of presentence investigation report. The practice of sharing the contents of the presentence investigation report with defendant and counsel.

discouragement. An effect that occurs when an effort made to eliminate one type of crime also controls others because it reduces the value of criminal activity by limiting access to desirable targets (e.g., pickpocketing). By placing more patrol officers on subway trains to discourage muggings, you have more police to prevent pickpocketing (nonviolent theft) and this discourages assaults, muggings, and other violent theft.

discovery. Procedure where prosecution shares information with defense attorney and defendant. Specific types of information are made available to defendant before trial, including results of any tests conducted, psychiatric reports, transcripts or tape-recorded statements made by the defendant. Also known as "Brady materials" after a specific court case.

discretion, general. In the criminal justice system, authority to make decisions based upon one's own judgment rather than on specified rules. Result may be inconsistent handling of offenders as well as positive actions tailored to individual circumstances.

discretion, police. In accordance with the dictates of an intuitive grasp of situational exigencies, police have authority to use force to enforce the law, if, in the officer's opinion, the situation demands it. *See also* legal approach, behavioral approach, and organizational approach.

discretionary release. Release of inmates from incarceration at the discretion of parole boards within the boundaries set by the sentence and the penal law.

discretionary review. Form of appellate court review of lower court decisions that is not mandatory but occurs at the option of the appellate court.

discriminatory (discriminative) power. A measure of each item's ability to separate persons who possess a characteristic to a high degree from those who possess the same characteristic to a low degree. Used in determining the internal consistency and/or reliability of an attitudinal measure.

disfranchisement. Withdrawing privileges and status from particular individuals, including prisoners who lose certain rights as the result of being convicted of a crime.

disinter, disinterment. The act of exhuming a previously buried body.

dismissal. A decision by a judicial officer to terminate a case without a determination of guilt or innocence.

dismissal for want of prosecution. Judicial decision to terminate proceedings against a criminal suspect because of the failure of prosecutors to present a case against the accused.

dismissal in the interests of justice. A judicial decision to terminate proceedings against a criminal defendant because such a prosecution is unwarranted, evidence is nonexistent, or a wrongful prosecution has been discovered and must be corrected.

disorderly conduct. Any illegal behavior that disturbs the public peace or order.

displacement. The transferral of an emotion, such as anger, to an object, person or action other than that which caused the emotion.

displacement effect. A change in the pattern of crime without a reduction in the total amount of crime that results from criminals' efforts to avoid punishment. Displacement may be from one target to another, from one area to another, or from one kind of offense to another.

disposition. Action by criminal or juvenile justice court or agency signifying that a portion of the justice process is completed and jurisdiction is relinquished or transferred to another agency or signifying that a decision has been reached on one aspect of a case and a different aspect comes under consideration, requiring a different kind of decision.

disposition hearing. Hearing in juvenile court, conducted after an adjudicatory hearing and a finding of delinquency, status offender, dependent/neglected, to determine the most appropriate punishment/placement/treatment for the juvenile.

disputatiousness. In the subculture of violence, it is considered appropriate behavior for a person who has been offended to seek satisfaction through violent means.

dispute resolution centers. Informal hearing infrastructures designed to mediate interpersonal disputes without the need for more formal arrangements of criminal trial courts.

disqualification. Withdrawing or removing someone from a proceeding. *See also* recusal.

dissent, dissenting opinion. Any judicial opinion disavowing or attacking the decision of a collegial court.

dissident. Someone holding a contrary view from the majority.

dissolve. To render null and void.

district attorney. City, county, state prosecutor who is charged with bringing offenders to justice and enforcing the laws of the state.

district courts. Trial courts at the state or federal level with general and original jurisdiction. Boundaries of their venue do not conform to standard political unit boundaries, but generally include several states or counties.

distringas writ. Writ issued to sheriff to seize defendant's goods as well as defendant. Designed so that sheriff can have defendant in custody when it is time for defendant to appear before a judicial officer.

disturbing the peace. Any act that disrupts the public decorum or neighborhood equilibrium; any noise or physical altercations sufficiently loud to warrant police officers to intercede.

diversion. Removing a case from the criminal justice system, while a defendant is required to comply with various conditions (e.g., attending a school for drunk drivers, undergoing counseling, performing community service). May result in expungement of record. Conditional removal of the prosecution of a case prior to its adjudication, usually as the result of an arrangement between the prosecutor and judge.

diversion, juvenile. Directing of youths from juvenile justice system, where they can remain with their families or guardians, attend school, and be subject to limited supervision on a regular basis by a juvenile probation officer.

diversion program(s). One of several programs preceding formal court adjudication of charges against defendants; defendants participate in therapeutic, educational, other helping programs. *See also* diversion.

diversion to civil court. Procedure whereby a crime is reduced in seriousness to that of a tort action and placed for disposition in civil court rather than in criminal court. *See also* alternative dispute resolution.

diversity jurisdiction. Type of jurisdiction used by United States Supreme Court when attempting to resolve suits between residents of different states.

divertee. Person who participates in a diversion program or who is otherwise granted diversion.

divestiture of jurisdiction. Juvenile court relinquishment of control over certain types of juveniles, such as status offenders.

dizygotic (DZ) twins. Fraternal twins who develop from two separate eggs fertilized at the same time. *See also* monozygotic twins.

DNA fingerprinting. Deoxyribonucleic acid (DNA) is an essential component of all living matter which carries hereditary patterning. Suspects can be detected according to their unique DNA patterning, as each person has a different DNA pattern. Similar to fingerprint identification, in which no two persons have identical fingerprints.

DNA profiling. The identification of criminal suspects by matching DNA samples taken from their person with specimens found at crime scenes.

DOB. Date of birth. Used in various documents at time of booking, arrest.

docket. A court record of the cases scheduled to appear before the court.

doctrine of *parens patriae. See parens patriae.*

document. Any written paper, official or unofficial, having potential evidentiary importance.

documentary evidence. Any written evidence.

document examiner. Expert who can determine the authenticity of a writing or written document.

Doe, John or Jane. Anonymous name given to an unidentified body; also name given to someone who wishes to remain anonymous.

domestic relations courts. Courts dealing with family problems, divorce, separations.

domestic violence. Any spousal altercation or intrafamilial conflict of sufficient nature to justify law enforcement intervention; spousal abuse is most frequently cited example. May involve parent-child conflict, either physical or psychological.

double-bunking. Placing two or more inmates in a cell originally designed to accommodate one inmate.

double-celling. *See* double-bunking.

double jeopardy. Subjecting persons to prosecution more than once in the same jurisdiction for the same offense, usually without new or vital evidence. Prohibited by the Fifth Amendment.

double marginality. The social burden African-American police officers carry by being both minority group members and law enforcement officers.

drift, drift theory. David Matza's term denoting a state of limbo in which youths move in and out of delinquency and in which their lifestyles embrace both conventional and deviant values.

driving record. Department of Motor Vehicles for particular jurisdiction maintains record of one's driving, number and type of tickets issued, driver's license suspensions, revocations.

driving while intoxicated (DWI) or driving under the influence (DUI). Operating a motorized vehicle under the influence of alcohol.

dropsy testimony. Perjured testimony made by police officers in an attempt to solidify a weak case. Defendants are often alleged to have "dropped" drugs on ground during automobile stop for traffic violation; hence, "dropsy testimony." More prevalent after exclusionary rule became search and seizure standard following case of *Mapp v. Ohio* (1963).

drug. Any chemical substance used for psychological or physical purposes.

drug abuse, drug abuse violations. Any offenses involving the use, possession, manufacture, or distribution of illegal or controlled substances (e.g., marijuana, cocaine or crack, heroin, and methamphetamine).

drug addiction. Any dependency upon a given substance, including narcotics, alcohol, prescription medicines.

drug courier profile. Way of identifying drug runners based on their personal characteristics. Police may stop and question individuals based upon the way they fit the characteristics contained in the profile.

drug czar. A cabinet-level position, originally created during the Reagan presidency, that functions to organize federal drug-fighting efforts.

Drug Enforcement Administration (DEA). Agency established to investigate violations of all federal drug trafficking laws. Regulates the legal manufacture of drugs and other controlled substances.

drug testing. Various means for determining whether someone has consumed various types of drugs in a recent period of time.

Drug Use Forecasting. A Department of Justice program which compiles data on drug use by arrestees in selected cities.

drunkard. One who is drunk in public.

drunkenness. Public intoxication other than driving under the influence.

druzhiny. People's volunteers functioned as tribunals for Soviet offenders.

dual citizenship. Possessing citizenship in two or more jurisdictions.

dual court system. A system consisting of a separate judicial structure for each state in addition to a national structure. Each case is tried in a court of the same jurisdiction as that of the law or laws broken.

dual procedure offense. Similar to British hybrid offenses, in which the prosecutor decides whether prosecution should proceed either by summary conviction or by indictment.

DUBAL. Driving with an unlawful blood alcohol level.

duces tecum. Legal term and court order obligating an attorney to bring to court all materials related to a given piece of evidence.

ducking stool. Sixteenth-century colonial corporal punishment device. Offender is placed in a chair at end of long lever and dunked in nearby pond until almost drowned. Punishment often for gossiping or wife-beating.

dueling. Illegal practice of settling an argument between two parties by determining a time and place where parties will fight to the death. In eighteenth and nineteenth centuries, dueling was accomplished by pistols or swords.

due process. Basic constitutional right to a fair trial, presumption of innocence until guilt is proven beyond a reasonable doubt, the opportunity to be heard, to be aware of a matter that is pending, to make an informed choice whether to acquiesce or contest, and to provide the reasons for such a choice before a judicial official. Actual due process rights include timely notice of a hearing or trial that informs the accused of charges, the opportunity to confront one's accusers and to present evidence on one's own behalf before an impartial jury or judge, the presumption of innocence under which guilt must be proved by legally obtained evidence and the verdict must be supported by the evidence presented, the right of accused persons to be warned of their constitutional rights at the earliest stage of the criminal process, protection against self-incrimination, assistance of counsel at every critical stage of the criminal process, and the guarantee that individuals will not be tried more than once for the same offense.

due process model. Model of the criminal justice system that assumes that freedom is so important that every effort must be made to ensure that criminal justice decisions are based on reliable information. Emphasizes the adversarial process, the rights of defendants, and formal decision-making procedures.

due process of law. A right guaranteed by the Fifth, Sixth, and Fourteenth Amendments of the United States Constitution, and generally understood to mean the due course of legal proceedings according to the rules and forms which have been established for the protection of private rights. *See also* due process.

Dugdale, Richard (1841-1883). Wrote *The Jukes: A Study in Crime, Pauperism, Disease and Herdity* (1877), advocating that heredity is responsible for the genetic transmission of criminal traits.

dumdum. Bullet designed to expand greatly upon impact, thus causing severe tissue damage. Illegal to use or possess.

duress. Affirmative defense used by defendants to show lack of criminal intent, alleging force, psychological or physical, from others as stimulus for otherwise criminal conduct.

duress and consent. Any unlawful constraints exercised upon individuals forcing them to do some act that would not have been done otherwise.

Durham rule. Insanity test requiring that it be shown that accused person had either a mental disease or defect at the time a criminal act was committed; such a showing would cause the accused not to have to requiste *mens rea*, and thus criminal responsibility and liability could be avoided.

Durkheim, Emile (1858-1917). French sociologist and positivist influenced by Auguste Comte. Believed crime to be prevalent as an integral part of human nature and even functional; thus, crime is inevitable. Wrote *Suicide*, an elaborate theoretical scheme about various types of suicide originating from different conditions, such as anomie and either close, loose attachments, social bonds with others in society. Wrote *The Division of Labor in Society*, wherein he described various types of society, growing from rural, mechanistic society to more complex organic systems characteristic of urban environments.

duty. An obligation that a person has by law or contract.

DWI. *See* driving while intoxicated.

dyathanasia. Mercy killing by withdrawal of life support machinery from a dying patient.

Dyer act. Act prohibiting interstate transportation of stolen motor vehicles.

E

early onset. A term referring to the assumption that a criminal career begins early in life and that people who are deviant at a very young age are the ones most likely to persist in crime.

early release. *See* parole.

eavesdropping. Surveillance of various forms designed to intercept communications between others.

Ebbinghous, Hermann (1850-1909). Psychologist who sought to quantify intelligence by designing tests to measure one's ability to memorize. Believed a correlation exists between criminality and IQ.

ecclesiastical. Pertaining to religious laws or institutions.

economic compulsive behavior. Behavior that occurs when drug users resort to violence to gain funds to support their drug habit.

economic crime. An act in violation of the criminal law designed to bring financial gain to offenders.

economism. Policy of controlling white-collar crime through monetary incentives and sanctions.

ecotage. Civil disobedience targeting environmental agencies or companies that exploit natural resources.

ectomorph. Body type described by Sheldon. Person is thin, sensitive, delicate.

educational release. Temporary unescorted leaves from prison or jail to attend courses at nearby schools. *See also* work release.

educator. *See* enabler.

EFT crime. Any violation of the law that would not have occurred except for the presence of an electronic fund transfer system.

elaboration. A method of introducing other variables to the analysis in order to determine the links between the independent and dependent variables.

electrocution. Means whereby offenders convicted of murder and sentenced to death are killed. Convicted offenders are strapped into chairs wired to an electrical power terminal and given a prolonged jolt of electricity that will kill them.

electroencephalogram (EEG). A device that can record the electronic impulses given off by the brain, commonly called brain waves.

electronic monitoring, electronic monitoring devices. The use of electronic devices (usually anklets or wristlets) which emit electronic signals to monitor offenders, probationers, and parolees. The purpose of their use is to monitor an offender's presence in a given environment where the offender is required to remain or to verify the offender's whereabouts.

element of the offense. Any conduct, circumstance, condition, or state of mind which in combination with other conduct, circumstances, conditions, states of mind constitutes an unlawful act.

Elizabeth Fry Center. Diversion program for female offenders operated in San Francisco, California.

Elliott, Delbert. Developed integrated theory together with David Huizinga and Suzanne Ageton. Persons experience perceptions of strain, suffer from inadequate socialization, and live in socially disorganized areas. When these factors exist simultaneously, youths develop weak bonds with conventional groups and some seek out delinquent persons to emulate, to receive approval. Eventual bonding with delinquent peer groups completes the process whereby one becomes a delinquent. Extensively discussed in *Explaining Delinquency and Drug Use* (1985).

Elmira Reformatory. First true reformatory, built in 1876. First superintendent was Zebulon Brockway, a rehabilitation and reformation advocate. Promoted educational training and cultivation of vocational skills and believed in prisoner reformation. Questionably successful.

emancipation. Giving up the care, custody, welfare, and financial support of a minor child by renouncing parental duties.

embargo. Any governmental effort to restrict the flow of commerce, usually from a foreign country.

embezzlement. Crime involving withholding or withdrawing, converting, or misappropriating, without consent, funds entrusted to an agent, such as a bank or bank officer.

emergency release procedures. A legal means to reduce prison population when it reaches a certain size (usually defined as a percent of capacity). Will permit earlier than normal consideration for parole, or earlier than specified mandatory release dates through the award of additional good time.

emergency searches. Searches conducted by police officers without a warrant, that are justified on the basis of some immediate and overriding need, such as public safety, the likely escape of a dangerous suspect, the removal or destruction of evidence.

eminent domain. Legal authorization for government to commandeer private property for its own use.

emotional numbing. Condition in which officers distance themselves from a stressful incident and make an effort not to feel anything. They deny having an emotional component, and therefore give the appearance that they are in a state of shock, but usually say, however, that they are in control and are having no problems dealing with the situation.

empirical data. Data based upon observation, experience, experiment.

employee assistance program. Program used by some police departments to help police officers or their family members with problems such as drug abuse, alcoholism, emotional difficulties.

employment prison. Prison for low-risk offenders. Inmates work at jobs outside the prison dur-

ing the day but must return to prison after work. *See also* work release.

empowerment. Empowerment is the essence of both organizational mission and value statements. Permits employees the latitude to perform at their highest levels, authorizing them to make any decisions within the scope of their work or employment.

en banc. "In the bench." Refers to a session of the court, usually an appellate court, where all of the judges assigned to the court participate.

enabler. Probation/parole officer who seeks to instruct and assist offenders to deal with problems as they arise in the community; assists clients to find support groups and necessary therapy to overcome personal problems.

endomorph. Body type described by Sheldon. Person is fat, soft, plump, jolly.

enforcement. *See* law enforcement.

enforcement costs. The financial cost of crime that results from the money spent on various criminal justice agencies.

enforcer. Probation/parole officer work-role orientation in which officers see themselves as enforcement officers charged with regulating client behaviors.

Engels, Friedrich (1820-1895). Associate of Karl Marx who collaborated in the formulation of economic determinism and the conflict perspective and in writing of the *Communist Manifesto* (1848). Wrote *The Condition of the Working Class in England* in 1844. A German social revolutionary and member of the Communist League who viewed society as a class struggle between those who own the means of production (the bourgeoisie) and those who work for them (the proletariat). Conflict arises between these two classes because of conflicting vested interests—profit vs. survival. Crime is also a function of social demoralization: workers become caught up in a milieu of frustration leading to violence and crime; thus, the capitalist system turns workers into criminals despite their will to act in conventional ways.

English common law. *See* common law.

English Penal Servitude Act. Act passed by British Parliament in 1853 authorizing establishment of rehabilitative programs for inmates and gradually eliminating transportation as a form of punishment.

enterprise syndicate. An organized crime group that profits from the sale of illegal goods and services, such as narcotics, pornography, and prostitution.

entrapment. Activity by law enforcement officers which suggests, encourages, or aids others in the commission of crimes that would ordinarily not have occurred without officer intervention. Defense used by defendants to show otherwise criminal act would not have occurred without police intervention, assistance, and/or encouragement.

entrepreneur. One willing to take risks for profit in the marketplace.

entry, gaining entry. Accessing any automobile, home or business, legally or otherwise.

episodic criminal. Person who only occasionally engages in criminal conduct.

epistemology. The study of the foundations of knowledge, especially with reference to its limits and validity.

equal employment opportunity. The policy of selection and advancement of personnel on the basis of merit, without regard to criteria such as race or gender. Equal Employment Opportunity Commission (EEOC) created in 1964 by Congress under Title VII of the Civil Rights Act of 1964 to enforce civil rights of employees.

equal protection. Clause of Fourteenth Amendment of United States Constitution guaranteeing to all citizens equal protection of the law, without regard to race, color, gender, class, origin, religion.

equity. The concept that the relationships between men, women, and society should be just and fair and in accordance with contemporary morality.

equivalent group hypothesis. Similar to the victimization explanation of crime that suggests a high-risk lifestyle places certain persons in positions where they may be victimized more easily. This notion is that victims and criminals share similar characteristics because they are not actually separate groups; thus, retaliation by one victimized group or person is great because both victim and offender are equivalent in their power to victimize each other.

error in fact. Any error made in a court of law which may or may not affect a judicial decision or judgment.

error in law. Any error made by the court which may affect the case outcome (e.g., permitting the prosecution to show numerous bloody photographs of a crime scene to inflame the jury and enhance a defendant's likelihood of being convicted and sentenced harshly). *See also* reversible error, harmless error.

escape. Any flight of a confined person from any type of criminal supervision facility, such as a jail or prison, community corrections agency, probation or parole department, halfway house, or electronic monitoring/house arrest program.

espionage. Illegal acquisition of secret government information by a citizen who transmits such information to a foreign power. *See also* industrial espionage.

essoiuner. Person who appears in court to present an excuse for the absence of the defendant.

estoppel. A legal means of preventing someone from doing something.

ethics, law enforcement. Codes of honor tacitly or overtly observed by law enforcement officers, upholding both the spirit and letter of the law and fulfilling the mission statement of police agencies.

ethnocentrism, ethnocentricity. The perception that one's own culture or cultural group is the best culture or group.

etiology. The study of the origins of events, such as crimes.

eugenics. Science based on principle of heredity, having for its purpose the improvement of the human race.

euthanasia. Also known as "mercy killing"; causing the death of persons suffering from incurable illnesses by administering lethal injections of deadly substances or withdrawing life-support systems from such persons. Intent of euthanasia is to bring an end to pain and suffering of those who have incurable illnesses.

evidence. All materials or means admissible in a court of law to produce in the minds of the court or jury a belief concerning the matter at issue.

evidence, corroborating. Any collateral evidence that enhances the value of other evidence.

evidence, prejudicial. Any evidence presented in court which may overwhelm jurors in ways that cause them to view the case subjectively rather than objectively.

evidentiary. Pertaining to the rules of evidence or the evidence in a particular case.

evil-causes-evil fallacy. A faulty belief that evil products, such as delinquent behavior, must have evil antecedents, such as child abuse or emotional trauma.

ex parte. A hearing or examination in the presence of only one party in the case.

ex post facto **laws.** Laws making criminal any act committed before they were passed or which retroactively increase the penalty for a crime. Such laws are unconstitutional.

ex rel. Latin term used in case citations to designate parties for whom others are acting.

examination, direct and cross. *See* direct examination and cross examination.

exception. An objection to a ruling, comments made by the judge or attorneys.

exceptional circumstances doctrine. Under this policy, courts hear only those cases brought by inmates in which the circumstances indicated a total disregard for human dignity, while denying hearings to less serious abuses. Cases allowed access to the courts usually involve situations of total denial of medical care.

excessive force. Any exceptional force extending beyond that necessary to disable suspects or take them into custody through arrest.

exchange. A mutual transfer of resources. A balance of profits and deficits that flow from behavior based on decisions as to the values and costs of alternatives.

exclusionary rule. Rule which provides that where evidence has been obtained in violation of the privileges guaranteed by United States Constitution, such evidence may be excluded at the trial.

exclusive jurisdiction. Specific jurisdiction over particular kinds of cases. United States Supreme Court has authority to hear matters involving the diplomats of other countries who otherwise enjoy great immunity from most other courts. Family court may have exclusive jurisdiction to hear child custody cases.

exculpate, exculpatory. Tending to exonerate a person of allegations of wrong-doing.

excusable homicide. Death from accident or misfortune that may occur during some lawful act.

excuse. A defense to a criminal charge in which accused persons maintain they lacked the intent to commit the crime.

execution. A legal enforcement of the death penalty as a sentence against an offender convicted of a capital crime.

execution of a warrant. Action by court officers to serve a warrant on a defendant in a court action.

executive branch. That segment of government responsible for the administration, direction, control, and performance of government. Examples of executives are the president of the United States, state governors, city mayors. Police and correctional subsystems are under the executive branch.

executive clemency or pardon. The removal of punishment and legal disabilities of a person by order of an executive, usually the president or a governor. *See also* pardon.

executive model of sentencing. A formal statement of goals, a codification of criminal penalties consistent with the goals, and an explicit structure and stated process for implementing sentencing goals.

executive order. Any presidential proclamation which becomes a law and legally binding.

executive privilege. A preventive measure designed to protect the president or the president's staff from Congressional inquiries and interrogation.

exemplar. A sample of material evidence which may be used to verify the authenticity of other similar evidence.

exhibitionism, exhibitionist. Exposure of one's sexual organs to others in a public place. One who exposes oneself in this fashion.

exigent circumstances. Circumstances in which quick action is necessitated, such as searches for drugs and other contraband that might be destroyed easily. Exception to exclusionary rule.

exiting. A successful disengagement from a previous pattern of criminal behavior.

ex-offender. A probationer or parolee. Usually someone who has been processed by criminal justice system, been tried and convicted, has served sentence, and is no longer under jurisdiction of criminal justice system.

exonerate. To absolve of blame, usually through trial and a finding of "not guilty."

expert power. Influence based on personal expertise or skills (e.g., we might listen to an expert on gangs and gang prevention in order to eliminate gangs). A concerned parent might not have expert power here.

expert testimony. Any oral evidence presented in court by someone who is considered proficient and learned in a given field where such evidence is relevant. Testimony provided by an expert witness.

expert witness. Witnesses who have expertise or special knowledge in a relevant field pertaining to the case at trial. Witness who is qualified under the Federal Rules of Evidence to offer an opinion about the authenticity or accuracy of reports, who has special knowledge which is relevant to the proceeding. Sometimes called "hired guns."

expiation. Offender punishments.

expiration of a sentence. Completing the time imposed by a judge. An inmate who serves the entire sentence imposed following conviction experiences an expiration of that sentence.

explanation. The systematic and empirical analysis of the antecedent factors that are responsible for the occurrence of an event or behavior.

explicit sentencing policy. A formal statement of goals, a codification of criminal penalties consistent with the goals, and an explicit structure and stated process for implementing sentencing goals.

explosive. Any volatile material capable of detonating and causing considerable destruction.

expressive crime. A crime having no purpose except to accomplish the behavior at hand, as opposed to creating monetary gain.

expressive violence. Violence intended not for profit or gain but to vent rage, anger, or frustration.

expropriation. State seizure of personal property.

expunge, expungement. Deletion of one's arrest record from official sources. In most jurisdictions, juvenile delinquency records are expunged when one reaches the age of majority or adulthood.

expungement orders. Juvenile court orders to seal juvenile records.

extenuating circumstances. Conditions under which offenders might be excused from culpability in criminal conduct.

extinction. Condition in which a crime prevention effort has an immediate impact that then dissipates as criminals adjust to new conditions.

extortion. Unlawfully obtaining or attempting to obtain property of others by threats of eventual injury or death to others, or harm to one's property.

extradition. Surrender of a person by one jurisdiction to another for the purpose of a criminal prosecution.

extralegal factors. Any element of a nonlegal nature. In determining whether law enforcement officers are influenced by particular factors when encountering juveniles on the streets, extralegal factors might include juvenile attitude, politeness, appearance, dress. Legal factors might include age, specific prohibited acts observed by the officers.

extroversion. Hans Eysenck's term meaning a dimension of the human personality describing individuals who are sensation-seeking, dominant, and assertive.

eye witness. Witness who actually saw the crime committed.

Eysenck, Hans. Criminologist and psychologist who studied criminal personality systems. Wrote *Crime and Personality* (1977). Regards criminal behavior as conditioned reflexes in response to apprehension of either pleasure or pain.

F

facsimile. A copy of an original object or document.

fact. A true statement. An actual event.

fact-finder. The jury in a case, criminal or otherwise.

fact-finding hearing. As applied to juvenile court, any hearing to determine whether the allegations in a petition are supported. *See also* adjudication hearing.

factual question. A question designed to elicit objective information from respondents regarding their background, environments, and habits.

false arrest. Unlawful physical restraint of someone by a law enforcement officer. May include confinement or brief detention in a jail for no valid legal reason.

false imprisonment. Act of unlawfully detaining or restraining a person.

false negative error. In research, a prediction that an event, such as delinquency, will not occur, but it does occur. *See also* false positive error.

false negatives. Offenders who are predicted to be nonviolent or not dangerous according to various risk prediction devices, but who turn out to be dangerous or pose serious public risk.

false positive error. In research, a prediction that an event, such as delinquency, will occur, but it does not occur. *See also* false negative error.

false positives. Offenders who are predicted to be dangerous or who pose serious public risk according to various prediction devices and instruments, but who are not dangerous and do not pose public risks.

false pretenses, obtaining property by. Inducing victims to part with their property through trickery, deceit, or misrepresentation.

family courts. Courts of original jurisdiction that typically handle the entire range of family problems, from juvenile delinquency to divorce cases.

Farrington, David. Criminologist who has developed a theory of delinquent development describing both nonoffenders and desisters. Wrote about this theory in the *Cambridge Study in Delinquent Development* (1983), which was an examination of 411 London boys. Unemployment was found related to certain forms of offending. Desisting was associated with physical relocation. Considerable stress is given to childhood factors as predictors of teenage antisocial behavior. Adolescents are "energized" to act in deviant ways, and their life events influence their behavior. Offending is viewed as situational, and criminality is variable over time, as one ages. Adult behavior is a function of both internal and external factors.

feasance. Performing an act.

Federal Bureau of Investigation (FBI). Established in 1908 through Department of Justice Appropriation Act as department's enforcement arm. Investigative agency that enforces all federal criminal laws and compiles information for the *Uniform Crime Reports* annually. Maintains extensive files on criminals. Assists other law agencies. (Initials FBI also stand for fidelity, bravery, and integrity.)

Federal Bureau of Prisons. Established in 1930. Charged with providing suitable quarters for prisoners and safekeeping of all persons convicted of offenses against the United States. Also contracts with local jails and state prisons for confinement of federal prisoners where there are insufficient federal facilities in the geographical area where the person has been convicted.

federal court system. The four-tiered structure of federal courts, including the United States Supreme Court, the Circuit Courts of Appeal, the United States District Courts, and the United States Magistrate.

federal district court. Basic trial court for federal government. Tries all criminal cases. Has extensive jurisdiction. District judges are appointed by the President of United States with the advice, counsel and approval of the Senate.

Federal Firearms Act. Congressional action in 1938 to limit interstate shipment of firearms or ammunition.

Federal Habeas Corpus Statute. Title 28, Section 2241 of the United States Code, permitting probationers, parolees, and inmates of prisons and jails to challenge the fact, length, and conditions of their confinement, placement in particular facilities, programs.

Federal Law Enforcement Training Center. Interagency organization which provides basic training for law enforcement officers at all state and federal levels. Also provides advanced training and specialist activities for criminalistics, criminal investigation, forensics and firearms training.

Federal Prison Industries. Profitable, government-owned corporation that markets goods produced by prisoners in confinement. *See also* UNICOR.

Federal Tort Claims Act of 1946. Title 28, Section 2674, United States Code, provides that the United States shall be liable, respecting the provisions of this title relating to tort claims, in the same manner and to the same extent as a private individual under like circumstances, but shall not be liable for interest prior to judgment for punitive damages.

Federal Witness Protection Program. Program established under the Organized Crime Control Act of 1970 whereby those who give evidence against criminals and thereby place their lives in jeopardy are relocated under new names and identifications to other parts of the country in order to avoid retaliation or death from offenders convicted by their testimony.

fee system. System whereby county government pays a modest amount of money for each prisoner per day as an operating budget.

felon. One who commits a felony.

felonious. Of or pertaining to felonies. Intent to commit a felony.

felony. Crime punishable by incarceration, usually in a state or federal prison, for periods of one year or longer.

felony murder, felony-murder doctrine. Imposition of criminal liability upon anyone who participates in a crime in which one or more victims are killed. Accomplices in a criminal scheme resulting in death do not actually have to be those who have killed others to be liable.

felony probation. Procedure of not requiring felons to serve time in jail or prison, usually because of prison overcrowding. Involves conditional sentence in lieu of incarceration.

Felson, Marcus. Developed routine activities theory, together with Lawrence Cohen. *See also* Cohen, Lawrence.

fence, fencing. Receiver of stolen property who resells the goods for profit. Negotiating the sale of stolen property.

Ferracuti, Franco. Criminologist who collaborated with Marvin Wolfgang to devise term, subculture of violence.

Ferri, Enrico (1856-1929). Student of Cesare Lombroso. Believed that certain physical characteristics indicate a particular criminal nature and that forces external to the individual are responsible for criminal conduct. Wrote *Criminal Sociology* (1917).

feticide. An abortion prohibited by law.

fetish, fetishism. Any strong sexual attachment to particular objects, such as shoes or women's hose.

fetus. An unborn child still in the womb.

fiction. Anything untrue or false, imaginary, hypothetical.

fiduciary. Someone authorized to act on behalf of another, in a position of trust, usually involving financial transactions.

field citation. Citation and release in the field by police as an alternative to booking and pretrial detention. Practice reduces law enforcement costs as well as jail costs.

field interview, interrogation law enforcement. A question-answer session conducted between a law enforcement officer and a citizen.

field training officer (FTO). A senior police officer who trains other officers in the field, overseeing their on-the-job training.

Fielding, Sir Henry (1707-1754). Eighteenth-century British novelist who laid the foundation for the first modern police force. Originated the Bow Street Runners, an early version of police.

Wrote *An Inquiry into the Cause of the Late Increase of Robbers* (1748).

fighting gangs. *See* conflict gangs.

filing. The commencement of criminal proceedings by entering a charging document into a court's official record.

filtering process. Screening operation, a process whereby criminal justice officials screen certain cases while advancing other cases to the next level of decision making.

financial/community service model. Restitution model for juveniles which stresses the offender's financial accountability and community service to pay for damages.

finding. A holding or ruling by the court or judge.

finding of fact. Court's determination of the facts presented as evidence in a case, affirmed by one party and denied by the other.

fine. Financial penalty imposed at time of sentencing convicted offenders. Most criminal statutes contain provisions for the imposition of monetary penalties as sentencing options.

fingerprint classification, identification. System for classifying and identifying fingerprints according to unique patterns of whirls and ridges on the fingertips.

firearm. Any weapon capable of discharging a projectile, usually through an explosive mechanism.

first offender, first-time offender. Person who has never been convicted of a criminal offense prior to the current conviction.

"fish." Prison slang for new inmate in a jail or prison.

fixed indeterminate sentencing. Sentencing scheme whereby judge sentences offenders to single prison term which is treated as the maximum sentence for all practical purposes. Parole board may determine early release date for offender. *See also* indeterminate sentencing.

fixed sentence. *See* determinate sentencing.

fixed-time rule. A policy in which people must be tried within a stated period after their arrest. *See also* statute of limitations.

flash houses. Eighteenth-century term describing public meeting places and taverns where thieves, pickpockets and other criminals could congregate and exchange stolen goods.

flashover. Arson term describing fire phenomenon in which temperatures in a room reach 2,000 degrees, clothing and furniture burst into flame spontaneously. In past years, arson was suspected whenever such spontaneous combustion occurred, since it almost always was related to the use of arsonist's gasoline or explosives. Currently, it may occur accidentally.

flat term. A specific, definite term for a conviction, not necessarily known in advance of sentencing.

flat time. Actual amount of time required to be served by a convicted offender while incarcerated.

fleeing felon rule. Rule rendered unconstitutional by United States Supreme Court in 1985 whereby law enforcement officers were permitted to use deadly force to apprehend felons attempting to escape apprehension. *See also Tennessee v. Garner,* 1985.

FLETC model. Graduated or escalating amounts of force, applied in accordance with the nature of suspect cooperation or resistance. Suspects who are cooperative are given verbal orders by officers, whereas other suspects may require varying degrees of force to subdue them.

flight. Any escape, fleeing from justice, especially if alleged offenders have been charged with an offense or are awaiting sentencing following conviction.

flogging. Whipping with a lash as a form of corporal punishment.

focal concerns. According to Walter Miller, value orientations of lower-class cultures whose features include the need for excitement, trouble, smartness, fate, and personal autonomy (1958).

folkways. Ways of doing things that are current in a society. Generally followed customs without moral values attached to them, such as not interrupting persons whenever they are speaking.

foot patrol. Originating in Flint, Michigan and elsewhere, programs in which officers walk in communities to patrol them have been moderately successful in bringing community residents into closer touch with patrolling officers. *See also* community policing.

force continuum. Subjective measure of the amount of force law enforcement officers apply in making arrests.

force, reasonable. Any amount or degree of force necessary for persons to protect themselves from aggressive suspects. Law enforcement officers may use force no greater than that which is necessary to subdue crime suspects.

forcible entry. *See* breaking and entering.

forcible rape. Sexual intercourse with persons forcibly and against their will. Assaults or attempts to commit rape by force or threat of force are also included.

forensics. The study and identification of the causes of crimes, deaths, and crime scene investigations.

forfeiture. Seizure by the government of property and other assets derived from or used in criminal activity.

forgery. Creation or alteration of a document such as a negotiable instrument. Intent to defraud by means of trickery and alteration of written documents that, if validly executed, would be legally binding transactions.

formal control. A social control governed by written rules and usually employing formal organizations for implementation.

formal social control. An effort to bring about conformity to the law by agents of the criminal justice system such as the police, the courts, and correctional institutions.

fornication. Sexual intercourse between unmarried persons. An offense in some jurisdictions.

foster family. Any surrogate family used temporarily to provide shelter to unsupervised youths.

foster home, foster group home. A blend of group home and foster home initiatives. Foster home provides a "real family" concept and is run by a single family, not a professional. Group home facility is an unlocked facility, licensed by the state or local jurisdiction and operated by a person or couple, to provide care and maintenance for children, usually one to four such children.

frankpledge. System requiring loyalty to the King of England and shared law and order responsibilities among the public. System directed that neighbors should form into small groups to assist and protect one another if they were victimized by criminals.

fratricide. Killing one's sister or brother.

fraud. Act of trickery or deceit, especially involving misrepresentation.

fraud offense. Any crime involving the use of misrepresentation or deception with the intent of depriving persons of money or valuables.

freedom of assembly. One of a United States citizen's constitutional rights involving the right to meet with others and discuss political issues.

free venture system. Privately run industries in prison settings where inmates work for wages and goods are sold for profit. *See also* UNICOR.

freeway patrol. Law enforcement assignment of patrolling major highways and interstate thoroughfares.

Freud, Sigmund (1856-1939). A psychologist who pioneered extensive work on psychoanalysis and psychological theory. Theorized Oedipus complex, Electra complex, and devised terms, such as the id, ego, superego, and libido or sex drive. Studied psychoses and neuroses as related to criminal conduct.

frisk. Patting down or running one's hands quickly over a person's body to determine whether the person has a weapon.

front-door solution, corrections. Solution to prison or jail overcrowding occurring at beginning of criminal justice process. Includes plea bargaining resulting in diversion, probation, community service, intermediate punishment or some other nonincarcerative alternative.

frottage. Compulsive act whereby persons derive sexual satisfaction by rubbing the clothing of another, particularly the clothing of strangers. Persons who commit frottage are called "frotteurs." Criminally, a mild form of battery.

fruits of the poisonous tree doctrine. United States Supreme Court decision in *Wong Sun v. United States* holding that evidence which is spawned or directly derived from an illegal search or an illegal interrogation is generally inadmissible against a defendant because of its original taint.

frumentarii. First professional criminal investigative units in western history. Had three principal duties: to supervise grain distribution to Rome's needy, oversee the personal delivery of messages among government officials, and detect crime and prosecute offenders.

Fry, Elizabeth Gurney (1780-1845). English Quaker women's prison reformer, toured United States and other countries in early 1800s attempting to implement prison reforms. Encouraged separate facilities for women, religious and secular educa-

tion, improved classification systems for women, reintegrative and rehabilitative programs.

fugitive. Person who has concealed him or herself, has fled a given jurisdiction in order to avoid prosecution or confinement.

fugitive warrant. Any written judicial order authorizing officers to arrest a particular person named in the warrant.

full enforcement. A policy whereby the police are given the resources and support to enforce all laws within the limits imposed by the injunction to respect the civil liberties of citizens.

functional approach to prison culture. Explanation of the prison culture that focuses on the shared experience within the prison, such as inmate responses to the pains of imprisonment.

functional incompetence or illiteracy. The inability to read well enough to perform the basic skills necessary in a modern society.

functionalism. Sociological perspective that suggests that each part of society makes a contribution to the maintenance of the whole. Stresses social cooperation and consensus of values and beliefs among a majority of society's members.

fundamental error. In a judicial proceeding, an error that affects the substantial rights of the accused is an affront to the integrity of the court.

fundamental fairness. Legal doctrine supporting the idea that so long as a state's conduct maintains the basic elements of fairness, the Constitution has not been violated.

"funnelling effect." The reduction occurring between the number of crimes committed annually, the number of arrests, prosecutions, and convictions. Only about 25 percent of all arrests in the United States result in convictions annually.

furlough, furlough program. An authorized unescorted or unsupervised leave granted to inmates for home visits, work, or educational activity, usually from 24 to 72 hours. Temporary release program. First used in Mississippi in 1918.

G

Gall, Franz Joseph (1758-1828). Phrenologist who studied shapes of skulls in an effort to predict the type of criminality exhibited by persons possessing certain physical characteristics.

gambling, gaming. Operating or playing a game for money in the hope of gaining more than the amount played. Any wager between two or more persons.

gang. A group who forms an allegiance for a common purpose and engages in unlawful or criminal activity. Any group gathered together on a continuing basis to engage in or commit antisocial behavior.

gang killing. Any murder involving members of teenage gangs where violence is a part of their group activity.

gaols. Fifteenth-century English jails.

garnish, garnishment. A legal means of attaching one's wages in order to pay a debt.

Garofalo, Raffaelo (1852-1934). Student of Cesare Lombroso who believed that physical characteristics or attributes are indicative of different types of criminal conduct. Wrote *Criminology* (1914).

garrote. To strangle a person, usually by a rope device or wire. The device itself which is used to strangle someone.

gauge. The means of measuring the bore of shotguns, such as 16 gauge or 20 gauge. Typically the larger the gauge, the smaller the bore diameter.

gay. Homosexual.

general court martial. Highest level of tribunal in the military, in which the most serious offenses are tried.

general deterrence. *See* deterrence.

general intent. Actions that on their face indicate a criminal purpose (e.g., breaking into a locked building, trespassing on someone's property).

general jurisdiction. Power of a court to hear a wide range of cases, both civil and criminal.

general strain theory. An expanded version of anomie theory that focuses upon both positive and negative sources of strain, the various dimensions of strain, strategies for coping with strain, and factors that determine whether strain will be coped with in a delinquent or nondelinquent fashion. Described by sociologist Robert Agnew (1992).

general verdict. A finding of guilty or not guilty.

generation gap. A once widely held belief, particularly during the 1960s, of extreme differences in attitudes between adults and adolescents. Later evidence suggests that this gap has been exaggerated.

gentrification. The process of reclaiming and reconditioning deteriorated neighborhoods by refurbishing depressed real estate and then renting or selling properties to upper-middle-class professionals.

Georgia Intensive Supervision Probation Program. Program commenced in 1982 that established three phases of punitive probation conditions for probationers. Phases moved probationers through extensive monitoring and control to less extensive monitoring, ranging from six to twelve months. Program has demonstrated low rates of recidivism among participants.

glandular theory. Theory linking abnormal and/or criminal behavior with thyroidal, adrenal, or other glandular malfunctions.

Glueck, Eleanor and Sheldon. Studied the life cycle of delinquent careers in their classic work, *Unraveling Juvenile Delinquency* (1950). Regarded family relations as primary factors in whether youths adopted delinquent behaviors. Believed that the earlier the onset of delinquency, the more deeply rooted would be the path of eventual criminal careers. Antisocial youths were more prone toward adult criminal careers than non-antisocial youth. Research has influenced risk instruments and dangerousness forecasts for probation, parole board early-release decision making and institutional placement, where higher risk scores are ordinarily assigned to younger ages when delinquency is first observed.

Goddard, Henry H. (circa 1880-1920). Studied "feebleminded" persons in institutions in 1920s, concluding that a majority of juvenile delinquents were feebleminded. Studies were later discounted for their lack of scientific integrity. Wrote *The Kallikak Family: A Study in the Heredity of Feeblemindedness* (1912).

Goffman, Erving. Criminologist and social psychologist who has investigated the impact of stigma on social behavior. Wrote *Presentation of Self In Everyday Life* (1959), *Asylums* (1961). Suggested that others' reactions to one's stigma, such as a facial deformity, trigger deviant conduct among those with various stigmata. Thus, stigma itself is not a direct cause of deviant or criminal conduct.

going rate. Local view of the appropriate sentence or punishment for a particular offense, the defendant's prior record, and other factors.

golf cart patrolling. A method of officer surveillance of neighborhoods or city areas using golf carts as transportation instead of cruisers; golf carts are used, especially in Tampa, Florida where golf cart patrolling was pioneered, in order to bring officers into closer touch with neighborhood and area residents. Such patrolling is often classified as a part of community-oriented policing.

"good faith" exception. Exception to exclusionary rule when police officers with good or honest intentions conducted search and seizure on basis of faulty warrant. Acting in "good faith" presumably excuses conduct.

good marks. Credit obtained by prisoners in nineteenth century England where prisoners were given "marks" for participating in educational programs and other self-improvement activities.

"good time," "good time" credits. An amount of time deducted from the period of incarceration of a convicted offender, calculated as so many days per month on the basis of good behavior while incarcerated. Credits earned by prisoners for good behavior. Introduced in early 1800s by British penal authorities, including Alexander Maconochie and Sir Walter Crofton. *See also* good marks.

"good-time" laws. Laws that allow a reduction of a portion of a prisoner's sentence for "good behavior" while in prison.

Goring, Charles (1870-1919). British criminologist who wrote *The English Convict* (1902), an examination of the characteristics of 3,000 English convicts and their comparison with college students, hospital patients, and soldiers. Concluded that criminals were shorter and weighed less, and they also were "mentally defective."

GOSSlink. *See* electronic monitoring devices.

graduate entry scheme. England and Wales special course where prospective police recruits are selected on the basis of their performance of in-service work and law enforcement education.

graffiti. Any wall writing, indoors or outdoors. Outdoors it is sometimes referred to as the "newspaper of the street."

graft. Bribes accepted in the course of one's police role in exchange for favors or concessions usually involving violations of the law.

grand jury. Investigative bodies whose numbers vary among states. Duties include determining probable cause regarding commission of a crime and returning formal charges against suspects. *See also* true bill and no true bill.

grand larceny. Theft of property with a value in excess of a given amount, such as $5000. There is interstate variation on what the amount is. *See also* petit larceny.

granny bashing. Abuse of the elderly, particularly one's parents.

grant of probation. Any court declaration sentencing a convicted person to probation.

"grass eaters." Slang term used for police officers who accept payoffs when their everyday duties place them in a position to be solicited by the public.

gratuity. Any present in exchange for a service.

Great Law of Pennsylvania. Established by William Penn in 1682. Designed to make prison and jail conditions more humane by banning branding, stocks and pillories, and other forms of corporal punishment. Repealed when Penn died, restoring corporal punishments.

Greenwood, Peter, Greenwood Scale. Researcher at RAND Corporation in Santa Monica, California. Devised "Greenwood scale" to measure future dangerousness, which is used as a classification measure for determining the level of custody for certain persons who are to be incarcerated. Advocates selective incapacitation as a crime-reduction strategy. Conducted empirical investigations of the effectiveness of the "three strikes and you're out" strategy for crime prevention and control.

grid search. Technique for searching crime scenes for evidence. Areas are searched by means of a strip method, whereby plots of land area are marked off by tape at right angles and searched in minute detail.

grievance, grievance procedure. Formalized arrangements, usually involving a neutral hearing board, whereby institutionalized individuals have the opportunity to register complaints about the conditions of their confinement.

grooves. The spiraling lines within the barrel of a firearm. Grooves are examined by forensic specialists to determine whether a particular firearm fired a particular projectile.

gross negligence. A tort wherein someone fails to provide the standard of care required in any given situation.

grounded-theory approach. In field research, the development of a theory that is closely and directly relevant to the particular setting under study whereby the researcher first develops conceptual categories from data and then makes new observations to clarify and elaborate these categories. Concepts and tentative hypotheses are then developed directly from data.

group counseling, group therapy. A treatment program that allows several inmates to be treated at the same time and at a low cost. Involves the discussion of feelings or attitudes in an effort to create mutual acceptance and a supportive environment. Group interaction is used as a therapeutic device.

group homes. Facilities for juveniles that provide limited supervision and support. Juveniles live in home-like environment with other juveniles and participate in therapeutic programs and counseling. Considered nonsecure custodial. *See also* foster home.

grouping. A collective of individuals who interact in the workplace, but, because of shifting membership, do not develop into a workgroup.

group process. A perspective applied to juvenile gangs that sees this form of delinquency as being produced primarily by status strivings within the gang itself, rather than by external strains or lower-class focal concerns.

guard. Once the preferred term to refer to those who supervise inmates in prisons, penitentiaries, jails. Currently, preferred term is "correctional officer."

guardian. Any person placed in legal control of another either temporarily or permanently and who is responsible for the other person's welfare.

guardian *ad litem.* A court-appointed attorney who protects the interests of children in cases involving their welfare and who works with the children during the litigation period.

Guardian Angels. New York-based organization consisting of young men and women who monitor subways and city streets to protect citizens from muggers.

Guerry, Andre-Michel (1802-1866). Did work to assist in the establishment of the cartographic school of criminology, which posited that social factors, including gender and age, influenced crime rates significantly. Factors such as season, climate, population composition and poverty also were believed to be correlated with criminality.

guided group interaction. A group dynamics treatment process stressing the use of youth reference group and changes in group norms to change behavior. Used in the Highfields and Provo experiments.

guilt by association. Any inference of one's culpability as the result of being in the company of someone who has committed a crime or is suspected of having committed a crime.

guilty plea. A defendant's formal affirmation of guilt in court to charges contained in a complaint, information, indictment claiming that they committed the offenses listed.

guilty verdict. Decision by a judge in a bench trial or jury in a jury trial of the guilt of defendants, based on evidence beyond a reasonable doubt for a conviction.

gun control, gun control laws. Any regulatory mechanism governing the sale, transfer, manufacture, exchange of firearms, including screening mechanisms for determining one's background and possible disqualifications for acquiring a firearm.

H

habeas corpus. Writ meaning "produce the body"; used by prisoners to challenge the nature and length of their confinement.

habeas corpus **petition.** Petition filed, usually by inmates, challenging the legitimacy of their confinement and the nature of their confinement. Document commands authorities to show cause why an inmate should be confined in either a prison or jail. Also includes challenges of the nature of confinement. A written order by the court to any person, including a law enforcement officer, directing that person to bring the named individual before the court so that it can determine if there is adequate cause for continued detention.

habitual criminal statutes, laws. *See* habitual offender statutes.

habitual offender. Any person who has been convicted of two or more felonies and may be sentenced under the habitual offender statute for an aggravated or longer prison term.

habitual offender statutes, laws. Statutes vary among states. Generally provide life imprisonment as a mandatory sentence for chronic offenders who have been convicted of three or more serious felonies within a specific time period.

halfway house. Community-based centers or homes operated either publicly or privately, staffed by professionals, paraprofessionals, volunteers, which are designed to provide housing, food, clothing, job assistance, and counseling to ex-prisoners and others in order to assist parolees in making the transition from prison to the community.

Hallcrest Report. Government-sponsored survey of the private security industry conducted by the Hallcrest Corporation.

haloperidol. Nonaddictive drug used for treatment programs involving withdrawal from drugs such as heroin.

"hands-off" doctrine, policy. Doctrine practiced by state and federal judiciary up until 1940s whereby matters pertaining to inmate rights were left up to jail and prison administrators to resolve. These were considered "internal" matters, where no court intervention was required or desired. In juvenile matters, doctrine was typical of United States Supreme Court toward appeals stemming from juvenile court decisions; tendency was to let juvenile courts manage themselves until *Kent v. U.S.*

hanging. A method of administering the death penalty in capital punishment cases. Condemned offenders are placed on a scaffold with a rope around their neck and a trap door causes them to fall a designated distance, at which time the rope tightens and their necks break, causing death.

harassment. Any act that annoys or alarms another person.

harmful errors. Errors made by judges that may be prejudicial to a defendant's case. May lead to reversals of convictions against defendants and to new trials.

harmless errors, harmless error doctrine. Errors of a minor or trivial nature and not deemed sufficient to harm the rights of parties in a legal action. Cases are not reversed on the basis of harmless errors.

hashish. A product of the hemp plant used for its hallucinogenic effects. Similar to but more powerful than marijuana. May be smoked or chewed to produce desired effects. Depressant acting on the central nervous system.

hate crimes. Crimes committed against victims because of their membership in specific ethnic or racial categories.

Hayes, Rutherford B. First president of the American Correctional Association (originally

called National Prison Association). Later United States President.

Healy, William. Together with Augusta Bronner, studied delinquent boys and IQ in Chicago and Boston in 1926. Found that delinquents were five to ten times more likely to have subnormal intelligence compared with nondelinquents.

hearing. Any formal proceeding in which the court hears evidence from prosecutors and defense and resolves a dispute or issue.

hearing, probable cause. A proceeding in which arguments, evidence, or witnesses are presented and in which it is determined whether there is sufficient cause to hold the accused for trial or whether the case should be dismissed.

hearsay evidence. Evidence that is not first-hand but is based on an account given by another.

hearsay rule. Courtroom precedent that hearsay cannot be used in court. Rather than accepting testimony on hearsay, the trial process asks that persons who were the original source of the hearsay information be brought into court to be questioned and cross-examined. Exceptions to the hearsay rule may occur when persons with direct knowledge are either dead or otherwise unable to testify.

hedonism. Jeremy Bentham's term indicating that people avoid pain and pursue pleasure.

hematoporphyrin test. A test for traces of blood (e.g., on clothing retrieved from a crime scene).

hereditary criminal propensities. Biological transmission of criminal inclinations or tendencies.

heredity theory. Postulates behaviors are result of characteristics genetically transmitted; criminal behaviors would be explained according to inherited genes from parents or ancestors who are criminal or who have criminal propensities.

heroin. Highly addictive opiate. Usually injected into the bloodstream with syringes by drug users.

Herrnstein, Richard. Criminologist who collaborated with James Q. Wilson to write *Crime and Human Nature* (1985). Argues that personal traits, such as genetic makeup, intelligence and body build, may actually outweigh social variables as predictors of criminal conduct. Proposes integrated theory of criminal behavior including biosocial makeup, personality, rational choice, structure and social process.

hierarchy rule. A standard *Uniform Crime Reports* scoring practice in which only the most serious offense is counted in a multiple-offense situation.

higher courts. Appellate courts and sometimes trial courts of record, as distinguished from lower courts.

High Street Jail. First jail constructed under the Great Law of Pennsylvania on High Street in Philadelphia.

Highway Patrol. State law enforcement agency whose primary function is to enforce motor vehicle laws on state and interstate highways.

highway statistics. A compilation of accident information, driver's license information, and any other information relating to automobile travel on the nation's highways.

hijacking. Taking over any mode of transportation by force. Most often automobiles and aircraft, although trains and buses have also been hijacked.

Hindelang, Michael. Criminologist who has studied juvenile delinquency and its causes. Described delinquents as extroverted. Generally finds support for the studies and theories of Hans Eysenck. Has investigated relation between IQ and criminality, collaborating with Travis Hirschi, and has found support for the association between IQ and criminal behavior.

Hirschi, Travis. Criminologist who has examined delinquency in his work, *The Causes of Delinquency* (1969) and the processes whereby persons acquire deviant behaviors. Described social control theory, positing that social ties and bonds in society become weakened. All persons in society are assumed to be potential law violators, but most are law-abiding because of fear of loss of close relations with friends, employment, neighbors; without such strong bonds, persons become detached from others and are more willing to engage in behaviors that will damage their reputations. Individual differences among society's members cause differential reaction to society's moral and ethical codes, thus some persons become more susceptible to criminal conduct. Social bond elements include attachment (person's sensitivity to and interest in others), commitment (time, energy, and effort expended in conventional activities), involvement (social inclusion in ongoing group activities), and belief (sharing a common set of moral values with others). Wrote *A General Theory of Crime* (1990) with Michael Gottfredson which examined self-control as an essential feature in their refinement of social control theory. The criminal offender and criminal act are separate concepts. Crime may be situational and impulsive for some persons predisposed to criminal conduct, but self-control is a stabilizing force. Effective parenting and early socialization are mechanisms that influence how one decides to engage in criminal conduct.

historical research. A research strategy that examines the same society at different times and looks at the way crime has changed with economic and social development.

history. All events occurring during the time of the research that might affect the individuals studied and provide a rival explanation for the change in the dependent variable.

holding. The legal principle drawn from a judicial decision. Whatever a court, usually an appellate court, decides when cases are appealed from lower courts. When an appellate court "holds" a particular decision, this may be to uphold the original conviction, set it aside, overturn in part and uphold in part.

Homans, George. Sociologist who developed modern social exchange theory, based on principles elaborated by George Herbert Mead and Georg Simmel. Wrote *The Human Group*. Considered social exchange as a primary ingredient to establishing societal conformity, viewing interactions in terms of rewards and costs.

home confinement, incarceration. Housing of offenders in their own homes with or without electronic monitoring devices. Reduces prison overcrowding and prisoner costs. Sometimes an intermediate punishment involving the use of offender residences for mandatory incarceration during evening hours after a curfew and on weekends. Also called "house arrest."

homicide. The killing of one person by another.

homicide, criminal. Causing the death of another without justification or excuse.

homicide, excusable. Intentional but justifiable causing of death; a noncriminal action.

homicide investigation. Any law enforcement inquiry into the death of one or more persons who have been killed.

homicide, justifiable. Intentional causing of another's death in the legal performance of one's duty or under circumstances defined by law as constituting legal justification.

homicide, willful. The intentional causing the death of another, with or without legal justification.

homophobia. Fear of homosexual persons.

hooliganism. Term used by Soviets in defining a broad range of criminal conduct including disorderly conduct, alcohol or drug abuse, prostitution, and loitering.

Hooton, Earnest (1887-1954). Neo-Lombrosian and anthropologist who wrote *Crime and the Man* (1939), in which it was claimed that on the basis of various physical characteristics, criminals could be differentiated from noncriminals. Believed that criminality was caused by physical inferiority.

Hoover, J. Edgar (1895-1972). Former director of the Federal Bureau of Investigation, where he started out as director in 1924. Renamed Bureau of Investigation "Federal Bureau of Investigation" in 1935. Created FBI Academy for training federal agents in 1935. Required early agents to be attorneys or certified public accountants as prerequisites for Special Agent positions.

Horney, Julie. Wrote about premenstrual syndrome (PMS) in 1978 and established a link between PMS and criminality. Believes that psychological and physical stress trigger early menstruation and violent conduct rather than simply menstruation.

hot pursuit. Circumstance involving chase of suspects by law enforcement officers. Often used to justify searches and seizures when suspect is eventually apprehended.

hot spots of crime. According to Lawrence Sherman, significant portion of police calls originate from only a few city locations, including taverns and housing projects.

houdoud. Islamic punishment as a crime deterrent. May involve amputation of thief's hand.

house arrest. *See* home confinement.

house of corrections. Any county correctional institution generally used for the incarceration of more serious misdemeanants, whose sentences are usually less than one year.

houses of refuge. Workhouses, the first of which was established in 1824 as a means of separating juveniles from the adult correctional process.

Howard, John (1726-1790). Early English prison reformer. Sheriff of Bedfordshire, England. Influenced by other European countries such as France to lobby for prison reforms.

hudud **crimes.** Serious violations of Islamic law regarded as offenses against God including such behavior as theft, adultery, sodomy, drinking alcohol, and robbery.

hue and cry. In 1500's, warning shouted by village watch men if crime was observed.

Hull House. Settlement home established by Jane Addams, a reformer. Financed by philanthropists. Operated as a home for children of immigrant families in Chicago who were taught religious principles, morality, and ethics.

hulks. Mothballed ships that were used to house prisoners in eighteenth-century England.

humanitarianism. In penal philosophy, the doctrine advocating the removal of harsh, severe, and painful conditions in penal institutions.

human relations. School of organizational behavior stressing personal qualities of those in roles such as police officers. Apart from impersonal relations with citizens, human relations stresses persons as personality systems with emotional components.

human relations model. Model of organizations devised by Elton Mayo in early 1930s, emphasizing recognition of individual differences among employees. Individual motivation is critical, human dignity and personality characteristics are important. Often contrasted with bureaucracy. *See also* bureaucracy for comparison.

hundred. In medieval England, a group of one hundred families that had the responsibility to maintain order and try minor offenses.

hung jury. Jury that cannot agree on a verdict.

hustle. The underground prison economy. An attempt to defraud.

hybrid offense. May be heard either by magistrates or by crown courts, depending upon prosecutorial discretion. May or may not be indictable and are influenced greatly by situational factors, such as a defendant's lack of a prior record, circumstances surrounding the commission of the offense, and harm inflicted upon victims.

hyperactivity. Excessive activity characterized by symptoms such as impulsiveness, restlessness, fighting, short attention span, erratic behavior, and aggressiveness.

hypoglycemia. Condition occurring in susceptible individuals in which level of blood sugar falls below an acceptable range, causing anxiety, headaches, confusion, fatigue, and aggressive behavior.

hypothesis. Statement derived from theory which is subject to empirical test. Statement of theory in testable form. Proposition set forth for some specific phenomenon.

hypothetical construct. An entity that cannot be observed directly with our present technology (e.g., love, motivation, short-term memory).

hypothetical question. A question based on an assumed set of facts.

hysteria. A psychological reaction to a shocking event, characterized by extreme fear, laughter, or some other highly emotional outburst.

I

id. Sigmund Freud's term to depict that part of personality concerned with individual gratification. The "I want" part of a person, formed in one's early years.

identification. In psychology, the incorporation in one person's personality of the features of another person's personality.

identification numbers. Numbers used to designate a file for a person charged with a crime. FBI use of such numbers is for fingerprint identification.

identification record. One's criminal record.

identify. To determine the identity of someone. In criminal investigations, to recognize something or someone relating to a crime.

ideology. A tightly knit set of beliefs, often with political implications, that justify a particular action system.

ignorance. A weak defense to a crime charge. Similar to mistake of fact.

illegal detention. Similar to false arrest, when one has been detained by law enforcement officers without probable cause or reasonable suspicion.

illegal expenditures. The costs of crimes that divert money from the legitimate economy and represent a loss of potential revenue for people who produce and supply legal goods and services.

illegal search and seizure. Any act in violation of the Fourth Amendment of the United States Constitution, which guarantees the right of individuals to be secure in their persons, houses, papers and effects, against unreasonable searches and seizures, shall not be violated, and that no warrants shall issue but upon probable cause, supported by oath or affirmation, and particularly describing the place to be searched and the persons or things to be seized.

illegitimacy. The condition of a child being born out of wedlock.

Illinois Juvenile Court Act (1899). Legislation establishing first juvenile court in United States

immunity, immunity from prosecution. Exemption from a civil suit or criminal prosecution, usually through an agreement with prosecutors to testify or give evidence of value to a prosecutor's case.

immunity, transactional. A grant of immunity applying to offenses to which a witnesses' testimony relates (e.g., one who conspires with others to commit a crime may testify against the co-conspirators without fear of being prosecuted for the crime contemplated).

immunity, use. A grant of immunity forbidding prosecutors from using immunized testimony as evidence against witnesses in criminal prosecutions.

impanel. To select and swear in a jury in a civil or criminal case.

impeach, impeachment. Attempt by prosecution or defense to question the credibility or veracity of each others' witnesses.

impersonating an officer. A crime, usually committed by a citizen who wears the clothing of and pretends to be a police officer for a variety of reasons. May involve simply carrying a badge and identifying oneself as a police officer in order to gain entry to a dwelling or seduce a victim.

implicit plea bargaining. Occurs when defendant pleads guilty with the expectation of receiving a more lenient sentence. *See also* plea bargaining.

implicit sentencing policy. A legislative orientation to sentencing that must be inferred from its other actions.

importation hypothesis. Explanations of the prison culture that focus on the background of inmates rather than current prison experience as a source of values and attitudes.

importation model. View that violent prison culture reflects the criminal culture of the outside world and is neither developed in nor unique to prisons.

imprisonment. Incarceration of a convicted offender.

impulse, irresistible. A type of insanity, in which the offender is acting under a compulsion over which he or she has little or no control.

impulsivity. Theory component that a particular trait produces criminal behavior. Impulsive people lack self-control.

impunity. State of not being subject to retaliation or consequences.

in camera. In a judge's chambers.

in delicto. Fault, as to a crime or happening; a finding that one is at fault in causing an accident or committing a crime.

in flagrante delicto. Caught in the act. The fact that the perpetrator of a crime was caught during the crime's commission is direct evidence of guilt.

in forma pauperis. "In the manner of a pauper." Refers to waiver of filing costs and other fees associated with judicial proceedings in order to allow indigent persons to proceed with their case.

in loco parentis. "In the place of the parents." Refers to someone other than a parent acting on behalf of a juvenile in any juvenile proceeding.

in re. "In the matter of." Refers to cases being filed for juveniles who must have an adult act on their behalf when filing motions or appeals.

in toto. Completely, entirely.

inadmissible. Evidentiary term used to describe something which cannot be used as evidence during a trial.

incapable. Unable to act in a particular way (e.g., unable to strangle a victim because of paralysis in hands or arms).

incapacitation, isolation. Philosophy of corrections espousing loss of freedom proportional to seriousness of offense. Belief that the function of punishment is to separate offenders from other society members and prevent them from committing additional criminal acts.

incarceration. Imprisonment in either a jail or prison.

incendiary. Any highly flammable device. A bomb intended to cause a fire.

incest. Sexual relations between close relatives other than husband and wife.

inchoate offenses. Conduct made criminal even though it has not yet produced the harm that the law seeks to prevent. Offenses preparatory to committing other crimes (e.g., conspiracy, attempt, or solicitation).

incidence. The frequency with which offenders commit crime, or the average number of offenses per offender. Measured by dividing the number of offenses by the number of offenders.

incident. Specific criminal act involving one or more victims.

incident-based reporting. A less restrictive and more expansive method of collecting crime data (as opposed to summary reporting) in which all the analytical elements associated with an offense or arrest are compiled by a central collection agency on an incident by incident basis.

incident-driven policing. A technocratic product, whereby police officers have traditionally responded or reacted to calls for service.

incite. To provoke or set in motion.

inciting a riot. The crime of instigating persons to riot, usually against some governmental policy or issue.

included offense. An offense that is made up of elements that are a subset of the elements of another offense having a greater statutory penalty, and the occurrence of which is established by the same evidence or by some portion of the evidence that has been offered to establish the occurrence of the greater offense.

incompetent evidence. Evidence inadmissible because it is flawed in various respects (e.g., a copy of an original document that appears to have been altered to project a particular viewpoint favorable to one side or the other).

incompetent to stand trial. The finding by a criminal court that defendants are mentally incapable of understanding the nature of the charges and proceedings against them, of consulting with an attorney, and of aiding in their own defense.

incorporation. Extension of due process clause of Fourteenth Amendment to make binding on state governments the rights guaranteed in the first ten amendments to the United States Constitution.

incorrigible, incorrigibility. Unmanageable. Term applicable to unruly children who are often placed in foster care, under nonsecure, secure circumstances where they can be governed, controlled, supervised.

incriminate, incrimination. To indicate guilt.

inculpate, inculpatory. To incriminate or show one's possible guilt; incriminating factors are inculpatory.

indecent exposure, exhibitionism. Exposure of one's sexual organs to others in a public place.

indefinite sentence. *See* indeterminate sentencing.

indemnify, indemnification. To compensate for losses or injuries in a tort action or actual compensation for such losses or injuries.

indentured servant system. System whereby persons paid for their passage to the American colonies from England by selling their services for a period of seven years. Also considered a "voluntary slave" migration pattern.

indeterminate punishment. *See* indeterminate sentencing.

indeterminate sentencing. Sentencing scheme in which a period is set by judges between the earliest date for a parole decision and the latest date for completion of the sentence. In holding that the time necessary for treatment cannot be set exactly, the indeterminate sentence is closely associated with rehabilitation.

index crimes, offenses. Specific felonies used by the Federal Bureau of Investigation in the *Uniform Crime Reports* to chart crime trends. Eight index offenses listed prior to 1988 are: aggravated assault, larceny, burglary, vehicular theft, arson, robbery, forcible rape, murder.

indictable offense. Offense in either Canada or Great Britain that includes violations of the criminal code or federal statutes.

indictment, bill of. A charge or written accusation found and presented by a grand jury that a particular defendant probably committed a crime.

indigent, indigent client/defendant. Poor. Anyone who cannot afford legal services or representation.

indirect control. Behavioral influence arising from an individual's identification with noncriminals and desire to conform to societal norms.

indirect costs. Costs to support an operation, such as central office administration and expenses incurred by other departments in supporting corrections.

individual rights. In criminal justice, any rights guaranteed to criminal defendants facing formal processing by the system. The preservation of the rights of criminal defendants is important to society because it is through the exercise of such rights that the values of our culture are most clearly and directly expressed.

individual therapy. A method of treatment commonly used in prison in which psychiatrists, psychologists, or psychiatric social workers help offenders solve psychological problems that are thought to be the cause of criminal behavior.

induction. Creating a general rule by seeing similarities among several specific situations.

industrial espionage. Giving away company secrets or formulae for a product or idea to another company. Usually committed by a company employee or officer.

industrial prison. Any prison in which the principal activity is industrial labor by the inmates, and also prisons in the period 1900 to 1930, when the focus of most prisons in the United States was the production of goods.

industrial school. A secure facility designed for juvenile delinquents where the principal functions are to equip youths with employable work skills.

inevitable discovery, inevitable discovery rule. Rule of law stating that evidence will almost assuredly be found and independently discovered and can be used in a court of law even though it was obtained in violation of certain legal rules and practices.

infamous crime. Any crime that is so heinous in its commission as to deserve national, even international, notoriety; any crime involving a highly visible public or private figure.

infant. Legal term applicable to juveniles who have not attained the age of majority. In most states, age of majority is 18.

infanticide. Killing of a newborn baby.

inference. A way of concluding something from a given set of facts. Juries make inferences about things based upon facts presented by both sides in a criminal case.

inferior courts. Lower courts, courts of limited jurisdiction.

informal social control. The reactions of individuals and groups that bring about conformity to norms and laws, including peer and community pressure, bystander intervention in a crime, and collective responses such as citizen patrol groups.

informant. Person who supplies information to police officers about others who are engaged in illegal activities.

information. Written accusation made by a public prosecutor against a person for some criminal offense, without an indictment. Usually restricted to minor crimes or misdemeanors. Sometimes called criminal information.

informed consent. Agreement to participate in an activity based upon full knowledge and understanding of what will take place.

infraction. An offense punishable by a fine or other penalty, but not normally by incarceration.

inherent coercion. Those tactics used by police interviewers that fall short of physical abuse but nonetheless pressure suspects to divulge information.

initial appearance. Formal proceeding during which the judge advises the defendant of the charges, including a recitation of the defendant's rights and a bail decision.

initial classification. The classification of newly received inmates, usually in a reception center, often with heavy reliance on previous records or tests.

initial classification analysis. Classification device used by Missouri Department of Corrections for determining the treatment plan and institutional assignments for both male and female offenders. Created in 1983.

initial plea. At a time of the initial appearance, defendant's declaration of guilt or innocence in response to the charges against defendant.

injunction. Court order prohibiting someone from doing some specified act or commanding someone to undo some wrong or injury.

injunction order. A written notice by the court to a party, prohibiting that party from committing some act.

inmate. Prisoner of jail or prison.

inmate code/subculture. Informal set of rules reflecting values of the prison culture or society.

inmate control model. Scheme which proposes the establishment of inmate grievance committees and inmate boards to investigate and decide issues pertaining to inmate grievances.

inmate dispute resolution. Internal inmate grievance procedures established by inmates themselves in either prisons or jails.

inmate grievance procedure. Mandatory administrative grievance procedure in all state and federal prisons where inmates may bring grievances to attention of wardens and other supervisory personnel.

inmate litigation explosion. *See* litigation explosion.

inmate self-government. Any prison management system that provides formal inmate participation or control over some decisions regarding routine, discipline, and program.

inmate social code. Informal set of rules that governs inmates.

innovation. The mode of adaptation in which cultural goals are accepted, but the means used to achieve these goals are considered unacceptable, possibly criminal.

Innovations Project. Project implemented by Ninth Circuit Court of Appeals in which cases are presented without oral argument. "Submission-without-argument" program, streamlining case processing and backlogs.

innovative adaptation. An alternative name for Merton's anomie theory that stresses the "innovation" mode of adaptation in the goals/means relation.

in-presence requirement. Legal principle that police officers cannot make an arrest in a misdemeanor case unless the crime is committed in their presence.

inquisitory system. System in which defendants must prove their innocence, as opposed to adversary system, which presumes defendant innocent until proven guilty by the prosecutor.

insane. Legal term meaning that offenders did not understand that what they were doing was wrong or were operating under such compulsion that they could not change their behavior or conform their behavior to the requirements of the law.

insanity. Degree of mental illness that negates the legal capacity or responsibility of the affected person.

insanity defense. Defense that seeks to exonerate accused persons by showing that they were insane at the time they were believed to have committed a crime.

Insanity Defense Reform Act of 1984. An act aimed to obligate the defense to prove the defendant insane as an affirmative defense. Previously, prosecutors in federal district courts bore the burden of showing that the defendant was not insane. This Act was triggered by the attempted assassination of President Ronald Reagan by John Hinckley, who pleaded insanity and was acquitted thereby.

insanity plea. A plea entered as a defense to a crime. The defendant admits guilt but assigns responsibility for the criminal act to the condition of insanity presumably existing when the crime was committed.

inside cells. Prison cells constructed back-to-back, with corridors running along the outside shell of the cell house.

insider trading. Using material nonpublic financial information to obtain unfair advantage over others when trading securities and stocks.

institutional capacity. The rated capability of a prison or other facility indicating the number of persons or bedspace available and how many individuals can be lawfully accommodated.

institutional child abuse. Includes approved use of force and violence against children in the schools and in the denial of children's due process rights in institutions run by different levels of government.

institutional orders. Also known as court decrees, the judicial orders applied to an institution to correct the conditions or practices that infringe on inmate rights.

instrumental crimes. Illegal acts whose purpose is to obtain funds to secure goods and services. Offenses in which committing the act is not an end in itself.

instrumental Marxist theory. Instrumental Marxism. View that capitalist institutions, such as the criminal justice system, have as their main purpose the control of the poor in order to maintain the hegemony of the wealthy.

instrumental violence. Violence that is designed to improve the financial or social position of the criminal.

insufficient evidence. Inadequate evidence to show one's guilt beyond a reasonable doubt. Prosecutors present a case and the case may be dismissed because of a lack of sufficient incriminating evidence.

intake decision. Review of a case by a court (juvenile or criminal) official. Screening of cases includes weeding out weak cases. In juvenile cases, intake involves the reception of a juvenile against whom complaints have been made. Decision to proceed or dismiss the case is made at this stage.

intake, intake officer. Process of screening juveniles who have been charged with offenses. Officer who conducts screening of juveniles. Dispositions include release to parents pending further juvenile court action, dismissal of charges against juvenile, detention, treatment by some community agency.

intake screening. A critical phase where a determination is made by a juvenile probation officer or other official whether to release juveniles to their parent's custody, detain juveniles in formal detention facilities for a later court appearance, release them to parents pending a later court appearance.

intake unit. A government agency that receives juvenile referrals from police, other government agencies, private agencies, or persons and screens them, resulting in closing of the case, referral to care or supervision, filing of a petition in juvenile court.

intangible property. Property with no tangible value, such as bonds, promissory notes, and stock certificates.

integrated structural theory. Criminologists Mark Colvin and John Pauly have devised this theory which views crime as the direct result of socialization within families (1983). Families characterized by despair and coercive relations are criminal behavior antecedents. Negative social relations at home carry over into one's school relations and scholastic performance is adversely affected, feelings of alienation and strain develop, and delinquency is a result.

integrated theory, theoretical model. A perspective that seeks to expand and synthesize earlier positions into a modern analytical device with great explanatory and predictive power. A blend of seemingly independent concepts into coherent explanations of criminality. *See also* multifactor theory.

intensive offender. A person who engages in criminal activity that begins at an early age, and is sustained over time, consciously planned, persistent, skilled, and frequent.

intensive probation supervision. *See* intensive supervised probation/parole.

intensive supervised probation/parole (ISP). No specific guidelines exist across all jurisdictions, but ISP usually means lower caseloads for probation officers, less than 10 clients per month, regular drug tests, and other intensive supervision measures.

intensive supervision program. Probation or parole program in which the officer-offender ratio is low, offenders receive frequent visits from their officer-supervisors, and continuous communication is maintained by the supervising agency or authority

intent. A state of mind, the *mens rea*, in which a person seeks to accomplish a given result, such as a crime, through a given course of action.

inter alia. "Among other things."

interactional or interactionist theory. Interaction with institutions and events during the life course determines criminal behavior patterns. Crimogenic influences evolve over time. Terance Thornberry applies this concept in describing the onset of delinquency and criminality. Viewed as age-graded and couched in a cognitive developmental context, since deviance either emerges or doesn't emerge during various stages where reasoning and sophistication develop and mature.

interactionist perspective. View that one's perception of reality is significantly influenced by one's interpretations of the reactions of others to similar events and stimuli.

interaction process analysis. A set of 12 categories used to code interaction in groups. A highly structured observational technique, using both structured observational categories and a structured laboratory setting.

interdict. To intercept, prohibit, prevent.

interest groups. Private organizations formed to influence government policies so that they will coincide with the desires of their members.

interlocutory appeal. An appeal during a trial proceeding in which the judgment of the trial court is suspended pending the successfulness of an appeal.

interlocutory decision. A temporary judgment pending the resolution of the facts at issue.

intermediate appellate courts. The third level of state courts. Appellate courts between trial courts and courts of last resort.

intermediate punishments, sanctions. Punishments involving sanctions existing somewhere between incarceration and probation on a continuum of criminal penalties. May include home confinement and electronic monitoring.

intermittent confinement, sentence. Imposed punishment where offender must serve a portion of sentence in jail, perhaps on weekends or specific evenings. Considered similar to probation with limited incarceration. *See also* split sentencing.

intermittent offender. Persons who engage in irregular and opportunistic crimes with low payoffs and great risks, and who do not think of themselves as professional criminals.

internal affairs unit. Department within police agencies charged with the responsibility to investigate misconduct and possible criminal behavior on the part of police officers.

internalized control. Self-regulation of behavior and conformity to societal norms through guilt feelings arising from the conscience.

internal process model. A perspective on organizations that places high value on predictability and control and uses structures which make activities more predictable.

International Court of Justice. Formed to establish some degree of jurisdiction over international crime.

international crimes. Major criminal offenses so designated by the community of nations for the protection of interests common to all world citizens.

international law. A global body of rules and regulations which the principal nations of the world abide by. A pact among nations to respect and observe particular laws governing trade, commerce, and trafficking in illegal contraband. Agreement to condemn terrorism and give up terrorists who seek asylum in particular countries.

internships. These programs generally are three-unit, upper-division offerings for graduating seniors to allow them practical exposure to the criminal justice system. Several universities make the internship a mandatory subject requiring up to 160 contact hours per 16-week semester.

interobserver reliability. An index of the degree to which different raters give the same behavior similar ratings.

INTERPOL. International Criminal Police Organization. The idea is attributed to Baron Pasquier, the prefect of the Paris police in 1809.

interpretive approach. Belief that the phenomena of focal concern to the sociobehavioral scientist are far less stable than those of interest to the natural scientists.

interrogation. Method of acquiring evidence in the form of information or confessions from suspects by police. Questioning, which has been restricted because of concern about the use of brutal and coercive methods and interest in protecting against self-incrimination.

interrogatories. A set of questions prepared by both prosecution and defense and administered to potential witnesses for either side.

interstate compact. Agreement between two or more states to transfer prisoners, parolees, or probationers from the supervisory control of one state to another.

intersubjectivity. A norm of scientific methodology that states that knowledge must be transmittable so that scientists can understand and evaluate the methods of other scientists and perform similar observations in order to verify empirical generalizations.

intoxication. The state of being incapable of performing certain tasks legally, such as operating motor vehicles or boats. Can be induced through consumption of alcoholic beverages, inhaling toxic fumes from petroleum products, or consumption of drug substances.

intoximeter. Device used to test breath for determining presence of alcohol.

intrinsic evidence. Actual information or documentation. Any inculpatory or exculpatory information or material that is self-explanatory or requires no elaboration or comment (e.g., fingerprints on a murder weapon).

invalidate. To annul, negate, set aside.

investigation. Inquiry concerning suspected criminal behavior for purposes of identifying offenders or gathering information or further evidence to assist the prosecution of apprehended offenders.

investigatory stage. That stage of a criminal investigation in which law enforcement officers are collecting information and evidence and in which no charges have been brought against any particular suspect.

involuntary manslaughter. Homicide in which the perpetrator unintentionally but recklessly causes the death of another person by consciously taking a grave risk that endangers a person's life.

involvement. A variable used by Travis Hirschi to describe an individual's participation in conventional activities.

ipso facto. "By the mere fact." By the fact itself (e.g., "We can assume, *ipso facto*, that if the defendant was observed beating another person in a bar by ten witnesses, then he is likely guilty of the beating inflicted on the victim.").

Irish system. Sir Walter Crofton's correctional methods involving tickets-of-leave for prisoners serving long sentences. Prisoners could gain early release (parole) through acquisition of tickets-of-leave. A method of obtaining compliance from inmates and rewarding them by releasing them short of serving their full sentences.

irresistible impulse, irresistable impulse test. A desire that cannot be resisted due to impairment of the will by mental disease or defect. A compulsion to commit a crime. The "irresistable impulse test" is an insanity defense requiring a showing that although accused persons knew right from wrong, they were unable to control their irresistible impulse to commit the crime.

isolated organizations. Correctional organizations that have weak ties to both centralized and local sources of policy and resources.

isolation. A sentencing philosophy seeking to remove the offender from other offenders when confined by placing prisoner in a cell with no communication with others. Also known as solitary confinement, which originated in Walnut Street Jail in Philadelphia, Pennsylvania in the late 1700's. Another usage of this term is to segregate offenders from society through incarceration.

isomorphism. Similarity or identity in structure.

issuance of warrants, writs. Any authorization by a judicial officer directing a law enforcement officer to act. May include search warrants, seizure orders.

issue. A legal fact to be resolved.

Italian school. "School of thought" developed by Cesare Lombroso linking criminal behavior with abnormal, unusual physical characteristics.

J

jail. City or county operated and financed facility to contain those offenders who are serving short sentences, are awaiting further processing. Jails also house more serious prisoners from state or federal prisons through contracts to alleviate overcrowding. Jails also house witnesses, juveniles, vagrants, and others.

jail as a condition of probation. Sentence in which judge imposes limited jail time to be served before commencement of probation. *See also* split sentencing.

jail commitment. A sentence of commitment to the jurisdiction of a confinement facility system for adults which is administered by an agency of local government and of which the custodial authority is usually limited to persons sentenced to a year or less of confinement.

jail confinement rate. The number of persons confined in jails, both as detainees awaiting trial and as misdemeanants serving short sentences, per 100,000 persons in the general civilian population.

jail house lawyer, jailhouse lawyer. Inmate in a prison or jail who becomes skilled in the law. Inmate who learns about the law and assists other prisoners in filing suits against prison or jail administration.

jail house turnouts, jailhouse turnouts. Inmates who are introduced to homosexuality while in prison.

jail sentence. Penalty of commitment to a jail facility for a specified period.

Jim Crow laws. Any number of ordinances that were passed, primarily in southern states and municipalities in the 1880s, legalizing segregation of blacks and whites. *Plessy v. Ferguson* (1896) was a major "separate, but equal" ruling, in which the United States Supreme Court actually endorsed the legality of such laws.

"jive bitches". Inmates who tend to be manipulative and unstable, causing problems for other inmates and staff.

job satisfaction. Degree of contentment with work performed.

John Doe warrant. Warrant issued when suspect's name is unknown, but an otherwise accurate description and location of suspect have been provided.

joinder. Coupling two or more criminal prosecutions (e.g., in a case in which two or more persons have allegedly committed a crime together, they may be tried in a single trial proceeding through a joinder).

joint trial calendar system. Method of case processing used by judges in certain jurisdictions, in which several judges share common court calendar with shared objective and responsibility of trying all cases on calendar within a specified period.

joyriding. Temporary taking a motorized vehicle without intent to permanently deprive the owner of same.

judge. A political officer who has been elected or appointed to preside over a court of law, whose position has been created by statute or by constitution and whose decisions in criminal and juvenile cases may only be reviewed by a judge or a higher court and may not be reviewed *de novo*.

judgment. Final determination of a case. A proclamation stating one's guilt or innocence in relation to criminal offenses alleged. In tort law, a finding in favor of or against the plaintiff. The amount of monetary damages awarded in civil cases.

judgment suspending sentence. A court-ordered sentencing alternative that results in the convicted offender being placed on probation.

Judicial Act of 1789. Act of the United States creating three tiers of courts: thirteen federal district courts, three higher-level circuit courts, and a supreme court.

judicial activism. United States Supreme Court's use of its power to accomplish social goals.

judicial adjuncts. Lawyers and others who assist courts and judges on a temporary basis in minor offense cases. Judicial adjuncts maintain law practice while performing these temporary duties.

judicial branch. That segment of government charged with interpreting the law and administering justice. Examples include the United States Supreme Court, state supreme, superior, and appellate courts; county courts; and magistrates' courts. Court subsystem falls under this branch of government.

judicial circuit. A specific jurisdiction served by a judge or court, as defined by given geographical boundaries.

judicial model of sentencing. Sentencing scheme in which control over type and duration of sentence is left in hands of trial judge.

judicial notice. An exclusively judicial determination or acknowledgment of facts in evidence apart from any persuasion by defense or prosecution.

judicial officer. A judge or magistrate who presides in a given jurisdiction.

judicial plea bargaining. Recommended sentence by judge who offers a specific sentence and/or fine in exchange for a guilty plea. *See also* plea bargaining.

judicial powers. Court jurisdiction to act in certain cases and decide punishments.

judicial process. The sequence of procedures designed to resolve disputes or conclude a criminal case.

judicial reprieve. Temporary relief or postponement of the imposition of a sentence. Commenced during Middle Ages at the discretion of judges to permit defendants more time to gather evidence of their innocence, to allow them to demonstrate that they had reformed their behavior.

judicial restraint. United States Supreme Court's deference to legislative and executive decision unless a clear constitutional right has been violated.

judicial review. Authority of a court to limit the power of the executive and legislative branches of government by deciding whether their acts defy rights established by the state and federal constitutions.

Judicial Sentencing Institute. An educational or training session for judges on issues relevant to sentencing.

judicial waiver. Decision by juvenile judge to waive juvenile to jurisdiction of criminal court.

Judiciary Act of 1891. Also known as "Evarts Act," created contemporary United States circuit court scheme for federal appellate review.

jump bail. Act by defendant of leaving jurisdiction where trial is to be held. Attempt by defendant to avoid prosecution on criminal charges.

jural postulates. Propositions developed by jurist Roscoe Pound holding that the law reflects the shared needs without which members of society could not co-exist. Pound's jural postulates are often linked to the idea that the law can be used to engineer the structure of society in order to predetermine certain kinds of outcomes, such as property rights as embodied in the law of theft do in capitalistic societies.

jurisdiction, court. The power of a court to hear and determine a particular type of case. Also refers to territory within which court may exercise authority such as a city, county, state.

jurisdiction, original. The lawful authority of a court or an administrative agency to hear or act upon a case from its beginning and to pass judgment on it.

jurisdiction, police. The established geographical boundaries in which the police of a political subdivision have authority.

jurisprudence. The application of the law in any jurisdiction.

jurist. A person who is skilled or well-versed in the law, usually lawyer or judge.

jurist value system. Category of decision making by parole boards in which parole decisions are regarded as a natural part of the criminal justice process in which fairness and equity predominate.

jury. *See* petit jury.

jury deliberations. Discussion among jury members concerning the weight and sufficiency of witness testimony and other evidence presented by both the prosecution and defense. An attempt to arrive at a verdict.

jury, grand. *See* grand jury.

jury, hung. *See* hung jury.

jury nullification. Jury refuses to accept the validity of evidence at trial and acquits or convicts for a lesser offense (e.g., although all of the elements for murder are proved, a jury may acquit defendants who killed their spouses allegedly as an act of mercy killing).

jury panel. A list of jurors summoned to serve on possible jury duty at a particular court. From the jury panel, the petit jury is selected.

jury poll. A poll conducted by a judicial officer or by the clerk of the court after a jury has stated its verdict but before that verdict has been entered into the record of the court, asking each juror individually whether the stated verdict is his or her own verdict.

jury size. Traditional twelve-member jury at federal level and many state and local levels; may vary between six-member jury and twelve-member jury at state and local level.

jury trial. Trial where guilt or innocence of defendant is determined by jury instead of by the judge.

"just-deserts" model. Correctional model stressing equating punishment with the severity of the crime. Based on Cesare Beccaria's ideas about punishment.

justice. A judge, particularly a supreme court judge. An ideal concerning the maintenance of right and the correction of wrong in the relations of human beings.

justice model. Philosophy which emphasizes punishment as a primary objective of sentencing, fixed sentences, abolition of parole, and an abandonment of the rehabilitative ideal.

justice of the peace (courts). Minor judicial official overseeing trivial offenses. A court, usually rural, possessing special original jurisdiction in most instances and certain quasi-judicial powers.

justifiable homicide. A homicide, permitted by law, in defense of a legal right or mandate.

justification. Defense to a criminal charge in which defendants maintain that their actions were appropriate or noncriminal according to the circumstances, and therefore, they should not be held criminally liable.

juvenile disposition. Decision by a juvenile court, concluding a disposition hearing, that an adjudicated juvenile be committed to a juvenile correctional facility, be placed in a juvenile residence, shelter, care or treatment program, required to meet certain standards of conduct, released.

juvenile justice agency. Any publicly or privately operated agency involved in the processing of infants or minors. Usually includes law enforcement, intake officers, juvenile court prosecutors, judges, and juvenile corrections.

juveniles. Persons who have not as yet achieved their eighteenth birthday or the age of majority.

juvenile court(s). A term for any court that has original jurisdiction over persons statutorily defined as juveniles and alleged to be delinquents, status offenders, or dependents.

juvenile court judgment. Juvenile court decision terminating an adjudication hearing, that the juvenile is delinquent, status offender, dependent, or that the allegations in a petition are not sustained.

juvenile court jurisdiction. Authority to decide juvenile matters by juvenile court. Usually applies to juveniles between 10 or 12 and 18 years of age, although ages vary among states.

juvenile delinquency. The violation of criminal laws by juveniles. Any illegal behavior or activity committed by persons who are within a particular age range and which subjects them to the jurisdiction of a juvenile court or its equivalent.

juvenile delinquent. Any minor who commits an offense that would be a crime if committed by an adult.

juvenile diversion. *See* diversion, juvenile.

juvenile diversion/non-custody intake program. California juvenile program implemented in 1982 targeted for more serious juvenile offenders. Characterized by intensive supervised probation, required school attendance, employment, and counseling.

juvenile diversion program. Any program for juvenile offenders that temporarily suspends their processing by the juvenile justice system. Similar to adult diversion programs. Also program established in 1981 in New Orleans, Louisiana by District Attorney's Office in which youths could receive treatment before being petitioned and adjudicated delinquent. *See also* diversion.

juvenile justice agency. Any governmental or private agency of which the functions are the investigation, supervision, adjudication, care, or confinement of juveniles whose conduct or condition has brought or could bring them within the jurisdiction of a juvenile court.

Juvenile Justice and Delinquency Prevention Act of 1984. Act passed by Congress in 1974 and amended numerous times, including 1984, encouraging states to deal differently with their juvenile offenders. Promotes community-based treatment programs and discourages incarceration of juveniles in detention centers, industrial schools, or reform schools.

juvenile justice system, process. The system through which juveniles are processed, sentenced, and corrected after arrests for juvenile delinquency.

juvenile record. An official record containing, at a minimum, summary information pertaining to an identified juvenile concerning juvenile court proceeding, and if applicable, detention and correctional processes.

K

Kales plan. 1914 version of Missouri Plan, in which committee of experts creates a list of qualified persons for judgeships, makes recommendations to governor. *See also* Missouri Plan.

Kansas City Preventive Patrol Experiment, Kansas City study. Controversial study conducted in early 1970s in Kansas City, which showed no relation between crime and the intensity of police patrolling in various city areas.

Katz, Jack. Criminologist who has devised term, seductions of crime, to indicate immediate benefits accruing from criminal activity. Situational inducements may propel persons otherwise exhibiting conventional behavior toward criminal conduct if they perceive sufficient rewards. Possibly related to need-fulfillment and doing something pleasurable and exciting, regardless of whether it is criminal.

Kefauver Committee. A special Senate committee targeting organized crime in the United States With exciting courtroom drama, its disclosures demonstrated the extent to which racketeers had established themselves in American society.

kidnapping. Felony consisting of the seizure and abduction of someone by force or threat of force and against victim's will. Under federal law, victims of a kidnapping are those who have been taken across state lines and held for ransom.

Kirchheimer, O. A critical criminologist who has written extensively about Marxist criminology. Views internal societal clashes as the result of unequal distribution of wealth and power. Collaborated with Georg Rusche in investigating societal conflict.

kleptomania. A psychological compulsion to steal.

Knapp Commission. A public body created in 1970 in New York City that led the investigation into police corruption and uncovered a widespread network of payoffs and bribes among regular patrol officers, detectives, and administrators.

known groups technique. Determining the validity of a measure by seeing whether groups known to differ on a characteristic differ on a measure of that characteristic (e.g., ministers should differ from atheists on a measure of religiosity).

Kohlberg, Lawrence. Developed stages of cognitive development as an explanation for why persons adopt conventional and nonconventional behaviors in their early years. Different stages of moral development are crucial in determining whether or not someone acquires the cognitive means to avoid unconventional conduct and to realize that whatever conduct is contemplated might be criminal or wrong.

Kretschmer, Ernst. Criminologist and anthropologist who believed that physical characteristics were highly correlated with criminality. Wrote *Physique and Character* (1926). Advocated that various body types were associated with various forms of criminality.

Krisberg, Barry. Criminologist who has declared as a part of a conflict theoretical perspective that crime is a function of privilege, in which crimes are created by powerful interests to perpetuate their domination of those less powerful or powerless. Elaborated in book, *Crime and Privilege: Toward a New Criminology* (1975).

KRUM. A Swedish association for advancing the cause of more humane treatment for prisoners, formed in 1966 to provide legal assistance for furtherance of inmate rights.

L

labeling theory, labeling. Theory attributed to Edwin Lemert that persons acquire self-definitions that are deviant or criminal. Persons perceive themselves as deviant or criminal through labels applied to them by others, thus the more people are involved in the criminal justice system, the more they acquire self-definitions consistent with the criminal label.

landmark decision. Decision handed down by United States Supreme Court that becomes the law of the land and serves as a precedent for subsequent similar legal issues in lower courts.

larceny, larceny-theft. Unlawful taking, carrying, leading or riding away of property from the possession or constructive possession of another; includes shoplifting, pocket-picking, thefts from motor vehicles, and thefts of motor vehicle parts or accessories.

laser. Acronym for Light Amplification by Stimulated Emission Radiation. A very narrow beam of light, useful for detecting speeds of motorists on highways.

latency theory. Theory that various needs are hidden in one's subconscious state, until they are triggered or activated by an event. A person may have latent homosexuality which may manifest itself in a situation in which the suggestion of a homosexual relation is made or under conditions which are conducive to such a liaison.

latent trait theory. Explanation of crime over time throughout the life cycle. Assumes that persons possess a dormant characteristic controlling their propensity to offend, and when opportunities arise which awaken such characteristics they cause manifestations of criminal behavior. Thus, the predisposition to act in criminal ways is a stable phenomenon, while the opportunity to commit crime fluctuates depending upon situational circumstances. Term is associated with David Rowe, D. Wayne Osgood, and W. Alan Nicewander (1990).

Laub, John. Criminologist who collaborated with Robert Sampson to devise age-graded theory and the significance of turning points throughout the life course. Marriage and career are viewed by these researchers as crucial in enabling adults to refrain from engaging in criminal activity. Theory elaborated in *Crime in the Making* (1993).

Lavater, J.K. (1741-1801). Physiognomist who believed that facial features of criminals could be used to predict their potential for criminal conduct.

law. The body of rules of specific conduct, prescribed by existing, legitimate authority, in a particular jurisdiction, and at a particular point in time.

law and order. A political ideology and slogan that seeks a return to the morality and values of earlier times and rejects the growing permissiveness in government and social affairs.

law assessor. Swedish citizens under age 70, with or without legal training, who sit with judges in hearing certain cases.

law enforcement. The activities of various public and private agencies at local, state, and federal levels that are designed to ensure compliance with formal rules of society that regulate social conduct.

law enforcement agency. Local, state, federal organizations and personnel who uphold the laws of their respective jurisdictions.

Law Enforcement Assistance Administration (LEAA). An outgrowth of the President's Crime Commission during the period 1965-1967, a time of great social unrest and civil disobedience. Created by Congress in 1968 and terminated in late 1970s. Designed to provide resources, leadership, and coordination to state and local law enforcement agencies to prevent and/or reduce adult crime and juvenile delinquency. Allocated millions of dollars to researchers and police departments over the next decade for various purposes. Many experiments were conducted with these monies, which led to innovative patrolling strategies in different communities.

law enforcement officer. An employee of a local, state, or federal governmental agency sworn to carry out law enforcement duties. A sworn employee of a prosecutorial agency who primarily performs investigative functions.

law enforcer. An officer policing style characterized by playing it by the book and enforcing all laws.

law guardian. Persons with legal authority and duty of taking care of someone and managing their property and rights, if the person is incapable of administering his or her affairs personally.

law of precedent. *See stare decisis.*

Law Reform Commision Act 1. Implemented by Canadian legislature to keep pace with changing Canadian society and to make appropriate reform recommendations to the legislature.

laws of imitation. An explanation of crime as learned behavior. Individuals are thought to emulate behavior patterns of others with whom they have contact.

lay witness. An eyewitness, character witness, or any other person called upon to testify who is not considered an expert. Lay witnesses must testify to the facts alone and may not draw conclusions or express opinions.

leading question. Question structured to lead respondent to the answer the questioner wants (e.g., "You like this book, don't you?").

learning theories. Any explanation for human behavior that suggests that behaviors are the product of associating with others and acquiring behaviors from the process of social interaction and social experience.

lease system. A form of prison industry under which contractors assumed complete control over prisoners.

left realism. Branch of conflict theory that holds that crime is a "real" social problem experienced by the lower classes. Radical criminologists have ignored the victimization of the working class to focus on upper-class crime. Fear of violence among the lower classes has allowed the right wing to seize the law-and-order issue for political control. Lower-class concerns about crime must be addressed by radical scholars. Community-based crime prevention strategies are regarded as desirable as crime control techniques which do not disenfranchise any particular societal aggregate.

legal aid. Any form of assistance wherein an agency or person assists another, usually indigent, in a legal matter by providing legal representation.

legal approach. Police discretion type characterized by codifications of discretion according to legal proscriptions. Discretionary behavior is measured by amount of deviation from proscribed rules.

legal ethics. Generally accepted code of conduct accepted by those admitted to the bar for the purpose of practicing law. One ethic is to avoid a personal and intimate relation with a client, another is to avoid assisting a client in violating the law by conspiring with the client to taint evidence or fabricate evidence to make the defense case stronger.

legalistic model. Emphasized the importance of written procedure and limited individual officer discretion. Promoted a 'Joe Friday' or 'strictly-by-the-book,' 'only the facts' mentality among law enforcement officers.

legalization. Removal of all criminal penalties from a previously outlawed act.

legal-rational authority. Max Weber's concept wherein authority is based in law, whereby persons are vested with rights to order others to comply with directives. Most common authority form for bureaucracies.

legal responsibility. The accountability of persons for a crime because of perpetrator's characteristics and the circumstances of the illegal act.

legal screening. An investigation to determine the nature of the offense, whether the child has previously committed offenses, and whether he or she is currently under some type of probationary supervision.

legal sufficiency. Presence of minimum legal elements necessary for prosecution of a case. When prosecutor's decision to prosecute a case is based on legal sufficiency, most cases are accepted for prosecution, but the majority of them are disposed of by plea bargaining or dismissal.

legislative branch, legislature. That segment of government responsible for the consideration, drafting, and enactment of the law (e.g., United States Congress, state legislatures, county commissioners, and city councils).

legislative exclusion. The legislature excludes from juvenile court jurisdiction certain offenses usually either very minor, such as traffic or fishing violations, or very serious, such as murder or rape.

legislative model, legislative model of sentencing. A sentencing structure in which the legislature retains most discretion, and does not permit a great deal of judicial or executive flexibility in fixing terms.

legislative waiver. Provision that compels juvenile court to remand certain youths to criminal courts because of specific offenses that have been committed or alleged.

legitimate power. Power form based on belief that superior has a right to compel subordinates to follow orders.

Lemert, Edwin M. Sociologist who wrote *Social Pathology* (1951) and *Human Deviance, Social Problems, and Social Control* (1967). Promoted labeling theory, which posits that persons acquire deviant perceptions of themselves through labels applied to them by others; labeling process includes primary deviance which may not be serious, but may nevertheless trigger the labeling process and secondary deviance. One's chances of becoming labeled are enhanced as the result of being of lower socioeconomic status, racial and ethnic minority status and other factors.

lesbianism. Female homosexuality.

lesser-included offense. A less important crime that is also a part of a more serious offense (e.g., in a vehicular homicide charge, if the defendant had been drinking alcoholic beverages a DWI charge might be a lesser-included offense).

letter of the law. Strictly legalistic approach to law enforcement. Zero-tolerance interpretation of the law.

level of government. The federal, state, regional, local county or city location of administrative and major funding responsibility of a given agency.

lewd and lascivious conduct. Moral depravity, immorality, gross depravity.

lewdness. Degenerate conduct in sexual behavior that is so well known that it may result in the corruption of public decency.

Lewis, Oscar. Sociologist who wrote about the culture of poverty in 1966. As a part of the culture of poverty, "at-risk" children were described, who were economically and culturally disadvantaged, conditions tending to generate violence and criminality.

lex non scripta. "The unwritten law" or common law. Law not written down in some codified form.

lex talionis. The law of retaliation or retribution. A form of revenge dating back to the Apostle Paul and used up until the Middle Ages.

libel. A tort of defamation through published writing or pictures critical of others.

liberal approach. The perspective that crime can be reduced by attacking its underlying causes through social reforms.

liberal feminist theory. Freda Adler, who has written *Sisters in Crime* and Rita Simon, who has written *The Contemporary Woman and Crime*, have both advocated that low crime rates among women are attributable to their "second class" economic and social position relative to men, and that as these economic and social positions converge over time, because of greater rights and opportunities for women, crime rates for both men and women will tend to converge. Their writing has given rise to "the new female criminal," a disputed term to depict today's female offender population.

liberal policing ideals. Liberalism as an ideology and related policies aimed at social reform designed to increase equality and democratic participation in governance. Liberals advocate the use of state power to aid disadvantaged individuals and groups, and believe that much criminal activity has roots in the social fabric.

libido. Sigmund Freud's term describing the sex drive he believed innate in everyone.

lie detector. An apparatus which records one's blood pressure and various other sensory responses and records one's reactions by means of a moving pencil and paper. Designed to determine whether one is telling the truth during an interrogation. Also known as polygraphs. Results of tests are not admissible in court.

"life." Habitual female offender in prison who engages in deviant behavior with little or no regard for punitive consequences.

life course, life course theory. Study of changes in criminal offending patterns over a person's entire life. Are there conditions or events that occur later in life that influence the way people behave, or is behavior predetermined by social or personal conditions at birth? Studied by Rolf Loeber and Marc LeBlanc, who endorsed a developmental view of criminal conduct (1990). They focus criminological attention on questions such as "Why do people begin to act antisocially?" or "Why do some persons escalate to more serious forms of crime?"

life history. A research method using experiences of persons as the unit of analysis (e.g., using the life experience of individual gang members to understand the natural history of gang membership).

limited jurisdiction. Court is restricted to handling certain types of cases such as probate matters or juvenile offenses. Also known as special jurisdiction.

limited risk control model. Model of supervising offenders based on anticipated future criminal conduct. Uses risk assessment devices to place offenders in an effective control range.

Lindbergh Law. Named for Charles Lindbergh, whose baby was kidnapped in the early 1930s. Forbids interstate transportation of anyone who has been kidnapped. Violating this law is a capital crime.

linear. A relationship between an independent and dependent variable that is graphically represented by a straight line.

line functions. Police work including patrol, traffic, juvenile, and detective investigation.

line units. Police components that perform the direct operations and carry out the basic functions of patrol, investigation, traffic, vice, and juvenile.

lineup. A procedure in which police ask suspects to submit to being viewed by witnesses to a crime together with others who resemble their personal characteristics. Identification in a lineup can later be used as evidence in court.

liquor law violations. State or local law violations relating to alcohol, except drunkenness and driving under the influence (e.g., consuming alcoholic beverages on the streets is prohibited in some cities).

litigation. Civil prosecution in which proceedings are maintained against wrongdoers, as opposed to criminal proceedings.

litigation explosion. Sudden increase in inmate suits against administrators and officers in prisons and jails during late 1960s and continuing through 1980s. Suits usually challenge nature and length of confinement or torts allegedly committed by administration, usually seek monetary or other forms of relief.

lividity. In forensics, a term describing the condition of tissue of a dead person, including the possible position in which the person was reclining when found, the time of death, and other factors.

loan shark. Anyone who lends money to others at various interest rates, usually above what are lawfully prescribed.

local legal culture. Norms shared by members of a court community as to case handling and a participant's behavior in the judicial process.

lockdown. Complete removal of inmate privileges and permanent confinement in cells. Usually follows prison riot or other serious prison disturbance.

Locke, John (1632-1704). English philosopher who wrote *Essay Concerning Human Understanding* and *Second Treatise on Government*. Advocated the application of reason, humanitarianism and secularism to problems of philosophy and political theory.

lockups. Facilities sometimes counted as jails, intended to hold prisoners for public drunkenness for short periods such as 24 or 48 hours.

loco parentis. See in loco parentis.

Loeber, Rolf. Criminologist who has suggested pathways to crime theory, holding that persons follow different roads or paths as a means of acquiring criminal behaviors (1993).

log. A record of events, meetings, visits, and other activities of an individual over a given period of time.

loitering. Standing around idly, "hanging around." Often used as a provocation by police officers to stop and question citizens who appear "suspicious," to describe vagrants, persons who are in public places with no visible means of support.

long-term facility. Any incarcerative institution for either juveniles or adults that is designed to provide prolonged treatment and confinement, usually for periods of one year or longer.

loose protocol effect. Variations in procedure because the written procedures (the protocol) is not detailed enough. These variations in procedure may result in researcher bias.

lower-class culture. *See* focal concerns.

lower courts. Courts of special original jurisdiction and sometimes trial courts, as opposed to higher or appellate courts.

LSD. Lysergic acid diethylamide, a substance derived from rye, which acts as an hallucinogenic drug.

lust murder. A form of homicide that is primarily motivated by aberrant sexual fantasies.

lynch, lynching. To hang without a trial. Mobs in the 1930s and 1940s and earlier lynched persons suspected of committing crimes. Often associated with hanging African-Americans in the South during a period of great racial tension and discord.

M

machismo. The demonstration of masculinity through the manipulation and exploitation of women.

Maconochie, Alexander (1787-1860). Prison reformer and superintendent of the British penal colony at Norfolk Island and governor of Birmingham Borough Prison. Known for humanitarian treatment of prisoners and issuance of "marks of commendation" to prisoners that led to their early release. Considered the forerunner of indeterminate sentencing in the United States

MADD. Mothers Against Drunk Driving, founded in 1980 by Candy Lightner after her daughter was killed by a drunk driver with multiple drunk-driving convictions.

mafia. Name given to organized crime syndicates in the United States and elsewhere, where such syndicates originated in Italy or Sicily; means "our family" or "our thing."

Magdelen Society. A women's prison reform society formed in 1830.

magistrate. A judge who handles cases in pre-trial stages. Usually presides over misdemeanor cases. An officer of the lower courts.

magistrate courts. Courts of special jurisdiction, usually urban.

Magna Carta. The "Great Charter" signed by King John in 1215 guaranteeing the legal rights of English subjects. Generally considered the foundation of Anglo-American constitutionalism.

mail fraud. Use of the United States mails to commit a crime, such as fraudulent advertising, shipping stolen merchandise by mail, or sending threatening letters to others.

maim. To inflict bodily injury on another willfully, usually resulting in loss of an organ or limb.

main effects. The overall or average effect of an independent variable.

make-believe families. Peer units formed by women in prison to compensate for the loss of family and loved ones that contain mother and father figures.

mala fides. Bad faith.

mala in se **crimes.** Illegal acts that are inherently wrong or intrinsically evil (e.g., murder, rape, or arson).

mala prohibita **crimes.** Illegal acts that have been codified or reduced to writing. Offenses defined by legislatures as crimes. Many state and federal criminal statutes are *mala prohibita.*

malfeasance. Misconduct by public officials. Engaging in acts which are prohibited while serving in public office.

malice. Intent to commit a wrongful act without a legitimate reason or legal justification.

malice aforethought. The *mens rea* requirement for murder, consisting of the intention to kill with the awareness that there is no right to kill. *See also mens rea.*

malicious mischief. Crime of willfully destroying the property of another.

malicious prosecution. Prosecutorial action against someone without probable cause or reasonable suspicion.

mamertine prison. Ancient prison constructed about 640 B.C. under the Cloaca Maxima, the main sewer of Rome, by Ancus Martius. Consisted of a series of dungeons constructed to house a variety of offenders.

management by objectives (MBO). Organizational strategy used in early 1970s whereby administrators could cope successfully with various organizational problems. MBO achieved by effective goal-setting and creating a system of accountability whereby one's performance could be measured over time. Feedback from higher-ups considered essential.

mandamus. *See* writ of mandamus.

mandate. A command or an order (e.g., a governor has a mandate to approve emergency legislation in state disaster situations).

mandatory conditional release. Usually refers to conditional release of prisoners through accumulation of good time credits.

mandatory release. Required release of inmates from incarceration upon the expiration of a certain time period, as stipulated by a determinate sentencing law or parole guidelines.

mandatory sentencing, mandatory sentence. Sentencing where court is required to impose an incarcerative sentence of a specified length, without the option for probation, suspended sentence, or immediate parole eligibility.

Manhattan bail project. Experiment in bail reform that introduced and successfully tested the concept of release on own recognizance.

Manhattan Court Employment Project. Project operated by Vera Institute between 1967-1970 in New York City, providing vocational training and job placement services for petty offenders and some minor felons. Discontinued after high recidivism rates were observed.

manifest function. Intended or recognized functions. In probation and parole, manifest function is to permit offender reintegration into society.

manipulation. A procedure allowing the researcher in experimental settings to have some form of control over the introduction of the independent variable; this procedure allows for the determination that the independent variable preceded the dependent variable.

Mann Act. Act passed in 1910 to prohibit the importation of women from the United States to serve in brothels in other countries. Also prohibited using women from other countries in United States brothels and coerced prostitution generally. A federal act prohibiting transporting persons across state boundaries for purposes of prostitution.

manslaughter. Criminal homicide without malice, committed intentionally after provocation (voluntary manslaughter) or recklessly (involuntary manslaughter).

manslaughter, involuntary. *See* involuntary manslaughter.

manslaughter, vehicular. Causing the death of another by grossly negligent operation of a motor vehicle.

manslaughter, voluntary. *See* voluntary manslaughter.

marginal deterrent effect. The extent to which crime rates respond to incremental changes in the threat of sanctions.

marijuana. Substance from the leaves of the hemp plant. Ingestion through eating or smoking causes euphoria. A "downer" in the drug community.

mark system. System devised by Sir Walter Crofton in which inmates earned credit for time served, which applied against original sentence, thereby permitting prisoners to gain early release.

marshal. Sworn officer who performs civil duties of the courts, such as the delivery of papers to begin civil proceedings. Some jurisdictions obligate these persons to serve papers for the arrest of criminal suspects and escort prisoners from jail to court or into the community when they are permitted to leave the jail or prison temporarily.

martial law. Usurpation of civilian authority by the military. Usually invoked during disasters or riot situations to prevent looting of demolished businesses and unruly crowds.

Martinson, Robert. Criminological critic who has written numerous essays about the futility of rehabilitative and reintegrative programs. Advocate of "nothing works" philosophy and of belief that correctional programs are only as good as the persons who run them and the adherence to policies that guide such programs.

Marx, Karl (1818-1883). European theorist who believed that society was a continuous class struggle between those who own the means of production (the bourgeoisie) and those who work for those who own the means of production (the proletariat). Different vested interests between these two "classes" (survival for the proletariat and profit for the bourgeoisie) make class conflict inevitable and perpetual. Ideas also known as economic determinism, since economics and their control were viewed as governing social interaction. Collaborated with Friedrich Engels in writing *The Communist Manifesto* (1848). Marx's ideas were later adopted, interpreted, and described by subsequent generations of scholars known as critical crimi-

nologists, Marxists, and conflict theorists or radical criminologists.

Marxian ideology of punishment. Contains the beliefs that capitalist society has built-in conflicts between capital and labor, that deviance is a result of class structure, and that the punishment system protects the unequal distribution of resources.

Marxist criminology. *See* radical criminology.

Marxist feminists. Those who view gender inequality as stemming from the unequal power of men and women in a capitalist society. Gender inequality stems from exploitation of females by fathers and husbands. Female criminality is a response to subordination of women and male aggression.

masculinity hypothesis. View that women who commit crimes have biological and psychological traits similar to those of men. Cesare Lombroso believed that a few "masculine" females were responsible for the handful of crimes committed by women.

Maslach Burnout Inventory. An inventory measuring a disorder, "burnout," characterized by a loss of motivation and commitment related to task performance. Burnout among police is measured by Maslach Burnout Inventory and other psychological devices which test degree of commitment to the job and the level of motivation to be successful.

Massachusetts model. Centralized model in which a high degree of control over offenders is exercised. Less than 15 percent recidivism. Requires additional conditions besides close monitoring, including community service, victim restitution, curfew, drug and alcohol tests. Limited clientele because of stringent selection criteria.

Massachusetts Prison Commission. Investigative body appointed by governor in 1817 to examine prison conditions and prisoner early release options and to make recommendations about policy issues. Noted for originating concept of halfway house.

mass murder. Killing of more than one person as a part of a single act or transaction, by one or more perpetrators.

master status. The situation in which other aspects of a person's behavior become submerged in a particular social identity, such as that of a deviant.

material. An important, relevant fact. A necessary element. Evidence which is relevant to a criminal case.

material witness. Any witness who has relevant testimony about a crime.

matricide. The murder of one's mother.

maturation. Biological, psychological, or social processes that produce changes in the individuals or units studied with the passage of time. These changes could possibly influence the dependent variable and lead to erroneous inferences.

Matza, David. In collaboration with Gresham Sykes, developed neutralization theory (1957), which posits that criminal behavior is learned. While persons acquire and inculcate societal values are considered normal, they are able to neutralize these normal values with illegitimate and unconventional behaviors; such persons can drift between conventional, law-abiding behavior and criminal conduct for varying periods of time.

maximum expiration date. The date when one's sentence has been served in its entirety.

maximum-security, maximum-security prisons. Designation given to prison where inmates are maintained in the highest degree of custody and supervision. Inmates are ordinarily segregated from one another and have restricted visitation privileges.

maximum sentence. Under law, the most severe sentence a judge can impose on a convicted offender.

maxi-maxi prison(s). Prison such as federal penitentiary at Marion, Illinois, where offenders are confined in individual cells for up to 23 hours per day, under continuous monitoring and supervision, with no more than three prisoners per guard.

mayhem. In common law, the crime of injuring someone so as to render them less able to fight.

McKay, Henry. Sociologist who collaborated with Clifford R. Shaw in describing social disorganization theory in the 1920s, positing a link between transitional slum areas and crime rates. Strongly influenced by the Chicago School and the work of Ernest Burgess and Robert E. Park.

McNaughten's Rule, case. Insanity defense in which defense claims insanity because when he committed the act, he didn't know what he was doing, or if he did know, he didn't know what he was doing was wrong. Currently, persons raising such a defense claim they did not know the difference between right and wrong.

Mead, George Herbert (circa 1930s). Sociologist who elaborated the term, "symbolic interactionism" (developed earlier by Georg Simmel) a view that explains social behaviors as responses to social stimuli. Developed term, "generalized other," as an abstract conformity medium, as "our impression of what we think others think of us and how we ought to behave," "a generalized conception of other's expectations of us" regardless of whether such conceptions are true or false.

meaninglessness. Lack of clarity about what one ought to believe, uncertainty about criteria for making important decisions.

meat eaters. Term used to describe police officers who actively solicit bribes and vigorously engage in corrupt practices.

mechanical jurisprudence. Suggests that everything is known and that therefore, the laws can be made in advance to cover every situation.

mechanical prevention. Directed toward target-hardening to make it difficult or impossible to commit particular offenses.

mechanical solidarity. A unity based upon shared values and norms and on the similarity of functions performed by all members of a society.

mediation. Informal conflict resolution through the intervention of a trained negotiator who seeks a mutually agreeable resolution between disputing parties.

mediation committees. Chinese civilian dispute resolution groups found throughout the country. Mediation committees successfully divert many minor offenders from handling by the more formal methods of justice.

mediator. Probation or parole officer who seeks to intervene in disputes between clients and others (e.g., client may not be able to pay rent on time and the mediator (probation officer) may negotiate with landlord to permit client to make periodic payments until rent is paid).

medical examiner. Qualified physician who examines bodies and performs autopsies. Usually employed by state or local agencies, such persons examine those who have been killed in violent crimes or conduct examinations into how deaths resulted.

medical model. Considers criminal behavior as an illness to be treated. Also known as "treatment model."

medium-security, medium-security prisons. Term applied to prisons where some direct supervision of inmates is maintained but prisoners are eligible for recreational activities and visitation privileges are more relaxed than in maximum security prisons.

Megargee inmate typology. Measure of inmate adjustment to prison life devised from items from the Minnesota Multiphasic Personality Inventory, a psychological personality assessment device; permits classification of prisoners into different risk levels.

mens rea. Intent to commit a crime. Guilty mind.

mentally ill. Persons who cannot conform their conduct according to the law, who don't know the difference between right and wrong, who possibly have a mental disease or defect.

mercy killing. Killing someone because of their intense pain and suffering as a part of a terminal illness or condition. A potentially criminal act whereby life-support system maintenance of a person is removed so that the person dies.

mere evidence. Evidence collected at a crime scene that is cumulative to show one's possible guilt but which does not show any material gain.

merit selection. Reform plan in which judges are nominated by a committee and appointed by the governor for a given period. When the term expires, the voters are asked to signify their approval or disapproval of the judge for a succeeding term. If judge is disapproved, the committee nominates a successor for the governor's appointment.

Merton, Robert K. (1910-). Written extensively about the theory of anomie and strain (1938). Influenced by Emile Durkheim and his theory of anomie. Wrote *Social Theory and Social Structure* (1957). Argues that societal emphasis on success goals cannot be achieved by all persons; thus, those who are less successful than others will turn to alternative means, perhaps criminal, to achieve these culturally desirable and approved goals.

mesomorph. Body type described by Sheldon. Person is strong, muscular, aggressive, tough.

Messner, Steven F. Criminologist who has written about social ecologyecology and its relation to suicide (1985). Also has collaborated with Richard Rosenfeld in describing the American Dream, a phenomenon not altogether different from Robert Merton's discussion of anomie and its link with crime.

methadone. A synthetic narcotic that is used as a substitute for heroin in drug-control efforts.

methadone maintenance. A treatment program for heroin addicts that uses an addictive drug (methadone) that does not produce euphoria if taken orally in regular doses, but that does block the euphoric effects of any heroin that is used.

methodology. A system of explicit rules and procedures on which research is based and against which claims for knowledge are evaluated.

Metropolitan Police Act of 1829. Act that empowered Sir Robert Peel to select and organize the Metropolitan Police of London.

Metropolitan Police Force Project Act of 1981. Law authorizing Toronto complaint review to investigate citizen complaints against police.

Metropolitan Police of London. Organized in 1829 by Sir Robert Peel, a prominent British government official. Included duties that emphasized close interaction with the public and maintenance of proper attitudes and temperament.

middle-class measuring rods. According to Albert Cohen, the standards by which teachers and other representatives of state authority evaluate lower-class youths. Because they cannot live up to middle-class standards, lower-class youths are bound to fail, which gives rise to frustration and anger at conventional society.

milieu therapy. A treatment that capitalizes on environmental conditions or persons in the surroundings as instruments of rehabilitation. This strategy is used to create a supportive, caring atmosphere so as to encourage the formation of constructive values, a positive self-concept, and behavioral change.

military syndrome. Propensity of police organizations to organize and operate police departments according to military organization and protocol, including use of ranks and similar hierarchies of authority.

Miller, Walter. Criminologist who has investigated gang delinquency (1958). Describes unique value system of lower-class culture and focal concerns. Value system gradually develops or evolves to fit conditions in slum areas.

mini-stations. Small police stations strategically located in high-crime-rate neighborhoods, staffed by one or more police officers.

minimal brain dysfuction (MBD). An attention-deficit disorder that may produce such antisocial behaviors as impulsivity, hyperactivity, and aggressiveness.

minimum due process. *See* due process.

minimum-security, minimum-security prisons. Term applied to prisons where inmates are housed in efficiency apartments and permitted extensive freedoms and activities, under little supervision by correctional officers. Designated for nonviolent, low risk offenders.

Minnesota Multiphasic Personality Inventory (MMPI). Personality assessment measure that purportedly assesses a number of personality traits including anxiety, authoritarianism, and sociability.

Minnesota sentencing grid. Sentencing guidelines established by Minnesota legislature in 1980 and used by judges to sentence offenders. Grid contains criminal history score, offense seriousness, and presumptive sentences to be imposed. Judges may depart from guidelines upward or downward depending upon aggravating or mitigating circumstances.

minor. Any person not of legal age or age of majority; any juvenile or infant.

Miranda warning, rights. Warning given to suspects by police officers advising suspects of their legal rights to counsel, to refuse to answer questions, to avoid self-incrimination, and other privileges.

miscarriage of justice. Decision by a court that is inconsistent with the legal rights of a party in the case.

miscegenation laws. Outmoded laws forbidding interracial marriages. Declared unconstitutional in 1967.

misdemeanant. Person who commits a misdemeanor.

misdemeanor. Crime punishable by fines and/or imprisonment, usually in a city or county jail, for periods of less than one year.

misprision of felony. The crime of concealing a felony committed by another.

misrepresentation. An untrue statement of fact made to deceive or mislead.

missing persons. Any persons who are unaccounted for following a 24-hour period.

mission statements. Goals and orientation statements of organizations designed to disclose their purposes and responsibilities. Used to vest employees with direction and motivation.

Missouri Plan. Method of selecting judges in which merit system for appointments is used. Believed to reduce political influence in the selection of judges.

mistake. Affirmative defense which alleges that an act was not criminal because the person charged did not know the act was a prohibited one.

mistake of fact. Unconscious ignorance of a fact or the belief in the existence of something that does not exist.

mistake of law. An erroneous opinion of legal principles applied to a given set of facts. A judge may rule on a given court issue and the ruling may be wrong because the judge misunderstands the meaning of the law and how it should be applied.

mistrial. A trial that cannot stand, is invalid. Judges may call a mistrial for reasons such as errors on the part of prosecutors or defense counsel, the death of a juror or counsel, a hung jury.

mitigating circumstances, factors. Circumstances about a crime that may lessen the severity of sentence imposed by the judge. Cooperating with police to apprehend others involved, youthfulness or old age of defendant, mental instability, and having no prior record are considered mitigating circumstances.

mittimus. An order by the court to an officer to bring someone named in the order directly to jail.

mixed control organization. A correctional organization in which policy-making and resource supply are shared by centralized and local resources.

mixed sentence. Two or more separate sentences imposed after offenders have been convicted of two or more crimes in the same adjudication proceeding. *See also* split sentence.

MMPI. *See* Minnesota Multiphasic Personality Inventory.

M'Naghten Rule. *See* McNaughton's Rule.

mob. Any violent crowd with a nefarious purpose.

mobile command post. Law enforcement vehicle containing communications equipment permitting unit to control activities of officers in other vehicles operating in the same geographical area.

model. An abstraction that serves to order and simplify reality while still representing its essential characteristics.

model penal code. Code developed by the American Law Institute clarifying crimes and accompanying punishments. No jurisdictions are obligated to adhere to it.

mode of adaptation. A way that persons who occupy a particular social position adjust to cultural goals and the institutionalized means to reach those goals. *See also* strain theory.

modus operandi. The characteristic method a person uses in the performance of repeated criminal acts.

Moffitt, Terrie. Wrote about neurophysiology in 1990, a study of brain activity, in which it is believed that neurological and physical abnormalities are acquired during the fetal stage and then control behavior throughout one's life span.

Mollen Commission. An investigative unit set up to inquire into police corruption in New York in the 1990s.

Molly Maguires. A powerful secret police organization in 1870s Pennsylvania.

monetary restitution. *See* restitution.

money laundering. Process whereby money derived from illegal activities is placed in secret bank accounts and subsequently transferred as "legal funds" to United States banks or institutions.

monitored release. Any form of recognizance release with the additional minimal supervision of service (e.g., defendants may be sworn to keep a pretrial services agency informed of their whereabouts, and the agency reminds these defendants of court dates and verifies their subsequent court appearance).

monogamy. Having only one spouse, as distinct from bigamy or polygamy.

monozygotic (MZ) twins. Identical twins who develop from a single fertilized egg that divides into two embryos.

Montesquieu, Charles-Louis de Secondat, Baron de La Brede et de (1689-1755). Lawyer, philosopher, and writer. Author of *The Spirit of the Laws*. Penal reformer who wrote about inhuman punishments at Devil's Island in French Guiana.

moonlighting. Practice of police officers holding after-hours jobs in private security or other related professions.

moot. Term used to describe a controversy that has ended or evolved to the stage where a court decision on that particular case is no longer relevant or necessary. This is a limitation on the power of courts to decide cases.

moot court. A court created and used by law students to practice what they have learned in class. A mock court in which students act as witnesses, the judge, jury, and prosecutors and defense counsel.

moot question. Because of situational factors, a question that is no longer relevant. During testimony, a question may have been answered indirectly, thus rendering it moot.

moral crusades. Efforts by interest-group members to stamp out behavior that they find objectionable. Typically, moral crusades are directed at public order crimes, such as drug abuse or pornography.

moral development theory. A view of criminality which holds that criminals have an underdeveloped moral sense preventing them from making the correct behavior choices in a given situation.

moral enterprise. The process undertaken by an advocacy group in order to have its values legitimated and embodied in law.

moral entrepreneurs. Persons who use their influence to shape the legal process in ways they see fit.

moral turpitude. Depravity or baseness of conduct.

mores. Ways of behaving in a society with a moral connotation attached.

MOSOP. Missouri Sexual Offender Program targeted to serve needs of incarcerated, non-psychotic sexual offenders.

motion. An oral or written request to a judge that asks the court to make a specific ruling, finding, decision, or order. May be presented at any appropriate point from an arrest until the end of a trial.

motion for a bill of particulars. An action before the court asking that the details of the state's case against a defendant be made known to the defense. *See also* discovery.

motion for continuance. An action before the court asking that the trial or hearing or proceeding be postponed to a later date.

motion for summary judgment. Request granted by judges who have read the plaintiff's version and defendant's version of events in actions filed by inmates, and a decision is reached holding for the defendant, usually prison authorities.

motion in limine. A pre-trial motion, generally to obtain judicial approval to admit certain items into evidence that might otherwise be considered prejudicial or inflammatory.

motion to dismiss. An action before the court requesting that the judge refuse to hear a suit. Usually granted when inmates who file petitions fail to state a claim upon which relief can be granted.

motor vehicle theft. Stealing or attempting to steal an automobile or any other mode of trasportation powered by gasoline or diesel fuel; includes snowmobiles, trucks, buses, motorscooters, and motorcycles.

Mount Pleasant Female Prison. First prison for female offenders, established in 1835 in New York.

mug shot. A photograph of a criminal suspect taken by police when suspect is booked following an arrest.

mules. Name given to couriers and smugglers of drugs and other illegal contraband, especially from other countries and into the United States. "Mules" often swallow large quantities of heroin or cocaine in glassine envelopes in an originating country. After crossing United States borders, they defecate and the illegal contraband is retrieved. Mules are paid nominal amounts for such smuggling.

multifactor theories. Explanations of criminal behavior that combine the influences of structural, socialization, conflict, and individual variables. *See also* integrated theories.

municipal courts. Courts of special jurisdiction whose jurisdiction follows the political boundaries of a municipality or city.

municipality. Any local jurisdiction, such as a town or county.

municipal liability theory. Theory that says city is liable when its police officers or other agents act to cause unreasonable harm to citizens. Theory of agency whereby city assumes responsibility for the actions of its employees, including the police.

murder. Intentionally causing the death of another without reasonable provocation or legal justification, or causing the death of another while committing or attempting to commit another crime.

murder in the first degree. A killing done with premeditation and deliberation or, by statute, in the presence of other aggravating circumstances.

murder in the second degree. A killing done with intent to cause death but without premeditation and deliberation.

murder transaction. Concept that murder is usually a result of behavior interactions between victims and offenders.

mushrooms. Term given by youth gang members to innocent-bystander victims of drive-by shootings. Term comes from popular video game, Centipede, in which the object is to "kill" or "mash" mushrooms that grow into threatening game enemies. When gang members discuss how many rival gang members were shot, they may say, "We got a few mushrooms too," meaning that they hurt or killed innocent bystanders as well.

mutual agreement program. Any formal agreement between inmates and penitentiary and/or parole board administrators or members whereby the inmate voluntarily enters a course of study and/or therapy designed for self-improvement such that a definite parole date can be established; if the inmate complies with the requirements of the agreement, through completing educational, vocational, or any other prescribed endeavor, the parole board will be influenced favorably to consider the inmate's early release from prison.

mutual pledge. Alfred the Great's system of internal policing that organized the people into tithings, hundreds, and shires; persisted between 1100-1500 A.D.

Myrdal, Gunnar. Scandinavian sociologist who wrote *An American Dilemma* in 1944. Contended that race relations could be understood best from the point of view of persons outside of United States who might be more objective in their assessments. Myrdal's own biases were evident from his work, strongly suggesting that cultural differences may not outweigh racial ones when evaluating race relations in other cultures.

N

naive check forgers. Edwin Lemert's term for amateurs who forge checks and do not believe that their actions will harm anyone. They are often from middle-class families and resort to forgery as a hasty reaction to some financial setback, often rationalizing their conduct. This latter behavior is called "closure."

naline test. A test administered to persons to detect narcotics.

narc. Slang for "narcotics officer."

narcoterrorism. A political alliance between terrorist groups and drug-supplying cartels. The cartels provide financing for the terrorists, who in turn provide quasi-military protection to the drug dealers.

narcotic. Any drug which is capable of producing euphoria, pain relief, or some other psychologically desirable condition, which is also a controlled substance and prohibited without a prescription.

narrative. A portion of a presentence investigation report prepared by a probation officer or private agency which provides a description of offense and offender. Culminates in and justifies a recommendation for a specific sentence to be imposed on the offender by judges.

National Advisory Commission on Criminal Justice Standards and Goals. Promulgated several important goals for police departments in order to clarify their policing functions, including maintenance of order, enforcement of the law, prevention of criminal activity, detection of criminal activity, apprehension of criminals, participation in court proceedings, protection of constitutional guarantees, assistance to those who cannot care for themselves or who are in danger of physical harm, control of traffic, resolution of day-to-day conflicts among family, friends, and neighbors, creation and maintenance of a feeling of security in the community, and promotion and preservation of civil order.

National Commission on Law Observance and Enforcement. Created by Herbert Hoover in 1929 to investigate law enforcement practices and standards.

National Council on Crime and Delinquency. A private national agency that promotes efforts at crime control through research, citizen involvement, and public information efforts.

National Crime Information Center (NCIC). Established by the FBI in 1967. Central information source for stolen vehicles, accident information, stolen property, arrested persons, fingerprint information, criminal offenses, and criminal offenders and their whereabouts.

National Crime Panel Reports, National Crime Panel Survey Reports. Criminal victimization surveys conducted for the Law Enforcement Assistance Administration by the United States Bureau of the Census, which gauge the extent to which persons age twelve and over, households, and businesses, have been victims of certain types of crime, and describe the nature of the criminal incidents and their victims. *See also National Crime Survey.*

National Crime Survey. Published in cooperation with the United States Bureau of the Census, a random survey of 60,000 households, including 127,000 persons 12 years of age or older and 50,000 businesses. Measures crime committed against specific victims interviewed and not necessarily reported to law enforcement officers. In 1991 survey became known as *National Crime Victimization Survey* to more accurately reflect the nature of the data collected.

National Crime Victimization Survey. See *National Crime Survey.*

National Incident-Based Reporting System (NIBRS). A reporting system in which the police describe each offense in a crime incident together with the data describing the offender, victim, and property.

National Institute of Corrections' Model Classification Project. Risk and needs assessment project established by the federal government to enable juvenile judges to make more informed sentencing decisions.

National Institute of Justice. Created in 1979 to provide for and encourage research to improve federal, state, and local criminal justice systems, prevent or reduce incidence of crime, and identify effective programs.

National Ombudsman. Swedish representative of the people elected by the Parliament for a four-year term. Oversees and intercedes in prisoner complaints and public grievances. May resolve disputes about judicial sentencing decisions and conduct inspections of Swedish prisons.

National Police Agency. Japanese national police and recentralized police operations throughout the 47 prefectures, including three additional prefecture-equivalent agencies in Tokyo and Hokkaido.

National Prison Association. Founded in 1870. First president was future United States President Rutherford B. Hayes. Later became American Prison Association, then American Correctional Association. *See also* American Correctional Association.

National Youth Survey (NYS). Program for gathering data on crime by interviewing adolescents over a five-year period. Program has been structured to overcome many of the criticisms of other self-report studies.

naturalization. Means whereby persons may attain United States citizenship, usually after completing various requirements, swearing allegiance to the United States, agreeing to obey its laws.

natural law. A body of principles and rules imposed by some higher power than person-made law that are considered to be uniquely fitting for and binding on any community of rational beings.

NCVS. Acronym for *National Crime Victimization Survey*.

necessarily included offense. An offense committed for the purpose of committing another offense (e.g., trespass committed for the purpose of committing burglary).

necessity. A condition that compels someone to act because of perceived needs. An affirmative defense (e.g., when someone's automobile breaks down during a snowstorm and an unoccupied cabin is nearby, breaking into the cabin to save oneself from freezing to death is acting out of "necessity" and would be a defense to breaking and entering charges later).

needs-based supervision. A form of community supervision in which interventions by the correctional staff are designed to meet specific needs attributed to or claimed by the offender.

negative affective states. Sociologist Robert Agnew has described strain theory with this variant condition (1992), characterized by failure to achieve positively valued goals, disjunction of expectations and achievements, removal of posi-

tively valued stimuli from individuals, and exposure to negative stimuli.

negative reinforcements. Punishments administered by superiors to subordinate police officers to prevent particular kinds of undesirable conduct.

neglected child, children. Infant(s) adjudged in need of supervision by the juvenile court if abandoned, without proper care, without substance, education, or health care because of neglect or refusal of a parent, guardian, or custodian.

negligence. Liability accruing to prison or correctional program administrators and probation or parole officers as the result of a failure to perform a duty owed clients or inmates or the improper or inadequate performance of that duty. May include negligent entrustment, negligent training, negligent assignment, negligent retention, or negligent supervision (e.g., providing probation or parole officers with revolvers and not providing them with firearms training).

negligent assignment. Placement of correctional officers, probation or parole officers, or other staff members in a position for which they are unqualified.

negligent entrustment. Administators' failure to monitor guards supplied with items they have not yet been trained to use, such as firearms.

negligent hiring and selection. Basis for civil lawsuit in which incompetent persons have been selected to perform important tasks, such as police work, and in which injuries to victims are caused by such incompetent persons.

negligent retention. Administrators' maintaining officers determined unfit for their jobs in those jobs.

negligent training. Basis for civil lawsuit in which clear duty to train employees (e.g., to use firearms) is not met.

negotiable instrument. Any written document promising to pay a certain amount of money (e.g., a check, money order, or promissory note).

Neighborhood Police Posts. Police posts in Singapore, similar to mini-stations or substations such as those found in Detroit, Michigan.

neighborhood policing. Any law enforcement patrol style emphasizing "beats" or regular patrols of the same city blocks or town territories for the purpose of becoming acquainted with the public served.

Neighborhood Watch, neighborhood watch programs. Organization of residents maintaining surveillance over a given area, where neighbors are encouraged to report suspicious circumstances to police and take precautions to prevent crime.

neoclassical school. School of thought which maintained that the accused should be exempted from conviction if circumstances prevented the exercise of free will.

nepotism. Practice of hiring one's relatives or close friends, regardless of qualifications.

net widening. Pulling anyone into a program who would not otherwise be targeted for such a program. Also known as "widening the net." Under ordinary conditions when police officers confront people on the street, the officers may be inclined to issue verbal warnings and release them; however, if a community program is created that caters to particular kinds of clients, officers may arrest these same people and involve them in these programs simply because the programs exist, thus needlessly bringing these people into the program.

networks. Ties among individual members of groups or among different groups.

neurophysiology. The study of brain activity. *See also* Terrie Moffitt.

neuroticism. Personality disorder characterized by low self-esteem, high anxiety, and variable mood swings.

neutralization theory. Explanation holds that delinquents experience guilt when involved in delinquent activities and that they respect leaders of the legitimate social order. Their delinquency is episodic rather than chronic, and they adhere to conventional values while "drifting" into periods of illegal behavior. In order to drift, the delinquent must first neutralize legal and moral values.

New Jersey Intensive Probation Supervision Program. Plan commenced in 1983 to serve low-risk incarcerated offenders, drawing clients from inmate volunteers. Program selectivity limits participants through a seven-stage selection process. Participants must serve at least four months in prison or jail before being admitted to program which monitors their progress extensively. Similar to Georgia Intensive Probation Supervision Program in success and low recidivism scores among participants.

New Police. Also known as the Metropolitan Police of London, formed in 1829 under the command of Sir Robert Peel. Became the model for modern-day police forces throughout the Western world.

new trial. Tribunal *de novo*. After a hung jury or a case is set aside or overturned by a higher court, a new trial is held to determine one's guilt or innocence.

next-of-kin. Nearest living relative to an arrested, injured, or deceased person.

Nicewander, W. Alan. Proposed concept of latent trait theory together with David Rowe and D. Wayne Osgood.

niche. Way of adapting to the prison community that stresses finding one's place in the system, rather than fighting for one's individual rights.

night court. A court so-called because it presides over many arrestees arrested for public drunkenness or lewdness, offenses which occur at night. Such courts hear and resolve petty offenses and make bail decisions. Some courts, such as exist in New York City, are called "after hours" courts, but arrestees also refer to them as "night courts."

nightstick. A baton used by police officers as a defensive device against suspects who assault them.

night watch. Early English watchman program designed to report crime.

night watchman. A thirteenth-century untrained citizen who patrolled at night on the lookout for disturbances. Currently, usually a privately employed officer who maintains a vigilance on the premises of private or public buildings.

1980 Refugee Act. Radically expanded the definition of those eligible for political asylum, but because it has been poorly enforced and easily abused, it helped bring on today's growing demand for new limits on aliens.

no bill. *See* no true bill.

"no knock" law. Regulation empowering law enforcement officers to enter homes or public places with a proper court order without knocking or announcing their intent to enter, in order to obtain evidence that might otherwise be destroyed or to protect themselves against persons who might otherwise imperil their safety.

"no pros." *See nolle prosequi.*

no true bill. Grand jury decision that insufficient evidence exists to establish probable cause that a crime was committed and a specific person committed it.

nolle prosequi. An entry made by the prosecutor on the record in a case and announced in court to indicate that the specified charges will not be prosecuted. In effect, the charges are thereby dismissed.

nolo contendere. Plea of "no contest" to charges. Defendant does not dispute facts, although issue may be taken with the legality or constitutionality of the law allegedly violated. Treated as a guilty plea.

nominal disposition. Juvenile court outcome in which juvenile is warned or verbally reprimanded, but returned to custody of parents.

nonavertable recidivist. Offender whose prior sentence would not have affected the commission of new crimes.

nonintervention. Justice philosophy that emphasizes the least intrusive treatment possible. Among its central policies are decarceration, diversion, and decriminalization.

nonjudicial disposition. A decision in a juvenile case by an authority other than a judge or court of law (e.g., an intake officer). Usually an informal method of determining the most appropriate disposition in handling a juvenile.

nonlethal weapons. Instruments that are designed to incapacitate rather than kill (e.g, "stun-guns" or TASERS, or pistols that shoot rubber bullets).

nonpartisan election. An election in which candidates who are not endorsed by political parties are presented to the voters for selection.

nonresidential program. Plan allowing youths to remain in their homes or foster homes while receiving services.

nonsecure facility, setting. A facility which emphasizes the care and treatment of youths without the need to place constraints to ensure public protection.

nonsuit. A judgment in favor of a defendant because of the failure of the plaintiff to state a case upon which relief can be granted.

nonviolent offense. Crime against property in which no physical injury to victims is sustained (e.g., embezzlement, fraud, forgery, larceny, burglary, vehicular theft).

norm. Societal expectations concerning behavior.

normlessness. A situation in which social guideposts or rules have eroded, or become ineffective for regulating conduct. In this condition, sometimes called anomie, delinquent behavior or criminal activities may be seen as justifying illegitimate routes to goal achievement. *See also* Emile Durkheim, Robert Merton.

notary, notary public. A person empowered by law to administer oaths, to certify things or documents as true, and to perform various minor official acts.

not guilty by reason of insanity. The plea of defendants or the verdict of a jury or judge in a criminal proceeding, that defendants are not guilty of the offense(s) charged because at the time the crimes were committed, the defendants did not have the mental capacity to be held criminally responsible for their actions.

notice. An official document advising someone of a proceeding which usually requires their attendance.

nuisance. An unlawful or unreasonable use of a person's property resulting in injury to another or to the public (e.g., someone who lets his dog roam freely about the community where it may bite someone or cause physical harm would be considered a nuisance).

nullen crimen, nulla poena, sine lege. "There is no crime, there is no punishment, without law."

numbers-game model. Caseload assignment model for probation or parole officers in which total number of offender/clients is divided by number of officers.

O

objective parole criteria. General qualifying conditions that permit parole boards to make nonsubjective parole decisions without regard to an inmate's race, religion, gender, age, or socioeconomic status.

objective test. Experiment for identifying entrapment. Test assumes suspects have criminal records and/or are disposed to particular type of crime, whatever means police wish to use to elicit behavior are acceptable.

obscenity, obscene material. Current legal theory suggests that sexually explicit material that lacks a serious purpose and appeals solely to the prurient interest of viewers is obscene. While nudity *per se* is not usually considered obscene, open sex behavior, masturbation, and exhibition of the genitals are banned in many communities. Local community standards often define obscenity.

observation. A research strategy that involves the careful and systematic watching of behavior.

obstruction of justice. Impeding or preventing law enforcement officers from doing their job. Interfering with the administration of justice.

OBTS. Acronym for Offender-based Transaction Statistics. A new means of reporting crime information in a more systematic way, by establishing interagency networks of information exchange.

occasional criminals. Persons who do not define themselves as criminals but who commit infrequent crimes, usually property crimes.

occupational crime. Offenses committed by persons for their own benefit in the course of performing their jobs.

offender, alleged. Person who has been charged with a specific offense by a law enforcement agency or court but has not been convicted.

offender, convicted. An adult who has been found guilty of one or more criminal offenses.

offender rehabilitation. Condition achieved when criminals are reintegrated into their communities and refrain from further criminal activity. *See also* rehabilitation.

offense escalation. Progression of less serious adult or juvenile offenders to more serious types of crimes.

offenses known to the police. Reported occurrences of offenses in the *Uniform Crime Reports* which have been verified at the police level.

offenses, Part I. *See* Part I offenses.

offenses, Part II. *See* Part II offenses.

Office of Justice Assistance, Research and Statistics (OJARS). Federal criminal justice funding agency comprised of the National Institute of Justice, the Bureau of Justice Statistics, and the Law Enforcement Assistance Administration. Prior to 1979, known as the Law Enforcement Assistance Administration.

Office of Justice Programs. Created in 1984 to replace the Law Enforcement Assistance Administration, and holds with similar powers and duties. Administers grants designed to assist criminal justice systems.

Office of Juvenile Justice and Delinquency Prevention. Established by Congress under the Juvenile Justice and Delinquency Prevention Act of 1974; designed to remove status offenders from jurisdiction of juvenile courts and dispose of their cases less formally.

official crime. Criminal behavior that has been recorded by the police.

official criminal statistics. Enumerations of crimes that come to the attention of law enforcement agencies. Arrest compilations and characteristics of offenders and crimes based on arrest, judicial, and prison records.

official data. Any data collected by law enforcement agencies, courts, and other governmental sources. The principal sources of official juvenile delinquency and crime data are the *Uniform Crime Reports* and *National Crime Survey*.

Ohlin, Lloyd. Criminologist who collaborated with Richard Cloward to write *Delinquency and Opportunity* (1960), which described strain theory and opportunity theory. They posit that deviance, delinquency, and crime are precipitated whenever disadvantaged youths are deprived of or lack the legitimate means to achieve culturally approved or desired goals. Described criminal gangs, conflict gangs, and retreatist gangs.

ombudsman. *See* National Ombudsman.

omission. The failure to do whatever the law prescribes or requires a person to do.

Omnibus Crime Control and Safe Streets Act. A piece of federal law and order legislation that was viewed by some as a political maneuver aimed at allaying fears of crime rather than bringing about criminal justice reform.

180 Degrees, Inc. Program operated by Minnesota Department of Corrections, comparable to a halfway house for sex offense parolees with no previous treatment for their sex offenses, who are willing to admit that they have committed one or more sex offenses, and who can function as group members in productive discussions about their sexual conduct.

on the pad. Expression denoting a police officer who receives regular payoffs for ignoring vice-related cases.

open court. Any court where spectators may gather.

opening statement. Remarks made by prosecution and defense attorneys to jury at the commencement of trial proceedings. Usually these statements set forth what each side intends to show by evidence to be presented.

open institutions. Prisons without walls, such as correctional camps, ranches, and farms.

open-systems model. A perspective on organizations that places high value on resource acquisition and growth through the use of flexible structures that can respond to opportunities.

operant conditioning theory. Explains behavior by reference to overt action and its conditioning by external stimuli, particularly the reinforcing or punishing consequences of one's actions.

operational capacity. Total number of inmates that can be accommodated based on size of jail or prison facility's staff, programs, and other services.

Operation Blockade. An Immigration and Naturalizaton Service (INS) experiment launched with $250,000 in extra overtime funds and agents stationed in inland posts in El Paso, Texas to prevent the influx of illegal aliens into the United States

Operation Identification. Sponsored by local police and other agencies to assist citizens in identifying their personal property if stolen. Includes fingerprinting children for later identification if lost or kidnapped.

opiate. Any drug capable of relieving pain and creating a psychological euphoria.

opinion. The official announcement of a court's decision and the reasons for that decision. In research methods, the verbal expression of an attitude.

opinion of the court. Opinion summarizing the views of the majority of judges participating in a judicial decision; a ruling or holding by a court official.

opium. Substance derived from the poppy plant. Used to manufacture heroin, a highly addictive narcotic.

opportunity theory. Proposes that individuals of low socioeconomic status are more likely to engage in criminal acts because they have fewer legitimate opportunities.

opportunist robber. Someone who steals small amounts whenever a vulnerable target presents itself.

oral argument. Verbal presentation made to an appellate court by prosecution or defense in order to persuade the court to affirm, reverse, or modify a lower court decision.

order. Any written declaration or proclamation by a judge authorizing officials to act.

order maintenance. Police function of preventing behavior that disturbs or threatens to disturb the public peace or that involves face-to-face conflict between two or more persons. In such situations, police exercise discretion in deciding whether a law has been broken.

ordinance. Any enactment of a local governing body such as a city council or commission.

Oregon boot. Correctional device used to disable prisoners who work on chain gangs. Usually consists of metal anklets linked by a short chain to impede walking or running.

Oregon model. Probation development project devised by the Edna McConnell Clark Foundation. Uses risk scores for selecting clients, relying heavily on former drug abuse and violence as criteria which exclude offenders from participation. Attempts selection of middle-range offenders, who are subject to "shock incarceration" for 30 days or more as part of the program. *See also* shock probation.

organic solidarity. A unity based upon an independence of functions, much as in a complex biological organism. *See also* Max Weber.

organizational approach. Type of police discretion whereby police administrators provide officers with a list of priorities and explicitly clarify how police should handle encounters with citizens.

organizational crime. Crime that involves large corporations and their efforts to control the marketplace and earn huge profits through unlawful bidding, unfair advertising, monopolistic practices, and other illegal means.

organizational development. An organizational change strategy that seeks to revitalize the culture of the organization by developing teamwork and sensitivity to workers' needs while improving organizational performance. Usually starts at the top of the organization and uses expert outside consultants to assist in the change process.

organizational values. Standards imparted by organizations to membership designed to instill them with work motivation and goals.

organized crime. Those self-perpetuating, structured associations of individuals and groups combined for the purpose of profiting in whole or in part by illegal means, while protecting their activities through a pattern of graft and corruption.

Organized Crime Drug Enforcement Task Force Program. A joint federal, state and local law enforcement initiative against high-level drug trafficking organizations.

organized robbery and gang theft. Highly skilled criminal activities using or threatening to use force, violence, coercion, and property damage, and accompanied by planning, surprise, and speed to diminish the risks of apprehension.

original jurisdiction. First authority over a case or cause, as opposed to appellate jurisdiction.

Osgood, D. Wayne. Proposed latent trait theory, together with David Rowe and W. Alan Nicewander.

outreach centers. Substations or satellite offices of regular probation and parole agencies.

overbreadth doctrine. First Amendment doctrine holding that a law is invalid if it can be applied to punish people for engaging in constitutionally protected expression, such as speech or religious rituals.

overcharging. Filing charges against a defendant more serious than the ones the prosecutor believes are justified by the evidence and charging more or more serious counts than those on which the prosecutor wants a conviction.

overcriminalization. The use of criminal sanctions to deter behavior that is acceptable to substantial portions of society.

overcrowding. Condition that exists when numbers of prisoners exceed the space allocations for which the jail or prison is designed. Often associated with double-bunking.

overrule. To reverse or annul by subsequent action (e.g., judges may overrule objections from prosecutors and defense attorneys in court, nullifying these objections; lower court decisions may be overruled by higher courts when the case is appealed).

P

pains of imprisonment. The deprivations associated with imprisonment, including loss of freedom, autonomy, goods and services, security, and heterosexual relationships.

panel. A set of jurors or prospective jurors. A set of judges assigned to hear a case. In research, a design in survey research that offers a close approximation of the before-after condition of experimental designs by interviewing the same group at two or more points in time.

panhandle, panhandler. To beg for money in a public place. One who begs for money in public.

paraffin test. A test to determine whether there is gunpowder residue on one's body or clothing.

paralegal. Person with some legal training who assists attorneys with their business; may look up legal cases, brief cases, and conduct interviews and interrogatories.

paranoia. Psychotic behavior wherein paranoiacs (1) have delusions of grandeur and (2) are fearful of others and feel persecuted.

paraphilias. Bizarre or abnormal sexual practices that may involve recurrent sexual urges focused on objects, humiliation, or children.

paraprofessional. Person who works in a community agency or public organization. Has some skills relating to corrections, but is not certified or has not completed any formal course of study culminating in a corrections certificate or degree.

pardon. Unconditional release of inmate, usually by governor or chief executive officer of jurisdiction.

parens patriae. "Parent of the country." Refers to doctrine that state oversees the welfare of youth, originally established by King of England and administered through chancellors.

Park, Robert Ezra (1864-1944). Assisted in developing the "Chicago School" in which theorists focused upon the functions of social institutions and their breakdown. Closely associated crime with particular neighborhoods and neighborhood conditions. Some neighborhoods form "natural areas" of affluence or poverty. Further, different types of crime could be associated with different types of neighborhoods. Examined "concentric zones" adjacent to Chicago and its suburban communities. Considered areas of urban renewal as "interstitial areas" or zones of transitions. The concentric zone hypothesis was one defining feature of the Chicago School, where different neighborhood zones emanating away from the "Loop," or downtown Chicago, exhibited different characteristics as well as different forms of criminal behavior. Collaborated with Edwin Sutherland, Louis Wirth, and Ernest W. Burgess.

parole. Prerelease from prison short of serving a full sentence. The status of an offender conditionally released from a confinement facility prior to the expiration of the sentence and placed under the supervision of a parole agency.

parole board, paroling authority Body of persons either appointed by governors or others or elected which determines whether those currently incarcerated in prisons should be granted parole or early release.

parole evidence. Oral testimony given in court.

parolee. Convicted offender who has been released from prison short of serving the full sentence originally imposed; usually must abide by conditions established by the parole board or paroling authority.

parole officer. Correctional official who supervises parolees.

parole prediction. An estimate of the probability of violation or nonviolation of parole on the basis of experience tables, developed with regard to groups of offenders with similar characteristics.

parole program. The specific conditions under which inmates are granted early release.

parole revocation. Two-stage proceeding that may result of a parolee's reincarceration in jail or prison. First stage is a preliminary hearing to determine whether parolee violated any specific parole condition. Second stage is to determine whether parole should be cancelled and the offender reincarcerated.

parole rules. The conditions upon which an inmate is granted early release. These may require them to report regularly to parole officers, to refrain from criminal conduct, to avoid contact with other convicted offenders, to maintain and support their families, to abstain from alcoholic beverages and drugs, or to remain with the jurisdiction. Violating any one or more of these rules may result in parole revocation.

parole supervision. Guidance, treatment, or regulation of the behavior of a convicted adult who is obliged to fulfill conditions of parole or conditional release. Parole supervision is authorized and required by statute, performed by a parole agency, and occurs after a period of prison confinement.

parole supervisory caseload. The total number of clients a parole agency or officer has on a given date or during a specified time period.

parole violation. A parolee's act against or failure to act in relation to the conditions of his or her parole program.

parricide. Murder of one's guardian, mother, or father.

parsimonious. Explaining a broad range of phenomena with only a few principles.

Part I offenses. Crimes designated by the FBI as "most serious" and compiled in terms of the number of reports made by law enforcement agencies and the number of arrests reported. Includes homicide, robbery, forcible rape, aggravated assault, burglary, motor vehicle theft, arson, and larceny.

Part II offenses. Crimes designated by the FBI as "less serious" and compiled in terms of the number of reports made to law enforcement agencies and the number of arrests made. Includes simple assault, fraud, embezzlement, disorderly conduct, vagrancy, runaways, curfew and loitering violations, suspicion, drunkenness, liquor law violations, drug abuse violations, gambling, prostitution, and several other offenses.

partial confinement. An alternative to traditional jail sentences consisting of "weekend" sentences that permit offenders to spend the work week in the community or in school. *See also* work release, study release, furloughs.

partial deterrent. Legal measure designed to restrict or control, rather than to eliminate, an undesirable act.

participation hypothesis. Proposes that the more subordinates participate in decision making affecting their work, the more they will like their work and comply with orders from superiors.

participant observation. Collecting information through involvement in the social life of a group the researcher is studying.

participative management. Theory of organizations in which employees have some input or "say" regarding departmental operations.

particularity. Requirement that a search warrant must state precisely where the search is to take place and what items are to be seized.

parties to offenses. All people associated with the crime, either before or after it was committed, whether they actually committed the crime or assisted in some way in its planning; may include those who assist criminals in eluding capture.

partisan election. An election in which candidates endorsed by political parties are presented to the voters for selection.

passive sensor. Alcohol detection device used by Japanese police and others to detect presence of alcohol in exhaled breath. Used in drunk driving investigations.

paternalism. Male domination. A paternalistic family, for instance, is one in which the father is the dominant authority figure.

pathologist. Expert trained in pathology, involving the study of the etiology and development of a disease.

pathways, pathways to crime. A part of life course theory suggesting that more than one road leads to criminal conduct. "Authority conflict pathway" proposes that criminal conduct begins in one's early years with parental defiance and stubborn behavior. "Covert pathway" proposes that crime begins with minor offending and status offending. "Overt pathway" proposes that various acts escalate from less to more serious, and eventually to criminal violence. Pathway theory suggested by Rolf Loeber (1993).

patriarchy. Male-dominated system. *See also* paternalism.

patricide. The killing of one's father.

patrol. Means of deploying police officers in ways that give them responsibility for policing activity in defined areas and that usually requires them to make regular circuits of those areas.

patrol car video cameras. Videotape units in police vehicles used for various purposes (e.g., to tape arrests of suspected drunk drivers, to illustrate causes for stops and arrests of motorists for various charges).

patrol officer, patrolman. A police officer whose duties include peacekeeping, service, and law enforcement in a particular area of a jurisdiction. May include foot, car, air, or other ways of covering a jurisdiction.

patterns of crime. A research strategy that involves the use of data to determine where crime is committed, who commits crime, who is victimized, and what are the major dimensions of the criminal act.

pauper. One without money or means to support him- or herself.

Peace Officer Standards and Training (POST). Commission established to administer training programs for prospective law enforcement officers nationwide. Includes mandatory training requirements for hiring police officers and those entering other aspects of law enforcement.

peace officer. Any law enforcement officer at the state or local levels whose primary responsibility is to enforce and preserve the public peace. May include sheriffs and their deputies, constables, and members of city police forces.

peacekeeping, peacekeeping role. Function of police involving keeping order within communities and seeing that societies operate in a smooth and conventional fashion.

peacemaking criminology. View that main purpose of criminology is to promote a peaceful and just society. Attempts to find humanistic solutions to social problems and crime rather than punishment and imprisonment.

pederasty. Anal intercourse, usually between a man and a boy.

pedophile, pedophilia. A molester of children. An unnatural fondness for children, particularly for sexual intercourse.

Peel, Sir Robert (1788-1850). British Home Secretary in 1829, founded the Metropolitan Police of London, one of the first organized police forces in the world.

Peeping Tom. One who looks in windows of others for the purpose of sexual gratification. *See also* voyeurism.

peer. An "equal." In a jury trial of one's peers, theoretically a trial composed of persons with characteristics similar to the defendant.

peer counseling program. Plan utilized by some police departments in which certain police officers are used to counsel others. They are intended to be non-threatening and to assist officers overcome their problems.

penal. Of or pertaining to punishment.

Penal Code of 1907. Initially defined a broad range of crimes and punishments in Japan. Although there is no formal distinction between felonies and misdemeanors, such as the distinction made in the United States, the Japanese Penal Code defines traditional crimes, including homicide, rape, burglary, robbery, and vehicular theft. The age of criminal responsibility has been set at 14, although persons age 20 or over are considered adults. Those between the ages of 14 and 19 are usually treated as juveniles in independent juvenile proceedings.

penal servitude. Put to work at hard labor under conditions of confinement.

penalty. Punishment prescribed by law or judicial decision for the commission of a particular offense, which may be death, imprisonment, fine, or loss of civil privileges.

penitentiary. Used interchangeably with "prison" to refer to long-term facilities where high custody levels are observed, including solitary confinement or single-cell occupancy, where prisoners are segregated from one another during evening hours.

Penitentiary Act. Legislation passed by House of Commons in England in 1779, authorizing creation of new facilities to house prisoners, where they could be productive. Prisoners would be well-fed, well-treated, well-clothed, housed in safe and sanitary units, and trained to perform skills.

penitentiary movement. Political and social attention focused on debates about the most effective penitentiary design. During this time (1790-1830) the first major prisons were built in the eastern United States.

Penn, William. Established "Great Law of Pennsylvania." Quaker, penal reformer, and founder of Pennsylvania. Abolished corporal punishments in favor of fines and incarceration, using jails to confine offenders.

Pennsylvania system. Devised and used in Walnut Street Jail in 1790 to place prisoners in solitary confinement. Predecessor to modern prisons. Used solitude to increase penitence and prevent cross-infection of prisoners. Encouraged behavioral improvements.

penologist. Social scientist who studies and applies the theory and methods of punishment for crime.

penology. A branch of criminology dealing with the management of prisons and inmate treatment.

Pepinsky, Harold (Hal). Advocated peacemaking as the primary function of criminology. Proposed that establishing social justice would eliminate all forms of predatory behavior.

per curiam. "By the court." Phrase used to distinguish an opinion rendered by the whole court as opposed to an opinion expressed by a single judge.

per diem. "By the day." The cost per day, here the daily cost of housing inmates.

per se. "By itself." In itself (e.g., the death penalty is not unconstitutional *per se*, but a particular method of administering the death penalty may be unconstitutional in some states).

percentage bail. A publicly managed bail service arrangement that allows defendants to deposit a percentage (about 10 percent) of the amount of bail with the court clerk.

peremptory challenge. Rejection of a juror by either prosecution or defense in which no reason needs to be provided for excusing juror from jury duty. Each side has a limited number of these challenges. The more serious the offense, the more peremptory challenges are given each side.

perjury. Lying under oath in court.

perpetrator. One who commits or attempts to commit a crime.

persistent felony offenders. Habitual offenders who commit felonies with a high recidivism rate.

persisters. Criminals who do not age out of crime. Chronic delinquents who continue offending into their adulthood. *See also* recidivism.

person. A human being considered a legal unit with rights and responsibilities who may litigate claims or be prosecuted or adjudicated.

person in need of supervision. A youth characterized as ungovernable, incorrigible, truant, or habitually disobedient. *See also* PINS.

personally secured bond. Security that is put up by defendant or defendant's family; this arrangement is generally out of reach of less affluent defendants.

personal choice. A perspective that sees all delinquent and criminal behavior as emanating from responsible individuals rather than from the social conditions in which they reside. Such persons must be held accountable for their actions, and their defective thinking must be corrected by firm and consistent approaches.

Pestalozzi, Henrich (1746-1827). Swiss educator who developed private institutions dedicated to the reform and training of wayward and destitute children.

petition. A document filed in juvenile court alleging that a juvenile is a delinquent, a status offender, or a dependent and asking that the court assume jurisdiction over the juvenile or that the juvenile transferred to a criminal court to be prosecuted as an adult.

petition not sustained. Finding by juvenile court at an adjudicatory hearing that there is insufficient evidence to sustain an allegation that a juvenile is a delinquent, status offender, or dependent.

petitioner. Person who brings a petition before the court.

petit jury. The trier of fact in a criminal case. The jury of one's peers called to hear the evidence and decide the defendant's guilt or innocence. Varies in size among states.

petit larceny. Also petty larceny, any theft of small amounts. A misdemeanor.

petty offenses. Minor infractions or crimes, misdemeanors. Usually punishable by fines or short terms of imprisonment.

peyote. The substance from a cactus of the same name. Used for hallucinogenic effects. A narcotic and an illegal substance.

phantom effect. Belief of burglars and thieves that police may be patrolling a particular area causing them to avoid area. Used to explain findings of Kansas City Preventive Patrol Experiments.

phenolphthalein test. A crude test to determine if a substance is blood.

phenomenological criminology. A perspective on crime causation that holds that the significance of criminal behavior is ultimately knowable only to those who participate in it. Central to this school of thought is the belief that social actors endow their behavior with meaning and purpose. Hence, a crime might mean one thing to the person who commits it, quite another to the victim, and something far different still to professional participants in the justice system.

Philadelphia House of Industry. Halfway house established in Philadelphia in 1889.

Philadelphia Society for Alleviating the Miseries of Public Prisons. Society made up of prominent Philadelphia citizens, philanthropists, and religious reformers who believe prison conditions ought to be changed and made more humane. Established in 1787.

phrenology. Outmoded system of analysis which determined one's character and development of faculties based on the shape and protuberances of one's skull.

physical location analysis. A simple observation that focuses on the ways in which individuals use their bodies in a social space.

physiognomy. Outmoded study of facial features and their relation to human behavior.

picaresque organization. A relatively permanent gang under the leadership of a single person who sometimes relies on the support and advice of a few officers.

pickpocketing. The theft of money or valuables directly from the garments of the victim.

piece-price system. A variation of the contract system of prison industry in which the contractor supplies the raw material and receives the finished product, paying the prison a specified amount for each piece produced.

pilferage. Theft by employees through stealth or deception.

pimp. A procurer or manager of prostitutes who provides access to prostitutes, protects them, and lives off of their proceeds.

Pinkerton Rule. Test enunciated by the United States Supreme Court in *Pinkerton v. United States* (1946) holding that a member of a conspiracy is liable for all offenses committed in furtherance of the conspiracy.

PINS, CINS, JINS. Acronyms for "person in need of supervision," "child in need of supervision," and "juvenile in need of supervision." Terms refer to juveniles who either are status offenders or are thought to be incorrigible or on the verge of becoming delinquent.

pirate. One who steals from another. Early meaning referred to robbery on high seas; today, a "film pirate" is one who traffics in stolen and copyrighted motion pictures or videotapes.

PKPA. The Parental Kidnapping Prevention Act, designed to deter or prevent "child snatching" by noncustodial parents.

placement. A sentence or disposition involving confinement to a facility or institution.

plain sight. *See* plain view.

plaintiff. The person or party who initiates a legal action against someone or some party in a civil court.

plain view, plain view doctrine, rule. Authorizes officers conducting a search to seize any contraband or illegal substances or items if they are in the immediate vision of officers. Evidence may be introduced in a trial whether original search was lawful or unlawful.

Platt, Anthony. Wrote that criminologists themselves have helped to reinforce stereotypical notions about poor and minority-group criminals. Believed that criminology must redefine its goals and definitions more in line with humanistic properties and accept the reality of a legal system founded on power and privilege. Wrote *The Child Savers* (1969).

plea. Answer to charges by defendant. Pleas vary among jurisdictions. Not guilty, guilty, *nolo contendere*, not guilty by reason of insanity, and guilty but mentally ill are possible pleas.

plea, guilty. A defendant's formal answer in court to the charges in a complaint, information, or an indictment where defendant states that the charges are true and that he or she has committed the offense(s) as charged.

plea, initial. The first plea entered in response to a given charge entered in a court record by or for a defendant.

plea, not guilty. A defendant's formal answer in court to the charges in a complaint or information or indictment, in which defendant states that he or she has not committed the offense(s) as charged.

plea agreement hearing. Meeting presided over by trial judge to determine accuracy of guilty plea and acceptability of general conditions of plea bargain agreement between prosecution and defense attorneys.

plea bargaining/negotiating. A preconviction deal-making process between the state and the accused in which the defendant exchanges a plea of guilty or *nolo contendere* for a reduction in charges, a promise of sentencing leniency, or some other concession from full, maximum implementation of the conviction and sentencing authority of the court. Includes implicit plea bargaining, charge reduction bargaining, sentence recommendation bargaining, and judicial plea bargaining.

plea negotiation. *See* plea bargaining.

plea *nolo contendere*. *See nolo contendere.*

plead. To respond to a criminal charge.

pledge system. An early method of law enforcement following the Norman Conquest in 1066 that relied on self-help and mutual aid.

pluralistic ignorance. A situation in which witnesses in a group fail to help the victim of an emergency or a crime because they interpret the failure of other witnesses to help as a sign that no help is needed.

plurality opinion. An opinion of an appellate court that is joined by more judges than have joined any concurring opinion, although not by a majority of judges in the court.

PMS. *See* premenstrual syndrome.

podular direct. A process of inmate supervision that requires correctional officers to be in direct contact with inmates who are not confined to cells.

podular indirect. A process of supervision wherein inmates are not confined to cells, and correctional officers can observe inmates but are physically separated from them.

points of identification. In fingerprint identification, a matching of ridges for particular fingers. Usually a minimum of 12 points of identification are required to show that someone's fingerprint matches one found at a crime scene.

police advisory board. A board made up of citizens from the community to oversee police policies and the administration of police procedures.

Police and Criminal Evidence Act of 1984. British Act authorizing the establishment of an independent Police Complaints Authority in 1985.

police brutality. Any unnecessary physical force used by police officers against citizens from which injuries to citizens are sustained.

police cautioning. Verbal warning by law enforcement officer to person who may have committed or attempted to commit a crime.

police-community awareness academies. T h e formation of "Citizens Police Academy" to teach citizens how police agencies operate originated in England, specifically from the Devon and Cornwall Constabulary, Middlemoor Exeter at the request of local citizens. In 1977, two small British municipal police agencies established a "Police Night School," a concept that has come in the United States to be known as "The Citizens Police Academy."

police-community relations. A generic concept including any program designed to promote or make more visible law enforcement strategies that are aimed at crime prevention and control and in which varying degrees of proactive citizen involvement are solicited.

Police Complaints Authority. An independent English investigative body to examine the validity of citizen complaints against police and capable of imposing appropriate administrative sanctions against the offending officers.

police corruption. Misconduct by police officers in the forms of illegal activities for economic gain. Accepting gratuities, favors, or unlawful payment for services that police are sworn to carry out as a part of their peacekeeping role. Not applied to officer conduct while off duty.

police court. Municipal tribunal trying those accused of violating city ordinances (e.g., vagrancy or public drunkenness).

police cynicism. The notion held by some police officers that all people are motivated by selfishness and evil.

police department. A local law enforcement agency directed by a chief of police or a commissioner.

police discretion. Choices by police officers to act in given ways in citizen-police encounters. Selection of behaviors among alternatives.

police diversion. A program that allows the police to recommend to juvenile suspects that they enroll in a program that offers counseling or training.

police misconduct. Any one of several different types of illegal and/or improper behavior of police officers, including acceptance of graft, falsifying police reports, and perjury.

police mission. Either implicit or explicit statements of general goals and objectives of police departments and officers.

police officer. A local law enforcement officer employed by a police department.

police officer style. Belief that the large aggregate of police officers can be classified into ideal personality types. Popular style types include: supercops who desire to enforce only serious crimes, such as robbery and rape; service-oriented officers, who see their job as that of a helping profession; and avoiders, who do as little as possible. The actual existence of ideal police officer types has never been conclusively proven.

police power. Influence of government to legislate to protect public health, safety, welfare, and morality.

police presence. The almost certain presence of police officers in places of business for the crime deterrent effects it affords.

police probation. A program requiring juvenile troublemakers to report to police regularly, attend school, make restitution, and maintain a neat personal appearance.

police professionalism. Increasing formalization of police work, and the rise in public acceptance of the police which accompanies it. A well-focused code of ethics, equitable recruitment and selection practices, and informed promotional strategies among many agencies.

police-school liaison program. Places law enforcement officers within schools to help prevent juvenile delinquency and to improve community relations. In some jurisdictions, program is referred to as "adopt-a-cop."

police state. A government where special powers are given to police to investigate private individuals and obtain information about them. Police powers are extensive, while citizen rights and powers are minimal.

police subculture. The result of socialization and bonding among police officers because of their stress and job-related anxiety; unofficial norms and values possessed by coteries of police in different agencies, formed by peculiar working hours and job stress.

police working personality. *See* working personality.

policy-level sentencing decisions. Sentencing decisions by the legislature or its delegate about the goals and structure of sentencing.

political considerations. Matters taken into account in the formulation of public policies and the making of choices among competing values. The distribution of the good (justice) produced by the system, when, and how.

political crimes. Acts that constitute threats against the state, including treason, sedition, or espionage.

polling the jury. *See* jury poll.

polygamy. Plural marriage. Having more than one spouse.

polygraph test. *See* lie detector.

poor laws. Seventeenth-century laws binding out vagrants and abandoned children as indentured servants.

pornography. Portrayal, by whatever means, of lewd or obscene sexually explicit material prohibited by law.

positive reinforcements. Rewards given by administrators to lower-level police officers for good conduct or otherwise conforming to the requirements set forth in the police mission.

positive school (of criminology). School of criminological thought emphasizing analysis of criminal behaviors through empirical indicators such as physical features compared with biochemical explanations. Postulates that human behavior is a product of social, biological, psychological, or economic forces. Also known as "Italian School".

positivism. Branch of social science that uses the scientific method of the natural sciences and that suggests that human behavior is a product of social, biological, psychological, or economic factors.

positivist criminology. *See* positive school.

posse. A group of persons empowered by a law officer to pursue criminal suspects.

post-conviction relief. Term applied to various mechanisms whereby offenders may challenge their conviction after other appeal attempts have been exhausted.

post-conviction remedies. Various means convicted persons have of seeking redress for their incarceration or conviction.

post-trauma strategies. Officer support programs designed to provide individual or group counseling for officers involved in stressful events, such as shootings.

post-traumatic stress disorder (PTSD). A severe disorder suffered by those who have experienced such traumatic, violent stress, such as combat, that they later lose orientation and kill or engage in other violent behavior, believing that they have returned to the traumatic situation. Some argue that victims of this disorder should not be held criminally responsible for crimes committed as a result of it.

Pound's model. Plan of court organization with three tiers: supreme court, major trial court, and minor trial court.

power. Person's ability to influence another person to carry out orders.

power groups. Criminal organizations that do not provide services or illegal goods but trade exclusively in violence and extortion. *See* power syndicates.

power of attorney. Authority given to another to act in one's place.

power rape. A rape motivated by the need for sexual conquest.

power syndicates. Organized crime groups that use force and violence to extort money from legitimate businesses and other criminal groups engaged in illegal business enterprises. *See* power groups.

powerlessness. A person's belief or expectation that his or her actions cannot determine outcomes or the future. A perception of the loss of personal influence over one's life or destiny, which is viewed as being controlled by powerful external forces.

praxis. The application of a theory to action. Marxist criminology applies this idea to explain revolution.

prearraignment lockup. Preventive detention. A place for preventive detention.

prebriefing conference program. Method of streamlining case processing in court, in which attorneys file appeals and discuss the structure and length of these appeals prior to their presentation before appellate courts.

precedent. Principle that the way a case was decided previously should serve as a guide for how a similar case currently under consideration ought to be decided.

precinct community councils (PCCs). Established as liaisons between police officers and local residents, these face-to-face councils have done much to foster better police-community cooperation and create better conditions of community crime control.

predictions of risk, predictions of dangerousness. Any device or instrument that purports to estimate an offender's chances of posing serious public danger if released from custody.

predisposition report, investigation. Report prepared by juvenile intake officer to furnish juvenile judge with background about juvenile so judge can make a more informed sentencing decision. Similar to presentence investigation report.

prejudicial error. Wrongful procedure that affects the rights of parties substantially and thus may result in the reversal of a case.

preliminary hearing, preliminary examination. Hearing by magistrate or other judicial officer to determine if person charged with a crime should be held for trial. Proceeding to establish probable cause. Does not determine guilt or innocence.

premeditation. Deliberate decision by perpetrator to plan to commit a crime. Any kind of planning beforehand to commit or carry out a crime.

premenstrual syndrome (PMS). A set of symptoms associated with the onset of menstruation, including fatigue, tension, nervousness, irritability, and depressed moods. A defense to criminal conduct based upon chemical or hormonal imbalances.

preplea conference. A discussion in which all parties participate openly to determine ways of bringing about an agreement on a sentence in return for a plea of guilty.

preponderance of evidence. Civil standard whereby the weight of the exculpatory or inculpatory information is in favor of or against the defendant; the greater the weight of information favoring the defendant, the greater the likelihood of a finding in favor of the defendant.

pre-release classification. The final classification decisions prior to release for the purpose of allocating inmates to transition programs.

pre-release programs in prison. Programs within the institution that are designed to prepare the inmate for release, usually including assistance in applying for a job and locating a suitable residence.

prescriptive guidelines. Sentencing guidelines in which the sentence values are determined on the basis of value judgments about appropriateness, rather than on the basis of past practice.

presentence investigation. Examination of convicted offender by a probation officer, usually requested or ordered by the court, including a victim impact statement, prior arrest records, and the offender's employment and educational history.

presentence investigation report, presentence report (PSI). Report filed by probation or parole officer appointed by court containing background information, socioeconomic data, and demographic data relative to defendant. Facts in the case are included. Used to influence sentence imposed by judge and by parole board considering an inmate for early release.

presentment. An accusation, initiated by the grand jury on its own authority, from their own knowledge or observation, which functions as an instruction for the preparation of an indictment.

President's Commission on Law Enforcement and the Administration of Justice. Created in 1967 to establish and promote standards for the selection of police officers and correctional employees. Led to the establishment of the Law Enforcement Assistance Administration.

presiding judge. The title of the judicial officer formally designated for some period as the chief judicial officer of the court.

presumption of innocence. Premise that a defendant is innocent unless proven guilty beyond a reasonable doubt. Fundamental to the adversary system.

presumption of validity. In constitutional law, premise that a statute is valid until it is demonstrated otherwise.

presumptive fixed sentence. A fixed determinate sentence within a limited range established by statute.

presumptive parole date. Presumed release date stipulated by parole guidelines should the offender serve time without disciplinary or other infractions or incidents.

presumptive sentencing, presumptive sentences. Statutory sentencing method which specifies normal sentences of particular lengths with limited judicial leeway to shorten or lengthen the term of the sentence.

pretrial conference. A meeting between opposing parties in a lawsuit or criminal trial, for purposes of stipulating things that are agreed upon and thus narrowing the trial to the things that are in dispute, disclosing the required information about witnesses and evidence, making motions, and generally organizing the presentation of motions, witnesses, and evidence.

pretrial detention. See preventive detention.

pretrial discovery. See discovery.

pretrial diversion. See diversion.

pretrial motion. See Motion in Limine.

pretrial publicity. Any media attention given to a case before it is tried in court.

pretrial release. The release of an accused person from custody, for all or part of the time before or during prosecution, upon his or her promise to appear in court when required.

prevalence. The proportion of a population that commits crime in a given period, measured by the number of offenders divided by the size of the population.

prevention. Philosophy of corrections which believes that the aim of punishment should be to prevent crime.

prevention and protection costs. The financial costs of crimes that result from expenditures on alarm systems, spotlights, locks, other target-hardening devices, and the money people spend on insurance premiums to cover their potential theft losses.

preventive detention. Constitutionally approved method of detaining those charged with crimes, when the likelihood exists that they either pose a serious risk to others if released or will flee the jurisdiction to avoid prosecution.

preventive patrol. Scheme by police officers inspired by the belief that high police officer visibility will effectively deter crime.

prima facie **case.** A case for which there is as much evidence as would warrant the conviction of defendants if properly proved in court. A case that meets the evidentiary requirements for a grand jury indictment.

primary deviance, deviation. Minor violations of the law that are frequently overlooked by police (including "streaking" or swimming in a public pool after hours).

primary evidence. First-hand evidence, eye-witness testimony, tangible incriminating evidence.

primary group. Charles Horton Cooley's term denoting a small and relatively permanent group characterized by intimate relationships.

primary prevention. *See* corrective prevention.

primitive term. A concept so basic that it cannot be defined by any other concept.

principals. Perpetrators of a criminal act.

prior record. Criminal history record information concerning any law enforcement, court or correctional proceedings that have occurred before the current investigation of or proceedings against a person. Statistical descriptions of the criminal histories of a set of persons.

prison. State or federally operated facility to house long-term offenders; usually designed to house inmates serving incarcerative terms of one or more years; self-contained facilities; some-times called total institutions. *See also* penitentiary.

prison argot. The slang characteristic of prison subcultures and prison life.

prison capacity. The size of the correctional population an institution can effectively hold.

prison commitment. The period of time a sentence offender must serve, imposed by a judge following the conviction for a crime. Time may be served in either jail or prison, depending upon the offense seriousness and space availability. Usually expressed in terms of months or years.

prison incarceration rate. The number of persons serving sentences in federal and state prisons per 100,000 people in the general population.

prison industries. Employment of prisoners in a business enterprise, often with market restrictions.

prison labor. Any manufacture of goods or performance of services by prisoners.

prison reform. Any activity designed to improve prison conditions. Usually sponsored or initiated by organized groups interested in prisoner welfare and rehabilitation.

prison riot. Any uncontrolled mob action by inmates in prisons. Refusal by inmates to submit to authority. Sometimes results in deaths of inmates and prison personnel.

prison sentence. *See* prison commitment.

prison subculture. Inmate code of conduct independent from prison rules and regulations; characterized by special hand or verbal signals and gestures, particular conduct, and a pecking-order system of status from high to low, depending upon one's strength and/or access to scare goods or contraband.

prisoner. Anyone who is held in either a county or city jail, prison, or penitentiary.

prisoner's rights movement. Diffuse movement among prisoners and groups supporting prisoner's rights in which means are examined whereby prisoners can exercise their legal rights in court and challenge jail and prison administration policies. Started in the late 1960s and continues, with growing numbers of petitions filed by inmates in state and federal courts annually.

prisonization. Social process whereby inmates determine where other inmates should be placed in the inmate subculture according to their strength, fighting ability, attractiveness, age, social connections, race, ethnicity, and other criteria.

privacy, right to. A constitutional right of all United States citizens relating to the Fourth Amendment which protects persons against unreasonable searches and seizures of their persons and homes.

private police. All non-public law enforcement officers including guards, watchmen, doorkeepers, crossing guards and bridge tenders, private detectives, and investigators.

private prisons. Correctional facilities operated by private firms on behalf of local and state governments.

private sector. People or businesses not affiliated with the government (the "public sector").

private security, private security agencies. Those self-employed individuals and privately funded businesses and organizations providing security-related services to specific clientele for a fee, for the individual or entity that retains or employs them, or for themselves, in order to protect their persons, private property, or interests from various hazards. Organizations that provide security for individuals and organizations.

privately secured bail. An arrangement similar to the bail bondsman system except that bail is provided without cost to the defendant. A private organization may provide bail for indigent arrestees who meet its eligibility requirements.

privatization. Trend in prison and jail management and correctional operations generally in which private interests are becoming increasingly involved in the management and operations of correctional institutions.

privatization of prison management. Delegation of the ownership and operation of prisons and jails to private corporations. Believed to be more economical than public ownership and operation methods.

privilege. Term associated with instrumental Marxism. Defined as the possession of that which is valued by a particular social group in a given historical period, including life, liberty and happiness, material goods and wealth, luxuries, and land. Barry Krisberg has written extensively about this phenomenon in his book, *Crime and Privilege: Toward a New Criminology* (1975).

privileged communication. Verbal exchange between two or more people that the court cannot require either to disclose.

pro bono. Literally "for the good," in legal terms, legal services provided at no cost to the defendant (e.g., indigent clients receive assistance from defense attorneys on a *pro bono* basis).

pro forma. According to form or a matter of policy or procedure; following specific rules.

pro se. Acting as one's own defense attorney in criminal proceedings. Representing oneself.

proactive, proactive police work, proactive patrol. An active search for offenders by police in the absence of reports of violations of the law. Arrests for crimes without victims are usually proactive, as opposed to reactive.

probable cause. Reasonable suspicion or belief that a crime has been committed and that a particular person committed it.

probatio. A period of proving, trial, or forgiveness.

probation. An alternative sentence to incarceration in which the convict stays under state's authority. Involves conditions and retention of authority by the sentencing court to modify the conditions of sentence or to resentence the offender if the offender violates the conditions. Such a sentence should not involve or require suspension of the imposition or execution of any other sentence.

probation agency, department. Any correctional agency of which the principal functions are juvenile intake, the supervision of adults or juveniles placed on probation status, and the investigation of adults or juveniles for the purpose of preparing presentence or predisposition reports to assist the court in determining the proper sentence or juvenile court disposition.

probationer. Convicted offender sentenced to a nonincarcerative alternative including supervised release in the community, restitution, community service, fines, or other conditions.

probation, juvenile. Sentence of supervised, conditional release of juvenile for a specified period. Usually under supervision of a juvenile probation officer.

probation officer. Professional who supervises probationers.

probation revocation. Process of declaring that a sentenced offender violated one or more terms of a probation program imposed by the court or probation agency. If probation involved a suspended prison or jail sentence, the revocation may mean that the original sentence is invoked and the individual is sent to prison or jail.

probation termination. The ending of the probation status of a probationer because of routine expiration of the probationary period, early termination by the court, or some program violation involving probation revocation.

probation violation. Any act or failure to act of a probationer that does not conform to the conditions of his or her probation.

probation workload, caseload. The total set of activities required in order to carry out the probation agency functions of intake screening of juveniles cases, referral of cases to other service agencies, investigation of juveniles and adults for the purpose of preparing predisposition or presentence reports, supervision or treatment of juveniles and adults granted probation, assisting in the enforcement of court orders concerning family problems such as abandonment and nonsupport cases, and such other functions as may be assigned by statute or court order. Caseload identifies the number of persons supervised by a probation officer.

probative. Tending to prove the truth or falsehood of a proposition. A witness may give testimony that has probative value if it shows the truthfulness or the untruthfulness of another witness or defendant.

probing. The technique used by an interviewer to stimulate discussion and obtain more information.

problem behavior syndrome (PBS). A view that considers a clustering of antisocial behaviors that involve substance abuse, smoking, precocious sexuality and early pregnancy, educational underachievement, suicide attempts, and thrill-seeking. A precursor to criminality.

problem-oriented policing. Policing technique employing citizen involvement in defining community crime problems and suggesting solutions for them.

procedural (criminal) law, procedural law. Rules that specify how statutes should be applied against those who violate the law. Procedures whereby the substantive laws may be implemented.

procedural due process. Constitutional requirement that all persons be treated fairly and justly by government officials. Accused persons can be arrested, prosecuted, tried, and punished only in accordance with procedures prescribed by law.

proceeding. Any official meeting, such as court, for the purpose of settling a case or dispute or finding guilt or innocence. An official inquiry.

process. A summons requiring the appearance of someone in court.

procuratorate, procuracy. Term used in many countries to refer to agencies with powers and responsibilities similar to those of prosecutor's offices in the United States.

productivity. Either measured or unmeasured output by officers, including numbers of arrests, time on duty, tickets issued, and participation in public events.

profession. Any career for which a recognized specialized course of study is required in order to belong to a special class known as professionals.

professional criminals. *See* career criminals.

Professional Education Council. Created by American Correctional Association for purpose of devising common curriculum leading to associate degree in corrections for corrections officers including jail guards. Degree not obligatory in most jurisdictions.

professional model. Plan of organization considered a blend of bureaucracy and human relations, in which personality and regulations are both considered important. Persons selected according to their professional skills and ability to adapt.

professional thief, theft. Skilled offender who is committed to crime as an occupation and thinks of him or herself as a criminal. Such an offender's criminal actions.

professionalization. Process of acquiring increased education, more in-service "hands-on" training, practical work experience, and using higher selection standards (physical, social, and psychological) for officer or staff appointments.

professionalization movement. Efforts by various interests to encourage higher standards of selection for police officers, including more formal education and training.

profit-making firm. An organization that charges greater than cost for services rendered and returns the surplus value to its owners.

programmed contact devices. Electronic monitoring system in which telephonic contact is made at random times with the offender, whose voice is electronically verified by computer.

progressives. Early twentieth-century American reformers who believed that state action could relieve human ills.

prohibition. Era between 1919 and 1933 when liquor was prohibited in the United States.

projection. A psychological defense mechanism by which the blame for unacceptable thoughts or behavior is directed at another person or group.

Project New Pride. Established in Denver, Colorado in 1973, blending education, counseling, employment, and cultural education for children ages 14 through 17. Eligible juveniles include those with two prior adjudications for serious misdemeanors and/or felonies. Goals are to reintegrate juveniles into their communities through school participation and employment and thereby reduce recidivism.

project organization. A group of several criminals who come together to commit one or a series of acts of robbery, burglary, fraud, or smuggling.

proletariat. In Marxism, the working class, which is dominated by the bourgeoisie in a capitalist society. Under socialism, the working class would ideally also be the owners of production, thus leading to a classless society.

promulgate. To officially put forth, as in a document containing rules and regulations.

proof beyond a reasonable doubt. Standard of proof to convict in criminal case.

property bond. Setting bail in the form of land, houses, stocks, or other tangible property. In the event the defendant absconds prior to trial, the bond becomes the property of the court.

property crime. Nonviolent felony involving criminal acts against property including but not limited to larceny, burglary, and vehicular theft.

property in service. Eighteenth-century practice of selling control of inmates to shipmasters who would then transport them to colonies for sale as indentured servants.

proscribe. To forbid or prohibit.

prosecuting attorney. *See* prosecutor.

prosecution. Carrying forth of criminal proceedings against a person, culminating in a trial or other final disposition such as a plea of guilty in lieu of trial.

prosecution agency, prosecutorial agency. Any local, state, or federal body charged with carrying forth actions against criminal. State legal representatives, such as district attorneys or United States Attorneys and their assistants, who seek to convict persons charged with crimes.

prosecutor. Court official who commences civil and criminal proceedings against defendants. Represents state or government interest, prosecuting defendants on behalf of state or government.

prosecutorial bluffing. Attempt by prosecution to bluff defendant into believing case is much stronger than it really is. Used to elicit guilty plea from defendant to avoid lengthy trial where proof of defendant's guilt may be difficult to establish.

prosecutorial discretion. The decision-making power of prosecutors based upon the wide range of choices available to them in the handling of criminal defendants, the scheduling of cases for trial, and the acceptance of bargained pleas. The most important form of prosecutorial discretion lies in the power to charge or not to charge a person with an offense.

prosecutorial information. A criminal charge against someone filed by the prosecutor.

prosecutorial waiver. Authority of prosecutors in juvenile cases to have those cases transferred to the jurisdiction of criminal court.

prosecutrix. A female prosecutor. A female victim who makes a criminal complaint against a perpetrator of a crime.

prostitution. The practice of engaging in sexual activities for hire.

protective neighboring. A combination of cooperative surveillance and willingness to intervene in a crime by the residents of a community.

protective sweep doctrine. The rule that when police officers execute an arrest on or outside private premises, they may conduct a warrantless examination of the entire premises for other persons whose presence would pose a threat, either to their safety or to evidence capable of being removed or destroyed.

Provo Experiment. Community-based delinquency rehabilitation program in Provo, Utah designed to curb recidivism through group therapy and other group activities.

provocation. Any action by one party designed to cause another person to act in a particular way, such as assault.

proximate cause. The factor that is closest to actually causing an event, such as the death of a victim.

proximity hypothesis. View devised by Rodney Stark and others that persons become crime victims because they live or work in high-crime areas with large criminal populations.

proxy. Someone acting on behalf of someone else in any legal proceeding, civil or criminal.

prurient interest. An excessive or unnatural interest in sex.

psychedelic drugs. Any narcotics capable of creating hallucinogenic experiences and/or euphoria.

Psychiatric Emergency Coordinating Committee. Formulated a comprehensive Memorandum of Agreement that took effect on April 1, 1985. The administrator of each participating agency agreed in writing to a list of specific actions. Designed to divert mentally ill persons involved in minor criminal behavior from the criminal justice system into the health care system, where they can receive more appropriate care.

psychoactive drug. A chemical substance that affects cognition, feeling, and/or awareness.

psychoanalysis. Method of dealing with human behavior, based upon writings of Sigmund Freud, that views personality as a complex composite of interacting mental entities.

psychoanalytic theory, perspective. Sigmund Freud's theory of personality formation through the id, ego, and superego at various stages of childhood. Maintains that early life experiences influence adult behavior.

psychological school. A perspective on criminological thought that views offensive and deviant conduct as the products of dysfunctional personality systems. The conscious, and especially the subconscious, contents of the human psyche are identified by psychological thinkers as major determinants of behavior.

psychological screening. Administration of tests or assessment devices designed to exclude potential police officers whose personal behaviors and personalities may be unsuitable for police work.

psychological theories. Explanations linking criminal behavior with mental states or conditions, antisocial personality traits, and early psychological moral development.

psychoneurosis. Any one of a number of emotional disorders thought to stem from problems of tension or anxiety. Commonly shortened to "neurosis".

psychopath. Person whose personality is characterized by a lack of warmth and feeling, inappropriate behavior responses, and an inability to learn from experience.

psychopathic behavior. Chronic asocial behavior rooted in severe deficiencies in the development of conscience. Virtually lacking in conscience.

psychopathy. A condition in which a person appears to be psychologically normal but in reality has no sense of responsibility, shows disregard for others, is insincere, and feels no sense of shame, guilt, or humiliation.

psychopharmacological. Descriptive term used to depict actions of persons who have ingested mood-altering drugs (e.g., violence may be psychopharmacological if perpetrator ingested LSD or PCP).

psychosis. A mental illness characterized by a loss of contact with reality.

psychoticism. A dimension of the human personality describing persons who are aggressive, egocentric, and impulsive.

psychotics. Persons whose id has broken free and now dominates their personality. Psychotics suffer from delusions and experience hallucinations and sudden mood shifts.

public defender. Attorney appointed by the court to represent an indigent defendant.

public defender agency. Any local, state, or federal organization, public or private, established to provide a defense to indigent clients or those who otherwise cannot afford to pay for their own defense against criminal charges. Because everyone is entitled to counsel, whether or not counsel can be afforded, such services exist to meet the needs of those without funds to hire their own private counsel.

public disclosure. Information about police agencies and officers disseminated by a public relations officer.

public intoxication. The condition of being severely under the influence of alcohol or drugs in public places to the degree that one may endanger persons or property.

public law. General classification of law consisting of constitutional, administrative, international, and criminal law.

public nuisance. Any action or condition that adversely impacts the public in a community.

public order crimes, offenses. Any breach of the peace or disturbance of community order. Includes sit-in demonstrations at abortion clinics, rioting behavior, and disturbing the peace.

public relations. Persons or bureaus involved in creating more effective and pleasant interactions and working associations between citizens, police officers, and agencies.

public safety department. Any agency organized at the state or local level to incorporate various emergency service functions in potential disaster situations.

public safety doctrine. Holding that police can legally question an arrested suspect without giving the Miranda warning if the information they need is essential for maintaining public safety.

punitive intent standard. A standard that distinguishes incarceration from other forms of confinement, such as detention, on the grounds of a demonstrable alternative purpose for the confinement, and reasonable relationships between the confinement practice and the alternate purpose.

punitive prevention. Relies on the threat of punishment to forestall criminal acts.

purge. The complete removal of arrest, criminal, or juvenile record information from a given record system.

pyromania, pyromaniac. A psychological condition including the compulsion to start fires, often for sexual gratification. Someone who sets fires.

Q

qualified immunity. A defense to a Civil Rights Act suit that claims the right violated was not clearly enunciated and therefore the violation was unintentional and the official should not be liable for damages.

quality circles. An application of total quality management. Approach encourages workers classified similarly (e.g., dispatchers, detectives, or patrol) to interact with one another in group settings to resolve problems common to their particular work specialties. Acting as a team, these personnel can often offer recommendations lead-

ing to savings in labor and time, enhanced service, and/or improved working conditions.

quality of work life. Organizational change projects that seek to improve conditions of workers on the job through the use of joint management labor communities for decisions about the conditions or process of work.

quarter session courts. Originally, courts that met four times a year, usually to try serious cases. Where this old title is still used, it is in connection with a higher or trial court.

quash. To vacate a sentence or annul a motion.

quasi-experiment. A study resembling an experiment except that random assignment played no role in determining which subjects got which level of treatment. Usually have less internal validity than experiments.

Queer Nation. Organization of gay men formed in 1990 in New York City following the terrorist bombing of an allegedly gay nightclub. Advocates gay rights and promotes demonstrations to further gay rights.

Quetelet, Lambert Adolphe Jacques (1796-1874). Belgian mathematician who was one of the first to pioneer the use of statistics to analyze social data, particularly criminological data. Founded the cartographic school of criminology, in which factors such as season, climate, gender and age were believed to be relevant variables influencing the occurrence of crime. Wrote *Treatise on Man and the Development of His Faculties* (1835).

Quinney, Richard. Wrote *The Social Reality of Crime* (1970). Theory consists of six propositions: (1) definition of crime (crime is a definition of human conduct created by authorized agents in a politically organized society); (2) formulation of criminal definition (such definitions describe behaviors that conflict with interests of that segment of society interested in shaping public policy); (3) application of criminal definitions (criminal labels are applied by persons who have political power); (4) development of behavior patterns in relation to criminal definitions (people engage in actions likely to be defined as criminal); (5) construction of criminal conceptions (conceptions of crime are diffused in the segments of society by communication); and (6) the social reality of crime (constructed by the formulation and applications of criminal definitions, the development of criminal behavior patterns, and the construction of criminal conceptions).

Also known for viewing criminology for its peacemaking potential. Sees peacemaking as a key criminology goal. Believes that the establishment of social justice is the way to eliminate all forms of predatory behavior.

R

race relations. Process of bringing members of different ethnic or genetic backgrounds together to promote harmony and goodwill. Area of study focusing upon the behaviors and customs of particular ethnic groups as a means of understanding them better to improve relations between police and members of these different groups.

Racketeer Influenced and Corrupt Organizations Act (RICO). Passed by Congress in 1970 to attack organized crime and prosecute it. Also authorizes both civil and criminal asset forfeiture.

racketeering. Any organized crime (e.g., organized gambling, prostitution, illegal regulation of commerce).

radar. Radio-frequency energy used to measure distance, depth, or altitude. Police officers use radar systems to detect speeders in vehicles on highways.

radial design. The physical design associated with the Pennsylvania system of prison housing units, usually untiered cells on outside walls radiating from a central control hub.

radical approach. A perspective that focuses on crime by both the underprivileged and the privileged, and attributes crime by both groups to the conditions of a capitalist society.

radical criminology. Stresses control of the poor by the wealthy and powerful. Crime is defined by those in political and economic power in such a way so as to control lower socioeconomic classes (e.g., vagrancy statutes are manifestations of control by wealthy over the poor).

radical nonintervention. Principle of doing the minimum legally possible to a criminal offender. This approach attempts to minimize the stigma attached by the justice system (e.g., diversion instead of a formal criminal procedure).

Rand Corporation. Private institution that conducts investigations and surveys of criminals and examines a wide variety of social issues. Distributes literature to many criminal justice agencies.

Contracts with and conducts research for other institutions. Located in Santa Monica, California.

ransom. Money or valuable property demanded in exchange for something of value in someone else's possession.

rape, rape, forcible. Traditionally, the felony of sexual intercourse forced by a man upon a woman (not his wife) against her will by the violence or threat of violence. The stipulation that the woman not be the man's wife is omitted in modern statutes. Sexual intercourse or attempted sexual intercourse with persons against their will, by force or threat of force.

rape shield law. Regulation protecting identity of a rape victim or preventing disclosure of a victim's sexual history.

rape, statutory. Sexual intercourse with a person who has consented in fact but is deemed, because of age, to be legally incapable of consent.

rape trauma syndrome. Predictable reactions of rape victims, including an initial acute reaction in which the victim's life is disrupted seriously, followed by a long-term phase in which victim's symptoms decrease and a period of readjustment and reconstruction follows.

rated capacity. The number of beds or inmates assigned by a rating official to various jails or prisons.

rational choice theory, rational choice. States that crime is the result of a decision-making process in which offenders weigh the potential penalties and rewards of committing a crime.

rational goal model. A perspective on organizations that places high values on productivity and efficiency and achieves these through goal planning, technological development, and evaluation.

rationalism. A school of thought that holds that the totality of knowledge can be acquired only by strict adherence to the forms and rules of logic.

RCMP. *See* Royal Canadian Mounted Police.

reaction formation. Individual response to anxiety in which persons react to a stimulus with abnormal intensity or inappropriate conduct.

reactive, reactive police, reactive patrols. Police activity occurring in response to a stimulus, such as a reported crime incident or notification that a crime has been committed. As opposed to proactive police work.

real evidence. Physical evidence such as a weapon, records, fingerprints, or stolen property.

real property. Land and buildings permanently attached thereto.

rearrest. One indicator of recidivism. Consists of taking parolee or probationer into custody for investigation in relation to crimes committed. Not necessarily indicative of new crimes committed by probationers or parolees as it may be the result of police officer suspicion.

reasonable competence. Standard by which legal representation is judged gauging whether the defendant received a reasonable level of legal aid.

reasonable doubt. Standard used by jurors to decide if the prosecution has provided sufficient evidence for conviction. Jurors vote for acquittal if they have reasonable doubt that the accused committed the crime.

reasonable suspicion. Warranted suspicion (short of probable cause) that a person may be engaged in criminal conduct.

rebellion. A mode of strain adaptation in which people reject cultural goals and develop a new set of goals, and reject institutionalized means to reach cultural goals and develop a new set of means. Behavior by which a person seeks to create a new social structure that will more effectively allow people to meet what the rebel considers appropriate goals.

rebutting testimony, evidence. Any questioning or presentation of evidence designed to offset, outweigh, or overwhelm evidence presented by the other side or question the veracity or truthfulness of witnesses.

reception center. A separate unit on prison grounds apart from regular prison cells and inmate population which receives inmates from the court for their initial classification.

recidivism. Return to criminality including rearrest, reconviction, and reincarceration of previously convicted felons or misdemeanants.

recidivism rate. Proportion of offenders who, when released from probation or parole, commit further crimes.

Reckless, Walter. Criminologist who has described containment theory (1957, 1961), which suggests that youths have the ability to resist criminal inducements ("containments"), but there are prevalent crime-inducing forces at work: "internal pushes" (discontent, anxiety, rebellion, mental conflict), "external pressures" (relative deprivation, limited opportunities, un-employment, insecurity), and "external pulls" (deviant peer group influence, mass media).

reclassification. Periodic reassessment of an inmate during the period of incarceration.

recognizance. Personal responsibility to return to court on a given date and at a given time.

reconviction. Measure of recidivism when former convicted offenders are found guilty of new crimes by a judge or jury.

recoupment. Forcing indigents to repay the state for at least a part of their legal fees.

recusal. Act of judges excusing themselves from proceedings, especially where they have an apparent conflict of interest in the case being tried.

Red Hannah. Whipping post used by Delaware prison authorities to flog inmates until corporal punishment statute in Delaware was repealed in 1973.

red light district. Any neighborhood in a community where prostitution is known to exist and flourish. In early times, red lights were hung outside of homes known for having prostitutes on premises.

redirect examination. Questioning of a witness following the adversary's questioning under cross-examination.

reductionism. British procedure for removing petty offenders from imprisonment to make room for more serious offenders.

Reeves. Chief law enforcement officers of English shires or counties. Forerunners of county sheriffs.

reference relationship. A person, group, or entity that a person takes into account when making decisions. These relationships are key sources of values, norms, attitudes, and aspirations.

referent power. Form of influence based on friendship, in which subordinates comply because they like or identify with their superior.

referee. A lawyer who serves part-time or full-time to handle simple routine juvenile cases.

referral to intake. Process of transferring a juvenile from custody of law enforcement officers or a social welfare agency to the custody of an intake officer or juvenile probation officer who will conduct a preliminary screening to determine whether the juvenile should move forward to juvenile court and be charged.

reform school. Antiquated term designating a juvenile facility geared to improve the conduct of those forcibly detained within.

reformatory. Detention facility designed to change criminal behavior or reform it.

reformatory concept. A late-nineteenth-century correctional model based upon the use of the indeterminate sentence and belief in the possibility of rehabilitation, especially of youthful offenders. Faded with the emergence of industrial prisons around the turn of the century.

reformatory model. Plan of custody for women stressing reformation, reintegration, skill acquisition, and moral and social improvement.

refreshing one's memory, reminding. During testimony, witnesses may have their memories refreshed by re-reading some document or looking at pictures to enable them to recall with greater clarity something that happened some time ago.

Regimented Inmate Discipline Program (RID). Oklahoma Department of Corrections program operated in Lexington, Oklahoma for juveniles, stressing military-type discipline and accountability. Facilities are secure and privately operated.

rehabilitation, rehabilitative ideal. Correcting criminal behavior through educational and other means, usually associated with prisons.

rehabilitation model. Plan of corrections emphasizing the provision of treatment programs designed to reform offenders.

rehabilitation policy. A correctional system with high concern for the individual offender and low concern for the community, using identification strategies to help the offender mature.

Rehnquist Court. The United States Supreme Court under the leadership of Chief Justice William Rehnquist.

Reiman, Jeffrey. Criminologist who advocates a conflict perspective model. Believes that criminalized acts are threats to the wealthy and powerful and that such acts are prevalent among the poor, the criminal justice system fails in its attempt to deal with street crime, and that white-collar offenses should be punished equally harshly as street crime. Wrote *The Rich Get Richer and the Poor Get Prison* (1984).

reincarceration. Return to prison or jail for one or more reasons including parole or probation violations and revocations, rearrests, and reconvictions.

reinforcement. In social learning theory, strengthening or increasing the likelihood of the future occurrence of some voluntary act. Positive reinforcement is produced by rewarding behavior, negative reinforcement by an unpleasant or punishing stimulus. Differential reinforcement is produced when a person comes to prefer one behavior over another as the result of more rewards and less punishment. Self-reinforcement refers to self-imposed positive or negative sanctions.

reintegration. Punishment philosophy that promotes programs that lead offenders back into their communities. Reintegrative programs include furloughs, work release, and halfway houses.

reintegration model. Correctional model that emphasizes the maintenance of offender ties with family and community as a method of personal reform, in recognition of the fact that the offender will be returning to the community.

reintegrative shaming. A method of correction that encourages offenders to confront their misdeeds, experience shame because of the harm they caused, and then be brought back into society. Elaborated in a book by John Braithwaite, *Crime, Shame, and Reintegration* (1989).

relation. A joint occurrence or covariation between two or more variables.

relative deprivation. Condition existing when people of wealth and poverty live in close proximity. Feelings of envy or envious indignation whenever persons see others with goods or lifestyles that they feel they deserve but don't have. Some criminologists attribute crime-rate differentials to relative deprivation.

release from detention. The authorized exit from detention of a person subject to criminal or juvenile justice proceedings.

release from prison. Any lawful exit from federal or state confinement facilities primarily intended for adults serving sentences one year or longer, including all conditional and unconditional releases, deaths, and transfers to other jurisdictions.

Release on bail. Release by a judicial officer of an accused person who has been taken into custody, upon the accused's promise to pay a certain sum of money or property if they fail to reappear later in court as required, a promise that may or may not be secured by the deposit of an actual sum of money or property.

release, pretrial. A procedure whereby accused persons who have been taken into custody may be allowed to be free before and during their trial.

release to third party. The release by a judicial officer of an accused person who has been taken into custody to a third party who promises to return the accused to court for criminal proceedings.

released on own recognizance. Allowing a person to leave given their word they will return to court to appear as required. Used in connection with bail determination in initial appearance proceedings, preliminary examinations, and arraignments.

relevant evidence. Information tending to prove or disprove a fact.

remand. To send back (e.g., the United States Supreme Court may remand a case back to the lower trial court where the case was originally tried).

remedy. Any declared solution to a dispute between parties (e.g., if someone is found guilty of slashing another's automobile tires, the remedy may be to cause the convicted offender to compensate the victim with money for the full value of the destroyed tires).

removal of landmarks. The relocation of monuments or other markings that designate property lines or boundaries for the purpose of fraudulently reducing the owner's interest in lands and estates.

reparole. The process of placing an inmate on parole who has previously been on parole. Parolee has violated one or more parole conditions, has had his parole program terminated, but has qualified to be paroled again.

repeal. A legislative act removing a law from the statute books.

replevin. An action by someone to recover previously unlawfully seized property.

reprieve. An executive act temporarily suspending the execution of a sentence, usually a death sentence. Differs from other suspensions of sentence not only in that it almost always applies to temporary withdrawing of a death sentence, but also in that it is usually an act of clemency intended to provide the prisoner with time to secure amelioration of the sentence.

res judicata. "Things judged." Refers to matters already decided in court, not subject to relitigation.

residential child care facility. A dwelling other than a detention or shelter facility providing care, treatment, and maintenance for children.

residential commitment. Any sentence of an offender to a halfway house or other community home where the offender/client may come and go freely during daytime hours for purposes of work or education; offender/client must return and remain in community home during evening hours, where curfew is observed.

residential treatment center. A government facility serving juveniles whose behavior does not necessitate the strict confinement of a training school, often allowing them greater contact with the community.

resisting arrest. The crime of obstructing or opposing a police officer making an arrest.

respondeat superior. Doctrine under which liability is imposed upon an employer for the acts of his employees that are committed in the course and scope of their employment.

respondent. A person asked to respond in a lawsuit or writ.

responsible. Legally accountable for one's actions and obligations.

restitution. Stipulation by court that offenders must compensate victims for their financial losses resulting from crime. Compensation to victim for psychological, physical, or financial loss. May be imposed as a part of an incarcerative sentence.

restoration. A goal of criminal sentencing that attempts to make the victim "whole again."

restraining order. Requirement by the court prohibiting contact between one person and another.

restraint policy. A correctional system with low concern for the offender and the community, using no strategy to influence offender behavior. A holding strategy.

restrictive deterrence. The effect of a penalty that causes people to limit their violations of the law in order to minimize the risk of punishment.

retained counsel. An attorney, not employed or compensated by a government agency or subunit or assigned by the court, who is privately hired to represent a person in a criminal proceeding.

Retired Senior Volunteer Program. A national effort that places retirees in community volunteer positions. Has been received in many quarters as one approach to augment police manpower shortages.

retreatism. A mode of strain adaptation in which cultural goals are abandoned and institutionalized means are also rejected.

retreatist subculture. A concept from opportunity theory in which youths relinquish cultural goals by withdrawing from society. Rejected by members of both criminal and conflict subcultures, these youngsters seek status and outlets such as drugs.

retribution. Philosophy of punishment that says offenders should be punished for purposes of revenge.

retroactive. Referring to things past (e.g., making a new law applicable to a previous time period.) Currently an unconstitutional action.

reverse, reversal. Action by a higher court to overturn, set aside, or vacate a particular conviction of matter being appealed.

reverse certification. When the criminal court has exclusive jurisdiction and transfers a case to the juvenile court.

reversible error. Errors committed by judges during trial that may result in reversal of convictions against defendants.

review. The procedure whereby a higher court examines one or more issues emanating from a lower court on an appeal by the prosecution or defense.

revocation, probation or parole. *See* probation or parole revocation.

revocation hearing. Two-stage proceeding conducted to determine whether a probationer's or parolee's program should be terminated or modified; first stage determines whether an infraction occurred and whether it is a violation of one or more of the probationer's or parolee's program conditions; the second stage determines the punishment, which for probationers may be: termination or modification of probation, transfer to a more intensive supervised probation program, placement in a jail; for parolees, it may be: return to prison, more intensive parole supervision, transfer to a different type of parole program.

revoke. To terminate a probation or parole order because of either a rule violation or commission of a new offense, and force offenders to begin or continuing serving their sentence.

revolutionary science. The abrupt development of a new paradigm that is accepted only gradually by a scientific community.

reward power. Influence based on ability of superior to reward subordinates.

Reynolds, James Bronson. Early prison reformer, established The University Settlement in 1893 in New York. Settlement project ultimately abandoned after Reynolds and others could not demonstrate its effectiveness at reform to politicians and the public generally.

RICO. *See* Racketeer Influenced Corrupt Organization Act.

right guy. An inmate code referring to any inmate who honors the prisoners' social codes.

right of allocution. Right of defendant to speak before sentence is pronounced.

rights of defendant. Constitutional guarantees to all persons charged with crimes. Includes representation by counsel at various critical stages, such as being charged with crimes, preliminary hearings, arraignments, trial, and appeals.

right to bear arms. Controversial right under the Second Amendment to carry firearms. United States Supreme Court has maintained that this is not a specific individual right, but rather a right of a state to maintain an armed militia. Individual states regulate whether persons may possess and use firearms.

right to counsel. Right to be represented by an attorney at critical stages of the criminal justice system. Indigent defendants have the right to counsel provided by state.

right to privacy. The freedom of individuals to choose for themselves the time, circumstances, and extent to which their beliefs and behavior are to be shared or withheld from others.

right to treatment. Assumption, usually by prison inmates, that inmates must be maintained in sanitary and comfortable settings, receive therapy or counseling if mentally imbalanced, and receive medical attention if injured.

Riksdagen. Swedish Parliament.

riot. Civil or public disturbance involving acts of violence, usually by three or more persons.

risk assessment, risk assessment device. The process of forecasting one's likelihood of reoffending if released from prison on parole or placed on probation by a judge. Any instrument designed to predict or anticipate one's future behavior based upon past circumstances or answers given to questions on questionnaires.

ritualism. A mode of strain adaptation in which cultural goals are scaled down or given up, while norms about the institutionalized means to reach cultural goals are accepted.

robbery. The taking or attempt to take anything of value from the care, custody, or control of a person or persons by force or threat of force or violence and/or by putting the victim in fear.

role ambiguity. Lack of clarity about work expectations. Unfamiliarity with correctional tasks.

role conflict. Clash between personal feelings and beliefs and job duties as probation, parole, or correctional officer.

ROR. *See* release on own recognizance.

Rosenfeld, Richard. Criminologist who has collaborated with Steven F. Messner and wrote about the American Dream, a concept not altogether different from Robert K. Merton's discussion of anomie and its association with criminality.

rotten pocket. Corrupt police officers who band together for illegal gain.

rout. At common-law disturbance of the peace similar to riot but without carrying out the intended purpose.

routine activities perspective, approach. Theory devised by Lawrence Cohen and Marcus Felson which states that an increase or decrease in crime rates can be explained by changes in the daily habits of potential victims. Based upon the expectation that crimes will occur where there is a suitable target unprotected by guardians. Theory suggests that motivation to commit crime and numbers of offenders are rather constant; thus, it is inevitable that in every society there will be someone willing to commit crime for diverse reasons. Thus, predatory crime, a vital component of their theory, rests upon the existence of suitable targets (victims), capable guardians (police), and motivated offenders (criminals). "Routine activities" refers to the activities of the normal American lifestyle.

Rowe, David. Proposed latent trait theory together with D. Wayne Osgood and W. Alan Nicewander.

Royal Canadian Mounted Police. Federal police of Canada. A national police force with general jurisdiction in all provinces.

Rule of Four. United States Supreme Court rule whereby the Court grants *certiorari* only on the agreement of at least four justices.

rule of law. Describes willingness of persons to accept and order their behavior according to rules and procedures that are prescribed by political and social institutions.

Rules of Civil Procedure. Rules governing civil cases where compensatory damages are sought. Rules governing courts of equity.

Rules of Criminal Procedure. Rules legislatively established by which a criminal case is conducted. Law enforcement officers, prosecutors, and judges use rules of criminal procedure in discretionary actions against suspects and defendants.

runaway. Any juvenile who leaves his or her home for long-term periods without parental consent or supervision.

Rusche, Georg. Criminologist and conflict theorist. Views society as consisting of two basic classes, those with power and those without it. Extends Marxist theory to include an unequal distribution of wealth and power.

Rush, Dr. Benjamin (1745-1813). Quaker penal and religious reformer and physician. Helped organization and operation of Walnut Street Jail for benefit of prisoners. Encouraged humane treatment of inmates.

S

sabotage. Any act willfully committed by someone against either an organization or government. May involve destruction of property or transmittal of information to parties not entitled to possess this information.

sadistic rape. Illegal sexual intercourse by force and motivated by offender's desire to torment and abuse the victim.

sadomasochism. Psychosexual condition whereby sexual partners inflict pleasure and pain upon one another simultaneously, usually for sexual gratification.

Salient Factor Score, SFS 81. Score which is used by parole boards and agencies to forecast an offender's risk to the public and future dangerousness. Numerical classification that predicts the probability of a parolee's success if parole is granted.

Samenow, Stanton. Criminologist who advocates rational choice theory in his work, *Inside the Criminal Mind* (1984). Believes that criminals are characterized as chronic liars, having intense anger, and artful at manipulativeness; also wrote with S. Yochelson, *The Criminal Personality* (1976, 1977).

Sampson, Robert. Criminologist who collaborated with John Laub to develop age-graded theory and highlight the significance of turning points. Life course theory elaborated in *Crime in the Making* (1993).

sanction. A penalty or punishment that is imposed on persons in order to enforce the law.

sanctioner value system. Plan used by parole boards in early release decision making in which amount of time served is equated with seriousness of conviction offense.

sanguinary laws. Laws in late 1600s and early 1700s providing for harsh punishments, including capital punishment, for burglary, rape, maiming, and witchcraft.

sanity hearing. A formal proceeding designed to determine whether a criminal defendant is sane or insane.

satanism. Belief in the occult, centering on the worship of the devil.

scale of patrol. Refers to the scope of a police officer's routine geographical patrol responsibilities.

Scared Straight. A delinquency deterrent program whose purpose is to scare youthful offenders in ways that will deter them from committing further delinquent acts or pursuing crime as adults. Juvenile offenders are taken through a prison where they are confronted by prisoners on a first-hand basis and told about the harshness of prison life.

scavenger gangs. Juvenile coalitions formed primarily as a means of socializing and for mutual protection.

schizophrenia. A type of psychosis often characterized by bizarre behavior, hallucinations, loss of thought control, and inappropriate emotional responses.

scientific police management. The application of social scientific techniques to the study of police administration for the purpose of increasing effectiveness, reducing the frequency of citizen complaints, and enhancing the efficient use of available resources. The heyday of scientific police management probably occurred during the 1970s, when federal monies were far more readily available to support such studies than they are currently.

scope of sentencing policy. The breadth of sanctions covered by sentencing policy. The most important distinction is between broad policies that address probation as well as prison terms and narrow policies that address only length of incarceration, but not whether to incarcerate.

screening. Procedure used by prosecutor to define which cases have prosecutive merit and which ones do not. Some screening bureaus are made up of police and lawyers with trial experience.

seal. To close from public inspection any record of an arrest, judgment, or adjudication, either criminal or juvenile.

search and seizure. Legal term contained in Fourth Amendment of United States Constitution referring to the searching for and carrying away of evidence by police during a criminal investigation.

search incident to an arrest. Authority of an arresting law enforcement officer to search immediate areas within control of arrestee. If suspect is arrested in his living room, police authority does not extend to searches of other areas not immediately within the control of the arrestee, such as an attic or back porch, detached garage, or basement.

search warrant. An order of the court directing law enforcement officers to search designated places for specific persons or items to be seized.

secondary deviance, secondary deviation. Law violations that have become incorporated into person's lifestyle or behavior pattern.

secondary group. A group that is usually larger, more complex, and less intimate than a primary group.

secondary prevention. Focuses on changing the behavior of individuals likely to become delinquent. Includes punitive prevention.

Secret Service. Agency created in 1860 with the primary function of guarding United States presidents. Other functions subsequently include investigations of counterfeiting United States currency and other illegal activities.

Section 1983 actions. Title 42, Section 1983 of the United States Code, setting forth grounds for legal actions involving civil rights violations by police officers against citizens.

secure confinement. Incarceration of juvenile offender in facility which restricts movement in community. Similar to adult penal facility involving total incarceration.

secure setting. Environment that places constraints on youths for their care and treatment and protection of the public.

security. The degree of restriction of inmate movement within a correctional facility, usually divided into maximum, medium, and minimum levels.

security and privacy standards. Sets of principles and procedures developed to ensure the security and confidentiality of criminal or juvenile record information in order to protect the privacy of persons identified in such records.

security classification. Internal corrections system of categorizing offenders into different supervisory or custody levels (e.g., minimum, medium, and maximum security).

seduction. Common-law crime of inducing an individual of previously innocent character to have sexual relations.

seductions of crime. The visceral and emotional appeal that the situation of crime has for those who engage in illegal acts. *See also* Jack Katz.

segregation. Correctional practice whereby certain types of offenders are separated either according to their institutional violations or for their own safety.

Seidmann, Robert. Criminologist who collaborated with William Chamblis in the writing of *Law, Order and Power*. A conflict theorist who has extended Marxist philosophy to explain in greater detail how rich and powerful economic and political interests dominate the lower classes.

selective enforcement. Act by police officers of prioritizing particular offenses or offenders and enforcing some laws and not enforcing others.

selective incapacitation. Process of incarcerating certain offenders who are defined by various criteria as having a strong propensity to repeat serious crimes. Belief that offenders who are recidivists or who have prior criminality should be incapacitated with relatively long prison sentences.

self-defense. Affirmative defense in which defendants explain otherwise criminal conduct by showing necessity to defend themselves against aggressive victims.

self-estrangement. A form of alienation in which persons see themselves as "aliens" or "strangers." Such individuals tend to view their actions in terms of external consequences instead of intrinsic pleasure or self-satisfaction and to see themselves as falling far short of what might have been high personal ideals.

self-fulfilling prophecy. Occurs whenever persons live up to the labels they are given by others.

self-incrimination. The act of exposing oneself to prosecution by answering questions that may demonstrate involvement in illegal behavior. Coerced self-incrimination is not allowed under the Fifth Amendment. In any criminal proceeding, the prosecution must prove the charges by means of evidence other than the testimony of the accused.

self-made person. A social myth that glorifies individual accomplishment to the exclusion or underestimation of the relevance of social structure to a person's life chances.

self-report crime, self-report data. Information disclosed by persons who have committed crimes of which police are unaware. Any statistical compilations of crimes reported by persons and where such persons have not been caught and prosecuted for committing these crimes.

self-report survey. Method whereby researchers ask persons directly about various types of offenses they have committed, regardless of whether they have been arrested and/or charged with committing those offenses.

self-representation. *See pro se.*

Sellin, Thorsten. Criminologist who investigated and described culture conflict theory, positing that different values present in segments of society may lead to persons engaging in criminal conduct. In turn, this serves as the basis for conflict. Normative conflict between various ethnic groups might generate criminal conduct, as diverse ethnic norms clash. Wrote *Culture Conflict and Crime* (1938). Collaborated with Marvin Wolfgang and Robert Figlio in studying the Philadelphia birth cohorts of 1945 and 1958.

sense of community. Psychological milieu established between police officers and citizens in which citizens acquire feel of security and safety among their own in individual neighborhoods.

sense of inequity. The belief that one's social position is not in as great a ratio to one's efforts as the social positions and efforts of others.

sentence. Penalty imposed upon a convicted person for a crime. May include incarceration, fine, both, or some other alternative. *See also* Mandatory Sentencing, Presumptive Sentencing, Indeterminate Sentencing, Determinate Sentencing.

sentence bargaining. Any negotiation between prosecutors and defense attorneys for the prosecutor's recommendation of a reduced sentence in exchange for a guilty plea to a lesser charge from a defendant.

sentence, determinate. *See* determinate sentencing.

sentence disparity. *See* sentencing disparity.

sentence hearing. *See* sentencing hearing.

sentence, indeterminate. *See* indeterminate sentencing.

sentence recommendation bargaining. Negotiation in which the prosecutor proposes a sentence in exchange for a guilty plea. *See also* plea bargaining.

sentence review. The reconsideration of a sentence imposed on a person convicted of a crime, either by the same court that imposed the sentence or by a higher appellate court.

sentencing alternatives. Range of possibilities the judge or jury has in sentencing persons (e.g., probation, suspended sentence, or prison).

sentencing commission. A group commissioned by the legislature to determine sentencing policy and usually to monitor implementation of that policy.

sentencing conference. An informal meeting prior to the sentencing hearing involving judge, prosecutor, defense attorney, and probation officer to discuss sentence recommendations.

sentencing council. The meeting of a panel of judges in a multi-judge court to discuss sentencing of pending cases; designed to temper individual decisions by comparison to group norms.

sentencing disparity. Inconsistency in sentencing of convicted offenders, in which those committing similar crimes under similar circumstances are given widely disparate sentences by the same judge. Usually based on gender, race, ethnic, or socioeconomic factors.

sentencing dispositions. Any punishments imposed by judges following a conviction or adjudication. May include probation, incarceration of some specified duration, fines, and/or other conditions (e.g., attending counseling or Alcoholics Anonymous meetings, or victim compensation).

sentencing guidelines. Instruments developed by the federal government and various states to assist judges in assessing fair and consistent lengths of incarceration for various crimes and past criminal histories. Referred to as presumptive sentencing in some jurisdictions.

sentencing hearing. Optional hearing held in many jurisdictions in which defendants and victims can hear contents of presentence investigation reports prepared by probation officers. Defendants and/or victims may respond to report orally, in writing, or both. Hearing precedes sentence imposed by judge.

sentencing memorandum. Court decision that furnishes ruling or finding and orders to be implemented relative to convicted offenders. Does not necessarily include reasons or rationale for sentence imposed.

Sentencing Reform Act of 1984. Act which provided federal judges and others with considerable discretionary powers to provide alternative sentencing and other provisions in their sentencing of various offenders.

sentencing structure. The division of decision authority at the individual case level of sentencing. Provides the formal relationships by which to implement policy.

separate confinement, separate system. A penitentiary system developed in Pennsylvania, whereby each inmate was held in isolation from other inmates. All activities, including craftwork, were carried out in individual cells. Solitary confinement in an isolated cell for the purpose of eliminating evil association in congregate quarters.

separation of powers doctrine. The principle that power is distributed among three branches of government—the judicial, legislative, and executive—for the purpose of ensuring that no one person will make the law, interpret the law, and apply the law.

sequester, sequestration. The insulation of jurors from the outside world so that their decision making cannot be influenced or affected by extralegal factors.

sequestered jury. A jury that is isolated from the public during the course of a trial and throughout the deliberation process.

serial murder. The killing of a large number of people over time by an offender who seeks to escape detection. Homicides that are committed over a period of time and involving a sequence of victims killed by the same perpetrator.

service. The police function of providing assistance to the public, usually with regard to matters unrelated to crime.

service model. Designed to meet community needs and expectations and therefore shaped by them.

service of process. The act of serving a summons on someone notifying them to be in court at a particular time.

service style. A style of policing that is marked by a concern with helping rather than strict enforcement. Service-oriented agencies are more likely to take advantage of community resources, such as drug treatment programs, than are other types of departments.

settlement houses. Homes or shelters established during 1886 and 1900 to furnish food, clothing, and temporary lodging to wayward or disadvantaged youths. Operated by charitable and religious organizations and staffed by volunteers.

severance. Separation of related cases so that they can be tried separately in different courts.

sex offender. Individual who commits a sexual act prohibited by law. Includes rapists, prostitutes, voyeurs, child molesters, etc.

sexual abuse. Refers to illegal sex acts performed against a minor by a parent, guardian, relative, or acquaintance.

sexual assault. *See* sexual battery.

sexual battery. In modern statutes, the unlawful oral, anal, or vaginal penetration by or union with the sexual organ of another.

sexual harassment. Unequal or offensive treatment in the workplace on the basis of gender.

shakedown. Intensive search conducted of inmate cells for the purpose of discovering weapons or contraband. Also a form of police corruption where money or valuables are extorted from criminals by police officers in exchange for the criminals not being arrested.

shared-powers model. Plan of prison administration stressing prisoner participation in administration of prison affairs.

Shaw, Clifford R. Sociologist who collaborated with Henry McKay in developing social disorganization theory, positing a relation between transitional slum areas and high crime rates during the 1920s.

Sheldon, William. A physician who wrote about the relation between physique and criminal behavior. Developed somatotype notion that different physiques tend to manifest different criminal behaviors. Typology included mesomorphs, who are well-developed and muscular, tending to commit robbery and assault; endomorphs, heavily built persons who are sluggish and have a propensity toward sex crimes; and ectomorphs, tall and thin persons believed to have a propensity toward embezzlement and property crimes.

shelter. A confinement or community facility for the care of juveniles, usually those held pending adjudication.

shelter care facility. A nonsecure or unlocked place of care and custody for children awaiting court appearances and those who have already been adjudicated and are awaiting disposition.

sheriff. Chief executive officer of county. Appoints jailers and other jail personnel, hires deputies to enforce county laws.

sheriff, deputy. A law enforcement officer employed by a county sheriff's department.

sheriff's department. A law enforcement agency organized and exercising its law enforcement functions at the county level, usually within unincorporated areas, and operates the county jail in most jurisdictions.

Sherman Antitrust Act. An 1890 act of Congress prohibiting any contract, conspiracy, or combination of business interests in restraint of foreign or interstate trade.

Sherman Report. The national review of law enforcement education programs that found that a liberal arts-related curriculum was the most appropriate one for training police officers.

shield laws. *See* rape shield laws.

shire reeve. In early England, the senior law enforcement figure in a county. The forerunner of today's sheriff.

shires. Early English counties.

shock incarceration. *See* shock probation.

shock parole. *See* shock probation.

shock probation. Sentencing offenders to prison or jail for a brief period, primarily to give them a taste or "shock" of prison or jail life, and then releasing them into the custody of a probation or parole officer through a resentencing project.

shoplifting. Stealing goods from stores or markets.

short-run hedonism. According to Albert Cohen, the desire of lower-class gang youths to engage in behavior that will give them immediate gratification and excitement but in the long run will be dysfunctional and negativistic.

short-term facility. Any incarcerative institution for either adults or juveniles where confinement is for a period of less than one year. Jails are considered short-term facilities.

shouts and rattles. Early New Yorkers who were equipped with actual noise-making rattles and who were expected to shout and rattle their rattles in the event they observed crimes in progress or fleeing suspects.

show cause, show cause order. Any order to appear in court and indicate to the court why an event has not occurred or why some disposition should not be made in a given case.

showup. *See* lineup.

siege mentality. Term developed by Elijah Anderson, who wrote *Streetwise: Race, Class and Change in an Urban Community* (1990). Refers to general mistrust of social institutions, such as businesses, schools and government, to deal effectively with poverty. Aggregates in neighborhoods, such as African-Americans, might believe generally that secret plans exist for their eradication through dispersion of drugs, AIDS, police brutality, and other adverse phenomena. The outside world is viewed as the "enemy" when, in fact, such may not be the case. Reinforced when police ignore crime in poor areas, whenever they are violent or corrupt, or whenever policies are enacted that adversely impact the poor and the communities in which they live.

silencer. Any device capable of suppressing the sound of a firearm when discharged. Such devices attach to the barrels of firearms, either by screwing on or by overlapping barrels and being tightened by screws on the silencers themselves.

silent system. *See* Pennsylvania System.

silver platter doctrine. Doctrine derived from the fact that federal authorities must obtain a search warrant before seizing property or conducting searches in criminal cases. When they conduct such searches and seizures without warrant, their collected evidence is inadmissible in federal court, but they may give their evidence "on a silver platter" to state officials, and the state officials can use this evidence against the same persons legally in state proceedings. Discarded as the result of *Mapp v. Ohio* (1961). *See also* exclusionary rule.

Simon, Rita. Sociologist who has written about feminist criminology in her work, *Women and Crime* (1975). Argues that women's movement has created greater economic opportunities for women. A "liberation hypothesis" suggests that women are in positions of committing the same types of crimes as men.

simple assault. An attack inflicting little or no physical harm on a victim.

simultaneity. A reciprocal cause-effect relation between two variables (e.g., sanctions by the criminal justice system may affect the crime rate, but the crime rate may also affect the sanctions that are meted out by the criminal justice system).

situational crime prevention. A method of crime prevention stressing tactics and strategies to eliminate or reduce particular crimes in narrow settings (e.g., reducing burglaries in a housing project by increasing lighting and installing security alarms).

situational inducements. Opportunities that maximize one's likelihood of engaging in criminal conduct. Where risk-taking is unlikely to result in apprehension and arrest, criminal conduct may occur for various incentives, usually monetary or thrill-seeking.

situationally based discretion. Options exercised by police officers during police-citizen encounters. May or may not include letter-of-law interpretations of events.

situational offender. First-offenders who commit only one offense for which they were apprehended and prosecuted, but who are unlikely to commit future crimes.

skeezers. Prostitutes who trade sex for drugs, usually crack.

Skinner, B.F. Psychologist who promoted behavior modification as a way of regulating criminal conduct. Through positive or negative reinforcement of behaviors, desirable or undesirable behaviors can be encouraged or discouraged.

skip tracer. Person who tracks down alleged offenders who have fled the jurisdiction to avoid prosecution. *See also* bounty hunter.

slander. The tort of defaming one's character through verbal statements.

Small, Albion. Sociologist and originator of the "Chicago School" in 1892.

smuggling. Unlawful movement of goods across a national frontier or state boundary or into or out of a correctional facility.

social capital. Positive relations with individuals and institutions that are life-sustaining. Relations include positive interpersonal relations with other persons and institutions. Marriage and a career are considered integral features of social capital.

social conflict theories. Explanations that assume criminal law and the criminal justice system are primarily means of controlling the poor and disenfranchised.

social control. Informal and formal methods of getting members of society to conform to norms, folkways, and mores.

social control theory. Explanation of criminal behavior which focuses upon control mechanisms, techniques and strategies for regulating human behavior, leading to conformity or obedience to society's rules, and which posits that deviance results when social controls are weakened or break down, so that individuals are not motivated to conform to them.

social disorganization theory, social disorganization. Proposes that criminal behavior is caused by a breakdown of neighborhood solidarity and community organization. Most often observed in zones in transition, such as areas of urban renewal, or areas in inner cities suffering decay and economic decline, where conditions are created which increase the incidence of crime.

social injustice. Collective sense of social inequality perceived by the poor toward the wealthy in describing relative deprivation.

social isolation. Feelings of loneliness, rejection, or social distance from others. A sense that one does not belong and that no one cares.

social justice. Fair distribution of important goods and services, such as housing, education, and health care.

social learning theory. Applied to criminal behavior, theory stressing importance of learning through modeling others who are criminal. Criminal behavior is a function of copying or learning criminal conduct from others.

social norm. *See* norms.

social process theories. View criminality as normal behavior. Everyone has the potential to become a criminal, depending upon the influences that impel them toward or away from crime and how they are regarded by others.

social psychological school. A perspective on criminological thought which highlights the role played in crime causation by weakened self-esteem and meaningless social roles. Social psychological thinkers stress the relationship of the individual to the social group as the underlying cause of behavior.

social screening. The acquisition of the case history, consisting of the child's relationship with his or her family, the child's demeanor, school records, and medical and psychological history.

social structure. Recurrent, stable patterns of interaction among persons.

social structure theories. Explain criminal conduct according to the creation of lower-class culture based upon poverty and deprivation, and the response of the poor to this situation.

socialization. Learning through contact with others.

socialized delinquency. Youthful behavior that violates the expectations of society but conforms to the expectations of other youths, particularly delinquent ones.

sociobiology. Scientific study of causal relation between genetic structure and social behavior.

socioeconomic. Level of income of neighborhood residents and general social standing or prominence.

sociological explanations. Theories of criminal conduct that emphasize social conditions that bear upon the individual as the causes of criminal behavior.

sociopath. *See* psychopath.

sodomy. Sexual penetration of the mouth or anus. A felony at common law.

solicitation. The inchoate offense of requesting or encouraging someone to engage in illegal conduct.

solitary confinement. *See* isolation.

somatotype, somatotype school of criminology. Body type that results from embryonic development. A criminological perspective that relates body build to behavioral tendencies, temperament, susceptibility to disease, and life expectancy.

Son of Sam laws. Legislated rules prohibiting criminals from profiting from their crimes through sales and/or publications of their stories to or through the media. "Son of Sam" comes from notes left by David Berkowitz at the scene of murders he committed.

SOS. "See Our Side" juvenile "aversion" program in Prince George's County, Maryland designed to prevent delinquency.

sovereign immunity. Principle that the state cannot be sued in its own courts or in any other court without its consent and permission.

special court martial. The military court that is second in the three grades of court martial in terms of the severity of the penalty that can be imposed.

specialized caseloads model. Probation or parole officer caseload model based on officer's unique skills and knowledge relative to offender drug or alcohol problems. Some probation and parole officers are assigned particular clients with unique problems that require more than average officer expertise.

Specialized Offender Accountability Program (SOAP). Program operated by the Lexington Correctional Center in Oklahoma for juveniles under 22 years of age. Based upon military disciplinary model. Individualized treatment is provided, although a strict military regimen is observed.

specific deterrence. *See* deterrence.

specific intent. The intent to accomplish a specific purpose as an element of a crime (e.g., breaking into someone's house for the purpose of stealing jewelry).

speedy trial. Defined by federal law and applicable to federal district courts, where a defendant must be tried within 100 days of an arrest. Every state has speedy trial provisions that are within reasonable ranges of the federal standard. Originally designed to comply with Sixth Amendment of United States Constitution. Longest state speedy trial provision is in New Mexico, which is 180 days.

Speedy Trial Act of 1974 (Amended 1979, 1984). Compliance with Sixth Amendment provision for citizen to be brought to trial without undue delay 30 to 70 days from date of formal specification of charges, usually in arraignment proceeding.

Spencer, Herbert (1820-1903). British sociologist who wrote *Social Statics* (1855). Was a devotee of Charles Darwin and thus believed in social evolution in a similar context as Darwin discussed biological evolution. Thus, "survival of the fittest" was a dominant theme in Spencer's writing. Society is governed by laws of conflict, out of which emerge criminality or conformity as competing interests.

spirit of the law. Efforts by police officers to exhibit leniency where law violations are observed. Usually first-offenders may receive leniency because of extenuating circumstances.

Spitzer, Stephen. A structural Marxist contending that laws are used to maintain long-term interests of the powerful and to control those persons who oppose or threaten these interests. Deviants are considered by structural Marxists as anyone who calls into question or criticizes capitalist modes of appropriating the product of human labor, social conditions under which capitalist production occurs, patterns of distribution and consumption in capitalist society, the process of socialization for productive and nonproductive roles, and the ideology supporting capitalist society.

split sentencing. Procedure whereby judge imposes a sentence of incarceration for a fixed period, followed by a probationary period a fixed duration. Similar to shock probation.

spontaneous declaration. An excited utterance, such as confessing to a crime during emotional stress at the crime scene.

spree murder. Killing of three or more persons within 30 days. Often associated with felony homicides.

Spurzheim, Johann K. (1776-1832). Phrenologist who studied head shapes and bumps and contours of the head in an effort to predict the types of criminal behaviors persons might manifest with such physical characteristics.

"squares." Inmates who are noncriminal types and considered situational offenders. This type of inmate does not conform to the inmate code.

stability of punishment hypothesis. The hypothesis that the rate of punishment in a given society will remain stable, despite fluctuations in the crime rate.

staff functions. Civilian work including clerks and professionals who coordinate internal organizational activities in police departments.

standard diversion. *See* unconditional diversion.

standardization of personnel. The selection and training of personnel to increase uniformity in knowledge, skill, or decisions.

standardization of work. The planning of work routines and practices to increase uniformity of processes and outcomes.

standard probation. Probationers conform to all terms of their probation program, but their contact with probation officers is minimal. Often, their contact is by telephone or letter once or twice a month.

standing. A doctrine mandating that courts may not recognize a party to a suit unless that person has a personal stake or direct interest in the outcome of the suit.

Star Chamber. An early English court which met secretly to try and punish offenders, usually in political matters.

stare decisis. Legal precedent. Principle whereby lower courts issue rulings consistent with those of higher courts, where the same types of cases and facts are at issue. The principle of leaving undisturbed a settled point of law or particular precedent.

Stark, Rodney. Criminological theorist who has devised the proximity hypothesis, which posits that persons who live in socially disorganized, high-crime areas have the greatest risk of coming into contact with criminal offenders, regardless of their own behavior or lifestyle. Victims do not encourage crime, but rather, are simply in the wrong place at the wrong time. "Deviant" places are depicted by Stark as poor, densely populated, highly transient neighborhoods in transition. In a sense, an offshoot of the concentric zone hypothesis devised by the Chicago School and Ernest Burgess and Robert Park.

state account system. A form of prison industry in which inmate production is directed by prison officials, goods are sold on the open market, and inmates receive a share of the profits.

state action doctrine. The traditional legal principle that only government officials or their representatives in the criminal justice process could be held accountable for the violation of an individual's constitutional civil rights.

state attorney general. Chief legal officer of a state responsible for both civil and criminal matters.

State Highway Patrol, state highway patrol officer. State law enforcement agency whose principal functions are the prevention, detection, and investigation of motor vehicle offenses and the apprehension of motor vehicle traffic offenders.

State Police, state police officer. State law enforcement agency whose principal functions may include police communications, aiding local police in criminal investigations, training police, guarding state property, and patrolling highways.

state-use system. A form of inmate labor in which items produced by inmates are salable only by or to state offices. Items that only the state can sell include such things as license plates and hunting licenses. Items sold only to state offices include furniture and cleaning supplies.

station house adjustments. Decisions by police officers to deal informally with arrestees, often at the police station. Actions often do not involve arrests, but warnings.

station house citation. An alternative to pretrial detention, whereby the arrestee is escorted to the precinct police station or headquarters rather than the pretrial detention facility. Release which may occur before or after booking is contingent upon the defendant's written promise to appear in court later as specified on the release form.

status frustration. Feelings of anger and hopelessness brought about by membership in a powerless segment of society. Linked to lower socioeconomic status.

status offender. Any juvenile who has committed an offense that would not be considered a crime if committed by an adult (e.g., a curfew violation would not be criminal action if committed by an adult, but such an act is a status offense if engaged in by a juvenile).

status offense. Any act committed by a juvenile that would not be a crime if committed by an adult.

statute of limitations. Period of time after which a crime that has been committed cannot be prosecuted. No statute of limitations exists for capital crimes.

statutes. Laws passed by legislatures. Statutory definitions of criminal offenses are embodied in penal codes.

statutory law. Authority based on enactments of state legislatures. Laws passed by legislatures.

statutory rape. *See* rape, statutory.

stay. A court order suspending proceedings or the enforcement of an order (e.g., a stay of execution for a prisoner who is about to be put to death).

stay of execution. Temporary cessation of capital sentence to be carried out against a person sentenced to the death penalty. Ordinarily issued by appellate judges or governors until issue or issues resulting in delay of sentence of death can be heard and resolved.

stereotype. A preconceived perception of a group, regardless of individual differences. Stereotypes may be either negative or positive, but they are often emotional and groundless.

stigmatization. Social process whereby offenders acquire undesirable characteristics as the result of imprisonment or court appearances. Undesirable criminal or delinquent labels are assigned those who are processed through the criminal and juvenile justice systems.

sting, sting operation. An undercover program wherein police officers attract likely perpetrators by posing as criminals.

stock manipulation. An illegal practice among brokers, in which they lead their clients to believe the price of a particular stock will rise, thus creating an artificial demand for it.

stolen property offenses. Any crime involving the exchange or transfer of property or contraband that has been taken by theft. Persons accepting such property and who know it has been obtained by illegal means may be prosecuted for receiving and concealing such contraband or merchandise.

Stonewall riots. Considered the beginning of the gay rights movement, this riot began when the New York City Police Department conducted a raid of a gay bar in Greenwich Village. A warrant stated that liquor was being sold in violation of the existing premises permit, but patrons of the bar resisted, claiming routine harassment. In the ensuing melee that became the Stonewall riots, four police officers were seriously injured and thirteen patrons were arrested.

stoopers. Petty criminals who earn their living by retrieving winning tickets that are accidentally discarded by race track patrons.

stop-and-frisk. Situation in which police officers who are suspicious of individuals will run their hands lightly over suspects' outer clothing to determine if persons possess a concealed weapon. Also called a "pat-down" or "threshold inquiry." Intended to stop short of any activity that would be considered a violation of the Fourth Amendment clause pertinent to reasonable searches and seizures.

strain. Emotional turmoil and conflict caused when persons believe they cannot achieve their desires and goals through legitimate means.

strain theory. A criminological theory positing that a gap between culturally approved goals and legitimate means of achieving them causes frustration which leads to criminal behavior.

stranger homicide. Criminal homicide committed by a person unknown and unrelated to the victim.

strategic analysis. A perspective holding that delinquency is best explained by assuming that human beings are rational individuals seeking to further personal interests and fulfill their goals by the most efficient means.

stratified society. View that society can be separated into levels based upon socioeconomic factors, ranging from the wealthy classes to the permanent underclass.

straw theory. An oversimplified version of an existing theory. Opponents of a theory may present and attack a "straw" version of that theory, but claim they have attacked the theory itself.

street crime. Illegal acts designed to prey on the public through theft, damage, and violence. Includes mugging and robbery.

street justice. When police decide to deal with a status offense in their own way, usually by ignoring it.

stress, police stress. The body's non-specific response to any demand placed upon it. Police stress refers to negative anxiety accompanied by an alarm reaction, resistance, and exhaustion. Anxiety contributes to heart disease, headaches, high blood pressure, and ulcers.

stressors. Factors that cause stress including boredom, constant threats to officer health and safety, responsibility for protecting the lives of others, and the fragmented nature of police work.

stress vs. non-stress training. Teaches police officers methods of coping with stress caused by role strain and conflict.

strict liability. Responsibility for a crime or violation imposed without regard to the actor's guilt. Criminal liability without *mens rea.*

strict-liability crimes. Illegal acts whose elements do not contain the need for intent or *mens rea.* Usually acts that endanger the public welfare, such as illegal dumping of toxic wastes.

structural Marxist theory. The view that the legal and justice system are designed to maintain the capitalist system and that members of both the owner and worker classes whose behavior threatens the stability of the system will be sanctioned. Stephen Spitzer has elaborated these views as an extension of the Marxian theory of deviance.

structured discretion. Term applied to judicial sentencing decisions for which guidelines exist to limit the severity or leniency of sentences imposed. Intention is to standardize sentences and create greater fairness in the courts. Also applies to early release decisions by parole boards.

study release. *See* work release.

subculture. Social clique and behavior patterns of a selected group, such as a gang.

subculture of violence. Subculture with values that demand the overt use of violence in certain social situations. Marvin Wolfgang and Franco Ferracuti devised this concept to depict a set of norms apart from mainstream conventional society, in which the theme of violence is pervasive and dominant. Learned through socialization with others as an alternative lifestyle.

subjective test. Way of determining whether entrapment has occurred. Test assumes that whatever record suspect may have is irrelevant. Police conduct is reprehensible *per se* and should not be tolerated as a means of eliciting crime.

subject matter specialization. Term applied when certain judges have exclusive jurisdiction over particular crimes.

subjudicial officer. Any judicial officer who is invested with certain judicial powers and functions but whose decisions in criminal and juvenile cases are subject to *de novo* review by a judge.

sublimation. The channeling of energy, such as that generated by hostility, into socially acceptable or culturally creative outlets.

Submission-Without-Argument Program. Plan designed to streamline case processing. Cases are presented without oral argument.

suboptimization. The practice by organizational subunits of valuing unit objectives over organizational objectives.

subornation of perjury. The crime of procuring someone to lie under oath.

subpoena. Document issued by a judge ordering a named person to appear in court at a particular time to either answer to charges or to testify in a case.

sub-rosa economic system. Informal economic system among inmates in which contraband dealings and gambling exist under a strict set of inmate-created rules.

substantial capacity test. Definition of insanity which has as its core the view that insane persons lack the ability to understand the wrongfulness of their acts.

substantive criminal law. Legislated rule that governs behaviors that are required or prohibited. Usually enacted by legislatures. Such law also specifies punishments accompanying such law violations.

substantive due process. Refers to practice of having substantive law conform to the principles of fairness set forth in the United States Constitution.

substantive law. Body of law that creates, discovers, and defines the rights and obligations of each person in society. Prescribes behavior, whereas procedural law prescribes how harmful behavior is handled.

subterranean behaviors, values. A value or ideal that is subordinate or below the surface in the dominant value system and is sought by most people only occasionally and in appropriate circumstances (e.g., 60's deviance, social problems, beatniks, hippies, drug culture, gangs).

suitable target. According to routine activities theory, a target for crime that is relatively valuable, easily transportable, and not adequately guarded.

summary court martial. The military court that is the lowest of the three grades of court martial in terms of the severity of the penalty that it can impose.

summary judgment. Any granted motion following the presentation of a case against a defendant in a civil court. Any argument countering the plaintiff's presented evidence. Usually the result of failing to state a claim upon which relief can be granted.

summary justice. Trial held by court of limited jurisdiction, without benefit of a jury trial.

summary offense. In Britain, minor offenses, equivalent to misdemeanors, which may decided by a local magistrate in lieu of trial. Least serious British law violations, involving petty criminal infractions.

summons. Same form as a warrant, except it commands a defendant to appear before the magistrate at a particular time and place.

Sumner, William Graham. Sociologist who developed terms "folkways" and "mores," ways of doing things in a society, without moral attachment (folkways) and with moral attachment (mores). A functionalist and consensus theorist who wrote *Folkways* (1906).

superego. Sigmund Freud's label for that part of personality concerned with moral values.

superior courts. The courts of record or trial courts.

supervised pretrial release. The release of defendants without bail but under the supervision of a pretrial release agency or other supervising party.

supervised release. A type of release requiring more frequent contact than monitored release does. Typically, various conditions are imposed and supervision is aimed at enforcing these conditions and providing services as needed. Some form of monetary bail may also be attached as a condition of supervised release, especially in high-risk cases.

Supreme Court. The federal court of last resort as specified by the United States Constitution. Any court of last resort in most kinds of cases at the state level.

suppression doctrine. *See* exclusionary rule.

suppression hearing. Session held before a judge who presides at one's trial. Purpose of session is to determine which evidentiary documents and/or statements will be permitted later at trial. Motions are heard from both the defense and prosecution to keep out or put in particular evidence, and the judge decides which evidence can and cannot be introduced at trial.

supra. "Above." In United States Supreme Court written opinions, references are made to earlier statements (e.g., in the case of *Doe, supra,* the matter was concluded in a particular way).

surety, sureties. During the Middle Ages, people who made themselves responsible for the behavior of offenders released to their care.

surety bond. A sum of money or property that is posted or guaranteed by a party to ensure the future court appearance of another person. *See also* bail bond.

surplus value. The Marxist view that laboring classes produce wealth that far exceeds their wages and goes to the capitalist class as profits.

surrebuttal. Introducing witnesses during a criminal trial in order to disprove damaging testimony by other witnesses.

surveillance. Visual or electronic eavesdropping for the purpose of monitoring one's presence and/or conversation, behaviors.

survey. Systematic collection of data or information by asking questions in questionnaires or interviews.

suspect. Any person believed by a law enforcement agency to have committed a crime.

suspended sentence. A jail or prison term that is delayed while defendants undergo a period of community treatment; if treatment is successful, jail or prison sentence is terminated.

suspicion. Reasonable belief that a crime has been committed and that a particular person or persons have committed the crime; however, the level of incriminating evidence is such that probable cause cannot be established for the purpose of making an arrest.

suspicionless searches. Those searches conducted by law enforcement officers without a warrant and without suspicion. Only permissible if based upon an overriding concern for public safety.

sustain. To uphold (e.g., the conviction was sustained by a higher appellate court).

Sutherland, Edwin H. (1883-1950). Known primarily for originating and elaborating differential association theory in his book, *Principles of Criminology.* This theory posits that persons acquire criminal behaviors not simply by associating with other criminals, but rather, their associations are characterized as intense, of long duration, frequent, and with greater priority. Thus, intensity, duration, frequency, and priority are key concepts. Believed that criminal behavior is learned, and it is acquired by a fairly elaborate interplay of factors noted above. Also described various types of career criminals in his classic work, *The Professional Thief* (1937).

SWAT. Acronym for Special Weapons and Tactics. SWAT teams are used in high-crime areas to conduct anti-terrorist activities, rescue hostages, and eliminate public danger posed by dangerous armed persons.

sworn officers. Police employees who have taken an oath and been given powers by the state to make arrests, use force, and transverse property, in accordance with their duties.

Sykes, Gresham. Developed naturalization theory in collaboration with David Matza.

symbolic interaction. Sociological view that people communicate through symbolic exchange. People interpret symbolic communication and incorporate it within their personality. Their view of reality, then, depends on their particular interpretation of symbolic gestures.

synnomie. A societal state, opposite of anomie, marked by social cohesion achieved through the sharing of values.

system. Complex whole consisting of interdependent parts whose operations are directed toward goals and are influenced by the environment within which they function.

systematic forgers. Edwin Lemert's term for professionals who earn their living by forging checks or passing bad or bogus negotiable instruments.

system boundaries. The division between a system and its environment. In human systems, the boundary is often permeable and changing.

system components. The separate subroutines or activities that contribute to total system objectives.

system efficiency. Operation of the prosecutor's office in such a way so as to effect speedy and early dispositions of cases in response to caseload pressures within the system. Weak cases are screened at intake, and other nontrial alternatives are used as primary means of disposition.

systemic link. Violent behavior that results from the conflict inherent in the drug trade. A bond between violent crime and substance abuse forged by drug sellers and users.

system objectives. The measured performance of a total system, rather than its parts. The joint products of system components.

system resources. Items a system may change and use to achieve objectives.

systems approach. An analytical method that focuses upon systemic properties and processes.

T

take into custody. Police action to physically apprehend a child engaged in status offending or delinquent conduct.

tangible property. Possessions that have physical form and substance and value in and of themselves (e.g., houses, automobiles, jewelry).

Tannenbaum, Frank. Criminologist who has investigated labeling theory. Believes that socially powerful groups define and react to deviant conduct. The act itself is not inherently criminal until defined as such by a particular power aggregate, therefore deviant behavior is defined according to particular times and places, as are the consequences of such conduct. Wrote *Crime and the Community* (1938).

Tarde, Gabriel (1843-1904). French sociologist who promoted the view that imitation was a crucial factor in influencing various forms of conduct, including suicide and criminality. Espoused theory of imitation holding that criminals imitate "superiors" they admire and respect in the The Laws of Imitation (1903). Also wrote *Penal Philosophy* (1912).

target-hardening. Making residences, businesses and people less susceptible to breaking and entering through better security measures.

TASER. Acronym for Tom Swift's Electronic Rifle, a nonlethal weapon used to disable a suspect by sending an electrical charge through wires that are fired into the suspect's skin with a pistol-like weapon.

taxonomy. A level of theory consisting of a system of categories constructed to fit the empirical observations so that relationships among categories can be described.

tazirat **crimes.** Minor violations of Islamic law, which are regarded as offenses against society, not God.

team policing. When investigative teams of police officers, detectives, and other personnel are assigned to a particular community area to work together in solving crimes that occur in that area.

technical parole violation. An infraction relating to the terms and conditions of one's parole program and behavioral conditions (e.g., violating curfew or testing positive for drugs or alcohol).

technical violation. In probation or parole programs, infractions of program rules unrelated to commission of crimes (e.g., curfew violation, testing positive for alcohol use, or leaving work early without permission).

techniques of neutralization. According to neutralization theory, the ability of delinquent youths to neutralize moral constraints so that they may drift into criminal acts. Such techniques include denial of responsibility, denial of injury, denial of victim, condemnation of the condemners, and an appeal to higher loyalties.

telephone pole design. Prison design that replaced the block design for maximum security units. A long central corridor is crossed by several shorter living unit and program buildings.

TEMPEST. A standard developed by the United States government that requires electromagnetic emanations from computers designed as "secure" to be below levels that would allow radio receiving equipment to "read" the data being computed.

temporal precedence. The coming or happening of one thing before another in time. In attempting to establish causality, one must establish temporal precedence, that is, that the causal factor was introduced before the effect occurred.

termination of parental rights. Termination by the court, upon petition, of all rights to minors by their parents. Parents may be judged incapable and their rights terminated because of the following: debauchery, use of drugs and alcohol, conviction of a felony, lewd or lascivious behavior, or mental illness.

territorial district courts. Federal trial courts corresponding to the United States district courts but located in the territories.

terrorism. A violent act or an act dangerous to human life in violation of the criminal laws of the United States or of any state to intimidate or coerce a government, the civilian population, or any segment thereof, in furtherance of a political or social objective.

terrorist, terrorist group. Politically or socially motivated person with diverse goals, but who most often attempts to cause public incidents and promote fear among people through deadly acts, including bombing airplanes, public transportation, public buildings, and assassinations. Any one of several loosely organized factions that commit acts of terrorism.

Terry-stop. Reference to the case of *Terry v. Ohio* (1968) involving the stop-and-frisk of a suspicious person.

tertiary prevention. The third level of prevention of recidivism. Focuses upon preventing further delinquent acts by youths already identified as delinquents.

testimony. Oral evidence provided by legally competent witnesses during trial proceedings.

Texas model. Also known as the "traditional" model of state court organization. Two "supreme" courts, one for civil appeals, one for criminal appeals. Has five tiers of district, county, and municipal courts.

Texas Rangers. Founded by Stephen Austin in 1823, the first territorial police agency in the United States.

thanatos. Sigmund Freud's concept of an instinctual drive towards aggression and violence.

theft. The crime of taking the property of others without permission.

theft of computer time, software, and hardware. The unauthorized use of computer time and software services, unauthorized copying of software programs, or outright theft of computer equipment.

theoretical range. The units or levels of analysis and explanation that might be sought by a particular theory.

theoretical system. Systematic combinations of taxonomies, conceptual frameworks, descriptions, explanations, and predictions in a manner that provides structure for a complete explanation of empirical phenomenon.

theory. A set of propositions from which a large number of new observations can be deduced. An integrated body of definitions, assumptions, and propositions related in such a way to explain and predict relations between two or more variables.

therapeutic community. Residential treatment unit that promotes change through communal processes of norm building, inmate participation in decisions, and group responsibility.

therapeutic intervention. Strategy by juvenile probation officer, in which officer may make visits to juvenile's home, inspect premises, and check with school officials on juvenile's progress.

thief-takers. Persons who were "fleet of foot" in early England, selected to pursue and apprehend fleeing criminals for a fee. Citizens who receive a reward for the apprehension of criminals.

Thomas, W.I. (circa 1900-1950). Wrote *Unadjusted Girl*. Developed concept of "Four Wishes," including response (love), recognition, new experience, and security. Used term "definition of the situation," meaning that "whatever is perceived as real will be real in its consequences." Four-wishes conception used to explain both conventional and unconventional (deviant) conduct, in which one form of new experience is conceivably criminal conduct.

Thornberry, Terence. Criminologist who has proposed an age-graded view of crime contending that crime emerges as social bonds deteriorate in one's early years. Serious delinquent youths form belief systems that are consistent with their deviant life style. They seek out others like them and adopt their behaviors. They reinforce the delinquent behaviors of others through their own social approval and emulation of them. Age-gradation is a key component closely attached to cognitive developmental stages, as one acquires reasoning ability and greater sophistication. Family attachment is crucial in one's early years in order to avoid delinquent and criminal behavior patterns.

three-strikes-and-you're-out philosophy. A crime prevention and control strategy that proposes to incarcerate those offenders who commit and are convicted of three or more serious or violent offenses; usual penalty is life imprisonment or the life-without-parole option. Intent is to incarcerate high-rate offenders to reduce crime in society. *See also* **habitual offender statutes.**

threshold inquiry. *See* stop-and-frisk.

thrill killing. Impulsive violence motivated by a murderer's decision to kill a stranger during a moment of recklessness or daring.

ticket-of-leave. An early form of conditional release used in the English and Irish prison systems.

tier system. Method of establishing various floors for cells where prisoners of different types can be housed. Started at Auburn State Penitentiary in 1816.

time, place and manner doctrine. First Amendment doctrine holding that government may impose reasonable limitations on the time, place and manner of expressive activities.

time served. Total time spent in confinement by a convicted adult before and after sentencing, or only the time spent in confinement after a sentence of commitment to a confinement facility.

tithing. In Anglo-Saxon law, an association of ten families bound together by a frankpledge for purposes of crime control.

Tonnies, Ferdinand. German sociologist who pioneered the terms *gemeinschaft* and *gesell-schaft* to depict two societal forms. The former characterizes societies founded on kinship and family, the latter is founded on contractual relations and formality. Criminal conduct is controlled through social ostracism in *gemeinschaft*-type societies, whereas crime is formally punished with specific sanctions and penalties in *gesellschaft* society.

topical autobiography. A private record that focuses upon a limited aspect of a person's life.

torch. A professional arsonist.

tort. A private or civil wrong or injury, other than breach of contract, for which the court will provide a remedy in the form of an action for damages. A violation of a duty imposed by law. Existence of a legal duty to plaintiff, breach of that duty, and damage as a result of that breach.

total enforcement. A policy whereby the police are given the resources and support to enforce all laws without regard to the civil liberties of citizens.

total institution. Erving Goffman's term describing places that completely encapsulate the lives of those who work and live within them. Rules govern behavior, and the group is split into two parts, one of which controls the lives of the other.

total quality management (TQM). An organizational method of involving subordinates in decision-making procedures to give them greater responsibility and encourage greater loyalty and devotion among them toward the company (e.g., in policing, encouraging rank-and-file police officers to take a more active role in decision-making about their jobs and work assignments and become more involved in community activities).

totality circumstances. Exception to exclusionary rule, whereby officers may make warrantless searches of property and seizures of illegal contraband on the basis of the entire set of suspicious circumstances.

totality of conditions. *See* totality of circumstances.

tracking. In education, the practice of assigning students to groups or classes based on an assessment of the student's ability or potential. Tracks are classified by level of difficulty, which can result in the stigmatization of the lower-track children and snobbery by the higher-track children, who are likely to be college-bound.

traditional rehabilitation model. *See* rehabilitation.

training school. A correctional facility for juveniles adjudicated to be delinquents or status offenders and committed to confinement by a juvenile court.

transactional immunity. *See* immunity, transactional.

transcript. A written record of a trial or hearing.

transfer hearing, proceeding. Proceeding to determine whether juveniles should be certified as adults for purposes of being subjected to jurisdiction of adult criminal courts where more severe penalties may be imposed. Also known as "certification" or "waiver."

transfer of property. The cost of crimes in which property is transferred from one person to another, such as from the victim of a theft to the thief.

transfer to adult court. *See* transfer.

transferred intent. If an illegal yet unintended act results from the intent to commit a crime, that act is also considered illegal.

transitional neighborhood. An area undergoing a shift in population and structure, usually from middle-class residential to lower-class mixed use.

transnational crime. A criminal act or transaction violating the laws of more than one country, or having an impact on a foreign country.

transportation. *See* banishment.

transportation officers. Authorized persons in charge of transporting inmates to other correctional institutions, usually to the state prison system after sentencing.

Trasler, Gordon. Criminologist and psychologist who wrote *The Explanation of Criminality* (1962). Student of B.F. Skinner who believed that conditioned anxiety or fear of punishment inhibits persons from engaging in criminal behavior.

treason. The crime of attempting by overt acts to overthrow the government, or of betraying the government to a foreign power.

treater value system. Parole board decision-making system where emphasis is upon rehabilitation, and where early release decisions are made on the basis of what will best suit the offender.

treatment model. *See* medical model.

trespass. Any unlawful interference with one's person or property.

trial. An adversarial proceeding within a particular jurisdiction, in which a judicial examination and determination of issues can be made, and in which a criminal defendant's guilt or innocence can be decided impartially by either a judge or jury. *See also* bench trial, jury trial.

trial court of general jurisdiction. Criminal court that has jurisdiction over all offenses, including felonies, and may in some states also hear appeals from lower courts.

trial court of limited jurisdiction. Criminal court where trial jurisdiction either includes no felonies or is limited to some category of felony. Such courts have jurisdiction over misdemeanor cases, probable-cause hearings in felony cases, and sometimes, felony trials that may result in penalties below a specific limit.

trial *de novo*. A new judicial hearing or proceeding. A new adversarial proceeding occurring as though there had never been a first trial or proceeding, usually granted to defendants where egregarious wrongs or misconduct occurred to nullify former adjudicatory proceedings.

trial judge. *See* judge.

trial jury. *See* petit jury.

trial sufficiency. Presence of sufficient legal elements to ensure successful prosecution of a case. When prosecutor's decision to prosecute a case is customarily based on trial sufficiency, only cases that seem certain to result in conviction at trial are accepted for prosecution. Use of plea bargaining is minimal. Good police work and court capacity are required.

tribunal. A court. A place where judges sit. A judicial weighing of information leading to a decision about a case.

truant. A juvenile who absents him or herself from school without a valid excuse.

truant officer. An officer of the juvenile court who apprehends truants.

true bill. Grand jury decision that sufficient evidence exists that a crime has been committed and that a specific suspect committed it. A charge of an alleged crime. An indictment.

true crimes. Extremely serious offenses in France. Comparable to serious felonies in United States Violent offenses.

truly disadvantaged. A term created by William Julius Wilson to describe those at the lowest level of the underclass. Such persons are described as victims of discrimination dwelling in urban inner cities. They live in areas where social disorganization has affected housing, schools, and employment, and which manifest a ghetto culture and behavior marked by criminality and violence. Since they seldom come into contact with the politically powerful, the source of their plight, they direct their rage and frustration inward toward others around them.

trustee. Any person entrusted to handle the affairs of another.

"trusty," trusty system. Plan whereby a prisoner is entrusted with authority to supervise other prisoners in exchange for certain privileges and status.

Turk, Austin. Sociologist and criminologist who has written extensively about the conflict perspective. Suggests that persons are different in their understandings and commitments, that divergence leads to conflict, that each conflicting party manifests diverse and conflicting interests, that persons with similar beliefs join forces to counter those with opposing views, that continuing conflicts lead to routinization of activities, which in turn foster economic exploitation, and that continual conflict is inevitable.

turning points. Life events that alter the development of a criminal career. A part of age-graded theory devised by Robert Sampson and John Laub in the work *Crime in the Making* (1993). Turning points include marriage and career, which tend to function as deterrents to criminal conduct or cause predisposed persons to desist from criminal behavior. Social capital is also important.

turnkey approach. Contracts with private interests to design, finance, construct, and operate facilities for the detention of juveniles, illegal aliens, and others.

tutelage. Instruction or socialization in criminal motives and skills, including how to spot opportunities for theft, how to plan thefts, and how to carry out thefts.

Tweed, William Marcy. Known as "Boss Tweed," an influential, corrupt political figure who dominated Tammany Hall in Democratic Party politics in New York City from 1866-1871.

Twinkie defense. Used by Dan White, the confessed killer of San Francisco Mayor George Moscone and city councilman Harvey Milk, who claimed he killed because of his addiction to sugar-laden junk foods, such as Twinkies. A biochemical explanation for criminal conduct.

Type I offenses. *See* index crimes.

Type II offenses. *See* index crimes.

typology. A set of categories.

U

u curve. The graphed pattern of inmate value distance from staff values as prison sentence progresses. Inmates first entering prison have values most similar to those of staff. Inmates in the middle of sentence have values least like those of staff. Inmates preparing for release have values closer to staff, but not as similar as those just entering prison. Also known as the J curve.

UCR. See *Uniform Crime Reports.*

ultra vires. Beyond the scope of one's prescribed authority.

unconditional discharge. A post-trial disposition, essentially the same as unconditional diversion. No savings obtained in criminal justice processing costs, but jail populations may be reduced. Conditions of release are imposed for an offense in which the defendant's involvement has been established.

unconditional diversion (standard diversion) program. Diversion program requiring minimal or no contact with probation department. May include minimum maintenance fee paid regularly for specified period such as one year. No treatment program is indicated.

unconditional release. The final release of an offender from the jurisdiction of a correctional agency. Also, a final release from the jurisdiction of a court.

unconstitutionally vague. A term used by the United States Supreme Court to declare a particular law lacking in specificity, failing to describe specific actions or behaviors that are prohibited, such as municipal vagrancy laws.

underclass. According to Gunnar Myrdal, permanent lower class that becomes institutionalized in a welfare state.

underworld. A broad class of criminals who operate outside of public view, such as organized prostitution or gambling. Racketeers.

UNICOR. Federal prison industry that manufactures goods for profit. Workers are prisoners who are paid prevailing wage. Considered a rehabilitative tool.

unification. Effort to organize all courts in a jurisdiction under a single administrative head.

Uniform Crime Reports. Annual publication by Federal Bureau of Investigation that describes crime from all reporting law enforcement agencies in the United States. New format in 1988 identifies incident-based reporting compared with other reporting schemes used in past years.

unit cost. The cost to provide services or products expressed in some standard measure (e.g., such as cost of probation supervision per probationer per year).

United Kingdom model. A rigorous recruitment and training program used in England and Wales for the purpose of police officer selection and training.

United States attorneys. Officials responsible for the prosecution of crimes that violate the laws of the United States. Appointed by the President and assigned to a United States district court jurisdiction.

United States Code Annotated. Comprehensive compendium of federal laws and statutes, including landmark cases and discussions of law applications.

United States Commissioners. *See* United States Magistrates.

United States Courts of Appeals. The federal circuit courts of appellate jurisdiction. As of 1996, there were 13 Circuit Courts of Appeal zoned throughout the United States and its territories.

United States Customs Service. Agency authorized to conduct searches and inspections of all ships, aircraft, and vehicles entering United States borders.

United States District Courts. The basic trial courts for federal civil and criminal actions.

United States Magistrates. Judges who fulfill the pretrial judicial obligations of the federal courts. Formerly, United States Commissioners.

United States Parole Commission. Established in 1930. Responsible for the management and monitoring of all federal prisoners released on parole, as well as the classification and placement of parolees and maintenance of reports of their progress.

United States Sentencing Guidelines. Rules implemented by federal courts in November 1987 obligating federal judges to impose presumptive sentences on all convicted offenders. Guidelines are based upon offense seriousness and offender characteristics. Judges may depart from guidelines only by justifying their departures in writing.

University Settlement. Privately operated facility in New York commenced in 1893 by James Bronson Reynolds to provide assistance and job referral services to community residents. Settlement involved in probation work in 1901. Eventually abandoned after considerable public skepticism, and when political opponents withdrew their support.

unlawful entry. Illegally opening an unlocked door without permission and entering the premises. A lesser-included offense of burglary, or breaking and entering.

unreasonableness. A search by law enforcement officers not conforming to the boundaries of propriety as prescribed by the courts, (e.g., pumping a suspect's stomach in order to retrieve evidence).

unreported crime. The amount of crime that occurs in any jurisdiction but is not reported to law enforcement agencies.

unsecured bail. A form of release differing from release on own recognizance only in that defendants are subject to paying the amount of bail if they default. Unsecured bail permits release without a deposit or purchase of bondsman's services.

unsolved crime. Any crime for which a perpetrator has not been either apprehended or convicted.

upperworld crime. Conduct in violation of the law engaged in during the course of business activity (e.g., tax evasion, price fixing). Perpetrators often view offenses as shrewd business practices that are not really criminal.

urbanization. Increasing population density in urban centers. The spread of industry and business in small geographical areas.

urban renewal. Destruction of older buildings and run-down properties and the construction of modern buildings, businesses, and residences.

use immunity. *See* immunity, use.

usury. The taking of or contracting to take interest on a loan at a rate that exceeds the level established by law.

utilitarianism. A criminological theory that crime prevention and criminal justice must serve the end of providing the greatest good for the greatest number. Based upon the rationality of lawgivers, law enforcers, and the public-at-large.

utilitarian justification of punishment. Justifications that promise an empirical benefit from the exercise of punishment, such as deterrence, incapacitation, and rehabilitation.

uttering a forged instrument. The crime of passing a false or worthless instrument, such as a check, with the intent to defraud or injure the recipient.

V

vacate. To annul, set aside, or rescind.

vacated sentence. Any sentence that has been declared nullified by action of a court.

vagrancy. The offense of living without any visible means of support. Most vagrancy laws have been declared unconstitutionally vague.

value. Something that is considered worthy, desirable, or proper.

value isolation. Sometimes considered cultural estrangement. Low rewards are attached to commonly held social values such as good grades, a high school diploma, or a steady job.

vandalism. Destroying or damaging, or attempting to destroy or damage, the property of another without his or her consent, except by burning, which is arson.

vehicular homicide. Death resulting from the unlawful and negligent operation of a motorized vehicle.

vengeance. A private and personal response to a wrong, not involving an established authority.

venire, veniremen list, veniremen. List of prospective jurors made up from registered voters, vehicle driver's licenses, tax assessors' records. Persons must reside within particular jurisdiction where jury trial is held. Persons who are potential jurors in a given jurisdiction.

venue. Area over which a judge exercises authority to act in an official capacity. Place where a trial is held.

venue, change of. Relocation of a trial from one site to another, usually because of some pretrial publicity making it possible that a jury might be biased and that a fair trial will be difficult to obtain.

verdict. Decision by judge or jury concerning the guilt or innocence of a defendant.

verdict, guilty. In criminal proceedings, the decision made by a jury in a jury trial, or by a judicial officer in a bench trial, that defendants are guilty of the offense(s) for which they have been tried.

verdict, not guilty. In criminal proceedings, the decision made by jury in jury trial, or by the judge in a bench trial, that defendants are not guilty of the offense(s) for which they have been tried.

verstehen. Understanding. The notion that social scientists can understand human behavior through empathy.

vicarious liability. Doctrine under which liability is imposed upon an employer for the acts of employees that are committed in the course and scope of their employment.

vice squad. Police officers assigned to enforce morally tinged laws, such as those on prostitution, gambling, and pornography.

victim. Person who has either suffered death or serious physical or mental suffering, or loss of property resulting from actual or attempted criminal actions committed by others.

victim assistance program. One of many programs in various states seeking to compensate victims of crimes for their losses.

victim compensation. Any financial restitution payable to victims by either the state or convicted offenders.

victim compensation programs. Any plans for assisting crime victims in making social, emotional, and economic adjustments.

victim impact statement. Information or version of events filed voluntarily by the victim of a crime, appended to the presentence investigation report as a supplement for judicial consideration in sentencing the offender. Describes injuries to victims resulting from convicted offender's actions.

victim/offender mediation model. Meeting between criminal and person suffering loss or injury from criminal whereby third-party arbiter, such as a judge, attorney, or other neutral party decides what is best for all parties. All parties must agree to decision of third-party arbiter. Used for both juvenile and adult offenders.

victim precipitation. The situation that exists when a person who suffers eventual harm from a crime plays a direct role in causing the crime.

victim proneness. The tendency for certain people to be victimized repeatedly. *See* victim precipitation, victim precipitated.

victim restitution. Having criminals pay back the victims of their crimes as an alternative to more serious sanctions.

Victim/Reparations model. Restitution model for juveniles in which juveniles compensate their victims directly for their offenses.

victim-witness assistance program. Plan available to prospective witnesses to explain court procedures and inform them of court dates, and to assist witnesses in providing better testimony in court.

victimization. Basic measure of the occurrence of a crime. A specific criminal act affecting a specific victim.

victimization data. Information collected about persons who are targets of criminal activity.

victimization rate. The number of victimizations per 1,000 persons or households as reported by the *National Crime Survey*.

victimization risk. Amenability to aggressive actions from others because of particular lifestyles (e.g., attending neighborhood high school with high crime rate).

victimization survey. A survey of respondents who have been victimized. Measures the extent of crime by interviewing persons about their experiences as victims.

victimless crime. Crime committed in which there are no apparent victims, or in which victims are willing participants in the criminal activity (e.g., gambling and prostitution).

victimology. A criminological subdiscipline that examines the role played by the victim in a criminal incident and in the criminal process.

Victims Bill of Rights. Entitlements established by New York State Compensation Board, outlining specific rights of crime victims, including notification of offender status and custody, case disposition, and incarceration/non-incarceration details.

vigilante, vigilante justice. Person who is alert, a watchman, on guard, cautious, suspicious, or ready to take action to preserve the peace. Currently refers to citizens who take the law into their own hands in an effort to apprehend and punish criminals.

violation. Minor criminal offense, usually under city ordinances, commonly subject only to fines.

violation of privacy. Any unlawful trespass, interception, observation, eavesdropping, or other surveillance that serves to infringe on the private rights of others.

violent crime, violent personal crime. Law violation characterized by extreme physical force including murder or homicide, forcible rape or child sexual abuse, assault and battery by means of a dangerous weapon, robbery, and arson.

Virginia Plan. Scheme deriving from England's royal court system, projecting superior and inferior courts; also called "Randolph Plan."

virulency. Stage in a violent career in which criminals develop a violent identity that makes them feared. They consequently enjoy hurting others.

visible crimes. Offenses against persons and property committed primarily by members of the lower class. Often referred to as "street crime" or "ordinary crime," these are the offenses most upsetting to the public.

visiting cottage program. Scheme established by Massachusetts Department of Corrections in which female offenders with children may have lengthy visits with their children in "cottages" on the prison premises.

vocational training. Education in a specific marketable skill.

void-for-vagueness doctrine. *See* unconstitutionally vague.

voir dire. "To speak the truth." Interrogation process whereby prospective jurors are questioned by either the judge or by the prosecution or defense attorneys to determine their biases and prejudices.

Vold, George. Conflict theorist who believed in a definite link between conflict theory and crime. Considered the primary contributor of this particular view. Law is created by the ruling class to dominate lower classes. Thus, Marxist philosophy fits Vold's view of society well. Conflict between classes is pervasive, fundamental, and persistent, and crime occurs when different classes clash over competing and opposing vested interests. Wrote *Theoretical Criminology* (1958).

Vollmer, August. Chief of Police of Berkeley, California. Professionalized policing by recommending educational training for police officers. Relied heavily on academic specialists in various forensics areas. Pioneered informal academic regimen of police training, including investigative techniques, photography, fingerprinting, and anatomy, among other academic subject areas.

Volstead Act. Legislation passed in 1919 to prohibit possession and/or consumption of alcoholic beverages. Repealed in 1933.

voluntariness. Willingness of defendant to enter a plea or make an agreement in a plea bargain proceeding. Judges must determine the voluntariness of the plea to determine that it was not coerced.

voluntarism. The freedom of participants to choose whether or not to take part in a research experiment or project and the guarantee that exposure to known risks is voluntarily undertaken.

voluntary manslaughter. Homicide in which the perpetrator intentionally, but without malice, causes the death of another person, as in the heat of passion, in response to strong provocation, or possibly under severe intoxication.

volunteer. Any citizen who wishes to donate time to assist in the supervision, education, counseling, or training of probationers, parolees, or divertees.

volunteerism. Propensity of citizens to become actively involved in various auxiliary police functions, such as Neighborhood Watch.

Von Hentig, Hans (circa 1940s). Proponent of physical characteristics as indicative of criminal propensities. Wrote a treatise on this subject in 1948.

Von Hirsch, Andrew. Criminologist and classicist who wrote *Doing Justice*. Advocate of "just-desert" philosophy, in which punishment is designed to fit the crime committed. Blameworthiness of the offense should not be changed for different persons who commit the same offense. Thus, committing the same offense should result in identical punishments, regardless of one's past criminal record, race, ethnicity, gender, or age.

voyeurism. The surreptitious observance of an exposed body or sexual act. *See also* Peeping Tom.

W

waiver, waiver of jurisdiction. Made by motion, the transfer of jurisdiction over a juvenile to a criminal court where the juvenile is subject to adult criminal penalties. Includes judicial, prosecutorial, and legislative waivers. Also known as "certification" or "transfer."

waiver motion or hearing. Motion by prosecutor to transfer juvenile charged with various offenses to a criminal or adult court for prosecution, making it possible to sustain adult criminal penalties.

Walnut Street Jail. Considered first American prison seeking to correct offenders. Built in 1776 in Philadelphia, Pennsylvania. One of first penal facilities which segregated female from male offenders and children from adults. Introduced solitary confinement of prisoners. Separated prisoners according to their offense severity. Operated on basis that inmates could perform useful services to defray the costs of confinement. Operated one of first prison industry programs. Inmates grew much of their own fruit through gardening.

warden. Chief administrator of a prison or penitentiary.

warehousing. An imprisonment strategy based upon the desire to prevent recurrent crime but which has abandoned any hope of rehabilitation.

warrant. A written order directing a suspect's arrest and issued by an official with the authority to issue the warrant. Commands suspect to be arrested and brought before the nearest magistrate.

warrant, arrest. Document issued by a judge that directs a law enforcement officer to arrest a person who has been accused of an offense.

warrant, bench. Document issued by a judge directing that a person who has failed to obey an order or notice to appear be brought before the court without undue delay.

warrant, search. Any document issued by a judicial official, based upon probable cause, directing law enforcement officers to conduct an inspection of an individual, automobile, or building with the intent of locating particular contraband or incriminating evidence as set forth in the document.

warrantless search and seizure. Examination of dwelling unit, person, or automobile without obtaining a search warrant from a magistrate or judge based upon probable cause and under oath.

Warren court. United States Supreme Court under the leadership of Chief Justice Earl Warren.

watchman style. A style of policing that is marked by a concern for order maintenance. Characteristic of lower-class communities where informal police intervention into the lives of residents is employed in the service of keeping the peace.

watchmen. Citizens in early England who were paid to observe in their neighborhoods for possible criminal activity.

watch system. During the Middle Ages in England, men were organized in church parishes to guard at night against disturbances and breaches of the peace under the direction of the local constable.

Watson, John. Psychologist who promoted the concept of behavior modification. Believed in operant conditioning, viewing behavior as the result of chains of stimuli and responses. Criminality is one response to stimuli that are found rewarding in connection with criminal conduct.

weapons offenses. Unlawful sale, distribution, manufacture, alternation, transportation, possession, or use or attempted sale, distribution, manufacture, alternation, transportation, possession, or use of deadly or dangerous weapons or accessories.

Weber, Max (1864-1920). German sociologist who wrote many works, including *The Protestant Ethic and the Spirit of Capitalism* (1906). Elaborated on the concept of *verstehen*, which is interpreted literally as meaning "at the level of understanding." Thus, through *verstehen*, sociologists can acquire a better understanding of their social world. Also pioneered work on bureaucracy, an organizational model which has been used in establishing police and correctional systems. Bureaucracy incorporates characteristics including selection by test, pre-arranged hierarchy of authority, expertise, non-overlapping functional departments or limited spheres of competence, abstract rules, and promotion according to ability. Advocated a value-free approach to research.

Wehrli, Jakob (? - 1855). Swiss educator who helped to establish early private institutions for wayward and destitute children.

werdgild. Under medieval law, the money paid by offenders to compensate victims and the state for a criminal offense.

Wharton's rule. Named after Francis Wharton, a well-known commentator on criminal law, this rule holds that two people cannot conspire to commit a crime such as adultery, incest, or bigamy, inasmuch as these offenses involve only two participants.

white-collar crime. Law violation committed by those persons of higher socioeconomic status in the course of their businesses, occupations, or professions (e.g., a banker who embezzles).

white slavery. Exploitation of females who are kidnapped and coerced into lives of prostitution.

Wichern, Johann Hinrich (1808-1881). Swiss educator who assisted in developing private institutions for wayward and destitute children.

Wickersham Commission, Wickersham Reports. 1929 Commission established to investigate police agencies and the state of training and education among police officers. Generally critical of contemporary methods of police organization and operation. Conclusions published by the National Commission on Law Observance and Enforcement, chaired by George W. Wickersham.

widening the net. *See* net widening.

Wilson, Edmund O. Espoused the influence and interplay of biological and genetic factors on perception and learning such that one's conduct, including criminal conduct, is influenced to a great degree by one's genetic make-up. Societal factors exist to create conventional behavior patterns, but the genetic element is strong. Wrote *Sociobiology* (1975).

Wilson, James Q. Political scientist and criminologist who wrote *Thinking About Crime* (1975) which is a policy analysis approach to crime. Critical of positivist thought in which crime is believed to be a function of external forces. Rather, believes that crime can be controlled more effectively by reducing criminal opportunities and selectively incapacitating known chronic recidivists. Chaired numerous videotaped panels as a part of an educational series for the National Institute of Justice during mid- to late 1980s focusing upon crime prevention strategies and the effectiveness of current tactics to deal with criminals at different phases of criminal justice processing. Has also authored *The Moral Sense* (1993), which details how hormones, enzymes, and neurotransmitters might be keys to understanding human behavior. He suggests that testosterone levels help to explain aging-out process among criminals, and that there is a relation between violence and hormonal imbalances. Collaborated with Richard Herrnstein to write *Crime* *and Human Nature* (1985), a controversial work linking criminal conduct with genetic factors. Maintains an integrated theoretical view attributing criminality to biosocial makeup, personality, rational choice, social structure and process.

Wilson, O.W. A former police chief in Wichita, Kansas and Chicago, Illinois. First Dean of the School of Criminology at the University of California, Berkeley in 1950. Successfully in centralized police administration and created command decision making, not only in Berkeley, but in many other cities during the 1950s and 1960s.

Wilson, William Julius. Criminologist who wrote *The Truly Disadvantaged* (1987). Discusses persons who are isolated in urban society and who are at the bottom rung of the social ladder. "Truly disadvantaged" cannot attack the source of their frustration, the elite society, and thus direct their rage and frustration at others around them. This becomes a vicious cycle of loss of self-confidence, frustration, anger, helplessness, and violence.

Wirth, Louis (1897-1952). Helped to establish the Chicago School during the 1920s, examining zones in and around Chicago, rings emanating from the city center outward toward the suburbs, where different social patterns existed and different types of crime were observed. Zones undergoing urban renewal or rapid social change were increasingly disorganized and ripe for high degrees of criminality. Collaborated with Edwin Sutherland, Robert Park, and Ernest Burgess.

wite. Portion of the wergild that went to the victim's family.

without undue or unnecessary delay. Standard used to determine whether suspect has been brought in a timely manner before a magistrate or other judicial authority after arrested. Definition of undue delay varies among jurisdictions. Circumstances of arrest, availability of judge, and time of arrest are factors that determine reasonableness of delay.

witness. Person who has relevant information about the commission of a crime; any person who has seen or heard inculpatory or exculpatory evidence that may incriminate or exonerate a defendant.

Wolfgang, Marvin. Wrote *Patterns in Criminal Homicide.* A landmark analysis of homicide and the relation between offenders and their victims. Has elaborated on the white-collar crime concepts of Edwin Sutherland. Also published *De-*

linquency in a Birth Cohort with Thorsten Sellin and Robert Figlio. Work examined two male birth cohorts from Philadelphia in 1945 and 1963. Led these researchers to conclude that 6 percent of these persons accounted for 54 percent of all delinquency and criminal activity, and they became known as the "chronic 6 percent." Also formulated the subculture of violence, a concept depicting a culture within a culture, in which the theme of violence is an integral part of one's lifestyle and one learns through socialization to value this conduct more highly than conventional behavior. Albert Cohen is credited with elaborating the subculture notion to delinquent behavior.

Woman's Self-Help Center Justice Outreach Program. Intermediate punishment program for females offering diversion and other supervisory services, located in St. Louis, Missouri.

work furlough. *See* work release.

workgroup. A collectivity of persons who interact in the workplace on a continuing basis, share goals, develop norms regarding how activities should be carried out, and eventually establish a network of roles that serve to differentiate this group from others.

workhouse. Early penal facilities designed to use prison labor for profit by private interests. Operated in English shires in mid-sixteenth century and later.

working personality. Term used to describe police officers as having similar and distinctive cognitive tendencies and behavioral responses, including a particular "life style."

work (and educational) release. Community-based program whereby persons about to be paroled work in community at jobs during day, return to facility at night. Limited supervision. Any program that provides for prison labor in the community, under conditions of relaxed supervision, and for which prisoners are paid adequate wages.

writ. A document issued by a judicial officer ordering or forbidding the performance of a specific act.

writ of *certiorari.* An order of a superior court requesting that the record of an inferior court (or administrative body) be brought forward for review or inspection. Literally, "to be more fully informed."

writ of error. A writ issued by an appellate court for the purpose of correcting an error revealed in the record of a lower court proceeding.

writ of *habeas corpus*. *See habeas corpus.*

writ of mandamus. An order of a superior court commanding that a lower court, administrative body, or executive body perform a specific function. Commonly used to restore rights and privileges lost to a defendant through illegal means.

writ of prohibition. An appellate court order that prevents a lower court from exercising its jurisdiction in a particular case.

writs of assistance. Ancient writs issuing from the Court of Exchequer ordering sheriffs to assist in collecting debts owed to the British Crown. Prior to the American Revolution, the writs of assistance gave agents of the Crown in the American colonies the unlimited right to search for smuggled goods. In modern practice, judicial orders to put someone in possession of particular property.

xenophobe. Person who is afraid of anyone from a foreign country.

XYY chromosome complement. A rare biological trait of some men that has been linked to a tendency to violate the law, or at least to be arrested for such violations.

XYY syndrome. Theory of criminal behavior suggesting that some criminals are born with extra "Y" chromosome, characterized as the "aggressive" chromosome compared with the "passive X" chromosome. Extra Y chromosome produces greater agitation, greater aggressiveness, and criminal propensities.

Yablonsky, Lewis. Criminologist who has studied gangs and gang patterns. Particularly known for observations of fighting gangs in studies of New York City gangs during late 1950s and early 1960s.

Yochelson, S. Criminologist who has conducted extensive studies of the criminal personality in his co-authored work with Stanton Samenow, *The Criminal Personality* (1976, 1977).

youth, youthful offender. Any person who is an infant, juvenile, or minor, who has not yet reached the age of majority or adulthood, and over which the juvenile court has jurisdiction. Varies according to each jurisdiction.

youth gangs. Self-formed associations of youths distinguished from other types of youth groups by their routine participation in illegal activities.

youth services bureau. A diversion program for juvenile courts that eliminates noncriminal cases and petty first offenses from the courts' consideration by providing a resource to help young persons become less troubled or less troubling. A neighborhood agency that coordinates all community services for young people, especially designed for the pre-delinquent or early delinquent.

Z

zero tolerance. A federal anti-drug measure that permits the confiscation of planes, vessels, or vehicles found to be carrying a controlled substance. No amount of drugs or illegal contraband is allowable or acceptable.

zone search. Method of searching crime scenes where area for search is divided according to sectors and each is carefully examined.

References

Abadinsky, Howard. (1994). Probation and Parole: Theory and Practice, 5/e. Upper Saddle River, NJ: Prentice-Hall.

Abadinsky, Howard and L. Thomas Winfree, Jr. (1992). Crime and Justice, 2/e. Chicago: Nelson-Hall Publishers.

Andenaes, J. "General Prevention Revisited: Research and Policy Implications." *Journal of Criminal Law and Criminology*, 66:338-365.

Anderson, Patrick R. and Donald J. Newman. (1993). Introduction to Criminal Justice, 5/e. New York: McGraw-Hill.

Bartollas, Clemens. (1993). Juvenile Delinquency, 3/e. New York: Macmillan.

Bartollas, Clemens and John P. Conrad. (1992). Introduction to Corrections, 2/e. New York: Harper Collins.

Black, Henry Campbell. (1989). Black's Law Dictionary. St. Paul, MN: West Publishing Company.

Champion, Dean J. (1990). Corrections in the United States: A Contemporary Perspective. Upper Saddle River, NJ: Prentice-Hall.

Champion, Dean J. (1990). Criminal Justice in the United States. Upper Saddle River, NJ: Prentice-Hall.

Champion, Dean J. (1990). Probation and Parole in the United States. Upper Saddle River, NJ: Prentice-Hall.

Champion, Dean J. (1992). The Juvenile Justice System: Delinquency, Processing, and the Law. New York: Macmillan.

Champion, Dean J. (1993). Research Methods for Criminal Justice and Criminology. Upper Saddle River, NJ: Prentice-Hall.

Cole, George F. (1995). The American System of Criminal Justice, 7/e. Belmont, CA: Wadsworth Publishing Company.

Drowns, Robert W. and Karen M. Hess. (1995). Juvenile Justice, 2/e. St. Paul, MN: West Publishing Company.

Eskridge, Chris W. (1996) Criminal Justice: Concepts and Issues, 2/e. Los Angeles: Roxbury Publishing Company.

Fox, Vernon B. and Jeanne B. Stinchcomb. (1994). Introduction to Corrections, 4/e. Upper Saddle River, NJ: Prentice-Hall.

Inciardi, James A. (1993). Criminal Justice, 4/e. New York: Harcourt, Brace, and Jovanovich.

LaGrange, Randy L. (1993). Policing American Society. Chicago: Nelson-Hall.

Peak, Kenneth J. and Ronald W. Glensor. (1996). Community Policing and Problem Solving: Strategies and Practices. Upper Saddle River, NJ: Prentice-Hall.

Scheb, John M. and John M. Scheb II. (1994). Criminal Law and Procedure, 2/e. St. Paul, MN: West Publishing Company.

Simonsen, Clifford E. (1991). Juvenile Justice in America, 3/e. New York: Macmillan.

UNITED STATES SUPREME COURT CASES

The United States Supreme Court cases listed in this section, as well as cases from United States District Courts, Circuit Courts of Appeal, and state courts, are cited by the names of persons involved in the cases as well as the volume numbers and page numbers where the cases can be found. A hypothetical citation might appear as follows:

Smith v. Jones, 358 U.S. 437, 112 S.Ct. 229 (1993)

Or a citation might appear as:

Smith v. Jones, 226 F.Supp. 1 (1992) or
Smith v. Jones, 442 P.2d 433 (1989)

These "cites" are important to anyone interested in legal research or learning about what the law says and how it should be interpreted or applied. They specify particular sources or *reporters* where these cases can be found. A reporter is a collection of books containing published opinions of different courts. In the cases discussed in this book, *most* are United States Supreme Court cases, while several are from state supreme courts. The first numbers in each citation above specify a *volume number*, the second number is a *page number* in the volume. In the hypothetical example above, *Smith v. Jones* is found in the 358th volume of the *United States Reports* on page 437. Also, the same case can be found in volume 112 of the *Supreme Court Reporter* on page 229. Below are several rules or guidelines governing citations and information about what is contained them.

U.S. Supreme Court

All Supreme Court opinions and decisions are printed in various sources. The official source for all Supreme Court opinions is the *United States Reports*, abbreviated as *U.S.*, and it is published by the United States Government Printing Office. The Supreme Court convenes annually for a *term*, such as the 1995 term or 1996 term, where cases are heard and decided. All Supreme Court actions are recorded in the *United States Reports*. There is a substantial time lag between the time the Supreme Court delivers its opinions and when cases are published in the *United States Reports*, however. This lag time may be up to a year. Other sources distribute these opinions in a more timely fashion to interested lawyers and researchers.

Parallel Citations and Unofficial Sources

Unofficial sources also print Supreme Court opinions in bound volumes on an annual basis. These include West Publishing Company's *Supreme Court Reporter* and the Lawyer's Cooperative *United States Supreme Court Reports, Lawyer's Edition*. The *Supreme Court Reporter* published by West is abbreviated as *S.Ct.*, while the *United States Supreme Court Reports, Lawyer's Edition* is abbreviated as *L.Ed*. Within days following a particular ruling by the United States Supreme Court, unofficial versions of the entire text of Supreme Court opinions are published by West Publishing Company and the Lawyer's Cooperative. For instance, West Publishing Company distributes *advance sheets*, booklets published every two or three weeks that contain recent Supreme Court actions, to its subscribers. During any given Supreme Court term, as many as 24 booklets or advance sheets will be sent to subscribers.

Another source is *United States Law Week*, which is published by the Bureau of National Affairs, Inc., and the *United States Supreme Court Bulletin*, published by Commerce Clearing House, Inc. The *United States Law Week* is abbreviated as *U.S.L.W.* Its major strength is that the most recent opinions are made available within days following decisions.

Whenever a Supreme Court opinion is cited, many scholars use *parallel citations* to indicate where any given case can be found. For instance, a case with typical parallel citations might be *Brewer v. Williams*, 430 U.S. 387, 97 S.Ct. 1232, 51 L.Ed.2d 424 (1977). According to the Harvard Law Review Association in Cambridge, Massachusetts, as well as Kunz, et al. *The Process of Legal Research* (1992), it is proper to rely exclusively upon the official reporter, which would be the *United States Reports* in Supreme Court cases. Thus, we would only need to cite *Brewer v. Williams*, 430 U.S. 387 (1977), and this cite would be sufficient to comply with legal protocol. However, because of the time lag between Supreme Court opinions and the publication of the *United States Reports*, it is proper to cite the next most recently available unofficial source. This would involve a citation from the *Supreme Court Reporter* published by West. Thus, if we didn't know the *United States Reports* cite yet, but we knew the *Supreme Court Reporter* cite, we could cite as follows: *Brewer v. Williams*, ___U.S.___, 97 S.Ct. 1232 (1977). The blank spaces indicate that we do not know yet what volume or page number *Brewer v. Williams* will be listed in the *United States Reports*. Later, when the *United States Reports* is published as the official version, we can supply the appropriate page numbers.

There are several hundred volumes of each of these reporters. Obviously, it would be very expensive for any college or university library to acquire each of these compendiums. Many libraries subscribe to the *United States Reports*, others receive the *Supreme Court Reporter*. Some might subscribe to the *United States Supreme Court Reports, Lawyer's Edition*. Large law school libraries have all of these volumes and more. However, many colleges and universities cannot afford to maintain all three versions, and since these are *parallel citations* and virtually identical opinions, it makes little sense for an average library to purchase three different compendiums of opinions which say the same thing. Scholars sometimes give three standard parallel citations whenever cases are cited. Thus, researchers can look up the same opinion in any one of these sources, depending on which version is maintained by their libraries.

Legal Citations in Introductory Criminal Justice and Criminology Textbooks

When students read introductory textbooks in criminology or criminal justice, it should not be considered unusual or confusing to see the *same* case in different books with *different* citations. For example, one criminology book may cite *Brewer v. Williams*, 97 S.Ct. 1232 (1977), while another will refer to *Brewer v. Williams*, 430 U.S. 387 (1977). Yet another book may use the Lawyer's Cooperative version and cite *Brewer v. Williams*, 51 L.Ed.2d 424 (1977). All of these citations are considered proper. When an author provides *all three* parallel citations, it may not be necessary, but it can be helpful to those with access to only particular sets of Supreme Court volumes.

The Meaning of 2d and 3d

When "2d" or "3d" follow a reporter, this does not indicate that a new edition of the source has been published. Rather, it means that the publishing company has "started over" with a fresh numbering system. For instance, the *Brewer v. Williams*, 51 L.Ed.2d (1977) denotes that the case can be found in volume 51 of the *United States Supreme Court Reports, Lawyer's Edition, Second Series*. There are no fixed rules governing when publishing companies commence new series for their volume renumbering.

Lower Federal Court and State Supreme Court Opinions

There are *no* official sources for reporting the opinions of lower *federal* courts, such as the different Circuit Courts of Appeal or United States District Courts. However, West Publishing Company publishes the *Federal Reporter*, abbreviated as *F*, or *F.2d*, to indicate where various opinions can be found for the United States Circuit Courts of Appeal. Not all of these opinions are published each year. The selection of opinions is at the discretion of the publisher, and often the decision to include or not to include particular Circuit Court of Appeals opinions is influenced by their constitutional relevance. Another source, also published by West, is the *Federal Supplement*, abbreviated as *F. Supp.* This source publishes selected opinions from United States District Courts, United States Customs Courts, and the United States Court of International Trade.

Separate state supreme court reporters are published. Several publishing companies, including West, publish these state supreme court opinions. The chart provided below shows which outlets publish which state supreme court opinions and the abbreviations used for such compilations.

The Inconsistency of U.S. Supreme Court Case Coverage

Is There Consistency to How the Supreme Court Reports Its Opinions? Yes, more or less. Each case contains a consistent citation format, a summary of what the Court decided, and names of justices concurring or dissenting. However, concerning the actual presentation of each case, there is as much variation as there are cases.

Does Each Supreme Court Case Have the Same Amount of Factual Detail? No. Most cases in this book have been summarized from original cases reported in the *Supreme Court Reporter*. Opinions written by the Supreme Court vary in length and complexity from one case to the next. Because all of these cases are appeals, summaries of original trial proceedings are not reproduced. Thus, there is considerable variation in the amount of detail provided. With many exceptions, reported cases contain a *syllabus*, or synopsis, of the facts leading to the appeal. Some cases have extensive and informative syllabi, while others offer scant information.

REPORTER	STATES INCLUDED
Atlantic Reporter (A or A.2d)	New Hampshire, New Jersey, Pennsylvania, Rhode Island, Vermont, and District of Columbia
North Eastern Reporter (N.E. or N.E. 2d)	Illinois, Indiana, Massachusetts, New York, and Ohio
North Western Reporter (N.W. or N.W.2d)	Iowa, Michigan, Minnesota, Nebraska, North Dakota, South Dakota, and Wisconsin
Pacific Reporter (P or P.2d)	Alaska, Arizona, California, Colorado, Hawaii, Idaho, Kansas, Montana, Nevada, New Mexico, Oklahoma, Oregon, Utah, Washington, and Wyoming
South Eastern Reporter (S.E. or S.E.2d)	Georgia, North Carolina, South Carolina, Virginia, and West Virginia
South Western Reporter (S.W. or S.W.2d)	Arkansas, Kentucky, Missouri, Tennessee, Texas, and Indian Territories
Southern Reporter (So. or So.2d)	Alabama, Florida, Louisiana, and Mississippi

Is the Criminal Justice Significance of a Case Outlined by the United States Supreme Court? No. The Supreme Court does not articulate the significance of each case for criminal justice. This chore is left for those who read and interpret these cases. Very often, the cases deal with a single question or issue.

Can Different Scholars Make Different Interpretations of the Same Case? Yes. It is entirely possible for two or more people reading a given case to have different opinions about the case and its significance. The decision rendered by the Supreme Court is only about the single question addressed. And the Court does not elaborate and say why a particular case is significant. The Court decides and interprets impartially and confines itself to the facts. The Court is supposedly devoid of emotion when rendering its opinions, although scholars cite ample instances of emotionally written opinions by various justices about different constitutional issues.

A good example of how different individuals interpret the same case differently is as follows. It is popularly assumed that in the case of *Furman v. Georgia* (1972), the Supreme Court declared the death penalty in Georgia to be "cruel and unusual" punishment and unconstitutional. This is not entirely true. Actually, the Court declared that the death penalty, as it was then being adminis-

tered in Georgia, constituted cruel and unusual punishment because it was applied in a racially discriminatory manner. Besides Georgia, all other states with death penalties suspended them until their legislatures could examine closely the procedures leading to death sentences. These investigations were geared to determine whether their particular death-penalty provisions were racially discriminatory. California commuted all death sentences at the time to life imprisonment. Charles Manson was one California inmate spared the death penalty, largely because of the *Furman* decision (see below). The fact is that no other state wanted to be criticized by the Supreme Court as Georgia had been. Quite simply, the Supreme Court found something wrong with the way the death penalty was being applied in Georgia. All other states with death penalties wished to comply with whatever the Court believed to be a constitutional application of the death penalty.

A solution to this problem was found in 1976, again in Georgia, when the Court decided the case of *Gregg v. Georgia*, wherein new procedures for death sentences were implemented. The Court declared that the new procedures enacted by the Georgia legislature did not violate constitutional rights. Specifically, the *Gregg* case established a two-stage trial proceeding in which guilt or innocence would be established in the first phase and the punishment would be decided in the second phase. In the second phase, specific aggravating and mitigating factors would be considered and weighed. If the number of aggravating circumstances were greater than the number of mitigating circumstances, then the jury would recommend the death penalty. If the mitigating circumstances were equal to or greater than the aggravating ones, then the jury would recommend life imprisonment. This new procedure was approved by the Supreme Court, in part because it removed race as a consideration in whether the death penalty should be imposed.

Therefore, the United States Supreme Court did *not* say in *Furman v. Georgia*, "the death penalty is hereby unconstitutional and abolished." Further, the Court did *not* say in *Gregg v. Georgia*, "The death penalty is hereby constitutional and can be used." The death penalty has *never* been abolished by the United States Supreme Court, despite the many different and conflicting interpretations scholars have attributed to the *Furman* decision. The question decided by the United States Supreme Court at the time was again a very narrow one: Is the application of the death penalty in Georgia constitutional? Yes or no? If yes, why? If no, why not?

Does the Supreme Court Reverse Itself Often in Deciding Cases? No. Only rarely does the Court rule an opinion rendered by an earlier Court as wrong. Usually the Court modifies, shapes, and focuses opinions by earlier Courts. One area undergoing continual modification and refinement is the Fourth Amendment provision against unreasonable searches and seizures. The Court is always considering different "search and seizure" scenarios that are considered "unreasonable" by appellants. All convicted offenders sentenced to death automatically become appellants, as all death penalties are appealed.

A good example of how the Supreme Court does not reverse itself, particularly on a sensitive issue, is the case of *Plessy v. Ferguson* (1896). In 1896, the Court decided that a black man's (Plessy's) rights were not violated in Louisiana when he was denied entry to a railroad dining car designated for whites only. The Court said then that as long as "separate but equal" facilities were provided for blacks as well as for whites (the railroad company provided all-black dining cars as well as all-white), then blacks could not claim that their Fourteenth Amendment rights were being violated under the "equal protection" clause.

Later, in 1954, the Court decided the case of *Brown v. Board of Education*, where the issue was that black children were denied admission to all-white schools in violation of their Fourteenth Amendment equal-protection clause rights because "separate but equal" educational facilities were provided for black children. In a landmark decision, the Court ruled that the "separate but equal" doctrine *does not apply to schools*. The Court did *not* say that the concept or doctrine of "separate but equal" was unconstitutional, just that it did not apply to schools. Later, the Court declared that the "separate but equal" doctrine did not apply to many other issues, such as public transportation, drinking fountains, and housing.

Interestingly, the "separate but equal" doctrine, inherently discriminatory, has *never* been reversed by the Court. No subsequent Court has proclaimed that the 1896 Court was wrong and that the "separate but equal" doctrine was unconstitutional. Rather, later Courts have stated that the "separate but equal" doctrine does not apply to this or that situation. Such is the narrowness of opinions delivered by the Court.

What About Cases Decided by State Supreme Courts? Some of the cases in this compilation are *state* supreme court cases. Whenever there is no United States Supreme Court case law to cite, the next best source is a state supreme court decision. While the decisions of state supreme courts are not binding on other states, these decisions provide other state jurisdictions with guidance whenever similar issues are addressed by appellants.

Abbreviations Used

The following abbreviations are used in the cases in this book:

Abbreviations:	Meaning:
BIA	Board of Immigration
DEA	Drug Enforcement Administration
DUI	Driving Under the Influence (of Alcohol or Drugs)
DWI	Driving While Intoxicated
FBI	Federal Bureau of Investigation
INS	Immigration and Naturalization Service
IRS	Internal Revenue Service
LEA	Law Enforcement Agency
NAACP	National Association for the Advancement of Colored People
RICO	Racketeer Influenced and Corrupt Organizations
SC	United States Supreme Court
USC	United States Code

Cases

A

Abel v. United States, 362 U.S. 217, 80 S.Ct. 683 (1960) **(Law Enforcement Officers or Agencies; Searches and Seizures).** Abel was a foreign spy living in a New York hotel and who was suspected of espionage. Reliable informants gave FBI and INS agents sufficient information to incriminate him. INS agents obtained an administrative deportation warrant seeking to deport him as an undocumented or unregistered alien. They went to Abel's hotel with their warrant, seeking first to obtain his cooperation regarding his espionage activities. FBI agents accompanied INS agents but without a search or arrest warrant. When INS agents entered Abel's apartment, they placed him under arrest and proceeded to search the premises. The search, with FBI agents acting only as "observers," yielded a false birth certificate and other forged identities used by Abel in his espionage activities. This evidence was subsequently turned over to the United States Attorney for investigation and prosecution. Abel was subsequently convicted. He appealed, alleging that the items seized should have been suppressed because the FBI had not obtained a valid search warrant. The SC upheld Abel's conviction, contending that the INS had every right to search his premises following reliable evidence of his culpability as an unregistered alien and spy. The INS justified the search based upon the administrative deportation warrant. As the evidence was obtained by INS agents during the lawful discharge of their responsibilities, it was not subject to suppression.

Adams v. Texas, 448 U.S. 38, 100 S.Ct. 2521 (1969) **(Death Penalty).** Adams was charged in Texas with killing a police officer. He maintained his innocence, but he was prosecuted and found guilty in a two-stage jury trial. The second phase of the trial led to the jury considering whether (1) Adams's act was deliberate, (2) his conduct in the future would cause a continuing threat to society, and (3) his conduct in the killing of the victim was unreasonable, given the victim's provocation, if any. If the jurors responded yes to all three questions, then the death penalty would be imposed. In this case, they did respond yes to all questions, and Adams was sentenced to death. He sought to have his conviction overturned because certain jurors had been excluded from his jury when they expressed opposition to the death penalty and their belief that their opposition might impair their judgment when deciding his case. The SC upheld

Adams's murder conviction. (Years later, exculpatory circumstances concerning Adams's involvement in the murder were discovered. In 1989, his conviction was overturned, and he was released from the Texas Department of Corrections).

Adams v. Williams, 407 U.S. 143, 92 S.Ct. 1921 (1972) **(Law Enforcement Officers or Agencies; Search and Seizure)**. An informant known to a police officer told the officer that Adams, who was seated in his car, was carrying narcotics and, further, had a gun in his waistband. The officer approached the car and asked Adams to roll down his window. After Adams complied, the officer saw the gun in plain view, where the informant had said it would be. He therefore made an arrest, which then led to a "search incident to an arrest," in which he discovered heroin and other weapons in Adams's possession. Adams was convicted. He appealed on the grounds that the officer had not seen him do anything wrong and so should not have arrested him. Police officers may not have sufficient *probable cause* to arrest a defendant but they must have *reasonable cause* to stop and frisk suspects for an officer's safety. Stop-and-frisk procedures need not be based on an officer's personal observation but on information supplied by another person. Because the officer was acting on information given by someone known to him, the SC upheld the conviction. The significance of the case is that officers do not always have to observe illegal conduct before making an arrest. Rather, informants who have been reliable in the past may justify an officer's investigation of suspicious suspects.

Adamson v. California, 332 U.S. 46, 67 S.Ct. 1672 (1947) **(Corrections; Death Penalty)**. Adamson was charged with murder in California. During his trial, he elected not to testify in his own defense, inasmuch as to do so would open the door for the prosecutor to question him about his past criminal record. Nevertheless, his refusal either to explain or deny the accusations against him was commented on by the judge and considered by the jury, who convicted him. He was sentenced to death. Adamson appealed to the SC, contending that this California court provision was unconstitutional under the Fourteenth Amendment. The SC upheld Adamson's death sentence and declared that the California provision was *not* unconstitutional.

Adickes v. S.H. Kress and Company, 398 U.S. 144, 90 S.Ct. 1598 **(Damages; Civil-Rights Actions)**. A white school teacher, Adickes accompanied several black people to a Kress store in Hattiesburg, Mississippi, to have lunch. Kress employees refused to serve Adickes because she was in the company of black people. She became belligerent, left the store, and was subsequently arrested for vagrancy by Hattiesburg police, who were alleged to be in a conspiracy with a Kress manager. The court found for Kress, denying a petition filed subsequently by Adickes wherein she alleged racial discrimination. Subsequently, however, the SC overturned the summary judgment and ordered a new trial for Adickes, in which she would have the opportunity to show that (1) a state-enforced custom of segregating the races in public eating places existed at the time of the incident, and (2) Kress was motivated to refuse her service as the result of that state-enforced custom. The SC declared that if such circumstances were found, then Kress would be in violation of Adickes's civil rights under Title 42, U.S.C., Section 1983.

Addington v. United States, 441 U.S. 418, 99 S.Ct. 1804 (1979) **(Evidentiary Standards)**. Addington's mother filed a petition in civil court for Addington's indefinite commitment to a mental institution. The state trial court determined that based upon *clear and convincing* evidence, Addington was mentally ill and should be indefinitely confined. Addington appealed, arguing that the *beyond-a-reasonable-doubt* standard should have been used to determine whether he was mentally ill and whether he should be indefinitely committed. The SC set aside Addington's commitment, holding that although the *beyond-a-reasonable-doubt* standard is not required in a civil proceeding, proof *stronger than preponderance of the evidence* is required. For this reason, the SC held that a standard stronger than preponderance of the evidence but less than "beyond a reasonable doubt" should govern whether juries may indefinitely commit individuals accused of being mentally ill.

Aguilar v. Texas, 378 U.S. 108, 84 S.Ct. 1509 (1964) **(Law Enforcement Officers or Agencies; Search and Seizure)**. On the basis of an informant's information, police in Texas obtained a search warrant to search the home of Aguilar for possible heroin, marijuana, and other narcotics. The police searched Aguilar's home, finding large quantities of narcotics. After Aguilar was convicted, he appealed, contending that there was no probable cause upon which a valid search warrant could be issued. The SC overturned Aguilar's conviction, saying that whenever information supplied by informants is used as the basis for search warrants, some information must be provided to the issuing magistrate that supports the credibility and reliability of the informant. That is, in what capacity do officers know the informant, and has the informant provided reliable information in the past? This, in short, is the *two-pronged test of informant reliability*. Thus the SC established that the standard for obtaining a search warrant by state officers is the same as applies under the Fourth and Fourteenth Amendments; a search warrant may be defective when it does not specify any factual basis for the magistrate to form a decision regarding issuance; officers need to outline the factual basis for the search. This test of informant reliability as the basis for a valid search warrant was effectively rejected in the case of *Illinois v. Gates* (1983), which opened the door to a totality-of-circumstances test where the identity of the informant was unknown to police.

Ake v. Oklahoma, 470 U.S. 68, 105 S.Ct. 1087 (1985) **(Death Penalty; Sentencing; Aggravating and Mitigating Factor Considerations)**. Ake was charged with two counts of first-degree murder. He declared that he was indigent, and counsel was appointed for him. He also requested the assistance of a competent psychiatrist to determine whether he was sane. Ake's defense was that he was insane, and thus it would be the state's obligation to furnish him with a psychiatrist to examine him and make a determination. A psychiatrist did so and found Ake to be incompetent to stand trial. He was confined in a mental hospital for a period of time. After six weeks of treatment, he was found to be competent to stand trial. His attorney asked for another psychiatric evaluation, independent of the state-provided one, but the judge denied this request, claiming that the expense was prohibitive. He was convicted. No testimony was given by psychiatrists during the sentencing phase of his trial. The death penalty was imposed when the state psychiatrist indicated that Ake's future dangerousness warranted it. Ake appealed. The SC reversed his conviction, holding that when a defendant has made a preliminary showing that his sanity at the time of the offense is likely to be a significant factor, then the state must provide access to a psychiatrist's assistance on this issue if the defendant cannot otherwise afford one.

Alabama v. Smith, 490 U.S. 794, 109 S.Ct. 2201 (1989) **(Plea Bargaining)**. A grand jury indicted Smith for burglary, rape, sodomy, and assault. He entered a guilty plea in exchange for a 30-year sentence and the dropping of the sodomy charge. He was convicted of first-degree burglary and rape. The judge sentenced Smith to concurrent terms of 30 years in prison on each of the other charges. Later, Smith was successful in having his guilty plea vacated and a trial was held on the three original charges. The jury found him guilty on all counts, and this time the judge sentenced him to life imprisonment for the burglary and sodomy convictions and to a 150-year term for the rape conviction. The judge explained the different sentence this time because he had not previously been fully aware of the circumstances under which these terrible crimes had occurred. Smith appealed, alleging the sentence was vindictive. The SC rejected Smith's claim that the new sentence was vindictive, since it could not be demonstrated that the judge deliberately enhanced these sentences because of the previous vacating of Smith's earlier guilty plea. The SC also stressed that in cases that go to trial, greater and more detailed information is available to sentencing judges compared with the information received as a part of a plea bargain agreement.

Alabama v. White, 496 U.S. 325, 110 S.Ct. 2412 (1990) **(Law Enforcement Officers or Agencies; Stop and Frisk)**. An anonymous tipster told police that a woman, White, would be leaving her apartment at a particular time with a brown briefcase containing cocaine and that she would get in a particular type of car and drive to a particular motel. Watching her apartment, police saw White emerge and enter the described vehicle. They followed her to the motel and stopped her car. They advised her that she was suspected of carrying cocaine. At their request, she permitted them to search her vehicle, where they discovered the described briefcase. They asked her to open it, where they found some marijuana, and arrested her. A search of her purse incident to her arrest disclosed a quantity of cocaine. She was charged and convicted of possessing illegal substances. She appealed, arguing that the police lacked *reasonable suspicion* to stop her initially and therefore the discovered drugs were inadmissible as evidence against her. The SC disagreed, holding that the anonymous tip and the totality of circumstances of subsequent police surveillance more than satisfied the less demanding standard of *reasonable suspicion* contrasted with the more demanding standard of *probable cause*. (*See especially Illinois v. Gates* [1983]) for a more extensive discussion of anonymous informants and the totality of circumstances justifying police stops and searches of suspicious persons and their effects.)

Alderman v. United States, 394 U.S. 165, 89 S.Ct. 961 (1969) **(Searches and Seizures)**. Government officials had obtained information through unauthorized wiretaps of offices where Alderman did business. Alderman himself was not a party to the conversations, in which others conspired to transmit murderous threats in interstate commerce, but because he owned the premises, he as well as the others was considered culpable. He sought to overturn his conviction, alleging that the information used against him had been obtained illegally, through unauthorized wiretaps without probable cause. The SC overturned Alderman's conviction, concluding that it had resulted from an illegal wiretap and surveillance. Furthermore, no evidence existed to show that Alderman actually participated in these illegally obtained conversations. Any surveillance records illegally obtained by the government, said the SC, should be turned over to the petitioners before being presented to a trial judge.

Alexander v. Louisiana, 405 U.S. 625, 92 S.Ct. 1221 (1972) **(Indictments)**. Alexander, a black man, was convicted of rape and sentenced to life imprisonment. He had been indicted by a grand jury consisting of men, mostly white, women having been excluded. The SC heard the case. Electing not to decide the key constitutional issue of whether the grand jury was discriminatory by excluding black jurors, and noting that Alexander's conviction was set aside on other grounds, the SC said that it was up to the state to decide whether Alexander should be retried, whether a *properly constituted grand jury* would return a new indictment, and whether Alexander might be convicted again.

Alexander v. United Sates, 507 U.S. ___, 113 S.Ct. 2766 (1993) **(Eighth Amendment; Fines; Asset Forfeiture)**. Alexander ran a store selling sexually explicit materials. He was charged with tax and obscenity offenses and violating the RICO statute governing racketeer influenced and cor-

rupt organization activities. Alexander ran a store selling sexually explicit materials. He was subsequently convicted and his assets were seized. He appealed, arguing that the seizure of his assets was unusually severe, in violation of the Eighth Amendment right against cruel and unusual punishments and "excessive fines." The SC reversed his conviction, saying that the appellate court should have considered whether the asset forfeiture in his case was "excessive." The significance of this case is that convicted offenders who have their assets seized can appeal the severity of their sentences under the "excessive fines" provision of the Eighth Amendment.

Allen v. Illinois, 478 U.S. 364, 106 S.Ct. 2988 (1986) **(Fifth Amendment, Self-Incrimination)**. Allen was charged with committing crimes of unlawful restraint and deviant sexual assault. The state filed a petition to have him declared a sexually dangerous person within the meaning of the Illinois Sexually Dangerous Persons Act, and the court ordered a compulsory psychiatric examination. When two examining psychiatrists testified later about Allen's sexual propensities, on the basis of information he disclosed to them, Allen sought to suppress this testimony, claiming it violated his Fifth Amendment right against self-incrimination. The court allowed the psychiatric testimony, and Allen himself did not testify. He was found to be "sexually dangerous" by the trial court and appealed on Fifth Amendment grounds. The SC heard his case and upheld the trial finding, holding that proceedings under the Illinois Sexually Dangerous Persons Act are not "criminal" within the meaning of the Fifth Amendment's guarantee against compulsory self-incrimination. Thus, the Fifth Amendment attaches only in criminal proceedings, not civil ones.

Allen v. Wright, 468 U.S. 737, 104 S.Ct. 3315 (1984) **(School Segregation)**. Allen and other parents of black children attending private schools under court order brought a class-action suit against those schools to remove racially discriminatory policies and procedures. They alleged that their children had not been receiving quality instruction from certain public schools because the IRS had failed to apply standards to, and remove tax-exempt status from, private institutions with discriminatory policies that indirectly hinder black children in public schools. In hearing this class-action suit, the SC held that the parents had *no standing* in suits against private schools filed on behalf of public schools.

Almeida-Sanchez v. U.S., 413 U.S. 266, 93 S.Ct. 2535 (1973) **(Law Enforcement Officers or Agencies; Vehicle Searches)**. Almeida-Sanchez, a Mexican citizen with a valid work permit, was driving 25 miles from the Mexican border. Border Patrol officers stopped his car without probable cause or consent, not even "reasonable suspicion," discovered marijuana, and charged him with possession of a controlled substance. He was subsequently convicted. When he appealed, the SC overturned his conviction, holding that the Border Patrol had not been conducting a "border search" because the highway he was traversing ran east–west, not north–south, and did not approach Mexico. Almeida-Sanchez's right against unreasonable searches and seizures had been violated when these officers, without warrant, probable cause, or even "reasonable suspicion," stopped his automobile for no reason and searched it extensively. The fact that marijuana was discovered did not justify this warrantless and groundless search.

Amos v. U.S., 255 U.S. 313, 41 S.Ct. 266 (1921) **(Law Enforcement Officers or Agencies; Consent Searches)**. Amos, a suspected bootlegger of illegal whiskey, was under surveillance by local authorities. One day these "deputy collectors of internal revenue" went to his home without an arrest or search warrant. Amos was not there, but his wife admitted them, after they advised her that they were there to "search for violations of the revenue law." They found some bottled whiskey, evidence that was used to bring Amos to trial. A jury was selected, but before the case actually started, Amos petitioned the court for the "return of illegally seized property," namely his whiskey. The court denied the motion and Amos was convicted. The SC heard Amos's appeal and reversed the conviction. The officers admitted that they had gone to Amos's home without an arrest or search warrant. The SC said that the officers were not entitled to continue with their search, despite the wife's permitting them to enter. The wife could not waive her husband's constitutional right against an unreasonable search and seizure, particularly since the search was conducted under "implied coercion."

Anderson v. State, 624 So.2d 362 (1993) **(Corrections; Probation Fees)**. Anderson, a probationer, failed to pay his monthly supervisory fees imposed by the court. He was employed and able to pay these fees. He simply elected *not* to pay them. In this case, because of his ability to pay, his probation was revoked by the judge. When Anderson appealed, a higher court declared that the judge was justified.

Andresen v. Maryland, 427 U.S. 463, 96 S.Ct. 2737 (1976) **(Law Enforcement Officers or Agencies; Searches Incident to Arrest)**. Andresen, a settlement attorney in Maryland who represented certain real estate interests, knowingly sold property to another individual where the title to the property was not clear because of two outstanding property liens. Investigating authorities asked for warrants to search Andresen's business premises, looking particularly for documents pertaining to "Lot 13T," the lot allegedly sold without clear title. Interviews with the purchaser and mortgage holder had been used as the basis for probable cause to obtain the search warrants. Andresen and his attorney were present at his office when the authorities conducted their search and seized the relevant documents. Andresen was tried and convicted of fraudulent misappropriation of funds. He appealed his conviction, alleging among other things that the search warrants were vague and that his presence constituted a form of self-incrimination, in violation of his Fifth Amendment rights. The SC upheld his conviction, holding the warrants to be proper. It ruled that statements voluntarily committed to writing by Andresen could be used against him. He was not compelled to say anything to officers while they conducted their search; thus his Fifth Amendment right was preserved.

Apodaca v. Oregon, 406 U.S. 404, 92 S.Ct. 1628 (1972) **(Jury Voting; Unanimity)**. Apodaca and others were found guilty of various serious crimes by less-than-unanimous jury verdicts. Oregon has a statute mandating a conviction or acquittal on the basis of a 10 to 2 vote, or what is referred to by the Oregon Legislature as a 10 of 12 vote. In Apodaca's case, the vote favoring conviction was 11 to 1. Apodaca challenged this vote as not being unanimous, and the SC heard the case contemporaneously with the case of *Johnson v. Louisiana* (1972) on an identical issue. In Apodaca's case, the SC upheld the constitutionality of the Oregon jury voting provision, declaring that votes of these kinds do not violate one's right to due process under either the Sixth or the Fourteenth Amendment. The significance of this case is that less-than-unanimous jury votes among the states are constitutional and do not violate one's right to due process.

Arave v. Creech, 507 U.S. 463, 113 S.Ct. 1534 (1993) **(Death Penalty; Habeas Corpus)**. Creech, confined in the Idaho Penitentiary, was convicted of the murder of another inmate. At his trial, the judge sentenced him to death, basing his decision, in part, on aggravating circumstances. He used the phrases "utter disregard" and "the cold-blooded pitiless slayer." Creech appealed the sentence, contending that the phrase "utter disregard" was invalid. The SC upheld Creech's conviction, holding that the phrase "utter disregard" did not violate any constitutional provisions.

Argersinger v. Hamlin, 407 U.S. 25, 92 S.Ct. 2006 (1972) **(Right to Counsel)**. Argersinger was an indigent charged with carrying a concealed weapon. In Florida, this crime is a misdemeanor punishable by imprisonment of up to six months and a $1,000 fine. Argersinger was not allowed to have court-appointed counsel, as required for a *felony,* because his crime was not a felony (*see Gideon v. Wainwright* [1963]). He was convicted of the misdemeanor and sentenced to 90 days in jail. He appealed, and the SC overturned his misdemeanor conviction. The SC said that any indigent defendant is entitled to counsel for *any* offense involving imprisonment, regardless of the shortness of the length of incarceration. Thus it extended the *Gideon* decision to include misdemeanor offenses, holding that no sentence involving the loss of liberty (incarceration) can be imposed where there has been a denial of counsel; defendants have a right to counsel when imprisonment might result.

Arizona v. Evans, ___U.S.___, 115 S.Ct. 1185 (1995) **(Law Enforcement Officers or Agencies; Exclusionary Rule; "Good Faith" Exception)**. Evans was arrested by Phoenix police during a routine traffic stop when it was discovered there was an outstanding arrest warrant against him. In the search incident to his arrest, police found marijuana in his trunk and charged him with marijuana possession. He was convicted. Later, it was determined that computer errors had implicated him wrongly by associating an outstanding arrest warrant for another person with a similar name. Thus, police officers had arrested the wrong man and had searched the wrong man's automobile trunk. Evans sought to have his conviction overturned, because, he said, his Fourth Amendment right against an unreasonable search

and seizure had been violated. After various appeals to the state court and an appeal to the Ninth Circuit Court of Appeals, Evans's conviction was overturned. The government appealed to the SC, which reinstated Evans's original conviction, saying simply that the "good faith" exception to the exclusionary rule was in effect, inasmuch as arresting officers had been acting appropriately and not engaging in misconduct. The police had had no knowledge of computer errors. The significance of this case is that even if an arrest is later found to be illegal or unsubstantiated by the facts, such as computer errors, if police, acting in "good faith," discover contraband or controlled substances incident to their arrest of the wrong person, the evidence they discover may be admissible against the suspect later in court. The primary function of the exclusionary rule is to guard against police misconduct. In this case, there was no police misconduct, only clerical error unattributable to police.

Arizona v. Fulminante, 499 U.S. 279, 111 S.Ct. 1246 (1991) **(Law Enforcement Officers or Agencies; Confessions)**. Fulminante was suspected of killing his daughter. Insufficient evidence existed to charge him, and he left the state of Arizona and traveled to New Jersey, where he was arrested and convicted for another crime. In prison, his cellmate, Sarivola, advised Fulminante that other inmates had heard that Fulminante was a "child murderer," and thus, his life was in jeopardy. Sarivola offered him protection in exchange for his confession to the murder of Fulminante's daughter. Fulminante confessed to Sarivola and later to Sarivola's wife. Later, he was charged in Arizona with the murder of his daughter, and the Sarivolas, who were also government informants, testified against him. Fulminante was convicted. He appealed on the ground that his confession had been coerced because Sarivola had implied a threat. The SC overturned his conviction on the basis of this argument. It ordered a new trial without the use of the confessions he had given to the Sarivolas. The SC stressed that the "harmless error" doctrine exists to govern involuntary confessions. However, the government had failed to show harmless error beyond a reasonable doubt. The trial judge had erred by permitting a coerced confession to be used against Fulminante. The judge's error would not have resulted in a reversal of a conviction, but it must be judged as harmless by using the "beyond a reasonable doubt" standard.

Arizona v. Hicks, 480 U.S. 321, 107 S.Ct. 1149 (1987) **(Law Enforcement Officers or Agencies; Searches; Searches Incident to Arrest; Plain View Rule; Open Field Searches).** One evening, persons in an apartment reported that someone from an above apartment had fired a bullet through their ceiling, injuring one of the lower apartment's occupants. Police investigated the upstairs apartment, rented by Hicks. While investigating, they discovered weapons and a stocking cap mask. Also, they noted that the apartment was run down but new stereo equipment stood in plain view. They wrote down serial numbers on the stereo equipment. In order to see the serial numbers, however, they had to move the equipment. Later, when compared with another crime report, these stereo items were found to have been stolen. A search warrant was obtained for Hicks's apartment. Hicks was arrested, charged with robbery, and convicted. He sought to suppress the evidence against him, alleging that his Fourth Amendment rights had been violated. The SC overturned Hicks's conviction, saying that in order for police officers to invoke the plain-view rule regarding the stereo equipment, they required probable cause to believe the equipment was stolen. Because the police used reasonable suspicion when moving the equipment, their act became a search requiring a proper warrant based upon probable cause. Reasonable suspicion does not, however, rise to the level of probable cause.

Arizona v. Mauro, 481 U.S. 520, 107 S.Ct. 1931 (1986) **(Confessions; Exceptions).** Mauro went into a store and said he had killed his son. When the police arrived, Mauro admitted the killing and led officers to his son's body. The police arrested Mauro and took him to the police station for questioning. They advised him of his Miranda rights twice, and he told them that he did not wish to answer further questions without an attorney present. His wife arrived and asked to speak with him. The police agreed, saying that they would tape-record the conversation with an officer present in the room. Despite a plea of temporary insanity, nullified by a number of statements in the conversation with his wife, Mauro was subsequently convicted of murder. He appealed, contending that his conversation with his wife should have been suppressed as evidence against him. The SC disagreed, saying that the conversation had not been an interrogation, despite the officer's presence and the taping of the conversation by po-

lice, because it had not been initiated by the police. Thus, the evidence was constitutionally proper and admissible. The significance of this case was that it further delineated what is or is not a custodial interrogation.

Arizona v. Roberson, 486 U.S. 675, 108 S.Ct. 2093 (1988) **(Law Enforcement Officers or Agencies; Confessions).** Roberson was arrested for a burglary and advised of his Miranda rights. He said he wanted to remain silent until he could speak with an attorney. A few days later, another officer approached Roberson in jail and asked to speak with him about another unrelated crime. The officer gave Roberson his Miranda warning before beginning that interrogation. Roberson made a full confession and was subsequently convicted. On appeal, he requested that his confession be suppressed. The prosecution countered by saying that he had confessed to another separate crime after being given his Miranda warning by another officer. However, the SC set aside Roberson's conviction, saying that police may not interrogate a suspect following his invocation of the right to silence and without his attorney present. The fact that the confession involved another crime did not matter. This second interrogation constituted a police-initiated custodial interrogation following an initial right invoked by the defendant to remain silent. The decision did not, however, bar defendants from initiating further conversation with police on their own, where their confessions and incriminating statements would be admissible in court.

Arizona v. Rumsey, 467 U.S. 203, 104 S.Ct. 2305 (1984) **(Death Penalty; Reconvictions and Resentencing Proceedings).** Rumsey, convicted of murder, was sentenced to life imprisonment by the judge. His case was overturned and set for retrial. A new trial also resulted in a conviction for murder. This time, the death penalty was imposed by the judge, who cited aggravating factors that outweighed mitigating ones. Rumsey appealed on the ground that the second penalty was stiffer than the first. The SC overturned the death-penalty sentence, saying that in capital cases in resentencing proceedings, the punishment cannot be greater than that imposed in the first sentencing. Thus, states cannot impose the death penalty on convicted murderers following prior trials where life imprisonment was imposed. The SC declared that the first judge's refusal to impose the death penalty operated as an acquittal of that punishment, not the offense itself. Thus, judges who impose life sentences in lieu of the death penalty cannot later impose the death penalty as a greater punishment. (*See Bullington v. Missouri* for a comparative case involving a *jury* decision about the same issue.)

Arizona v. Washington, 434 U.S. 497, 98 S.Ct. 824 (1978) **(Double Jeopardy).** Washington was convicted of murder, but an Arizona court granted him a new trial because the prosecution had withheld exculpatory evidence. At the beginning of the second trial, the defense counsel made various remarks about "hidden" information from the first trial. The prosecutor moved for a mistrial, which was granted. Washington was subsequently convicted in a third trial. Later, as a prison inmate, he filed a habeas corpus petition seeking to have his conviction overturned because the second judge's decision to declare a mistrial had been erroneous and had led to his being placed in double jeopardy by a third trial. The SC rejected Washington's arguments, holding that the mistrial had been proper. Thus, no previous trial had been concluded with an acquittal and so Washington was not being tried again for the same offense.

Arizona v. Youngblood, 488 U.S. 51, 109 S.Ct. 333 (1988) **(Evidence Preservation).** Youngblood was accused of child molestation, kidnapping, and sexual assault. Earlier, a 10-year-old boy had been sodomized by a middle-aged man, later identified as Youngblood (on the basis, in part, of semen samples collected from the child's anus). After a laboratory analysis, the semen samples had not been preserved by the police. Expert witnesses who testified on Youngblood's behalf at the trial said that he might have been exonerated if the samples had been preserved for more careful analysis. Youngblood was convicted. He appealed to have his conviction overturned, because, he argued, the police had showed bad faith in failing to preserve crucial evidence in his defense. The SC rejected Youngblood's appeal, holding that the failure of the police to preserve potentially useful evidence was not a denial of due process unless the defendant could actually show bad faith on the part of police. Youngblood's conviction stood, since he was unable to demonstrate this.

Arkansas v. Sanders, 442 U.S. 753, 99 S.Ct. 2586 (1979) **(Law Enforcement Officers or Agencies; Search and Seizure).** Sanders was stopped in a cab after leaving an airport. An in-

formant had provided a tip to police to watch out for a person carrying a green suitcase containing marijuana. A description of Sanders was also provided. When Sanders arrived at the airport, he was carrying a green suitcase. He entered a cab and the suitcase was placed in the trunk. When police stopped the cab, they opened the suitcase and discovered marijuana. This evidence was used to convict Sanders of marijuana possession. Sanders appealed his conviction, contending that police should have obtained a warrant before opening his luggage. The SC agreed, overturned Sanders conviction, and said that absent exigent circumstances, police are required to obtain a search warrant before searching luggage taken from an automobile properly stopped and searched for contraband. The SC said that one's luggage is a repository for one's personal effects, and thus some expectation of privacy exists. Therefore, a search warrant is required for such luggage searches. Thus, the significance of this case is that there were no compelling circumstances for police officers to act quickly. They had had time to obtain a warrant and had failed to do so. (*See also California v. Acevedo* [1991] where this doctrine has since been modified to include warrantless searches of large containers, including luggage).

Ashcraft v. Tennessee, 322 U.S. 143, 64 S.Ct. 921 (1944) **(Law Enforcement Officers or Agencies; Confessions).** Ashcraft and another man, Ware, allegedly conspired to kill Ashcraft's wife. They were arrested following her murder and interrogated at length. Specifically, officers interrogated Ashcraft first for about 8 hours, from 6:00 a.m. on the day of the murder until about 2:00 a.m. the next morning. Several days later on a Saturday, officers again took Ashcraft into custody and interrogated him in "relays" from Saturday evening at 7:00 p.m. until Monday morning at 9:30 a.m. During this period of intensive interrogation, Ashcraft was given no rest and only one five-minute respite. He confessed and was convicted. He appealed, alleging that his confession was coerced. The SC reversed Ashcraft's conviction, saying that his confession was not voluntary, but rather, compelled after 36 hours of interrogation. Thus, it was not admissible during his trial.

Ashe v. Swenson, 397 U.S. 436, 90 S.Ct. 1189 (1970) **(Double Jeopardy).** Several armed men broke into a room and robbed Roberts and five other men who were playing poker. Later, four men, including Ashe, were arrested and charged with robbery. Ashe was subsequently acquitted of the robbery because of weak identification evidence and contradictory testimony. Six weeks later, he was charged again with robbing Roberts. This time, Ashe was convicted, despite his contention that this was a clear case of double jeopardy. He appealed to the SC, which heard his case and agreed, reversing his conviction, holding that one cannot be tried for the same offense by using each and every victim of the robbery as a separate trial target. If that had been done, Ashe conceivably could have faced six separate trials for robbery involving each of the six poker players. After having been acquitted of the robbery charge involving at least one player, Ashe became effectively insulated from further prosecutions under the double-jeopardy clause of the Fifth Amendment.

Austin v. United States, 509 U.S. 602, 113 S.Ct. 2801 (1993) **(Asset Forfeiture)**. The Austin case decided by the SC declared that there are limits on governmental authority to use forfeiture laws against drug criminals, finding that seizure of their property must not be excessive when compared with the seriousness of the offense charged. Austin was convicted of cocaine possession with intent to distribute. The federal government seized his mobile home and body shop as a part of their "asset forfeiture" program, where one's assets used in the furtherance of the crime can be seized. Austin thought the seizure of his property and business was excessive in proportion to the amount of cocaine he had possessed. He also believed that the asset forfeiture violated his Eighth Amendment right against excessive fines. The government held that asset forfeiture in criminal cases should not be relevant for the "Excessive Fines" Clause of the Eighth Amendment; Austin argued that it *is* relevant. The SC reversed the judgment against Austin and sent the case back to the United States District Court to determine if the seizures of his home and business were excessive and cruel and unusual punishment.

B

Bailey v. United States, ___U.S.___, 116 S.Ct. 501 (1995) **(Law Enforcement Officers or Agencies; Search and Seizure; Sentence Enhancements)**. A police officer stopped Bailey's vehicle in the District of Columbia because it lacked an inspection sticker and a front license plate. When he failed to produce a valid driver's license, Bailey was ordered from the car. At that time the officer saw something in plain view between the two front seats. A bag was produced, yielding 30 grams of cocaine. Bailey was subsequently convicted of drug charges. His sentence was enhanced by a federal district court judge when it was determined that during the discovery of the cocaine the police had found a firearm in the vehicle trunk. An appeal to the SC resulted in the sentence enhancement being overturned. The SC noted that the federal provision allowing enhancing sentences for using firearms during the commission of a federal crime refers to an active employment of the firearm by the defendant. In this case, the firearm, though loaded, was in a bag inside the locked vehicle trunk. Thus, the prosecution would have had to prove that Bailey was actively using his firearm during his possession and transportation of cocaine. The prosecution failed to show that Bailey intended such active employment of the firearm. (*See Robinson v. United States* [1995] for a similar opinion).

Baker v. McCollan, 443 U.S. 137, 99 S.Ct. 2689 (1979) **(Corrections; Inmate Rights)**. McCollan was stopped in Dallas, Texas, for running a red light. A cursory check of records revealed that he was wanted in another county on separate charges. He was transported to the other county, where he was jailed for several days. Initially, he protested that this arrest and detention was a case of mistaken identity. Eventually, photographs of the wanted man and McCollan were compared and it was obvious that police had arrested the wrong person. They released McCollan and he sued for false imprisonment under a civil-rights statute. Initially, the court gave him a summary judgment against the county sheriff, and the government appealed. The SC heard the case and reversed the lower court. In sum, they ruled *against* McCollan, declaring that the Constitution does not guarantee that only the guilty will be arrested. McCollan had failed to state a claim upon which relief could be granted. As long as police were acting in good faith and provided the accused with due process rights, then the arrest and detention were lawful. As soon as they recognized their mistake, they had corrected it immediately.

Baldasar v. Illinois, 446 U.S. 222, 100 S.Ct. 1585 (1980) **(Sixth Amendment; Right to Counsel)**. Baldasar was convicted in a theft of property not exceeding $150 in value. Although this offense was a misdemeanor, it was Baldasar's second offense, and therefore, it became a felony. He was sentenced to one to three years in prison. He appealed, claiming that he had not been represented by counsel at the time of his first conviction. Therefore, the enhanced penalty from the second conviction was not constitutional. The SC agreed with Baldasar and overturned his conviction, holding that no indigent criminal defendant shall be sentenced to a term of imprisonment unless the state has afforded him the right to assistance of counsel. Baldasar had requested but had been denied counsel in the trial for his original misdemeanor, which became a crucial step in enhancing the penalty resulting from his second conviction.

Baldwin v. Alabama, 472 U.S. 372, 105 S.Ct. 2727 (1985) **(Death Penalty; Cruel and Unusual Punishment).** Baldwin and another man, both of whom had escaped from a North Carolina prison, came upon a 16-year-old girl who was having car difficulty. They forcibly took her with them in their car, attempted to rape her, committed sodomy, and attempted to choke her to death. Then they ran over her with their car, locked her body in the trunk, and drove on through Georgia and Alabama. Twice on their journey when they heard her cry out, they opened the trunk and stabbed her repeatedly with knives. They took the still-living girl from the trunk and ran over her again in a truck Baldwin had stolen. Finally, they cut her throat with a hatchet and she died after the 40-hour ordeal. Baldwin was convicted of robbery and murder. Alabama's 1975 statute concerning the death penalty (later repealed) required that penalty to be recommended if specified aggravating factors existed. Accordingly, the jury recommended the death penalty, and the judge, after considering the recommendation, imposed it. Baldwin appealed both verdict and penalty to the SC, contending that the "mandatory" nature of the sentence violated his constitutional rights, and that the judge's consideration of various background factors in his life was capricious and arbitrary as well. The SC rejected these arguments and affirmed Baldwin's death sentence, holding that judges may consider death-penalty recommendations from juries but are not obligated to follow them. These judges may weigh the mitigating and aggravating factors accordingly and decide on the best sentence. This procedure is constitutional.

Baldwin v. New York, 399 U.S. 66, 90 S.Ct. 1886 (1970) **(Jury Trials).** Baldwin was arrested and prosecuted for "jostling" (picking pockets), a Class A misdemeanor punishable by a maximum term of imprisonment of one year in New York. According to New York law at the time, this was a petty offense not entitling a defendant to a jury trial. Baldwin asked for and was denied a jury trial. He then appealed. The SC declared that petty offenses carrying a one-year prison term are serious in that jury trials are required if requested. Specifically, the months of imprisonment constituted serious time. The SC said that a potential sentence in excess of six-month imprisonment is sufficiently severe by itself to take an offense out of the category of "petty" as respects right to jury trial (at 1886, 1891). The SC overturned Baldwin's conviction and sent the case back to the lower court for a jury trial.

Ballew v. Georgia, 435 U.S. 223, 98 S.Ct. 1029 (1978) **(Jury Size).** Ballew was a theater manager in Atlanta. He showed a sexually explicit movie, *Behind the Green Door*, in his theater in violation of an Atlanta ordinance. The film was seized, but Ballew obtained another copy of the film and continued to exhibit it. He was arrested, charged, and convicted of violating a Georgia ordinance prohibiting distribution of obscene materials. He appealed, alleging his Sixth and Fourteenth Amendment rights were violated, since his conviction was by a five-member jury. The SC reversed Ballew's conviction, holding that a five-member jury deprived him of the right to a trial by jury guaranteed by the Sixth and Fourteenth Amendments. The significance of *Ballew* is that the SC effectively set the lower limit of a jury size at six. No upper limit of a jury size has ever been determined by the SC.

Barber v. Page, 390 U.S. 719, 88 S.Ct. 1318 (1968) **(Right to Confront Witnesses; Cross-Examination of Accusers).** Barber was convicted of a crime in Oklahoma in part from testimony given from a transcript taken from a preliminary hearing. A witness, Woods, was a prisoner in a federal prison in Texas. Oklahoma officials made no effort whatsoever to secure the witness to testify and used his transcripted testimony instead. Barber, represented by counsel, objected and appealed the conviction, contending that the right of cross-examination as set forth in the Sixth Amendment had been violated. The SC overturned the conviction, because the state had made no effort to secure Woods in court and had treated lightly Barber's right to cross-examine his accuser.

Barclay v. Florida, 463 U.S. 939, 103 S.Ct. 3418 (1983) **(Death Penalty).** Barclay and others had driven around Jacksonville, Florida, streets looking for white people to kill. It was their intention to start a race war. In the process, they killed a white hitchhiker. Barclay was convicted of murder by a jury trial. In a second phase of the jury deliberations, the jury advised the judge to give Barclay life imprisonment; however, the judge noted from the presentence investigation report various statutory aggravating factors, and he imposed the death penalty. Among the aggravating factors were an extensive prior criminal record, committing the murder during an act of kidnapping, and knowingly creating a risk of death to many persons. The Florida Supreme Court vacated the judgment of the lower court and the case was retried, in order to give Barclay the opportunity to rebut the aggravating factors cited by the sentencing judge. One of the aggravating factors cited, the prior record of Barclay, was not an aggravating factor, according to statute. The other factors, however, were. The second trial ended like the first. Barclay was convicted and sentenced to death. The SC heard the case and upheld the death sentence, saying that although the original judge had erred by listing a nonstatutory aggravating factor, the other factors were aggravating according to statute and thus, the death penalty was proper. There was no reversible error in citing nonstatutory aggravating factors, as long as there were one or more statutory aggravating factors not outweighed by any mitigating ones.

Barefoot v. Estelle, 463 U.S. 880, 103 S.Ct. 3383 (1983) **(Habeas Corpus Petitions).** Barefoot was convicted of murder following a jury trial. A two-stage proceeding was conducted, where the second stage of jury deliberations determined his punishment. A part of this phase involved psychiatrist testimony about Barefoot's potential for dangerousness in the future. The testimony concluded that Barefoot would pose a threat to others, so he was given the death penalty. He appealed, contending that such psychiatric testimony was unconstitutional. The SC disagreed, saying that the use of such testimony at sentencing hearings is constitutional. Thus, the testimony of psychiatrists about Barefoot's future dangerousness was not a violation of his due-process rights.

Barker v. Wingo, 407 U.S. 514, 92 S.Ct. 2182 (1972) **(Speedy Trials).** Barker and Manning were alleged to have shot an elderly couple in Kentucky in July 1958. They were arrested later and a grand jury indicted them in September 1958. Kentucky prosecutors sought 16 continuances to prolong Barker's trial. Manning was subjected to five different trials, each with a hung jury until the fifth trial, in which Manning was convicted. Then, Barker's trial was scheduled. During these five trials, Barker made no attempt to protest or to encourage a trial on his own behalf. After postponement for various reasons, his trial was finally held in October 1963, when he was convicted. He appealed, alleging a violation of his right to a speedy trial. The SC heard the case and declared that since from every apparent circumstance, Barker did not want a speedy trial, he was not entitled to one. The principle is that defendants must assert their desire to have a speedy trial in order to invoke the speedy-trial provision and to have Amendment rights be enforceable.

Barron v. Baltimore, 7 Pet. 243 (1833) **(Bill of Rights).** The owner of a wharf in Baltimore challenged a local action that seriously impaired the value of his wharf. He maintained that the government had taken his property without providing just compensation, in violation of the Fifth Amendment. At that time, state and local governments were exempt from the Bill of Rights, which pertained only to encroachments by the federal government, so he lost the case. Later, the Fourteenth Amendment (1868) changed this considerably and through the equal-protection clause and due-process provision extended the Bill of Rights and other amendments to all government levels.

Batson v. Kentucky, 476 U.S. 79, 106 S.Ct. 1712 (1986) **(Juries, Jury Selection, Use of Peremptory Challenges).** In Kentucky, a black man, Batson, was convicted by an all-white jury of second-degree burglary. The prosecutor had used all of his peremptory challenges to exclude the few black prospective jurors from the jury pool. Ordinarily, peremptory challenges may be used to strike particular jurors, without the prosecutor's having to provide a reason for doing so. In this case, the use of peremptory challenges was rather transparent, and Batson appealed. In a landmark case, the SC decided that peremptory challenges may not be used for a racially discriminatory purpose. Thus, creating an all-white jury by deliberately eliminating all prospective black candidates was discriminatory. The SC ruled in favor of Batson.

Baxstrom v. Herold, 383 U.S. 107, 86 S.Ct. 760 (1966) **(Corrections)**. Baxstrom was convicted of second-degree assault and sentenced to two and a half years in prison. Later, he was certified as insane and placed in a state institution for the mentally ill. When his original sentence was about to expire, the doctor in charge of the institution filed a petition seeking a civil commitment of Baxstrom for a prolonged period. Eventually, Baxstrom filed an appeal, which reached the SC. The SC ruled that Baxstrom had been denied equal protection of the laws under the Fourteenth Amendment. Thus, the case was remanded in order for a jury review to determine his mental condition and the prospects for a civil commitment.

Baxter v. Palmigiano, 425 U.S. 308, 96 S.Ct. 1551 (1976) **(Corrections; Inmate Rights)**. In a Rhode Island prison, a convicted murderer, Palmigiano, was serving a life sentence. During his confinement, he allegedly incited other prisoners to riot, and he was summoned before the Prison Disciplinary Board. He was advised that he might be prosecuted independently by the state for inciting other prisoners to riot, but for the time being, the board would hear and determine the factual nature of the charges against him. He was advised that his attorney could not be present during this hearing but that he himself could consult counsel-substitutes. Palmigiano was forbidden to cross-examine persons giving testimony against him. He was also advised that he could remain silent but that his silence could lead the board to regard him unfavorably. He remained silent, evidence was presented, and the board placed him in punitive segregation for 30 days. He filed a Title 42, U.S.C. Section 1983 civil-rights action, contending that the disciplinary hearing had violated his due process rights. The SC upheld the decision of the board, declaring that prison inmates do not have a right to court-appointed or private counsel in disciplinary hearings. Also, they cannot confront and cross-examine witnesses at all times. Although criminal defendants usually have the right to remain silent without incurring negative inference, in an inmate's case, silence is incriminating.

Bearden v. Georgia, 461 U.S. 660, 103 S.Ct. 2064 (1983) **(Corrections; Probation Revocation)**. Bearden's probation was revoked by Georgia authorities because he failed to pay a fine and make restitution to his victim as required by the court. He claimed he was indigent, but the court rejected his claim. The SC disagreed. It ruled that probation may not be revoked in the case of indigent probationers who have failed to pay their fines or make restitution. It further suggested alternatives for restitution and punishments that were more compatible with the abilities, and economic resources of indigent probationers; for example, community service. In short, the probationer should not be penalized where a reasonable effort has been made to pay court-ordered fines and restitution.

Beck v. Alabama, 447 U.S. 625, 100 S.Ct. 2382 (1980) **(Death Penalty; Reversible Error)**. Beck was charged with murder during the course of a robbery. When the judge issued instructions to the jury, he did not advise it that felony murder is a lesser included offense than the capital crime of robbery with intentional killing. Rather, he gave instructions that the jury must either convict Beck of first-degree murder or acquit him. The jury convicted him. Beck appealed to the SC, contending that the judge should have issued instructions to the jury on the lesser included charge, for which evidence existed. The SC reversed Beck's conviction, saying that the judge erred in failing to issue such a jury instruction. The death penalty may not be imposed constitutionally after a jury verdict of guilt in a capital trial where the jury was not permitted to consider a verdict of guilt of a lesser included offense.

Beck v. Ohio, 379 U.S. 89, 85 S.Ct. 223 (1964) **(Law Enforcement Officers or Agencies; Search and Seizure)**. Beck, having a prior record of criminal activity, was driving down a street in Cleveland, Ohio, when police officers stopped him without probable cause. They did not have a warrant, nor was Beck doing anything to arouse suspicions of criminal activity. They took him to the police station, where they searched him and his car. Some betting slips were found in his socks. He was charged with possessing "clearing house" (betting) slips in violation of state law and convicted. Beck appealed, contending that the clearing house slips had been illegally seized since no lawful search warrant had been obtained and the officers had had no probable cause to stop him initially. The SC agreed with Beck and overturned his conviction, saying that the officers had no probable cause to stop him, search him or his car, or detain him for any length of time at the police station. That something illegal was discovered as the result of this warrantless search lacking probable cause did not justify the search. Police must have probable cause before stopping anyone and conducting any sort of search of the person or the automobile.

Beckwith v. U.S., 425 U.S. 341, 96 S.Ct. 1612 (1976) **(Internal Revenue Service and Miranda Warnings; Exceptions).** Beckwith was interviewed in his home by visiting IRS agents. During this noncustodial questioning, he made various incriminating statements that were later used against him in a case involving criminal income tax evasion. Beckwith was convicted. He sought to suppress the statements he had made to IRS agents earlier, because, he alleged, they had failed to give him the Miranda warning. The SC disagreed and said that IRS interviews in field offices do not constitute custodial interrogations for purposes of administering the Miranda warning to taxpayers. Being interviewed in one's home and without mention of criminal charges does not constitute custodial interrogations for Miranda purposes. While Beckwith may have felt that the interview was coercive, it wasn't.

Beecham v. United States, ___U.S.___, 114 S.Ct. 1669 (1994) **(Citizenship: Civil Rights of Convicted Felons).** Beecham was a convicted felon who had a prior felony conviction in Tennessee and a federal conviction for interstate transportation of stolen property. Subsequently, Tennessee reinstated Beecham's civil rights for purposes of voting and other matters. However, he was apprehended by federal agents for being a convicted felon in possession of a firearm. He was convicted and he appealed, arguing that the fact that Tennessee had reinstated his civil rights entitled him to possess a firearm. The SC disagreed, saying that while the State of Tennessee had restored his civil rights, his loss of rights stemming from his federal conviction for interstate transportation of stolen property had not been restored; thus, Beecham was in violation of a federal statute. His restoration of rights in Tennessee had nothing to do with his federal felony conviction. The significance of this case is that states can restore a convicted offender's civil rights, but if they are convicted federal felons, they are still in violation of federal laws such as "being a convicted felon in possession of a firearm."

Bell v. Wolfish, 441 U.S. 520, 99 S.Ct. 1861 (1979) **(Corrections; Prisoner Rights).** This case involved the minimum-security Metropoli-

tan Correctional Center in New York City, a facility operated by the United States Bureau of Prisons and designed to accommodate 449 federal prisoners, including many pretrial detainees. It had been constructed in 1975 and was considered architecturally progressive and modern, generally a comfortable facility. Originally, the facility was designed to house inmates in individual cells. But soon, the capacity of the facility was exceeded by inmate overpopulation. Inmates were obliged to share their cells with other inmates. This double-bunking and other issues related to overcrowding eventually led to a class-action suit against the facility by several of the pretrial detainees and prisoners, including Bell. A lower court ruled in favor of the prisoners, holding that "compelling necessity" had not been demonstrated by prison officials in their handling of the overcrowding situation. But the SC overturned the lower court and said that the "intent" of prison officials should decide whether double-bunking was intended as "punishment" or a simple deprivation because of necessity. Since no "intent" to punish pretrial detainees could be demonstrated, there was no punishment. Hence, the Eighth Amendment was not violated.

Bennis v. Michigan, ___U.S.___, 116 S.Ct. 994 (1996) **(Asset Forfeiture; Innocent Owner Defense).** Tina Bennis jointly owned an automobile with her husband, John Bennis. John Bennis was observed by Detroit police officers engaging in a sexual act with a prostitute in his car on a Detroit city street in public view. He was arrested and convicted of gross indecency. The automobile was seized as a public nuisance under a Michigan statute. Tina Bennis sued for recovery of her jointly owned vehicle, claiming that she was an innocent owner of the car and didn't know that it would be used for illegal purposes. The SC heard the case and upheld Michigan's seizure of the vehicle as a public nuisance, defined as any object or place which was kept for the use of prostitutes. The SC referred to a long and unbroken line of cases (as precedent) that hold that an owner's interest in property may be forfeited by reason of the use to which the property is put, even though the owner did not know that it was to be put to such use.

Benton v. Maryland, 395 U.S. 784, 89 S.Ct. 2056 (1969) **(Self-Incrimination; Double Jeopardy).** Benton was tried and convicted of burglary in a Maryland state court. He was acquitted on a larceny charge. Because of grand and petit jury irregularities, he was given the option of being re-tried by jury on both counts, burglary and larceny. He sought to have his burglary conviction set aside. A subsequent jury found him guilty of *both* burglary and larceny, the same larceny count of which he had been acquitted in an earlier trial. He appealed, contending that his right against double jeopardy had been violated. The SC reversed his conviction for larceny, saying that this was a clear case of double jeopardy. The state cannot set aside acquittals resulting from void grand jury indictments.

Berger v. New York, 388 U.S. 41, 87 S.Ct. 1873 (1967) **(Law Enforcement Officers or Agencies; Electronic Surveillance).** Berger was a conspirator who was suspected of attempting to bribe a member of the New York State Liquor Authority. His telephone calls were monitored and recorded, according to a New York State statute authorizing such electronic eavesdropping. Placements of bugs or electronic wiretaps of telephones could be authorized by any police officer at the rank of sergeant or above. Nothing was specified in the order in the Berger case, only to record whatever was said. Berger was ultimately indicted and convicted. He appealed, contending that the wiretap was a violation of his Fourth Amendment rights. The SC overturned Berger's conviction because the New York statute was overly broad and contained little to safeguard the public against unreasonable searches and seizures. The SC declared that in order to be valid, a search warrant obtained for wiretapping purposes must be based upon probable cause, specific as to conversation to be recorded, and for a limited period during which a suspected crime is committed. In addition it must include a provision for reporting to the court what, if any, information was recorded, must name the person or persons to be wiretapped, and must end whenever the incriminating information has been recorded. In 1968, the Omnibus Crime Control and Safe Streets Act was passed by Congress, which spelled out these basic requirements for search warrants authorizing wiretaps or electronic surveillance of criminal suspects.

Berkemer v. McCarty, 468 U.S. 104, 104 S.Ct. 3138 (1984) **(Law Enforcement Officers or Agencies; Confessions; Custodial Interrogations).** McCarty was stopped on suspicion of DUI by the Ohio State Highway Patrol. He made several incriminating statements to police, including the facts that he had formerly consumed two beers

and smoked some marijuana. He was then placed under arrest and taken to the Highway Patrol station for further interrogation. At no time was he administered the Miranda warning. Police subsequently checked his blood-alcohol content (BAC) and found no alcohol. Nevertheless, McCarty pleaded "no contest" and was convicted of DUI. He appealed, arguing that his incriminating statements to police should have been suppressed as evidence against him. His conviction was overturned by a lower court and the SC affirmed the reversal, holding that while an ordinary traffic stop does not constitute a custodial interrogation for purposes of giving Miranda warnings to DUI suspects, subsequent interrogation when the suspect is in custody does require such a warning. In McCarty's case, this warning was never given; thus, his incriminating statements were inadmissible against him later in court. This Berkemer Rule, as it is known (named after Sheriff Harry J. Berkemer of Franklin County, Ohio) states that routine traffic stops do not constitute custodial interrogations for purposes of issuing Miranda warnings to persons suspected of driving while intoxicated or under the influence of drugs.

Betts v. Brady, 316 U.S. 455, 62 S.Ct. 1252 (1942) **(Death Penalty; Provision of Counsel to Indigent Clients).** Betts claimed that he was indigent and thus demanded a court-appointed attorney to defend him on a robbery charge. The court said that Betts could be appointed counsel only in rape or murder cases, and denied his request. He appealed. The SC ruled that felony cases in which life or death is not an issue, the states are not required to furnish counsel in every case; many states at this time, however, provide counsel because it is required by their own constitution or by court rulings in state courts. This decision was overturned as the result of the ruling in *Gideon v. Wainwright* (1963), where the SC concluded that in all felony cases, state or federal, indigent defendants are entitled to counsel.

Bivens v. Six Unknown Named Agents of Federal Bureau of Narcotics, 403 U.S. 383, 91 S.Ct. 1999 (1971) **(Search and Seizure; Damages to Other Parties).** Bivens and others were subjected to an illegal search by federal narcotics agents who broke into his apartment, arrested Bivens and others, and searched the apartment for narcotics, all without a warrant. Bivens was convicted, but the conviction was reversed because of the warrantless arrest and search. Bivens and others then filed suit against federal narcotics officers, seeking damages. Their original suit was dismissed because the trial court said that they "lacked standing" and had failed to state a cause of action. The SC overturned the decision of the lower court, saying that in a federal cause of action, damages are recoverable upon proof shown of injuries resulting from agents' violation of the Fourth Amendment. (*See Carlson v. Green* [1980] for a similar case).

Black v. Romano, 471 U.S. 606, 105 S.Ct. 2254 (1985) **(Corrections; Probation Revocation).** Romano, a probationer, had his probation revoked by the sentencing judge because of alleged program violations. The defendant had left the scene of an automobile accident, a felony in the jurisdiction where the alleged offense occurred. The judge gave reasons for the revocation but did not indicate that he had considered any option other than incarceration. The SC ruled that judges are not generally obligated to consider alternatives to incarceration before they revoke an offender's probation and place him in jail or prison. Probationers and parolees have obtained substantial rights since 1985. Supreme Court decisions have provided them with several important constitutional rights that invalidate the arbitrary and capricious revocation of their probation or parole programs by judges or parole boards. The two-stage hearing is extremely important to probationers and parolees, in that it permits ample airing of the allegations against the offender, cross-examinations by counsel, and testimony from individual offenders.

Blackburn v. Alabama, 361 U.S. 199, 80 S.Ct. 274 (1960) **(Confessions).** Blackburn, a mentally ill person, was charged with robbery in an Alabama court. He pled not guilty by reason of insanity. In fact, he had been absent from a mental ward in a hospital at the time the robbery was committed. Doctors and other experts confirmed that he was incompetent. Nevertheless, he confessed to the crime after an extensive interrogation, and on that basis he was convicted. Blackburn appealed, maintaining that he had been forced into making the confession. The SC heard the case, including evidence that the confession had been extorted after eight or nine hours of intense interrogation in a crowded sheriff's room. The SC overturned the conviction, saying the coercive conditions under which it had been obtained were unconstitutional and violated the due-process clause under the Fourteenth Amendment. Involuntary confessions to crimes are inadmissible as evidence against criminal suspects.

Blanton v. North Las Vegas, 489 U.S. 538, 109 S.Ct. 1289 (1989) **(Petty Offenses and Jury Trials).** Blanton was convicted in Nevada of operating a motor vehicle while under the influence of alcohol, a petty offense. He then demanded a jury trial. Defendants can obtain jury trials in petty-offense cases only when they can show that the additional penalties (e.g., community service, fines) viewed together with the maximum prison term are so severe that the legislature clearly determines that the offense is a "serious one." Blanton had been convicted under Nevada law, where the maximum prison term is six months. That he lost his driver's license for 90 days, that he was required to attend courses on alcohol abuse, and that he had to pay a fine of $1,000 and perform 48 hours of community service did not amount to severe punishment. The SC declared Blanton's offense to be petty and not deserving of a jury trial. (*See United States v. Nachtigal* [1993] for a comparative case).

Block v. Rutherford, 468 U.S. 576, 104 S.Ct. 3227 (1984) **(Corrections; Inmate Rights; Visitation).** Rutherford and other pretrial detainees at the Los Angeles County Jail protested that they were being denied contact visits with their spouses and that they were not permitted to observe shakedowns of their cells by jail correctional officers. A Title 42, U.S.C. Section 1983 action was filed against the county sheriff by Rutherford. The SC ruled that jail inmates have no constitutional right to contact visits with others and no constitutional right to observe correctional officers conducting cell shakedowns (searches for contraband). A primary consideration of the SC is whether a significant penological interest, such as security and safety of the institution, is served by such regulations. In this case, the SC said a significant penological interest existed for the Los Angeles County Jail to maintain such a policy.

Blockburger v. United States, 284 U.S. 299, 52 S.Ct. 180 (1932) **(Double Jeopardy).** Blockburger was charged with violating the Harrison Narcotic Act. Specifically, he allegedly sold morphine to particular persons over several days, and he was charged on each separate offense. He was convicted of each offense and appealed to the SC, arguing that his sales represented a single, continuous transaction, and therefore, only one offense should be punishable under the law rather than several offenses. The appeal sought to overturn the separate convictions for morphine sales under the double-jeopardy clause of the Fifth Amendment, which prohibits successive prosecutions for the same criminal act or transaction under two criminal statutes whenever each statute does not "require proof of a fact which the other does not." The SC upheld Blockburger's separate convictions, holding that separate sales of morphine to the same purchaser on successive days are separate offenses for purposes of punishment, and double jeopardy does not attach.

Bloom v. Illinois, 391 U.S. 194, 88 S.Ct. 1477 (1968) **(Sixth Amendment; Right to Counsel).** Bloom was held in contempt of court for allegedly filing a false will for probate. He was sentenced to imprisonment for 24 months. He requested a jury trial but was denied. Then he appealed to the SC, which reversed his conviction for contempt, holding that whether a jury trial is a constitutional right turns on the seriousness of the penalty actually imposed. A 24-month incarcerative term is indeed serious. It was clear that Bloom was entitled to a jury trial and it was constitutional error to deny him that right.

Blystone v. Pennsylvania, 494 U.S. 299, 110 S.Ct. 1078 (1990) **(Corrections; Death Penalty).** Blystone was convicted of first-degree murder, robbery, and criminal conspiracy to commit homicide. The sentencing jury was instructed to consider aggravating and mitigating circumstances and to impose the death penalty if aggravating circumstances outweighed the mitigating ones. The death penalty was imposed on Blystone, and he appealed, contending that the weighing procedure of aggravating and mitigating circumstances made the death penalty a mandatory penalty and thus unconstitutional. The SC rejected Blystone's argument, saying that the Pennsylvania statute of weighing the aggravating and mitigating circumstances was not unconstitutional.

Board of Pardons v. Allen, 482 U.S. 369, 107 S.Ct. 2415 (1987) **(Corrections; Probation and Parole).** Allen was a Montana state prison inmate who filed suit against the Board of Pardons for denying him due process by failing to apply statutorily mandated parole criteria and failing to explain in writing the reasons for his denial of parole. The parole law in Montana said that the parole board shall release on parole certain persons who qualify according to specified criteria. Allen believed

that he was parole-eligible and should be granted a parole, according to the phraseology of the Montana statute. Montana authorities disagreed. Allen appealed. The SC upheld Allen's right to have a substantial liberty interest in the statute as stated. Thus, Montana was obligated because of "shall" to apply the standards established for early release in Allen's case. At the very least, it became incumbent upon Montana to provide Allen with full due process to determine whether he should receive early release.

Booth v. Maryland, 482 U.S. 496, 107 S.Ct. 2529 (1987) **(Corrections; Death Penalty; Victim Impact Statements).** Booth was convicted of first-degree murder in a Baltimore court. During his sentencing, a victim-impact statement (VIS) was read so that his sentence might be intensified. Following the sentence of death, Booth appealed, alleging that the VIS was a violation of his Eighth Amendment right against cruel and unusual punishment. The SC agreed and said that during sentencing phases of capital murder trials, the introduction of VIS is unconstitutional. Among its reasons for this opinion, the SC said that a VIS creates an unacceptable risk that a jury may impose the death penalty in an arbitrary and capricious manner. Thus, VIS information may be totally unrelated to the blameworthiness of the offender.

Bordenkircher v. Hayes, 434 U.S. 357, 98 S.Ct. 663 (1978) **(Courts and Prosecution; Plea Bargaining).** Hayes was indicted for check forgery in Fayette County, Kentucky. The punishment for such an offense was from 2 to 10 years, while a Habitual Offender Statute carried a mandatory life imprisonment sentence upon conviction. Hayes also had several prior felony convictions; thus he qualified as an habitual offender and could be prosecuted under that statute. The prosecutor told Hayes that if he pled guilty to the forgery charge, the prosecutor would not charge him with violating the Habitual Offender Statute. Hayes decided to plead not guilty and was convicted of the forgery charge. Then, however, the prosecutor brought habitual-offender charges against Hayes, who was ultimately convicted and sentenced to life imprisonment. He appealed, alleging that he had been coerced to plead guilty by the threat of prosecution as an habitual offender. The SC disagreed with Hayes, saying that it is not a violation of due process for a prosecutor to threaten defendants with other criminal prosecutions so long as the prosecutor has probable cause to believe that the accused has committed an offense defined by statute. The significance of the case is that prosecutors may use additional charges as threats in plea bargaining with criminal defendants, as long as there is a basis for these charges. It would be improper and unconstitutional if a prosecutor threatened to bring charges for which there was no probable cause.

Bounds v. Smith, 430 U.S. 817, 97 S.Ct. 1491 (1977) **(Corrections; Inmate Rights).** Prison inmates have the right of access to adequate law libraries or to the assistance of those trained in the law. In a landmark case in North Carolina in 1977, Bounds and other prisoners alleged that prison officials were denying them reasonable access to the courts and equal protection by failing to provide them with adequate legal library facilities. The state then proposed to create seven libraries for offenders to be available to 13,000 prisoners housed in 77 prison units in 67 counties. The SC said this plan was not proper because it did not create a library for each prison, but the SC offered prison systems alternatives or forms of legal assistance besides law libraries. They can provide paralegals, train inmates to become paralegals working under a lawyer's supervision, hire attorneys on a part-time basis, or actually hire full-time attorneys for inmates on site. The case is significant because it declared these other avenues of access to the law acceptable.

Bourjaily v. United States, 483 U.S. 171, 107 S.Ct. 2775 (1987) **(Sixth Amendment; Confrontation of Witnesses).** Bourjaily was charged in United States district court of conspiring to distribute and of possession of cocaine. Various friends of Bourjaily were implicated, and he had become a suspect through evidence obtained in tape-recorded telephone conversations between him and undercover FBI agents. An FBI informant, Lonardo, also implicated Bourjaily. At his trial, Bourjaily protested that the government had accepted Lonardo's statements as proof of a conspiracy to distribute cocaine. Further, he argued that Lonardo's statements supported the conspiracy only according to a preponderance of the evidence standard. Finally, Lonardo himself had not testified, but his statements had been read into the record against Bourjaily. Bourjaily was convicted. He appealed, alleging that his Sixth Amendment rights had been violated because he had been unable to cross-examine Lonardo. He also alleged that Lonardo's statements amounted to hearsay

and were thus excludable as evidence against him. The SC decided otherwise and upheld his conviction. The SC declared that evidence of a coconspirator, Lonardo, is not hearsay if such evidence is obtained during the course and in the furtherance of a conspiracy. Thus Lonardo's out-of-court statements were admissible against Bourjaily. Further, out-of-court statements may be proven by the offering party (the prosecution) only on the basis of the preponderance of the evidence.

Boyd v. United States, 116 U.S. 616, 6 S.Ct. 524 (1886) **(Law Enforcement Officers or Agencies; Self-Incrimination).** Fraudulently imported goods were seized by customs inspectors, and Boyd, one of the owners of the goods, requested to have his goods returned. The court required him to produce evidence, specifically invoices for previous shipments, in order to determine the value of the seized property in question. Boyd objected to having to produce such documents, because, he alleged, some of the documents might be incriminating. Nevertheless, he produced the documents under protest, and the court ruled against him. He appealed. The SC overturned the lower court decision, saying that the notice to produce the invoices in this case, the order by virtue of which it was issued, and the law which authorized the order, were unconstitutional and void. The owner of property may be cited as a witness in a proceeding to forfeit his property. A witness, as well as a party, is protected by law from being compelled to give evidence that tends to incriminate him. Thus, persons who are subject to property forfeiture should be entitled to all privileges given to someone charged with committing a criminal offense.

Boyde v. California, 494 U.S. 370, 110 S.Ct. 1190 (1990) **(Eighth Amendment; Aggravating and Mitigating Circumstances).** Boyde was charged with robbery, kidnapping for robbery, and first-degree murder; convicted; and sentenced to death. During the sentencing phase of the trial, the jury was given instructions by the judge including the phrase, "shall consider, take into account and be guided by" in determining whether the death penalty ought to be imposed. Boyde appealed, challenging this phrase as mandatory phraseology and thus illegal in death-penalty cases, because mandatory death penalties are illegal (in that aggravating and mitigating circumstances cannot be weighed by the jury). Boyde also claimed that such instructions were "ambiguous and erroneous." The SC upheld Boyde's conviction and death sentence, holding that the judicial instruction did not violate the Eighth Amendment claim made by Boyde that the mandatory nature of the phraseology prevented the jury from making an individualized assessment of the death penalty's appropriateness. States are free to structure and shape consideration of mitigating evidence to achieve a more rational and equitable administration of the death penalty.

Boykin v. Alabama, 395 U.S. 238, 89 S.Ct. 1709 (1969) **(Death Penalty).** Boykin was arrested for common-law robbery. At his trial, which had no jury, he entered a guilty plea. He was convicted and sentenced to death. He appealed. The SC overturned Boykin's conviction, largely because there was no evidence to show whether his guilty plea was voluntary or made knowingly. As the SC declared, it was reversible error for the trial judge to accept the petitioner's guilty plea without an affirmative statement showing that it was intelligent and voluntary. Thus, the significance of this case is that when guilty pleas are entered by criminal defendants, judges must determine from them whether their pleas are knowingly entered and completely voluntary; that is, that they are effectively waiving various rights to confront their accusers and cross-examine them and to give testimony in their own behalf.

Bowers v. Hardwick, 478 U.S. 186, 106 S.Ct. 2841 (1986) **(Laws Prohibiting Sodomy).** There is no fundamental right to commit sodomy among homosexuals. State laws prohibiting such behavior are constitutional if they otherwise meet constitutional standards.

Brady v. Maryland, 373 U.S. 83, 83 S.Ct. 1194 (1963) **(Discovery).** Brady was charged with murder. He took the stand in his own defense and admitted to participating in the crime, but he declared that his confederate, Boblit, was the one who actually killed the victim. Various statements had been made to police and prosecution by Boblit. The prosecutor denied Brady access to these statements, alleging confidentiality. Following Brady's conviction, some of this evidence came to light and proved favorable and exculpatory to Brady. He sought an appeal, claiming that he had been denied due process because these important statements had been withheld during his trial. The SC agreed with Brady and overturned his murder conviction, saying that "suppression by prosecution of evidence favorable to an ac-

cused upon request violates due process where evidence is material either to guilt or to punishment, irrespective of good faith or bad faith of prosecution."

Brady v. United States, 397 U.S. 742, 90 S.Ct. 1463 (1970) **(Plea Bargaining).** Brady and a codefendant were charged with kidnapping. The offense carried a maximum penalty of death. Brady initially entered a not-guilty plea, but his codefendant pleaded guilty under a plea-bargain arrangement. When Brady learned that his companion had confessed and agreed to testify against him, Brady changed his plea to guilty, in exchange for a lengthy prison sentence. He knew that if the case proceeded through trial, the jury could impose the death penalty. After he received a 50-year sentence, it was commuted to 30 years. Brady appealed, claiming that his plea of guilty had been involuntarily given, that he had done so only to avoid the possible imposition of the death penalty. The SC upheld Brady's conviction and sentence, saying that the guilty plea had not been coerced. The SC stated that a plea of guilty is not invalid merely because it is entered to avoid the possibility of a death penalty. Thus, although Brady's plea of guilty may well have been motivated in part by a desire to avoid a possible death penalty, the court was convinced that his plea was voluntary and intelligently made and it had no reason to doubt that his solemn admission of guilt was truthful.

Branzburg v. Hayes, 408 U.S. 665, 92 S.Ct. 2646 (1972) **(Media Rights in Grand Jury Proceedings).** Newspaper persons have no constitutional right to maintain the confidentiality of their news sources when subpoenaed before grand juries and are compelled to give testimony. They must disclose the identity of their sources if questioned about them.

Braxton v. United States, 500 U.S. 344, 111 S.Ct. 1854 (1991) **(Guilty Pleas; U.S. Sentencing Guidelines; Acceptance of Responsibility Statements).** Braxton entered guilty pleas to charges of assaulting federal officers but pled not guilty to the more serious charge of intent to kill a United States marshal. The government accepted these pleas, but when applying the United States Sentencing Guidelines, it applied an enhancement more applicable to the charge to which Braxton had pled not guilty. Thus Braxton was sentenced as though he had actually committed the crime of "intentionally attempting to kill a United States marshal." The government argued that Braxton had "stipulated" to the essence of the charge, that he had deliberately fired a shotgun through his front door when United States marshals came to arrest him. Braxton appealed the more severe sentence. The SC heard the appeal and vacated the sentence, holding that there was nothing in Braxton's stipulation that he ever intended to kill a United States marshal. Because this was a necessary element of an "intent to kill a United States marshall" charge, the sentence had to be vacated and the case remanded for resentencing.

Brecht v. Abrahamson, 507 U.S. 619, 113 S.Ct. 1710 (1993) **(Prosecutorial Misconduct).** At a murder trial in a Wisconsin court, Brecht admitted shooting the victim but claimed it was accidental. State prosecutors in their jury arguments cited Brecht's pre-Miranda statements that he failed to tell anyone of the accidental nature of the shooting. More important, a prosecutor commented on his silence following the Miranda warning. The jury convicted Brecht and he appealed, arguing that the errors committed by the prosecutor were prejudicial. The SC upheld Brecht's conviction, holding that the prosecution statements did not have a substantial or injurious effect or influence in determining the jury's verdict.

Breed v. Jones, 421 U.S. 519, 95 S.Ct. 1779 (1975) **(Juvenile Law; Double Jeopardy).** On February 8, 1971, in Los Angeles, Jones, 17 years old and armed with a deadly weapon, allegedly committed robbery. He was apprehended and an adjudicatory hearing in juvenile court was held on March 1. Jones was declared delinquent for robbery. The judge transferred him to criminal court to stand trial on these same charges. Jones was subsequently convicted of robbery. He appealed the decision and the SC reversed the conviction, concluding that the robbery adjudication in juvenile court was considered the equivalent of a criminal trial on the same charges. The juvenile court judge should either have placed Jones in secure confinement following his adjudication or simply have waived jurisdiction over Jones initially to criminal court. To find a juvenile delinquent in juvenile court and then waive him to criminal court on the same charges was unconstitutional because it put him in double jeopardy.

Brewer v. Williams, 430 U.S. 387, 97 S.Ct. 1232 (1977) **(Law Enforcement Officers or Agencies; Custodial Interrogations; Confessions).** Williams was a suspect in the disappearance of a ten-year-old girl from a YMCA building on Christmas Eve, in Des Moines, Iowa. He was seen leaving the building with something wrapped in a blanket, with skinny legs sticking out. Williams's car was spotted later about 150 miles from Des Moines, and he was apprehended in Davenport. Des Moines police went to Davenport to bring Williams back to Des Moines, and during their return trip they asked him various questions. As it was beginning to snow heavily, they speculated out loud that a small girl's body would be difficult to find out in the snow and that the girl should at least have a proper "Christian burial." Williams broke down, admitted to the crime of murder, and led police to the girl's body. He was subsequently convicted of murder, but he appealed and his conviction was overturned because police had interrogated him without an attorney present during their trip back to Des Moines. A subsequent retrial resulted in Williams's conviction on other grounds, as there was additional incriminating evidence in his automobile. But the Christian burial case, as it is known, clearly illustrates that police officers may not conduct interrogations of suspects without first advising them of their right to counsel. (*See the follow-up case of Nix v. Williams* [1984]).

Brinegar v. United States, 338 U.S. 160, 69 S.Ct.1302 (1949) **(Law Enforcement Officers or Agencies; Search and Seizure).** Brinegar was known by police to be a bootlegger of illegal liquor and to transport it frequently across state lines. Federal revenue agents observed him driving his car in Oklahoma, five miles west of the Missouri line. They noticed that it was weighed down in the back and was speeding. After a short chase, they forced Brinegar off of the road and observed in plain view a case of liquor in his car. Twelve more cases of untaxed liquor were found under the car seats. Brinegar was convicted of transporting illegal liquor across state lines. He appealed, arguing that the officers had lacked probable cause to stop him and search his vehicle. The SC disagreed and adopted a totality-of-circumstances type of test in this situation. The officers who surveilled Brinegar's car knew who he was and what he did from past observation and experience. They knew various contact points where illegal liquor was obtained. Given all the events they observed, combined with reasonably trustworthy information, the SC believed that the officers had had probable cause to intercept Brinegar and search his vehicle.

His conviction was thus upheld. (*See Carroll v. United States* [1925] for a comparative case).

Briscoe v. Lahue, 460 U.S. 325, 103 S.Ct. 1108 (1983) **(Legal Liabilities of Police Officers).** Briscoe was convicted of burglary. He later sued a police officer who had given perjured testimony against him, according to Title 42, U.S.C. Section 1983, a civil-rights section. The SC held that police officers enjoy *absolute immunity* from civil prosecutions when they have given testimony, even perjured testimony, against criminal defendants. Officers who allegedly commit perjury are not immune from possible criminal penalties against them if their testimony is determined to be perjured.

Brooks v. Tennessee, 406 U.S. 605, 92 S.Ct. 1891 (1972) **(Defendant Testimony at Trial; Order of Defense Case Presentation).** Brooks was charged with armed robbery and unlawful possession of a pistol. At his trial, he desired to give testimony. Tennessee law mandated that if a defendant in a criminal case wishes to give testimony, he must do so before any other defense witnesses are called. After Brooks was convicted, he appealed, alleging that this protocol had violated his due process rights as well as his right against self-incrimination under the Fifth Amendment. The SC heard his appeal and reversed his conviction, saying that the Tennessee statute is unconstitutional. Criminal defendants may or may not wish to testify after hearing other defense witnesses testify. It is the privilege of defendants to decide whether to testify in their own behalf. Thus, compelling a defendant who wishes to testify to speak first violates his right against self-incrimination. The significance of this case is that defendants in criminal cases may testify at any stage of the defense case or not testify at all, if they so choose.

Brower v. County of Inyo, 489 U.S. 593, 109 S.Ct. 1378 (1991) **(Law Enforcement Officers or Agencies; Seizures).** Brower was a suspect who had stolen a car, leading police on a 20-mile chase down a major highway. In an effort to stop him, police caused an 18-wheel tractor-trailer rig to be placed across the highway ahead of him. Police headlights were turned toward Brower, thus preventing him from seeing the truck across the road. He crashed into the truck and was killed. His family filed a Title 42, U.S.C. Section 1983 civil rights action against police, alleging that Brower had been the subject of an unreasonable seizure. Liability was not decided by this case, but the SC declared that the roadblock established by police in this case was unreasonable and thus constituted an unreasonable seizure, violating Brower's Fourth Amendment rights. The police measures clearly exceeded the reasonableness necessary to stop a fleeing thief. It was a property crime, the punishment for which would probably have been a short prison term, certainly not the death penalty. Because the officers knew or should have known that the roadblock and blinding headlights would probably cause Brower's death, they were clearly using excessive force, which was unconstitutional.

Brown v. Board of Education, 347 U.S. 483, 74 S.Ct. 686 (1954) **(Separate but Equal Educational Facilities; Racial Discrimination; Consent Decrees).** In 1954, Brown brought a class-action suit challenging the separate-but-equal doctrine as it pertained to elementary schools. At the time, especially in the South, separate educational facilities were provided black children that were allegedly the same quality as the schools provided while children. White and black children could not, however, attend the same schools. The SC heard the case and decided that as far as education is concerned, the separate-but-equal doctrine does not apply. Thus, the original *Plessy v. Ferguson* (1896) decision on this matter was partially set aside. It is unconstitutional to have separate but equal schools for blacks and whites.

Brown v. Illinois, 422 U.S. 590, 95 S.Ct. 2254 (1975) **(Law Enforcement Officers or Agencies; Arrests).** Brown was arrested in Illinois without probable cause or a warrant and taken to a police station, where he was told his Miranda rights. While at the police station, he gave at least two incriminating statements, linking him with a murder. At his trial, he sought to suppress these statements. However, they were ruled admissible and Brown was convicted. He appealed, and the SC overturned his conviction, concluding that because his arrest was warrantless and lacking probable cause, the Miranda warning and Brown's statements were inadmissible. It cited the fruits-of-the-poisonous-tree doctrine, which says that if the arrest was illegal, its illegality taints the "fruits" of the arrest, or confessions given later.

Brown v. Mississippi, 287 U.S. 278, 56 S.Ct. 461 (1936) **(Law Enforcement Officers or Agencies; Confessions).** Brown was a suspect in a murder. He was visited at his home by a deputy sheriff and brought to the murder scene. He denied committing the murder. The deputy and others hanged him from a tree, let him down, and then hanged him again. Later they tied him to a tree and beat him. A few days later the deputy came to his home again and arrested him. Brown was taken to jail, where he was beaten repeatedly and told that the beatings would continue until he confessed. He confessed to the murder and was subsequently convicted and sentenced to death. He filed an appeal on the grounds that he had been denied due process. The SC agreed. It argued further that the brutality of police officers had rendered his confession and other statements inadmissible in court against him. Coerced confessions to crimes are unconstitutional. His conviction was overturned.

Brown v. Texas, 443 U.S. 47, 99 S.Ct. 2637 (1979) **(Law Enforcement Officers or Agencies; Arrests).** Brown was stopped by two Texas police officers, who asked him to identify himself and explain his presence to them. The officers had no suspicion that Brown was involved in anything illegal. He refused their request and was charged with refusing to cooperate with police and was convicted. He appealed. The SC overturned his conviction, because persons may not be punished for refusing to identify themselves if police have no suspicion of their being involved in any type of criminal or suspicious activity.

Bruton v. United States, 391 U.S. 123, 88 S.Ct. 1620 (1968) **(Sixth Amendment Right to Cross-Examine One's Accusers).** Bruton and Evans were charged with armed postal robbery. The accomplice, Evans, gave police a confession implicating Bruton. Evans was not called to testify, although his confession was admitted against Bruton. Thus, Bruton's attorney could not cross-examine Evans. The trial judge instructed the jury that Evans's confession was significant evidence against Evans but should not be considered evidence against Bruton. Bruton was convicted. He appealed, and the SC overturned the conviction, saying that the jury instructions by the trial judge to disregard that part of Evans's confession implicating Bruton were insufficient to cure the error of not permitting Evans to be cross-examined. The significance of this case is that a defendant is entitled to cross-examine his accuser, even if it is an accomplice who confesses and implicates the defendant. It is insufficient for a judge to permit a confession into evidence where a party other than the confessor is implicated, without giving the other party an opportunity to confront his accuser in court. Bruton's Sixth Amendment right to cross-examine witnesses against him had clearly been violated in this case. (*See Harrington v. California* [1969] for a similar case with a different holding under different circumstances).

Buchanan v. Kentucky, 483 U.S. 402, 107 S.Ct. 2906 (1987) **(Fifth and Sixth Amendments; Self-Incrimination).** Police discovered the body of Barbel Poore in an automobile; she had been shot twice in the head and sexually assaulted. (*See Stanford v. Kentucky* [1989] for a discussion of the crime's details). Three persons were subsequently arrested, including Buchanan, a juvenile. Confessions from the other participants implicated Buchanan as the criminal events were reconstructed. He and an accomplice, Stanford, were transferred to criminal court for trial on the murder charges. The two were tried jointly. A "death-qualified" jury was selected. Objections from defense counsel were overruled. During the trial, Buchanan raised a mental-status defense, and the state used the results of a psychiatric report about him to rebut this defense. Both suspects were convicted. Buchanan appealed, alleging that his Fifth and Sixth Amendment rights had been violated, first because the jury was "death-qualified" and thus did not represent a fair cross-section of the community, and second because the report from the state psychiatrist was based upon an evaluation of Buchanan where his attorney was not present. The SC rejected both of Buchanan's claims. It said that the use of a death-qualified jury for a joint trial in which the death penalty was sought only against Stanford, the codefendant, did not violate Buchanan's Sixth Amendment right to an impartial jury. Further, the state's use of a psychiatric report about Buchanan solely to rebut Buchanan's mental-status defense did not violate Buchanan's Fifth or Sixth Amendment rights.

Buck v. Bell, 274 U.S. 200, 47 S.Ct. 584 (1927) **(Sterilization of Mentally Ill).** Carrie Buck was an 18-year-old feebleminded woman who was committed to a mental-health facility in Virginia. A Virginia statute declared at that time that such mentally deficient persons should be sterilized. Buck's lawyer appealed, arguing that the Virginia statute was unconstitutional. The SC upheld the constitutionality of that statute, saying that "it is far better to prevent those who are manifestly unfit from continuing their kind...three generations of imbeciles are enough" (at 585). (*See*

Skinner v. Oklahoma [1942] for an opinion about another type of sterilization issue and a contrary holding on grounds involving the equal protection clause of the Fourteenth Amendment).

Buckley v. Fitzsimmons, 507 U.S.___, 113 S.Ct. 2606 (1993) **(Prosecutorial Misconduct).** Buckley was charged with murder. Prosecutors made various statements surrounding the indictment of Buckley for the murder, including several untrue statements. Subsequently, the charges against Buckley were dropped, and he sued the prosecutors under Title 42, U.S.C. Section 1983, alleging that his civil rights had been violated by this prosecutorial misconduct. The prosecutors sought absolute immunity from this suit and the SC heard the case. The SC upheld Buckley's right to sue the prosecutor, who only enjoyed qualified immunity from such suits. Prosecutors are liable for statements they make publicly if such statements are false and they result in harm to defendants who are innocent of criminal wrong-doing.

Bullington v. Missouri, 451 U.S. 430, 101 S.Ct. 1852 (1981) **(Death Penalty; Resentencing Hearings).** Bullington was charged with capital murder. His case was heard by a jury, who found him guilty. In the sentencing phase, the jury had to decide between the death penalty and life imprisonment as a punishment, and they recommended the latter. Subsequently, Bullington's conviction was reversed and a new trial resulted. Bullington was again convicted. This time, the jury decided in favor of the death penalty. Bullington appealed and the SC heard his case. It set his death-penalty sentence aside, saying that the first jury's refusal to impose the death penalty was an acquittal for that form of punishment. A subsequent trial cannot result in a punishment greater than that imposed by the first in a capital case. (*See Arizona v. Rumsey* [1984] and *Caspari v. Bohlen* [1984] for comparative cases).

Bumper v. North Carolina, 391 U.S. 543, 88 S.Ct. 1788 (1968) **(Law Enforcement Officers or Agencies; Search and Seizure).** Bumper was a suspect in a rape case. Police went to his home and advised his grandmother that they had a search warrant and wanted to come in and look around. The police did *not* have any warrant. Nevertheless, the grandmother gave her consent, and police entered the home and found evidence later incriminating Bumper in the rape. He was convicted. He appealed, arguing that the evidence, a rifle, should have been suppressed since police did

not have a warrant. The prosecutor countered by saying that they were conducting a valid search of Bumper's premises consistent with the consent to search given by the grandmother. The SC disagreed with the prosecutor, holding that misrepresentation by police that they have a valid search warrant and the giving of consent as the result of that misrepresentation do not justify a subsequent warrantless search. The incriminating evidence was suppressed and Bumper's conviction was overturned.

Burch v. Louisiana, 441 U.S. 357, 99 S.Ct. 1623 (1979) **(Sixth Amendment; Right to Counsel).** Burch was convicted 5–1 by a six-person jury on charges of exhibiting obscene motion pictures. He appealed to the SC, which overturned his conviction. The SC used precedent to justify its action where a less-than-unanimous six-person jury is unconstitutional (*See Duncan v. Louisiana* and *Ballew v. Georgia*). After an overly lengthy opinion (in view of the fact that the matter had already been settled in two landmark cases earlier), the SC said, again, that six-person juries must be unanimous; if they are not, then the defendant has been deprived of the right to a fair jury trial under the Sixth and Fourteenth Amendments.

Burks v. United States, 437 U.S. 1, 98 S.Ct. 2141 (1978) **(Double Jeopardy).** Burks was charged with robbery in a United States district court in Tennessee. During his trial expert testimony of his insanity was offered. The government rebutted with expert and lay testimony of Burks' sanity. The jury found Burks guilty. A motion by Burks for a new trial was denied. However, an appellate court found that the government's proof to counter Burks's claim of insanity was insufficient, and his conviction was reversed. The appellate court sent the case back to the district court, where the judge could determine whether a directed verdict of acquittal was in order or if a second trial should be held. Burks contested the notion of a second trial. An appeal from Burks to the SC resulted in the following decision. The SC said that for the purposes of determining whether the double jeopardy clause precludes a second trial after the reversal of a conviction, a reversal based on insufficiency of evidence is tantamount to an acquittal. This is to be distinguished from reversal due to trial error. In holding that evidence is insufficient to prove guilt beyond a reasonable doubt, the appellate court is giving the requirements for an entry of a judgment of acquittal. Burks was thereby acquitted of the robbery.

Butterworth v. Smith, 494 U.S. 624, 110 S.Ct 1376 (1990) **(Grand Juries).** Smith, a reporter for a Florida newspaper, gave evidence before a grand jury in a criminal matter involving certain public officials. Subsequently, he wanted to write an article about his testimony and the subject matter of the events. However, a Florida statute barred him from disclosing grand jury statements he made publicly, and Smith sued, alleging a violation of his First Amendment right of free speech. The SC eventually ruled that laws prohibiting disclosures of grand jury testimony are unconstitutional to the extent that they pertain to witnesses who wish to speak about their own testimony after the grand jury has been terminated.

C

Cabana v. Bullock, 474 U.S. 376, 106 S.Ct. 689 (1986) **(Death Penalty; Jury Instructions).** Bullock and a friend, Tucker, were offered a ride by Dickson. An argument developed and Dickson was subsequently killed by Tucker. Bullock and Tucker disposed of Dickson's body, but subsequently, they were apprehended and charged with first-degree murder and robbery in a Mississippi court. Bullock was convicted, and during the sentencing phase of his trial, the judge issued confusing instructions to the jury. According to Mississippi law, Bullock could receive the death penalty if he had been found by the jury to have killed Dickson, intended to kill him, and/or intended to use lethal force against him. This factual prerequisite was not made clear to the jury; rather, mere presence at a scene involving a murder makes the partner equally guilty with the perpetrator who commits the murder, in this case, Tucker. The jury sentenced him to death. Bullock filed a habeas corpus petition challenging his sentence, contending that the jury instructions had been faulty and that his role had been insufficient to warrant the death penalty. The SC heard his case and vacated the death sentence, remanding the case back to a Mississippi trial court, where the jury could be given the choice of either imposing a sentence of life imprisonment on Bullock or determining the factual question of whether Bullock had killed, attempted to kill, or intended to use lethal force

against Dickson. If it was determined that Bullock possessed the requisite culpability, then the death sentence could be reimposed.

Cabell v. Chavez-Salido, 454 U.S. 432, 102 S.Ct. 735 (1982) **(Corrections; Probation and Parole).** Several resident aliens, including Chavez-Salido, attempted to secure jobs as probation officers in California. California has a statute requiring that all public employees declared by law to be police officers must be United States citizens. The resident aliens filed suit, alleging that they were constitutionally entitled to these jobs. The SC upheld the right of California to impose such a statute as a requirement for holding these law enforcement positions. That right does not mean that resident alien status disqualifies persons from any public positions. Rather, it pertains to law enforcement and probation and parole work.

Cady v. Dombrowski, 413 U.S. 433, 93 S.Ct. 2523 (1973) **(Law Enforcement Officers or Agencies; Vehicle Searches).** Dombrowski was a Chicago police officer who became drunk and had an automobile accident in Wisconsin. He was transported from his disabled vehicle by another party to a nearby town, where he called the police and had them drive him back to his vehicle. The Wisconsin police officers were aware of Dombrowski's status as a police officer from Chicago and knew that officers carried firearms. Thus, when they returned to his car, they searched it for a weapon. Dombrowski had been drinking heavily and they considered him drunk. They arrested him for drunken driving and jailed him. In the meantime, the wrecked vehicle was towed to a garage, where its contents were inventoried. A revolver was found, together with some bloody clothing. Further investigation linked this clothing and pistol with a murder recently committed in nearby Fond du Lac County. Dombrowski was charged with murder and convicted, largely on circumstantial evidence. He sought to suppress the evidence resulting from the officer's inventory search of the vehicle. The SC upheld Dombrowski's conviction, saying that the warrantless search for the pistol was legitimate on the basis of what the officers knew about Dombrowski's police officer status, and that a subsequent search with a warrant disclosing incriminating bloody clothing was also valid. The original search of the vehicle by police was valid because the officers had exercised a form of custody over the car and removed it from the road as a possible traffic hazard. Police had also acted to protect innocent citizens who might have discovered Dombrowski's service revolver by accident and become injured.

Cage v. Louisiana, 498 U.S. 39, 111 S.Ct. 328 (1990) **(Death Penalty; Jury Instructions).** Cage was convicted of first-degree murder in a New Orleans court. The judge issued instructions to the jury concerning the interpretation of "beyond a reasonable doubt." His definition of the phrase included words such as "it must be such doubt as would give rise to a grave uncertainty," "an actual substantial doubt," and "a moral certainty." Cage was sentenced to death. He appealed the conviction and sentence, and the SC overturned his conviction. The SC concluded by saying that phrases such as "grave uncertainty" and "moral certainty" suggest a higher degree of doubt than is required for acquittal under the reasonable doubt standard (at 329-330).

Caldwell v. Mississippi, 472 U.S. 320, 105 S.Ct. 2633 (1985) **(Death Penalty; Executions).** Caldwell had shot and killed the owner of a small grocery store while robbing it. After he was apprehended and tried, the defense and prosecution gave their summations. The prosecution told the jury not to view itself as finally determining whether Caldwell would die, because a death sentence would be reviewed for correctness by the Mississippi Supreme Court. He was convicted and sentenced to death. Caldwell appealed, arguing that the prosecutor's remarks during summation had been improper and had misled the jury into believing that they would not be responsible for the death of Caldwell. The SC reversed his conviction, holding that the prosecutor's remarks had been improper because they were inaccurate and misleading in a manner that diminished the jury's sense of responsibility. Thus, the SC concluded, these prosecutorial remarks and the jury's subsequent recommendation for the death penalty had violated Caldwell's Eighth Amendment right to due process.

California v. Acevedo, 500 U.S. 565, 111 S.Ct. 1982 (1991) **(Law Enforcement Officers or Agencies; Vehicle Searches).** DEA agents discovered a Federal Express package shipped from Hawaii to California that contained a large quantity of marijuana. They allowed Federal Express personnel to deliver the package to a house and placed the house under surveillance. Subsequently, a man entered the house and left later

carrying a tote bag. They intercepted him and found about a pound of marijuana in the bag. Later they observed Acevedo arrive at the house and leave later carrying a brown paper bag about the size of the tote bag. Police officers stopped Acevedo's car thereafter, searched the brown paper bag without a warrant, and discovered marijuana. The police lacked probable cause to search the vehicle itself, although they did have probable cause to believe that the paper bag held marijuana. Acevedo was convicted and he appealed. The SC upheld Acevedo's conviction, saying that probable cause to believe that a container has contraband may enable officers to search that container, even if it is in a vehicle that they lack probable cause to search. This case modified greatly two other cases, *United States v. Chadwick* (1977) and *Arkansas v. Sanders* (1979), because it permitted officers to open containers, even large ones, if there was probable cause to do so, even if those containers were in vehicles that police lacked probable cause to search in their entirety.

California v. Brown, 479 U.S. 538, 107 S.Ct. 837 (1987) **(Eighth Amendment; Jury Instructions).** Brown was convicted of forcible rape and first-degree murder of Susan J., a 15-year-old girl in Riverside, California. During the penalty phase of the two-phased trial, the judge issued the following jury instruction: "You must not be swayed by mere sentiment, conjecture, sympathy, passion, prejudice, public opinion or public feeling." The jury imposed the death sentence. An automatic appeal resulted in the California Supreme Court reversing Brown's conviction on the grounds that the judge's jury instruction had violated Brown's Eighth and Fourteenth Amendment rights to due process. The SC heard the state's appeal and reversed the California SC, reinstating Brown's conviction and death sentence. The SC held that since the jury instruction had been given during the sentencing phase of Brown's trial, it did not violate either the Eighth or Fourteenth Amendment rights of Brown. Further, the jury instruction was reasonable because it emphasized to jurors the extraneous nature of factors unrelated to the factual circumstances of the murder itself. The instructions from the judge merely limited the jury's sentencing considerations to "record evidence."

California v. Byers, 402 U.S. 424, 91 S.Ct. 1535 (1971) **(Confessions; Interrogations).** Byers was involved in an automobile accident and left the scene without first giving his name and address to the police. He claimed the privilege under the Fifth Amendment that such information given would be self-incriminating and thus would violate his rights. A California court granted an appeal of a writ of prohibition, preventing the court from proceeding against Byers on the hit-and-run charge. The government appealed and the SC vacated the judgment, holding that the constitutional privilege against compulsory self-incrimination had not been infringed by the state statute that required motorists involved in accidents to stop at the scene and give their name and address.

California v. Carney, 471 U.S. 386, 105 S.Ct. 2066 (1985) **(Law Enforcement Officers or Agencies; Vehicle Searches).** Carney was believed to be exchanging marijuana for sex in a motor home parked in a vacant lot. Police had heard rumors, not from reliable informants, about his activities, and placed his motor home under surveillance. They observed a young boy enter it and leave a while later. They intercepted the boy and asked him whether Carney was exchanging sex for marijuana. The boy admitted it, so police entered Carney's motor home without a warrant and without Carney's consent. They found marijuana and arrested Carney. They impounded his motor home and searched it extensively at the police station, discovering more marijuana. He was subsequently convicted. He appealed, alleging that police had made an unlawful search of his vehicle in violation of his Fourth Amendment rights. The SC upheld Carney's conviction, stating in brief that it considered his motor home, for all practical purposes, to be the same as an automobile; thus, police were entitled to search it, with probable cause and without a warrant. This case is significant because it caused motor homes to fall under the so-called *automobile exception* to warrantless searches of vehicles whenever probable cause is present.

California v. Ciraolo, 476 U.S. 207, 106 S.Ct. 1809 (1986) **(Law Enforcement Officers or Agencies; Searches; Plain View; Open Field Searches).** Ciraolo was growing marijuana in his backyard, according to an anonymous tip received by police. The yard could not be seen from the street, so police flew over Ciraolo's home in an airplane and photographed the backyard. After viewing photographs and detecting marijuana plants, officers obtained a search warrant for Ciraolo's premises, where they found growing marijuana plants. Ciraolo was convicted of cultivating mari-

juana. He appealed, contending that he had a reasonable expectation of privacy, which included his backyard, and that planes flying over his yard viewing it constituted a Fourth Amendment unreasonable search. The SC upheld the aerial use of photography in identifying illegal contraband, such as growing marijuana. It declared that one's property, such as a backyard, cannot be barred from public view from the air; thus, anything, such as marijuana or other illegal contraband, is subject to being viewed and seized.

California v. Greenwood, 486 U.S. 35, 108 S.Ct. 1625 (1988) **(Law Enforcement Officers or Agencies; Searches).** Greenwood, a suspected drug dealer, was under surveillance by the police. They observed that from time to time, he would place out trash for trash collectors. They inspected some of his trash and discovered sufficient incriminating evidence to obtain a search warrant of the premises based upon probable cause. A search yielded large quantities of cocaine and hashish and resulted in Greenwood's arrest and conviction for various drug violations. He appealed, contending that his trash should have been subject to a search warrant before police inspected it, and thus, the evidence later discovered and used against him in court should have been excluded. The SC disagreed and said that warrantless searches of trash or garbage are permissible, because persons give up their right to privacy of refuse whenever they place it in public places in trash containers, readily accessible to others.

California v. Hodari D., 499 U.S. 621, 111 S.Ct. 1547 (1991) **(Law Enforcement Officers or Agencies; Arrests).** Hodari was a juvenile who was observed by police late at night with others huddled around a vehicle in a high-crime neighborhood of Oakland. Everyone fled in different directions when seeing the approaching police vehicle. One officer, Pertoso, drove around the block to intercept one of the fleeing persons, Hodari. Hodari ran into Pertoso and a brief scuffle ensued. Hodari broke free, began to run away again, and threw away what appeared to be a small rock. The officer tackled Hodari and arrested him. The recovered rock turned out to be crack cocaine. After Hodari was convicted, he appealed, contending that he had been seized unreasonably and that Petroso had lacked probable cause to arrest him and use the thrown-away cocaine against him. The SC disagreed with Hodari and upheld his conviction, saying that the thrown-away cocaine constituted *abandonment*, that Petroso had not *seized* Hodari before this abandonment, and thus, that the cocaine was admissible against Hodari. If Petroso had tackled Hodari and arrested him before Hodari threw away the crack cocaine, then the eventual discovery of cocaine would have been excluded as evidence against Hodari because Petroso would not have been able to establish probable cause for his arrest.

California v. Prysock, 453 U.S. 355, 101 S.Ct. 2806 (1981) **(Confessions; Exceptions).** In January 1978, Prysock and another man murdered a woman, Erickson. Prysock and his companion were arrested shortly thereafter and taken to a police station for questioning. The questioning was preceded by an extemporaneous Miranda warning, in which the officers covered the general points. Prysock indicated a desire to talk with police but without a tape recorder. He also asked if he could have an attorney present *later*, after talking with police. They said he could have one. He gave incriminating statements to police without the attorney present, at his own insistence, and he was subsequently convicted. He appealed, arguing that the Miranda warning had not been recited precisely and thus his confession ought to have been excluded and his conviction overturned. An appellate court agreed, and the government appealed. The SC reinstated his murder conviction, holding that the Miranda warning need not be a virtual incantation of the precise language contained in the Miranda opinion; such a rigid rule is not mandated by Miranda or any other decision of the SC. Essentially, Prysock's constitutional rights had not been violated when police gave him the *Miranda* warning in a general way.

California v. Ramos, 463 U.S. 992, 103 S.Ct. 3446 (1983) **(Death Penalty vs. Life-Without-Parole Sentences).** Ramos was convicted of murder, robbery, and attempted murder. During the penalty phase of his trial, the judge was obligated to advise the jury that a sentence of life imprisonment without possibility of parole may be commuted by the governor to a sentence that includes the possibility of parole, known as the *Briggs Instruction*. Subsequently, the jury gave the death penalty. Ramos appealed, claiming that the jury instruction had violated his due-process rights and constituted cruel and unusual punishment under the Eighth and Fourteenth Amendments. The SC rejected Ramos's appeal outright, holding that there is no federal prohibition against a judge in-

structing a jury to consider the governor's power to commute a life sentence without parole to one where parole is a possibility. A further assertion by Ramos concerned a statement given by a psychiatrist about Ramos's future dangerousness. The claim that such commentary by a psychiatrist is unconstitutional was also rejected (*See Jurek v. Texas*).

California v. Trombetta, 467 U.S. 97, 104 S.Ct. 2528 (1984) **(Law Enforcement Officers or Agencies; Preservation of Evidence).** Trombetta was stopped on suspicion that he was driving while intoxicated (DWI). Police administered a breath-analysis test to Trombetta to determine his blood-alcohol level. Contrary to custom, the breath sample they took was not preserved. Trombetta later sought to suppress the breath-analysis results, claiming that an independent examination of the sample might have led other experts to different conclusions about his alleged level of intoxication. A lower appellate court ruled in favor of Trombetta, obligating California officers to preserve breath samples that they planned to use against motorists on DWI charges in court. However, the SC reversed the lower court and ruled that it is not in violation of the Fourteenth Amendment due-process clause for law enforcement agencies not to preserve breath samples from DWI suspects. Put another way, it is not necessary for California or any other state to preserve breath samples taken from DWI suspects. This practice does not violate any constitutional right of DWI defendants to due process. Currently, California law advises DWI suspects that breath samples will not be preserved, but their results may be used against them in DWI court actions later. California offers defendants a urinalysis test and a blood test as options to a breath test to determine their level of intoxication for prosecution purposes. Defendants may choose their option, although a refusal to take any of the options will result in automatic revocation of their driver's licenses.

California Department of Corrections v. Morales, ___U.S.___, 115 S.Ct. 1597 (1995) **(Corrections; Parole Hearings; Parolee Rights).** Morales had shot his girlfriend in the head, neck, and abdomen. He was convicted of first-degree murder in 1971 and was sentenced to life in prison. In 1980, he was paroled to a halfway house, where he became acquainted with a 75-year-old woman, Washabaugh. He married her shortly thereafter. The couple planned to move to

Los Angeles. Washabaugh's family didn't hear from her and reported her missing after several days. A human hand was found on the Hollywood Freeway in Los Angeles was later identified as Washabaugh's. The body was never recovered, and Morales was subsequently arrested and charged with her murder. He pleaded nolo contendere to second-degree murder and was sentenced to 15 years to life. Morales became eligible for parole in 1990. At his parole-eligibility hearing in July 1989, the Board of Prison Terms found him unsuitable for release in 1990, citing numerous aggravating factors to justify their denial of parole. When Morales was originally convicted for Washabaugh's murder in 1980, California had a policy of reviewing a person's parole eligibility on an annual basis. However, in 1981 the policy changed to allow these reviews every three years. Thus, when Morales was denied parole in 1989, the board set his next hearing for 1992. He appealed, seeking an annual parole review and arguing that his three-year review resulted from an ex post facto policy decision. The SC upheld the California policy decision as applied to Morales, saying that the ex post facto clause is aimed at laws that retroactively alter definition of crimes or increase punishment for criminal acts. The policy change in California only altered the method to be followed in fixing parole release dates.

Campbell v. United States, 365 U.S. 85, 81 S.Ct. 421 (1961) **(Discovery).** Campbell was charged with bank robbery. During the testimony of a government witness, it became known that a previous statement had been made by that witness. The defense sought to obtain that statement, but the court denied them access to it. The government also denied the *existence* of the statement, when, in fact, it actually existed. Campbell was convicted. He appealed, arguing that under the Jencks Act, he was entitled to discovery of the prior statement given by the government witness in order to impeach the witness. The SC overturned his conviction and held that under the Jencks Act, such information is discoverable and should be turned over to the defense by government attorneys. Thus, Campbell had been deprived of the right to a fair trial.

Camara v. Municipal Court of the City and County of San Francisco, 387 U.S. 523, 87 S.Ct. 1727 (1967) **(Law Enforcement Officers or Agencies; Arrests; Probation and Parole).** In November 1963, the Division of Housing Inspec-

tion of the San Francisco Department of Public Health entered an apartment building to make a routine annual inspection of possible violations of the city's housing code. Camara rented an apartment on the ground floor. Housing inspectors advised him that under the city building code, ground floor apartments were not for residential purposes and asked to enter the apartment. Camara denied them entry, saying that they needed a search warrant. Later, they attempted to enter his apartment without a warrant and were again refused. They charged him under a criminal code for refusing to permit a lawful inspection of a dwelling. Camara appealed. The SC supported Camara, holding that administrative searches of the kind at issue in this case are significant intrusions upon the interests protected by the Fourth Amendment. Further, no immediate need for such a search had been stated by city officials. The significance of the case is that Camara had a constitutional right to demand a search warrant from the city officials and could not be convicted of a crime for refusing to consent to a city inspection.

Cannon v. State, 624 So.2d 238 (1993) **(Corrections; Probation).** In open court in Alabama, Cannon was convicted of criminally negligent homicide and probation was imposed. He refused the sentence and demanded to be incarcerated instead. The judge insisted he accept the probation sentence. Cannon appealed. In an Alabama court of appeals decision, the court upheld Cannon's right to refuse probation, and he was remanded to prison instead. This is not as bad as it sounds, however. Cannon had been incarcerated for many months prior to his conviction. By accepting probation, he would have been obliged to adhere to certain restrictive conditions for a period of time far in excess of the time remaining to be served. In effect, he had only a few more months to serve of his original sentence. Thus, a probation sentence would have involved a longer term of conditional freedom than the number of months remaining before his unconditional release from prison. The court said that "Our holding merely recognizes a convict's right to reject the trial court's offer of probation if he or she deems it to be more *onerous* than a prison sentence."

Cardwell v. Lewis, 417 U.S. 583, 99 S.Ct. 2464 (1974) **(Law Enforcement Officers or Agencies; Vehicle Searches).** Lewis was suspected of a murder. Police interviewed him five days later and viewed his automobile, which was thought to have been used to accomplish the crime. While the automobile was in a public parking lot, police obtained an arrest warrant for Lewis and towed his car to the police station, where they made plaster casts of the car's tires, as well as obtained some paint scrapings from the outside of the car. Nothing was obtained from the interior. All of this external examination of the car was done without a warrant. Subsequently, Lewis was charged with the murder and convicted. He appealed, arguing that the search of his automobile without warrant had violated his Fourth Amendment rights. A lower court excluded the evidence police had obtained. The SC reversed this decision, upholding Lewis's conviction, concluding that the external view of Lewis's car was not unreasonable; that its towing to a lot for further search, based upon probable cause, was not unreasonable; thus, Lewis's Fourth Amendment rights had not been violated.

Caribbean International News Corporation v. Puerto Rico, No., 92-949, May 17, 1993 **(Press Access to Preliminary Hearings; Territories Under United States Control).** The SC has held that the press may be permitted access to preliminary hearings in criminal trials in United States territories as well as states.

Carlson v. Green, 446 U.S. 14, 100 S.Ct. 1468 (1980) **(Corrections; Damages).** Jones suffered personal injuries while incarcerated in a federal prison in Indiana. Prison officials failed to give him proper medical attention, and he died. His mother, Green, as administratrix of his estate, filed suit, alleging that prison officials had subjected him to cruel and unusual punishment, violating his due-process, equal-protection, and Eighth Amendment rights. The trial court dismissed the complaint, saying Green had no right to sue on behalf of her dead son. Green appealed, and the Seventh Circuit Court of Appeals reversed the dismissal and remanded the case. The government appealed. The SC ruled in favor of Green, holding that a remedy was available to the administratrix, even though her allegation could also support a suit against the United States under the Federal Tort Claims Act and survival of her cause of action was governed by federal common law rather than state statute. In short, Green had the right to sue as established by *Bivens v. Six Unknown Federal Narcotics Agents* (1971).

Carnley v. Cochran, 369 U.S. 506, 82 S.Ct. 43 (1962) **(Sixth Amendment Right to Counsel).** Trial judges must advise defendants of their right to counsel in plea-bargain proceedings, and a defendant's failure to request counsel is not equivalent to a waiver of that right to counsel.

Carroll v. Board of Parole, 859 P.2d 1203 (1993) **(Corrections; Parole Boards).** Carroll had been convicted of murder and had served the minimum sentence prescribed by law. However, the Oregon Parole Board, considering the seriousness of the crime and other factors, voted to override the minimum sentence and continue the inmate's incarceration. He contested this action, but the Oregon Parole Board is vested with the power to override any minimum-sentence provision that might otherwise provide a means whereby an offender might be paroled automatically. The Oregon Court of Appeals upheld the board's action as legitimate, as a unanimous vote was required to override the minimum sentence and the board had voted unanimously.

Carroll v. United States, 267 U.S. 132, 45 S.Ct. 280 (1925) **(Law Enforcement Officers or Agencies; Arrests).** Carroll was a suspected bootlegger of illegal liquor. Police had tried several times to stop his car but had failed to do so. One evening officers saw Carroll's car returning to Grand Rapids from Detroit. They stopped the car and proceeded, without warrant, to search it extensively. Eventually, after tearing apart seats and other automobile components, they discovered illegal whiskey. Carroll was convicted of transporting intoxicating liquor. He appealed, arguing that the whiskey evidence was the result of an illegal search of his vehicle without probable cause and also without a valid search warrant. The SC upheld his conviction, saying that officers did, indeed, have probable cause to stop him and did not need a search warrant. It stressed that automobiles, unlike houses, are highly mobile entities, and therefore the police were authorized to search it before its occupants could destroy any illegal contraband.

Carter v. Kentucky, 450 U.S. 288, 101 S.Ct. 1112 (1981) **(Sixth Amendment; Prosecutorial Misconduct).** Carter was charged with a serious crime. He requested the judge to instruct the jury that the defendant's refusal to testify should not lead to an inference of guilt nor prejudice the jury against him in any way. The judge refused, and Carter was found guilty. He appealed, alleging that he had been denied a fair trial because the trial judge failed to issue those instructions to the jury after being asked to do so in a timely manner. The SC agreed with Carter and overturned his conviction on those grounds. It said that the state trial judge has a constitutional obligation, upon proper request from defense, to give a no-adverse-inference instruction to the jury before they deliberate on his guilt or innocence.

Carter v. People of State of Illinois, 329 U.S. 173, 67 S.Ct. 216 (1946) **(Corrections; Death Penalty).** In 1928, Carter pleaded guilty to murder and was sentenced to a 99-year prison term. At the time he entered his plea, he was advised of his right to counsel, but he gave up that right knowingly and voluntarily. He also waived other rights normally waived during plea bargaining and the entering of guilty pleas. In 1945, Carter filed a writ of habeas corpus, alleging that he had been denied counsel during the sentencing phase of his trial. A reading of the 1925 record is clear, that Carter knowingly and intelligently gave up his right to an attorney when entering his initial guilty plea. Only many years later did he express a concern about the absence of counsel, which he had never requested, at his sentencing. The SC upheld Carter's murder conviction, holding that his due-process rights had not been violated when he was sentenced without the presence of counsel. His own waiver of counsel, knowingly, intelligently, and voluntarily, defeated his contention that he was denied counsel.

Caspari v. Bohlen, ___U.S.___, 114 S.Ct. 948 (1994) **(Double Jeopardy).** Bohlen and others were convicted of robbing a jewelry store in Missouri in 1981. The judge determined that Bohlen was also a persistent offender and was thus in violation of Missouri's persistent-offender statute. The jury convicted him of first-degree robbery, and the judge sentenced him to three consecutive terms of 15 years in prison. Bohlen appealed and the Missouri Supreme Court overturned his conviction, because no proof of his being a persistent offender had been presented at his trial. The case was retried, this time to allow the prosecution the opportunity of showing proof of Bohlen's four prior felony convictions and his status as a persistent offender for a commensurate sentence. Again, the trial judge sentenced Bohlen to three consecutive terms of 15 years in prison. Again, Bohlen appealed on the grounds that the second trial had violated his Fifth Amendment right against double jeopardy. Bohlen's conviction and consecutive sentences were upheld by the SC,

who said that it is well established that there is no double-jeopardy bar to the use of prior convictions in sentencing persistent offenders (at 954). The significance of this case is that the double-jeopardy issue does not apply in re-sentencing proceedings in noncapital cases. (*See comparative cases such as Bullington v. Missouri* [1981] and *Arizona v. Rumsey* [1984]).

Chambers v. Florida, 309 U.S. 227, 60 S.Ct. 472 (1940) **(Confessions).** Following a murder and robbery in May 1933, Florida police arrested Chambers and other black men without warrants and confined them in the Broward County Jail for investigation. They underwent persistent questioning from the afternoon of May 20 until the sunrise of May 21. Chambers had also been questioned during the daytime all week leading up to the overnight interrogation. Others involved in the murder apparently implicated Chambers, who was subsequently indicted for the murder. He confessed under intensive pressure from the sheriff's investigators, who used physical violence against him. He was sentenced to death. He appealed, alleging that his confession had been coerced. The SC agreed and overturned his conviction, ruling that his due-process rights had to be preserved at all times, and that dragnet methods of arrest on suspicion without warrant, protracted questioning and cross-questioning, and physical violence against a person being questioned over a five-day period are unconstitutional. Chambers was black and the murder victim was white. The equal protection clause of the Fourteenth Amendment should have protected Chambers but had been violated. Chambers's case was sent back to the originating trial court for a possible retrial, this time without the benefit of a coerced confession from Chambers.

Chambers v. Maroney, 399 U.S. 42, 90 S.Ct. 1975 (1970) **(Law Enforcement Officers or Agencies; Exclusionary Rule; Vehicle Searches).** Chambers and three other men in a station wagon fit the description given to the police by eye-witnesses following a gas station robbery. The police stopped Chambers's car and placed them under arrest, asserting probable cause based on the profile of the perpetrators and their escaping vehicle. The officers had the car towed to the police station, where it was more extensively searched. The search yielded the money from the gas station, some weapons, and other incriminating material. The police then obtained a search warrant for Chambers' home where they found further incriminating evidence of his involvement in the robbery. Chambers was convicted. He appealed, seeking to suppress the evidence disclosed by the search of his car by police at the police station. The SC upheld his conviction, saying that police may search vehicles, at their convenience, when they have arrested criminal suspects with probable cause that they are the likely perpetrators. The police were entitled to search the vehicle when they initially stopped Chambers on the highway as a search incident to an arrest. The fact that they chose to search the car at the police station did not nullify the legality of their search.

Chambers v. Mississippi, 410 U.S. 284, 91 S.Ct. 499 (1973) **(Fair Trials).** Chambers was charged with murdering a police officer. It was known during the trial that three witnesses had heard another man, McDonald, admit to killing the officer. However, a Mississippi law prohibited the testimony of these witnesses because it considered such testimony to be hearsay. Chambers then sought to call McDonald so that he could cross-examine him. The Mississippi law also forbade calling McDonald because he was not considered to be an adverse witness. Chambers was convicted. He appealed. The SC overturned his conviction, saying that the Mississippi law was unconstitutional and had deprived Chambers of a fair trial by denying him the opportunity of cross-examining material witnesses.

Chandler v. Florida, 449 U.S. 560, 101 S.Ct. 802 (1976) **(Fair Trials; Media Coverage).** The Florida Supreme Court placed a ban on televised broadcasting of judicial proceedings, respecting the right of criminal suspects to a fair trial. The ban was challenged. The SC ruled that a defendant must show something more than the jurors' awareness that a trial has attracted media attention in order to prevent broadcasting that might prejudice jurors.

Chapman v. California, 386 U.S. 18, 87 S.Ct. 824 (1967) **(Law Enforcement Officers or Agencies; Exclusionary Rule; Judicial or Prosecution Commentary on Defendant's Refusal to Testify).** Chapman and a confederate, Teale, were charged with robbing, kidnapping, and murdering a bartender. During the trial, Chapman did not testify. At that time, California had a statute permitting the judge and prosecutor to comment on the fact that the defendant did not testify in his or her own defense and that inferences about guilt could be drawn from the defendant's failure to testify. The trial judge told the jury that they could draw adverse inferences from the defendant's failure to testify. Chapman was convicted. Before he appealed, the SC decided another case, *Griffin v. California* (1965), which held that commentary by a judge or prosecutor about a defendant's refusal to testify in a criminal case must not infringe on his right not to be compelled to be a witness against himself, guaranteed by the Fifth Amendment. The California Supreme Court, therefore, admitted that Chapman had been denied a federal constitutional right because of the judge's instructions to the jury about that silence, but it held that the error was *harmless*. Chapman appealed. The SC reversed Chapman's conviction, holding that the error was *not harmless* when the state prosecutor's argument and the trial judge's jury instructions continuously and repeatedly impressed the jury that the refusal of the defendant to testify required inferences to be drawn in the state's favor. Chapman was granted a new trial, where judicial and prosecutorial commentary on her refusal to testify in her own case were prohibited.

Chapman v. United States, 365 U.S. 610, 81 S.Ct. 776 (1961) **(Law Enforcement Officers or Agencies, Consent Searches).** Chapman rented a dwelling in a wooded area near Macon, Georgia. The landlord went to the house to invite him to church. Chapman wasn't home and the landlord smelled "sour mash," a whiskey odor. He advised police, who went to the house and entered it through a window, without a warrant, although the landlord had given his permission for police to enter. The police found a distillery and 1,300 gallons of whiskey. Subsequently, federal officers were summoned to the house. Their investigation led to Chapman's arrest and conviction of making illegal whiskey. He appealed, alleging that the police should have obtained a valid warrant before entering his premises, and that the landlord had no right to admit officers to the dwelling he was renting. The SC reversed Chapman's conviction, holding that the warrantless search was unjustified. The federal officers had had time to obtain a warrant but had failed to do so. Even the search by Georgia police was in violation of the Fourth Amendment provision against unreasonable searches and seizures, because they had not known at the time that the premises were being used for illegal whiskey manufacture. A Georgia ordinance provides that an information must be filed by the solicitor-general before a "public nuisance" can be abated, such as the dwelling where the whiskey was being manufactured illegally. (*See Weeks v. United States* [1914] for a comparative case).

Cheek v. United States, 498 U.S. 192, 111 S.Ct. 604 (1990) **(Good-Faith Beliefs and Criminal Law)**. Cheek was charged with income-tax evasion in a federal district court. He protested, citing his reasonable belief that the income-tax laws are unconstitutional because he had formerly been told so by a group believing the tax laws are unconstitutional. Thus, he had not paid income tax for various years. The judge instructed the jury that an honest but unreasonable belief that tax laws violate one's rights does not constitute a good-faith misunderstanding of the law. Cheek appealed. The SC overturned his conviction, saying that it was error to instruct the jury to disregard evidence of defendant's understanding about whether to pay income taxes. The Court held that a good-faith misunderstanding of the law or a good-faith belief that one is not violating the law negates willfulness, whether or not the claimed belief or misunderstanding is objectively reasonable.

Chimel v. California, 395 U.S. 752, 89 S.Ct. 2034 (1969) **(Law Enforcement Officers or Agencies; Exclusionary Rule)**. Chimel was suspected of being involved in the burglary of a coin company in California. Police officers obtained a valid arrest warrant and went to his home to arrest him. When Chimel returned from work, police were waiting for him. They placed him under arrest and then proceeded to search his entire house, as a "search incident to an arrest." In Chimel's attic, they found some of the stolen coins, which were used against him in court. He was convicted of burglary. Chimel appealed. The SC overturned his conviction, arguing that the police search of Chimel's residence was well beyond the scope of the *arrest* warrant. The police should have obtained a *search* warrant, but they had not. The SC said that in a search incident to an arrest under the circumstances in *Chimel*, police are permitted to search only the defendant's person and the area within the immediate vicinity. Thus, they may search the room where the suspect is arrested but cannot extend their search to other areas of his residence without a valid search warrant. (*See Cupp v. Murphy* [1973] and *Schmerber v. California* [1966] for related issues.)

City of Canton v. Harris, 489 U.S. 378, 109 S.Ct. 1197 (1989) **(Legal Liabilities of Police Of-**ficers)**. Harris was arrested and taken to a police station in a patrol wagon. During the trip, she apparently fell to the floor and was observed sitting on the floor when the police arrived at the station. While at the station, Harris fell several times, was incoherent, and eventually was left on the floor unattended. Police officials never gave her aid or medical attention. Her family later arrived and transported her to a hospital, where she was diagnosed with several emotional ailments and hospitalized. They later sued police officials and the municipality under Title 42, U.S.C. Section 1983, alleging that her civil rights had been violated because of deliberate indifference by police to her emotional and physical condition. The municipality claimed immunity from such a suit and alleged inadequate police training, for which the municipality denied responsibility. The SC disagreed, saying that the municipality was liable to such suits. However, the SC said that in order for plaintiffs to prevail, they must show that the city (1) had deliberately failed to train their officers; (2) such training was municipality policy; and (3) the identified deficiency in officer training must be shown to be directly related to injuries sustained by victims.

Cleavinger v. Saxner, 474 U.S. 193, 106 S.Ct. 496 (1985) **(Corrections; Inmate Rights; Prison Disciplinary Councils)**. Saxner was an inmate at the Federal Correctional Institution in Indiana. He was found guilty by a prison disciplinary board of encouraging work stoppage by other inmates. He was placed in administrative detention and had to forfeit a certain number of "good-time" days that are normally used to reduce the maximum sentence to be served. Saxner was subsequently paroled. He filed suit against the prison disciplinary board and was awarded damages. Board members appealed, alleging they were entitled to absolute immunity in such suits. The SC said that these board members were not the equivalent of parole board members and did not have absolute immunity; although they had qualified immunity, it did not protect them from such suits as that instigated by Saxner.

Clemons v. Mississippi, 494 U.S. 738, 110 S.Ct. 1441 (1990) **(Death Penalty; Mental Incapacity)**. Clemons was accused of capital murder. During the sentencing phase of the trial, the judge instructed the jury that if the act was "especially heinous, atrocious or cruel," then this fact would be considered as a statutory aggravating factor.

Clemons was convicted. When the appellate court in Mississippi heard his appeal, it re-weighed the aggravating and mitigating circumstances, essentially upholding the originally imposed death sentence. Clemons then appealed to the SC, which reversed the Mississippi appeals court on the grounds that it was "unclear" from the record as to how the Mississippi court intended to reinterpret and reweigh the aggravating and mitigating factors and the judge's instructions to the jury. Thus, the death sentence was vacated and the case remanded to the Mississippi Supreme Court to clarify its intent relative to its decision and the harmless-error analysis of the case.

Coker v. Georgia, 433 U.S. 584, 97 S.Ct. 2861 (1977) **(Corrections; Death Penalty; Cruel and Unusual Punishment; Eighth Amendment).** Coker was convicted of raping a woman and he was sentenced to death. He appealed. The SC overturned his death sentence, saying that death sentences are inappropriate punishments for rape where the life of the rape victim is not taken.

Coleman v. Alabama, 399 U.S. 1, 90 S.Ct. 1999 (1970) **(Indigents; Appointment of Counsel).** Several defendants, including Coleman, were accused of assault with intent to commit murder. As indigents, they were denied counsel at their preliminary hearing, with the Alabama judge declaring that nothing that happened at the preliminary hearing would influence the trial later. Coleman was convicted. He appealed. The SC ruled that preliminary hearings are critical stages. Since indigent defendants are entitled to counsel at critical stages, which Coleman had been denied, his conviction was overturned.

Colombe v. Connecticut, 367 U.S. 568, 81 S.Ct. 1860 (1961) **(Self-Incrimination).** Colombe was suspected of committing several burglaries and homicides. He was taken into custody on unrelated charges of disturbing the peace and held for four days, during which he was extensively interrogated about the burglaries and homicides. His detention for disturbing the peace was admitted by police to be a ruse to keep him in custody to interrogate him. Eventually, he confessed to the crimes and was convicted. He appealed. The SC ruled that his confession had been involuntarily given. It said that when an interrogation is so lengthy and protracted, the process becomes the equivalent of extortion to obtain a confession; thus, such an exploitation of questioning,

whatever its usefulness, is not permitted. Colombe's conviction was reversed.

Colorado v. Bertine, 479 U.S. 367, 107 S.Ct. 738 (1987) **(Law Enforcement Officers or Agencies; Consent Searches).** Bertine was arrested for DWI. Police officers conducted a "routine" inventory of his van's contents, which yielded illegal drugs. The van was towed to the police impound lot, and Bertine was subsequently convicted of cocaine possession. He appealed. The police argued that the departmental policy and routine investigation without warrant was to protect a car owner's property and to insure against any claims of loss following a car's impoundment. The SC upheld Bertine's conviction, thus condoning police policy of conducting warrantless inventories of impounded vehicles.

Colorado v. Connelly, 479 U.S. 157, 107 S.Ct. 515 (1986) **(Confessions; Exceptions).** Connelly approached a uniformed Denver police officer and began to confess to a murder committed in 1982. The officer advised him of his Miranda rights, but Connelly acknowledged that he understood and he continued his confession. Later, a detective arrived and advised Connelly of his Miranda rights again; Connelly continued to confess. In fact, he led officers to where the murder had been committed and furnished them with incriminating details. He said that he was "following the advice of God" by confessing. Psychiatrists examined Connelly and found him incompetent to assist in his own defense, but they also found him competent to stand trial. He was convicted and appealed, contending that his mental state rendered him incompetent to be properly advised of his Miranda rights. The SC disagreed and upheld his conviction, saying that his belief that he was confessing because of God's advice did not automatically exclude his confession as admissible evidence against him.

Colorado v. Spring, 479 U.S. 564, 107 S.Ct. 851 (1987) **(Confessions; Exceptions).** Spring was involved in a shooting of a man during a hunting trip in Colorado. Furthermore, he was involved in an illegal enterprise involving interstate transportation of stolen firearms. He was arrested in Kansas City by the FBI, who advised him of his Miranda rights and interrogated him about the stolen firearms. At various points during the interrogation, Spring was read his Miranda rights again, and he signed several statements to that effect. Subsequently, visiting Colorado officers continued to interrogate Spring, asking him if he had been involved in the murder of the man on the hunting trip earlier. Spring confessed and signed a written confession. He was convicted of murder. He appealed, arguing that his confession to the murder ought to have been suppressed as evidence against him, since his Miranda warnings had been given only in relation to the stolen firearms charges. The SC disagreed and upheld his murder conviction. It said that once Miranda warnings have been given, police are not limited to maintain the scope of questioning only to one crime but can ask about other crimes. A waiver of a person's Miranda rights while police are asking questions about one crime continues and applies when police ask suspects about other crimes, during the same custodial interrogation.

Conley v. Gibson, 355 U.S. 41, 78 S.Ct. 99 (1957) **(Law Enforcement Officers or Agencies; Seizures).** A black railway employee, Conley was among those who suffered a loss of protection and seniority from a renewed contract between the railroad and the union. Conley sued, claiming that jobs had been "abolished" resulting in many blacks losing their jobs, while whites were hired as "new employees" to perform these old "abolished" jobs. The suit was dismissed by a lower court, but the SC heard Conley's case. The SC overruled the lower court and stated that the complaint filed against the union sufficiently alleged breach of contract and the union's statutory duty to represent fairly and without hostility all of the employees in the union, including Conley.

Connecticut v. Barrett, 479 U.S. 523, 107 S.Ct. 828 (1987) **(Confessions; Exceptions).** Barrett was a suspect in a sexual assault. He was arrested and told his Miranda rights. He acknowledged his Miranda rights, asked for an attorney, and advised police that he would not make any kind of written statement but wanted to make an oral statement. He was told his Miranda rights several times at different points during the interrogation. A defective tape recorder meant that the police had only one written record of the conversation, which was compiled by one of the interrogating officers. Subsequently, the oral confession was used against Barrett in obtaining a conviction. He appealed, contending that the "writings" kept of his oral and voluntary incriminating statements should have been excluded, because he had never waived his right to an attorney or to make written statements about what he had done. The SC up-

held his conviction, saying that voluntary confessions are admissible even though a suspect has not waived his right to an attorney or to making a written confession. Therefore, if suspects wish to discuss their involvement in crimes with police voluntarily after they have heard their Miranda rights, their incriminating statements may, indeed, be used against them in a court of law.

Connecticut Board of Pardons v. Dumschat, 452 U.S. 458, 101 S.Ct. 2460 (1981) **(Corrections; Visitation).** Dumschat was a prisoner serving a life term for murder in 1964. The Connecticut Board of Pardons was vested with the authority to commute such sentences and parole inmates after they had served minimum terms. Dumschat applied numerous times to have his sentence commuted, but the board refused. At no time were reasons given for these refusals. Dumschat filed suit against the board, alleging that his due-process rights under the Fourteenth Amendment were being violated because the board was not giving reasons for refusing to commute his sentence. He also noted that the board had granted commutations to more than three-fourths of prior applicants. The SC upheld the Connecticut Board of Pardons, saying that inmates eligible for commutations of their sentences are not guaranteed such commutations because of previous board actions. Furthermore, inmates are not entitled to a statement of reasons for the rejection of their applications. However, inmates seeking parole are entitled to statements from their parole boards about why their parole is denied.

Connally v. Georgia, 429 U.S. 245, 97 S.Ct. 546 (1977) **(Law Enforcement Officers or Agencies; Issuance of Search Warrants by Unsalaried Justices of the Peace).** During a drug investigation, an informant had given the Georgia police information about Connally's involvement in marijuana distribution. Police officers secured a search warrant from an unsalaried justice of the peace, who received a fee for issuing search warrants but who did not receive any fee for denying them. Connally was convicted. He appealed, alleging that the particular fee system used in Georgia led to the issuance of a warrant without probable cause and that the judge was biased in issuing one because of the fee he would be paid. The SC agreed with Connally and reversed his conviction on these grounds. It said that a situation where a judge benefits financially from issuing search warrants is in violation of the Fourth and Fourteenth Amendments.

Coolidge v. New Hampshire, 403 U.S. 443, 91 S.Ct. 2022 (1971) **(Law Enforcement Officers or Agencies; Search and Seizure).** Coolidge was a suspect in the murder of a 14-year-old girl. She had been called by a man who wanted her to work as a babysitter. She soon was missing but her body was not discovered until 13 days later. Coolidge was questioned by police and took a lie-detector test. Simultaneously, as the result of a search warrant issued by the state attorney general, police seized his vehicle, which they searched several times over a period of days. They also went to Coolidge's home and asked his wife for any guns in the home and for the clothes Coolidge was wearing the night the girl disappeared. Coolidge's wife turned several guns over to police as well as the clothes. This evidence, together with trace evidence from Coolidge's vehicle, was sufficient to convict him of the girl's murder. Coolidge appealed, contending that *all* evidence seized should have been excluded. The SC agreed in part and disagreed in part. It suppressed the evidence seized on the basis of the search warrant because it had not been issued by a neutral and detached magistrate. The SC stressed the fact that the attorney general was not a "neutral and detached" party and thus was not in the position of issuing a valid search warrant in this particular case. However, it allowed the evidence provided by Coolidge's wife, because it was the result of consent and did not require a warrant. Coolidge's conviction was upheld.

Cooper v. California, 386 U.S. 58, 87 S.Ct. 788 (1967) **(Law Enforcement Officers or Agencies; Search and Seizure).** Cooper was suspected of selling heroin. A police informant provided sufficient information for police to arrest Cooper. About a week later, his vehicle was impounded by police, who routinely searched it for inventory purposes. Such a search yielded a piece of a brown paper sack that matched a sack containing heroin that the police had earlier seized from Cooper. This evidence was introduced at Cooper's trial and he was convicted. He appealed, contending that the impoundment of his vehicle and subsequent warrantless search of it had violated his right under the Fourth Amendment against unreasonable searches and seizures. The SC upheld his conviction, noting that the nature of the inventory and warrantless search was not

unreasonable or in violation of Cooper's Fourth Amendment rights.

Cooper v. Pate, 378 U.S. 546, 84 S.Ct. 1733 (1964) **(Corrections; Civil Rights; Inmate Rights).** Cooper, a prisoner in the Illinois State Penitentiary, desired to purchase some religious periodicals. The warden refused, and he sued, alleging a violation of his First Amendment religious rights. Appeals courts denied his petition, but the SC vacated these lower court rulings. Prisoners are entitled to the protection of the Civil Rights Act of 1871 and may challenge conditions of their confinement in federal courts. The SC held that Cooper was entitled under the First and Fourteenth Amendments to purchase religious materials.

Costello v. United States, 350 U.S. 359, 76 S.Ct. 406 (1956) **(Hearsay Evidence; Grand Jury Indictments).** Racketeer and mobster Costello was indicted by a federal grand jury following hearsay statements from various FBI agents who estimated his net worth and gave scenarios they derived from their informants. He was convicted. Later, he appealed, alleging that the hearsay statements should not have been included in grand jury testimony and thus the indictments were defective and the conviction should be overturned. The SC disagreed and upheld his conviction, saying that grand juries may hear and consider hearsay evidence to determine whether to indict particular persons.

Couch v. United States, 409 U.S. 322, 93 S.Ct. 611 (1973) **(Law Enforcement Officers or Agencies; Searches).** A taxpayer, Couch, was investigated by the IRS for possible tax fraud. When her records were requested, she told investigators that her records were in the possession of an accountant and had been for several years. When a summons was delivered to the accountant, the accountant said that the records had been delivered to Couch's attorney. Couch invoked the right against self-incrimination under the Fifth Amendment as a reason for refusing to turn over her records to the IRS. The SC heard the case and decided in the government's favor, holding that the right of self-incrimination doesn't exist where records are in the hands of a third party, such as an accountant. Thus, there is no reasonable expectation of privacy once a defendant has turned over records to an accountant or an attorney. There is no confidential accountant-client privilege.

County of Riverside v. McLaughlin, 500 U.S. 44, 111 S.Ct. 1661 (1991) **(Law Enforce-**

ment Officers or Agencies; Arrest and Jail Detention; 48-Hour Provision). McLaughlin was arrested without a warrant and detained for several days over a weekend in the Riverside County Jail in California. The policy of arrest and detention in Riverside County provided for arraignments, without unnecessary or undue delay, within 48 hours after persons are arrested, excluding weekends and holidays. The SC heard the case and determined that a 48-hour period is presumptively reasonable, provided that an arraignment immediately follows. If not, then the government bears the burden of showing why a period beyond 48 hours is reasonable detention of an accused person. If the period is less than 48 hours, the burden shifts to the accused to show unreasonable delay.

Cox v. Louisiana, 379 U.S. 536, 85 S.Ct. 453 (1965) (**First and Fourteenth Amendments; Picketing**). The First and Fourteenth Amendments do not afford the same kind of freedom to those who communicate ideas by marching, picketing, or patrolling on streets and highways that they do to those who communicate by speech alone.

Coy v. Iowa, 487 U.S. 1012, 108 S.Ct. 2798 (1988) (**Sixth Amendment; Confrontation of Witnesses**). Coy was arrested for sexually assaulting two 13-year-old girls who were camping in a neighboring yard. The girls identified him as their attacker, and he was arrested. During the trial, a screen was erected between the witness stand and the defense table, so that Coy could not observe the girls directly when they testified against him. Following his conviction on two counts of lascivious acts with children, he appealed, alleging that his Sixth Amendment right to confront his accusers and cross-examine them in open court had been violated. The SC overturned his conviction, holding that his constitutional right to face-to-face confrontation was violated when the Iowa court placed a screen between him and his accusers.

Crane v. Kentucky, 476 U.S. 683, 106 S.Ct. 2142 (1986) (**Law Enforcement Officers or Agencies; Custodial Interrogations**). In August 1981, Crane allegedly shot to death a liquor store clerk in Louisville. He was 16 years old and was taken into custody by police for an unrelated charge. During interrogation by police, "out of a clear blue sky," Crane began to confess numerous crimes, including the murder of the liquor store clerk. Subsequently, Crane was indicted for mur-

der, but he moved to suppress his confession to police on the grounds that it had been "coerced." The court denied his motion, noting that it had been given voluntarily, and Crane was convicted. He appealed, claiming that the judge had denied him the opportunity to present evidence that his confession had been coerced. A portion of that testimony would have been the circumstances under which Crane was interrogated, the size of the interrogation room, the number of officers present, the time interval over which the interrogation occurred, and other environmental factors. The SC heard the case and reversed Crane's murder conviction on the grounds that the judge had erred by denying the admissibility of evidence about the confession circumstances. The SC declared that evidence about the circumstances under which the confession had been given was central to the defense's case, as there was no physical evidence linking Crane with the murder and his confession was the only evidence presented by the state. Thus, the defense is entitled to rebut the credibility of a confession, particularly where such evidence is so central to the defendant's claim of innocence.

Crist v. Bretz, 437 U.S. 28, 98 S.Ct. 2156 (1978) (**Corrections; Habeas Corpus Petitions; Double Jeopardy**). Bretz and a codefendant, Cline, were charged with grand larceny, offering false evidence, and obtaining money and property under false pretenses. After the jury was selected, but before any witnesses could testify, Bretz filed a motion to have one of the charges dropped, since the Montana legislature had repealed the law they were accused of violating two weeks before they actually violated it. Actually, a typographical error had made the date appear as 1974 when, in fact, the year of their alleged illegal act was 1973. Thus, their act *would* fall within the repealed statute. The false-pretenses charge was dropped against a prosecutorial protest. Bretz then made a motion to dismiss the entire criminal information so that a new charge could be filed. The motion was granted, and the judge dismissed the jury. Subsequently, prosecutors filed revised charges against Bretz and Cline based on new information. After a second jury had been impaneled, Bretz sought to have the case against him dismissed on the grounds of double jeopardy. The motion was denied, and Bretz was subsequently convicted and sentenced. He then filed a habeas corpus petition. The SC overturned his conviction, holding that jeopardy attaches in a jury trial when the jury is impaneled and sworn, and not before any witnesses testify. The Montana statute reading that "jeopardy does not attach until the first witness is sworn in a jury trial" is unconstitutional under the Fifth and Fourteenth Amendments. Thus, Bretz was freed because of double jeopardy.

Crooker v. Metallo, 5 F.3d 583 (1993) **(Corrections; Parole Officer Powers).** Parole officers conducted a "sweep" of a parolee's premises on the basis of a search incident to an arrest for alleged parole violations. The "sweep" included a quick search between the box springs and mattress of his bed, where illegal contraband was found. The First Circuit Court of Appeals held for the officer, indicating that they had possessed qualified immunity while conducting the search, and that their search had been objectively reasonable.

Crosby v. United States, 506 U.S. 255, 113 S.Ct. 748 (1993) **(Trials of Persons in Absentia).** Crosby and others were indicted by a federal grand jury in Minnesota on charges of mail fraud. Crosby appeared and posted a $100,000 bond. His trial was scheduled for a date in October, 1988, but he failed to appear. He was tried in absentia and was convicted, together with another codefendant. He was not apprehended until six months later in Florida, where he was returned to Minnesota. He was sentenced to 20 years in prison and appealed his conviction in absentia. The SC heard his appeal and overturned his sentence, holding that persons may not be tried in absentia, even if their absence is the result of fleeing the jurisdiction or escape.

Cruz v. Beto, 405 U.S. 319, 92 S.Ct. 1079 (1972) **(Corrections; First Amendment Inmate Rights).** Cruz, a Buddhist, was a prisoner in the Texas Department of Corrections. He was prohibited from using the prison chapel, from communicating with his prison inmate Buddhist representative, and from reading newspapers or obtaining news from any other sources. He was placed in solitary confinement on a diet of bread and water for a two weeks as a punishment for sharing some magazines about Buddhism with other inmates. He filed suit against the Texas Department of Corrections under Title 42, U.S.C. Section 1983 for violating his First Amendment freedom of religion rights. The SC agreed with Cruz that indeed, the Texas Department of Corrections had violated his religious rights. Thus, inmates with unconventional religious beliefs must be given a reasonable opportunity to exercise these beliefs, comparable to the opportunities of other inmates to exercise their own religious beliefs.

Cruz v. New York, 481 U.S. 186, 107 S.Ct. 1714 (1987) **(Sixth Amendment; Confrontation of Codefendants).** Two brothers, Eulogio and Benjamin Cruz, were implicated in the second-degree murder of a Bronx gas station attendant in 1982. They were tried jointly, despite Eulogio's request that he be given a separate trial. Although Benjamin did not testify, he had previously implicated Eulogio in a videotaped confession that was used in court. Eulogio's earlier confession was also read into the court record. The judge instructed the jury to disregard those portions of Benjamin's testimony that pertained to Eulogio. Eulogio Cruz was convicted. He appealed, alleging that his Sixth Amendment right to confront and cross-examine a witness had been violated when his brother's videotaped confession was played in front of the jury. The SC reversed his conviction, holding that Eulogio Cruz's Sixth Amendment right had been violated. The Court said that the confrontation clause bars admission of a nontestifying codefendant's confession incriminating the defendant at their joint trial, even if the jury is instructed not to consider it, and even if the defendant's own confession is admitted against him. Eulogio was entitled to a new trial without Benjamin's confession read into the record.

Cupp v. Murphy, 412 U.S. 291, 93 S.Ct. 2000 (1973) **(Law Enforcement Officers or Agencies; Arrests).** Murphy voluntarily went to a police station for questioning after his estranged wife had been found dead. At the station, he was questioned by police, who noted a dark spot on one of his fingers. They asked him what it was, and Murphy began to wipe it off. Police asked him if they could take some scrapings of the dark spot from under his fingernails and examine them. Murphy refused and continued to rub off the dark spot. Police moved immediately to restrain him and obtain samples of the dark substance without his permission or a warrant. The specimens turned out to be blood matching his wife's blood as well as bits of fabric from her nightgown. Murphy was charged with second-degree murder on the basis of this evidence and convicted. He appealed, arguing that since he had not been formally arrested while at the police station, police officers should have obtained a valid search warrant to seize samples of the dark substance on his fingers. The SC upheld Murphy's conviction, saying that exigent circumstances existed and police had to move quickly before Murphy could remove or destroy these specimens. The delay involved in getting a warrant could have given him time to get rid of the incriminating evidence. (*See Chimel v. California* [1969]).

Custis v. United States, ___U.S.___, 114 S.Ct. 1732 (1994) **(Habeas Corpus; Challenges of State Convictions Following Federal Conviction; Sentencing Enhancements).** Custis was convicted in federal court for possession of firearms and cocaine. He had three previous state convictions, and under the Armed Career Criminal Act, he received an enhanced sentence. He appealed, contending that the convictions in Maryland had been the result of ineffective assistance of counsel. Thus, his federal sentence should not have been enhanced. The SC upheld his conviction and sentence enhancements, noting that Custis had not raised the issue of attorney competence at either of his previous Maryland convictions. Further, he had plea bargained and knowingly and intelligently waived his rights when entering guilty pleas. Thus, the SC declared, only if Custis had been convicted and denied counsel at those times could he challenge such convictions. Defendants in federal proceedings have no right collaterally to attack validity of previous state convictions used to enhance their sentences under the Armed Career Criminal Act. However, if Custis wished to challenge his state convictions, he could do so not in federal court but rather in state court through federal habeas corpus review.

Cuyler v. Adams, 449 U.S. 433, 101 S.Ct. 703 (1981) **(Inmate Transfers and Hearings).** Adams was a prisoner in a Pennsylvania prison. As part of an Interstate Agreement on Detainers, an order was issued to try him in New Jersey for other crimes, and he was scheduled for transfer to a New Jersey prison. He appealed the transfer order. The SC ruled that inmates are entitled to a hearing on the matter of whether they should be transferred from one prison in one state to another prison in another state under the Interstate Agreement on Detainers. Thus Adams was entitled to a hearing.

Cuyler v. Sullivan, 446 U.S. 335, 100 S.Ct. 1708 (1980) **(Multiple Defendants and Defense Attorneys; Conflict of Interest).** Cuyler was one of three defendants charged with a crime. The three defendants were represented by two different attorneys. Cuyler was convicted. He appealed, alleging conflict of interest because of two different attorneys representing three clients. The SC declared that trial courts are obligated to investigate allegations of conflicts of interest provided that they are made in a timely fashion. In this case, the timeliness of appeal was poor, and no evidence was presented to cause serious question whether multiple counsel amounted to a conflict of interest.

D

Dalia v. United States, 441 U.S. 238, 99 S.Ct. 1682 (1979) **(Law Enforcement Officers or Agencies; Searches).** Dalia was suspected by FBI agents of transporting stolen goods in interstate commerce. Armed with a court order, they entered Dalia's office late one evening and planted bugging equipment. On the basis of subsequent incriminating statements obtained through such surveillance, Dalia was convicted. He appealed, contending that the incriminating evidence against him ought to have been suppressed since the issuing judge had not specifically authorize unlawful entry into his office when approving the initial surveillance. The SC held that such specific authorization was not required under a separate warrant and upheld Dalia's conviction. Thus, when courts authorize bugging of suspect offices or dwellings, such orders do not need to contain separate provisions for how entry into these offices or dwellings should be conducted.

Daniels v. Williams, 474 U.S. 327, 106 S.Ct. 662 (1986) **(Corrections; Inmate Rights).** Daniels was an inmate at the Richmond, Virginia, Jail. He slipped on a pillow left on some stairs and injured his back. He filed a lawsuit (Title 42, U.S.C. Section 1983 civil-rights action) against Williams, a sheriff's deputy who worked at the jail and had left the pillow on the stairs. Daniels alleged that Williams's negligence had deprived him of his "liberty" interest and due process according to the Fourteenth Amendment. The SC disagreed, saying that due process is not violated merely because of an official's negligent act that causes an unintentional loss of life, liberty, or property.

Darden v. Wainwright, 477 U.S. 168, 106 S.Ct. 2464 (1986) **(Sixth Amendment; Prosecutorial Misconduct).** Darden was a convicted murderer under sentence of death. He filed a habeas corpus petition challenging the exclusion of a juror from his earlier trial, allegedly improper remarks made by the prosecutor during his summation to the jury, and ineffective assistance of counsel. One prospective juror had been excused by the judge when the juror declared a moral and religious opposition to the death penalty, which was one option in Darden's case. The prosecutor had referred to him as an "animal." Darden thought the one-half hour preparation by his attorney between the trial's guilt phase and the penalty phase insufficient to prepare an adequate mitigation statement. The SC rejected all of Darden's arguments. It held that jurors may be excused from death-penalty cases where their religious views or moral feelings would render them unable to vote for such a penalty. Further, the emotional rhetoric from the prosecutor was insufficient to deprive Darden of a fair trial. Finally, evidence showed that the defense counsel had spent considerable preparatory time for both the trial and mitigation statement during the penalty phase.

Davidson v. Cannon, 474 U.S. 344, 106 S.Ct. 668 (1986) **(Corrections; Standard of Negligence)**. Davidson, a New Jersey prison inmate, was threatened with assault by other inmates. He alerted the warden and other officials of the impending harm from these other prisoners. The officers failed to act on the warning, and subsequently Davidson was injured. He brought a Title 42, U.S.C. Section 1983 civil-rights action against prison authorities for negligence that led to his injuries under the theory of "deliberate indifference." The SC rejected Davidson's argument that the prison officers had been abusively negligent. It held that the officers had not regarded the matter as particularly serious, in their opinion, and a lack of due care does not approach the seriousness of deliberate indifference.

Davis v. Alaska, 415 U.S. 308, 94 S.Ct. 1105 (1974) **(Juvenile Law; Confidentiality)**. Davis was charged with grand larceny in an Alaska court. A key witness against him was a juvenile, Green. Green was protected from extensive cross-examination by Davis's defense counsel through a special Alaska confidentiality law protecting a juvenile's status. Specifically, the defense counsel was barred from asking Green about his juvenile delinquency history. Green had previously been judged delinquent on a burglary charge. Davis was convicted. He appealed. The SC decided that Davis's attorney should have been able to cross-examine the juvenile witness, despite the Alaskan

law to the contrary. Thus, in a criminal trial, the accused is guaranteed the right to cross-examine and confront witnesses against him under both the Sixth and Fourteenth Amendments. These rights prevail over state policies or laws to the contrary.

Davis v. Georgia, 429 U.S. 122, 97 S.Ct. 399 (1976) **(Sixth Amendment; Right to Counsel)**. Davis was charged with murder. When his jury was being selected, one prospective and eligible juror expressed some doubt as to whether he could vote for the death penalty. After some questioning, he said that he could vote for the death penalty, although he didn't particularly favor it. He was excluded by the prosecutor. Davis was convicted and given a death sentence. He appealed, alleging that his Eighth Amendment right had been violated when an eligible juror had deliberately been excluded by the prosecution. The SC agreed with Davis and reversed his death sentence, holding that unless a prospective juror is irrevocably committed before trial to vote against the death penalty regardless of the facts and circumstances of the case, he may not be excluded, and if the juror is improperly excluded even though not so committed, any subsequently imposed death penalty cannot stand.

Davis v. Mississippi, 394 U.S. 721, 89 S.Ct. 1394 (1969) **(Law Enforcement Officers or Agencies; Arrests)**. Davis was one of 25 black youths who were picked up for questioning about a rape in December 1965 in Meridian, Mississippi. The rapist had been described as black. Police began a systematic process of picking up black men, without arrest warrants or probable cause, taking them to police headquarters, interrogating and fingerprinting them, and then releasing them. Davis became a suspect when his fingerprints matched those of the rapist that had been left on the woman's home window. He was convicted on the testimony of the rape victim and the fingerprint evidence. He appealed, seeking to suppress the fingerprint evidence. The SC overturned his conviction, holding that where fingerprints are obtained without a warrant or probable cause, they are invalid as evidence against criminal suspects. Thus, the SC determined that Davis' Fourth Amendment right against unreasonable searches and seizures had been violated.

Davis v. State, 422 S.E.2d 546 (1992) **(Corrections; Powers of Probation Officers)**. Davis, a probationer convicted of possessing a controlled substance, was away from his home one evening when his 10-year-old son found drugs in the house, dialed 911, and summoned police. These drugs were later used as evidence against Davis to revoke his probation. He appealed to a Georgia court of appeals, which argued that a 10-year-old, regardless of his motives, has no authority to give police permission to enter his father's home and search his bedroom for illegal contraband. In this instance, the police intrusion into Davis' home constituted unlawful entry, and no basis could be shown upon which to issue a warrant on probable cause. Police would have to find some other way to use the illegally seized evidence. The case against Davis was thrown out and his probation was reinstated.

Davis v. United States, 328 U.S. 582, 66 S.Ct. 1256 (1946) **(Law Enforcement Officers or Agencies; Consent Searches).** Davis owned a gas station in New York City under a company named Davis Auto Laundry Corporation. He was suspected of selling gasoline on the black market without rationing coupons, which were required during World War II. Two federal agents purchased gasoline from an attendant at Davis' gas station without using the required coupons. The attendant was arrested and Davis was later ordered to open his gasoline pumps so that agents could verify whether he had sufficient coupons to cover the gasoline purchases. He said that his records were in a locked office, and the federal agents threatened to knock the door down unless Davis permitted them to enter. Later, because of evidence seized as a result of a warrantless search of Davis's office, he was convicted of unlawful possession of gasoline coupons. He appealed, saying that the evidence from his office should have been obtained with a warrant. The SC upheld his conviction, saying that insufficient evidence existed to support his contention that he was forced into disclosing the contents of his office records. Thus, the SC held that the search was consensual rather than coerced. The officers also wanted to inspect public documents, not private ones. Thus, their demand of Davis was within their right.

Dawson v. Delaware, 503 U.S. 159, 112 S.Ct. 1093 (1992) **(Eighth Amendment; Aggravating Factors; Death Penalty).** Dawson was convicted of first-degree murder. During the penalty phase of his trial, a stipulation was read into the record about his membership in the Ayran Brotherhood, a white racist prison gang. The jury found sufficient aggravating factors outweighing the mitigat-

ing ones and recommended the death penalty. On appeal, Dawson contended that his First Amendment right had been violated when it was disclosed that he was a member of the Ayran Brotherhood; therefore, his death sentence ought to be reversed. The SC agreed with Dawson, holding that his First and Fourteenth Amendment rights had been violated by the admission of the Aryan Brotherhood evidence in the case, because the evidence had no relevance to the issues being decided and serious prejudicial effects had stemmed from it. His death sentence was vacated.

Deal v. United States, 507 U.S.___, 113 S.Ct. 1993 (1993) **(Sentence Enhancements).** Deal was convicted of six different bank robberies. He was also convicted of possessing and using a firearm in each of the six robberies. These convictions yielded sentences of 20 years and 5 years for each of the offenses to run consecutively. Deal appealed, arguing that the convictions and sentences were excessive. The SC upheld the constitutionality of the 105-year sentence, saying that it is not glaringly unjust to refuse to give the offender a lesser sentence merely because he escaped apprehension and conviction until the sixth crime had been committed. Thus, convicted offenders may incur sentence enhancements for various crimes they have committed but for which they have not been caught or convicted.

Delaware v. Fensterer, 474 U.S. 15, 106 S..Ct. 292 (1985) **(Sixth Amendment; Confrontation Clause).** Fensterer was accused of killing his fiancee. Circumstantial evidence was used, including a cat leash used to strangle the woman and hair fibers that matched those of Fensterer. FBI Special Agent Robillard testified at Fensterer's trial about the hair analysis but could not recall precisely which detection method had been used to establish the hair match. An expert for the defense gave a contrary opinion. Fensterer was convicted. On appeal to the Delaware Supreme Court, he argued that he had been denied adequate cross-examination of the FBI agent, because the agent could not recall the method for examining the hair fibers. The Delaware Supreme Court overturned Fensterer's conviction on the ground that "Fensterer was denied his right to effectively cross-examine a key state witness." The state appealed. The United States SC reversed the Delaware SC by holding that the agent's testimony should be evaluated according to its weight, not according to its admissibility. The expert opinion was admissible, and the fact that the agent couldn't recall the precise method of hair determination did not bar such an opinion from the jury; rather, the jury could give that opinion more or less weight in their determination of facts relevant to Fensterer's guilt or innocence. Fensterer's right to a fair trial and to cross-examination of witnesses against him had not been infringed.

Delaware v. Prouse, 440 U.S. 648, 99 S.Ct. 1391 (1979) **(Law Enforcement Officers or Agencies; Arrests; Vehicle Searches).** Prouse was randomly stopped by a police officer, who observed nothing illegal about Prouse's vehicle or the way Prouse was driving it. The officer asked Prouse for his driver's license and vehicle registration. While doing so, the officer smelled marijuana and saw it in plain view on the floor of the vehicle. Prouse was subsequently convicted of marijuana possession. He appealed, contending that the officer had had no probable cause to stop him in the first place, so all evidence found should have been suppressed. The SC agreed with Prouse, saying that officers must have probable cause in order to stop vehicles; they may not stop vehicles randomly for spot checks. This case did not make spot checks of vehicles unconstitutional. The SC allowed for states to devise schemes whereby spot checks could be made less intrusively, such as DWI stops, which are currently permitted.

Delaware v. Van Arsdall, 475 U.S. 673, 106 S.Ct. 1431 (1986) **(Sixth Amendment; Cross-Examination Rights).** Epps was stabbed to death following a New Year's Eve party in Smyrna, Delaware. On the basis of circumstantial evidence, Van Arsdall was charged with first-degree murder, because he had been one of two remaining guests at the party when Epps was killed. Various witnesses testified for the state, and evidence was introduced to show that Van Arsdall had blood-stained clothing matching the blood of the victim. A witness, Fleetwood, gave incriminating testimony against Van Arsdall. On cross-examination, the defense counsel attempted to question Fleetwood about a deal he had made with prosecutors to give testimony in the case in exchange for dropping public drunkenness charges. The court permitted the cross-examination but outside of the jury's presence. Van Arsdall was convicted of murder. He appealed on the grounds that he had been denied a fair trial because of the violation of the confrontation clause of the Sixth Amendment.

The Delaware Supreme Court reversed his conviction and the state appealed. The United States SC heard the case and vacated the Delaware SC judgment, remanding the case back to the lower court for a determination as to whether the potential bias of the prosecution witness was actually harmless error or sufficiently important to have denied Van Arsdall a fair trial. Thus, the SC said, the correct inquiry was whether, assuming that the damaging potential of the cross-examination was fully realized, a reviewing court might nonetheless say that the error was harmless beyond a reasonable doubt.

Delo v. Lashley, 507 U.S. 272, 113 S.Ct. 1222 (1993) **(Eighth Amendment; Jury Instructions; Death Penalty).** Lashley, aged 17, had brutally beaten and stabbed to death his 55-year-old physically impaired cousin. He was tried and found guilty of capital murder. At a conference held before the sentencing phase of his trial, the defense counsel sought to have the judge instruct the jury that Lashley had no significant history of prior criminal activity as a mitigating circumstance. At the same time, the counsel moved to have Lashley's juvenile record barred from the jury. The judge did not expressly rule on the latter motion. However, the judge indicated that Lashley would not be entitled to the requested assertion about his lack of prior criminal activity without appropriate evidence. Subsequently, the jury heard *no* evidence about Lashley's lack of prior criminal history. It gave the death sentence. Lashley filed a habeas corpus petition alleging that his due-process rights had been violated by the judge when he failed to issue this jury instruction. The SC rejected Lashley's appeal, holding that he was not entitled to the punishment-phase instruction that he was presumed innocent of other crimes as a mitigating factor without some proof offered by defense counsel.

Delo v. Stokes, 495 U.S. 320, 110 S.Ct. 1880 (1990) **(Eighth Amendment; Habeas Corpus).** Stokes was convicted of capital murder and sentenced to death. Following several habeas corpus petitions where Stokes raised several issues on appeal, he was granted a stay of execution. Missouri prosecutors appealed to the SC. The SC reversed the United States district judge's stay of execution. It was determined that Stokes had raised four habeas corpus petitions earlier and that he could have raised the present issue as a part of one of his earlier petitions. Thus, the SC said, it was abuse of judicial discretion for the federal judge to grant a stay of execution to Stokes when he filed his fourth petition. Thus, the application from the state to vacate the stay of execution was granted.

Demarest v. Manspeaker, 498 U.S. 184, 111 S.Ct. 599 (1991) **(Corrections; Witness Fees for Prisoners).** Demarest, a state prisoner in Colorado, was subpoenaed to appear as a witness in a federal trial. He was held in a local jail for eight days while waiting to testify. Later, he sought to be compensated for a *witness fee* of $30 per day ordinarily extended to other witnesses. He sought such fees as the result of being ordered to testify under a writ of *habeas corpus ad testificandum* ("you have the body to testify"). Lower courts rejected his claim, but the SC heard his case and ordered that the court must pay him the $30 per day witness fee, especially in view of the *habeas corpus ad testificandum* writ. The SC said that inmates are not otherwise excluded from collecting such fees, since they are subject to subpoena as any private citizen.

Demosthenes v. Baal, 495 U.S. 731, 110 S.Ct. 2223 (1990) **(Death Penalty, Stay of Execution).** Baal had attempted to rob a woman in Nevada and subsequently had stabbed her repeatedly, causing her death, stolen her car, and fled. Following Baal's subsequent arrest in Reno in February 1988, he was given his Miranda warnings and confessed. Two psychiatrists examined him in March 1988 and determined that he was competent to stand trial for the first-degree murder charges. He entered a plea of not guilty by reason of insanity. Before his trial, he was examined by other psychiatrists, who confirmed the earlier psychiatric diagnosis that Baal was "disturbed" but competent. Baal thus withdrew his not guilty by reason of insanity plea and pleaded guilty to first-degree murder and robbery, both with a deadly weapon. A three-judge Nevada panel accepted his guilty plea and sentenced him to death. On appeal he won a stay of execution from the Nevada Supreme Court. Then he tried to waive a federal review of his claim to insanity. In May 1990, Edwin and Doris Baal, his parents, filed a habeas corpus petition on his behalf, asserting that Baal was not "competent" to waive the federal review. The SC rejected the petition, concluding that federal habeas corpus statutes to interfere with the course of state proceedings must occur only in specified circumstances, which in this case were clearly lacking. The Nevada SC had granted the stay of execution without finding that Baal was not competent to waive further proceedings. The SC, therefore, vacated the stay of execution and entitled Nevada to proceed with his execution as scheduled.

Deshaney v. Winnebago County Department of Social Services, 489 U.S. 189, 109 S.Ct. 998 (1989) **(Corrections; Inmate Rights).** A four-year-old was severely beaten by his father. Custody of the child was awarded to the mother. The Winnebago County Department of Social Services was aware of the custody order but did nothing for a time to remove the boy from the home of the father, where the boy was beaten repeatedly. At one point, he was beaten so severely that he suffered permanent brain damage that left him severely retarded. The child was placed in an institution for life. The father was later tried and convicted of child abuse. The mother sued the county on behalf of her son, alleging under Title 42, U.S.C. Section 1983 that the county had violated the child's constitutional right to due process by failing to intervene to protect him against his own father. The trial court decided in favor of the county and the mother appealed. The SC upheld the original trial court decision, stating that the state does not have a duty to protect individuals who are not in state custody from harm by private individuals. Thus, there is no civil liability incurred by state officials for failure to act when persons are harmed by other members of the public. In short, the failure to protect does not result in civil damages against the state or its officials.

Dickey v. Florida, 398 U.S. 30, 90 S.Ct. 1564 (1970) **(Speedy Trials).** Dickey was charged in 1968 with various crimes allegedly committed in 1960. He tried several times to have an immediate trial, but for various reasons, his trial was delayed until 1968. Between 1960 and 1968, some witnesses died, others became unavailable. Also, some relevant police records were destroyed or misplaced. He was convicted. He appealed, arguing that his rights to a speedy trial had been violated. The SC overturned his conviction, saying that prompt inquiry is a fundamental right, and the charging authority has a duty to provide a prompt trial to ensure the availability of records, recollection of witnesses, and availability of testimony.

Dillingham v. United States, 423 U.S. 64, 96 S.Ct. 303 (1975) **(Speedy Trial).** Dillingham was arrested for a crime. After a 22-month interval, he was indicted, and 12 months after that, he was brought to trial and was convicted. He appealed, arguing that the 22-month interval between his arrest and indictment had violated his rights to a speedy trial under the Sixth Amendment. The SC declared that invocation of the speedy trial provision need not await indictment, information, or other formal charge. Thus, the delay between Dillingham's arrest, indictment, and trial was unreasonable under the Sixth Amendment; his conviction was overturned.

Dobbert v. Florida, 432 U.S. 282, 97 S.Ct. 2290 (1977) **(Eighth Amendment; Death Penalty; Penalty Phase).** Dobbert was convicted of first-degree murder, second-degree murder, child torture, and child abuse and sentenced to death. He appealed, alleging that changes in the jury decision to recommend mercy instead of the death penalty without review by a trial judge had jeopardized his chances of receiving a life sentence. Further, he claimed that there was no death penalty "in effect" in Florida at the time he was convicted, since an earlier death penalty statute had been held to be invalid when *Furman v. Georgia* (1972) had been decided. Dobbert also claimed that excessive pretrial publicity denied him the right to a fair trial. The SC rejected all of his arguments, saying that changes in the death-penalty statute were simply procedural, and thus there was no rights violation. Further, new statutes provided convicted offenders with *more* procedural safeguards rather than fewer of them. Dobbert's equal protection rights under the Fourteenth Amendment were not violated either, because the new statute did not deny him such protection. Finally, the pretrial publicity, in view of the "totality of circumstances," was insufficient to conclude that he was denied a fair trial. The SC upheld his conviction and sentence.

Doe v. Coughlin, (DCNY No. 88-CV-964) (1988) **(Corrections; Prisoners with AIDS).** A prisoner diagnosed with AIDS was placed in an isolation ward with other AIDS-positive inmates. The unnamed prisoner, Doe, filed a class-action suit alleging that his right to medical-record confidentiality had been violated as the result of such a transfer. The appellate court agreed with Doe and declared that his records were confidential and disclosure would lead to harassment and psychological pressures. This was a lower-court opinion, and other cases involving this issue have been treated and decided differently.

Doe v. United States, 487 U.S. 201, 108 S.Ct. 2341 (1988) **(Confessions; Exceptions).** An unnamed person, John Doe, was a target of a federal grand jury inquiry into possible federal offenses involving fraudulent manipulation of oil cargoes and receipt of unreported income. The grand jury compelled Doe to disclose records of bank accounts he maintained in Bermuda and the Cayman Islands. He refused to give additional information and was cited for contempt and jailed. The contempt charge stemmed from the fact that he was asked to order the banks in question to disclose bank account sums, not necessarily the names of persons on those bank accounts. Doe claimed that to have done so would have violated his right against self-incrimination under the Fifth Amendment. He appealed. The SC ruled that authorizing foreign banks to disclose records of accounts without identifying the actual documents or acknowledging their existence does not violate a person's Fifth Amendment privilege against self-incrimination.

Doggett v. United States, 505 U.S. 647, 112 S.Ct. 2686 (1992) **(Speedy Trials).** Doggett was charged in a United States district court with conspiracy to distribute cocaine. Because of various delays, mostly caused by the government, his trial was not held for 8 1/2 years. He was convicted. He appealed, contending that the 8 1/2 year delay before his case was tried violated his speedy-trial rights under the Sixth Amendment. The SC overturned Doggett's conviction, concluding that the 8 1/2 year delay in his trial, largely because of government causes, violated his Sixth Amendment rights.

Douglas v. Buder, 412 U.S. 430, 93 S.Ct. 2199 (1973) **(Corrections; Probation Revocation).** Douglas was a probationer whose probation was revoked because he had been in an automobile accident and had received a traffic citation. He did not report this citation for several days, and technically, he was in violation of his probation program, which required notification of his probation officer of any arrest without undue delay. Douglas appealed the revocation, contending that it was unreasonable. The SC reversed his revocation, holding that the issuance of a traffic citation is not an arrest, and thus the idea of reporting a traffic ticket is so devoid of evidentiary support as to be invalid under the due-process clause of the Fourteenth Amendment.

Douglas v. California, 372 U.S. 353, 83 S.Ct. 814 (1963) **(Corrections; Inmate Rights).** Douglas was convicted of several felonies. He appealed, alleging that because of indigence, an attorney had not been appointed to represent him. An appellate court ruled that appointment of counsel would have been of no value to him. The SC overturned the appellate court decision, saying that where defendants have exhausted their state remedies for appeals of convictions, they are entitled to further discretionary review by the SC of California. Further, Douglas' Fourteenth Amendment right of equal protection under the law had been violated when counsel was not provided for his state appeal.

Dow Chemical Co. v. United States, 476 U.S. 227, 106 S.Ct. 1819 (1986) **(Law Enforcement Officers or Agencies; Plain View Rule; Open Field Searches).** Dow Chemical brought suit against the United States government for conducting an unreasonable aerial surveillance of Dow's 2,000-acre property by the Environmental Protection Agency as a part of the Clean Air Act. Dow, which was subject to fines for various Clean Air Act violations, claimed that its Fourth Amendment right had been violated. The SC disagreed, holding that site inspections by aerial photography are reasonable and do not constitute a "search" in the context of the Fourth Amendment provisions.

Downum v. United States, 372 U.S. 734, 83 S.Ct. 1033 (1963) **(Double Jeopardy).** Downum was charged on six counts of stealing from the mail and forging checks. In April 1961, he appeared for trial, and a jury was sworn in. Before the actual process of witness testimony began, the prosecutor moved that the jury should be discharged since one of his crucial witnesses was not present. The jury was discharged. Two days later another jury was impaneled and trial was held, whereupon Downum was convicted. He appealed on the grounds that his right against double jeopardy under the Fifth Amendment had been violated. The SC agreed with Downum and overturned his conviction. (*See Christ v. Bretz* [1978] for a similar case and holding).

Doyle v. Ohio, 426 U.S. 610, 96 S.Ct. 2240 (1976) **(Self-Incrimination).** Doyle and another person were arrested for selling marijuana. At the time of their arrest, they were told their Miranda rights and elected to remain silent. However, during their trial, they gave exculpatory testimony that had been unknown by the prosecution. When cross-examined by prosecutors as to why they had not disclosed such exculpatory information at the time of their arrest, Doyle and his friend said that according to their Miranda rights, they had the right to remain silent. They were convicted. They appealed, alleging a violation of their due-process rights under the Fourteenth Amendment. The SC reversed their conviction, saying that the government had had no right to impeach their exculpatory testimony at trial because of their invocation of the silence privilege under *Miranda*. Thus, the due-process rights of Doyle and his co-defendant had been violated.

Draper v. United States, 358 U.S. 307, 79 S.Ct. 329 (1959) **(Law Enforcement Officers or Agencies; Search and Seizure).** An informant whose information had been reliable and accurate in the past gave a federal agent a description of Draper, time of arrival, and other information that was corroborated by the agent, which resulted in Draper's arrest. The subsequent search uncovered heroin in Draper's possession. He was convicted. He appealed, arguing that the information given by the informant, who died before Draper's trial and was unable to offer testimony, was hearsay and thus had not justified the eventual search incident Draper's arrest. However, the SC reasoned that such hearsay from a previously reliable informant was sufficient to establish probable cause to stop and search Draper.

Duckworth v. Eagan, 492 U.S. 195, 109 S.Ct. 2875 (1989) **(Confessions; Exceptions).** Duckworth, a murder suspect, was interrogated by Indiana officials, who gave him a general Miranda statement to sign. The form did not contain the full litany of the Miranda warning, but it was sufficiently specific to advise Duckworth of his right to an attorney, and that if he could not afford one, an attorney would be provided free if and when the case went to court. Duckworth made several incriminating statements. The following day, he was given another Miranda form to sign and did so. He was interrogated, confessed, and was convicted of the murder. He appealed, contending that his first waiver was not "valid" because it was not the exact Miranda warning carried by police officers for guidance when arresting suspects. Thus, he argued, his later confession was inadmissible as well, since it was prompted by his initial statements. The SC disagreed and said that the Miranda "general" warning was sufficiently specific to constitute a valid warning for lawful and constitutional police interrogations. The SC declared that the Miranda warning is not required to be read to suspects in the exact form as contained in the *Miranda* case. The evidence obtained against Duckworth in both interrogations was admissible against him, and his murder conviction was upheld.

Duckworth v. Serrano, 454 U.S. 1, 102 S.Ct. 18 (1981) **(Corrections; Inmate Rights).** A prisoner, Serrano, sought to challenge his conviction through a habeas corpus petition. He alleged that he had been denied effective assistance of counsel at his trial, and thus his due-process rights had been violated. Serrano had not sought relief in state courts *first*, however. The SC took significant notice of the fact that he had commenced his petition with the Seventh Circuit Court of Appeals, a federal appellate body, rather than in an Indiana state court. The SC dismissed his petition because he had failed to exhaust all state remedies. The significance of this case is that any petitioner who has been convicted of a state crime must first exhaust all state remedies before attempting to file petitions in federal courts. This is considered a landmark case because it obligates prisoners to direct their habeas corpus petitions first to state courts before they pursue federal remedies. This decision is no doubt calculated to reduce crowded federal court dockets.

Dumbra v. United States, 268 U.S. 435, 45 S.Ct. 546 (1925) **(Law Enforcement Officers or Agencies; Stop and Frisk).** During Prohibition, Dumbra operated a winery. Revenue agents observed an undercover Prohibition agent buy two gallons of wine from Dumbra. Several other transactions were completed with illegal liquor being exchanged for money. In each case, Dumbra was observed walking to the back of a store and returning with illegal liquor in gallon bottles. Subsequently, officials obtained a search warrant and raided Dumbra's premises, confiscating a large quantity of liquor. Dumbra was convicted. He appealed, saying that there was no probable cause as the basis for the search warrant issued. The SC disagreed with Dumbra and upheld his conviction, saying that under the circumstances of the ready availability of liquor on the premises and the frequent sales to agents by various Dumbra family members, sufficient probable cause existed to justify the issuance of the search warrant.

Dunaway v. New York, 442 U.S. 200, 99 S.Ct. 2248 (1979) **(Law Enforcement Officers or Agencies; Arrest; Exclusionary Rule).** Dunaway was involved in a murder according to a reliable informant; however, sufficient evidence could not be presented to obtain an arrest warrant. Police officers picked up Dunaway anyway (not formally arresting him) and took him to police headquarters, where he was interrogated for several hours. Subsequently, he made several incriminating statements that led to his being charged with and convicted of murder. Dunaway appealed, contending that police had lacked probable cause to arrest him initially. The SC agreed and overturned his conviction. The significance of *Dunaway* is that police officers cannot take persons into custody and interrogate them for purposes of criminal prosecution without showing probable cause. The SC declared that Dunaway's detention and interrogation at the stationhouse by police were both illegal, and thus his subsequent confession was inadmissible in court.

Duncan v. Louisiana, 391 U.S. 145, 88 S.Ct. 1444 (1968) **(Courts; Juries; Jury Trials).** Duncan was convicted in a bench trial of simple battery in a Louisiana court. The crime was punishable as a misdemeanor, with two years' imprisonment and a fine of $300. In Duncan's case, he was sentenced to only 60 days and a fine of $150. He appealed, saying that he had demanded a jury trial and none was provided. The SC agreed with Duncan, saying that a crime with a potential punishment of two years is a serious crime, despite the sentence of 60 days imposed. Thus, for serious crimes, under the Sixth Amendment, Duncan was entitled to a jury trial.

Dunn v. White, 45 CrL 2360 (1989) **(Corrections; Prisoners with AIDS).** A prisoner, Dunn, objected to a blood test to determine whether he was HIV-positive as violative of his right against an unreasonable search and seizure under the Fourth Amendment. The court of appeals ruled that drawing his blood in a hospital setting was the equivalent of drawing blood in hospital settings to determine DUI cases. There is no unreasonableness associated with such "seizures" of blood.

Duren v. Missouri, 439 U.S. 357, 99 S.Ct. 664 (1979) **(Sixth Amendment; Right to Counsel).** Duren was charged with various crimes in a Missouri court. At the beginning of his trial, a jury was selected under a jury system that automatically exempted women from jury duty if they so chose to be exempted. He was convicted. He appealed, contending that the jury-selection process that excluded women had deprived him of a fair trial, since it denied him the opportunity to be tried by a jury of his peers as a cross-section of the community. The SC agreed with Duren that he had indeed been deprived of a fair trial. Specifically, the SC said that if women, who are "sufficiently numerous and distinct from men," are systematically excluded from venires, the fair-cross-section requirement for jury selection cannot be satisfied. Thus, Duren's conviction was overturned on the basis of a deliberate pattern of underrepresentation of women on juries in Missouri.

E

Eddings v. Oklahoma, 455 U.S. 104, 102 S.Ct. 869 (1982) **(Juvenile Law; Death Penalty).** On April 4, 1977, Eddings and several other companions ran away from their Missouri homes. In a car owned by Eddings' older brother, they drove, without direction or purpose, eventually reaching the Oklahoma Turnpike. Eddings had several firearms in the car, including rifles that he had stolen from his father. At one point, he lost control of the car and was stopped by an Oklahoma State Highway Patrol officer. When the officer approached the car, Eddings stuck a shotgun out of the window and killed the officer outright. When Eddings was subsequently apprehended, he was sent to criminal court on a prosecutorial motion. Efforts by Eddings and his attorney to oppose that action failed. In a subsequent two-stage trial, several aggravating circumstances were introduced and alleged, while several mitigating circumstances, including Eddings' youth, mental state, and potential for treatment, were considered by the trial judge. However, the judge did not consider Eddings' "unhappy upbringing and emotional disturbance" as significant mitigating factors to offset the aggravating ones. Eddings' attorney filed an appeal that eventually reached the SC. Although the Oklahoma Court of Criminal Appeals reversed the trial judge's ruling, the SC reversed the Oklahoma Court of Criminal Appeals. The reversal pivoted on whether the trial judge had erred by refusing to consider the "unhappy upbringing and emotionally disturbed state" of Eddings. The trial judge had previously acknowledged the boy's youth as

a mitigating factor. The *fact* of Eddings' age, 16, was significant, precisely because the majority of justices did not consider it significant. Rather, they focused upon the issue of introduction of mitigating circumstances specifically outlined in Eddings' appeal. They decided Oklahoma could lawfully impose the death penalty on a juvenile who was 16 years old at the time he committed murder. The case raised the question of whether the death penalty as applied to juveniles was "cruel and unusual" punishment under the Eighth Amendment of the Constitution. The SC avoided the issue. The Justices did *not* say it was "cruel and unusual punishment," but they also did *not* say it wasn't. What they said was that the youthfulness of the offender is a mitigating factor of great weight that must be considered. Thus, many jurisdictions were left to make their own interpretations of the high court opinion.

Edwards v. Arizona, 451 U.S. 477, 108 S.Ct. 1880 (1981) **(Law Enforcement Officers or Agencies; Confessions).** Edwards was implicated in a crime by an accomplice who gave police a taped confession. Edwards was given his Miranda warning. He wanted to strike a deal with police, but he also wanted an attorney. At that point, his interrogation stopped and an attorney was appointed. The next day, two officers visited Edwards in his cell and gave him his Miranda warning again. They asked him if he would talk to them. After indicating that he didn't want to talk with them, he asked if he could hear the taped confession of his accomplice. After hearing this, he gave incriminating statements to police. Edwards was charged with and convicted of various crimes, with his confession used as evidence against him in court. He appealed, seeking to suppress his confession. The SC overturned his conviction and threw out the confession, saying that once he had requested an attorney, police interrogation should have ceased entirely, even though he had been told his Miranda rights a second time before he gave the incriminating statements. His attorney had not been present during the second custodial interrogation. Edwards had already advised police of his desire not to say anything, but they had persisted. Thus, police may not continue a custodial interrogation of a suspect represented by an attorney who requests to remain silent, even though the Miranda warning is given more than once and preceding any subsequent interrogation. Suspect-initiated conversation, however, may be used for incrimination purposes.

Elder v. Holloway, ___U.S.___, 114 S.Ct. 1019 (1994) **(Title 42, U.S.C. Section 1983 Civil Rights Action Against Police Officers for Excessive Use of Force).** Elder was arrested without warrant by Idaho police because they believed he was wanted in Florida on a criminal charge. At first, they planned to arrest him in his workplace, which was a public area, where an arrest warrant is not required. However, they found that Elder had left work early and gone home. They continued to his home, where they surrounded the dwelling and ordered him out of the house. Authorities instructed Elder to crawl out of the house, but Elder, who suffered from epilepsy, walked out of the house instead and immediately experienced an epileptic seizure. He fell to the ground, where his head struck the pavement, causing him to suffer permanent brain trauma and paralysis. Subsequently, Elder filed suit against the police officers under Title 42, U.S.C. Section 1983, alleging that the officers had violated his civil rights by arresting him in his home without a suitable warrant. The United States district court granted the officers a summary judgment on the grounds of their qualified immunity from such suits. Elder appealed. The SC overturned the summary judgment and ordered the case sent back to district court for a trial resolution of factual questions. However, it did not offer an opinion or ruling on the qualified immunity defense. Rather, it placed the matter in the circuit court of appeals to resolve the issue in light of all prevailing law and authority.

Elkins v. United States, 364 U.S. 206, 80 S.Ct. 1437 (1960) **(Law Enforcement Officers or Agencies; Search and Seizure).** The SC overturned the so-called silver-platter doctrine, which had previously allowed state authorities who discovered evidence of a federal crime in an illegal search to turn the evidence over to federal agencies for prosecution, as long as federal agents did not participate in the search.

Enmund v. Florida, 458 U.S. 782, 102 S.Ct. 3368 (1982) **(Corrections; Death Penalty; Eighth Amendment and Cruel and Unusual Punishment).** Enmund was the driver of a vehicle where his co-defendants committed first-degree murder. Under a felony murder statute, he was treated by the court as though he had committed the murder with the other two defendants, and he was convicted and sentenced to death. He ap-

pealed. The SC reversed Enmund's conviction, saying that where the defendant did not take life, or use, or attempt to use lethal force, the death penalty was too severe a punishment.

Escobedo v. Illinois, 378 U.S. 478, 84 S.Ct. 1758 (1963) **(Law Enforcement Officers or Agencies; Custodial Interrogations; Right to an Attorney).** An informant told police that Escobedo had murdered someone. Without an arrest warrant, the police arrested Escobedo and commenced to interrogate him, without benefit of counsel, on his way to the police station. Escobedo asked to speak with an attorney on several occasions during a subsequent long interrogation period. At certain points, he was escorted about the station to various rooms, and at these times, he would see his attorney at a distance down the hall. The attorney was denied access to his client, who was told that his attorney "did not wish to see him" or was "unavailable." After many hours of intensive interrogation, Escobedo eventually confessed to murder and was convicted. He appealed. The SC overturned the conviction on the grounds that Escobedo had been denied counsel and that interrogation had proceeded despite his plea to have counsel present. Thus, the denial of counsel to Escobedo when he requested it had violated his right to due process. The case is also significant because the SC stressed the fact that initially, police officers were merely investigating a murder. At some early point, their mode shifted to accusation, where they accused Escobedo of murder. Thus, whenever police officers shift their questioning from investigatory to accusatory, defendants are entitled to counsel and to refrain from conversing with officers unless counsel is present.

Espinosa v. Florida, 505 U.S. 1079, 112 S.Ct. 2926 (1992) **(Eighth Amendment; Aggravating Factors in Sentencing).** Espinosa was convicted of first-degree murder, second-degree murder, attempted murder, grand theft, and burglary, and was sentenced to death. He appealed. One of the aggravating circumstances articulated by the judge to the jury during the penalty phase of the trial included the words, "especially wicked, evil, atrocious or cruel." This particular phrase had been declared unconstitutionally vague in several prior cases, including *Stringer v. Black* (1992), *Clemons v. Mississippi* (1990), and *Maynard v. Cartwright* (1988). Thus, it was an invalid aggravating factor. Nevertheless, it was used and given "great weight" in finding Espinosa eligible for the death penalty. The SC held that the jury must not be permitted to weigh invalid aggravating circumstances and vacated the death penalty. Thus, Espinosa's due process rights had been violated.

Estelle v. Gamble, 429 U.S. 97, 97 S.Ct. 285 (1976) **(Corrections; Inmate Rights).** Gamble was an inmate in a Texas prison. He was injured while performing an inmate work assignment. During the next several months, he saw medical personnel on at least 17 occasions and subsequently was declared fit to work. He continued to refuse work assignments and eventually filed a Title 42, U.S.C. Section 1983, action alleging cruel and unusual punishment. Gamble alleged that personnel had not X-rayed his back and other body areas to determine whether bones were broken. The SC said that whenever prison authorities ignore a prisoner's medical ailments or complaints, this would constitute cruel and unusual punishment arising from deliberate indifference to inmate medical needs. But in Gamble's case, it was clear that officials had not expressed deliberate indifference to Gamble's medical complaints; they had *not* acted negligently.

Estelle v. Smith, 451 U.S. 454, 101 S.Ct. 1866 (1981) **(Death Penalty; Fifth and Sixth Amendment; Right to Counsel).** Smith was a Texas prisoner who had been convicted of murder and given a death sentence. He sought through habeas corpus to have his conviction and death sentence overturned on the basis that the prosecution, without his attorney's knowledge, had used statements from a psychiatrist who had examined Smith, and to whom Smith had confided various incriminating facts that would lead the psychiatrist to believe that Smith would pose a danger to others in the future. The SC reversed his conviction and death sentence, holding that the admission of the doctor's testimony at the penalty phase of the trial had violated Smith's Fifth Amendment right against self-incrimination, since he had not been advised before the examination that his statements could or would be used against him in court. Further, the fact that the doctor gave testimony about the future dangerousness of Smith without Smith's attorney's knowledge violated Smith's Sixth Amendment right to effective assistance of counsel.

Estelle v. Williams, 425 U.S. 501, 96 S.Ct. 1961 (1976) **(Corrections; Inmate Rights; Discovery).** Williams was charged with assault with intent to commit murder and stood trial for the offense in his prison clothing. After he was con-

victed, he appealed, contending that he should not have had to stand trial in such clothing because it biased the case against him and violated the equal protection clause of the Fourteenth Amendment. The SC agreed that Williams should not have been tried while wearing prison attire; however, because he had not objected during trial to wearing this clothing, his appeal was negated. This case is significant because although Williams didn't win his point, he caused subsequent courts to be sensitive to how defendants should be dressed during their trials. Currently, defendants cannot be compelled to wear prison clothing during their trials, but they must make timely and proper objections.

Evitts v. Lucey, 469 U.S. 387, 105 S.Ct. 830 (1985) **(Sixth Amendment; Right to Counsel).** Lucey was convicted in a Kentucky court of trafficking in controlled substances. He filed an appeal, without representation by counsel; it was later dismissed. Eventually, Lucey sought habeas corpus relief, contending that he had been denied the effective assistance of counsel on his first appeal. The SC granted his petition and reinstated his appeal as a matter of right, holding that as an integral part of due process, Lucey was entitled to be represented by an attorney in his initial appeal of his conviction. Because he had not been permitted counsel on the appeal, the dismissal of his appeal was unconstitutional.

Ex parte Crouse, 4 Wharton (Pa.) 9 (1838) **(Rights of Government Over Children).** A girl was committed to the Philadelphia House of Detention by the court because she was considered unmanageable. She was not given a trial by jury. Rather, her commitment was made arbitrarily by a presiding judge. The father tried to secure her release, claiming that parental control of children is exclusive, natural, and proper. A higher court rejected the father's claim, upholding the power of the state to exercise necessary reforms and restraints to protect children from themselves and their environments. In effect, children were temporarily deprived of any legal standing to challenge decisions made by the state in their behalf. Although this decision was only applicable to Pennsylvania citizens and their children, other states took note of it and sought to invoke similar controls over errant children in their jurisdictions.

Ex parte Hawk, 321 U.S. 114, 64 S.Ct. 448 (1944) **(Corrections; Inmate Rights).** Hawk was convicted in a Nebraska court of a crime. He filed a habeas corpus petition, alleging various trial irregularities. He first filed his action in federal court, which rejected his appeal. He then appealed to the SC, which also rejected him, holding that Hawk had not exhausted all of the state remedies at his disposal. Hawk should have sought relief first in Nebraska courts, but had not done so.

Ex parte Hull, 312 U.S. 546, 61 S.Ct. 640 (1941) **(Corrections; Inmate Rights).** In 1941, prison and jail officials carefully screened all outgoing inmate mail, including legal documents and petitions addressed to state or federal courts. Petitions by inmates to the court for virtually any grievance or complaint, founded or unfounded, were often conveniently trashed by prison officials, who claimed that these petitions were improperly prepared and thus ineligible for court action. Prison and jail policies permitted the disposal of such materials. In *Hull*, the SC declared that no state or its officers may abridge or impair a prisoner's right to have access to federal courts. The court, not prison or jail officials, would determine whether petitions were properly prepared. Although the original *Hull* decision pertained to a particular class of legal petitions, it was eventually extended to include access to the courts for all petitions.

F

Fare v. Michael C., 442 U.S. 707, 99 S.Ct. 2560 (1979) **(Law Enforcement Officers or Agencies; Juveniles and Confessions).** Trial court judges must evaluate the voluntariness of confessions by juveniles by examining the totality of circumstances. Michael C. was a juvenile murder suspect who was taken into custody by police, told his Miranda rights, and questioned. When asked if he wanted an attorney, he asked to have his probation officer present. Police advised him that they would contact his probation officer later, and then they asked him if he wanted to answer some of their questions. Michael C. made subsequent incriminating statements and police charged him with murder. He was convicted. He appealed, alleging that his request for a probation officer was the equivalent of asking for an attorney, and thus, his Fifth Amendment right against self-incrimination had been violated when police did not provide him with a probation officer. The SC disagreed and concluded that when he was told

his Miranda rights, he had given up his right to remain silent because he had not specifically asked for an attorney to be present during further questioning and he had given incriminating statements voluntarily. Probation officers do not perform the same functions as attorneys and so are irrelevant concerning the Miranda warning given to criminal suspects.

Faretta v. California, 422 U.S. 806, 95 S.Ct. 2525 (1975) **(Courts; Right to Counsel).** Faretta, who was charged with grand theft, desired to represent himself. The judge ruled that he had no constitutional right to represent himself in the case and appointed a public defender to defend him. Faretta was convicted. He appealed, arguing that he had a right to represent himself. The SC overturned his conviction, holding that Faretta indeed had a right knowingly and intelligently to waive his right to counsel and represent himself in the criminal proceeding. Thus, he had been denied his constitutional right to act as his own counsel.

Ferguson v. Georgia, 365 U.S. 570, 81 S.Ct. 756 (1961) **(Right to Counsel).** Ferguson was charged with murder. During his trial, he requested that his attorney should ask him questions while on the witness stand, but the Georgia court prohibited him from testifying according to an incompetency statute. Ferguson was subsequently convicted of murder. He appealed. The SC said that the denial of the right to have Ferguson's attorney ask him questions was a denial of counsel and in violation of his due-process rights guaranteed by the Fourteenth Amendment.

Fex v. Michigan, 507 U.S. 403, 113 S.Ct. 1085 (1993) **(Speedy Trials).** Fex, a prisoner in Indiana, was brought to trial in Michigan 196 days following his trial request to Michigan officials and 177 days after the request was received by Michigan prosecutors. He was convicted. He appealed, alleging that the 180-day limit for a speedy trial had been violated. The SC upheld his conviction, noting that the statutory 180-day period had not begun until the Michigan prosecutor received his request. The SC said that if the warden in Indiana delayed the forwarding of a prisoner's request for a speedy trial, that merely postponed the starting of the 180-day clock, which is triggered by the prosecutors' receipt of notice.

Fisher v. United States, 425 U.S. 391, 96 S.Ct. 1569 (1976) **(Law Enforcement Officers or Agencies; Searches).** Fisher was under investigation by the IRS for income tax fraud. His accountant placed Fisher's papers in the hands of Fisher's attorney, and the government subpoenaed the papers. Subsequently, Fisher was convicted. He appealed, alleging that his Fifth Amendment right against self-incrimination had been violated. The SC upheld his conviction, saying that there was no confidential disclosures made between Fisher and his attorney; thus Fisher's Fifth Amendment rights had not been violated as the result of some vague attorney-client privilege he presumed existed, simply by a possession of important documents. Fisher had merely sought legal advice, not an opportunity to make disclosures normally covered under the ideal attorney-client privilege scenario.

Fitzpatrick v. Bitzer, 427 U.S. 445, 96 S.Ct. 2666 (1976) **(Corrections; Inmate Rights).** Present and retired female employees of the State of Connecticut brought a suit against the state, alleging that a state benefit plan discriminated against them. The petitioners requested a back-pay award and reasonable attorney's fees for filing the suit. The lower court denied them relief, and the SC heard their case. The SC ruled in their favor, saying that under the Eleventh Amendment, they should not be prevented from seeking back-pay awards from the state. The SC held that the current version of the state's retirement plan was discriminatory against them because of their gender.

Fletcher v. Weir, 455 U.S. 603, 102 S.Ct. 1309 (1982) **(Sixth Amendment; Prosecutorial Misconduct).** Weir was in a fight with Buchanan outside a nightclub and stabbed Buchanan, who died. Weir fled the scene. Later, when apprehended by the police, he said nothing about the incident. However, during the trial, he took the stand in his own defense and for the first time alleged self-defense as the reason for stabbing Buchanan. The prosecutor sought to discredit him by referring to his pre-arrest silence. When Weir was convicted, he appealed, alleging a violation of his Fifth Amendment rights against self-incrimination by the prosecutor's effort to impeach his testimony in court. The SC ruled that for impeachment purposes, it is proper for prosecutors to make such comments about the defendant's pre-arrest silence, particularly if the defendant raises self-defense as his defense. Thus, Weir's right against self-incrimination had not been jeopardized by the prosecutor who cross-examined him regarding his pre-arrest silence.

Florida v. Bostick, 501 U.S. 429, 111 S.Ct. 2382 (1991) **(Law Enforcement Officers or Agencies; Seizures).** Bostick was a passenger on a bus from Miami to Atlanta. Florida police boarded the bus without any suspicion but rather with a simple intent to catch drug smugglers. They approached Bostick, asked him a few questions, asked to see his ticket, and then asked if they could search his bag. They advised Bostick he had a right to refuse, but he gave his consent. They discovered cocaine in his bag and he was subsequently convicted of cocaine possession. He appealed and the SC upheld the conviction, because given the totality of circumstances, Bostick had not been under arrest and had given his consent at the time of the search. Further, the fact that Bostick was on a bus did not constitute a "seizure" in the Fourth Amendment context. The SC concluded that the governing test is whether a reasonable person would feel free to decline the police offer to search his or her luggage, given the totality of circumstances.

Florida v. Jimeno, 499 U.S. 934, 111 S.Ct. 1801 (1991) **(Law Enforcement Officers or Agencies; Consent Searches).** Jimeno was overheard arranging a drug transaction over the telephone by a police officer. The officer followed Jimeno and stopped his car when Jimeno made an illegal traffic movement. He advised Jimeno that he believed Jimeno had narcotics in his possession and asked if he could search Jimeno's car. Jimeno consented, and the officer found narcotics in a closed container within the car. Later Jimeno was convicted. He appealed, moving to suppress the evidence in the closed container, arguing that it had been beyond the scope of the warrantless and consensual search of his vehicle. The SC upheld his conviction, stressing that police had had Jimeno's permission to search the car and that this permission had not been qualified to exclude containers that might contain illegal narcotics. (*See United States v. Ross* [1982]).

Florida v. Riley, 488 U.S. 445, 109 S.Ct. 693 (1989) **(Law Enforcement Officers or Agencies; Plain View Rule; Open Field Searches).** Riley was growing marijuana on his property, which was partially blocked from view by a greenhouse. A helicopter surveillance of Riley's yard by sheriff's officers revealed marijuana plants in plain view. A search warrant was obtained based upon these observations, and Riley's home was searched and the plants seized. Riley was subsequently convicted of growing marijuana. He appealed, contending that the helicopter surveillance constituted a "search" of his premises and thus a search warrant was required to conduct it. The SC upheld Riley's conviction, noting that helicopter observations of ground structures in plain view do not constitute searches as set forth in the Fourth Amendment. Thus, the warrant had been lawfully obtained on the basis of probable cause. Search warrants are not required by police who travel the airways and who observe contraband in plain view with the naked eye.

Florida v. Royer, 460 U.S. 491, 103 S.Ct. 1319 (1983) **(Law Enforcement Officers or Agencies; Search and Seizure).** Royer was an airline passenger in the Miami airport. DEA agents thought he fit a "drug courier profile", inasmuch as he bought a one-way ticket for cash and under an assumed name; he also was young, nervous, casually dressed, with heavy luggage. He gave police his driver's license with his correct name when requested. He also followed them to a room, again at their request, where they asked him if they could look through his luggage. He consented. They found marijuana, and Royer was eventually found guilty. He appealed, alleging that his Fourth Amendment rights had been violated because of the unreasonableness of his original stop and detention and the subsequent search. The SC agreed and overturned his conviction, saying that it is insufficient for police merely to have consent, without probable cause, to make a warrantless search of personal effects, such as luggage. The SC stressed Royer's lengthy detention and noted it was a serious intrusion into his privacy, especially as police had no probable cause to engage him in further searches. Consent given after an illegal act by police is tainted by the illegal act.

Florida v. Wells, 495 U.S. 1, 110 S.Ct. 1632 (1989) **(Law Enforcement Officers or Agencies; Vehicle Searches).** Wells was stopped and arrested for DWI. After his car was impounded by police, they asked him if they could inventory its contents. Wells gave them permission. They found and pried open a large trunk, where they discovered a large quantity of marijuana. Wells was convicted of possessing a controlled substance. He appealed. The SC overturned his conviction, saying that so-called inventory searches are not for the purpose of discovering evidence of a crime. Further, no department policy existed that would permit such intrusions into Wells' automobile.

Had there been such a policy in effect, it is likely that the marijuana evidence would have been successfully used against him. The SC stressed the significance of an absence of police department policy relating to inventory searches of impounded vehicles.

Ford v. Wainwright, 477 U.S. 399, 106 S.Ct. 2595 (1986) **(Corrections; Death Penalty).** Ford was convicted of murder in Florida in 1974 and sentenced to death. At no time during his trial had he shown any signs of being mentally incompetent. However, when he appealed in 1982, he was examined by two psychiatrists over a period of time and determined to be mentally incompetent. His condition deteriorated to such an extent that he was almost catatonic. Nevertheless, the governor of Florida appointed three other psychiatrists to examine Ford, and they found him sane enough to be executed. However, the SC decided in Ford's favor, holding that insane persons cannot be executed. Furthermore, the SC held that Florida's procedures for determining a person's competence were inadequate. This is an interesting case, because Ford was sane when he committed the offense and was convicted of it; he became insane afterwards.

Forrester v. White, 484 U.S. 219, 108 S.Ct. 538 (1988) **(Corrections; Probation and Parole).** Forrester, a female probation officer, was demoted and discharged from her job by a judge, White. Forrester alleged that the judge had fired her because of her gender, in violation of the Fourteenth Amendment equal-protection clause. White disagreed, saying that he had absolute immunity from such litigation by Forrester because of his judicial status. The SC said otherwise, concluding that the act of firing Forrester was not a judicial one, and thus White did not enjoy absolute immunity because of his judicial position. The judge was subject to suits by those employees under him who believe they were unfairly treated or discriminated against.

Forsyth County, GA, v. Nationalist Movement, 505 U.S. 123, 112 S.Ct. 2395 (1992) **(First Amendment Right of Assembly).** An ordinance in Forsyth County, Georgia, provided for the payment of variable fees depending upon events and the types of marches or assemblies planned. The Nationalist Movement filed suit to challenge the validity of this ordinance and the fees it imposed on a sliding scale. The SC declared the Forsyth County ordinance to be invalid, because it unconstitutionally tied the amount of fees to the content of speeches and lacked adequate procedural safeguards; no limit on such a fee could remedy these constitutional violations.

Foster v. California, 394 U.S. 440, 89 S.Ct. 1127 (1969) **(Law Enforcement Officers or Agencies; Lineups).** Foster confessed to police the day following a robbery and gave information about the other two robbers who had participated. He was placed in a subsequent lineup with other men, all of whom were shorter. Foster was wearing a jacket similar to the one he had worn in the robbery. The eyewitness couldn't be sure that Foster was the robber and asked police if he could speak with Foster. After conversing with him in a private room, the witness still could not positively identify him as one of the robbers. A week later, the witness viewed another lineup, this time with Foster and four different persons from those in the first lineup. This time the witness positively identified Foster. Foster was convicted of the robbery. He appealed. The SC overturned Foster's conviction (despite his admission) and said that the police methods used were improper, because such lineups biased witness identifications of suspects. In this case, the police had violated Foster's right to due process by biasing the lineup for an eyewitness.

Foucha v. Louisiana, 504 U.S. 71, 112 S.Ct. 1780 (1992) **(Insanity Pleas).** Foucha was charged with aggravated burglary and the discharge of a firearm. He pleaded not guilty by reason of insanity. Examining doctors found him lacking mental capacity, and he was acquitted on this basis. Subsequently, he was committed to the East Feliciana Forensic Facility until such time as doctors recommended that he be released or until further court order. Five years later, several doctors recommended to the judge that Foucha should be released from the mental health facility, but one doctor believed that Foucha continued to present a danger to either himself or to others. The judicial decision was to order the continued confinement of Foucha. He appealed. The SC ruled that the Louisiana statute requiring the continued confinement of someone acquitted by reason of insanity following a hospital review committee recommendation to release the person after a finding of no mental illness, was a violation of Foucha's due-process rights. Foucha was ordered released.

Francis v. Franklin, 471 U.S. 307, 105 S.Ct. 1965 (1985) **(Jury Instructions).** Franklin was convicted of murder by a Georgia court and sent to prison. He was awaiting treatment at a dentist's office outside the prison when he attempted to escape. He stole a pistol and shot and killed the resident of a nearby house, but he was apprehended shortly thereafter and charged with murder. When the trial was concluded and the jury was given instructions from the judge, the judge advised the jury, among other things, that Franklin's acts were "presumed to be the product of a person's will, but the presumption may be rebutted. A person of sound mind and discretion is presumed to intend the natural and probable consequences of his acts." This phraseology shifted the burden of proving at least one of the elements of the criminal offense of malicious murder to the defendant rather than the prosecution. He was convicted. The SC heard his appeal and overturned his conviction, holding that it had been a harmful and irreversible error for the judge to have instructed the jury as to Franklin's *intent* to commit the crime. The SC said that a jury instruction that creates a mandatory presumption, whereby the jury must infer the presumed fact if the state proves certain predicate facts violates the due-process clause if it relieves the state of the burden of persuasion on an element of an offense. The state, not the defendant, must prove intent.

Francis v. Henderson, 425 U.S. 536, 96 S.Ct. 1708 (1976) **(Corrections; Grand Juries; Sixth Amendment).** Francis, a black man, was convicted in Louisiana of felony murder. He did not appeal. But six years later he filed a habeas corpus petition, alleging that blacks had been excluded from the grand jury that had indicted him, and thus he had been deprived of a fair trial. The SC upheld his conviction, reasoning that his request failed to conform to the state requirement that any objection to the composition of the grand jury must be made in advance of the trial.

Franks v. Delaware, 438 U.S. 154, 98 S.Ct. 2674 (1978) **(Law Enforcement Officers or Agencies; Fourth Amendment; Search Warrants).** Franks was suspected of first-degree rape, second-degree kidnapping, and first-degree burglary. Authorities obtained a search warrant for Franks' premises. When police officers gave a sworn affidavit supporting the warrant, they gave misstatements and untruths. Franks's defense counsel sought to introduce evidence that the search warrant was illegally obtained on the basis of deliberate lies by police, but the judge denied his request. Franks was convicted. He appealed, contending that the search leading to the incriminating evidence against him had been prefaced by an illegal search warrant containing deliberate untruths from police officers under oath. The SC overturned his convictions on these grounds. The SC said if, after a hearing, Franks established by a preponderance of evidence that false statements led to the issuance of a search warrant and were intentionally made, and if the false statements were necessary to establish probable cause to justify the search warrant's issuance, then the search warrant had to be voided and the fruits of the search excluded from the trial to the same extent as if probable cause had been lacking on the face of the affidavit.

Frazier v. Cupp, 394 U.S. 731, 89 S.Ct. 1420 (1969) **(Law Enforcement Officers or Agencies; Consent Searches).** Frazier was indicted together with his cousin, Rawls, for murder in Oregon. Some question arose about whether Rawls, who pled guilty, would actually testify against Frazier, and whether the prosecutor ought to rely on such testimony. The prosecutor made statements to the jury about what they could expect to hear from Rawls. This and other statements by the prosecutor were regarded as prejudicial to Frazier, especially a reference to a "confession" made by Rawls implicating Frazier. Also, when Frazier was being questioned by police, he had said in passing, "I had better get a lawyer," but he had continued to answer questions. He was convicted. His appeal to the SC through a writ of habeas corpus was that his Miranda rights had not been observed and that there was prosecutorial misconduct and that his due-process rights had been violated. The SC upheld his conviction. The prosecutor's comments were harmless errors and Frazier had been advised of his Miranda rights but had simply failed to exercise them.

Frisbie v. Collins, 342 U.S. 519, 72 S.Ct. 509 (1952) **(Law Enforcement Officers or Agencies; Exclusionary Rule).** Collins, living in Chicago, was a suspect in a murder investigation in Michigan. Michigan authorities found Collins in Chicago and forcibly brought him back to Michigan to stand trial. Collins was convicted. He appealed, arguing that the officers had had no right to "kidnap" him in Chicago and strong-arm him back into Michigan. The SC heard Collins' case. Although the arrest appeared to be invalid, irregular, and perhaps illegal, Collins' return to Michi-

gan placed him within the jurisdiction where he stood accused of murder. The SC upheld Collins' conviction, saying that nothing permits a guilty person rightfully convicted to escape justice because he is brought to trial against his will. Bounty hunters perform similar tasks by bringing persons back into jurisdictions from which they have fled to avoid prosecution. Thus, the case significance is that unlawful arrests of criminal suspects do not jeopardize their convictions in subsequent trials where they have been brought forcibly into jurisdictions where criminal charges have been brought against them.

Fuller v. Oregon, 417 U.S. 40, 94 S.Ct. 2116 (1974) **(Indigents; Ability to Pay Attorney Fees and Court Costs).** Fuller was accused of third-degree sodomy. He entered a guilty plea and was sentenced to a five-year probation term, contingent upon his successfully completing a jail work-release program that permitted him to attend a nearby college and upon his reimbursing the county for fees involving an attorney and an investigator because of his indigency. Fuller appealed, alleging that the state could not constitutionally impose as a condition of his probation the repayment of legal fees and court costs. The SC upheld his conviction and probation program conditions, holding that Oregon's recoupment statute merely provides that a convicted person who later becomes able to pay for his counsel may be required to do so. This obligation may be imposed upon persons with a foreseeable ability to meet it, and it is enforced only against those who actually become able to meet it without hardship. Indigent offenders who cannot repay these court costs cannot have their probationary terms revoked simply because of their inability to pay. In Fuller's case, however, he had the ability to repay the costs incurred for his court activity, and thus Oregon was able to enforce the recoupment statute against him.

Furman v. Georgia, 408 U.S. 238, 92 S.Ct. 2726 (1972) **(Death Penalty).** Furman, a black man, was accused of murder. Evidence that he was mentally deficient was presented at his trial. Despite this defense and others, Furman was convicted and sentenced to death. He appealed the sentence on grounds that his Fourteenth Amendment rights were being violated. At the time, disproportionately more blacks were receiving the death penalty than white murderers. The SC set Furman's death penalty aside, saying that the racially discriminatory way in which the death penalty was being administered in Georgia constituted cruel and unusual punishment. It is important to note that the SC never said that the death penalty was per se unconstitutional; rather, the manner in which it was being administered was unconstitutional because it violated the Eighth and Fourteenth Amendments.

G

Gagnon v. Scarpelli, 411 U.S. 778, 92 S.Ct. 1756 (1973) **(Corrections; Probation Revocation).** Scarpelli pled guilty to a charge of robbery in July, 1965, in a Wisconsin court. He was sentenced to 15 years in prison. But the judge suspended this sentence on August 5, 1965, and placed Scarpelli on probation for 7 years. The next day, August 6, Scarpelli was arrested and charged with burglary. His probation was revoked without a hearing, and he was placed in the Wisconsin State Reformatory to serve his 15-year term. About 3 years later, Scarpelli was paroled. Shortly before his parole, he filed a habeas corpus petition, alleging that his probation revocation had been invoked without a hearing and without benefit of counsel. Thus he had been denied due process. Following his parole, the SC acted on his petition and ruled in his favor. Specifically, it said that Scarpelli had been denied his right to due process, because no revocation hearing had been held and he had not been represented by court-appointed counsel as an indigent. In effect, the Court, referring to *Morrissey v. Brewer* (1972), said that "a probation revocation, like parole revocation, is not a stage of a criminal prosecution, but does result in loss of liberty. . . . We hold that a probationer, like a parolee, is entitled to a preliminary hearing and a final revocation hearing in the conditions specified in *Morrissey v. Brewer*." The significance of this case is that it equated probation with parole as well as equating the respective revocation proceedings. Although the Court did not say that all parolees and probationers have a right to representation by counsel in all probation and parole revocation proceedings, it did say that counsel should be provided in cases where the probationer or parolee makes a timely claim contesting the allegations. No constitutional basis exists for providing counsel in all probation or parole revocation proceedings, but subsequent probation and parole revocation hearings usually involve defense counsel if legitimately requested. The SC declaration has been liberally interpreted in subsequent cases.

Gardner v. Broderick, 392 U.S. 273, 88 S.Ct. 1913 (1968) **(Self-Incrimination).** Gardner was a police officer who was dismissed from the force for refusing to waive his right against self-incrimination before a grand jury investigating police corruption. Gardner appealed his dismissal, alleging that the department had no right to dismiss him for invoking his Fifth Amendment privilege. The SC agreed, declaring it unlawful to compel testimony from persons where their jobs are in jeopardy for refusing to testify or give incriminating information. Thus attempts to compel testimony from persons at the expense of their constitutional rights are unconstitutional and a violation of their due-process rights.

Gardner v. Florida, 430 U.S. 349, 97 S.Ct. 1197 (1977) **(Corrections; Death Penalty).** Gardner was convicted of first-degree murder. Following the conviction, a sentencing hearing was held in which the jury recommended life imprisonment. However, the judge cited aggravating factors and imposed the death penalty. It was important that portions of the presentence investigation relied upon by the judge for his knowledge of aggravating factors were not given to the defense under discovery. Apparently, there were several mitigating factors cited in the report favorable to Gardner but ignored by the judge. Gardner appealed. The SC overturned his conviction, acknowledging that the government had not complied with the discovery law by failing to give Gardner a complete presentence investigation report. The report contained information to support a life sentence rather than the death penalty. The SC declared that the failure of the Florida Supreme Court to consider or even read the confidential portion of the report violated Gardner's right to due process under the Fourteenth Amendment.

Garner v. United States, 424 U.S. 648, 96 S.Ct. 1178 (1976) **(Corrections; Probation and Parole).** Garner was charged in a United States district court in California with violating various federal gambling statutes. His tax returns were introduced as evidence against him, showing him to be a "professional gambler." He was convicted. Garner appealed, arguing that his tax returns were privileged documents and that to reveal their contents to a jury would be self-incriminating. The SC upheld his conviction, saying that he should have exercised his right against self-incrimination at the time his tax returns were prepared and when he stated his profession as "gambling." Thus, the SC gave considerable significance to the timeliness of asserting the Fifth Amendment self-incrimination claim.

Garrity v. New Jersey, 385 U.S. 493, 87 S.Ct. 616 (1967) **(Public Employees; Self-Incrimination).** Garrity and other police officers were suspected of fixing traffic tickets. Garrity was advised that any statement he made could be used against him and that if he refused to answer any question, he would be fired. Therefore, Garrity made various incriminating statements. He was convicted of conspiracy to violate state traffic laws. He appealed, alleging that his Fifth Amendment right against self-incrimination had been violated because his disclosures had been inherently coerced. The SC overturned his conviction, saying that circumstances where a person may lose his job if he fails to give incriminating information are coercion. Thus the Fourteenth Amendment prohibits the use of such coerced evidence in a subsequent criminal proceeding if the statements were obtained under threat of removal from office; this privilege is extended to all public employees, including police officers.

Geders v. United States, 425 U.S. 80, 96 S.Ct. 1330 (1976) **(Sixth Amendment; Right to Counsel).** Geders was charged in a United States district court with possessing marijuana and illegally importing controlled substances. During a 17-hour overnight recess of his trial, Geders asked to speak with his attorney, but his request was denied by the federal district judge. He was convicted. He appealed, alleging a violation of his Sixth Amendment right to counsel. The SC agreed and overturned Geders's conviction, holding that the federal judge's order to deprive Geders of seeing his counsel between his direct examinations and cross-examination by the government had deprived Geders of the effective assistance of counsel. The federal judge had attempted to sequester the defendant, and though sequestration of witnesses is within the broad powers of federal judges, they are prohibited from sequestering defendants from seeing their own attorneys.

Gelbard v. United States, 408 U.S. 41, 92 S.Ct. 2357 (1972) **(Wiretaps).** Gelbard was subpoenaed to testify before a grand jury based upon information disclosed from a judge-authorized wiretap of Gelbard's home. Gelbard refused to answer grand jury questions, contending that he had a right to privacy in his telephonic communications. Because of the existence of a statute forbidding such intercepted telephonic transmissions, he was able to avoid a contempt charge for refusing to provide testimony to the grand jury.

Georgia v. McCollum, 505 U.S. 42, 112 S.Ct. 2348 (1992) **(Peremptory Challenges).** McCollum was indicted on charges of aggravated assault and simple battery. During jury selection, his attorney used his peremptory challenges to strike certain prospective jurors from jury duty because of their race. McCollum was acquitted. The state challenged the use of these peremptory challenges, arguing that they had created a biased jury as in *Batson v. Kentucky* (1986), where the prosecutor used peremptory challenges for racial-bias purposes. The SC agreed with the state and rejected the defendant's attorney's use of peremptory challenges for racial purposes. Thus, according to *Batson* and *McCollum*, neither prosecutors nor defense attorneys may deliberately use their peremptory challenges to excuse jurors on the basis of their race.

Gerstein v. Pugh, 420 U.S. 103, 95 S.Ct. 854 (1975) **(Law Enforcement Officers or Agencies; Arrest; Appointment of Counsel).** Pugh and Henderson were arrested in Dade County, Florida. They were charged with robbery and carrying a concealed weapon. The prosecutor alone determined the issue of probable cause in holding them without bail. Pugh and Henderson were convicted. They filed a habeas corpus petition with the court, declaring that a judge should have determined whether probable cause existed for pretrial detention in a hearing. The SC upheld their conviction, holding that it is not necessarily the case that judicial oversight to determine probable cause for pretrial detention is essential. The SC said that because of its limited function and its nonadversarial nature, the probable-cause determination is not a "critical stage" in the prosecution that would require appointed counsel. However, the Fourth Amendment requires a timely judicial determination of probable cause as a prerequisite to detention. It is not necessary, however, for counsel to be present in such a determination.

Gertz v. Robert Welch, Inc., 418 U.S. 323, 94 S.Ct. 2997 (1974) **(Corrections; Damages).** A Chicago police officer, Nuccio, was convicted of murder. The victim's family retained Gertz, a prominent attorney, to represent them in a civil action against Nuccio. An article appeared in a magazine shortly thereafter, alleging that the murder had been part of a Communist conspiracy to discredit local police. The article went on to blame Gertz, the attorney, for "framing" Nuccio. It further alleged that Gertz had a criminal record and it labeled him a "Communist-fronter." Gertz sued the magazine because of the defamatory statements that were not true. The trial court determined that Gertz had not proved that the defamatory statements were published with a knowledge of their falsity or in reckless disregard for the truth. The court decided in favor of the magazine. The SC overturned the lower court, holding that magazines may not claim constitutional privilege against liability arising from suits from persons who are not public officials or public figures. The media are not immune from suits from private individuals whom they have defamed.

Gideon v. Wainwright, 372 U.S. 335, 83 S.Ct. 792 (1963) **(Right to Counsel).** Gideon broke into a poolroom allegedly with the intent to commit larceny. This act was regarded as a felony in Florida. Gideon was indigent and asked for a lawyer to represent him. He was advised by the judge that counsel could only be appointed to persons if the offense involved the death penalty. Therefore, Gideon represented himself and was convicted. He appealed. The SC overturned his conviction, saying that all indigent defendants are entitled to court-appointed counsel in felony cases. (*See Argersinger v. Wainwright* [1972] for a narrowing of this provision to minor crimes or misdemeanor cases).

Gilbert v. California, 388 U.S. 263, 87 S.Ct. 1951 (1967) **(Self-Incrimination).** Gilbert was first arrested by an FBI agent on charges that he had robbed a bank in Alhambra, California, and had killed an investigating police officer. During the robbery, Gilbert had given the bank tellers a note demanding money. When the FBI agent interviewed Gilbert following his arrest, without an attorney present, Gilbert gave the agent some handwriting samples. These were incriminating, because they matched the writing in the note at the bank robbery scene. Gilbert was convicted. He appealed, arguing that his Fifth Amendment right against self-incrimination had been violated when he gave samples of his handwriting to the FBI agent. The SC upheld Gilbert's conviction and re-jected his Fifth Amendment claim, noting that handwriting samples are mere physical evidence, not evidence of "self-incrimination." Self-incrimination pertains to utterances and documents that contain incriminating statements or content-specific information.

Gilmore v. Utah, 429 U.S. 1012, 97 S.Ct. 436 (1976) **(Corrections; Death Penalty).** Gilmore, a convicted murderer, was ordered executed in Utah. Shortly thereafter, he waived his right to appeal and asked for a speedy execution. Several of his friends interceded on his behalf and moved for a stay of execution. The stay was granted, and Gilmore promptly moved to have the stay terminated. The SC heard Gilmore's case and removed the stay of execution, arguing that whenever a convicted murderer has been sentenced to death and has made a knowing and intelligent waiver of any and all federal rights that he might have asserted after the sentence was imposed, a stay of execution may be terminated over any objections from family members or friends. Thus, if death-row inmates wish intelligently and knowingly to waive their rights to appeal death sentences, they may do so over objections from friends and relatives.

Gitlow v. New York, 268 U.S. 652, 45 S.Ct. 625 (1924) **(Freedom of Speech; First Amendment).** Gitlow, a member of the Socialist Party, was convicted of violating a New York sedition law by distributing leaflets advocating the overthrow of the government. He appealed. Although the SC did not overturn Gitlow's conviction, it did specify that the First Amendment right of free speech was applicable to states as well as the federal government.

Go-Bart Importing Company v. United States, 282 U.S. 344, 51 S.Ct. 153 (1931) **(Law Enforcement Officers or Agencies; Searches).** Gowens and Bartels, owners of the Go-Bart Importing Company, were suspected of possessing, selling, and importing intoxicating liquor in violation of the Prohibition Act. Federal officers went to their place of business with arrest warrants. There, they told a secretary that they had a search warrant, a false statement since they had no such warrant. O'Brien, the government agent who falsely stated that he had a search warrant, proceeded to search the premises and discovered various incriminating documents, which led to the conviction of Gowens and Bartels. They appealed, arguing that no search warrant had been obtained and that this was an unreasonable search in violation of their Fourth Amendment rights. The SC overturned their conviction and ordered the prosecutor to suppress any seized evidence emanating from the illegal search.

Godfrey v. Georgia, 446 U.S. 420, 100 S.Ct. 1759 (1980) **(Corrections; Death Penalty).** Godfrey shot and killed his mother-in-law and wife by firing a gun through a window. He subsequently chased his daughter and beat her with the butt of the gun. Following his conviction, at his sentencing hearing, the judge said that his crimes were outrageously or wantonly vile, horrible, or inhuman in that they involved torture, depravity of mind, or aggravated battery of the victim (at 1760). Godfrey appealed, arguing that such phraseology was a violation of the cruel-and-unusual-punishment provision of the Eighth Amendment. The SC overturned his conviction, saying that this broad and vague construction of statutory aggravating circumstances suggested an arbitrary and capricious infliction of the death sentence. Thus, the judge's language in sentencing was interpreted as arbitrary and capricious, inconsistent with the defendant's rights under the Eighth Amendment. A state's responsibility, the SC said, was to authorize capital punishment in such ways as to provide clear, objective, and rational standards for such sentencing.

Godinez v. Moran, 507 U.S.___, 113 S.Ct. 2680 (1993) **(Death Penalty; Right to Counsel).** Moran was charged with several murders, although he had entered a plea of not guilty by reason of insanity. Several doctors reported test results that indicated Moran was competent to stand trial. Following these psychiatric reports, Moran advised the Nevada court that he wished to dismiss his attorneys and plead guilty to the multiple murders. The court determined that Moran made these guilty pleas knowingly, intelligently, and voluntarily. Further, Moran waived his right to assistance of counsel and other rights associated with guilty pleas. Subsequently, after he was convicted and sentenced to death, he filed a habeas corpus petition alleging that even though he had earlier requested to represent himself, he was incompetent to do so. The SC upheld the conviction and death sentence, holding that the competency standard for pleading guilty or waiving the right to counsel is the same as the competency standard for standing trial. Moran had been found competent in both instances and had knowingly and in-

telligently waived the rights he was now alleging had been violated.

Gomez v. United States District Court, 503 U.S. 653, 112 S.Ct. 1652 (1992) **(Eighth Amendment; Death Penalty).** Gomez was convicted of capital murder and sentenced to death in California. He was to die by the gas chamber, but he lodged an appeal with the SC, alleging that death by cyanide gas was cruel and unusual punishment. The SC heard his appeal and rejected it. It is significant to note that Gomez had made several prior habeas corpus appeals, where this particular allegation had not been included. Thus, the SC stressed Gomez's last-minute attempt to manipulate the judicial process as one reason for not ruling favorably for him. In effect, the SC did not rule precisely on whether death by cyanide gas was cruel and unusual; only that Gomez had not properly raised such an issue in his previous habeas corpus petitions.

Grady v. Corbin, 495 U.S. 508, 110 S.Ct. 2084 (1990) **(Fifth Amendment; Self-Incrimination; Grand Jury Indictments; Double Jeopardy).** Corbin was a motorist involved in the death of one person and injury to another. He pled guilty to driving while intoxicated. Subsequently, he was indicted by a grand jury on charges of reckless manslaughter, criminally negligent homicide, and third-degree reckless assault stemming from the same incident. It is important to note that driving while intoxicated is an element establishing each of these other offenses. Since Corbin had already pled guilty to DWI and been convicted, he sought to dismiss the indictment on the grounds of double jeopardy. An appellate court dismissed the indictment, and the state sought to challenge this dismissal with an appeal to the SC. The SC affirmed the dismissal on double-jeopardy grounds. The SC said that the double-jeopardy clause bars a subsequent prosecution if, to establish an essential element of an offense charged in that prosecution, the government will prove conduct that constitutes an offense for which the defendant has already been prosecuted.

Graham v. Connor, 490 U.S. 396, 109 S.Ct. 1865 (1989) **(Law Enforcement Officers or Agencies; Excessive Use of Force).** Graham was a diabetic who asked his daughter to drive him to the store to buy orange juice for his condition. When he entered the store, there were long lines, and Graham hurried back out and told his daughter to drive him to another store. A police officer observed Graham's quick entry and exit at the store, became suspicious, and stopped Graham's daughter as an "investigative stop" while he determined to find out "what happened" back at the store. In the meantime, Graham became belligerent and was handcuffed by police. He sustained further "injuries" while handcuffed. When police found that nothing had happened at the store, they released Graham, who filed a Title 42, U.S.C. Section 1983 civil-rights suit against the officers for using excessive force unnecessarily against him. The SC declared that police officers are liable whenever they use excessive force, and that the standard they should use is objective reasonableness rather than substantive due process when they subdue suspicious persons. This is tantamount to a totality-of-circumstances test applied to discretionary actions of police officers in the field when they are dealing with situations where only partial information exists that a crime may have been committed. The reasonableness of the situation and force used is determined on the spot, considering all circumstances.

Gray v. Mississippi, 481 U.S. 648, 107 S.Ct. 2045 (1987) **(Death Penalty; Juror Bias).** In June 1982, Gray was indicted for murder in the stabbing death of a man during a kidnapping. When the jury was being selected, the prosecution excluded for cause a prospective juror, who had equivocated but ultimately stated that she could consider the death penalty under appropriate circumstances. Gray was convicted of the murder and the death penalty was imposed. Gray appealed, alleging that he had been deprived of a fair trial since a prospective juror had been excused for cause, which was improper under the law. The SC overturned Gray's conviction on the grounds that the juror had been unlawfully and improperly excused from jury duty. Thus this exclusion was not only improper but potentially prejudicial to the trial outcome and death sentence.

Green v. Georgia, 442 U.S. 95, 99 S.Ct. 2150 (1979) **(Death Penalty).** Green was charged with the murder of a woman, Allen. During the trial, it was disclosed that he and an accomplice, Moore, had raped and murdered Allen. Green was convicted. Moore had been tried separately and convicted, receiving the death penalty. During the penalty phase of Green's trial, Green tried to introduce testimony from another party, Pasby, who had overheard Moore say that he (Moore) had killed Allen by shooting her twice after sending

Green on an errand. The judge refused to introduce Pasby's testimony, which would have mitigated Green's role in Allen's murder. Green appealed and the SC overturned the death sentence, holding that it was improper for the judge to exclude exculpatory testimony from a witness during the sentencing phase, as such testimony was relevant to the critical issue of the death penalty. Thus, Green had been denied a fair trial in regard to his punishment.

Greenholtz v. Inmates of Nebraska, 442 U.S. 1, 99 S.Ct. 2100 (1979) **(Corrections; Probation and Parole).** The Nebraska prison system annually reviews files of inmates who are parole-eligible, and the Nebraska Parole Board decides whether they should be released in a two-stage proceeding: one phase consists of an initial review, and the second phase is a final parole hearing. The Parole Board decides whether the inmate is a good or bad parole risk, partially on the basis of evidence presented at these hearings. Inmate rights given by the Parole Board include the right to present evidence, call witnesses, be represented by counsel, and receive a written statement of reasons in the event parole is denied. Inmates believed that they were entitled to more constitutional rights relating to their early release than those given by the Parole Board and appealed to the SC. The Court upheld the Nebraska Parole Board and declared that inmates have no inherent constitutional rights to be released conditionally before the expiration of their valid sentences. Parole is a *privilege,* not a *right.* Furthermore, parole is optional with each state. For instance, Maine and the federal prison system have abolished parole. These jurisdictions currently use a form of supervised release.

Greer v. Spock, 424 U.S. 828, 96 S.Ct. 1211 (1976) **(Corrections; Inmate Rights).** Spock and others were members of a political party in 1972 seeking to make speeches on a government reservation, Fort Dix, New Jersey. They were prohibited from making such speeches on the reservation and appealed to a federal district court, where they argued that their First and Fifth Amendment rights had been violated. Injunctive relief was granted by a New Jersey court, and the government appealed. The SC reversed the injunction, declaring that Spock and others had no constitutional right to make political speeches and distribute leaflets on a military reservation, that regulations banning such political speeches and demonstrations and governing the distribution of literature were not constitutionally invalid on their face, and that regulations had not been unconstitutionally applied to Spock. Thus politicians have no constitutional right to campaign on military installations.

Gregg v. Georgia, 428 U.S. 153, 96 S.Ct. 2909 (1976) **(Corrections; Death Penalty).** Gregg was convicted of robberies and murders in Atlanta and sentenced to death. According to newly enacted provisions by the Georgia legislature, death penalty cases required bifurcated trials (two-stage trials), where guilt or innocence could be determined in the first stage, and the penalty could be assessed in the second stage. The provisions further required that in the penalty phase the jury was to consider and weigh aggravating and mitigating circumstances, and if the former outweighed the latter, the death penalty was to be imposed. An automatic appeal of the death sentence was also prescribed by law. Gregg appealed his death sentence, but the SC upheld it, saying that the procedures Georgia had instituted for applying the death penalty were constitutional and were not in violation of either the Eighth or Fourteenth Amendments.

Griffin v. California, 380 U.S. 609, 85 S.Ct. 1229 (1965) **(Corrections; Inmate Rights).** Griffin was accused of a crime in California and decided during the trial not to take the stand or answer questions in his own defense. However, the prosecutor commented on the fact that Griffin failed to speak on his own behalf and that this failure was interpreted to reflect the guilt of the defendant, when in fact Griffin did not want his prior criminal record exposed. He was convicted. Griffin appealed, protesting the constitutionality of the California statute allowing prosecutors (and judges) the privilege of commenting about a defendant's decision not to testify in his own behalf. The SC ruled the California statute unconstitutional. Thus, prosecutors and others may not comment on the refusal of a defendant to testify as a Fifth Amendment right to avoid making incriminating statements. (*See Adamson v. California* [1947] for a similar case and prior ruling).

Griffin v. Illinois, 351 U.S. 12, 76 S.Ct. 585 (1956) **(Courts; Rights of Indigents).** Griffin and an accomplice were convicted of armed robbery in a Cook County court. Following their conviction and claiming to be indigent, Griffin requested a copy of the court transcript at no charge.

Under existing Illinois law, only persons sentenced to death and indigent could make such requests. Their request was denied by Illinois. Griffin appealed. The SC reversed the Illinois court, holding that the due-process rights of Griffin had been violated by denying him transcript. The SC further stated that it did not hold that Illinois must purchase a stenographer's transcript in every case where a defendant cannot buy it, but it believed the state should find other means of affording adequate and effective appellate review to indigent defendants.

Griffin v. Wisconsin, 483 U.S. 868, 107 S.Ct. 3164 (1987) **(Corrections; Probation and Parole).** Griffin was placed on probation after being convicted of resisting arrest, disorderly conduct, and obstructing a Wisconsin police officer in 1980. One condition of Griffin's probation was that he not possess a firearm. An informant advised Griffin's probation officer that Griffin had a weapon on his premises. Based on previous reliable information provided by the information, the officer believed that reasonable grounds existed to conduct a warrantless search. He went to Griffin's home, searched it without a warrant, and discovered a gun. Griffin was subsequently arrested, prosecuted, and convicted for being a convicted felon in possession of a firearm. He was sentenced to two years. He appealed on the grounds that the search of his premises should have been conducted with a properly issued warrant and based upon probable cause. The SC declared that probation officers are entitled to special consideration because of their demanding jobs. They should not be held to the more stringent standard of probable cause since they must often take immediate action to detect crimes or seize illegal contraband relating to their probationer or parolee clients. The reasonable grounds standard, a lesser standard than probable cause, is upheld to the extent that probation or parole agency policies make provisions for such warrantless searches of offender premises in their jurisdictions. The ruling was not intended as a blanket right to violate a person's Fourth Amendment rights on a whim.

Griffith v. Kentucky, 479 U.S. 314, 107 S.Ct. 708 (1987) **(Corrections; Death Penalty).** Griffith, a black man, was arrested for conspiracy to distribute marijuana. During his trial in Jefferson County, the prosecutor used four out of five peremptory challenges to strike from jury duty four out of five prospective black jurors. Griffith was convicted. He appealed, saying that the prosecutor had violated his right to due process by striking from jury duty most of the black candidates. He said the case of Batson v. Kentucky (1986) should be retroactively applied to his case. The SC overturned his conviction, holding that the *Batson* case, prohibiting prosecutors from using their peremptory challenges to give racial bias to a jury pool, should be retroactively applied where a showing exists that such conduct has occurred. Thus, Griffith's case qualified for a retroactive application of *Batson*. The SC held that a new rule for the conduct of criminal prosecutions is to be applied retroactively to all cases, state or federal, pending on direct review or not yet final, with no exception for cases in which the new rule constitutes a "clear break" with the past.

Grunewald v. United States, 353 U.S. 391, 77 S.Ct. 963 (1957) **(Corrections; Inmate Rights).** Grunewald was convicted of conspiring to defraud the United States government by influencing witnesses testifying in a grand jury hearing in a criminal case. The conspiracy was alleged to have occurred in 1948 and 1949, although prosecution for this conspiracy was not implemented until October 1954. Grunewald appealed, arguing that the statute of limitations had expired for prosecuting his case. The SC overturned his conviction, basically agreeing with Grunewald. The SC said that the government had failed to show that any overt acts had occurred since October 1951, three years prior to October 1954, the three-year statute-of-limitations period. In any case, government prosecutors must be mindful of the statute of limitations governing conspiracy cases, and even though they can demonstrate that a conspiracy might be continuing, their case fails if it cannot show any overt act associated with this conspiracy during the statute-of-limitations period.

Gustafson v. Florida, 414 U.S. 260, 94 S.Ct. 488 (1973) **(Law Enforcement Officers or Agencies; Searches Incident to Arrest).** Gustafson was driving in Brevard County when he was stopped for a traffic violation. He did not have a valid driver's license, so the officer arrested him. Then he was searched. A cigarette package was recovered, which contained marijuana cigarettes. He was charged for marijuana possession and convicted. He appealed, arguing that this search of his person had violated his rights against unreasonable searches and seizures under the Fourth Amendment. The SC upheld his conviction, saying that full searches of persons incident to lawful arrests do not violate Fourth or Fourteenth Amendment rights of arrestees. Thus, police may conduct a thorough search of a lawfully arrested person.

H

Hafer v. Melo, 502 U.S. 21, 112 S.Ct. 358 (1991) **(Legal Liabilities of Public Officials).** Melo was a government employee who was fired by Hafer, the auditor general of Pennsylvania. Melo sued Hafer underHam Title 42, U.S.C. Section 1983, seeking monetary damages. Hafer claimed immunity because of her official capacity. The suit was filed in federal court and Hafer was being sued in her personal capacity, not her official capacity. Thus, she was not immune from Section 1983 lawsuits. (*See Will v. Michigan Department of State Police* [1989] for a comparative opinion about this issue). Currently, state officials cannot be sued in state or federal courts in their official capacity, but they may be sued in their personal capacity.

Hagen v. Utah, ___U.S.___, 114 S.Ct. 958 (1994) **(Jurisdiction).** Hagen pled guilty to distributing drugs on a Utah Reservation for American Indians. He appealed, arguing that the State of Utah did not have jurisdiction over the reservation; rather, jurisdiction was properly placed in a United States district court. A Utah court of criminal appeals reversed Hagen's conviction on this ground, but the Utah Supreme Court reversed this reversal and reinstated Hagen's original conviction. He appealed to the United States SC, which upheld his conviction. The SC said that the reservation had once been a federally protected reservation, but it had been opened to non-Indians during the early 1900s; thus it was no longer a federally protected area. Therefore, Utah courts had exercised proper jurisdiction over Hagen.

Haines v. Kerner, 404 U.S. 519, 83 S.Ct. 1336 (1972) **(Corrections; Inmate Rights).** Haines, an inmate of the Illinois State Penitentiary, was involved in a fight with another inmate. He sustained various injuries and was placed in solitary confinement as a punishment. While in solitary confinement, he was forced to sleep on the floor with only a blanket. He had both a prior foot injury and circulatory ailments that were not treated by correctional officials during this time. He later sued the prison and state, but his case was dismissed outright by an appellate court without entitling Haines to show proof of his injuries or the harsh treatment. He appealed again. The SC reversed the decision of the lower court, holding that Haines had a right to show proof as a means of recovering damages from the state. This narrow SC holding means that prisoners seeking relief are entitled to show proof that they suffered damages. Courts may not bar them from showing such proof. The SC did not rule on the merits of Haines' arguments, only the procedural matter of being able to show proof in court to sustain his petition.

Haley v. Ohio, 332 U.S. 596, 68 S.Ct. 302 (1948) **(Juvenile Law; Confessions)**. A 15-year-old youth, Haley, suspected of being involved in a store robbery, was taken into custody one night for interrogation. The police questioned Haley for five hours, rotating their interrogator teams in shifts. They showed Haley confessions from some of his friends implicating him. Eventually, he confessed. At no time was he advised of his right to counsel; an attorney who tried to see him was rebuffed by police. Even his mother was unable to see him. Haley was subsequently convicted of murder and sentenced to life imprisonment. He appealed. Although this case was before the *Miranda* case and defendant's rights were not police priorities when conducting interrogations, the SC detected a high degree of coercion in Haley's case. The conviction was overturned, and the SC concluded that juvenile suspects may not be coerced into confessing to crimes. Involuntary confessions cannot be used in court.

Ham v. South Carolina, 409 U.S. 524, 93 S.Ct. 848 (1973) **(Jury Trials)**. Ham was convicted of a crime. When the jury was being selected, he was prohibited from asking prospective jurors if they harbored any sort of racial bias or any bias because Ham wore a beard. He was convicted. He appealed, arguing that he had the right to question jurors about their biases. The SC overturned Ham's conviction and declared that defendants have a right to inquire about possible juror bias against persons who wear beards. It is also permissible for *judges* to inquire of potential jurors whether they are racially prejudiced. (*See Ristaino v. Ross* [1976] for a comparative case.)

Hamilton v. Alabama, 368 U.S. 52, 82 S.Ct. 157 (1961) **(Corrections; Probation and Parole; Appointment of Counsel)**. Hamilton, an indi-

gent, was indicted for murder by a grand jury. At his arraignment following the indictment, he was not represented by counsel and he was subsequently convicted of murder. He appealed, contending that he had been disadvantaged by not having counsel present during the arraignment. The SC overturned his conviction, saying that arraignments are critical stages requiring the presence of a court-appointed attorney in indigent cases. In Alabama at the time, defendants were required to show that they were in need of counsel. Hamilton had not requested counsel at the time, but counsel had not been offered either.

Hammett v. Texas, 448 U.S. 725, 100 S.Ct. 2905 (1980) **(Death Penalty; Mental Competency)**. Hammett was convicted of murder and sentenced to death. On his behalf, an appeal was filed by his attorney. Hammett moved to have the petition withdrawn, so that his execution could proceed without any legal delay. The SC held that Hammett withdrew the petition knowingly and intelligently, and therefore granted his motion. The significance of this case is that persons sentenced to death can waive their appeal rights if they desire, with full knowledge of the consequences, including an execution.

Hampton v. United States, 425 U.S. 484, 96 S.Ct. 1646 **(Entrapment)**. Hampton was suspected of trafficking in narcotics. A paid government informant agreed to supply him with narcotics so that Hampton could, in turn, sell these drugs to another undercover agent, in this case a DEA agent. Hampton was arrested, charged with trafficking in narcotics, and convicted. He appealed, arguing that entrapment existed because the government had provided illegal narcotics to an acquaintance and that Hampton had never intended to sell heroin nor had even known that he was dealing in it at the time. The SC upheld Hampton's conviction, saying that entrapment does not exist, even when government agents supply heroin in arranging a situation meriting an arrest for narcotics trafficking. (*See United States v. Russell* [1973] for a similar case and holding.) The SC stressed the fact that Hampton had had a predisposition to traffic in narcotics at the time the government provided the illegal drugs to the paid informant. This was a very controversial case, because the government engaged in what many persons regarded as outrageous conduct by supplying a narcotic, heroin, to a paid informant to create its own crime scenario.

Harlow v. Fitzgerald, 457 U.S. 800, 102 S.Ct. 2727 (1982) **(Legal Liabilities of Police Officers; Good Faith).** Harlow was an aide to President Richard Nixon, and Fitzgerald was an Air Force official who was dismissed, based upon allegations by Harlow and others. Fitzgerald sued for unlawful discharge, alleging that Harlow was retaliating for Fitzgerald's intent to call attention to extravagant Air Force spending. Harlow claimed absolute immunity because of his position relative to President Nixon as a government official. The SC said that government officials are not entitled to absolute immunity, only to qualified immunity. It stressed the importance of official conduct relative to employee dismissals and whether such conduct violates clearly established statutory or constitutional rights of which a reasonable person should have known.

Harmelin v. Michigan, 501 U.S. 957, 111 S.Ct. 2680 (1991) **(Mandatory Sentences).** Harmelin, a convicted drug dealer, was apprehended with 672 grams of cocaine. He was convicted and a mandatory sentence of life imprisonment was imposed. Harmelin challenged the constitutionality of this sentence and also declared that it was disproportional to the crime. The SC disagreed and let his conviction and sentence stand, believing them to have not violated any of Harmelin's constitutional rights.

Harrington v. California, 395 U.S. 250, 89 S.Ct. 1726 (1969) **(Sixth Amendment Right of Cross-Examination of Witnesses Against Defendant).** Harrington was charged with murder. A co-defendant made a confession implicating Harrington, and this confession was introduced as evidence against him. The co-defendant also testified in court against Harrington and was cross-examined by Harrington's attorney. Confessions from two others involved in the murder were read into the record, but these two persons were not called to testify, inasmuch as there was already overwhelming evidence against Harrington. Harrington was convicted. He appealed, arguing that his Sixth Amendment right to cross-examine his accusers had been violated. In an unusual turn of events, the SC upheld Harrington's conviction, saying that because of the overwhelming inculpatory evidence against him, the judicial decision to disallow cross-examination of these other persons had not violated Harrington's Sixth Amendment rights. The SC considered not calling the accomplices to testify to be harmless error.

Harris v. Alabama, ___U.S.___, 115 S.Ct. 1031 (1995) **(Death Penalty; Judicial Consideration of Jury Recommendations in Sentencing).** Harris was convicted of capital murder. During the sentencing phase, the jury recommended life imprisonment to the judge, but the judge cited a preponderance of aggravating factors over mitigating ones and imposed the death penalty. Harris appealed, contending that the jury decision should have been honored by the judge. The SC upheld Harris' conviction and death penalty, saying that judges may impose the death penalty, despite a recommendation by the jury for a sentence of life imprisonment. Juries only "recommend" to judges, who need only consider the recommendation; judges make the final sentencing decision. This case is significant, because it underscores the power of sentencing judges to consider and weigh aggravating and mitigating circumstances. If the aggravating circumstances in a capital case outweigh the mitigating ones, then the death penalty is justified. In this case, the jury had been emotionally persuaded to recommend a life sentence; however, the judge had determined that specific aggravating circumstances far outweighed any mitigating ones, and he had imposed the death penalty.

Harris v. New York, 401 U.S. 222, 91 S.Ct. 643 (1971) **(Self-Incrimination).** Harris was indicted for selling heroin. During his trial, statements were admitted into evidence that Harris had made to police, both before and after he was told his Miranda rights. Some of these statements involved transactional details of his heroin sales. Harris was cross-examined by the prosecutor about these pre-Miranda statements. He was convicted. He sought to suppress these statements from his case and appealed to the SC. The SC affirmed Harris' conviction, saying that Harris could not invoke the Fifth Amendment concerning statements he had already made to police. Harris' past inconsistent and conflicting statements were within the proper scope of cross-examination by the prosecutor and unprotected by any Fifth Amendment claim.

Harris v. Oklahoma, 433 U.S. 682, 97 S.Ct. 2912 (1977) **(Double Jeopardy).** Harris and a companion robbed a grocery store, and the grocery store clerk was shot and killed by Harris' companion. Harris was charged with and convicted of felony murder. Subsequently, he was charged with robbery with a firearm and convicted. He appealed, alleging that his double-jeopardy rights had been violated, since he had already been convicted of felony murder, which included similar crime elements. The SC reversed his robbery conviction, holding that when conviction of a greater crime, murder, cannot be had without conviction of the lesser crime, robbery with firearms, the double-jeopardy clause bars prosecution for the lesser crime after conviction of the greater one.

Harris v. Pulley, 465 U.S. 37, 104 S.Ct. 871 (1984) **(Death Penalty).** Harris was convicted of murder in California and sentenced to death. He appealed, arguing that the court had neglected to compare his punishment with how other murderers in California have been punished. The SC upheld his conviction and sentence, saying that there is no constitutional requirement making it mandatory for judges to compare the proportionality of their sentences with those of similar cases.

Harris v. United States, 390 U.S. 234, 88 S.Ct. 992 (1968) **(Law Enforcement Officers or Agencies; Plain View; Searches and Seizures).** Harris' automobile had been observed leaving the scene of a bank robbery. Later, Harris was arrested by police and his car was impounded. The car was subjected to a routine search. Incriminating evidence was obtained from his car and later used against him in court, when he was convicted. He appealed, but the SC upheld his conviction, saying that anything in plain view in an automobile during an inventory search is subject to seizure and admissible in court later.

Hayes v. Florida, 470 U.S. 811, 105 S.Ct. 1643 (1985) **(Law Enforcement Officers or Agencies; Searches and Seizures).** Hayes was a suspect in a criminal case. He was visited by police, who asked him if they could take his fingerprints. Hayes refused, at which time the police advised him that if he didn't go to the police station voluntarily, he would be arrested. He reluctantly agreed to go, and his fingerprints were taken. They matched those at the crime scene and Hayes was subsequently convicted of the crime. He appealed. The SC overturned his conviction, however, holding that there had been no probable cause to arrest Hayes, he had given no consent to go to the police station, and there had been no prior judicial authorization for such fingerprinting. The subsequent investigative detention at the police station had violated Hayes' Fourth Amendment rights against unreasonable searches and

seizures. Police must have probable cause to take persons into custody for purposes of taking their fingerprints and subjecting them to interrogations.

Haynes v. Washington, 373 U.S. 503, 83 S.Ct. 1336 (1963) **(Confessions; Exceptions).** In December 1957, Haynes was arrested by Spokane police shortly after a gasoline station had been robbed. On the way to the police station, Haynes admitted the robbery orally. He was subsequently interrogated by a Spokane detective and was placed in a lineup for identification by gas station attendants and other witnesses later that evening. The following morning, Haynes was again questioned by detectives for about 1-1/2 hours. He gave two confession statements, signing one but not the other. The next day he was taken before a magistrate for a preliminary hearing. Police continued to insist that Haynes should sign the second confession, since he had already signed the first one. He persistently refused to sign the second confession. He was later convicted, with the first signed confession used against him as evidence. He appealed. The SC overturned Haynes's conviction, holding that the police interrogation methods had been improper and that Haynes had been subjected to coercive methods in signing the first confession. Thus, such evidence would be inadmissible in a retrial of the case.

Heath v. Alabama, 474 U.S. 82, 106 S.Ct. 433 (1985) **(Double Jeopardy).** Heath was charged by a Georgia jury for arranging to have his wife killed by two men from Alabama. They kidnapped his wife and transported her body across state lines into Georgia. Following his conviction in Georgia for murder with malice, an Alabama court also found him guilty of murder during a kidnapping and sentenced him to death. His convictions were affirmed by Alabama courts despite an appeal based on a double jeopardy claim. He appealed again. The SC upheld his murder convictions in both states, saying that the inherent sovereignty of both Alabama and Georgia as states meant that Heath had not been subjected to double jeopardy by being convicted of the same murder in two different jurisdictions. When Heath committed murder, he had violated the laws of two separate state jurisdictions, and thus the double-jeopardy provision does not apply to him.

Helling v. McKinney, 507 U.S.___, 113 S.Ct. 2475 (1993) **(Corrections; Inmate Rights; Eighth Amendment Violations).** McKinney was a prisoner in the Nevada state prison system. He filed suit against prison officials under Title 42, U.S.C. Section 1983, alleging that cigarette smoke from cellmates was jeopardizing his health and thus was subjecting him to cruel and unusual punishment under the Eighth Amendment. He also said officials had exhibited deliberate indifference to him when he asked for a smoke-free environment. The environmental tobacco smoke (ETS) could not be proved to cause future bodily harm or injury, although the SC declared that McKinney had plainly stated a case upon which relief could be granted. The SC remanded this case back to the originating court to determine whether deliberate indifference actually had been manifested by prison administrators. Since McKinney filed his suit, however, the Nevada prison system has created smoke-free areas and has implemented major policy changes regarding ETS throughout the Nevada prison system. These administrative changes may discourage any favorable decision for McKinney on the deliberate indifference issue.

Henderson v. Morgan, 426 U.S. 637, 96 S.Ct. 2253 (1976) **(Plea Bargaining)**. Morgan was convicted following a plea of guilty to second-degree murder in New York. He later filed a writ of habeas corpus, alleging that his plea had not been voluntary, since the nature and proof of actual charges were never explained to him and he had never admitted to committing the specific acts constituting the charge. The SC set aside the conviction, noting that Morgan was of unusually low mental capacity and had not admitted that he had intended to commit the crime. Further, the SC noted, neither defense counsel nor trial court had explained to Morgan that intent to cause death of his victim was an essential element of the offense of second-degree murder. Thus, it was impossible to conclude that Morgan's plea to the unexplained charge of second-degree murder was voluntary.

Henderson v. United States, 339 U.S. 816, 70 S.Ct. 843 (1950) **(Corrections; Inmate Rights)**. In 1942 Henderson, a black man, attempted to dine in a railroad car that had been partitioned by curtains, with 10 tables reserved for white passengers and 1 table reserved for black passengers. He sought to be accommodated in the white dining area, was refused, and brought suit against the railroad. The case was ultimately heard by the SC, who decided in Henderson's favor, holding that such divisions of dining conveniences in railroad

cars were discriminatory and violated the Interstate Commerce Act.

Henry v. United States, 361 U.S. 98, 80 S.Ct. 168 (1959) **(Law Enforcement Officers or Agencies; Search and Seizure)**. FBI agents who were conducting surveillance in a case totally unrelated to Henry happened to observe him and another person load several boxes into Henry's automobile. At a distance of 300 feet, FBI agents could see "Admiral" on the boxes being loaded. They approached Henry and his friend, inquired about the boxes, searched them, and detained the two men while they determined whether the merchandise was stolen. It was, and Henry and his friend were arrested for interstate transportation of stolen radios. A federal district court convicted the two men and they appealed. They claimed that the FBI agents had lacked probable cause to conduct a warrantless search of Henry's vehicle, because a visual inspection of the boxes and their contents was not definitive proof of their status as stolen merchandise. The United States attorney argued that because the radios were indeed stolen, the end (the arrest and conviction of Henry and his friend) justified the means (the warrantless search and lack of probable cause). The SC ruled against the government, overturning his conviction. It concluded that "an arrest is not justified by what the subsequent search discloses." It also said, "It is better, so the Fourth Amendment teaches, that the guilty sometimes go free than that citizens be subject to easy arrest." The case significance for police officers is that they cannot conduct warrantless searches lacking probable cause and justify their conduct if illegal contraband is uncovered as a result of their illegal search. (*See Terry v. Ohio* [1968] and *Sibron v. New York* [1968].)

Hernandez v. New York, 500 U.S. 352, 111 S.Ct. 1859 (1991) **(Sixth Amendment; Right to Counsel; Peremptory Challenges)**. Hernandez was convicted of various crimes. During the selection of his jury, the prosecutor used several peremptory challenges to strike from potential jury duty four Latinos. Following his conviction, Hernandez filed an appeal, alleging that the prosecutor had deliberately deprived him of a fair trial by eliminating persons like Hernandez. The argument was similar to the one made in *Batson v. Kentucky* (1986), where it was held that peremptory challenges cannot be used to create racially pure juries or to strike off members of a particular race. At the time, objections had been raised by defense counsel, but the prosecutor cited various valid reasons for using these challenges. The SC upheld his conviction, holding that an acceptable race-neutral explanation had been provided by the prosecutor for striking the Latino jurors in that case. No evidence to the contrary had been presented.

Herrera v. Collins, 506 U.S. 390, 113 S.Ct. 853 (1993) **(Death Penalty).** On the basis of a handwritten confession, two eyewitness accounts and identifications, and two additional and critical pieces of circumstantial evidence, Herrera was convicted of first-degree murder and sentenced to death in Texas in 1982. Ten years later, he initiated a habeas corpus petition alleging that he was innocent of these murders because of "newly discovered evidence." Texas statutes have provisions governing the time limits to bring new appeals on newly discovered evidence. Herrera had gone well beyond these limits, and considering his confession, eyewitnesses to the murders, and the incriminating circumstantial evidence, the threshold for questioning Herrera's original conviction had not been reached. The SC upheld Herrera's conviction and death sentence, although it did offer one other avenue of relief. The SC said that Herrera could appeal to the Texas governor for clemency on a post-trial demonstration of actual innocence. Thus, if Herrera could show that the newly discovered evidence was exonerating, then the governor could grant clemency.

Herring v. New York, 422 U.S. 853, 95 S.Ct. 2550 (1975) **(Counsel Right of Summation in Bench Trial Case).** In a bench trial, Herring's attorney was denied the opportunity to summarize the defense case before the New York judge. A New York statute gave the judge discretion to either hear a summation from the defense or not hear it. The judge convicted Herring after hearing the evidence. Herring appealed, saying that he had been denied the assistance of counsel because of this statute in violation of the Sixth Amendment and that his due-process rights had been violated under the Fourteenth Amendment. The SC overturned Herring's conviction, saying that the New York statute had violated Herring's Fourteenth Amendment rights by preventing defense counsel from presenting closing arguments.

Hester v. United States, 265 U.S. 57, 44 S.Ct. 445 (1924) **(Plain View Rule; Open Field Searches).** Hester was suspected of manufacturing illegal liquor. Revenue agents secreted themselves in bushes near Hester's house. When he

emerged carrying a large jug, he saw them in the bushes, panicked, dropped the jug, and ran. The agents picked up the jug and determined that it contained illegal whiskey. Hester was convicted of manufacturing moonshine whiskey. He appealed, arguing that the officers were trespassing on his land at the time he observed them. The SC disagreed, saying that the fact that officers were trespassing did not by itself nullify their observations. The officers had no warrant, but they didn't need one, since Hester had dropped the whiskey jug in plain view. Rather, officers had merely examined abandoned containers when Hester and his companions attempted to elude officers. Thus, there had been no Fourth Amendment violation and the evidence was properly admitted against Hester.

Hewitt v. Helms, 459 U.S. 460, 103 S.Ct. 864 (1983) **(Corrections; Solitary Confinement).** Following riots in a Pennsylvania prison, an inmate, Helms, was given several misconduct reports. He was placed in solitary confinement for a period of time. Subsequent misconduct reports resulted in his being placed in solitary confinement for six months. Helms filed suit under Title 42, U.S.C. Section 1983, alleging that his Fourteenth Amendment right to due process had been violated because he had been denied full hearings on the two punishments. The SC denied Helms relief, saying that administrative segregation (solitary confinement) requires no formal hearings and is often ordered to insure prisoner safety. Specifically, inmates are not entitled to hearings to determine whether administrative segregation should be imposed for *protection*. The SC stressed, however, that for purposes of *punishment,* inmates are entitled to hearings as set forth in *Wolff v. McDonnell* (1974). Thus, there is a difference between administrative segregation, where no hearing is required, and punitive segregation, where it is.

Hildwin v. Florida, 490 U.S. 638, 109 S.Ct. 2055 (1989) **(Death Penalty; Aggravating and Mitigating Circumstances).** Hildwin was convicted of first-degree murder. During the penalty phase of Hildwin's trial, the jury recommended the death penalty, citing four specific aggravating factors and no mitigating ones. Hildwin appealed the death sentence, contending that Florida's capital-sentencing scheme is unconstitutional because it permits the imposition of death without a specific finding by the jury that sufficient aggravating circumstances exist to merit it. The conviction and death sentence were upheld by the SC, which declared that Hildwin's rights had not been violated. The SC said that findings made by a judge rather than a jury did not violate the Sixth Amendment because there is no Sixth Amendment right to jury sentencing, even where the sentence turns on specific findings of fact.

Hill v. California, 401 U.S. 797, 91 S.Ct. 1106 (1971) **(Law Enforcement Officers or Agencies; Searches)**. Police in Los Angeles County arrested two men for narcotics possession. A search of the car in which they were driving disclosed incriminating evidence linking the men with an armed robbery and kidnapping that had occurred a few days earlier. The police obtained confessions from the two men implicating Hill, the owner of the car. On the basis of probable cause alone, the police went to Hill's apartment to arrest him, but they did not have an arrest or search warrant. A person answered the door who matched Hill's description but was not Hill and denied that he was. The police arrested him anyway, thinking he was Hill, and conducted a warrantless search of his apartment. They found guns, some stolen property, and some pages of Hill's diary, which contained incriminating information. The prosecutor used this seized evidence incident to an arrest to prosecute and convict the real Hill. Hill appealed, saying that the warrantless search of his apartment was not valid because the person in it was not the person police thought he was. Therefore, the wrong person had been arrested and this fact should have nullified any incriminating evidence later found by police. The SC heard Hill's appeal and upheld his conviction, using the good-faith exception to the exclusionary rule. Thus, the SC said, the police were entitled to do whatever the law would allow them to do, even under circumstances when they had the wrong arrestee in custody. The SC upheld their subsequent search incident to lawful arrest based on probable cause to be valid and reasonable.

Hitchcock v. Dugger, 481 U.S. 279, 107 S.Ct. 1821 (1987) **(Death Penalty; Nonstatutory Aggravating and Mitigating Factors During Penalty Phase)**. Hitchcock was convicted of capital murder in Florida. During the sentencing phase of his trial, the judge advised the jury on aggravating and mitigating circumstances, saying that certain nonstatutory mitigating circumstances "had no place" in the proceeding. Thus, the judge obli-

gated jurors to disregard any nonstatutory mitigating factors when considering whether Hitchcock should receive the death penalty. They decided that he should. He appealed, arguing this point as violative of his Eighth Amendment right against cruel and unusual punishment. The SC vacated his sentence, holding that Hitchcock had been sentenced to death in proceedings that did not comport with the requirement that the sentencer may neither refuse to consider nor be precluded from considering any relevant mitigating evidence. Thus juries may consider nonstatutory mitigating factors when deciding to impose the death penalty in capital cases.

Hobby v. United States, 468 U.S. 339, 104 S.Ct. 3093 (1984) **(Grand Juries)**. Hobby was charged with federal fraud charges in North Carolina. Prior to his trial, he was indicted by a grand jury. He moved to dismiss the indictment, alleging racial discrimination in the selection of the jury foreman. The motion was rejected and he was convicted. He again sought to overturn his conviction by claiming the grand jury foreman had been selected on racially discriminatory grounds. Hobby, a white man, made a general allegation that none of the 15 grand juries convened in North Carolina in the past seven years had had black or female foremen, and that only six grand jury members had been women. The SC observed that while discrimination is prohibited by law, there was insufficient evidence to support the idea that the grand jury in Hobby's indictment showed a purposeful discrimination pattern in regard to race or gender. Further, the SC declared, any discrimination evident in the grand jury had nothing whatever to do with his conviction in the fair trial that followed. Thus there was nothing presented by Hobby as evidence as to why his conviction should be overturned or his indictment dismissed.

Hoffa v. United States, 335 U.S. 293, 87 S.Ct. 408 (1966) **(Right to Counsel)**. Hoffa was suspected of jury tampering when it was alleged that he attempted to bribe jurors. One of his close friends, Partin, who was a government informant, agreed to ask him incriminating questions at the request of FBI agents. Based in part upon the testimony given by Partin, Hoffa was convicted. He appealed, alleging that his right to confidentiality under the Fourth Amendment had been violated. The SC upheld Hoffa's conviction, saying that he had had no reasonable expectation of privacy when he voluntarily confided his wrongdoing to a friend.

Holbrook v. Flynn, 475 U.S. 560, 106 S.Ct. 1340 (1986) **(Prosecutorial Conduct; Courtroom Decorum and Arrangement; Right to Fair Trial).** Flynn was indicted for armed robbery in Rhode Island and held without bail. Later in court, four uniformed state troopers were positioned behind him as a customary security force. He was convicted. Flynn appealed, alleging that the presence of the officers sitting behind him had prejudiced the jury, and thus his Sixth Amendment fair trial rights had been violated. Following a reversal of his conviction by a lower appellate court, the SC heard the case and reinstated Flynn's robbery conviction, holding that he had failed to show that the officers' presence in court prejudiced his case to the extent that his fair trial rights had been violated. The SC expressed serious doubts that the mere presence of these officers in court had posed an unacceptable threat to Flynn's right to a fair trial or that the jurors had regarded their presence as inherently prejudicial.

Holloway v. Arkansas, 435 U.S. 475, 98 S.Ct. 1173 (1978) **(Sixth Amendment; Right to Counsel).** Holloway was accused of robbery with the use of a firearm and rape. Before his trial, he and several co-defendants were being represented by the same counsel. Motions were made for appointment of separate counsel for each man because of confidential information one might give against another. The judge denied these motions, and Holloway was subsequently convicted. Holloway appealed on the grounds that he had been denied effective assistance of counsel and that the judge's ruling had created an unfair trial situation. The SC reversed Holloway's conviction and chided the judge for not having granted defense motions for separate attorney representation. The SC said that whenever judges improperly require joint representation of several defendants over a timely objection, reversal of the conviction is automatic. Thus, the SC declared, Holloway's case was unfairly prejudiced because the same counsel represented co-defendants with conflicting interests.

Horton v. California, 496 U.S. 128, 110 S.Ct. 2301 (1990) **(Law Enforcement Officers or Agencies; Searches).** A suspect in an armed robbery, Horton, was visited by police armed with a valid search warrant, specifically authorizing them to look only for stolen property, not the weapons used in the robbery. No stolen property

was found. However, the police discovered some weapons that were in plain view, and an officer seized them, correctly believing them to be the weapons used in the robbery. Horton was convicted. He appealed, contending that the weapons should have been excluded in the case against him, because the warrant had not specified them to be seized. The SC disagreed and said that an inadvertent discovery of incriminating evidence in plain view does not result in the exclusion of this evidence from trial later. Ordinarily, in plain-view cases as exceptions to the exclusionary rule, discovery by police of illegal contraband has to be "accidental." In the *Horton* case, however, the officers knew that they *might* find other incriminating evidence, such as weapons, even though weapons were not listed in the search warrant. The *Horton* case eliminated the "accidental" requirement for seizures of evidence in plain view known by police to be incriminating evidence for criminal suspects.

Houchins v. KQED, Inc., 438 U.S. 1, 98 S.Ct. 2588 (1978) **(Corrections; Inmate Rights).** A television station, KQED, reported the suicide of a jail inmate. Interviews were conducted with the sheriff and with a psychiatrist who was on call with the jail. KQED wanted a more extensive tour of the facility but was refused. However, the sheriff instituted a systematic tour of the jail for interested citizens, including the media. KQED was dissatisfied with this short tour and wanted a more extensive one. Sheriff Houchines denied this request, so KQED filed suit against him, alleging that he had violated the First Amendment rights of KQED by not granting it a more extensive tour of the jail. The SC upheld Houchins's decision and held that his policy had not violated the First Amendment rights of the media. (*See Saxbe v. Washington Post Co.* [1974] and *Pell v. Procunier* [1974] for similar rulings on similar issues.)

Hubbard v. United States, ___U.S.___, 115 S.Ct. 1754 (1995) **(False Statements; Judicial Authority).** Hubbard filed for bankruptcy in 1985. He gave various false statements in oral and written responses to the Bankruptcy Court. Later when his false statements were disclosed, he was charged with violating a federal law prohibiting false statements made to any department or agency of the United States knowingly and willfully. Hubbard was convicted under the statute. He appealed. The SC overturned his conviction regarding false statements made, holding that such false statements do not pertain to judicial proceedings, such as bankruptcy courts. This was a technical interpretation and should not be taken to mean that defendants may routinely commit perjury during trial proceedings. Rather, this specific statute, Title 18, U.S.C. Section 1001 does not apply to judicial proceedings. The United States attorney should have sought other charges falling under more appropriate criminal statutes of Title 18.

Hudson v. Louisiana, 450 U.S. 40, 101 S.Ct. 970 (1981) **(Double Jeopardy).** Hudson was convicted of first-degree murder. He filed a motion for a new trial with the original trial judge, who granted it, declaring that "the evidence presented by the prosecution in the first trial was legally insufficient to support the guilty verdict." Thus, a second trial was ordered. Hudson appealed, however, arguing that this would be double jeopardy. The SC agreed, stating that the double-jeopardy clause of the Fifth Amendment precludes a second trial once the reviewing court has found that the evidence [in the first trial] was legally insufficient to support a guilty verdict. Hudson was therefore freed.

Hudson v. McMillian, 503 U.S. 1, 112 S.Ct. 995 (1992) **(Corrections; Inmate Rights).** Hudson, a prison inmate in Louisiana, was beaten by two correctional officers as he was being transported between units on the penitentiary grounds. He suffered minor injuries but filed suit against the officers under Title 42, U.S.C. Section 1983. The trial court awarded Hudson damages, but a higher court reversed the trial court, ruling in favor of the officers by saying that the minor injuries to Hudson were not sufficient to constitute cruel and unusual punishment. The SC disagreed, saying the excessive force used by the correctional officers had indeed been cruel and unusual punishment even though only minor injuries to the prisoner had been sustained.

Hudson v. Palmer, 468 U.S. 517, 104 S.Ct. 3194 (1984) **(Corrections; Searches and Seizures).** Palmer was an inmate at Bland Correctional Center in Virginia, serving sentences for forgery and bank robbery. During a cell shakedown, where officers searched his cell, they discovered a torn pillow. They broke a few of Palmer's personal effects in the process of their search. Palmer sued the officers, alleging his Fourth Amendment right against an illegal search and seizure had been violated. He claimed that the officers needed probable cause and a search warrant to enter his cell and search it. The SC disagreed, saying that prisoners have no reasonable expectation of privacy; further, correctional officers do not need probable cause or a warrant to search inmate cells from time to time for illegal contraband. If personal items are broken, intentionally or unintentionally, this is not a violation of the inmate's due-process rights in violation of the Fourteenth Amendment.

Hughes v. Rowe, 449 U.S. 5, 101 S.Ct. 173 (1980) **(Corrections; Inmate Rights).** Hughes was a prisoner in Illinois. He allegedly consumed some alcohol made on prison grounds in violation of prison regulations. Without a hearing in the matter or any emergency conditions, he was placed in isolation for 10 days, and he lost 30 days of statutory "good-time" credit. Hughes filed a Title 42, U.S.C. Section 1983 civil-rights suit, alleging that his constitutional rights had been violated and that he had never been given a hearing before being penalized. Lawyers representing the attorney general for the State of Illinois were awarded $400 in counsel fees and Hughes was ordered to pay them. He appealed. The SC said that (1) no emergency conditions had existed to justify Hughes's isolation; (2) no hearing had been held; and (3) the assignment of $400 in fees was improper. Officials must give prisoners a hearing before administering punishments of any kind, barring any emergency conditions that might exist. In this case, administrators, as well as the district court judge, had acted improperly assessing counsel costs to Hughes.

Hurtado v. California, 110 U.S. 516 (1884) **(Death Penalty; Indictments).** In 1879, California dropped the grand jury system, replacing it with broad prosecutorial discretionary powers, such as filing information against minor offenders and felons. In 1884, absent an indictment, Hurtado was charged with murder through a piece of criminal information, convicted, and sentenced to death. He appealed. The SC upheld the death sentence, holding that the grand jury is merely a procedure that the states can abolish at will. The significance of this case is that grand juries are not required for death-penalty cases to be conducted in state courts.

Husty v. United States, 282 U.S. 694, 51 S.Ct. 240 (1931) **(Law Enforcement Officers or Agencies; Stop and Frisk).** Husty was a known bootlegger of illegal whiskey. His automobile was searched without warrant by federal officers who knew Husty and his reputation. Incriminating evidence was seized and Husty was convicted. His sentence greatly exceeded the actual statutory sentence for the offense. Husty appealed and the SC overturned his conviction and sentence, because the maximum sentence for the offense was exceeded by the sentence actually imposed. Nevertheless, the search of Husty's automobile was ruled reasonable under the circumstances, since a reliable informant had given police an accurate description of where the car would be parked and what it would contain. Essentially, the SC said that officers may search a vehicle for illegal liquor, if on probable cause, without a previous arrest, and if facts coming to their attention would lead a reasonably prudent man to believe that liquor was illegally possessed therein.

Hutto v. Davis, 454 U.S. 370, 102 S.Ct. 703 (1982) **(Corrections; Inmates Rights).** Davis was a Virginia inmate who had been sentenced to 40 years in prison and a $20,000 fine for a conviction for marijuana possession with intent to distribute. He sought habeas corpus relief, contending that the 40-year sentence was disproportionate to the crime and thus was cruel and unusual punishment. Ultimately, after considerable hearing and rehearing through the appellate process, the SC decided the matter by upholding Virginia authority to mandate sentences for crimes as they see fit without labeling such sentences "cruel and unusual." Davis' 40-year sentence had been legislatively mandated, and thus the SC believed that it would be improper to interfere with state legislative sanctions. Davis' sentence was therefore upheld.

Hutto v. Finney, 437 U.S. 678, 98 S.Ct. 2565 (1978) **(Corrections; Solitary Confinement).** In 1970, the Arkansas prison system was declared unconstitutional on various grounds and its conditions of confinement cruel and unusual, in violation of the Eighth Amendment. Subsequently, a check by federal officials revealed that the reforms to be implemented had not been completed. The court issued additional orders for prison official compliance. These orders included (1) limiting the number of prisoners who could reasonably be confined in one cell, (2) discontinuing particular types of nonnutritious meals, (3) maximizing the days of solitary confinement as punishment at 30, and (4) obligating the state to pay for attorneys' fees and expenses. Hutto, the Arkansas commissioner of corrections, appealed, contending that the 30-day confinement standard was too lenient and that the court had wrongfully assigned attorneys' fees to the state. The SC upheld the lower court on the 30-day limitation on solitary confinement and the assessment of attorneys' fees against the state.

Hutto v. Ross, 429 U.S. 28, 97 S.Ct. 202 (1976) **(Sixth Amendment; Confessions).** Ross was charged in an Arkansas court with embezzlement. He entered into a plea-bargain agreement with prosecutors where he would plead guilty in exchange for a 15-year sentence, with 10 years suspended. Before accepting the plea agreement, Ross was requested by prosecutors to make a statement confessing to the embezzlement, and Ross did so, after being advised by his attorney of his Fifth Amendment privilege against self-incrimination. Later, Ross withdrew from the plea bargain and demanded a jury trial, which he was granted. During the trial, the prosecutor admitted Ross' confession into evidence against him, and he was convicted. Ross appealed, contending that the confession "was a part of the plea bargain" and that as he had withdrawn from the plea bargain, the confession was thus inadmissible. The SC disagreed, holding that the existence of a plea bargain may well have entered into Ross' decision to give a confession, but Ross had been properly advised by his attorney of his Fifth Amendment right against self-incrimination. The plea agreement would be enforceable in any case, with or without Ross' confession. Thus, Ross confessed, and this confession was determined to be freely and voluntarily given, without an direct or implied promises or inducements or coercion from prosecutors. Ross' conviction stood.

I

Idaho v. Wright, 497 U.S. 805, 110 S.Ct. 3139 (1990) **(Sixth Amendment; Residual Hearsay Exception).** Wright was accused of lewd conduct with a minor. She and a boyfriend, Giles, had sodomized Wright's two daughters, age five and two. Giles had sexual intercourse with both girls, while Wright held them down and covered their mouths. At Wright's trial, the older daughter testified directly. It had previously been stipulated that the younger daughter would not testify, as she was not "capable of communicating to the jury."

Nevertheless, under an exception to the hearsay rule, the examining child-abuse specialist was able to relate what she had been told by the two-year-old victim. Wright was convicted. She appealed later, maintaining that such hearsay was not admissible under the confrontation clause of the Fifth Amendment. A reliability requirement provided that hearsay should be supported by a showing of "particularized guarantees of trustworthiness." The Idaho Supreme Court overturned Wright's conviction and the case was appealed to the United States SC, which affirmed the Idaho decision. The SC determined that the statements given by the two-year-old were not made under circumstances of reliability comparable to those required by law. The case was remanded for possible retrial.

Illinois v. Allen, 397 U.S. 337, 90 S.Ct. 1057 (1970) **(Fair Trials; Public Trials).** Allen was charged with robbery. He waived his right to counsel and elected to represent himself. During the jury selection and trial, he was abusive and argued constantly with the trial judge until eventually he was ordered removed from the courtroom. The trial was held anyway and he was convicted. Later, Allen appealed to the SC, arguing that his Sixth Amendment right had been violated because he was not present at his own trial when convicted. The SC upheld his conviction, saying that repeated warnings to Allen from the judge had had no effect on his conduct, which was so disruptive as to prevent the jurors from properly considering the evidence. Thus there was nothing unconstitutional about the judge's removing Allen from the courtroom.

Illinois v. Andreas, 463 U.S. 765, 103 S.Ct. 3319 (1983) **(Law Enforcement Officers or Agencies; Search and Seizure).** DEA agents in Illinois intercepted a large container from Calcutta and opened it. They found marijuana, resealed the container, and had it delivered to Andreas's home, where they placed the container under surveillance. Eventually, Andreas was seen with the container, and police moved in without a warrant. They seized it, arrested Andreas, and reopened the container, disclosing the marijuana. Andreas was convicted of possessing a controlled substance. He filed an appeal with the SC, arguing that his Fourth Amendment rights had been violated because police did not have a warrant when they reopened the container, which had been previously opened during a customs inspection. The

SC upheld his conviction, saying that warrants to open containers are not needed if the containers have first been opened by customs agents according to their statutory duty and rights. The SC also said that there was no substantial likelihood that the contents of the container had changed during the brief period that it was out of the sight of a surveilling officer, and thus reopening the container did not intrude on any legitimate expectation of privacy and did not violate the Fourth Amendment rights of Andreas.

Illinois v. Condon, 507 U.S. 948, 113 S.Ct. 1359 (1993) **(Fourth Amendment; Search and Seizures).** Condon was suspected of dealing in cocaine. An informant provided police in DuPage County with sufficient information to obtain a warrant to search Condon's home. One evening, a team of police officers stormed Condon's home without knocking or announcing their presence and found a large quantity of cocaine, marijuana, and several weapons. At a later trial, Condon was convicted. He appealed alleging that police had not knocked and first announced their intentions before conducting the search. Police countered that their unannounced entry and search were caused by exigent circumstances. Condon's conviction was overturned by the Illinois Supreme Court, which held that the unannounced entry had not been prompted by exigent circumstances and conflicted with the protocol to be followed in such instances of searches and seizures. The Illinois prosecutor appealed the ruling to the SC. The SC declined to hear Illinois's appeal in this ruling. However, some dissenting SC members suggested that because of the present conflict among the states about search-and-seizure protocol, the SC should hear the case and resolve the conflict.

Illinois v. Gates, 462 U.S. 213, 103 S.Ct. 2317 (1983) **(Fourth Amendment; Search and Seizure; Informants).** Based upon an anonymous letter received by police officers, a couple, Lance and Sue Gates, of Bloomingdale, was accused of selling drugs. A fairly detailed description of the Gates' activities was contained in the letter. Police placed the Gates under surveillance, and everything described in the letter was observed to occur. The Gates were moving large quantities of drugs between Florida and Illinois by automobile and air. The police obtained a search warrant from a judge and searched the Gates home, discovering large quantities of drugs. They were convicted. They appealed to the SC, arguing that the reliability of the informant could not be determined; thus, no basis existed to support the search warrant leading to the drug discovery. The Gates moved to suppress all drugs found as the result of this allegedly faulty search. The landmark decision in this case was that the totality of circumstances, not informant reliability (previously used in *Aguilar v. Texas*, [1964]), justified the search warrant issued. Thus it is now easier for police to obtain search warrants where they allege that a totality of circumstances suggests a crime is or has been committed and specific suspects have been named.

Illinois v. Krull, 480 U.S. 340, 107 S.Ct. 1160 (1987) **(Exclusionary Rule; Good Faith Searches).** Officers conducted a good-faith, warrantless search of an automobile in an auto wrecking yard. The Illinois statute permitting such search was unconstitutional, although the officers didn't know that and were acting in good faith. The incriminating evidence obtained from the search was admissible in court, however, because of the good-faith conduct of the officers.

Illinois v. Lafayette, 462 U.S. 640, 103 S.Ct. 2605 (1982) **(Law Enforcement Officers or Agencies; Searches Incident to Arrest).** Lafayette was arrested for disturbing the peace. While being booked at the local jail, he was searched along with his personal effects. His shoulder bag contained drugs in violation of the Illinois Controlled Substances Act. Lafayette was convicted. He moved to suppress the drugs because they had been the subject of a warrantless search. The SC upheld Lafayette's conviction, contending that it is perfectly reasonable to search an arrestee's personal effects if he or she is under arrest based upon probable cause. Further, the SC stressed the fact that it was administrative procedure for the jail to scan clothing and other personal possessions of arrestees to ensure that illegal contraband does not enter the inner jail facilities to become available to other inmates. Discoveries of illegal drugs during such searches are only incidental to these administrative searches.

Illinois v. Perkins, 496 U.S. 292, 110 S.Ct. 2394 (1990) **(Interrogations; Informants).** Perkins was being held in jail on an aggravated battery charge. An undercover officer entered the cell, pretending to be another arrestee. Soon Perkins gave him voluntary statements about an unrelated crime, a murder, and the statements were used later to obtain a murder conviction

against Perkins. Perkins appealed, contending that the officer should have told him his Miranda rights before interrogating him. The SC said that Miranda warnings are not required whenever suspects give voluntary statements to persons they do not believe are law enforcement officers.

Illinois v. Rodriguez, 497 U.S. 177, 110 S.Ct. 2793 (1990) **(Law Enforcement Officers or Agencies; Consent Searches).** A woman, Fischer, called police and reported that she had been beaten by her boyfriend, Rodriguez, who was living elsewhere. The police went with Fisher to Rodriguez's apartment. She allowed them entry, since she lived there with Rodriguez and had a key. Indeed, her clothes, furniture, and other personal effects were in the apartment as proof of her statements. When police entered, they saw in plain view containers of cocaine and drug paraphernalia and arrested Rodriguez. The seized evidence was used against him and he was convicted. He appealed, contending that Fischer had moved out weeks before she and the police came to his apartment, and that she did not have the right to permit police entry. In fact, Fischer had moved out. Nevertheless, the police were acting in good faith that she did, indeed, have the authority to admit them. Thus, the court upheld Rodriguez's conviction, saying that a warrantless entry and search based on the consent of someone they believed to possess common authority over the premises was valid, even if the person actually lacked that authority.

Illinois v. Sommerville, 410 U.S. 458, 93 S.Ct. 1066 (1973) **(Double Jeopardy).** Sommerville was tried for a crime. During the trial, a mistrial was declared, where the original indictment was ruled defective. A new trial was scheduled and Sommerville appealed, contending that it represented double jeopardy in violation of his Fifth Amendment rights. The SC disagreed, saying that the first trial was never completed, and that therefore, double jeopardy was not an issue. The significance of this case is that it legitimizes mistrials of defendants and does not place them in double jeopardy.

Illinois v. Vitale, 447 U.S. 410, 100 S.Ct. 2260 (1980) **(Double Jeopardy).** Vitale, driving his car, was convicted of "failing to reduce speed," resulting in the death of two children. Later, he was charged with involuntary manslaughter under a different Illinois statute. He sought to dismiss this charge on double-jeopardy grounds, since "failing to reduce speed" was an essential element of the manslaughter offense. The Illinois Supreme Court dismissed the charge, but prosecutors appealed to the United States SC. Vitale's case was remanded to the originating trial court in order to determine whether "failing to reduce one's speed" was an essential element of the manslaughter offense. If it was essential, then double jeopardy would attach and Vitale could not be prosecuted for manslaughter. This decision relied on the *Blockburger* test (*see Blockburger v. United States* [1932]), which said that the second of two successive prosecutions would be barred if the prosecution sought to establish an essential element of the second crime by proving the conduct for which the defendant had been convicted in the first prosecution.

Imbler v. Pactman, 424 U.S. 409, 96 S.Ct. 984 (1976) **(Legal Liabilities of Police Officers).** Imbler was convicted of murder. He subsequently filed for habeas corpus relief, alleging that the prosecutor had suppressed material evidence at his earlier trial and that he had been unlawfully prosecuted as a result. Further, he filed a civil suit under Title 42, U.S.C. Section 1983, alleging his civil rights had been violated. The SC upheld his conviction, stating that the state prosecuting attorney had been acting within the scope of his authority and duties in initiating and pursuing a criminal prosecution. The prosecutor had not violated Imbler's constitutional rights and possessed absolute immunity from suits from Imbler.

Ingraham v. Wright, 430 U.S. 651, 97 S.Ct. 1401 (1977) **(Corrections; Inmate Rights).** In January 1971 Ingraham and another junior high school student filed a complaint against the Drew Junior High School in Dade County, Florida. They complained that "paddling" youths as a punishment was cruel and unusual and violative of their Eighth Amendment rights. The SC determined that the cruel-and-unusual-punishment clause of the Eighth Amendment does not apply to school discipline, whatever its form.

In re Blodgett, 502 U.S. 236, 112 S.Ct. 674 (1992) **(Death Penalty; Eighth Amendment).** Blodgett was convicted of multiple murders and sentenced to death in the State of Washington. Numerous motions and appeals were filed to delay his execution while various issues were decided. The State of Washington filed a petition for a writ of mandamus (requiring officials to carry out the execution order), but did not file any appeals re-garding a court of appeals order staying Blodgett's execution. Blodgett filed a motion to proceed *in forma pauperis*. The SC denied the writ of mandamus, holding that a mandamus to the court of appeals from Washington would not issue, where Washington had failed to file any objection to court of appeals stay of execution order or to vacate or modify its order. Blodgett's execution was thus stayed while he continued litigating various issues relative to his conviction and sentence.

In re Gault, 387 U.S. 1, 87 S.Ct. 1428 (1967) **(Juveniles; Juvenile Rights).** Gault was a 15-year-old in Arizona who, with another boy, allegedly made an obscene telephone call to an adult neighbor, Mrs. Cook. Police arrested Gault and took him to jail for questioning. In several subsequent one-sided juvenile court proceedings, Gault was not permitted to cross-examine his accuser or to testify in his own behalf. He was not initially permitted counsel or advised of his rights. Later, the juvenile court judge adjudicated his case and confined him in the Arizona State Industrial School until he reached age 21. He appealed, and the SC reversed the decision. This landmark case established a juvenile's right to have counsel, to confront and cross-examine accusers, to have protection from self-incrimination, and to have adequate notice of charges when there is the possibility of confinement as a punishment.

In re Kemmler, 136 U.S. 436, 10 S.Ct. 930 (1890) **(Death Penalty; Electric Chairs; Eighth Amendment).** This case declared that the use of the electric chair for administering the death penalty is not cruel and unusual punishment.

In re Sindram, 498 U.S. 177, 111 S.Ct. 596 (1991) **(Corrections; Jailhouse Lawyers; Frivolous Lawsuits).** Sindram was convicted of speeding in Dorchester County, Maryland, in May 1987. Since then, he filed 43 separate petitions and motions with appellate courts, all of which were denied. The SC heard an extraordinary writ wherein Sindram requested the court to allow him to proceed *in forma pauperis*. Essentially, he asked the SC to declare him indigent so that the government would have to pay the costs and docking fees of his future petitions. Noting that this same motion had been made and denied on 12 previous occasions, the SC denied the writ, stating that Sindram had failed to show that no adequate relief could be had in any other form or from any other court and that there were no "drastic" circumstances that warranted extraordinary relief. The SC ordered the clerk of the SC not to accept any petitions from Sindram unless he paid the requisite docking fees. Further, the SC labeled his numerous motions and filings as "frivolous."

In re Winship, 397 U.S. 358, 90 S.Ct. 1068 (1970) **(Juvenile Law; Standard of Proof in Juvenile Proceedings).** Winship, age 12, purportedly entered a locker and stole $112 from a woman's pocketbook in New York City. He was charged with larceny. Under Section 712 of the New York Family Court Act, a juvenile delinquent is defined as "a person over seven and less than sixteen years of age who does any act, which, if done by an adult, would constitute a crime." Interestingly, the juvenile judge in the case acknowledged that the proof to be presented by the prosecution might be insufficient to establish the guilt of Winship beyond a reasonable doubt, although he did indicate that the New York Family Court Act provided that "any determination at the conclusion of [an adjudicatory hearing] that a [juvenile] did an act or acts must be based on a preponderance of the evidence" standard (397 U.S. at 360). Winship was adjudicated as a delinquent and ordered to a training school for 18 months, subject to annual extensions of his commitment until his 18th birthday. Appeals to New York courts were unsuccessful. The SC subsequently heard Winship's appeal and reversed the New York Family Court ruling because the beyond-a-reasonable-doubt standard had not been used in a case where incarceration or loss of freedom was likely. The standard of proof of beyond a reasonable doubt applies to juvenile delinquency proceedings where incarceration or incapacitation is a judicial adjudicatory option.

Irvine v. California, 374 U.S. 128, 74. S.Ct. 381 (1954) **(Law Enforcement Officers or Agencies; Wiretapping; Electronic Surveillance; Fourth Amendment).** Irvine was suspected of illegal gambling. Police officers, without a warrant, went to his home when he was not there and had a locksmith open the door. They placed various microphones throughout the home where they could record conversations later. They even bored a hole in the roof to install further wires, but no telephone lines were "tapped." Police reentered Irvine's home on several occasions and moved microphones about in order to listen to and record any incriminating statements. Later, at Irvine's trial, these statements were used as evidence against him and he was convicted. Irvine

appealed. The SC affirmed and limited the *Rochin* exception to the *Wolf* doctrine in situations involving violence, brutality, or shocking conduct to the defendant; the SC severely criticized the authorities in this case for their behavior, but it did uphold the conviction. At no time in the appeal had Irvine mentioned his constitutional rights. This is significant. The SC cannot act on a constitutional question if it is not initiated by the convicted offender. Without a constitutional issue to consider, the SC affirmed Irvine's conviction. However, it noted that the statute of limitations had not expired and that the conduct of the police in entering Irvine's home without a warrant and planting microphones was inexcusable and in need of rectification. Thus it appears that if Irvine had raised a Fourth Amendment search-and-seizure issue with the SC, his conviction might have been overturned as the information yielded by these illegal microphone plants would be declared inadmissible against him.

J

Jacobson v. United States, 503 U.S. 540, 112 S.Ct. 1535 (1992) **(Entrapment).** In early 1984, Jacobson ordered from an adult book store several books containing pictures of nude young boys. This was not illegal at the time, because the Child Protection Act of 1984 had not been passed. After the passage of this act, United States postal inspectors found Jacobson's name on an adult book store mailing list and began to send him fictitious catalogues and other materials, inviting him to subscribe. At the outset, however, Jacobson declared only his interest in observing only young nudes, not sex acts between them. He responded to many of these solicitations over the next three years. All of this activity was generated by United States postal inspectors as well as the United States Customs Office, as some of the materials were sent from other countries. Finally, in May 1987, United States postal inspectors sent Jacobson a catalogue offering photos of young boys in sexually explicit poses. Jacobson ordered a magazine from the catalogue, and when it was delivered by the United States postal inspector, Jacobson was arrested for receiving child pornography through the mail. He was convicted. He appealed, arguing the defense of entrapment. The SC agreed and overturned his conviction, saying that the government may not originate a criminal design, implant in an innocent person's mind the disposition to commit the criminal act, and then induce commission of the crime so the government can prosecute.

Jackson v. Denno, 378 U.S. 368, 84 S.Ct. 1774 (1966) **(Self-Incrimination)**. Jackson was wounded in a gunfight following an August 28, 1996, robbery of a hotel desk clerk. At the hospital later, he gave incriminating statements that were introduced at his trial, where he was convicted. At his trial, he declared that his confession had been coerced. In New York, judges may exclude involuntary confessions, but they may allow confessions that are *questionably voluntary* and allow juries to decide whether or not they are voluntary. Jackson appealed, contending that the confession should have been suppressed outright, and that the jury should not have been shown it as evidence. The SC reversed his conviction, saying that Jackson is entitled to an evidentiary hearing to determine whether the incriminating confession was voluntarily given or whether it was coerced. Thus judges may not decide to include or exclude a confession on their own authority, before allowing juries to hear it.

Jackson v. Indiana, 406 U.S. 715, 92 S.Ct. 1845 (1972) **(Prosecutions of Mentally Incompetent)**. Jackson was accused of two criminal offenses. He was a mentally defective deaf mute who could not read, write, or virtually otherwise communicate. In Indiana, a statute declares that mentally incompetent criminal defendants may be committed to a state institution on more lenient standards than those applied to civil commitment cases. Further, the standards for release of committed criminal defendants are more stringent than those for the release of others who have been committed through civil process. The judge exercised his power in this case by declaring Jackson mentally unfit and incapable of standing trial, thus committing him to an institution until such time as "he is cured." Since this cure was not a reasonable expectation for Jackson, the commitment was tantamount to a life sentence in a mental institution. Jackson appealed. The SC intervened and rejected the judge's commitment order, thus remanding the case back to the court to determine whether Jackson was criminally responsible for his alleged acts. The significance of this case is that Jackson's Fourteenth Amendment rights to due process and equal protection had been vio-lated by the Indiana court, because Jackson had been committed by a more lenient standard than those of others, and his release conditions were more stringent than those of others. This inequality of treatment was in conflict with the Fourteenth Amendment provision.

Jago v. Van Curen, 454 U.S. 14, 102 S.Ct. 31 (1981) **(Corrections; Probation and Parole)**. Van Curen was convicted of embezzling $6 million. During his confinement, he was interviewed to see if he was possibly eligible for parole under a new shock parole program. The interview went well and he was notified that he would soon be paroled. However, it was then discovered that Van Curen had lied to the parole board about the amount of money he had embezzled (he told the board that he had embezzled $1 million, not $6 million), and that he had also lied about his parole plan and where he was going to live and with whom. His parole was rescinded by the parole board without a hearing. Van Curen appealed, alleging that he had a right to a hearing to answer the charges leading to the rescission. The SC declared that inmates do not have a right to be heard in a proceeding to rescind parole. This type of hearing is different from a parole hearing, where inmates do have assorted rights.

James v. Illinois, 493 U.S. 307, 110 S.Ct. 648 (1990) **(Sixth Amendment; Impeachment Evidence)**. In August 1982, several boys were returning home from a party when they were confronted by three other boys who demanded money. A fight ensued, resulting in the shooting death of one boy and serious injury to another. Detectives from the Chicago Police Department discovered 15-year-old James in his mother's home under a hair dryer. They took him into custody as a suspect. His hair was black and curly. Detectives asked James about his prior hair color, and he said that the day before, his hair had been reddish brown and straight. He admitted to police that he deliberately changed his appearance. James' statements were made without his being given the Miranda warning, and he had been arrested without a warrant. Eyewitnesses to the murder said the shooter had reddish, straight hair and identified James as the shooter, although his hair was now a different color. During the trial, James elected not to testify, and his prior statements about changing his hair color were not admitted into evidence, as they had been illegally obtained by police. However, James called a family friend, Henderson, who testified that on the day of the shooting, she had driven James to school so that he could register, and that his hair had been "black and curly." In an effort to counter this obvious perjury, the prosecutor used James' illegally obtained statements for impeachment purposes in confronting Henderson. Ordinarily, illegally obtained statements can be used to impeach a defendant who testifies under oath, as an important exception to the exclusionary rule. In this case, however, these illegally obtained statements were instead used to impeach a witness for the defense. James was subsequently convicted, and he appealed, alleging that his Fourth Amendment right had been violated. The SC agreed and overturned his conviction, holding that the impeachment exception to the exclusionary rule that permits the prosecution to introduce illegally obtained evidence to impeach a defendant's own testimony would not be expanded to impeach testimony of all defense witnesses.

Jenkins v. Anderson, 447 U.S. 23, 100 S.Ct. 2124 (1978) **(Death Penalty).** Dennis Jenkins was accused of manslaughter in a Michigan court. During his trial, he claimed self-defense. Further, the prosecutor questioned Jenkins on the witness stand about the fact that Jenkins had not surrendered himself to authorities for at least two weeks following the killing. This failure to turn himself in was referred to as prearrest silence. The prosecutor, therefore, used Jenkins' prearrest silence to impeach his credibility and truthfulness about alleging self-defense, suggesting that Jenkins would have spoken out had he actually killed the other person in self-defense. He was convicted. He appealed, claiming that the comments by the prosecutor about his "prearrest silence" were prejudicial remarks and violated his Fifth Amendment right against self-incrimination. The SC upheld his manslaughter conviction, holding that although prosecutors cannot comment on a defendant's silence during the trial, they may use prearrest silence as a means of impeaching a defendant's testimony on cross-examination. This does not violate the Fifth Amendment rights of defendants.

Johnson v. Avery, 393 U.S. 483, 89 S.Ct. 747 (1969) **(Corrections; Jailhouse Lawyers).** The use of jailhouse lawyers may not be prohibited unless free counsel is provided by the state; in absence of any adequate substitute, inmates should be allowed to use legal assistance of other inmates. Johnson was serving a life sentence in Tennessee. He studied the law diligently and on numerous oc-

casions helped other inmates to prepare legal documents such as habeas corpus petitions, usually for a small fee or other reward. Tennessee had a statute prohibiting one prisoner providing legal aid to another. The statute read in part, "no inmate will advise, assist or otherwise contract to aid another, either with or without a fee, to prepare writs or other legal matters. . . . Inmates are forbidden to set themselves up as practitioners for the purpose. . .of writing writs." Thus Johnson was violating a Tennessee law, but he was also assisting other prisoners, many of whom were illiterate and could not prepare petitions themselves, in having access to the courts under the 1941 (*Ex parte Hull*) SC declaration. As a punishment for his legal assistance to other prisoners, Tennessee authorities placed Johnson in solitary confinement for a year. He appealed. Eventually, his case was heard by the SC, which ruled that neither Tennessee nor any other state can prohibit the exercise of legal strategies by inmates, either on their own behalf or on the behalf of other prisoners, as means of reaching the courts. All states are obligated to comply with this ruling unless they can demonstrate that prisoners have access to some alternative and equivalent form of legal assistance for those seeking *postconviction relief*. Such relief is an attempt by prisoners to obtain some satisfaction for a grievance such as a challenge about the nature of their confinement, their initial conviction, or some other matter. Thus, the SC ushered in the "new age in jailhouse lawyering."

Johnson v. Jones, ___U.S.___, 115 S.Ct. 2151 (1995) **(Law Enforcement Officers or Agencies; Excessive Use of Force; Qualified Immunity).** Five police officers arrested Jones, thinking he was drunk, when in fact he was a diabetic suffering from an insulin seizure. He later found himself in a hospital with several broken ribs. He sued. His allegations that police officers had used excessive force when arresting him and beating him at the station house were substantiated by other collateral factual information. The police officers asked for a summary judgment in Jones's suit against them, and the motion was denied by a district court. The officers appealed. The SC affirmed the denial of the motion, holding that police officers may not appeal a district court's summary judgment order insofar as that order determines whether or not the pretrial record sets forth a "genuine" issue of fact for trial. Jones was therefore entitled to a trial on the issue of whether his Title 42, U.S.C. Section 1983 civil rights had been violated.

Johnson v. Louisiana, 406 U.S. 356, 92 S.Ct. 1620 (1972) **(Jury Unanimity; Due Process; Reasonable Doubt Standard).** Johnson was arrested without a warrant at his home based upon a photograph identification by a robbery victim. He was later subjected to a lineup, where he was identified again. Johnson was represented by counsel. He was subjected to trial by jury for the robbery offense and convicted in a jury vote of 9 to 3. Johnson appealed, contending that the jury verdict should be unanimous. The SC affirmed his conviction, saying, in effect, that states have the right to determine whether conviction requires unanimity of jury votes or only a majority vote. The SC concluded by saying that the verdicts rendered by 9 out of 12 jurors are not automatically invalidated by the disagreement of the dissenting 3. Johnson was not deprived of due process or a fair trial because of the 9 to 3 vote. (*See also Apodaca v. Oregon* [1972] for a comparative case.) This SC decision applies to states only and does not affect federal jury voting, which must be unanimous in their verdicts. Federal criminal jury sizes of 12 may be reduced to 11 under special conditions with judicial approval; either size must be unanimous.

Johnson v. Mississippi, 486 U.S. 578, 108 S.Ct. 1981 (1988) **(Eighth Amendment; Aggravating and Mitigating Circumstances).** In December 1981, Johnson and several other men were stopped by a Mississippi highway patrolman for speeding. While the officer was searching the car, one of Johnson's companions stabbed the officer, seized his revolver, and shot him dead. Johnson and his companions were later arrested and charged with murder. They were convicted. During the penalty phase of the trial, the jurors found three aggravating circumstances, which, they said, outweighed the mitigating ones. One aggravating circumstance was an authenticated copy of a commitment order that showed Johnson's conviction and commitment to a Monroe County, New York, jail for the crime of second-degree assault in 1963. Although the New York Supreme Court had vacated Johnson's 1963 conviction, it had continued to function as an aggravating circumstance in the penalty phase of Johnson's 1988 trial. Johnson appealed and the SC reversed his conviction, holding that a death sentence that rests, in part, on a felony conviction that was later vacated violates

the Eighth Amendment prohibition against cruel and unusual punishment.

Johnson v. Texas, 507 U.S.___, 113 S.Ct. 2658 (1993) **(Death Penalty).** Johnson, age 19, was convicted of capital murder. During the sentencing phase of the trial, the judge instructed the jury to consider, in view of Johnson's age, his future dangerousness or threat to society. He was sentenced to death. Johnson appealed his conviction and death sentence on the grounds that the jury had been precluded from considering his youth because of the "future dangerousness" instruction. The SC rejected Johnson's appeal, since the jury had been instructed to consider all of the evidence, including Johnson's youthfulness. The future-dangerousness consideration was merely one additional factor to consider when recommending the death penalty.

Johnson v. Virginia, 373 U.S. 61, 83 S.Ct. 1053 (1963) **(Corrections; Inmate Rights).** Johnson, a black man, was given a traffic citation. He appeared in traffic court, where he was supposed to be seated in a section reserved for black persons. He elected to stand instead and thus was cited for contempt by the judge. He appealed. The SC held that the segregation of public facilities is unconstitutional and violated Johnson's Fourteenth Amendment rights to equal protection under the law. A state may not constitutionally require segregation of public facilities, including courtrooms.

Johnson v. Zerbst, 304 U.S. 458, 58 S.Ct. 1019 (1938) **(Assistance of Counsel).** The SC ruled that in all federal trials of a serious nature, counsel must be appointed for an indigent defendant unless he or she intelligently waives this right.

Jones v. Barnes, 463 U.S. 745, 103 S.Ct. 3308 (1983) **(Sixth Amendment; Right to Counsel).** Barnes was convicted of robbery and assault in a New York jury trial. He attempted to launch several appeals through a court-appointed attorney. The attorney advised him that most of his claims were groundless. Defense counsel advised Barnes of at least seven claims of error which he considered including in his brief, but when the case was eventually appealed, the counsel focused primarily on three of the claims. Barnes filed a habeas corpus petition, alleging ineffective assistance of counsel. The SC rejected his argument that his counsel had been ineffective. Rather, the SC declared, defense counsel assigned to prosecute an appeal from a criminal conviction does not have a constitutional duty to raise every nonfrivolous issue requested by Barnes. In the SC's opinion, the counsel was effective and had supported Barnes's claims to the best of his ability, which was reasonable.

Jones v. North Carolina Prisoners' Labor Union, Inc., 433 U.S. 119, 97 S.Ct. 2532 (1977) **(Corrections; Inmate Rights).** A North Carolina Prisoners' Labor Union was established in 1974 for various purposes, such as charity work, the improvement of prison conditions, and resolutions of inmate grievances. A year later, prison officials sought to limit the activities of this prisoners' union and declared certain of its activities prohibited. The union filed suit against the prison system, specifically protesting that they had a right to solicit the membership of other inmates in their union through bulk mailings and group meetings. The SC upheld the North Carolina prison officials' action and declared that a ban on prisoner union activities is constitutional. It does not violate either the First Amendment right of free speech and assembly or the Fourteenth Amendment rights of equal protection and due process.

Jones v. United States, 357 U.S. 493, 78 S.Ct. 1253 (1958) **(Law Enforcement Officers or Agencies; Arrests).** Federal alcohol agents received information from a reliable informant in April 1956 that Jones' farmhouse in Dawsonville, Georgia, was the site of an illicit distillery. In an area behind the house, they found mash and other discarded alcohol ingredients. The officers placed Jones' home under surveillance. During the evening hours, they observed a truck stop at the house and heard loud noises from the house. They approached the truck and saw Jones' wife and children. The truck appeared to be carrying illegal whiskey. Jones' wife ran to the house. Federal agents followed her, pushed by her, and entered the premises. When asked by Mrs. Jones if they had a warrant to search, the officers said a warrant was not required. They proceeded to conduct a thorough search and discovered considerable incriminating evidence used later in court against Jones. He was convicted of violating liquor laws and possessing an unregistered still. Jones appealed, arguing that the warrantless search of his home violated his Fourth Amendment right against an unreasonable search and seizure. The SC overturned Jones' conviction, saying that the federal officers could not make a warrantless

search of one's premises regardless of whether they had probable cause to believe that the premises contained illegal contraband. Probable cause for belief that certain articles subject to seizure are in a dwelling cannot of itself justify a search without a warrant.

Jones v. United States, 362 U.S. 257, 80 S.Ct. 725 (1960) **(Law Enforcement Officers or Agencies; Exclusionary Rule).** Officers in the District of Columbia executed a search warrant for drugs and entered an apartment where Jones was a guest. When the officers searched the apartment, they found illegal drugs on the premises and they also searched Jones and found drugs in his possession. Jones was convicted later after admitting that some of the drugs on the premises were his and that he had been living at the apartment for a time. Later, he sought to suppress the evidence against him, but his motion to do so was rejected, because he "lacked standing" as the owner of the apartment. Among other things, Jones had attacked the search warrant as being issued on the basis of "hearsay" and not probable cause, making it not a reliable or valid warrant. An appellate court denied his motion, but the SC decided in his favor that, at least, he had "standing" to file such a motion. The case was remanded back to the trial court where he could again challenge the admissibility of the original evidence.

Jones v. United States, 463 U.S. 354, 103 S.Ct. 3043 (1983) **(Insanity).** Jones was acquitted of a crime by reason of insanity and was committed to a mental hospital. Within 50 days, he was entitled to a hearing to show that he was eligible for release. The hearing disclosed that he was still mentally ill and should continue to be confined. He appealed. The SC affirmed the judgment of the lower courts, supporting Jones's continued confinement. The SC held that when a criminal defendant establishes by a preponderance of the evidence that he is not guilty of a crime by reason of insanity, the due-process clause permits the government, on the basis of the insanity judgment, to confine him to a mental institution until such time as he regains his sanity or is no longer a danger to himself or to society, and he can be confined to a mental hospital for a period longer than he could have been incarcerated had he been convicted.

Jurek v. Texas, 428 U.S. 262, 91 S.Ct. 2950 (1976) **(Corrections; Death Penalty).** Jurek was convicted of murder and sentenced to death. He challenged the constitutionality of the sentence, arguing that it was capricious and arbitrary. Specifically, Texas statutes provide that juries must decide three questions: (1) whether the conduct of the defendant causing the death was deliberate and had the reasonable expectation that death would result; (2) whether the defendant's conduct was an unreasonable response to provocation, if any, by the deceased; and (3) whether it is probable that the defendant would commit criminal acts of violence constituting a continuing threat to society. Jurek challenged the constitutionality of these questions as *unconstitutionally vague*. The SC upheld his death sentence, holding that there is nothing in the Texas statutes that violates one's rights under the Eighth and Fourteenth Amendments. Further, the imposition of the death penalty is not per se cruel and unusual punishment.

Justices of Boston Municipal Court v. Lydon, 466 U.S. 294, 104 S.Ct. 1805 (1984) **(Double Jeopardy)**. Lydon was convicted under the two-tiered trial system of breaking into an automobile and stealing property. Under Massachusetts law, the first tier consists of a bench trial, where a police-court judge decides the case. Then, if a defendant is convicted, he or she may demand and receive a subsequent jury trial in the second tier. Lydon believed the evidence against him insufficient to warrant conviction. He appealed to a higher Massachusetts court, which denied his appeal, contesting the insufficiency of evidence. Lydon believed that as long as his insufficiency-of-evidence claim was under appeal by another court, it would be double jeopardy for him to be tried later by a jury. Ultimately, the SC heard Lydon's case and held that the procedures in place in Massachusetts were such that it would not be double jeopardy for Lydon to be convicted in one court and tried again in a jury trial in the second tier. It was constitutional that Lydon could be retried *de novo* without any judicial determination of the sufficiency of evidence at his prior bench trial.

K

Kastigar v. United States, 406 U.S. 441, 92 S.Ct. 1653 (1972) **(Self-Incrimination; Fifth Amendment)**. Kastigar was subpoenaed before a grand jury to give self-incriminating testimony, despite his invocation of the Fifth Amendment against self-incrimination under a grant of immunity from subsequent prosecution. The government was of course obligated to prove that the witness's testimony was sufficiently in furtherance of government interests. The witness objected. The SC upheld the right of the government to compel self-incriminating testimony from witnesses under a grant of immunity. They must answer questions of grand jurers. However, they have some protection. Should a prosecution be carried out against the same witnesses, it must be demonstrated that incriminating information was gleaned about them from sources other than their self-incriminating testimony.

Katz v. United States, 389 U.S. 347, 88 S.Ct. 507 (1967) **(Law Enforcement Officers or Agencies; Exclusionary Rule)**. Katz was a bookmaker suspected of transmitting wagering information by telephone. Federal agents bugged a public telephone booth that Katz was known to use frequently. No warrant was issued for such an action. He was convicted, and he appealed. The SC ruled that telephone booths are constitutionally protected areas designed to avoid the "uninvited ear." Thus warrants based upon probable cause must be issued before any such intrusion can be made, and the requirements articulated in *Berger v. New York* (1967) must be observed. The *Katz* case overruled *Olmstead v. United States* (1928).

Kaufman v. United States, 394 U.S. 217, 89 S.Ct. 1068 (1969) **(Corrections; Searches and Seizures)**. Kaufman was convicted of armed robbery despite pleading insanity. He filed a motion to vacate the sentence because of evidence illegally seized in violation of his Fourth Amendment rights and because he had been denied the effective assistance of counsel. The lower appellate courts held that his claims were made too late and were not proper in a postconviction proceeding. The SC overturned the lower-court decision, saying that the claim of unconstitutional search and seizure was cognizable in postconviction proceedings.

Keeney v. Tamayo-Reyes, 504 U.S. 1, 112 S.Ct. 1715 (1992) **(Habeas Corpus Relief; Corrections)**. A prison inmate, Tamayo-Reyes, was a Cuban immigrant who entered a nolo contendere plea to a first-degree manslaughter charge. He claimed that the *mens rea* portion of the crime had not been adequately explained to him in Spanish. Lower courts denied his habeas corpus petition to seek a hearing on whether he had fully understood when he entered the nolo plea. The SC held, however, that Tamayo-Reyes was entitled to a hearing and thus remanded his case to the trial court for further proceedings.

Kennedy v. Mendoza-Martinez, 372 U.S. 144, 83 S.Ct. 554 (1963) **(Corrections; Inmate Rights).** Mendoza-Martinez, born in the United States in 1922, went to Mexico in 1942 to evade military service. He returned voluntarily to the United States in 1946. In 1947, he was convicted of having violated the Selective Service Act of 1940. He served a year. In 1953, he was served with an arrest warrant and deported as an alien. He appealed the deportation order, and a lower court entered a judgment in his favor. The government appealed, but the SC affirmed the lower-court decision, holding that statutes divesting an American of his citizenship for leaving or remaining outside of the country in time of war and national emergency for the purpose of evading military service are unconstitutional because they do not afford procedural safeguards under the Fifth and Sixth Amendments.

Kent v. United States, 383 U.S. 541, 86 S.Ct. 1045 (1966) **(Juvenile Law; Waiver Hearings).** In 1959, Kent, a 14-year-old in the District of Columbia, was apprehended and charged with several housebreakings and attempted purse snatchings. He was judged delinquent and placed on probation. Subsequently in 1961, an intruder entered the apartment of a woman, took her wallet, and raped her. Fingerprints at the crime scene were later identified as those of Kent, who had been fingerprinted in connection with his delinquency case in 1959. On September 5, 1961, Kent admitted the offense as well as other crimes, and the juvenile court judge advised him of his intent to waive Kent to criminal court. In the meantime, Kent's mother had obtained an attorney, who advised the court that he intended to oppose the waiver. The judge ignored the attorney's motion and transferred Kent to the United States district court for the District of Columbia, where Kent was tried and convicted of six counts of housebreaking by a federal jury, although the jury found him "not guilty by reason of insanity" on the rape charge. Kent appealed. His conviction was reversed by the SC. The SC held that a full hearing, with assistance of counsel, must be held concerning the question of transferring a juvenile case to an adult court; children or their attorneys must have full access to social records used to make de-

terminations, and the judge must state in writing the reasons for the transfer. The majority held that his rights to due process and to the effective assistance of counsel had been violated when he was denied a formal hearing on the waiver and his attorney's motions were ignored. The SC said that the matter of a waiver to criminal court was a "critical stage," relating to the defendant's potential loss of freedoms, and thus attorney representation was fundamental to due process. Because of the *Kent* decision, waiver hearings are now considered critical stages.

Kentucky v. Stincer, 482 U.S. 730, 107 S.Ct. 2658 (1987) **(Sixth Amendment; Competency of Testimony).** Sergio Stincer sodomized two minor girls and was arrested. In the early stages of his trial, the judge held an in-chambers hearing to determine whether the minor girls were competent to testify. Stincer's attorney was permitted to attend this hearing, but Stincer was not. The judge determined that both girls were competent to testify. Stincer was convicted. He appealed, alleging that his exclusion from the in-chambers hearing had violated his right to confront his accusers under the Sixth Amendment. The Kentucky Supreme Court reversed Stincer's conviction on these Sixth Amendment grounds, but the state appealed to the SC. The SC overruled the Kentucky high court and reinstated Stincer's sodomy convictions, holding that his exclusion from the competency in-chambers hearing had not violated his Sixth Amendment rights. There was no evidence to suggest that his attendance at the hearing would have affected the girls' testimony in any way to influence the trial outcome differently. It is not necessary that defendants are entitled to attend all in-chambers hearings between defense counsel, prosecutors, and judges as a means of preserving their due-process rights.

Kentucky Department of Corrections v. Thompson, 490 U.S. 454, 109 S.Ct. 1904 (1989) **(Corrections; Visitation Privileges).** In a Kentucky prison, several prisoners were denied visits from three women on separate occasions. Reasons given were that such visits would constitute a clear and probable danger to the safety and security of the institution and would interfere with its orderly operation. No hearings were held to determine whether the prisoners should have these visits. The prisoners filed suit alleging that their Fourteenth Amendment rights had been violated. The SC upheld Kentucky prison policy, holding that such a policy denying such visitation under those circumstances was not in violation of prisoner rights. The SC stressed the safety-and-security issue relative to maintaining prison orderliness and said that no hearings were required for such decisionmaking.

Ker v. California, 374 U.S. 23, 83 S.Ct. 1623 (1963) **(Search and Seizure)**. Ker was suspected of unlawful possession of marijuana on the basis of various sales of marijuana to undercover officers and information from another man, Murphy, also a drug dealer. Police placed Ker under surveillance. One day, police went to Ker's apartment and asked the building manager to admit them. Without either an arrest or search warrant, they quickly entered the apartment and found large quantities of marijuana. Ker was subsequently arrested and convicted. He appealed, arguing that his right against unreasonable searches had been violated by the officers who had failed to get a warrant. The SC upheld the warrantless search in Ker's case, since, they reasoned, marijuana is a substance that is easily destroyed. Thus, drug dealers are known to dispose of these substances quickly if they are alerted to a possible arrest and search. They can flush narcotics down their toilets or sinks or dispose of them in other ways. Thus, because of exigent circumstances, it was important for police to act quickly in Ker's case.

Kimmelman v. Morrison, 477 U.S. 365, 106 S.Ct. 2574 (1986) **(Sixth Amendment; Right to Counsel)**. In a bench trial in New Jersey, Morrison was accused of rape. During the trial, a police officer testified about a bed sheet found at the crime scene, which had been seized without a proper search warrant. The defense attorney objected and moved to suppress statements about the bed sheet. The judge, however, ruled that it was too late to register such an objection, that the proper time would have been during discovery, when the items seized and to be used as evidence against Morrison were disclosed to him. Morrison was convicted. He filed a habeas corpus petition, alleging incompetence of counsel relating to the bed sheet and the motion to suppress it. Because the defense attorney had not raised a motion at an earlier and more proper time, Morrison argued, he had been deprived of the effective assistance of counsel and thus had been convicted. An appellate court reversed his conviction on these grounds, and the state appealed to the SC. The SC affirmed the lower appellate court, concluding that Morri-

son's counsel had been ineffective due to his failure to conduct any pretrial discovery and determine what the state had planned to present as incriminating evidence. Further, the counsel clearly had failed to make a timely motion to suppress such evidence. On these grounds, Morrison's conviction was reversed.

Kirby v. Illinois, 406 U.S. 682, 92 S.Ct. 1877 (1972) **(Law Enforcement Officers or Agencies; Lineups)**. Kirby was stopped on the street by a police officer and asked for his identification. The identification shown the officer was that of another man who had been robbed of his wallet a few days earlier. Suspicious of Kirby, the officer asked him to accompany him to police headquarters where he would check the identification. This was not an arrest and the officer did not know of the earlier robbery. While checking records at the police station, the officer discovered the robbery report. He called the robbed man and asked him to come to the police station. When the victim saw Kirby in a police detention room, he identified Kirby as the robber. At that time, Kirby was arrested, charged, and subsequently convicted of the robbery. Kirby appealed, seeking to question the identification procedure used by police and claiming that he should have had an attorney present at such an identification. The SC disagreed with Kirby, holding that there is no right to counsel at police headquarters, at police lineups, or at identification sessions when suspects have not been formally charged with a crime. (*See United States v. Wade* [1967].)

Klopfer v. North Carolina, 386 U.S. 213, 87 S.Ct. 988 (1967) **(Speedy Trials)**. Klopfer was charged with criminal trespass. His case was eventually brought to court, at which time a mistrial was declared. Klopfer inquired as to whether the government was going to continue its prosecution, and it advised him that the state was filing a *nolle prosequi* with leave, which means that it was allowing itself an opportunity to retry Klopfer at a later date convenient for it. Klopfer sought relief from the SC, declaring that he believed that the *nolle prosequi* with leave left him in a vulnerable position relative to eventual prosecution, and that he was entitled to a speedy trial under the law according to the Sixth and Fourteenth Amendments. The SC agreed with Klopfer and endorsed a speedy-trial provision, saying that defendants are entitled to such because (1) witnesses are more credible through an early trial; (2) a defendant's ability to defend himself and trial fairness would not be jeopardized; and (3) a defendant's pretrial anxiety would be minimized.

Koon v. United States, _____ U.S. _____, 116 S.Ct. 2035 (1996) **(Law Enforcement; Police Misconduct; Excessive Use of Force).** Police officers Koon and Powell were convicted in federal court of violating constitutional rights of motorist, King, under color of law during arrest and sentenced to 30 months' imprisonment. United States district court trial judge used United States sentencing guidelines and justified a downward departure of 8 offense levels from "27" to "19" to arrive at a 30 to 37-month sentence. Government appealed, contending that downward departure of 8 offense levels from "27" was an abuse of judicial discretion and that the factors cited for the downward departure were not statutory. An original offense seriousness level of "27" would have meant imposing a sentence of 70 to 87 months. The 9th Circuit Court of Appeals rejected all of the trial court's reasons for the downward departure and Koon and Powell petitioned the SC. The SC upheld the Circuit Court of Appeals in part and reversed it in part. Specifically, the SC said that the primary question to be answered on appeal is whether the trial judge abused his discretion by the downward departure in sentencing. The reasons given by the trial judge for the downward departure from an offense level of "27" to "19" were that: (1) the victim's misconduct provoked police use of force; (2) Koon and Powell had been subjected to successive state and federal criminal prosecutions; (3) Koon and Powell posed a low risk of recidivism; (4) Koon and Powell would probably lose their jobs and be precluded from employment in law enforcement; and (5) that Koon and Powell would be unusually susceptible to abuse in prison. The SC concluded that a 5-level downward departure based on the victim's misconduct that provoked officer use of force was justified, because victim misconduct is an encouraged [by the United States Sentencing Commission] basis for a guideline departure. The SC said that the remaining 3-level departure was an abuse of judicial discretion. Federal district judges may not consider a convicted offender's career loss as a downward departure factor. Further, trial judges may not consider an offender's low likelihood of recidivism, because this factor is already incorporated into the Criminal History Category in the sentencing guideline table. Considering this fac-

tor to justify a downward departure, therefore, would be tantamount to counting the factor *twice*. The SC upheld the trial judge's reliance upon the offenders' susceptibility to prison abuse and the burdens of successive state and federal prosecutions, however. The SC remanded the case back to the district court where a new sentence could be determined. Thus, a new offense level must be chosen on the basis of the victim's own misconduct which provoked the officers and where offender susceptibility to prison abuse and the burden of successive state and federal prosecutions could be considered. The significance of this case for criminal justice is that specific factors are identified by the SC to guide federal judges in imposing sentences on police officers convicted of misconduct and violating citizen rights under color of law. Victim response that provokes police use of force, an officer's susceptibility to abuse in prison, and the burden of successive state and federal prosecutions are acceptable factors to be considered to justify downward departures in offense seriousness, while one's low recidivism potential and loss of employment opportunity in law enforcement are not legitimate factors to justify downward departure in offense seriousness.

Kremen v. United States, 353 U.S. 346, 77 S.Ct. 828 (1957) **(Law Enforcement Officers or Agencies; Searches Incident to Arrest).** Kremen owned a cabin in Twain Harte, California. Two men, Steinberg and Thompson, were fugitives from federal justice. They were in the company of Kremen and another person, Coleman. FBI agents conducted surveillance of Kremen's cabin for some 24 hours, observing Thompson and Steinberg. When Thompson and Steinberg left the cabin, they were placed under arrest by FBI agents. The agents then entered the cabin and arrested Kremen and Coleman for "relieving, comforting, and assisting a fugitive from justice." Without a warrant they proceeded to search the cabin and remove all the contents, including incriminating evidence that was used to convict Kremen. He appealed, contending that the search had been illegal. The SC overturned his conviction, saying that the seizure of the entire contents of a house and its removal some 200 miles away to the FBI offices for the purpose of examination were beyond the sanction of any of its cases (at 829). It is invalid to conduct a warrantless search and seize a home's entire contents. Such action renders guilty verdicts as a result of the seized evidence illegal.

Kuhlman v. Wilson, 477 U.S. 436, 106 S.Ct. 2616 (1986) **(Law Enforcement Officers or Agencies; Custodial Interrogations).** Wilson was charged with robbery and murder following a 1970 robbery of a taxi company and murder of the night dispatcher in the Bronx, New York. Following his arraignment, he was placed in a cell with Lee, a paid government informant. Wilson made various incriminating statements to Lee, which were reported to police and used against Wilson later in his trial. According to Lee, Wilson's incriminating statements to him were "unsolicited" and "spontaneous." Wilson was convicted. He filed a habeas corpus petition alleging that his incriminating statements to Lee should have been suppressed. He claimed that his Sixth Amendment right to counsel had been violated when police deliberately elicited statements from him through Lee acting on their behalf (*see Massiah v. United States* [1964]). The state court failed to vacate his conviction on those grounds and Wilson appealed to federal court. The Circuit Court of Appeals reversed his conviction on these grounds. New York appealed this ruling to the SC, which reversed the lower appellate court ruling, thus *reinstating* Wilson's murder and robbery convictions. The SC held that apart from any information derived from the informant, Lee, there was sufficient additional inculpatory evidence against Wilson to support his conviction anyway. Further, New York courts had determined that a police officer had merely instructed Lee to "listen" to Wilson and not to elicit statements from him. Thus, unsolicited statements or statements made voluntarily do not violate a person's Sixth Amendment right to counsel during "interrogations" by police-paid sponsored informants.

Kyles v. Whitley, ___U.S.___, 115 S.Ct. 1555 (1995) **(Death Penalty).** Kyles was accused in Louisiana of first-degree murder. During the trial, the prosecution failed to disclose to Kyles favorable and exculpatory evidence under discovery. For instance, eyewitness testimony and statements favorable to Kyles were withheld, as were statements made to police by an informant, Beanie. A computer printout of all car license numbers at or near the murder scene, which did not include Kyles's car license number, was in the possession of the prosecution but was not made available to Kyles or his attorney when they de-manded discovery. He was convicted and sentenced to death. Appeals by Kyles to higher state courts resulted in affirmation of his original conviction and sentence. Then he sought relief by an appeal to the SC. The SC overturned Kyles's conviction, holding that the prosecution had violated Kyles's *Brady* rights (*see Brady v. Maryland* [1963]) to have relevant exculpatory information made available to him by the prosecution. The significance of this case is that it is the constitutional duty of prosecutors to disclose favorable evidence to defendants in criminal prosecutions.

L

Lackey v. Texas, ___U.S.___, 115 S.Ct. 1421 (1995) **(Death Penalty).** Lackey was convicted of murder and remained on death row for 17 years. He filed an appeal to the SC, arguing that 17 years on death row was cruel and unusual punishment in violation of his rights under the Eighth Amendment. The SC denied Lackey's writ of certiorari, commenting that this particular question was a "novel one" that should benefit from further study (at 1422). Justice Breyer commented that the issue was "an important *undecided one*" [emphasis added]. The SC further elaborated that often, death-row inmates cause long delays because of frivolous filings of motions or through escape or other delays. In short, the 17-year death-row period was not decided either way as cruel and unusual punishment in this particular case.

Lakeside v. Oregon, 435 U.S. 333, 98 S.Ct. 1091 (1978) **(Death Penalty).** Lakeside escaped from the Multnomah County Correctional Institution. During his trial on the escape charges, his attorney introduced evidence to show that he was not responsible for his actions because he was mentally ill. Lakeside did not testify in his own behalf. The judge advised the jury that because Lakeside did not testify in his own behalf, no adverse inference should be drawn from that fact. However, before giving his jury instructions, the judge had been requested by the defense counsel not to mention the fact that Lakeside did not have to testify. The judge ignored this request and gave the instruction anyway. Lakeside was convicted. He appealed, alleging that his right against compulsory self-incrimination had been violated when the judge gave the jury that instruction despite the request from defense counsel. The SC rejected Lakeside's appeal, saying that while it may be wise for a trial judge not to give such a cautionary instruction over defense counsel's objection, trial judges may do so as a matter of law, unless their state instructs otherwise. Thus, Lakeside's Fifth Amendment and Fourteenth Amendment rights had not been infringed.

Lamont v. Postmaster General, 381 U.S. 301, 85 S.Ct. 1493 (1965) **(Corrections; Inmate Rights).** Mail from Communist countries, in the form of propaganda-like literature and leaflets, was being routinely destroyed by the United States Post Office and letter carriers under a statute that permitted that agency to destroy unsealed foreign mail determined to be Communist political propaganda. This statute was challenged, and the SC ruled it unconstitutional in violation of the First Amendment right of free speech.

Lanier v. South Carolina, 474 U.S. 25, 106 S.Ct. 297 (1985) **(Law Enforcement Officers or Agencies; Miranda Warnings; Fifth Amendment; Voluntariness of Confessions).** Lanier was suspected in a robbery and arrested, although no arrest warrant had been prepared beforehand. During police interrogation, he gave a voluntary confession after being told his Miranda rights. He was convicted. Lanier appealed, contending that since no arrest warrant had been issued, his arrest was illegal; thus his confession, tainted by the illegal arrest, had also been illegally obtained and should not have been admissible in court against him. Further review by the South Carolina Supreme Court led the court to conclude that Lanier's confession was admissible, despite the illegal arrest, because it was voluntarily given. He appealed again. The SC reversed the conviction, holding that voluntariness is insufficient on its own to purge the taint of an illegal arrest. Voluntariness is merely a threshold requirement for Fourth Amendment analysis.

Lankford v. Idaho, 500 U.S. 110, 111 S.Ct. 1723 (1991) **(Corrections; Death Penalty).** In this rather complicated case, Lankford and his brother were charged with first-degree murder but entered a guilty plea in exchange for a minimum 10-year term. The judge refused to approve the plea agreement and the case went to trial. The defense and prosecuting attorneys proceeded as though the 10-year minimum term was being sought as a punishment, and the death penalty was not contemplated. When the brothers were con-

victed of the murder, the judge asked whether either party wished to cite aggravating or mitigating circumstances to determine the type of sentence imposed. Neither side indicated this, and in the sentencing phase, the two brothers were recommended for long prison terms. The judge, however, decided that the punishment was too lenient and imposed the death penalty on both brothers, citing several aggravating circumstances in justification. The brothers appealed. The SC overturned the death penalty because neither side had been permitted to argue the merits of aggravating or mitigating circumstances. The judge's personal feelings in the matter had come too late in the proceeding for either side to address the aggravating and mitigating circumstances. Thus, the SC ruled that the sentences of death were unconstitutional because the judge had failed to provide adequate notice that they would be imposed.

Lascelles v. Georgia, 148 U.S. 537, 13 S.Ct. 687 (1893) **(Law Enforcement Officers or Agencies; Arrests).** Lascelles was a former resident of Georgia who was living in New York. While in New York, he was served with an extradition order to Georgia to face indictments for larceny and fraud. After he was extradited to Georgia on these charges, another Georgia grand jury indicted him on other charges, for which he was subsequently tried and convicted. He contested this new conviction, saying that he should have been permitted to return to New York rather than face new indictments in Georgia. The SC heard affirmed his conviction, noting that there is no requirement for any state to bar trying a defendant for new offenses after he has been extradited to that state for earlier alleged offenses. Defendants may be tried for any other offenses than those specified in the requisition in the extradition, and no constitutional right is thereby denied. In short, if a person is extradited to a state for a specific charge, nothing exists to prevent the extraditing state from bringing new charges against him.

Lee v. Florida, 394 U.S. 378, 88 S.Ct. 2069 (1968) **(Wiretapping).** Florida officials sought to intercept a telephone conversation between Lee and another party. Incriminating information was subsequently obtained implicating Lee in a crime. He was convicted. He appealed. The SC overturned its conviction, ruling that no one may intercept a telephone message, other than the sender, and no person shall disclose the contents of such messages. Thus, state agents were prohibited from conducting warrantless wiretaps against criminal suspects.

Lee v. Illinois, 476 U.S. 530, 106 S.Ct. 2056 (1986) **(Sixth Amendment; Cross-Examination Rights).** Lee and Thomas had both killed Lee's aunt and a friend by stabbing them to death. Later, Thomas confessed to police about his role in the murders and implicated Lee. During their subsequent joint trial neither testified in his or her own behalf. However, portions of Thomas' confession implicating Lee were read to the jury over the objections of Lee's attorney. They were both convicted. Lee appealed, arguing that she had been denied her Sixth Amendment right to confront her accuser, Thomas, as he had not testified. The SC held that uncorroborated confession from a co-defendant cannot suffice to satisfy the confrontation-clause requirements of the Sixth Amendment. Because Lee had not been permitted to cross-examine Thomas about the veracity of his confession, her right to a fair trial and to confront the witness against her had been violated. Hence, her conviction was overturned.

Lee v. Washington, 390 U.S. 333, 88 S.Ct. 944 (1968) **(Corrections; Inmate Rights).** In the early 1960s, the Alabama prison system was segregated racially, with black prisoners in one section and white prisoners in another. Prisoners filed suit alleging racial discrimination relative to where they were placed in the prison. The SC decided that the Alabama prison system practice of segregating prisoners was in direct violation of the Fourteenth Amendment and therefore unconstitutional.

Lefkowitz v. Turley, 414 U.S. 70, 94 S.Ct. 316 (1973) **(Corrections; Inmate Rights).** New York statutes provided that contractors must waive their immunity to testify concerning their state contracts in such hearings as grand jury proceedings. If contractors refuse to testify, then their contracts with the state are subject to cancellation. This statute was appealed by Turley and others as unconstitutional on various grounds, including the Fifth Amendment right against self-incrimination. A circuit court of appeals held the statute unconstitutional, and New York appealed. The SC affirmed the unconstitutionality of the statute, saying that a state may not insist that public employees or government contractors waive their Fifth Amendment privilege against self-incrimination and consent to the use of the fruits of the interrogation in any later proceeding. A significant infringement of constitutional rights, such as the right against compelled

self-incrimination, cannot be justified by the speculative ability of those affected to cover the damage.

Lego v. Twomey, 404 U.S. 477, 92 S.Ct. 619 (1972) **(Self-Incrimination).** Lego confessed to a crime after interrogation by police in Illinois. Some dispute arose during the trial to suggest that his confession was not voluntarily given. Lego was convicted. He appealed, alleging that the confession had not been voluntary. The SC upheld his conviction, saying that despite the fact that the voluntariness of the confession had been questioned, if the jury believed that it was freely given, then it might consider the confession in deciding Lego's guilt or innocence. In this case, the SC said it was only sufficient to demonstrate by a preponderance of the evidence whether Lego's confession was indeed voluntary, although states other than Illinois can establish stricter standards if they wish to do so.

Lemon v. State, 861 S.W.2d 249 (1993) **(Corrections; Probationer Community Service Orders).** Lemon, a probationer convicted of misappropriation of property, was required by a judge to perform community service at the orders or discretion of his probation officer. He appealed. The Texas Court of Appeals reversed this condition of his probation, because it is up to the judge, not the probationary officer, to determine the nature of one's community service to be performed under a sentence of probation with conditions.

Lewis v. Jeffers, 497 U.S. 764, 110 S.Ct. 3092 (1990) **(Eighth Amendment; Death Penalty).** Jeffers and his girlfriend, Cheney, were arrested and held in the Pima County Jail on charges of possessing narcotics and stolen property. While on bail, Jeffers determined that Cheney was cooperating with police and made arrangements to kill her. Under false pretenses, he invited her to his apartment, gave her an overdose of heroin, and when she didn't die immediately, used his belt to strangle her. Following her death, Jeffers and a friend injected her body with considerably more heroin and took numerous photographs of her dead body, wrapped her in newspapers and plastic bags, and buried her in a shallow grave. Later, when Jeffers was arrested, tried and convicted of her murder, the judge gave instructions to the jury during the penalty phase of the trial. The jury found two aggravating circumstances and no mitigating ones and recommended the death penalty for Jeffers. Jeffers appealed, alleging that the jury instruction containing the phrase, "especially heinous . . . and depraved" was overly broad and unconstitutionally vague. The SC heard Jeffers' appeal and upheld his conviction and death sentence, thus rejecting his various claims. The statutory circumstance that the crime was committed in "an especially heinous, cruel, or depraved manner" was not unconstitutionally vague, and further, the jury, a rational body, could have found that Jeffers had committed the murder in this manner. Thus, Jeffers' Eighth and Sixth Amendment rights had not been violated.

Lewis v. United States, 385 U.S. 206, 87 S.Ct. 424 (1966) **(Informants).** An undercover agent purchased marijuana from Lewis on two different occasions. In one instance, he entered Lewis' home and bought marijuana. Lewis was subsequently convicted, partially by the testimony given by the undercover agent. Lewis appealed, alleging his Fourth Amendment right against unreasonable searches and seizures had been violated. The SC disagreed and upheld his conviction, saying that the misrepresentation of the undercover agent's identity and Lewis' willingness to sell marijuana were insufficient to show that a Fourth Amendment rights violation had occurred.

Libretti v. United States, ___U.S.___, 116 U.S. 356 (1995) **(Asset Forfeiture).** Libretti was convicted in federal court of violating various drug laws, money-laundering, and firearms offenses. He entered a guilty plea and was convicted. The government then seized all his criminal-tainted assets, including assets Libretti believed were beyond the scope of forfeiture. He appealed the more extensive forfeiture, contending that he had not been advised of it during his plea-bargain hearing and that he should have been so advised by the judge and prosecutor. The SC upheld the conviction and the more extensive asset forfeiture, holding that a plea agreement does not obligate the judge to set forth all material possessions subject to forfeiture, that the plea agreement itself is designed to determine the voluntariness of the plea, among other things, and whether the offender is knowingly and intelligently waiving his rights to trial, confronting witnesses against him, and other provisions. When Libretti waived his right to a jury trial, he gave up the right to have a subsequent separate jury determination of which of his assets ought to be seized.

Linkletter v. Walker, 381 U.S. 618, 85 S.Ct. 1731 (1965) **(Exclusionary Rule).** Linkletter was arrested without a warrant in Louisiana. Police took him to the police station, where they searched him. Then the police went to his home and seized certain property and papers. Subsequently, they searched his place of business, finding incriminating information. All of these searches were conducted without a warrant. The searches were subsequently upheld as valid, based upon probable cause, and incident to an arrest. Linkletter was convicted of burglary. Some time later, in June 1961 *Mapp v. Ohio* was decided, thereby extending the exclusionary rule to all states to deter police misconduct in conducting warrantless searches of a defendant's premises similar to the searches of Linkletter's business and dwelling. Linkletter filed a habeas corpus petition, claiming that the evidence police seized in his case ought to have been suppressed, given the decision in the *Mapp* case. The SC heard his appeal and upheld his conviction, saying that the exclusionary rule cannot be applied retroactively because his conviction occurred prior to the *Mapp* decision. The significance of this case is that it demonstrates that subsequent SC decisions are not retroactively applied to prior cases. The exclusionary rule does not apply to cases decided before *Mapp*. The SC was careful to note, however, that such retrospective applications of rules *may* be made in future cases, depending upon the issue and law.

Lisenba v. People of the State of California, 314 U.S. 219, 62 S.Ct. 280 (1941) **(Corrections; Death Penalty).** Lisenba was accused of murder in California. He used an alias, Robert S. James. He was questioned extensively when he was first arrested. He confessed and was convicted. Later he appealed, claiming that his confession had been coerced. However, the SC noted that Lisenba had showed a self-possession, a coolness, and an acumen throughout his questioning and at his trial that negated the view that he had so lost his freedom of action that the statements made were not his but were the result of the deprivation of his free choice to admit, to deny, or refuse to answer. Accordingly, the SC upheld his murder conviction and dismissed his allegations of coercion.

Liteky v. United States, ___U.S.___, 114 S.Ct. 1147 (1994) **(Judicial Remarks as Bias or Prejudice Against Defendants).** Liteky and other persons were arrested for willfully injuring federal property. The indictment charged that Liteky and others had committed acts of vandalism, including the spilling of human blood on walls and various objects, at the Fort Benning Military Reservation. During the trial, the judge make frequent remarks interpreted as caustic, critical, or disapproving of, or hostile to, Liteky's counsel, Liteky, and his co-defendants. Liteky was convicted. He appealed, arguing that the judge should have excused himself from the case because of his bias and prejudicial remarks made during the trial. The SC rejected Liteky's argument, holding that the fact that the presiding judge may, upon completion of the evidence, be exceedingly ill disposed towards the defendant, who has been shown to be a thoroughly reprehensible person, does not make the judge excusable for bias or prejudice, as his knowledge and the opinion it produced were properly and necessarily acquired in the course of the proceedings and might be necessary to completion of the judge's task. The significance of this case, in part, is that federal judges have considerable latitude in their remarks made during criminal trials. It takes more than expressions of hostility or impatience or animosity to create conditions under which federal judges must excuse themselves from a federal district court criminal proceeding.

Lockett v. Ohio, 438 U.S. 586, 98 S.Ct. 2954 (1978) **(Corrections; Death Penalty).** Lockett was convicted of aggravated murder and robbery and sentenced to death. Because he had been primarily an "aider and abettor" rather than the perpetrator of the crime, he challenged his conviction on various grounds. He alleged that it was improper for the prosecutor to make remarks to the jury to the effect that the state's evidence was "unrefuted" and "uncontradicted"; that exclusion of prospective jurors who indicated that they could not be trusted to decide the death penalty because of their particular views was improper; that he had not been given adequate notice of the meaning of the statute under which he was convicted; and that the death penalty statute did not permit consideration of aggravating and mitigating circumstances. The SC heard the appeal and ruled negatively on the first three allegations. However, it overturned his death sentence on the fourth allegation, noting that Ohio had an unusual means of considering aggravating and mitigating circumstances in its present death-penalty sentencing procedures. Specifically, the limited range of mitigating circumstances that might be considered was in violation of both the Eighth and Fourteenth Amendments.

Lockhart v. Fretwell, 506 U.S. 364, 113 S.Ct. 838 (1993) **(Sixth Amendment; Right to Counsel).** Fretwell was convicted of capital murder in Arkansas and sentenced to death. Subsequently, the death penalty was vacated and Fretwell was sentenced to life-without-parole. That sentence was imposed after it was determined that there were several errors involving Fretwell's counsel. One of these "errors" involved failing to make a motion protesting the inclusion of an aggravating factor that duplicated one of the elements of the capital murder offense. Arkansas appealed and the SC heard the case. The SC reinstated the death sentence, holding that the defense attorney's actions had not been sufficiently prejudicial to warrant setting aside the death sentence. Prejudice in this instance referred to specific trial unreliability or irregularities, not to weighing aggravating and mitigating circumstances. Further, Fretwell would have had to show that the defense counsel's errors had been so prejudicial so as to render the trial fundamentally unfair or unreliable. Fretwell had failed to demonstrate this.

Lockhart v. McCree, 476 U.S. 162, 106 S.Ct. 1758 (1986) **(Corrections; Death Penalty).** McCree was charged with capital murder. During jury selection at McCree's trial, the judge dismissed for cause various jurors who voiced their opposition to the death penalty, which was a consideration in McCree's case. The jury eventually convicted McCree of murder, but they recommended life without parole. McCree appealed the sentence, contending that the judge had had no right to remove prospective jurors, simply because they opposed the death penalty. The SC upheld McCree's conviction, holding that it is constitutional in a capital murder case for jurors to be excused who oppose the death penalty in such a way so that their performance as jurors would substantially be impaired. This case upholds the right of the judge and prosecutors to strike prospective jurors who oppose the death penalty and whose judgment would be impaired as a result, without violating the constitutional rights of the accused to enjoy a fair and impartial trial. Thus the notion of a death-qualified jury is upheld here (compare this case with *Witherspoon v. Illinois* [1968] on a similar issue).

Lo-Ji Sales, Inc. v. New York, 442 U.S. 319, 99 S.Ct. 2319 (1979) **(Law Enforcement Officers or Agencies; Fourth Amendment; Search and Seizure).** A New York police investigator purchased two films from Lo-Ji Sales, an "adult" bookstore. He concluded that such films were in violation of a New York obscenity ordinance. He obtained a general search warrant, authorizing officers to seize anything "similar" to the first two films. A subsequent six-hour search by officers yielded numerous films, projectors, magazines, and other "adult" paraphernalia. Lo-Ji Sales was charged with and convicted of violating the state obscenity ordinance. A motion to suppress the seized materials was denied. An appeal was subsequently directed to the SC, where the obscenity conviction was overturned. Although police argued that the Lo-Ji Sales "adult" bookstore was a "public place" and thus open to inspection, including searches and seizures, and that the attendant at the store "gave his consent" for the subsequent search, the SC rejected these rationales as invalid. The store clerk had been placed under arrest and thus was not in a position to give his consent. Furthermore, the search warrant had failed to specify the places to be searched and the items to be seized; it failed because of its lack of specificity. Thus, the items seized as the result of the unreasonable and illegal search were suppressed and the Lo-Ji conviction reversed.

Long v. District Court of Iowa, 385 U.S. 192, 87 S.Ct. 362 (1966) **(Court Access).** Long was convicted of larceny. He was sentenced to a term "not to exceed five years." While serving his sentence in prison, Long filed for habeas corpus relief, alleging that his due-process rights had been violated because he had not been represented by counsel during his preliminary hearing and because the court would not give him, as an indigent, a free transcript of the habeas corpus proceeding. The Iowa court denied him the right to a free transcript and found his lack of attorney representation groundless. Long appealed to the SC, which overturned the Iowa court's decision denying him the right to a transcript. The SC said that to interpose any financial consideration between an indigent prisoner and his exercise of a state right to sue for his liberty is to deny that prisoner the equal protection of the laws.

Lopez v. United States, 373 U.S. 427, 83 S.Ct. 1381 (1963) **(Law Enforcement Officers or Agencies; Electronic Surveillance).** Lopez was under investigation by the IRS for income tax evasion. An IRS agent called Lopez and recorded a conversation during which Lopez offered the agent a bribe to ignore undeclared income. The in-

criminating statement was subsequently admitted into evidence against Lopez and he was convicted. He appealed, contending that no warrant had been obtained to conduct such electronic surveillance and that his incriminating statements ought to have been excluded. The SC heard the case and upheld Lopez's conviction, saying that the IRS agent, as a participant in the conversation, had been entitled to record it, without giving notice to the other party that such a recording was being made. The importance of this case is that it authorizes warrantless recordings of conversations, wherein *one* of the parties *consents* to the recording despite the other party's ignorance of the fact that the conversation is being recorded. Thus, if anyone wishes to tape-record a telephone conversation without the knowledge or consent of the other party, the recording will be admissible as evidence as long as *one* of the parties consents to the recording. This does not mean, however, that conversations between two parties can be recorded by a third party without a warrant based upon probable cause. (*See Berger v. New York* (1967) for a specific statement on intercepted recordings of conversations and lawful wiretaps.)

Los Angeles v. Lyons, 461 U.S. 95, 103 S.Ct. 1660 (1983) **(Law Enforcement Officers or Agencies; Arrests).** Lyons was stopped by Los Angeles police officers for a traffic violation. During the stop, police seized him and placed him in a chokehold. He offered no resistance, and the chokehold was applied without provocation or justification. It damaged Lyons's larynx. Lyons sued Los Angeles, but the city denied him relief. The SC heard the case and ruled that Lyons had failed to satisfy the case-or-controversy requirement to show that he had sustained immediate danger from the challenged official conduct (the chokehold). The case significance is that the federal court cannot entertain claims by any or all citizens who do no more than assert that certain practices of law-enforcement officers are unconstitutional.

Louisiana ex rel. Francis v. Resweber, 329 U.S. 459, 67 S.Ct. 374 (1947) **(Corrections; Inmate Rights; Death Penalty).** Francis was convicted of murder and sentenced to death in the state electric chair. On the appointed date, he was strapped in the electric chair and received a current of electricity designed to cause death. However, a chair malfunction caused the electrocution to be insufficient to kill Francis. Thus, Francis was returned to his prison cell and a new execution date was set, pending repair of the electric chair. Francis appealed, contending that a failed execution attempt made unconstitutional any subsequent execution attempt by the state. In short, Francis was declaring a case of double jeopardy. The SC disagreed, saying that a failed attempt to carry out a valid death sentence does not nullify or render unconstitutional any subsequent application of the death penalty as prescribed by law. This was not a case of double jeopardy.

Lowenfield v. Phelps, 484 U.S. 231, 108 S.Ct. 546 (1988) **(Death Penalty; Aggravating and Mitigating Circumstances).** Lowenfield murdered a woman with whom he lived, her three children, and one of her male friends. A trial was held in Louisiana, and a conviction resulted. During the sentencing phase of the trial, the judge gave the jury instructions about weighing the aggravating and mitigating circumstances. One element of the offense was that Lowenfield "intended to kill or inflict great bodily harm upon more than one person." The jury deliberated for many hours and could not arrive at a decision as to the recommended sentence. A note was sent to the judge for additional instructions, and the judge complied. The judge advised the jurors that one aggravating circumstance was the fact that death resulted to more than one person as the result of the defendant's actions. With this instruction, the jury quickly decided that the death penalty should be imposed and recommended it to the judge. Lowenfield was sentenced to death. He appealed, alleging that his due-process rights had been violated when one of the crime elements was the same as an aggravating circumstance. Further, he alleged that the judge's subsequent clarification instruction was inherently coercive. The SC heard the case and rejected both of Lowenfield's arguments. The SC determined that the judge's instruction was not so coercive as to deprive Lowenfield of any constitutional right. Further, the SC said that the death sentence was not invalidated merely because one element of the crime happened to coincide with one of the statutory aggravating circumstances.

Lozada v. Deeds, 498 U.S. 430, 111 S.Ct. 860 (1991) **(Sixth Amendment; Right to Effective Assistance of Counsel).** Lozada was convicted in Nevada on four counts of possession and sale of controlled substances. Following the trial proceedings, Lozada's attorney failed to notify him of his right to appeal, of the procedures and time limitations of an appeal, and of his right to court-appointed counsel. Further, Lozada alleged that his attorney had failed to file a notice of appeal or to ensure that Lozada received court-appointed counsel on appeal. Finally, he alleged that the attorney had misled Lozada's sister, and hence, Lozada, when he told her that the case had been forwarded to the public defender's office, which it hadn't. Lozada appealed on a subsequent habeas corpus petition on the grounds that he had had ineffective assistance of counsel as the result of these alleged events. Lower appellate courts dismissed his appeal. The SC found otherwise, however, and reversed his convictions, holding that Lozada had made a substantial showing that he had been denied the right to effective assistance of counsel.

Ludwig v. Massachusetts, 427 U.S. 618, 96 S.Ct. 2781 (1976) **(Double Jeopardy).** Ludwig was convicted first in a nonjury trial, and later in a new six-person jury trial *de novo*, of negligently operating a motor vehicle so that public safety was endangered. Under Massachusetts law, a two-tiered trial system exists. The first tier consists of a nonjury trial. If the defendant is convicted, then he may appeal the case to an actual jury trial. Ludwig believed that the fact that he had initially requested a jury trial and had not been given one violated his speedy-trial rights, and that his subsequent conviction by the jury trial was double jeopardy stemming from the first nonjury trial conviction. The SC upheld the two-tiered trial system of Massachusetts and declared that Ludwig's right against double jeopardy and to a speedy trial had not been violated. Further, the SC noted that Massachusetts guarantees defendants a jury trial as the direct result of an appeal from a nonjury proceeding where a conviction results. This fact is not held to be double jeopardy.

M

Maine v. Moulton, 474 U.S. 159, 106 S.Ct. 477 (1985) **(Law Enforcement Officers or Agencies; Confessions).** Moulton was suspected of burglary and theft. When he was arrested, he obtained counsel. Later, a friend of Moulton's, Colson, agreed with police to record his telephone conversations with Moulton. Incriminating evidence was obtained in this fashion and introduced later against Moulton in court. Following his conviction, he appealed, and the SC heard the case. The SC held that the incriminating statements made by Moulton to Colson had been recorded by request of police; thus this was an interrogation of sorts, where Moulton's attorney should have been present. Because Moulton was being represented by counsel, the "interrogation" and the incriminating evidence it yielded had to be suppressed as evidence against Moulton. The SC overturned Moulton's conviction on this basis. (*See Massiah v. United States* [1964] for a comparative case).

Maleng v. Cook, 490 U.S. 488, 109 S.Ct. 1923 (1989) **(Corrections; Jailhouse Lawyers; Frivolous Lawsuits).** Cook was convicted of robbery in Washington and sentenced to 20 years. This term expired in 1978. While on parole in 1976, Cook was convicted of assault and was sentenced to two life terms. He was also sentenced to 30 years imprisonment by a federal judge for bank robbery. In 1985, Cook filed a habeas corpus petition challenging his latest sentences and the enhancement of them resulting from his expired sentence from 1958. The SC ruled that Cook was entitled to file his petition because he was "in custody" through federal incarceration. This narrow ruling by the SC permitted Cook to proceed with his lawsuits against Washington and the federal government for their alleged illegal enhancements of his sentence.

Malinski v. New York, 324 U.S. 401, 65 S.Ct. 781 (1944) **(Confessions).** Through informants close to him (his girlfriend and an old friend), Malinski was implicated in the murder of a police officer. He was later arrested and interrogated by police. He made a confession to police after being confronted by witness statements. Malinski was also humiliated by police, who kept him in a state of undress. His arraignment was delayed for four days. He was held without being permitted to speak to anyone other than police, who, he alleged, beat him during the interrogation sessions. He was convicted. He appealed. The SC overturned his conviction, noting evident coercion and that other due-process rights had been violated during Malinski's processing.

Malley v. Briggs, 475 U.S. 335, 106 S.Ct. 1092 (1986) **(Legal Liabilities of Police Officers).** Malley was a police officer who obtained an arrest warrant against Briggs, a marijuana-dealing suspect. Briggs and others were arrested and charged with possession of marijuana. A grand jury subsequently failed to indict them and the charges were dropped. At that point, Briggs filed a Title 42, U.S.C. Section 1983 civil-rights suit against Malley, alleging that Malley had violated Briggs' constitutional rights against illegal searches and seizures. Malley raised the claim of absolute immunity, because he was a Rhode Island state trooper acting officially. The SC ruled that Malley was not entitled to *absolute* immunity but to *qualified* immunity in this case. The absolute-immunity defense does not extend to police officers when they are sued for damages under Title 42, U.S.C. Section 1983 claims.

Mallory v. United States, 354 U.S. 449, 77 S.Ct. 1356 (1957) **(Confessions; Custodial Interrogations).** In an apartment house in the early morning hours of April 7, 1954, a woman doing laundry in the basement encountered trouble with the washing machine. She called the janitor, Mallory, who lived in the building with his wife and two sons. The janitor fixed the washing machine, left the laundry room, and later reappeared masked with his two sons. These men raped the woman and left the apartment shortly thereafter. The victim gave an account of the rape to police and named Mallory as a key suspect. Later that afternoon, Mallory and his sons were arrested and taken to police headquarters and questioned. Mallory was subjected to intensive questioning and a lie detector test. At about 10 p.m. that evening, he confessed. Because a magistrate could not be found, Mallory was brought before a commissioner the following morning and arraigned. Because of various delays, Mallory's trial occurred a year later. He was convicted. He appealed, arguing that he had not been brought before a magistrate without undue delay and that his extensive interrogation by police had been without probable cause and of unreasonable duration. The SC heard Mallory's case and overturned his conviction, holding that police had had only reasonable suspicion when Mallory was originally arrested, and that the subsequent detention and interrogation yielded probable cause for which rape charges could be filed against Mallory. The SC also noted that during the afternoon when Mallory was first arrested, numerous magistrates had been available to police. Thus Mallory had not been brought before them without undue delay, a violation of his due-process rights. The SC said that it is not the function of police to arrest, as it were, at large and to use an interrogating process at police headquarters to determine whom they should charge before a committing magistrate on "probable cause."

Malloy v. Hogan, 378 U.S. 1, 84 S.Ct. 1489 (1964) **(Self-Incrimination).** Malloy was suspected of having knowledge about illegal gambling in Connecticut. He was subpoenaed to provide information about illegal gambling before a magistrate. He refused to testify on the grounds that his Fifth Amendment right against self-incrimination would be violated. He was jailed on a contempt citation for his refusal. He appealed. The SC overturned his contempt citation, saying that although Malloy was not a defendant in a criminal action, his testimony could have incriminated him in such illegal activity, and thus he had right to invoke his Fifth Amendment right against self-incrimination.

Maness v. Meyers, 419 U.S. 492, 95 S.Ct. 584 (1976) **(Corrections; Probation and Parole).** Maness is a lawyer in Temple, Texas. His client was accused of selling obscene magazines. During the early investigative proceedings, Maness and a co-counsel represented his client and another man on the same obscenity charges and were served with a notice to produce numerous obscene magazines in court. Maness elected not to comply with the order because of his client's Fifth Amendment claim against self-incrimination. Maness was cited for contempt by the judge. He appealed. The SC heard Maness' case and decided the very narrow question of whether a lawyer may be held in contempt for advising his client, during the trial of a civil case, to refuse to produce material demanded by a subpoena *duces tecum* when the lawyer believes in good faith the material may tend to incriminate his client. The contempt order was set aside. The SC stressed the good faith of Maness in defending his client and justifying his conduct.

Manson v. Braithwaite, 432 U.S. 98, 97 S.Ct. 2243 (1977) **(Law Enforcement Officers or Agencies; Lineups; Pretrial Identification).** An undercover officer, Glover, exchanged money for drugs with a man later described as Braithwaite. The exchange occurred in an apartment complex where Braithwaite was observed through a door open about 12 inches. Glover described the man to other officers, and they thought it might be Braithwaite, who fit that description and had a prior record of drug offenses. They showed a picture of Braithwaite to Glover, who identified Braithwaite as the drug dealer. Braithwaite was arrested and subsequently convicted. He ap-

pealed, seeking to suppress Glover's identification of him as biased, as other police officers had showed Glover Braithwaite's photograph and did not put him in a lineup. The SC upheld Braithwaite's conviction, holding that the identification procedure followed in Braithwaite's case was not a violation of due process, despite the suggestive nature of the photograph shown to Glover. Thus the photograph as well as Glover's direct identification of Braithwaite in court were not suppressed as evidence against him.

Mapp v. Ohio, 367 U.S. 1081, 81 S.Ct. 1684 (1961) **(Law Enforcement Officers or Agencies; Exclusionary Rule).** Police in Cleveland suspected someone of bomb making or possessing bomb materials. The suspect was believed to be at the home of Mapp, a woman friend. Officers went to Mapp's home and asked to come in. Mapp refused, suggesting that officers get a warrant. The officers left and Mapp called her attorney. The officers returned later, waving a piece of paper and saying that they had a warrant to conduct their search of her premises. Mapp's attorney arrived at the same time. Neither he nor Mapp was permitted to see the "warrant." Mapp grabbed the piece of paper and shoved it down her bosom. A police officer quickly retrieved it and handcuffed her. A thorough search of her home disclosed no bomb materials. However, a trunk in Mapp's basement yielded pencil sketches and drawings depicting what officers believed to be "pornography." Mapp was subsequently convicted of possessing pornographic material. She appealed to the SC, claiming that the officers had had no right to search her home. The SC agreed with Mapp and overturned her conviction. No warrant had ever been issued and it was unknown what the piece of paper was that police waved in front of Mapp and her attorney preceding their unlawful search of her premises. This is a landmark SC case, because it established the *exclusionary rule* to deter police misconduct in search-and-seizure cases. It made the rule applicable to *both* state and federal law-enforcement officers. Thus, any evidence seized illegally is inadmissible later in court against criminal suspects. Overruled cases relating to the exclusionary rule were *Weeks v. United States* (1914), *Wolf v. Colorado* (1949) and *Wong Sun v. United States* (1963). The Fourth Amendment protects citizens from unreasonable searches and seizures by the states; this decision by SC overturned the *Wolf* decision and made the Fourth

Amendment applicable to states through the due-process clause of the Fourteenth Amendment.

Marron v. United States, 275 U.S. 192, 48 S.Ct. 74 (1927) **(Law Enforcement Officers or Agencies; Searches).** Prohibition officers secured a search warrant for illegal liquors and entered Marron's premises. They found illegal liquor, but they continued their search and eventually discovered ledgers and other personal items unrelated to liquor. They arrested Marron and confiscated these materials, some of which were used to convict him of unlawfully selling liquor and operating a general nuisance. Marron appealed, arguing that the officers had had no right to seize his ledgers and that this evidence ought to have been suppressed. He also argued that his ledgers were a form of self-incrimination and that his Fifth Amendment right had been violated as the result of the officers violating his Fourth Amendment right against unreasonable searches and seizures. The SC heard the case and overturned his conviction, ruling that the illegal search warrant relating to his seized ledgers should have resulted in suppression of these documents as evidence against him. The SC further noted that the Fifth Amendment protects every person against self-incrimination by evidence obtained through search and seizure in violation of rights under the Fourth Amendment.

Marshall v. Lonberger, 459 U.S. 422, 103 S.Ct. 843 (1983) **(Death Penalty; Aggravating Circumstances).** Lonberger was accused of capital murder. During his Ohio trial, prosecutors introduced a document showing that he had entered a guilty plea to a crime in Illinois. He was convicted. Lonberger appealed on grounds that the Illinois conviction had been improperly introduced and that his guilty plea in the Illinois case had not been voluntary. The SC heard Lonberger's appeal and upheld his conviction, saying that the admission in the Ohio murder trial of Lonberger's Illinois conviction based upon a guilty plea had not deprived Lonberger of a fair trial or violated any federal right.

Martinez v. California, 444 U.S. 275, 100 S.Ct. 553 (1980) **(Corrections; Parole Officer Liabilities).** Thomas, a parolee, was convicted of rape in 1969 and sentenced to a 20-year term. He had previously been diagnosed as having mental problems and had spent some time in a state mental hospital. After serving only 5 years in prison, Thomas was paroled to the custody of his mother.

While on parole, he murdered a 15-year-old girl. A wrongful death action under Title 42, U.S.C. Section 1983 was filed by the victim's family, alleging that California was liable for her death and that she had been deprived of her life without due process of law. Essentially, this case represents a challenge of whether or not a state is liable for the actions of paroled persons. Are parole officers exempted from liability when parolees commit crimes that harm others? The SC said that California authorities were not liable in this case; the death caused by Thomas was not caused by state action.

Maryland v. Buie, 494 U.S. 325, 110 S.Ct. 1093 (1990) **(Searches Incident to Arrest).** Police suspected Buie of involvement in an armed robbery and went to his home with a valid arrest warrant. The officers fanned out and commenced searching the home for Buie, who was in the basement. He surrendered. While the police investigated the basement to see if anyone else was there who might pose a danger to them, they observed a red running suit like the one used in the armed robbery. This evidence was seized and used in a subsequent trial where Buie was convicted of armed robbery. He appealed, arguing that the police had had no business entering parts of his home searching for evidence without a valid search warrant. The SC disagreed and said that in this case, officers were merely attempting to determine whether anyone else might be on the premises who would pose a danger to them. The SC stressed that this was a protective sweep for the safety of officers, and that contraband or evidence seen in plain view during such a sweep was not immune from a Fourth Amendment reasonable seizure.

Maryland v. Craig, 497 U.S. 836, 110 S.Ct. 3157 (1990) **(Sixth Amendment; Trial Rights).** Craig was suspected of sexual offenses, including assault and battery arising from her operation of a preschool and sexual abuse of a six-year-old child. Under Maryland law, child witnesses may give testimony through one-way closed-circuit television, not directly in the courtroom in the presence of defendants, if it is believed that the child would suffer emotional distress from the courtroom appearance. This procedure is not regarded as denying defendants "the right to confront and cross-examine their accusers." Craig was convicted. She appealed, citing a violation of her Sixth Amendment right to confront and cross-examine her accuser as the result of the indirect, closed-circuit child testimony. The SC rejected her appeal, holding that the confrontation clause does not categorically prohibit child witnesses in child-abuse cases from testifying against defendants at their trials, outside of defendants' presence, by one-way closed-circuit television, especially a finding of "necessity" (child trauma and mental distress) made on a case-specific basis.

Maryland v. Garrison, 480 U.S. 79, 107 S.Ct. 1013 (1987) **(Law Enforcement Officers or Agencies; Searches).** Armed with a valid search warrant into an apartment rented by McWebb, police mistakenly entered an apartment rented by Garrison, where they found illegal drugs. Garrison was subsequently convicted under the Controlled Substance Act. He appealed, contending that the police had not had a valid search warrant or probable cause to enter his apartment to look for contraband. The SC disagreed, saying that if officers happen to search the wrong dwelling in the reasonable but mistaken belief that they are in the right dwelling, this action does not violate Fourth Amendment rights of those in the wrongly invaded dwellings. In this instance, it was determined that the search warrant originally obtained was overbroad; however, even this ambiguity did not invalidate the warrant. This ruling is similar to the good-faith exception to the exclusionary rule. (*See United States v. Leon* [1984]).

Maryland v. Macon, 472 U.S. 463, 105 S.Ct. 2778 (1978) **(Fourth Amendment; Illegal Searches and Seizures).** Bacon was convicted of knowingly distributing obscene material. He appealed, claiming that government agents, in this case county detectives without a warrant, had entered his place of business for the purpose of looking at his obscene material and that this was tantamount to a search under the Fourth Amendment. The SC disagreed, upholding his conviction. The SC said that the county detectives' action in entering his business was not a "search" in the Fourth Amendment sense, since his place of business was open to the public, including county detectives. Further, the county detectives had arrested Bacon following examination of the obscene material and had confiscated some of the material. The SC held that this material was not excludable as evidence against Bacon, since it was a reasonable seizure incident to a lawful warrantless arrest.

Massachusetts v. Sheppard, 468 U.S. 981, 104 S.Ct. 3424 (1984) **(Law Enforcement Officers or Agencies; Exclusionary Rule).** Sheppard, a murder suspect, was investigated by police. Officers attempted to obtain a search warrant articulating the places to be searched and things or items to be seized. For some reason, conventional search warrants were not available, so the officers decided to use alternative warrants used for searching for controlled substances. These warrants were in a different form from those of conventional search warrants. The officers crossed out certain phraseology and wrote in other pertinent phraseology so that the warrant would be worded correctly. After further modification by a judge, the contrived search warrant against Sheppard was signed. Incriminating evidence was obtained as the result of executing the search warrant. Sheppard's attorney made a pretrial motion alleging that the contrived search warrant was invalid; thus, according to the exclusionary rule, the evidence obtained by its execution ought to be suppressed. The trial judge allowed the evidence against Sheppard, who was convicted of first-degree murder. He appealed, but the SC upheld his conviction, despite the faulty nature of the search warrant. The SC declared that in a manner similar to *United States v. Leon* (1984) the police officers executing the search warrant had done so in good faith. The difference between *United States v. Leon* (1984) and *Sheppard* is that in *Sheppard*, it was alleged that the officers *knew* that the warrant was defective in advance, since it had been substantially revised and rewritten; whereas in *Leon*, officers *did not know* the defectiveness of the warrant. The SC concluded that the officers in *Sheppard believed* the warrant-issuing judge, who had advised them that the warrant was valid when, in fact, it wasn't.

Massiah v. United States, 377 U.S. 201, 84 S.Ct. 1199 (1964) **(Law Enforcement Officers or Agencies; Interrogations).** Massiah was believed to be transporting illegal drugs into the United States from South America. He was indicted by a federal grand jury on drug charges. While he was under indictment and awaiting trial, a friend of Massiah's was directed by FBI agents to sit in Massiah's car and elicit incriminating statements about the drugs from Massiah. Massiah's friend was wearing a wire transmitter, and an FBI agent was sitting in a car behind Massiah's car in order to record these incriminating statements. Massiah did make incriminating statements that were recorded and he was subsequently convicted. He appealed. The SC overturned his conviction, saying that the conversation he had with his friend in Massiah's car constituted an *interrogation*, since the friend was *acting on behalf of and at the instruction of the government*. Thus, because Massiah was under indictment and represented by counsel, who was entitled to be present during the interrogation but was not present, Massiah's constitutional rights had been violated.

Mathis v. United States, 391 U.S. 1, 88 S.Ct. 1503 (1968) **(Law Enforcement Officers or Agencies; Confessions).** Mathis was accused of filing false claims for income tax refunds. While he was awaiting his trial, IRS agents visited him at the jail and without issuing a Miranda warning, asked Mathis various self-incriminating questions about his tax returns, who prepared them, and other matters. He was not warned to remain silent if he wished, or told he had the right to an attorney. He made various incriminating statements that were later used against him in court. He appealed, alleging that he should have been told his Miranda rights before IRS agents interrogated him. The SC agreed with Mathis, holding that under incarcerative interrogations such as these, investigators, even IRS agents, must tell suspects of criminal activity such as income tax evasion their Miranda rights. Mathis's conviction was overturned.

Mathews v. United States, 485 U.S. 58, 108 S.Ct. 883 (1988) **(Entrapment).** Mathews allegedly provided a loan to a paid government informant who was sponsored by the FBI. The loan involved a kickback to Mathews for making the loan involving the Small Business Administration. The FBI arrested Mathews for accepting a bribe. At his trial, Mathews sought to raise the entrapment defense, but the judge ruled that Mathews could not do so unless he admitted to all elements of the bribery charge. Mathews wished to deny certain of these elements, but he also wanted to raise the entrapment defense. He was convicted. He appealed and the SC overturned his conviction, saying that defendants may raise the entrapment defense without admitting to one or more elements of the crimes with which they are charged. Previous courts had ruled narrowly that entrapment may be raised as an affirmative defense only if defendants admit to *all* elements of the offense initially. Thus the *Mathews* case broadens this entrapment issue and permits defendants to raise the entrapment defense and deny certain elements of their alleged crimes.

Mayberry v. Pennsylvania, 400 U.S. 455, 91 S.Ct. 499 (1971) **(Fair Trials).** Mayberry was convicted of a crime and was cited for 11 separate contempt-of-court charges by the judge. Mayberry had been verbally abusive to the judge and had engaged in continual disruptive behavior. The judge subsequently sentenced Mayberry to an additional 22 years for the contempt charges. Mayberry appealed. The SC reversed the contempt convictions and sentences, saying that another judge should have heard the inflammatory comments about the judge and the bases for contempt citations. The SC said that Mayberry's removal from the courtroom would have been the best remedy for his conduct, given the circumstances.

Mabry v. Johnson, 467 U.S. 504, 104 S.Ct. 2543 (1984) **(Plea Bargaining).** Johnson was convicted of burglary, assault, and murder in Arkansas. On appeal, the Arkansas Supreme Court set aside the murder conviction, and plea bargaining commenced between Johnson's defense counsel and the prosecution. In exchange for a guilty plea, the prosecution offered Johnson a 21-year sentence to be served *concurrently* with the other burglary and assault sentences. Eventually, Johnson accepted the state's offer. But instead of sentencing Johnson to concurrent sentences, the judge sentenced him to 21-year *consecutive* sentences, meaning that when he finished one sentence, he would have to begin another, and so on. He appealed in a habeas corpus finding, alleging that the first plea agreement containing the concurrent sentencing recommendation was enforceable in the present sentencing circumstance, and that the prosecutor should be held to honor that plea agreement. The SC heard Johnson's appeal and held that when Johnson ultimately accepted the prosecutor's first plea agreement, this did not create a constitutional right to have the bargain specifically enforced, and thus, he might not successfully attack his later guilty plea. The SC noted that prosecutors are obligated to honor their plea agreements; whenever defendants enter guilty pleas on false premises, they may withdraw their pleas and their convictions cannot stand. However, in this case, no such promises had been made to Johnson by the prosecutor, so the judge's ruling and sentencing were allowed to stand.

Mayer v. Chicago, 404 U.S. 189, 92 S.Ct. 410 (1971) **(Corrections; Inmate Rights).** Mayer, an indigent, was arrested and charged with disorderly conduct in Chicago. He was convicted and requested a transcript of his trial proceeding. Illinois statutes provided for issuances of transcripts for indigents only for felony cases. Mayer appealed, alleging his due-process rights had been violated. The SC heard the case and ordered Illinois to provide Mayer with a trial transcript. The SC said that the fact that the charges against Mayer involved fines only and not imprisonment were no excuse for the invidious discrimination against an indigent defendant.

Maynard v. Cartwright, 486 U.S. 356, 108 S.Ct. 1853 (1988) **(Eighth Amendment; Aggravating Circumstances).** Cartwright shot and killed a man and slit his wife's throat. These victims had formerly employed him. An Oklahoma jury found Cartwright guilty of first-degree murder. When the judge gave the jury instructions during the penalty phase of the trial, he used the phrase, "especially heinous, atrocious, or cruel" in describing various aggravating circumstances they were to consider. Cartwright challenged his death sentence on the grounds that such a statement was unconstitutionally vague. The SC agreed with Cartwright, and his death sentence was vacated, as the instruction, determined to be unconstitutionally vague, had not offered sufficient guidance to the jury in deciding whether to impose the death penalty.

McCarthy v. United States, 394 U.S. 459, 89 S.Ct. 1166 (1969) **(Plea Bargaining).** McCarthy, a 65-year-old man, was charged with income tax evasion. He pleaded not guilty at first, but later, following a debilitating illness, entered a guilty plea in exchange for government leniency. The judge, however, sentenced McCarthy to one year imprisonment and a $2,500 fine. The attorney for McCarthy objected strongly to the sentence and fine, and a subsequent appeal was filed, alleging the judge's violation of Rule 11 of the Federal Rules of Criminal Procedure. Among the crucial elements of Rule 11, which governs plea bargains and plea-bargain hearings, judges are supposed to address defendants who wish to plead guilty in open court and determine the voluntariness of their plea. Further, judges are ordered by statute to determine whether there is a factual basis for the plea, meaning, what would the prosecutor have introduced as evidence against the defendant if the case had gone to trial. Thus, if the prosecutor fails to furnish the judge with evidence that would have resulted in the defendant's guilt beyond a reasonable doubt, then the judge would be compelled to reject the guilty plea and dismiss the case against the defendant. Because the judge in McCarthy's case had failed to inquire as to the factual basis for the plea, and failed to inquire of McCarthy whether he understood the nature of the charges against him, the SC overturned McCarthy's conviction.

McCleskey v. Kemp, 481 U.S. 279, 107 S.Ct. 1756 (1987) **(Death Penalty; Disproportionality of Executions on the Basis of Race).** McCleskey, a black man, was convicted of murdering a police officer during a grocery store robbery in 1978. He was sentenced to death. McCleskey appealed, introducing evidence to show that statistically more black criminals receive the death penalty than white criminals and claiming that such disproportion is unconstitutional. The SC rejected McCleskey's claim. Georgia's death penalty, the SC said, was not arbitrary and capricious, nor was it being applied in a discriminatory manner, regardless of statistical evidence to the contrary.

McCleskey v. Zant, 499 U.S. 467, 111 S.Ct. 1454 (1991) **(Habeas Corpus Petitions; Death Penalty; Sixth Amendment; Effective Assistance of Counsel; Informants).** McCleskey was charged with murder and armed robbery. A cellmate of McCleskey's, Evans, was called to testify against him. Evans said that McCleskey had boasted about the killing and admitted it. McCleskey was convicted and sentenced to death. He appealed, claiming that the cellmate-induced conversations had been made without the assistance of his counsel. The SC rejected his claim, stating that they could have been made in an earlier appeal proceeding. The fact that McCleskey was making it in a subsequent proceeding nullified the claim. Thus, in order for such claims to be considered, they must be made at the right time, shortly after they occur, not after several appeals have been unsuccessfully lodged with state and federal courts.

McCray v. Illinois, 386 U.S. 300, 87 S.Ct. 1056 (1967) **(Law Enforcement Officers or Agencies; Search and Seizure).** In this case, a warrantless search incident to a warrantless arrest was based upon a reliable informant's information to police. Police refused to reveal the identity of the informant later at McCray's trial, where he was convicted. McCray appealed, alleging that the identity of the informant should have been revealed and that a warrant based upon probable cause should have been issued. The SC noted that in McCray's case, however, the use of the reliable informant was unrelated to McCray's guilt or innocence, a trial function. Rather, the informant had been used as a basis for investigating and conducting surveillance of McCray, who later exhibited sufficient incriminating conduct to justify his arrest by police. The court upheld the conviction.

McDonald v. United States, 335 U.S. 451, 69 S.Ct. 191 (1948) **(Law Enforcement Officers or Agencies; Searches Incident to Arrest; Consent Searches).** McDonald and others were suspected of operating a lottery from their home. Police conducted surveillance of them and then, without a warrant, entered McDonald's home through a window after hearing what they thought to be an "adding machine," a device often used in illegal lottery operations. Incriminating evidence was seized and McDonald was subsequently convicted because of it. Because the police had had no arrest or search warrants when they entered McDonald's residence and seized the illegal material and equipment, McDonald appealed, alleging his Fourth Amendment right against unreasonable searches and seizures had been violated. The SC summarily overturned McDonald's conviction, holding the evidence inadmissible since it had been illegally seized without probable cause or an arrest or search warrant.

McGautha v. California, 402 U.S. 183, 91 S.Ct. 1454 (1971) **(Death Penalty; Jury Decision).** McGautha was convicted of first-degree murder during an armed robbery. During the penalty phase of the trial, the judge gave the jury instructions, saying that the jury would fix a penalty at their absolute discretion and that the vote for a particular punishment must be unanimous. The jury returned the death penalty and McGautha was sentenced. McGautha appealed, contending that standardless jury sentencing was unconstitutional. The SC rejected McGautha's argument and upheld the sentence as valid, despite an absence of specific standards by which to impose the death penalty, maintaining that juries have total discretion in deciding death penalty or life imprisonment. The decision was later modified in *Gregg v. Georgia* (1976).

McGinnis v. Royster, 410 U.S. 263, 93 S.Ct. 1055 (1972) **(Corrections; Probation and Parole).** A New York statute provides that jail prisoners may not accrue their time in jail as pretrial detainees to be used in calculating their prison good-time credit later. A circuit court of appeals ruled the statute unconstitutional, but the government appealed. The SC reversed the circuit court decision, saying that the New York statute denying certain state prisoners good-time credit for parole eligibility for the period of their presentence county jail incarceration does not violate the equal protection clause of the Fourteenth Amendment. Thus there is no obligation for New York or any other state to provide prisoners with such credit for calculating good-time credit for parole eligibility.

McKeiver v. Pennsylvania, 403 U.S. 528, 91 S.Ct. 1976 (1971) **(Juvenile Law; Jury Trials for Juveniles).** In May 1968, McKeiver, age 16, was charged with robbery, larceny, and receiving stolen goods. He was represented by counsel, who asked the court for a jury trial "as a matter of right." This request was denied. McKeiver was subsequently adjudicated delinquent. On appeal to the SC later, McKeiver's adjudication was upheld. The case is important because the SC said that jury trials for juveniles are not a matter of constitutional right but rather at the discretion of the juvenile court judge. In about a fifth of the states today, jury trials for juveniles in juvenile courts are held under certain conditions.

McKnight v. State, 616 So.2d 31 (1993) **(Courts and Sentencing; Habitual Offender Statutes).** McKnight was convicted of being an habitual felony offender. Ordinarily, this conviction carries a mandatory life-without-parole penalty. However, the judge in McKnight's case imposed probation. Although the Florida Court of Appeals did not like the judge's decision, it upheld it anyway, supporting the general principle of judicial discretion.

McKoy v. North Carolina, 494 U.S. 433, 110 S.Ct. 1227 (1990) **(Eighth Amendment; Aggravating and Mitigating Circumstances).** McKoy was convicted of first-degree murder. During the sentencing phase of his trial, the jury made a "binding" recommendation for the death penalty, after finding two statutory aggravating circumstances, two of eight possible mitigating circumstances, that the mitigating circumstances did not outweigh the aggravating circumstances, and that the aggravating circumstances were "substantial" enough to justify recommending the death penalty. North Carolina had a procedure whereby jurors must find unanimously that specific aggravating and mitigating circumstances exist. Some jurors believed that other mitigating circumstances may have existed, but the jury was not unanimous as to those mitigating circumstances and thus, they were not considered as weight against the aggravating circumstances. McKoy appealed the death sentence on the grounds that the unanimity rule was unconstitutional and violative of his right against cruel and unusual punishment under the Eighth Amendment. The SC agreed with McKoy and overturned his conviction, holding that North Carolina's unanimity requirement impermissibly limited jurors' consideration of mitigating evidence and thus was contrary to prior case law decided by the SC. In effect, one holdout juror can exclude one or more mitigating circumstances from being weighed against the aggravating ones. Thus, the death sentence was vacated and the case was remanded.

McMann v. Richardson, 397 U.S. 759, 90 S.Ct. 1441 (1970) **(Plea Bargaining).** The defendant knowingly and voluntarily pleaded guilty to murder. He was sentenced to 30 years in prison. He appealed, alleging that his guilty plea had been coerced. The SC upheld his conviction, saying that no evidence existed to show that the guilty plea was coerced. A mere allegation of coercion is insufficient to overturn a conviction resulting from a plea bargain.

McMillan v. Pennsylvania, 477 U.S. 79, 106 S.Ct. 2411 (1986) **(Mandatory Sentencing).** Dynel McMillan was convicted of aggravated assault by shooting another man in the right buttock during an argument over a debt. Under Pennsylvania's Mandatory Minimum Sentencing Act of 1982, anyone convicted of certain felonies and who "visibly possesses a firearm" during the commission of a felony is subject to a mandatory minimum sentence of five years. This fact may determined by a preponderance of the evidence. McMillan appealed the conviction and five-year mandatory minimum sentence, arguing that such an issue ought to be decided by a jury trial, that the standard of proof should not be "preponderance of the evidence" but rather, "beyond a reasonable doubt," and that the act itself was invalid. The SC rejected all of McMillan's claims. First, the SC noted, the five-year mandatory minimum sentence is a *sentencing issue*, not a *jury issue*. Thus, a jury trial is not necessary for this factual determination. Further, because it is a sentencing issue, the standard of proof may be "preponderance of the evidence." The SC upheld the constitutionality of the mandatory minimum sentencing law.

McNabb v. United States, 318 U.S. 332, 63 S.Ct. 608 (1943) **(Law Enforcement Officers or Agencies; Exclusionary Rule).** The McNabb family in Chattanooga, Tennessee, was a clan of mountaineers dealing in illegal whiskey by operating an illegal still. Agents from the Alcohol Tax Unit raided their settlement one evening when it was learned that they planned to sell a large quantity of illegal liquor. During their raid, one federal officer was shot and killed. Later, federal agents visited the home of the McNabbs and arrested the brothers Freeman and Raymond. They took the men to the federal building in Chattanooga, where they were not brought before any United States magistrate or other judicial official but kept in a small room for 14 hours and not permitted to see relatives or lawyers. There is no evidence that they requested counsel. Neither had passed the fourth grade in school. Following intensive questioning by agents, they eventually confessed to the killing and were tried, convicted of murder, and sentenced to 45 years in prison. They appealed. The SC reversed their convictions, holding that coerced confessions are not admissible. Further, the officers had erred by not providing suitable counsel for these defendants and the interrogation conditions were inherently illegal and contrary to due process. Thus, their confessions had been improperly received as evidence against them.

McNeil v. Wisconsin, 501 U.S. 171, 111 S.Ct. 2204 **(Sixth Amendment Rights).** McNeil was charged with armed robbery in West Allis, Wisconsin. He requested and was represented by a public defender. While in police custody, McNeil signed a Miranda rights waiver and agreed to talk with police about the West Allis robbery; during that time, he made incriminating statements about his involvement in a murder in Caledonia, Wisconsin. He was then formally charged with the murder in Caledonia. In a pretrial motion, he moved to suppress his former incriminating statements. This motion was denied. He was convicted. He appealed on the grounds that his statements should have been barred from evidence, because he had requested counsel during his initial appearance and because police were initially telling him his Miranda rights concerning an unrelated crime. McNeil believed he must be told his rights for *each* of the crimes with which he had been charged. The SC heard McNeil's appeal and rejected it, holding that the assertion of the Sixth Amendment right to counsel does not imply invocation of the Miranda Fifth Amendment right; such a rule would seriously impede effective law enforcement by precluding uncounseled but uncoerced admissions of guilt pursuant to valid Miranda warnings.

Meachum v. Fano, 427 U.S. 215, 96 S.Ct. 2532 (1976) **(Corrections; Inmate Transfers).** Fano was one of several inmates transferred from the Massachusetts prison at Norfolk to a prison at Bridgewater, following a period of firesetting at the institution at Norfolk. The Bridgewater prison was a lesser facility in regard to amenities, and it had maximum-security and medium-security designations compared with the medium-security-only designation at Norfolk. Thus prisoners transferred from Norfolk to Bridgewater would be deprived of many benefits they earlier enjoyed. Fano and others filed a civil rights suit under Title 42, U.S.C. Section 1983, alleging that they were entitled to due process when subjected to interstate prison transfers. The SC disagreed and ruled simply that prisoners have *no* rights concerning where they are placed within the prison system. Prisoners cannot have a say regarding where the prison system decides to place them, as long as cruel and unusual punishment conditions do not exist. Thus, many state prisoners are confined in local jails (because of prison overcrowding) with far fewer amenities than prisons. These jail-confined state prisoners are now governed by the *Meachum v. Fano* ruling and thus cannot dictate where they should be placed in the prison system.

Mempa v. Rhay, 389 U.S. 128, 88 S.Ct. 254 (1967) **(Corrections; Probation Revocation).** Mempa was convicted of joyriding in a stolen vehicle on June 17, 1959. He was placed on probation for two years by a Spokane, Washington, judge. Several months later, Mempa was involved in a burglary on September 15. Mempa admitted participating in the burglary. The county prosecutor in Spokane moved to have Mempa's probation revoked. At his probation revocation hearing, the sole testimony about his involvement in the burglary came from his probation officer. Mempa was not represented by counsel, was not asked if he wanted counsel, and was not given an opportunity to offer statements in his own behalf. Furthermore, there was no cross-examination of the probation officer about his statements. The court revoked Mempa's probation and sentenced him to

10 years in the Washington State Penitentiary. Six years later in 1965, Mempa filed a writ of habeas corpus, alleging that he had been denied a right to counsel at the revocation hearing. The Washington Supreme Court denied his petition, but he appealed, and the United States SC elected to hear it. The SC overturned the Washington decision and ruled in Mempa's favor. Specifically, the SC said Mempa had been entitled to an attorney but had been denied one. While the Court did not question Washington authority to defer sentencing in the probation matter, it said that any indigent (including Mempa) is entitled at every stage of a criminal proceeding to be represented by court-appointed counsel, where "substantial rights of a criminal accused may be affected." Thus, the SC considered a probation revocation hearing to be a "critical stage" that falls within the due-process provisions of the Fourteenth Amendment. In subsequent years, several courts also applied this decision to parole revocation hearings.

Menna v. New York, 423 U.S. 61, 96 S.Ct. 241 (1975) **(Double Jeopardy).** A grand jury was investigating a murder conspiracy. On November 7, 1968, Steve Menna was summoned into the proceeding. He refused to answer questions after being granted immunity. He was summoned to the grand jury again in March 1969, where he again refused to answer grand jury questions. He was held in contempt and sentenced to 30 days in jail. Menna served his sentence. Subsequently, he was indicted for his refusal to answer questions before the grand jury on the November 7, 1968, date. He moved to have the indictment dismissed under the double-jeopardy clause of the Fifth Amendment. However, he was unsuccessful and convicted on this second contempt charge. He appealed, again claiming double jeopardy, this time to the SC. The SC overturned Menna's contempt adjudication on the grounds that it violated his double-jeopardy rights. Where a 30-day sentence is imposed following a contempt adjudication, a subsequent conviction stemming from the same contempt incident is clearly double jeopardy and unconstitutional.

Michigan Department of State Police v. Sitz, 496 U. S. 444, 110 S.Ct. 2481 (1990) **(Law Enforcement Officers or Agencies; Sobriety Checkpoints).** Michigan State Police established various sobriety checkpoints to determine whether certain drivers were intoxicated. Sitz was stopped at one of these checkpoints and cited for driving while intoxicated. He was convicted and he appealed. The SC heard his case, in which Sitz alleged that his Fourth and Fourteenth Amendment rights had been violated. Essentially, his argument was that sobriety checkpoints are unconstitutional because they constitute unreasonable searches and seizures. Although the SC said that there was "slight" intrusion in Sitz's case, the checkpoint system used by Michigan was constitutional. It noted that when Sitz was stopped, he was one of approximately 125 other drivers who were inconvenienced by a delay averaging 25 seconds. The SC stressed the insignificance of the minor intrusion involved in sobriety checkpoints, which did not violate Fourth Amendment and Fourteenth Amendment guarantees.

Michigan v. Chesternut, 486 U.S. 567, 108 S.Ct. 1975 (1988) **(Law Enforcement Officers or Agencies; Seizures; Stop and Frisk).** Chesternut was walking down a road when he saw a police patrol unit and began to run. Police officers in the unit followed him to see where he was going. As they pulled alongside Chesternut, who continued to run, they saw him throw to the ground numerous bags containing a white substance. They stopped and examined the bags, concluding tentatively that they might be illegal drugs. They stopped Chesternut and found additional bags of the same substance. It turned out to be narcotics and he was arrested and charged with narcotics possession. He was convicted. He appealed to the SC, arguing that the police officers had violated his Fourth Amendment right against unreasonable searches and seizures by following him and investigating without probable cause. The SC upheld Chesternut's conviction, concluding that the officers' investigatory pursuit had not constituted a seizure in violation of the Fourth Amendment. The SC stressed the reasonable-man notion and the contextual circumstances surrounding Chesternut's arrest. Given the existing circumstances, investigatory pursuits of suspects by police do not constitute illegal seizures.

Michigan v. DeFillippo, 443 U.S. 31, 99 S.Ct. 2627 (1979) **(Law Enforcement Officers or Agencies; Fourth Amendment; Warrantless Searches Incident to An Arrest).** One evening, Detroit police found DeFillippo in an alleyway with a woman who was in the process of lowering her slacks. DeFillippo was asked to produce ID, and when he gave vague replies, officers searched him and discovered illegal drugs in his pockets.

Later in court, his attorney moved to suppress the evidence seized by officers, contending that they had lacked probable cause to search DeFillippo. DeFillippo was subsequently convicted, but the Michigan Supreme Court held the Detroit ordinance to be unconstitutionally vague. The government appealed and the SC heard the case. The SC ruled that DeFillippo's conviction should be upheld, since the officers were acting in good-faith reliance on the Detroit ordinance. DeFillippo had been observed engaged in an illegal act, and his lawful arrest had justified the subsequent search of his person, producing the incriminating drugs. It would be unreasonable to expect that officers would either know or have reason to know that the Detroit ordinance would subsequently be declared to be unconstitutionally vague. The fact of a lawful arrest, standing alone, authorizes a search. In this case, there was "abundant" probable cause to believe that DeFillippo had committed or was committing an illegal act.

Michigan v. Harvey, 494 U.S. 344, 110 S.Ct. 1176 (1990) **(Law Enforcement Officers or Agencies; Custodial Interrogations).** Harvey was arraigned on rape charges, and counsel was appointed for him. Initially, he wanted to make a statement to police but didn't know whether he ought to have his attorney present. The police advised Harvey that he could make a statement *without* his attorney present, since the attorney would eventually get a copy of his statement anyway. Subsequently, Harvey signed a rights waiver form and made incriminating statements to police without his attorney present. Later in court, Harvey gave conflicting statements, and police used his earlier statement, given without the attorney present, to impeach his court testimony. Harvey was convicted of first-degree criminal sexual conduct. He appealed. A Michigan court overturned his conviction, saying that it is unconstitutional for prosecutors to use statements otherwise inadmissible under the *Jackson* rule (*see Michigan v. Jackson* [1986]) to impeach a defendant's later testimony in court. The State of Michigan appealed, and the SC reinstated Harvey's conviction, holding that a statement to police taken in violation of *Jackson* may be used to impeach a defendant's testimony (in court later). The important point here is that Harvey's statements had been initiated by Harvey, not by police, even though Harvey had invoked his Sixth Amendment right to counsel. This information *could not* be used by prosecutors in their case-in-chief against the defendant, but *it could* be used for impeachment purposes.

Michigan v. Jackson, 475 U.S. 625, 106 S.Ct. 1404 (1986) **(Law Enforcement Officers or Agencies; Confessions).** A woman planned the murder of her husband and spoke to Jackson and several other men about possibly carrying out this crime. Jackson was arrested and made various incriminating statements about the conspiratorial nature of the planned murder. At his arraignment, Jackson requested that counsel be appointed for him. A lawyer was provided. The following day, police initiated another interrogation of Jackson, without his attorney present, in which he admitted that he had murdered the woman's husband. Jackson was charged with murder and convicted. He appealed. The SC overturned his conviction because his due-process right had been violated when he was interrogated without the counsel that had been provided for him. The prosecution argued that Jackson's statement was voluntary, and that he had waived his right to have counsel present when giving his murder confession. The SC disagreed and said that custodial interrogations that are police-initiated require the presence of an attorney. Without an attorney present, the accused cannot effectively waive his right to be interrogated further. Thus defendants cannot be interrogated by police once they have invoked their right to silence and have an attorney. However, interrogations and confessions initiated by the suspect are permissible. Thus, if Jackson had requested to speak with officers and had admitted the murder, the confession would have been valid. This case established the *Jackson Rule*, which says that once a defendant invokes the Sixth Amendment right to counsel, any waiver of that right—even if voluntary, knowing, and intelligent under traditional standards—is presumed invalid if given in a police-initiated discussion, and that evidence obtained pursuant to that waiver is inadmissible in the prosecution's case-in-chief. However, suspect-initiated statements can be used to impeach testimony given by defendants on cross-examination.

Michigan v. Long, 463 U.S. 1032, 103 S.Ct. 3469 (1983) **(Law Enforcement Officers or Agencies; Stop and Frisk).** Long was driving erratically in an automobile and swerved into a ditch. Police observed this action and approached him. Long appeared intoxicated, but he produced a driver's license. When returning to his vehicle to obtain the registration, police observed a large

hunting knife on the floor of the car. At that point, they stopped Long and frisked him, finding no dangerous weapons. Nevertheless, one of the officers, for his own protection, shined his flashlight into Long's car and saw some marijuana. Long was arrested and his car trunk was then opened and searched, incident to an arrest. Approximately 75 pounds of marijuana were found in the trunk and Long was convicted. Long appealed, arguing that his Fourth Amendment right against unreasonable searches and seizures had been violated when police looked in his car. However, the SC upheld his conviction, saying that protective searches are permissible when police have reason to believe a suspect may pose some danger to them.

Michigan v. Lucas, 500 U.S. 145, 111 S.Ct. 1743 (1991) **(Sixth Amendment, Trial Rights and Evidentiary Issues; Rape-Shield Laws).** Lucas was charged with rape. Under Michigan's rape-shield law, which provides for exclusion of any testimony or evidence of the victim's past sexual conduct or history. In Lucas' case, however, he had had a prior sexual relationship with the victim and sought to introduce this evidence, which was excluded under the rape-shield law. Among other things, Lucas had failed to comply with a notice-and-hearing requirement of Michigan law to determine the admissibility of such testimony. Lucas was convicted of third-degree sexual conduct. He appealed. The SC upheld Lucas' conviction, holding that the preclusion of evidence of Lucas' past sexual conduct with the victim for Lucas' failure to comply with notice-and-hearing requirements of Michigan's rape-shield law was not per se a violation of Lucas' Sixth Amendment rights adequately to confront and cross-examine his accuser on this past sexual relationship.

Michigan v. Mosley, 423 U.S. 96, 96 S.Ct. 321 (1975) **(Law Enforcement Officers or Agencies; Confessions).** Mosley was a suspect in several robberies and was arrested by police. They advised Mosley of his Miranda rights, and he refused to talk to them. After two hours, another officer from another jurisdiction visited Mosley and asked him questions about a homicide, after giving him another Miranda warning. Mosley gave incriminating statements to the visiting detective and was subsequently convicted of murder. He appealed, alleging that his Fifth Amendment right had been violated because of the new questioning by the detective when he had said he didn't wish to discuss the robberies with police earlier. The SC disagreed, however, saying that Mosley had been properly told his Miranda rights and that in the first instance of questioning, officers had rigidly adhered to the letter of the Miranda warning and ceased questioning him. Further, the second interrogation by a visiting detective had been preceded by a new Miranda warning, and thus, Mosley's statements were considered voluntarily given.

Michigan v. Summers, 452 U.S. 692, 101 S.Ct. 2587 (1981) **(Law Enforcement Officers or Agencies; Stop and Frisk; Search Incident to Arrest).** Summers was leaving a house believed by police to be a drug contact point. Police had it under surveillance. They detained Summers while they entered the house with a valid search warrant based upon probable cause. They found large quantities of narcotics and also determined that Summers was the owner of the home. They arrested him and searched him, discovering a quantity of heroin. He was convicted of heroin possession, and he appealed, contending that his detention was a "seizure" because the police had lacked probable cause to detain him initially. The SC disagreed with Summers, noting that police officers had had a valid search warrant for Summers's premises, and that once contraband was found and it was determined that Summers was, indeed, the home owner, sufficient probable cause existed to arrest him and conduct a more thorough search of his person.

Michigan v. Thomas, 458 U.S. 259, 102 S.Ct. 3079 (1983) **(Law Enforcement Officers or Agencies; Fourth Amendment; Warrantless Vehicle Searches and Inventories).** An automobile was routinely stopped by police for failing to give a left-turn signal. Thomas was a passenger in the vehicle. When officers approached the vehicle, they saw in plain view an open bottle of malt liquor on the floorboard between Thomas's feet. The driver of the car, a 14-year-old, was cited for not having a driver's license. Thomas claimed that he (Thomas) owned the car. He was taken to a patrol car and his automobile was ordered towed to a police impound lot. Before it was towed, however, an officer searched the vehicle, the standard operating procedure when inventorying a car's contents. Two bags of marijuana were found in the glove compartment, which prompted the officer to search further. He found a loaded .38 revolver in the air vents under the dashboard. Thomas was arrested and eventually convicted of concealing

firearms. He appealed, claiming that the pistol had been discovered as the result of an unreasonable search and seizure in violation of his Fourth Amendment rights. The SC upheld the conviction, noting that when police officers have probable cause to believe there is contraband inside an automobile that has been stopped on the road, they may conduct a warrantless search of the vehicle, even after it has been impounded and is in police custody.

Michigan v. Tucker, 417 U.S. 433, 94 S.Ct. 2357 (1974) **(Confessions; Exceptions).** Tucker was under investigation by police for a crime and was given only a partial Miranda warning. He later made incriminating statements leading to his conviction at a subsequent trial. He appealed, alleging that his full Miranda warning had not been provided and thus the incriminating statements he made should have been excluded at the trial. The SC adopted a totality-of-circumstances and good-faith exception test in Tucker's case, saying that under the circumstances, and because police officers were acting in good faith, technical flaws in the Miranda warning Tucker was given were insufficient to overcome the presumption that his Fifth Amendment right against self-incrimination had been violated. Tucker's conviction was upheld.

Michigan v. Tucker, 417 U.S. 433, 94 S.Ct. 2357 (1974) **(Fifth Amendment; Miranda Warning; Statements of Witnesses).** Tucker, an indigent, was arrested by police as a rape suspect. He was told that he could remain silent and had a right to counsel, but he was not advised of his right to counsel if indigent. Tucker told police, without the presence of counsel, that he was with a friend, Henderson, at the time of the alleged rape. However, the police later determined from questioning Henderson that Henderson only had incriminating information about Tucker and did not support his alibi. Henderson was later called to testify in court against Tucker and gave the incriminating statements, nullifying Tucker's alibi. Tucker was convicted of rape. He sought an appeal through a habeas corpus petition, alleging that his Miranda rights had not been observed by police, and that Henderson's testimony ought to have been suppressed, inasmuch as Henderson came to police attention only after Tucker brought up his name as an alibi witness. A lower court agreed and reversed the conviction. The government appealed and the SC heard the case. The SC reinstated

Tucker's rape conviction, holding that the failure of police to advise Tucker of his right to appointed counsel had no bearing on the reliability of Henderson's testimony, which was subjected to cross-examination in a fair trial later. The use of testimony of a witness discovered by police as the result of Tucker's statements under these circumstances did not violate Tucker's Fifth, Sixth, and Fourteenth Amendment rights. The SC further declared that although the police failed to afford Tucker the full measure of procedural safeguards later set forth in Miranda, this failure did not deprive Tucker of his privilege against self-incrimination, since the record clearly indicates that Tucker's statements during the police interrogation were not involuntary or the result of potential legal sanctions. The evidence derived from the police interrogation was therefore admissible.

Michigan v. Tyler and Tompkins, 436 U.S. 499, 98 S.Ct. 1942 (1978) **(Law Enforcement Officers or Agencies; Fourth Amendment; Search Warrants).** The state alleged that Tyler and his companion, Tompkins, conspired to burn some property they owned in order to collect insurance on the property, a fraudulent act. Evidence introduced at their subsequent trial included photographs taken by arson investigators, who arrived early at the site of the burning building. Also, firemen had entered the building, together with police and others, and several plastic containers of flammable liquid were retrieved. This evidence was also used against Tyler and Tompkins in convicting them of the conspiracy and arson charges. Tyler appealed, seeking to suppress the incriminating evidence under the theory that investigators had not first obtained a valid search warrant before entering the premises. An appellate court reversed their convictions on these grounds and ordered a second trial. The state appealed. The SC heard the case and ruled partly in favor of the state and partly in favor of Tyler and Tompkins, holding that official entries into premises to investigate fires must be preceded by warrants. However, a burning building presents an "exigent circumstance" where a warrantless entry and search may be conducted; while on the premises and for a reasonable time thereafter, firemen and arson investigators may seize any evidence they believe relates to the fire's origin. Therefore, evidence seized the night of the fire in the course of extinguishing it and for a reasonable period afterward is admissible. However, evidence col-

lected from the fire scene by arson investigators and police a day or so later must be prefaced by a proper search warrant. In this case, the post-investigatory actions of police and investigators were warrantless, and therefore, the evidence subsequently obtained in these subsequent searches and seizures was inadmissible in a retrial of Tyler and Tompkins, which was ordered.

Miller v. California, 413 U.S. 15, 93 S.Ct. 2607 (1973) **(Obscenity Ordinances).** Miller was convicted of breaking a California obscenity ordinance prohibiting the mailing of obscene materials, in this case, photographs of men and women in couples or groups performing sex acts. He appealed, alleging that the statute was unconstitutional because of its vagueness and because no one knew how to measure obscenity. The SC upheld his conviction, settling the question of obscenity standards by placing these standards in the hands of individual state legislatures. Thus, obscenity is defined according to individual state statutes.

Miller v. Fenton, 474 U.S. 104, 106 S.Ct. 445 (1985) **(Self-Incrimination).** Miller was suspected of first-degree murder and subjected to a 58-minute interrogation in the New Jersey State Police Barracks. Eventually, he confessed and was convicted. He appealed, filing a habeas corpus petition challenging his conviction and his confession, which he alleged had been coerced. The SC overturned his conviction, saying that the habeas corpus petition was a proper means of challenging his conviction, and that the actions of police in obtaining Miller's confession had been inherently coercive. Substantial circumstances were prevalent in this case and the conditions under which Miller confessed indicated that the confession had not been voluntary. The SC referred the case back to trial court where it could be determined whether or not the confession was coercive or voluntary.

Mills v. Maryland, 486 U.S. 367, 108 S.Ct. 1860 (1988) **(Death Penalty; Aggravating and Mitigating Circumstances).** Mills was an inmate of the Maryland Correctional Institution in Hagerstown. He stabbed his cellmate to death with a homemade knife and was charged with murder. A trial was held and the jury found Mills guilty. Instructions from the judge at the beginning of the sentencing phase led jurors to believe that they must agree unanimously on mitigating circumstances before they could consider them in Mills' case. If they could not agree, then they had to render a death-penalty decision. Since they were not unanimous regarding any mitigating circumstances, they decided on the death penalty as required from the judge's instructions. Thus, a mandatory element was introduced into the penalty phase, which is unconstitutional in relation to death-penalty decisions. Mills appealed, arguing this very point to the SC. The SC overturned Mills' conviction, concluding that there was a substantial probability that reasonable jurors, upon receiving the judge's instructions, might well have thought they were precluded from considering any mitigating evidence unless all 12 jurors agreed on the existence of a particular such circumstance. The SC said the jurors must consider all the mitigating evidence. The possibility that a single juror could block such consideration, and consequently require the jury to impose the death penalty, was not to be risked. Therefore, the death-penalty sentence was vacated.

Mincey v. Arizona, 437 U.S. 385, 98 S.Ct. 2408 (1978) **(Law Enforcement Officers or Agencies; Fourth Amendment; "Murder Scene Exception").** Mincey was involved in a raid on his apartment by undercover police officers. One police officer was shot and killed, and Mincey was seriously wounded and taken to a hospital. During the next four days, his apartment was searched extensively by police, who tore it apart. They also interrogated Mincey while he was in the hospital, drugged, and in great pain. Mincey continually asked the police to discontinue their questioning, but they persisted. He eventually gave incriminating statements to police under this debilitating condition in the hospital. These incriminating statements, as well as newly discovered evidence from his apartment, were used against him. He was convicted of murder, assault, and various narcotics offenses. He appealed. The SC held that Mincey's Fourth Amendment right against an unreasonable search and seizure had been violated when police searched his apartment for four days without a warrant. Further, statements he gave while hospitalized had been given under coercive circumstances and were therefore inadmissible. Since his due-process rights had been violated, his conviction was overturned.

Minnesota v. Dickerson, 507 U.S. ___, 113 S.Ct. 2130 (1993) **(Law Enforcement Officers or Agencies; Stop and Frisk).** Dickerson emerged from a known "crack house" and was observed by police officers walking down an alley. When he saw the officers approaching him, he reversed direction and walked away from them. They decided to stop him for an investigative pat-down. They discovered no weapons, but one of the officers thrust his hand into Dickerson's pockets and found a small quantity of crack cocaine in a glassine envelope. He claimed that he had "felt a small lump that felt like crack cocaine" through Dickerson's clothing after the initial pat-down and frisk. Dickerson was charged with cocaine possession and convicted. He appealed, and the SC overturned his conviction on the ground that the search of Dickerson went well beyond the scope specified in *Terry v. Ohio*, where police officer pat-downs and frisks of suspects were used exclusively for the purpose of determining whether they possessed a dangerous weapon that might be used to harm the police. This specific type of incident is directly on point and consistent with a SC ruling in another case involving excessive officer intrusion into a suspect's pocket in a search for contraband: *Sibron v. New York* (1968).

Minnesota v. Murphy, 465 U.S. 420, 104 S.Ct. 1136 (1984) **(Law Enforcement Officers or Agencies; Confessions).** Murphy was serving a three-year probation term for criminal sexual conduct. One of his probation conditions was that he was to report regularly to his probation officer and answer all questions truthfully. Another condition was that he seek sexual therapy and counseling. During one of these counseling sessions, Murphy confessed to one of his counselors that he had committed a rape and murder in 1974. The counselor told his probation officer, who, in turn, interrogated Murphy at his residence. Murphy admitted the crime (responding truthfully) after extensive interviewing and interrogation. The probation officer gave this incriminating information to police, who arrested Murphy later and charged him with the 1974 rape and murder. Murphy claimed later that the probation officer had not advised him of his Miranda rights and thus, his confession should not be admitted later in court against him. As a general rule, criminal suspects who are the targets of a police investigation must be advised of their Miranda rights if undergoing an interrogation, whether or not they are in custody. A similar rule pertains to probationers. It might be argued, for instance, that the *fact* of their probation is a form of "custody." Thus all probationers (and parolees) might be considered "in custody" during the their program terms. However, "custody" implies being unable to leave the presence of the interrogator. When suspects conclude their interrogation, they may or may not be permitted to leave. If they leave, they are *not* considered to be in custody. Otherwise, they *are* in custody. Murphy was not in custody, however. Also, he had not been compelled to answer the probation officer's questions.

Minnesota v. Olson, 495 U.S. 91, 110 S.Ct. 1684 (1989) **(Law Enforcement Officers or Agencies; Exclusionary Rule).** Olson, a suspect in a robbery-murder, was believed to be staying at the home of two women, according to an anonymous tip. Police surrounded the house, called the women inside on a telephone, and advised them that Olson should surrender by stepping outside unarmed. A male voice was overheard to say, "Tell them I left." Hearing this, police officers forced entry into the house, without warrant or permission, and made a warrantless arrest of Olson, who was hiding in a closet. Later, incriminating statements made by Olson led to his conviction for the robbery-murder. He appealed, contending that the warrantless entry into the home of the women had been an unreasonable search and that exigent circumstances did not exist to justify it. The SC ruled that the search and subsequent arrest of Olson were invalid, and thus, his statements to police were inadmissible as evidence against him. This is an example of the fruits-of-the-poisonous-tree doctrine. (*See Wong Sun v. United States* [1963]).

Minnick v. Mississippi, 498 U.S. 146, 111 S.Ct. 486 (1990) **(Law Enforcement Officers or Agencies; Custodial Interrogations; Miranda Warnings).** A day after escaping from a Mississippi county jail, Minnick and an accomplice killed two men during the burglary of a trailer. Minnick fled to California, where he was arrested on Friday, August 22, 1986, by Lemon Grove police. On August 23, FBI agents advised Minnick of his right to counsel and his right not to answer their questions. Minnick made a partial confession to FBI agents, although he advised them to "come back Monday" when he would have an attorney present. The same day, Minnick was appointed an attorney, who advised him to say nothing to police. On Monday, August 25, a deputy sheriff from Mississippi, Denham, flew to the San Diego jail where Minnick was being held. Minnick was reluctant to talk to Denham, but jailers told him he "had to talk." Minnick related all the incidents following his jail escape and admitted

committing one of the murders. He was subsequently convicted on two counts of capital murder and sentenced to death. He appealed, moving to suppress his statements to FBI agents and to Denham. The SC reversed Minnick's conviction and sentence and remanded the case to a lower court, reasoning that once the Miranda warning had been given and an attorney appointed, further questioning by police might not resume without an attorney present, if the defendant had invoked the right to have counsel present.

Miranda v. Arizona, 384 U.S. 436, 86 S.Ct. 1602 (1966) **(Law Enforcement Officers or Agencies; Confessions, Exclusionary Rule).** Miranda was arrested on suspicion of rape and kidnapping. He was not permitted to talk to an attorney, nor was he advised of his right to one. He was interrogated by police for several hours, eventually confessing and signing a written confession. He was convicted. Miranda appealed, contending that his right to due process had been violated because he had not first been advised of his right to remain silent and to have an attorney present during a custodial interrogation. The SC agreed and set forth the *Miranda warning*. This monumental decision provided that confessions made by suspects who were not notified of their due-process rights cannot be admitted as evidence. Suspects must be advised of certain rights before they are questioned by police; these rights include the right to remain silent, the right to counsel, the right to free counsel if suspects cannot afford one, and the right to terminate questioning at any time.

Mistretta v. United States, 488 U.S. 361, 109 S.Ct. 647 (1989) **(Courts; United States Sentencing Guidelines).** Mistretta was convicted of selling cocaine. The United States Sentencing Guidelines were officially in effect after November 1, 1987. Mistretta's criminal acts and conviction occurred after this date, and thus he was subject to guidelines-based sentencing rather than indeterminate sentencing, which the federal district courts had previously followed. Under the former sentencing scheme, Mistretta might have been granted probation. However, the new guidelines greatly restricted the use of probation as a sentence in federal courts, and thus, Mistretta's sentence involved serving an amount of time in prison. Mistretta appealed his conviction, arguing that the new guidelines violated the separation-of-powers doctrine, as several federal judges were members of the United States Sentencing Commission and helped to formulate laws and punishments, an exclusive function of Congress. The SC upheld Mistretta's conviction and declared the new guidelines to be constitutional, not in violation of the separation of powers doctrine.

Monroe v. Pape, 365 U.S. 167, 81 S.Ct. 473 (1961) **(Corrections; Inmate Rights).** Monroe was a suspect in a Chicago murder. Thirteen Chicago police officers broke into his home one evening and made him and several others stand naked in a room while the police ransacked his residence searching for incriminating information. During the search, officers tore up mattresses, furniture, and emptied drawers. Monroe was taken to the police station, where he was held for several days on "open charges." Eventually, he was released without any charges being brought against him. He filed suit against the police department under Title 42, U.S.C. Section 1983, alleging that his civil rights had been violated. An Illinois court dismissed Monroe's complaint and Monroe appealed. The SC declared that the Illinois police had acted improperly and violated Monroe's rights under the Federal Civil Rights Act.

Montanye v. Haymes, 427 U.S. 236, 96 S.Ct. 2543 (1976) **(Corrections; Inmate rights).** Haymes, a prisoner at Attica Correctional Facility in New York, was involved in circulating a petition among other inmates protesting his removal as clerk in the Attica law library. Subsequently, he was transferred to Clinton Correctional Facility, another maximum-security prison. Haymes filed suit against the prison system in New York alleging that his transfer to another prison had violated his due-process rights. The SC said that such a transfer had not violated the inmate's due-process rights, and that prisoners do not have a right to determine where they are confined. (*See the ruling in Meachum v. Fano* [1976] for a scenario similar to *Montanye v. Haymes*).

Moody v. Daggett, 429 U.S. 78, 97 S.Ct. 274 (1976) **(Corrections; Probation and Parole).** Moody was a convict serving time in prison for rape. He was subsequently paroled, and while on parole, he killed two persons. He received a concurrent 10-year sentence for both murders. These murders also violated one or more of his original parole conditions stemming from the rape conviction. Moody asked that a prompt revocation hearing be held on this parole violation so that any additional time imposed for this parole violation

could run concurrently with his current 10-year sentence. The United States Parole Board rejected this request. Instead, it issued a *detainer warrant* such that whenever Moody was released subsequently, he would be returned to face the United States Parole Board and its own punishments imposed for the parole violation. Moody appealed this decision. The SC upheld the decision of the United States Parole Board. Thus, parole violators such as Moody are not entitled to a prompt revocation hearing in the event that they are incarcerated for other crimes.

Moore v. Illinois, 408 U.S. 786, 92 S.Ct. 2562 (1972) **(Fair Trials; Discovery).** Moore was accused of first-degree murder. Prior to his trial, written statements were obtained from witnesses by police. These statements as well as other information compiled by police were requested under discovery by Moore's attorney. Most information was given to Moore, with the exception of a diagram of the crime scene and several witness statements unknown to Moore. Moore was convicted. He appealed, arguing that the exclusion of some pieces of information by the prosecution had violated his discovery rights. He claimed that a specific request from him about unknown statements was unnecessary because he should not have been expected to request that which he did not know was in existence. The SC upheld his conviction, saying that the suppression of evidence did not amount to a denial of discovery by the defendant and therefore did not constitute a denial of due process.

Moore v. Illinois, 434 U.S. 220, 98 S.Ct. 458 (1977) **(Law Enforcement Officers or Agencies; Lineups).** Moore was suspected of rape and other crimes. He was arrested after police had shown the rape victim numerous photographs and she had picked out Moore's as that of a likely suspect. Moore was taken before a judge for a hearing. At the hearing, Moore was advised by the judge that Moore was being charged with rape and other crimes. At about the same time, the state's attorney brought the victim into the hearing, where she was advised in advance that a suspect was in custody and that she "ought to identify him if she could." The victim saw Moore and identified him as the rapist. Moore was not represented by counsel at any time from his arrest and through this hearing. Counsel for Moore was eventually appointed after a grand jury indicted him for the rape. Moore's attorney moved for suppression of the victim identification but the motion was denied. Moore was convicted of rape. He appealed, arguing that admission of the identification testimony at trial had violated his Sixth and Fourteenth Amendment rights. The SC overturned Moore's conviction, saying that his Sixth and Fourteenth Amendment rights had, indeed, been violated because of an absence of counsel to represent him at these earlier critical stages. The identification had been conducted illegally, as the direct result of an illegal lineup.

Moore v. Michigan, 355 U.S. 155, 78 S.Ct. 191 (1957) **(Corrections; Probation and Parole; Waiver of Counsel).** Moore was accused of murdering a woman in 1938. He entered a guilty plea through a plea bargain agreement and was convicted and sentenced to life imprisonment. In 1950, he filed a motion for a new trial, alleging that his guilty plea had been entered without benefit of counsel. The SC overturned his conviction for the following reasons. When Moore entered his guilty plea, he was 17 years old and had a seventh-grade education. The trial judge had Moore come into his chambers, where he interviewed Moore for 5 or 10 minutes. The judge said that Moore had told him that he (Moore) just "wanted to get it over with" and that as far as the judge was concerned, Moore had intelligently and knowingly and voluntarily given up his right to counsel and other rights normally waived during plea bargain agreements. The SC observed that several different kinds of defenses, including insanity, could have been raised to account for Moore's conduct when committing the murder. The SC declared that under these circumstances, Moore's rights could not have been fairly protected without the assistance of counsel to help him with his defense. Essentially, the SC advised Michigan that the state should have provided him with counsel despite his waiver of his right to counsel.

Moore v. State, 623 So.2d 842 (1993) **(Sentencing; Restitution).** Moore was convicted of purchasing a stolen truck. The original truck's owner, the victim, claimed that there were tools worth $500 in the truck when it was stolen by the person who had sold the truck to Moore. The judge imposed a sentence of probation, with a restitution condition that Moore repay the victim $500 for the loss of the tools. Moore appealed. A Florida court of appeals set aside this condition, since it did not show (1) that the loss had been caused by Moore's action and (2) that there was a significant relation between the loss and the crime of purchasing a stolen vehicle.

Morales v. New York, 396 U.S. 102, 90 S.Ct. 291 (1969) **(Law Enforcement Officers or Agencies; Arrest).** In October 1964, a murder occurred in an apartment building where Morales lived. His mother informed police that Morales had wished to talk with them and that they should come to her place of business that evening to do so. Morales was subsequently arrested, confessed to the murder, and was subsequently convicted. He appealed, alleging that his arrest had been improper and therefore his subsequent confession was invalid. The SC reversed his conviction, reasoning that although his detention was not a formal "arrest," he was not free to leave the custody of officers at the police station when his confession was given. However, no hearing was conducted to determine whether the circumstances surrounding Morales's confession were coerced or voluntary. The SC vacated the conviction and remanded the case back to the trial court, where the question of a coerced confession could be considered as a part of his due-process rights.

Moran v. Burbine, 475 U.S. 412, 106 S.Ct. 1135 (1986) **(Self-Incrimination).** Burbine, a murder suspect, was arrested by police and given the Miranda warning. The police, knowing that Burbine's sister had had counsel appointed for him and that the attorney was attempting to reach Burbine, elected to question Burbine for a few hours anyway, before he was allowed to see his counsel. Burbine did not know that his sister had appointed counsel for him or know that his counsel was attempting to reach him. Further, the police had advised Burbine's attorney that no interrogation was planned for the evening and that the attorney could see him "in the morning." Burbine made a confession to police about the murder and was subsequently convicted. He appealed, alleging that his Fifth Amendment right against self-incrimination had been violated when police forbade the attorney to talk to him. The SC upheld Burbine's conviction, saying that he had been properly told his Miranda rights and was in the position of knowingly giving or not giving incriminating statements to police, regardless of other events occurring around him and of which he was unaware. The SC said that events outside the defendant's knowledge could have no bearing on the defendant's invocation of his right to silence. Thus, when Burbine decided to talk with police about the murder and confess, he was knowingly waiving his right to silence.

Morgan v. Illinois, 504 U.S. 719, 112 S.Ct. 2222 (1992) **(Corrections; Death Penalty; Death-Qualified Juries).** Morgan was suspected of capital murder. Prior to the trial, he wanted the judge to ask prospective jurors whether they would automatically impose the death penalty regardless of the facts, but the judge refused. Eventually, Morgan was convicted and sentenced to death. He appealed, arguing that his due-process rights had been violated. The SC reversed the conviction and sent the case back to the lower court for retrial. The explanation was that it was unconstitutional for the judge *not* to ask such a question of jurors. Thus, Morgan's due-process rights had been violated. This case is distinguished from *Witherspoon v. Illinois* (1968), which had to do with a juror being impaired to function as a juror in view of his opposition to the death penalty. In *Morgan,* jurors who would automatically vote for the death penalty regardless of the facts would be excludable as jurors for cause.

Morris v. Mathews, 475 U.S. 237, 106 S.Ct. 1032 (1986) **(Double Jeopardy).** Mathews and another man, Dougherty, robbed a bank in Ohio and were pursued by police to a farmhouse, where they hid. Shortly thereafter, police heard shots from inside the house, and Mathews surrendered. Police found Dougherty dead and assumed he had committed suicide. Mathews pleaded guilty to the robbery and was convicted of aggravated robbery. A few days later, Mathews confessed to killing Dougherty and was indicted on aggravated murder charges stemming from the robbery incident. He moved to quash the indictment on the grounds of double jeopardy, since some of the aggravated murder elements were an integral part of the elements of the aggravated robbery of which he had been convicted. The state denied his motion. Later, the state concluded that the aggravated murder charge was indeed double jeopardy, and thus it reduced the charge to the lesser included offense of murder, which was clearly supported by independent elements not associated with the aggravated robbery conviction. Mathews sought habeas corpus relief from the SC, but the SC upheld his murder conviction, holding that since the state had changed his conviction from a jeopardy-barred offense to a nonjeopardy-barred offense, the burden would therefore shift to Mathews to prove that the trial outcome would have been somehow differ-

ent. Thus the SC declared that reducing Mathews' concededly jeopardy-barred conviction for aggravated murder to a conviction for murder that concededly was not jeopardy barred was an adequate remedy for the double-jeopardy violation.

Morris v. Schoonfield, 399 U.S. 508, 90 S.Ct. 2232 (1970) **(Corrections; Probation and Parole).** Morris was convicted of a crime in Maryland, fined, and sentenced to a prison term. When his prison term expired, Morris, an indigent, couldn't pay the fine imposed, and thus authorities continued to imprison him. Morris filed a habeas corpus petition, alleging that he could not be held beyond the statutory imprisonment period, simply because he was poor and couldn't pay the fine imposed by the sentencing court. The SC heard his case and vacated the sentence, holding that an indigent may not be imprisoned beyond the maximum term specified by statute solely because of his failure to pay a fine and court costs.

Morrissey v. Brewer, 408 U.S. 471, 92 S.Ct. 2593 (1972) **(Corrections; Parole Revocation).** Morrissey was a parolee who allegedly violated several parole conditions. The violations included (1) failing to report his place of residence to his parole officer, (2) buying an automobile under an assumed name and operating it without parole officer permission, (3) obtaining credit under an assumed name, and (4) giving false statements to police after a minor traffic accident. The paroling authority summarily revoked his parole, and he was returned to prison. Morrissey appealed the summary revocation and the SC heard his case. Among other things, the Court in this landmark case established the minimum due process requirements for parole revocation: (1) Two hearings are required: the first is a preliminary hearing to determine whether probable cause exists that a parolee has violated any specific parole condition; the second is a general revocation proceeding. (2) Written notice must be given to the parolee prior to the general revocation proceeding. (3) Disclosure must be made to the parolee concerning the nature of parole violation(s) and evidence obtained. (4) Parolees must be given the right to confront and cross-examine their accusers unless adequate cause can be given for prohibiting such a cross-examination. (5) A written statement must be provided containing the reasons for revoking the parole and the evidence used in making that decision. (6) The parolees are entitled to have the facts judged by a detached and neutral hearing committee.

Muhammad v. Carlson, 43 CrL 2131 (1988) **(Corrections, Prisoners with AIDS)**. Muhammad, a prisoner, was transferred to a United States medical center because he had lost his limb coordination. Blood examination indicated that he had AIDS. Upon such a diagnosis, Muhammad was transferred back to the general prison population after being isolated for a seven-month period. He appealed, claiming that his isolation had violated his due-process rights. An appellate court upheld the constitutionality of his isolation, saying that the transfer had not been to punish him and that the new conditions complied with constitutionally safe guidelines of prison policy.

Murphy v. Waterfront Commission, 378 U.S. 52, 84 S.Ct. 1594 (1964) **(Law Enforcement Officers or Agencies; Exclusionary Rule)**. Murphy and others were subpoenaed to appear before the Waterfront Commission of New York Harbor concerning a work stoppage. Murphy refused to answer questions on Fifth Amendment grounds against self-incrimination. Immunity was therefore granted to Murphy under New Jersey and New York law, but he continued to refuse to testify, claiming he had not been granted federal immunity. He was cited for contempt. He appealed. The SC had previously held that federal immunity was not granted whenever states granted immunity to testifying witnesses. However, the SC overturned that particular decision, holding that the federal government may not make use of answers given by witnesses in state proceedings. Thus Murphy was compelled to testify in New Jersey and New York hearings, but the federal government had to honor the immunity extended to Murphy by these states.

Murray v. Carrier, 477 U.S. 478, 106 S.Ct. 2639 (1986) **(Sixth Amendment; Right to Counsel)**. Murray was accused in a Virginia court of rape. Prior to his trial, Murray demanded statements made by the rape victim, but the trial judge refused to disclose them. After Murray was convicted of rape, his counsel filed an appeal but did not include the matter of the victim's testimony or the denial of the discovery motion pertaining to it. The appeal was denied. On his own, Murray filed a habeas corpus petition alleging ineffective assistance of counsel and a failure of the prosecution to disclose the victim's statement. The SC held that the mere fact that counsel had failed to recog-

nize the factual or legal basis for a claim or failed to raise it despite recognizing it did not constitute cause for procedural default. Nor did the fact that the defense counsel had inadvertently neglected to include the discovery matter in his later motion filed with the court. Thus, the SC rejected Murphy's appeal and dismissed his defaulted discovery claim.

Murray v. Giarrantano, 492 U.S. 1, 109 S.Ct. 2765 (1989) **(Corrections; Inmate Rights)**. Giarrantano was a Virginia prisoner sentenced to death for a murder. He was indigent and sought postconviction relief, asking Virginia officials to appoint him an attorney to assist him to file an appeal. Virginia denied him such appointed counsel, and he appealed on his own. The SC upheld the Virginia decision, saying that indigent death-row inmates are not entitled to prison-appointed counsel to pursue further appeals or other postconviction relief.

Murray v. United States, 487 U.S. 533, 108 S.Ct. 2529 (1988) **(Law Enforcement Officers or Agencies; Exclusionary Rule)**. DEA agents suspected Murray of dealing in illicit drugs. Placing him under surveillance, they observed him drive a camper into a warehouse. When Murray and an associate emerged from the warehouse 20 minutes later, other DEA agents observed a large tractor trailer with a long, dark container. When the truck departed, it was followed by DEA agents. They stopped the drivers searched the truck, discovering marijuana. When the DEA agents watching the warehouse heard about the marijuana, they quickly, without a warrant, forced their way into Murray's warehouse, where they found several large burlap bags of marijuana "in plain view." They left the warehouse, obtained a valid search warrant from a judge, and reentered the warehouse, where they seized the previously viewed marijuana bales. They also confiscated notebooks detailing Murray's drug trafficking and other illicit dealings. Murray was ultimately arrested, tried, and convicted of trafficking in illegal drugs. He appealed. The SC rejected Murray's idea that the evidence should have been suppressed because officers had acted in an illegal manner when they first forced entry into the warehouse. While the SC declared this initial action by police to be misconduct, it concluded that the subsequent search in the context of a valid warrant *was* a valid search.

Mu'Min v. Virginia, 499 U.S. 400, 111 S.Ct. 1364 (1991) **(Sixth Amendment; Right to Counsel).** Mu'Min was charged with and convicted of a murder while he was out on a prison work detail (where he was serving a term on another charge). There was considerable news publicity surrounding the killing, and when the case came to trial, Mu'Min's attorney made a motion for the judge during *voir dire* to ask whether any specific jurors had any knowledge of the pretrial publicity and if so, what effect would it have on their ability to hear and decide the case fairly. The judge denied the motion, and Mu'Min was subsequently convicted. He appealed, alleging that his right to an impartial jury as provided by the Sixth Amendment had been violated. The SC upheld his conviction, holding that the refusal of the judge to question jurors about specific contents of news reports to which they had been exposed had not violated Mu'Min's Sixth or Fourteenth Amendment rights to due process.

N

Nathanson v. United States, 290 U.S. 41, 54 S.Ct. 11 (1933) **(Law Enforcement Officers or Agencies; Search and Seizure).** Nathanson was suspected of selling illegal liquor. His arrest was preceded by a search warrant merely stating suspicion and belief of violation of tariff laws without disclosing supporting facts. He was convicted. He appealed on the grounds that the basis for the search warrant was insufficient and thus violative of the Fourth Amendment right against unreasonable searches and seizures. The SC agreed with Nathanson and overturned his conviction. The mere suspicion that the law has been violated, without clearly articulating the reasons for the suspicion, is held to be insufficient basis for a search warrant.

Neil v. Biggers, 409 U.S. 188, 93 S.Ct. 375 (1972) **(Law Enforcement Officers or Agencies; Lineups; Pretrial Identification).** Biggers was suspected of rape. At the time the rape occurred, it was full moonlight, and the victim had an opportunity to look at the rapist clearly. Prior to Biggers's arrest, the victim had been subjected to showups, lineups, and photographs of previous rape suspects. At no time did she identify any of them as her attacker. But when Biggers was pre-

sented in a lineup with others, the victim immediately said she had "no doubt" that he was the rapist. He was convicted, largely on her testimony. He challenged the conviction, contending that his identification by the victim had been "suggestive." The SC upheld his conviction, noting the totality of circumstances under which the victim had made her positive identification. The SC concluded that weighing all the factors, it found no substantial likelihood of misidentification, and that the evidence was properly allowed to go to the jury.

New Jersey v. Portash, 440 U.S. 450, 96 S.Ct. 2737 (1976) **(Self-Incrimination).** Portash was a public official who gave testimony before a grand jury investigating extortion and misconduct in office. He was granted immunity in exchange for his testimony. Later, he was charged with extortion and his grand jury testimony was used against him. He was convicted. He appealed, saying that his Fifth Amendment rights had been violated and that he had been granted immunity, thus barring admission of his grand jury statements, which were indeed incriminating. A New Jersey Supreme Court reversed his conviction on these grounds, and the government appealed to the SC. The SC upheld Portash's reversal of conviction, saying that his testimony in response to being granted immunity was the essence of coerced testimony and involved the Fifth Amendment in its most clear form.

New Jersey v. T.L.O., 469 U.S. 325, 105 S.Ct. 733 (1985) **(Juvenile Law; Search and Seizure).** A 14-year-old girl was caught smoking a cigarette in the school bathroom, violating school rules. When confronted by the principal, she denied that she had been smoking. The principal examined her purse and discovered a pack of cigarettes, some rolling papers, money, marijuana, and other drug materials. This information was turned over to police, who charged the girl with delinquency. She was convicted. The girl's attorney sought to exclude the seized evidence because it was believed to be in violation of her Fourth Amendment right against unreasonable searches and seizures. The SC heard the case and ruled in favor of school officials, declaring that they only need reasonable suspicion, not probable cause, in order to search students and their possessions while on school property. When students enter their schools, they are subject to a lower standard than that applied to adult suspects when suspected of wrongdoing or carrying illegal contraband in violation of school rules.

New York v. Belton, 453 U.S. 454, 101 S.Ct.2869 (1981) **(Law Enforcement Officers or Agencies; Vehicle Searches).** Police stopped a suspicious-looking car in which Belton was a passenger. When they approached the vehicle, the officers smelled marijuana, and they found that no occupant of the car had documents showing ownership of the car. They placed the occupants under arrest and proceeded to search the vehicle. The search turned up a jacket owned by Belton, which contained cocaine. Belton was convicted of cocaine possession. He appealed, arguing that the search of the vehicle had been a warrantless intrusion into his privacy and in violation of his Fourth Amendment rights. The SC upheld Belton's conviction, saying that searches of automobiles following arrests of suspects, based upon probable cause, are proper.

New York v. Burger, 482 U.S. 691, 107 S.Ct. 2636 (1987) **(Law Enforcement Officers or Agencies; Search and Seizure).** Burger was in an automobile-wrecking business, where he dismantled wrecked automobiles and sold parts for profit. In the course of his business, he dealt in stolen automobiles and unregistered vehicles. Following an investigation of his wrecking-yard activities, police visited the yard with the intent to conduct a routine, administrative inspection of a commercial enterprise. They discovered numerous stolen parts, which were seized and used later in court against Burger as evidence. Burger was convicted of criminal possession of stolen property. He appealed, alleging that the "search" for inventory purposes should have been preceded by a lawfully issued search warrant, and thus, items subsequently seized without such a warrant should have been suppressed as evidence against him. The SC disagreed, however, and upheld his conviction, noting that administrative inventory inspections and searches by police, which are authorized by statute, are legal and do not require search warrants.

New York v. Class, 475 U.S. 106, 106 S.Ct. 960 (1986) **(Law Enforcement Officers or Agencies; Fourth Amendment; Vehicle Searches; Warrantless Inventories).** Two New York City police officers stopped Benigno Class, who was speeding and driving with a cracked windshield. When they attempted to determine the vehicle identification number (VIN), it could not be seen directly. The officer reached into the automobile and moved some papers that were obscuring the VIN on the dashboard. In doing so, saw the butt of a pistol protruding from underneath the driver's seat and seized the weapon. Class was arrested and convicted of criminal possession of a weapon. He appealed. Lower courts reversed Class's conviction. It was effectively argued that the search of the automobile by the officer had overstepped the officer's bounds of proper conduct. However, the SC heard the government's appeal and reinstated Class's conviction, holding that the movement of the papers was sufficiently unintrusive as to not violate his Fourth Amendment rights. Class had no reasonable expectation of privacy with respect to his VIN, and thus, when police attempted to see it, their conduct was reasonable. Thus they saw the pistol handle in plain view. Not only were two traffic violations committed by the offender, but officer safety became an immediate concern when the pistol handle was observed lawfully.

New York v. Harris, 495 U.S. 14, 110 S.Ct. 1640 (1990) **(Law Enforcement Officers or Agencies; Exclusionary Rule).** Harris was suspected of committing second-degree murder in the death of Staton in New York City on January 11, 1984. Various facts gave police officers probable cause to believe that Harris was the perpetrator. Without an arrest warrant, police went to Harris's home, knocked, were admitted by Harris, read him his Miranda rights, and questioned him. Harris admitted killing Staton and was arrested. While at the police station, Harris made two additional inculpatory statements, one videotaped, and gave a written and signed confession to police, despite the fact that he had indicated he wanted to end their questioning of him. He was convicted. The SC said that because the police had acted without a warrant in the original arrest of Harris, his first statement made at home was inadmissible. Also, it ruled his third statement, which was videotaped, inadmissible, since Harris had declared his desire not to continue being interrogated but was interrogated anyway. The second statement, however, given at police headquarters, was ruled admissible, despite the fact that his arrest without a valid warrant was inconsistent with the SC's ruling in *Payton v. New York* (1980). The SC declared that when police have probable cause to arrest suspects, the exclusionary rule does not bar the state's use of a statement made by a defendant outside of his home, even though the statement is taken *after* an arrest made in the home in violation of *Payton*.

New York v. P.J. Video, 475 U.S. 868, 106 S.Ct. 1610 (1986) **(Law Enforcement Officers or Agencies; Probable Cause Standard).** Doing business as Network Video, P.J. Video was visited by investigators, who rented several videocassette movies and subsequently determined that they violated New York's obscenity laws. A search warrant was issued and Network Video's premises were searched. Large quantities of movies were seized and introduced later in a trial against P.J. Video. P.J. Video attorneys moved for the dismissal of charges on the grounds that the search warrant should have been issued according to a "higher" probable-cause standard than is ordinarily used, since books and films were the subject matter under investigation. The motion was granted, and the state appealed. The SC heard the case and ruled that for purposes of the Fourth Amendment, there is no "higher" standard to which search warrants should adhere; a mere finding of probable cause is sufficient to authorize a valid search warrant, and thus the materials seized were legally admissible against P.J. Video. The videocassettes should not have been suppressed as evidence.

New York v. Quarles, 467 U.S. 649, 104 S.Ct. 2626 (1984) **(Confessions; Exceptions).** A woman reported that she had just been raped by an armed man, who ran into a supermarket. Police went to the market and saw Quarles. They approached him and had him place his hands on his head. A pat-down led to the discovery of an empty shoulder holster. Fearing that a firearm was near Quarles, making the issue of public safety of paramount concern, police asked Quarles where the gun was. He identified where he had thrown it among some empty cartons. The officers retrieved the gun and then read Quarles his Miranda rights. He was charged with rape and convicted. Quarles appealed, arguing that the initial statements he gave about the whereabouts of his gun should have been excluded as evidence against him, since officers had not told him his rights prior to questioning him about the gun's whereabouts. The SC upheld Quarles's conviction, saying that officer concern for public safety, where a firearm was near a potentially dangerous suspect, overrides the matter of advising suspects of their right to silence and other Miranda warnings. Thus the SC created a public-safety exception to allow investigating officers to bypass the Miranda warning when public safety is believed to be in jeopardy.

Nix v. Williams, 467 U.S. 431, 104 S.Ct. 2501 (1984) **(Law Enforcement Officers or Agencies; Exclusionary Rule).** On Christmas Eve, a 10-year-old girl was missing from a YMCA building in Des Moines, Iowa. Eyewitnesses reported later observing Williams leaving the YMCA building carrying a large bundle wrapped in a blanket, with two skinny legs protruding. Officers found Williams's car the next day 160 miles east of Des Moines. At a rest stop between where the car was found and the YMCA building, they discovered items of clothing and other articles. They assumed that the girl's body was probably somewhere between Des Moines and where Williams's car was found. Williams was subsequently found in a nearby town and arrested. While he was being driven back to Des Moines in a police vehicle, police officers engaged him in conversation relating to the girl's whereabouts. Because it had recently snowed, finding her body would be difficult. Officers suggested to Williams that he ought to tell them where her body was so that they could give her a "Christian burial." (This became known as the *Christian Burial Case.*) Williams confessed and directed officers to the girl's body. Williams was charged with and convicted of first-degree murder. He appealed, and his conviction was overturned inasmuch as police officers had not advised him of his Miranda rights. He was subjected to a second trial, in which his original confession was excluded. He was convicted again, but this time because the prosecutor showed that the girl's body would have been discovered eventually, thus providing the conclusive evidence against Williams. The significance of this case is that it introduced the inevitable-discovery exception to the exclusionary rule, whereby prosecutors may argue that inculpatory evidence may be introduced against criminal suspects if it can be shown that police would have eventually discovered the incriminating evidence anyway.

Nixon v. United States, 506 U.S. 224, 113 S.Ct. 732 (1993) **(Impeachment Proceedings Against Federal District Court Judges).** Nixon was a federal district court judge who was impeached following a Senate committee and testimony session that disclosed evidence of judicial misconduct. Nixon appealed, alleging that the Senate had not given him a full evidentiary hearing and thus had violated its constitutional duty to "try" all impeachments. The SC heard the appeal and upheld Nixon's impeachment, holding that the Senate had sole discretion to choose impeachment procedures, and thus, controversy was a nonjudiciable political question.

North v. Russell, 427 U.S. 328, 96 S.Ct. 2709 (1976) **(Eighth Amendment; Use of Judges).** North was convicted of a DWI charge in Kentucky in July 1974 by a police-court judge. He had first demanded a jury trial and been denied one. Kentucky, like Massachusetts, has a two-tiered trial system, where the first trial is a nonjury trial. Following a conviction, an offender may appeal to have a jury trial and must be granted one. North did not request a subsequent jury trial following his conviction for DWI in the nonjury situation. He was sentenced to and served 30 days in jail and lost his driver's license for a temporary period. He appealed the conviction, alleging that his due-process rights had been violated when he was tried before a police-court judge. Further, he alleged that his equal-protection rights had been violated, because some police-court judges have legal training, and others do not. The SC upheld his conviction, holding that North had elected *not* to appeal his original conviction in a trial *de novo*, which was his right to do. The SC said that the Kentucky two-tier trial court system, with law judicial officers in the first tier in smaller cities and an appeal of right with a *de novo* trial before a traditionally law-trained judge in the second, does not violate either the due-process or equal-protection guarantees of the Constitution.

North Carolina v. Alford, 400 U.S. 25, 91 S.Ct. 160 (1970) **(Plea Bargaining).** Alford was indicted for first-degree murder. A subsequent plea agreement was approved wherein Alford entered a guilty plea to second-degree murder in exchange for life imprisonment (rather than the death penalty) in the event of a guilty verdict. The judge imposed a 30-year term. Alford appealed. A lower appellate court held that his plea of guilty had been involuntary, because it had been prompted by a fear of the death penalty, and vacated the sentence. The SC reversed the lower court, letting the 30-year term stand. The SC said that an accused may voluntarily, knowingly, and understandingly consent to the imposition of a prison sentence, even though he is unwilling to admit participation in the crime, or even if his guilty plea contains a protestation of innocence, when, as here, he intelligently concludes that his interests require a guilty plea and the record strongly evidences guilt. The significance of this case, known as the Al-

ford plea, allows defendants to enter a nolo contendere plea that is in their best interests (e.g., avoiding a likely death penalty through a jury trial); thus accused persons may be unwilling to admit guilt, but they may also waive their right to a jury trial and accept a sentence, such as that arranged through a plea bargain.

North Carolina v. Butler, 441 U.S. 369, 99 S.Ct. 1755 (1979) **(Law Enforcement Officers or Agencies; Custodial Interrogations).** Butler was charged with kidnapping, armed robbery, and felonious assault. He made incriminating statements to police officers after they had given him the Miranda warning. He was convicted. He appealed, arguing that he had not expressly waived his right to the presence of counsel. The North Carolina SC overturned his conviction. Another appeal was made. The United States SC vacated the lower court's decision, saying that an explicit statement of waiver is not invariably necessary to support a finding that the defendant waived his right to remain silent or the right to counsel guaranteed by the *Miranda* case.

North Carolina v. Pearce, 395 U.S. 711, 89 S.Ct. 2072 (1969) **(Reconvictions).** Pearce was convicted of assault with intent to commit rape and was sentenced to 12 to 15 years. Several years later, he filed a habeas corpus petition, alleging that an involuntary confession had been admitted as evidence against him at his trial. He was subsequently retried, was convicted, and this time was sentenced to 8 years. This sentence, when added to the time he had already spent in prison, amounted to a term longer than his original sentence. Pearce appealed, arguing that the additional time imposed was a punishment for having his original conviction set aside. The SC heard this appeal and set aside the sentence, saying that although nothing prohibits judges from imposing harsher sentences in retrials than sentences imposed in earlier trials, constitutional guarantees obligate the government to give full credit of previous time served against new sentence. The SC also said that any unexplained additional punishment is a violation of due process.

O

O'Connor v. Donaldson, 422 U.S. 536, 95 S.Ct. 2486 (1975) **(Corrections; Inmate Rights).** Donaldson was confined in a mental health treatment facility for nearly 15 years. He petitioned for release but was denied. He sought a Title 42, U.S.C. Section 1983 action against hospital authorities, alleging that his civil rights were being violated because of what he alleged to be an unlawful detention. The SC ultimately heard his case and held that states may not lock up persons against their will merely based on a finding of "mental illness" and where there is no constitutional basis to continue to confine them after the basis for their original commitment no longer exists. A state cannot confine nondangerous individuals who are capable of surviving safely in freedom by themselves with the help of willing and responsible family. The state officials have only qualified immunity from suits brought by their patients.

O'Connor v. Ortega, 480 U.S. 709, 107 S.Ct. 1492 (1987) **(Corrections; Probation and Parole).** A hospital administrator, Ortega, was suspected of sexual harassment of his employees. While he was on administrative leave during an investigation of these harassment allegations, officials inventoried and searched his property and computer. No warrant was ever obtained to conduct such a search, and the property of Ortega was never properly inventoried following the search. Ortega filed suit, alleging his Fourth Amendment rights had been violated. The SC heard his case and decided that the officials had needed a warrant to conduct such a search of his offices. The SC remanded the case back to a lower court to decide the justification for the search and seizure and evaluate the reasonableness of both the inception of the search and its scope.

Ohio v. Roberts, 448 U.S. 56, 100 S.Ct. 2531 (1986) **(Sixth Amendment Right to Cross-Examine One's Accusers).** Roberts was suspected of a crime. At his trial the prosecutor presented transcript testimony from a witness who had testified earlier at a preliminary hearing. In an effort to obtain the witness's presence in court to testify in person, the prosecutor had issued five different subpoenas over a five-month period, but the witness could not be located. Roberts was convicted. He appealed, arguing that his Sixth Amendment right to cross-examine his accuser had been denied. The SC upheld Roberts's conviction, saying that the state had made a good-faith effort to locate a state witness over several months by issuing five subpoenas, and that because the witness was constitutionally unavailable, the transcript of her testimony was admissible as evidence against

Roberts. (Compare this case with *Harrington v. California* [1969], *Pointer v. Texas* [1965], and *Barber v. Page* [1968].)

Oklahoma City v. Tuttle, 471 U.S. 808, 105 S.Ct. 2427 (1985) **(Legal Liabilities of Public Officials).** The widow of Tuttle sued Oklahoma City officials because a police officer had shot and killed her husband, Tuttle, outside a bar where he had been participating in a robbery. Her civil-rights action, under Title 42, U.S.C. Section 1983, alleged negligence on the part of Oklahoma City officials in training their officers in the use of firearms. The SC ruled that Oklahoma City was not liable for the death of Tuttle and that this shooting showed no sign of gross negligence or negligent training or deliberate indifference.

Olden v. Kentucky, 488 U.S. 227, 109 S.Ct. 480 (1988) **(Sixth Amendment; Cross-Examination of Witnesses).** Olden and Harris, both black, were in a bar in Princeton, Kentucky, that catered primarily to black customers. Earlier that evening two white women, Matthews and her friend, Patton, went to the same bar and began drinking. Matthews became nervous as more blacks entered the bar during the evening. She became intoxicated and lost track of her friend. Olden told her that her friend had left and had been involved in a car accident. He suggested that Matthews accompany him to the accident scene. When she left the bar, Olden and Harris threatened her with a knife and drove her to a remote location, where they allegedly raped her. She was later taken to a location near the home of a friend and released. She immediately advised her friend, a man named Russell, that she had just been raped by Olden, Harris, and two other men who had joined them later. Police subsequently arrested Olden and prosecuted him for sodomy. During the trial, Olden asserted the defense of consent, claiming that Matthews had wanted to have sex with him. Several men testified to corroborate Olden's version of events. During the trial, information came to the defense that Matthews had been having an extramarital affair with Russell. Thus, it was conjectured that she probably used the "rape" story to deceive Russell. The defense attempted to cross-examine Matthews about her living arrangement with Russell, but the judge barred such questioning. Olden was convicted of sodomy. He appealed, alleging that the trial court's refusal to allow him to impeach Matthews's testimony had deprived him of the right to confront and cross-examine his accuser. The SC overturned his conviction, holding that the trial court's refusal to permit Olden to cross-examine Matthews about her cohabitation arrangement with Russell had violated Olden's Sixth Amendment right to confront his accuser.

Olim v. Wakinekona, 461 U.S. 238, 103 S.Ct. 1741 (1983) **(Corrections; Visitation Privileges).** Wakinekona was a Hawaiian prisoner transferred to a California prison and reclassified to a higher custody level. He appealed, alleging his due-process rights had been violated because no hearing had been held to determine his new classification. The appeal was rejected by a lower court, but a state court of appeals reversed the lower-court decision. The government appealed, and the SC heard the case. The SC reversed the state appellate court decision, holding that the transfer of the prisoner from Hawaii to California did not implicate the due-process clause of the Fourteenth Amendment. Hawaii's prison system does not create a protected liberty interest that must be considered by California prisons. Prisoners have no rights relating to where they are confined or at what custody level.

Oliver v. United States, 466 U.S. 170, 104 S.Ct. 1735 (1984) **(Law Enforcement Officers or Agencies; Plain View Rule; Open Fields Searches).** Oliver grew marijuana on some land near his home. He had fenced in the property and posted a "No Trespassing" sign. Acting on reports from an informant that Oliver was growing marijuana in the field, officers went to the field and found a footpath. Without an arrest warrant or a search warrant, they followed it about a mile until they came to some marijuana plants growing in the middle of the field. Oliver was arrested and convicted of marijuana manufacturing. He appealed, contending that the "No Trespassing" sign required police to obtain a search warrant before they trespassed on his property. The SC disagreed with Oliver and upheld the conviction, saying that "No Trespassing" signs are not sufficient to create the reasonable expectation of privacy that requires police to have a warrant; further, the open field was such that the privacy expectation that an owner would have relating to it does not exist. Police may "trespass" and search any such open area without a warrant and without probable cause.

Olmstead v. United States, 277 U.S. 438, 48 S.Ct. 564 (1928) **(Law Enforcement Officers or Agencies; Electronic Surveillance).** During Pro-

hibition in the 1920s, Olmstead and others were involved in a conspiracy to distribute illegal liquor in violation of the National Prohibition Act. Federal agents had gathered most of their vital information about the conspiracy from wiretaps, (telephone intercepts) from which information about the conspiracy could be easily obtained. The wiretaps had been installed in the telephone lines outside of suspects' homes. Olmstead and others were convicted. They appealed, arguing that the wiretaps were an invasion of their right to privacy under the Fourth Amendment. The SC upheld their conviction, declaring wiretaps by government agents legal. The SC stressed the fact that there was no trespass by authorities into any constitutionally protected area, such as the home's interior. Thus, an unreasonable search and seizure of "conversation" had not occurred. This was the landmark case ruling on wiretaps and their constitutionality. Subsequently, this case was overruled in *Katz v. United States* (1967), which held that any form of wiretapping or electronic surveillance that violates one's reasonable expectation of privacy is a search, and thus a warrant is required based upon probable cause before such a "search" through electronic surveillance is conducted.

O'Lone v. Estate of Shabazz, 482 U.S. 342, 107 S.Ct. 2400 (1987) **(Corrections; Inmate Rights; Freedom of Religion).** Several Muslim prisoners in a New Jersey penitentiary filed suit under Title 42, U.S.C. Section 1983, alleging their First Amendment rights to religious freedom were being violated. Specifically, they objected to work assignments that interfered with their returning, during daytime hours, to buildings on prison grounds where religious services were observed. This was a prison policy based on security reasons. The SC disagreed with the men, saying that legitimate penological interests prevail over specific inmate religious interests, and that to accommodate the particular religious idiosyncrasies of inmates would jeopardize prison security in an unreasonable way. Thus, prison policies geared to maintain security of prisons, even though they prevent inmates from exercising their right to worship, are constitutional policies.

O'Neal v. McAninch, ___U.S.___, 115 S.Ct. 992 (1995) **(Judicial Jury Instructions).** O'Neal was accused of aggravated murder, kidnapping, and robbery. The trial judge gave the jury an incorrect instruction. O'Neal was convicted. He appealed. An appellate court ruled that the judge's error was harmless. However, a federal appellate judge expressed grave doubt whether the trial error was indeed harmless or rather had had substantial and injurious effects or influences in determining the jury's verdict. O'Neal appealed again. The SC said that whenever a federal judge expresses "grave doubt" about a jury instruction and its constitutionality or effects, this is not harmless error and thus the petitioner must win. The significance of this case is the stress on "grave doubt." If there is a grave doubt that such an error is harmless, then it is not harmless. O'Neal's conviction was overturned and a new trial was ordered.

On Lee v. United States, 343 U.S. 747, 72 S.Ct. 967 (1952) **(Law Enforcement Officers or Agencies; Electronic Surveillance).** On Lee owned a laundry and also provided opium, a controlled substance, to others illegally. A friend and federal undercover agent visited On Lee and with a hidden electronic microphone engaged On Lee in incriminating conversations about his drug sales. Later, the evidence obtained, including the conversations the agent had with On Lee, was admitted against him in a trial, in which he was convicted. On Lee appealed, seeking to have the conversational evidence suppressed as a violation of his Fourth Amendment guarantees. The SC upheld his conviction. Its reasoning is significant because it declared essentially that as long as one of the parties having a conversation with another "consents" to the recording of it, it is lawful under the Fourth Amendment. Thus, if someone called another person on the telephone and recorded the conversation without the other's knowledge, this would be lawful since the person recording the conversation was consenting to it. Therefore, *any* conversation between friends, even though one of the friends may be a police officer or informant, is subject to electronic surveillance as long as one of the parties agrees and if the recording is not in violation of state law.

Oregon v. Bradshaw, 462 U.S. 285, 103 S.Ct. 2830 (1988) **(Confessions; Exceptions).** Bradshaw wrecked his pickup truck, and a passenger in his truck was killed. During the police investigation, Bradshaw was told his Miranda rights, denied his involvement, and asked for an attorney. However, he continued to converse with the officer, eventually admitting that he had been driving the truck while intoxicated and under license suspension. In court later, Bradshaw moved to suppress the statements he had made to police, but his

motion was denied and he was convicted. He appealed. The SC upheld his conviction, saying that his own continued conversation with officers constituted knowing and intelligent waiver of his right to counsel. Thus, voluntary statements made by arrestees after they have been told their Miranda rights may be used against them despite the absence of counsel which they have formerly requested.

Oregon v. Elstad, 470 U.S. 298, 105 S.Ct. 1285 (1985) **(Confessions; Exceptions).** Elstad was suspected of burglary, and police officers went to his home with an arrest warrant. They entered the house at the mother's invitation and proceeded to Elstad's room, where they advised him that he was implicated in the burglary. Elstad told officers, "I was there," before being given his Miranda warning. He was placed under arrest and taken to the police station, where he requested to talk to officers. He gave a full and voluntary confession to the burglary and signed a typed statement. After he was convicted, he appealed, contending that his original statement was an inculpatory one, and because it had been given before he was told his Miranda rights, it should have been excluded as well as the confession he made later resulting from the incriminating statement. The SC disagreed with Elstad and upheld the burglary conviction. They noted that prior statements made by suspects before Miranda warnings are given are admissible so long as they are voluntary, especially if subsequent confessions are given following Miranda warnings, where earlier statements are substantiated.

Oregon v. Hass, 420 U.S. 714, 95 S.Ct. 1215 (1975) **(Confessions).** Hass was accused of taking bicycles from two house garages in Klamath Falls, Oregon, in August 1972. An automobile license number enabled police officers preliminarily to identify Hass as the thief. Hass was told his Miranda rights, and he gave police statements about the bicycle thefts in a confession. Hass said he would probably want to see a lawyer when he got to jail and he made other statements later to police. He was convicted of the theft and sentenced to two years' probation and a fine. He appealed, arguing that some of the testimony given by police officers should have been inadmissible, because of his statement about seeing an attorney after getting to jail. The SC upheld Hass's conviction, holding that his statements to Oregon police had been voluntary, despite the Miranda warning.

Oregon v. Kennedy, 456 U.S. 667, 102 S.Ct. 2083 (1982) **(Double Jeopardy).** Kennedy was accused of theft. During his trial, an expert witness for the state testified that he had never done business with Kennedy. The prosecutor asked him, "Is that because he is a crook?" Kennedy moved for a mistrial and was granted a new trial. In the retrial, a motion for dismissal on double-jeopardy grounds was rejected. Kennedy was convicted. Kennedy then appealed to the SC, asking it to consider whether the prosecution had deliberately provoked the mistrial by the remarks made to the witness. If these remarks reflected an intentional provocation, then a case of double jeopardy could be made and Kennedy could not be tried again on those same charges. The SC said that there was no apparent indication that the prosecutor intended to provoke a mistrial, and thus Kennedy was barred from making a double-jeopardy claim to prevent the retrial from occurring.

Oregon v. Mathiason, 429 U.S. 492, 97 S.Ct. 711 (1977) **(Confessions; Exceptions; Probation and Parole).** Mathiason, a parolee, was living at a residence where a burglary occurred. About a month later, a police officer left a card saying he would like to talk with Mathiason about the burglary. On his own volition, Mathiason went to the police station and entered voluntarily into a conversation with the officer and eventually confessed to the burglary. At no time prior to this confession did he receive a Miranda warning. He was convicted. He appealed, arguing that he should have been given the warning before confessing. The SC rejected his appeal, saying that he went to the police station merely to answer questions. He was not in custody, he had not been arrested, and he had given statements to police freely and voluntarily, including his confession. Thus his conviction was proper.

Orozco v. Texas, 394 U.S. 324, 89 S.Ct. 1095 (1969) **(Confessions; Exceptions).** Orozco was confined to a bed at the time he was questioned by police concerning his part in a crime. He gave incriminating statements about his part in the crime. Partial Miranda warnings had been given to him. He was convicted. He appealed. The SC declared that his bed-ridden condition and the presence of police had converted this "interview" into a full-fledged custodial interrogation where Orozco's right attached, and thus he was entitled to the full Miranda warning apprising him of his right to counsel and to silence. His conviction was overturned.

Osborn v. United States, 385 U.S. 323, 87 S.Ct. 429 (1966) **(Law Enforcement Officers or Agencies; Electronic Surveillance).** Osborn, a Nashville lawyer, had hired Vick, a Nashville police officer, to do some background checks on prospective jurors in a case Osborn was handing for Hoffa, a union official. Unknown to Osborn was the fact that Vick had agreed with the FBI to report any "illegal activities" in the case. Vick wore a recording device unknown to Osborn and was wearing it when Osborne made incriminating statements to Vick in Osborn's office. Osborn disclosed that one of the prospective jurors, Elliott, was his own cousin and that Vick ought to visit him and see whether he would be susceptible to receiving $5,000 for his pro-defense jury work. Osborn was convicted, largely on Vick's testimony and the recording made of the conversation between Osborn and Vick. Osborn appealed his conviction, alleging entrapment. The SC heard the case and upheld Osborn's conviction, holding that it was proper for Vick to record his conversation with Osborn. There was significant overt action on Osborn's part to sustain his conviction. No warrant had been required for the wire worn by Vick, because Osborn himself was not presently under indictment when the conversations were recorded, and the conversation was consensually recorded, because Vick, one of the conversants, agreed to record it. This was *not* a third-party scenario where FBI are intentionally "listening in" to discover incriminating evidence; rather, Osborn had instructed Vick to offer Elliott the bribe.

O'Shea v. Littleton, 414 U.S. 488, 94 S.Ct. 669 (1974) **(Corrections; Death Penalty).** Littleton and 17 other black residents of Cairo, Illinois, brought a Title 42, U.S.C. Section 1983 action against judges and police for allegedly engaging in discriminatory practices relating to bail-setting, sentencing, and jury-free practices in criminal cases. The SC heard the case and rejected their claims, holding that these persons had failed to show any actual case or controversy where such discrimination occurred, and that the simple assertions and inferences were only speculative and not grounded in fact. Further, Littleton had failed to show any likelihood of substantial and immediate irreparable injury, or the inadequacy of remedies under the law.

Owen v. City of Independence, Mo., 445 U.S. 622, 100 S.Ct. 1398 (1980) **(Legal Liabilities of Police Officers and City Officials).** Owen, the chief of police in Independence, was fired without explanation by the city manager, following citizen complaints about police misconduct. Owen sued the city under a Title 42, U.S.C. Section 1983 civil-rights claim. He alleged that he had not been permitted a hearing or given a statement of charges against him; thus his constitutional rights had been violated. Attorneys for the city manager claimed the city manager was acting in good faith and properly, according to existing city charter provisions. The SC declared that Independence did not have immunity from liability under the Section 1983 claim and might not assert the good-faith defense in response to such a Section 1983 complaint.

P

Palko v. Connecticut, 302 U.S. 319, 58 S.Ct. 149 (1937) **(Corrections; Death Penalty; Self-Incrimination).** Palko was convicted of second-degree murder in Connecticut, and a life sentence was imposed. Because of procedural errors, the conviction was overturned and a new trial was held. In the second trial, Palko was again convicted of first-degree murder, and the death sentence was imposed. Palko appealed, saying that his second trial was double jeopardy and in violation of his constitutional rights. The SC rejected his appeal, holding that none of his constitutional rights had been violated, when in fact, the state was merely seeking a fair trial for him.

Parke v. Raley, 506 U.S. 20, 113 S.Ct. 517 (1992) **(Standard of Proof).** In 1986, Raley was charged with robbery and with being a persistent felony offender, having been previously convicted of various felonies in 1979 and 1981. These previous convictions were the result of guilty pleas entered by Raley in different courts, where records of such events were not made. He was convicted. Raley sought to challenge Kentucky's persistent-offender statute by showing that the other convictions ought to have been suppressed as considerations, because it could not be determined from the absence of records whether Raley's guilty pleas in those instances were voluntary. The SC ultimately heard Raley's appeal and rejected

it, upholding the constitutionality of Kentucky's persistent-offender sentencing statute. Regarding Raley's earlier "guilty" pleas, the SC held that prior factual determinations by previous court convictions are entitled to the presumption of correctness.

Parker v. Dugger, 498 U.S. 308, 111 S.Ct. 731 (1991) **(Juries; Death Penalty; Two-stage Trials).** Parker was convicted of a double first-degree murder in Florida. At the sentencing hearing, the jury found numerous aggravating circumstances, but they also found considerable mitigating circumstances that outweighed the aggravating factors. Therefore, they recommended to the judge a sentence of life imprisonment. However, the judge overrode the jury recommendation and sentenced Parker to death, citing several statutory aggravating factors and *no* statutory mitigating factors. There was also a question as to the validity of some of the aggravating circumstances cited by the judge and evidence of their existence. Parker appealed. The Florida Supreme Court affirmed the death penalty, so Parker appealed to the United States SC. The SC overturned the death sentence, holding that the Florida Supreme Court had acted arbitrarily and capriciously by failing to treat adequately Parker's nonstatutory mitigating evidence. The Florida court had also erred when it declared that the trial judge had found no "mitigating factors" when in fact he had found such factors, although they happened to be nonstatutory. The SC declared Parker's death sentence to be invalid because of these factors and because the court had deprived Parker of his right to individualized treatment and consideration.

Parker v. Randolph, 442 U.S. 62, 99 S.Ct. 2132 (1979) **(Sixth Amendment Right to Cross-Examine One's Accuser).** Three defendants were tried and convicted of a crime in which they all participated. Some of them gave oral confessions, which were introduced as evidence against them. The judge instructed the jury to disregard any portion of those statements that implicated one or both of the other defendants. All three were convicted. They appealed, arguing that the interlocking nature of their cases and the confessions violated the Sixth Amendment. The SC overturned their convictions, saying that the accused's right to cross-examination had been violated in the joint trial where some of the defendants did not testify, but where one or more of their confessions were read into the record, despite the judge's instructions to the jury to disregard portions of confessions implicating one or both defendants. The case significance is that when codefendants are tried together, the admissibility of a confession is limited to the specific defendant who gives the confession. The court must be careful to control what portions of confessions may be used as evidence against specific defendants, if one or more defendants elect not to testify on their own behalf or subject themselves to cross-examination.

Parratt v. Taylor, 451 U.S. 527, 101 S.Ct. 1908 (1981) **(Corrections; Inmate Rights).** Taylor was an inmate at the Nebraska Penal and Correctional Complex. While confined, he ordered hobby materials from a company outside the prison. When his materials arrived, corrections officers signed for the package, but at that time, Taylor was in isolation and was not permitted to have these materials. Later, when Taylor was released from isolation, he sought to retrieve his package, but no one could locate it. He sued prison officials for the loss of his package under a Title 42, U.S.C. Section 1983 civil-rights allegation. The SC heard the case and rejected Taylor's argument for the following reasons: In order to prevail in a 1983 action, the inmate must prove that (1) prison officials committed an act against an inmate in their official capacity; and (2) the conduct deprived the inmate of rights, privileges, or immunities under the United States Constitution. The SC found that the prison employees had acted in their official capacity as hobby shop employees, there was not conduct apparent that caused Hughes to be deprived of his rights. In this case, what is apparent is that someone purloined Taylor's property, but no one could prove it. In any case, Taylor was advised that the "loss" he suffered did not constitute a violation of constitutional rights.

Patterson v. Illinois, 487 U.S. 285, 108 S.Ct. 2389 (1988) **(Confessions; Exceptions).** Patterson was a murder suspect. He was interrogated twice, and on each occasion he signed a waiver of his Miranda rights in order to converse with police voluntarily. He gave several incriminating statements during these interrogations and was subsequently convicted of murder. He appealed, contending that he had not been specifically advised of his right to counsel during interrogation. The SC disagreed and upheld his conviction, saying that the waiver of a right to counsel is included in the Miranda warning, and that Patterson had waived his right to counsel in both instances when

he signed this waiver. The Miranda warning is also a warning advising against self-incrimination.

Paul v. Davis, 424 U.S. 693, 96 S.Ct. 1155 (1976) **(Corrections; Inmate Rights).** Davis was a known shoplifter in Louisville, Kentucky. His name and photo were distributed to various retail outlets in a flyer of suspected or known shoplifters. Davis found out about this circular from his boss and filed a class-action Title 42, U.S.C. Section 1983 civil-rights suit against the chief of police of Louisville, alleging that he was being deprived of a liberty and property interest because of the circular. He asked the SC to declare unconstitutional the publication of such circulars as defamatory of his character and a violation of his right to privacy. The SC decided there was no constitutional basis for his claims against officials in Louisville, and his constitutional rights had not been violated by their circular actions.

Payne v. Tennessee, 501 U.S. 808, 111 S.Ct. 2597 (1991) **(Corrections; Death Penalty; Victim Impact Statements).** Payne was convicted of a double murder. At the sentencing hearing, he introduced various witnesses on his behalf to avoid the death penalty. During the same hearing, the victims' relatives introduced their victim impact statement, pressing the jury to impose the death penalty on Payne. The death penalty was imposed, and Payne appealed, contesting the introduction of damaging evidence and opinions expressed in the victim-impact statement. The SC upheld Payne's death sentence, holding that victim-impact statements do not violate an offender's Eighth Amendment rights. The significance of this case is that it supports and condones the use of victim impact statements against convicted offenders during sentencing hearings. (*See Booth v. Maryland* [1987] for a comparable case where victim-impact statements were suppressed. In the present situation, however, victim-impact statements were constitutional as a part of the sentencing hearing involving the death penalty and other crimes.)

Payton v. New York, 445 U.S. 573, 100 S.Ct. 1371 (1980) **(Law Enforcement Officers or Agencies; Exclusionary Rule).** Payton was suspected of the death of a gas station manager. Police went to Payton's apartment to arrest him without a warrant, although they had plenty of time to obtain one. No one was home, and police forced their way in with a crowbar. They found a .30 caliber rifle shell casing on the floor "in plain view."

This shell casing was incriminating evidence, and Payton was subsequently convicted of the murder. He appealed. The SC overturned Payton's conviction because police had not obtained a valid arrest warrant in a routine felony arrest situation. There were no exigent circumstances compelling police to act quickly. What evidence they later discovered as the result of their illegal entry into Payton's dwelling was inadmissible. The SC stressed that the governing factor here was whether there was reason for police to act quickly or whether the arrest of Payton was otherwise routine. The SC said the arrest was routine; thus, a lawful arrest warrant for Payton was required.

Pell v. Procunier, 417 U.S. 817, 94 S.Ct. 2800 (1974) **(Corrections; Inmate Rights).** Several professional journalists and California prison inmates filed suit against prison authorities under Title 42, U.S.C. Section 1983, alleging that they had been denied the First Amendment right of freedom of speech. Specifically, journalists had wanted to interview certain inmates following a prison riot. Prison policy was to refuse such interviews. The SC heard the case and decided in favor of prison authorities. Thus a prison regulation prohibiting media interviews with inmates neither violates the First Amendment nor the rights of inmates to be heard by media personnel.

Pembaur v. Cincinnati, 475 U.S. 469, 106 S.Ct. 1292 (1986) **(Legal Liabilities of Public Officials).** A physician, Pembaur, filed suit against the City of Cincinnati, whose police officers allegedly violated his Fourth and Fourteenth Amendment rights by forcing their way into his clinic to serve a *capias* on two of his employees. He was subsequently charged with obstruction of justice and convicted. Pembaur continued his suit against county officials, where they alleged that they were immune from such suits. Pembaur's claim was rejected and he appealed the case to the SC. The SC reinstated his claim against county officials, saying that the county is liable under Title 42, U.S.C., Section 1983.

Pennsylvania v. Bruder, 488 U.S. 9, 109 S.Ct. 205 (1988) **(Law Enforcement Officers or Agencies; Miranda Warnings During Routine Traffic Stops; Persons in Custody).** Bruder was stopped by police one evening because he appeared to be driving erratically and he ran a red light. Bruder left his vehicle and approached the police, who smelled alcohol. They also observed that Bruder was stumbling. He was administered several field sobriety tests, which he failed. Police asked Bruder if he had been drinking, and he said he had been drinking and was driving home. Police placed him under arrest, and told him his Miranda rights. He was subsequently convicted of DWI. He appealed, alleging that his statements before the Miranda warning should not have been admitted against him in court. The SC asked the critical question whether or not he was in a coercive situation when answering police questions before his arrest. The SC determined that he was not entitled to a Miranda warning. His statements made before his arrest were admissible against him and his DWI conviction was upheld.

Pennsylvania v. Finley, 481 U.S. 551, 107 S.Ct. 1990 (1987) **(Corrections; Inmate Rights).** Finley, an indigent, was convicted of second-degree murder in Pennsylvania. She appealed. An attorney was appointed to assist her in perfecting her appeal. The attorney inspected the trial record and other legal matters, concluded that there was nothing worth arguing in the appeal, and withdrew. A new lawyer was appointed to represent Finley. Her appeal efforts were fruitless, so she demanded a new attorney for a new appeal, alleging that the first attorney who withdrew had been incompetent and objecting to the conduct of the second lawyer. Finley appealed to the SC, alleging that her due-process rights had been violated by the attorney withdrawal and other attorney conduct. The SC rejected her appeal, holding that indigent prisoners have no equal-protection right to appointed counsel in postconviction proceedings after exhaustion of appellate process or in postconviction relief proceedings after exhaustion of appellate process. States have no obligation to provide post-conviction relief for collateral attack upon judgment, and when they do, fundamental fairness mandated by due process does not require them to supply a lawyer.

Pennsylvania v. Mimms, 434 U.S. 106, 98 S.Ct. 330 (1977) **(Law Enforcement Officers or Agencies; Vehicle Searches).** Mimms was stopped in his vehicle for having expired license plates. Officers observed a "bulge" in his clothing when he got out of the vehicle, and they patted him down, discovering a firearm. He was subsequently arrested and convicted of carrying a concealed weapon and possessing a firearm without a license. He appealed. The SC upheld his conviction, citing *Terry v. Ohio* (1968) and the fact that the officers did indeed have reasonable suspicion and exercised reasonable caution when they observed the bulge in his jacket. The officers were entitled to act in a manner to ensure their safety and security.

Pennsylvania v. Muniz, 496 U.S. 582, 110 S.Ct. 2638 (1990) **(Confessions; Exceptions).** Muniz was stopped by police on suspicion of drunken driving. He given various field sobriety tests and failed all of them. He even admitted to police that he failed because he had been drinking. The officers arrested Muniz. Later, they asked if Muniz would submit to taking these same tests again, only this time, the police would videotape his actions. He agreed, and again he failed the tests. Next, police asked Muniz to take a Breathalyzer test and Muniz refused. The police then read Muniz his Miranda rights for the first time and he admitted again that he had been drinking and driving. This evidence was admitted against him later in court, including the videotaped failing of the sobriety tests. He was convicted. He appealed, contending that the videotapings had been done before he had been told his Miranda rights. However, the SC upheld Muniz's DWI conviction, saying that the videotaping and questioning of Muniz before the Miranda warning was given constituted routine questioning and other procedures common to DWI stops and questioning. Police may videotape suspected drunken drivers and ask them routine questions, such as age, residence, and hair color, without specifically giving them the Miranda warning. Routine information of this sort may be used as evidence against them.

Pennsylvania v. Ritchie, 480 U.S. 39, 107 S.Ct. 989 (1987) **(Sixth Amendment; Due Process).** Ritchie was accused of rape, corruption of a minor, and involuntary sexual intercourse. Prior to trial, defense counsel sought to examine certain juvenile records maintained by Children and Youth Services (CYS). CYS policy forbade inspection by others, including defense counsel, of confidential juvenile information. Ritchie was tried and convicted. He appealed, alleging that he should have been allowed to examine the juvenile records, and thus he had been deprived of a fair trial. The Pennsylvania Supreme Court overturned his conviction on these grounds, and the state appealed to the United States SC. The SC reinstated Ritchie's convictions but remanded the case to a lower court to resolve other issues. The SC declared that under the rules of discovery, defendants are not authorized to have unsupervised

authority to search state records to make a determination of the materiality of confidential information. Thus, the state's compelling interest in safeguarding and protecting its child-abuse information outweighed Ritchie's discovery interests. The SC agreed that Ritchie was entitled to know whether the CYS information might have changed the outcome of his trial had it been disclosed. For this reason alone, a remand was necessary. But the SC disagreed with the notion that defense counsel is entitled to access to CYS files. Thus, an *in camera* review of file information would determine whether the information was relevant to Ritchie's case.

Penry v. Lynaugh, 492 U.S. 302, 109 S.Ct. 2934 (1989) **(Corrections; Death Penalty).** Penry was a mentally retarded inmate convicted of capital murder in Texas. He had an IQ of 54 and a mental age of 6 years old. He was 22 when the capital murder was committed, and he was sentenced to death. Penry appealed his death sentence, contending that mentally retarded persons cannot be executed. The SC upheld Penry's death penalty as constitutional, since Penry had to be judged competent to stand trial initially. Some people believe that this decision contradicts what the SC decided in *Ford v. Wainwright* (1986), that Ford was insane, and the SC held that no insane person can be executed. The SC distinguished between the two cases, however, indicating that Ford was unaware of what was going on around him and did not understand the purpose for his execution; Penry knew what he had done and that it was wrong. Therefore, Penry's execution was upheld as constitutional.

Penson v. Ohio, 488 U.S. 75, 109 S.Ct. 346 (1988) **(Sixth Amendment; Right to Counsel).** Penson, an indigent, was convicted of several serious crimes. He was appointed a new attorney for his appeal to a higher court, but his attorney filed a Certification of Meritless Appeal and Motion, which indicated that he had thoroughly examined the trial record and could find no sound basis for an appeal. The attorney asked to be removed as counsel for Penson. Later, Penson asked for but was denied a new attorney to launch yet another appeal. Subsequently, on its own, the Ohio Supreme Court discovered that Penson had several arguable claims in his case, and in fact, one of these claims might have resulted in reversible error. Nevertheless, the court rejected Penson's new request for counsel and his appeal, justifying its decision because the court had thoroughly examined the record and received the benefit of arguments from counsel who had represented Penson and a codefendant. Eventually, Penson's case reached the SC. The SC scolded the Ohio Supreme Court in various ways, by noting that it had erred in several respects. When Ohio judges determined that there were "arguable" issues in Penson's case, they erred when they decided not to hear his appeal. They also erred when they permitted Penson's counsel to withdraw, after he submitted a statement claiming that no arguable issues could be found. The SC noted that the most glaring error was the failure of the Ohio Supreme Court to appoint a new counsel for Penson after it had determined that there were several "arguable issues." Thus, the SC said, Penson's due-process rights had been violated and it overturned his convictions.

People v. Hipp, 861 S.W.2d 377 (1993) **(Sentencing; Plea Bargaining)**. Hipp was determined by the court to be addicted to gambling. That addiction combined with the offense for which he was convicted compelled the court under mandatory sentencing to prescribe a jail term as well as accompanying therapy for the addiction. The judge simply accepted the defendant's guilty plea in exchange for a term of probation. The New York Court of Appeals overruled the judge in this case, indicating that New York statutes do not authorize a trial court to ignore clearly expressed and unequivocal mandatory sentencing provisions of the New York Penal Law.

People v. Matthews, 23 Cal.Rptr.2d 434 (Cal.App.Sept.) (1993) **(Corrections; Pardons)**. Matthews completed a term of probation for a crime committed in California. He applied for a pardon and certification of rehabilitation from California but was denied. The denial was based on the fact that in order to qualify for the pardon and certification of rehabilitation, one must be a California resident for at least three years. Matthews didn't qualify.

Perry v. Leeke, 488 U.S. 272, 109 S.Ct. 594 (1989) **(Sixth Amendment; Right to Counsel)**. Perry was accused of murder, kidnapping, and sexual assault in South Carolina. During his trial, a 15-minute recess was declared by the judge, who advised Perry not to speak with anyone, including Perry's attorney. Subsequently, Perry was convicted of these crimes. He appealed through a habeas corpus petition, alleging that his Sixth Amendment right to counsel had been violated because of the prohibition against seeing his attorney during the recess. The SC upheld Perry's conviction, holding that the state trial court's order directing Perry not to consult his attorney during the afternoon recess had not violated Perry's Sixth Amendment right to assistance of counsel.

Pierson v. Ray, 386 U.S. 547, 87 S.Ct. 1213 (1967) **(Legal Liabilities of Public Officials)**. Fifteen white and black clergymen attempted to use white facilities at an interstate bus terminal in Jackson, Mississippi. Police officers arrested them for disturbing the peace. They waived a jury trial and were convicted, being sentenced to four months. Subsequently, they appealed the case and filed a civil-rights suit against the police officers who arrested them, alleging false imprisonment and civil-rights violations. Early appellate decisions resulted in favorable verdicts for the officers, so the clergymen appealed to the SC. The SC decided that the clergymen did indeed have standing to seek damages against the Jackson police officers. Their claim under Title 42, U.S.C. Section 1983 was thus upheld and sent back to a civil trial court for further proceedings.

Plessy v. Ferguson, 163 U.S. 537, 16 S.Ct. 1138 (1896) **(Racial Segregation)**. Plessy, a man who had some African-American ancestry, boarded an all-white railroad car. He refused to leave when asked by the railroad conductor. At the time, separate but equal facilities was the governing doctrine relating to white and black accommodations, particularly in Southern states. Plessy filed suit against the railroad, alleging discrimination. The SC heard the case and declared that as long as equal facilities were provided for blacks, separate accommodations for them did not violate the "separate but equal" concept. The significance of this case is that it set a precedent for racial discrimination patterns for the next 50 years, in virtually every social activity involving different races: separate but equal restrooms, bus seating, drinking fountains, housing. The doctrine was set aside on a piecemeal basis, beginning with *Brown v. Board of Education* (1954), where this separate but equal doctrine was determined *not* to apply to education. Thereafter, individual SC decisions addressed the separate but equal issue in each of the areas to which it applied. The SC never overturned the original decision rendered in *Plessy v. Ferguson*. This fact demonstrates an important principle about SC decisionmaking—it is narrow in its scope, and subsequent SC decisions almost never result in a total abandonment of prior SC decisions.

Pointer v. Texas, 380 U.S. 400, 85 S.Ct. 1065 (1965) **(Witness Confrontation by Defendant).** Pointer was accused of armed robbery. At a preliminary hearing where Pointer was not represented by counsel, a victim, Phillips, testified against him. Pointer did not cross-examine the victim. Later at Pointer's trial, the prosecutor offered for the record the transcript of testimony of Phillips during the preliminary hearing as evidence against Pointer, since the victim had left the state and indicated no intention to return to give testimony directly in Pointer's trial. Pointer was convicted. He appealed, arguing that he had not had an opportunity to cross-examine Phillips. The Texas Supreme Court rejected his argument and upheld his conviction. The SC eventually heard Pointer's case and overturned his conviction because his Sixth Amendment rights had been violated. The SC said that the statements given by Phillips during the preliminary hearing had afforded no defense attorney an opportunity to cross-examine Phillips. The use of Phillips's transcript of testimony had offered Pointer no right of cross-examination, and thus the conviction could not be proper unless Pointer were allowed the right to cross-examine his accuser. The significance of this case is that a transcript of testimony from an available witness and victim is insufficient as a basis for a conviction, because the right of cross-examination is denied.

Poland v. Arizona, 476 U.S. 147, 106 S.Ct. 1749 (1986) **(Double Jeopardy).** Patrick Poland and his brother, Michael, had robbed a bank and killed the bank guards, dumping them in a nearby lake and weighting them down with rocks. A trial resulted in their conviction of first-degree murder, and the death penalty was imposed. Subsequently, they appealed; their convictions were reversed, the death penalties were set aside, and a new trial was ordered. A second trial had the identical result, with new death penalties imposed. The Polands sought to overturn their second convictions on the grounds of double jeopardy stemming from their first trial. The SC upheld their convictions and death sentences, declaring that when a conviction is reversed on appeal, it is nullified and the "slate is wiped clean," so that if the defendant is convicted again, he may be constitutionally subjected to whatever punishment is lawful, including the death penalty. There was no "death penalty" acquittal in the first trial. Thus double jeopardy was not a consideration in the Polands' case.

Polk County v. Dodson, 454 U.S. 312, 102 S.Ct. 445 (1981) **(Attorney Competence; Sixth Amendment Rights).** Dodson was convicted of a crime after being defended by a public defender lawyer from Polk County, Iowa. Dodson filed suit under Title 42, U.S.C. Section 1983 that his Sixth, Eighth, and Fourteenth Amendment rights had been violated. First, he said, his attorney had failed to represent him adequately, and he was suing her under state law. Second, he further alleged that his attorney had subjected him to cruel and unusual punishment as the result of her desire to withdraw from the case, and that this withdrawal in turn had violated his due-process rights. Considering all claims against his lawyer and Polk County, the SC dismissed all of them, holding that Dodson had failed to show any right that was violated. The SC concluded that withdrawals from frivolous cases by attorneys do not in and of themselves violate a person's right to due process.

Ponte v. Real, 471 U.S. 491, 105 S.Ct. 2192 (1985) **(Corrections; Inmate Rights).** Real was a prisoner at the Massachusetts Correctional Institution at Walpole. He was charged with various prison regulation violations. During the disciplinary hearing, Real said that he wanted to call four witnesses. Only one of the witnesses appeared to offer testimony against Real. The other witnesses were not called, and the board did not advise Real why they were not called. Real was found guilty and given 30 days in isolation and had 150 days deducted from his good-time credit. He appealed, contending that the board should have provided its reasons in writing for refusing to call these other witnesses. The SC disagreed, saying that the board need not reduce to writing the reasons for not calling specific witnesses at prison disciplinary hearings.

Powell v. Alabama, 287 U.S. 45, 53 S.Ct. 55 (1932) **(Right to Counsel).** During a train trip in Alabama, two white women were allegedly raped by several young black men. At an unscheduled stop, the train was searched by police, who arrested nine black young men and charged them with rape. Not until the trial date did the judge assign an attorney to represent each man. In one-day trials, each young man was convicted and sentenced to death. They appealed. The SC overturned their convictions, citing several violations of constitutional rights. Among other things, the men had not been permitted the assistance of counsel in their own defense until the trial date. Additionally, unreliable and incompetent evidence had been admitted against the men, evidence that would not have been admitted in other courts. The charges had not been properly formulated or delivered to the men, so that they did not understand fully what it was they were supposed to have done and when. Considering the time of the incident, the late early 1930s, and race relations in the State of Alabama, their treatment by authorities was consistent with inequities against blacks in the South generally during that time period.

Powell v. Nevada, 507 U.S.___, 114 S.Ct. 1280 (1994) **(Warrantless Arrests; Probable Cause Determinations).** Powell was arrested on November 3, 1989, for felony child abuse. However, it was not until November 7 that a magistrate found probable cause to hold him for a preliminary hearing. Subsequently, the child, his girlfriend's four-year-old daughter, died, and Powell was accused of murder and convicted. He appealed, alleging that the four-day delay between his warrantless arrest and the finding of probable cause to conduct a preliminary hearing violated the 48-hour rule set forth in a subsequent case, *County of Riverside v. McLaughlin* (1991). The Nevada Supreme Court upheld his conviction, saying that because the McLaughlin 48-hour rule came about *after* Powell's conviction, it could not be retroactively applied to affect his case and conviction. Powell appealed to the SC, which overturned Powell's conviction and set aside his death sentence, saying that the McLaughlin rule had indeed been violated by the excessive delay between arrest and a finding of probable cause. The significance of this case is that certain rules, such as the McLaughlin 48-hour rule, may be retroactively applied in capital cases. Thus, the Nevada court had erred by allowing the presumptively unreasonable delay of four days between a warrantless arrest, detention, and finding of probable cause. The SC did not say, however, that Powell was automatically entitled to be set free. Rather, Nevada courts were encouraged to explore other remedies for their error and in violating the 48-hour rule under *McLaughlin*.

Powell v. Texas, 392 U.S. 514, 88 S.Ct. 2145 (1963) **(Cruel and Unusual Punishment).** Powell was convicted of public drunkenness. He appealed, arguing that his "status" of being a chronic alcoholic should remove his public drunkenness from that of criminal conduct. The SC heard his case, upheld his conviction, and held that presently, the state of drunkenness is substantially different from that of being addicted to a narcotic.

Powell v. Texas, 492 U.S. 680, 109 S.Ct. 3146 (1989) **(Sixth Amendment; Right to Counsel).** Powell was suspected of capital murder. When Powell was first arrested, the trial court ordered a psychiatric examination to determine his future dangerousness. Neither Powell nor his attorney was advised on at least four occasions that doctors would be examining Powell on the issue of his future dangerousness. During his trial, and during the penalty phase following a jury verdict of guilty, doctors for the state testified about Powell's future dangerousness and elaborated on their reports. Powell's attorney introduced the testimony of one doctor who examined Powell on the defense's behalf. Powell was convicted and sentenced to death. He appealed, alleging that his Sixth Amendment rights had been violated when he and his attorney were not notified about the state psychiatric examinations and their intended purposes. The state countered that since Powell had introduced psychiatric testimony of his own, his appeal should be rejected. The SC overturned Powell's conviction, saying that Powell had been deprived of his Sixth Amendment right to counsel when psychiatric examinations were performed by state experts, without notice to him or his attorney that the examinations would encompass the issue of future dangerousness, and that Powell's introduction of psychiatric testimony on his own behalf did not effectively waive his Sixth Amendment right to notification.

Powell v. United States, ___U.S. ___. 116 S.Ct. 2035 (1996) (*See Koon v. United States*).

Powers v. Ohio, 499 U.S. 400, 111 S.Ct. 1364 (1991) **(Sixth Amendment; Right to Counsel).** Powers was charged with murder, aggravated murder, and attempted aggravated murder, all with firearm specifications (calling for mandatory minimum sentences). A white man, he objected to the government's use of peremptory challenges to strike seven black prospective jurors from the jury. Subsequently, Powers was convicted. He appealed, alleging that his Fourteenth Amendment right had been violated under the equal-protection clause because of the alleged discriminatory use of peremptory challenges. The matter of excluding prospective black jurors by the use of peremptory challenges had already been decided in *Batson v. Kentucky* (1986), where it was declared unconstitutional to use peremptory challenges to achieve a racially pure jury. In the *Batson* case, however, the defendant was black, and government prejudice was obvious in the use of these peremptory challenges. In the *Powers* case, the defendant was white and prospective black jurors had been excluded. The SC heard Powers' appeal and overturned his conviction on the same grounds as *Batson*, holding that criminal defendants may object to race-based exclusions of jurors effected through peremptory challenges whether or not defendants and excluded jurors share the same race.

Preiser v. Rodriguez, 411 U.S. 475, 93 S.Ct. 1827 (1973) **(Corrections; Inmate Rights).** Rodriguez and others were state prisoners who were deprived of good-time credits by the New York Department of Correctional Services because of disciplinary proceedings. Rodriguez appealed under a habeas corpus petition. The lower courts dismissed the petition, saying that it was not relevant for challenging the fact and duration of one's confinement. The SC overturned the lower-court decision, holding that when state prisoners are challenging the very fact or duration of their physical confinement, and the relief sought is a determination that they are entitled to immediate release from that imprisonment, the sole federal remedy is a writ of habeas corpus.

Preiser v. Rodriguez, 411 U.S. 475, 93 S.Ct. 1827 (1973) **(Title 42, U.S.C. Section 1983 Claims; Corrections).** Although Section 1983 of the civil-rights act can be used by prisoners for constitutional claims against state prison officials or employees for the *conditions* of prison life, it cannot be used to challenge the *fact* and *length* of confinement.

Press-Enterprise Company v. Superior Court of California, 478 U.S. 1, 106 S.Ct. 2735 (1986) **(Fair Trials; Media Influence).** A newspaper sought to be present at a preliminary hearing in a criminal proceeding in a California court. The court declared that there is no First Amendment right of access to preliminary hearings. The SC overturned this opinion by the California court and said that the media have a right under the First Amendment to attend preliminary hearings.

Preston v. United States, 376 U.S. 364, 84 S.Ct. 881 (1964) **(Law Enforcement Officers or Agencies; Searches and Seizures).** Preston was

arrested for vagrancy. His car was towed from the arrest scene and searched. Police found two loaded revolvers in the glove compartment. Unable to open the trunk of the car, they entered it by removing the back seat, where they found additional incriminating evidence leading to Preston's conviction for various offenses. He appealed, alleging a violation of his Fourth Amendment right against an unreasonable search and seizure of contraband or illegal items. The government said that the warrantless search of his vehicle was incident to an arrest and therefore valid. Preston appealed again. The SC overturned Preston's conviction, saying that the warrantless search of Preston's vehicle had been too remote in time to be considered a search incident to an arrest. Therefore, the incriminating evidence should be suppressed.

Priest v. Cupp, 545 P.2d 917 (Ore.Ct.App.) (1976) **(Corrections; Deliberate Indifference).** The prohibition against cruel and unusual punishment for Oregon prisoners does not guarantee that an inmate will be free from, or cured of, all real or imagined medical problems while in custody.

Procunier v. Martinez, 416 U.S. 396, 94 S.Ct. 1800 (1974) **(Corrections; Inmate Rights).** Several California prison inmates brought a class-action suit against the California Department of Corrections alleging unreasonable mail censorship, specifically censorship of mail containing inmate complaints, grievances, and inflammatory views or beliefs. The SC agreed with the inmates and ruled that the mail censorship provisions used by the California Department of Corrections were unconstitutional, although any mail that is potentially disruptive of inmate discipline may be censored. Further, any censorship policy must demonstrate that such censorship furthers a particular government interest unrelated to such suppression. Thus authorities may not censor mail simply because it contains unflattering opinions about them or their staffs.

Procunier v. Navarette, 434 U.S. 555, 98 S.Ct. 855 (1978) **(Corrections; Damages).** A class-action suit was filed by California inmates under Title 42, U.S.C. Section 1983 civil-rights claim that correctional officers had failed to mail various letters and documents to legal aid groups, media, and other addressees. The prisoners alleged violations of their First and Fourteenth Amendment rights. The correctional officers sought protection under an absolute-immunity defense. The SC said that the officers were not entitled to *absolute* immunity, but rather to *qualified* immunity. According to the SC, qualified immunity is any action in the good-faith fulfillment of officers' responsibilities, and that such action will not be punished. Furthermore, at the time this case was filed, there was no existing or prevailing constitutional right specifically protecting a prisoner's correspondence. Thus, this case set a precedent for the current good-faith standard of immunity used in correctional settings.

Proffitt v. Florida, 428 U.S. 242, 96 S.Ct. 2960 (1976) **(Corrections; Death Penalty).** Proffitt was convicted of first-degree murder and sentenced to death. He appealed, saying that the Florida statute outlining eight statutory aggravating factors and seven statutory mitigating factors was flawed, because the aggravating and mitigating circumstances "lacked precision" of definition. The SC upheld his conviction and death sentence, maintaining that under Florida law, judges are required to impose the death penalty on all first-degree murderers where statutory aggravating factors outweigh the mitigating ones. Further, the death penalty is not per se cruel and unusual punishment in violation of the Eighth Amendment, as originally alleged by Proffitt.

Pulley v. Harris, 465 U.S. 37, 104 S.Ct. 871 (1984) **(Corrections; Death Penalty).** Harris was convicted of murder in a California court and sentenced to death. He appealed the sentence, alleging that the court had not considered his sentence of death in comparison with other similar situations where the death penalty was not imposed. Thus, Harris claimed, the California death-penalty statute was unconstitutional because it did not require judges to make such a comparison. The SC upheld Harris' death sentence, holding that the Eighth Amendment is not violated when states do not consider other sentences imposed in other capital cases to determine whether a particular sentence is proportionate.

Purkett v. Elem, ___U.S.___, 115 S.Ct. 1769 (1995) **(Juries; Peremptory Challenges).** Elem, a black man, was accused of second-degree robbery. During the selection of jurors, the prosecutor used one of his peremptory challenges to strike from the jury pool a prospective black juror. Elem appealed, alleging that this use of a peremptory challenge was in violation of a policy set forth in *Batson v. Kentucky* (1986) prohibiting the use of peremptory challenges for racial purposes. The SC heard Elem's habeas corpus petition and argu-

ment. It upheld Elem's conviction when it determined that the prosecutor had used the peremptory challenge in a racially neutral fashion. The reason given for striking this black prospective juror was that the man had long, unkempt hair and a moustache and beard. The SC accepted this explanation as being race-neutral. It held that opponents of peremptory challenges must carry the burden of proving that purposeful discrimination has occurred. The explanation given by those exercising their peremptory challenges need not be persuasive or even plausible; rather, these explanations are considered only in determining whether opponents have carried their burden of proof by showing that the peremptory strikes were discriminatory. In this case, the peremptory challenge was satisfactorily explained and Elem's conviction was upheld.

R

Rakas v. Illinois, 439 U.S. 128, 99 S.Ct. 421 (1978) **(Law Enforcement Officers or Agencies; Stop and Frisk; Plain View Rule; Open Field Searches).** Rakas was a passenger in a car believed by police to be the getaway vehicle in a recent robbery. They stopped the car and conducted a warrantless search of it. They found incriminating evidence, including a sawed-off shotgun and ammunition, later used as evidence against Rakas, who was convicted of the robbery. Rakas appealed, attempting to suppress the evidence found in the vehicle because it was a result of violation of his Fourth Amendment right against unreasonable searches and seizures. The SC upheld the conviction, saying that Rakas did not own the vehicle; thus, he could not interfere with the police search of it. In the SC's words, Rakas did not have a possessory interest in the car, and therefore, he could not claim a reasonable expectation of privacy in it.

Ralston v. Robinson, 454 U.S. 201, 102 S.Ct. 233 (1981) **(Juvenile Law).** Robinson, age 17, was convicted of second-degree murder and sentenced to 10 years' imprisonment under the Federal Youth Corrections Act (FYCA). While incarcerated, he assaulted a corrections officer and was convicted in a later trial on this new offense. The judge in this case sentenced Robinson as an adult and committed him to the Federal Bureau of Prisons for confinement to run consecutively with his earlier sentence. Robinson appealed, contending that he should remain under the FYCA and receive rehabilitative treatment. The judge declined to consider the FYCA an option in Robinson's case. Robinson appealed again, alleging that the judge had had no right to sentence him in such a way as to deprive him of the "rehabilitative milieu of the FYCA." The SC upheld the judge's sentence, declaring that the second judge had made a sufficient finding that the respondent would not benefit from YCA treatment during the remainder of his youth term.

R.A.V. v. City of St. Paul, Minn., 505 U.S. 377, 112 S.Ct. 2538 (1992) **(City Ordinances Prohibiting Racially Motivated Activities).** R.A.V. allegedly burned a cross on a black family's lawn. He was charged under a St. Paul ordinance that forbids such acts that "arouse anger, alarm, or resentment in others on the basis of race, color, creed, religion or gender." Following conviction, R.A.V. challenged the St. Paul ordinance as being invalid under the First Amendment. The SC reversed his conviction, saying that such an ordinance was overbroad and was facially invalid under the First Amendment.

Rawlings v. Kentucky, 448 U.S. 98, 100 S.Ct. 2556 (1980) **(Law Enforcement Officers or Agencies; Searches Incident to Arrest).** Rawlings placed illegal drugs in the purse of a female friend. He later was convicted of possession of illegal drugs. He appealed, saying that the police had no right to search his friend's purse. The SC disagreed and upheld his conviction, saying that Rawlings had no reasonable expectation of privacy relative to putting illegal contraband into someone else's purse or personal property.

Reid v. Georgia, 448 U.S. 438, 100 S.Ct. 2752 (1980) **(Law Enforcement Officers or Agencies; Search and Seizure).** Reid was observed at the Atlanta airport with another person. They fit a profile of a particular drug carrier and were approached by a suspicious DEA agent. The agent asked them if they would accompany him to another airport area; during this walk, Reid fled, discarding his luggage. The DEA agent inspected the luggage and found that it contained drugs. Reid was arrested and eventually convicted. He appealed, alleging his Fourth Amendment rights had been violated. The SC overturned his conviction, noting that the DEA agent had had no reasonable suspicion, based on the totality of circumstances,

to believe that Reid and the other person were engaging in any criminal activity. The SC said that the DEA agent's suspicions were more in the nature of an inchoate and unparticularized suspicion or hunch. This was too slender a reed to support the seizure in this case. Reid's case was vacated and remanded to the trial court. DEA agents need more than the factual information in this case to require persons in airports to stop and accompany them for further investigation.

Reno v. Koray, ___U.S.___, 115 S.Ct. 2021 (1995) **(Corrections; Bail Time as Flat Time).** Koray was arrested for laundering monetary instruments in violation of a federal statute. He was convicted and sentenced to 41 months in prison. Between his arrest and conviction, Koray was ordered "confined to the premises" of the Volunteers of America community treatment center, without authorization to leave unless accompanied by a government special agent. Koray appealed his 41-month sentence, arguing that he should be given credit for the time he had spent "in detention" in the community treatment program. The Third Circuit Court of Appeals reversed his conviction on those grounds, and the government appealed. The SC reversed the Third Circuit, upholding Koray's original 41-month sentence. The SC said that ordinarily, defendants might be entitled to time spent in official detention. However, the assignment of Koray to the community agency did not constitute official detention in the formal sense, and thus, the time he spent in this agency could not be counted as time against his 41-month sentence. This decision may seem like hairsplitting, but the SC said that official detention pertains only to those defendants placed in a penal or correctional facility and subject to the control of the Federal Bureau of Prisons (at 2021).

Rhode Island v. Innis, 446 U.S. 291, 100 S.Ct. 1682 (1981) **(Law Enforcement Officers or Agencies; Confessions).** Innes was suspected of an abduction and murder of a taxi driver. He was arrested by police, taken into custody, and told his Miranda rights. Two other officers arrived at that point and gave Innes his Miranda warning again. He was then driven to the police station. Both times after receiving the Miranda warning, Innes was asked if he wanted to speak with officers about the crime. Innes said he wanted an attorney and did not want to speak with the officers. While the officers were driving to the station, they talked among themselves, not with Innes. They spoke of how a shotgun was used in the murder and that it would be too bad if school children might find the shotgun and hurt themselves, as the murder occurred near a school. Innes interrupted the officers and asked them to drive him back to the murder scene, where subsequently he showed them where the shotgun was found. This evidence helped to convict Innes of the murder. He appealed, contending that his statements were inadmissible against him, as he had already asked for an attorney and had not wished to speak to police. The SC disagreed, saying that Innes had initiated the conversation on his own, that it had not been coerced by police, and that they had been talking among themselves, not to Innes. Thus, the conversation among the officers was not the functional equivalent of an interrogation, because the officers did not know that Innes would make a self-incriminating response and there was no express questioning of him.

Rhodes v. Chapman, 452 U.S. 337, 101 S.Ct. 2392 (1981) **(Corrections; Inmate Rights).** Kelly Chapman and Richard Jaworski, two inmates of the Southern Ohio Correctional Facility, were housed in the same cell. They objected, contending that double-celling violated their constitutional rights. Furthermore, in support of their claim, they cited the facts that their confinement was *long-term* and not *short-term* as it was in *Bell v. Wolfish* (1979), that physical and mental injury would be sustained through such close contact and limited space for movement, and that the Ohio facility was housing 38 percent more inmates than its design capacity specified. The SC ruled that double-celling in this long-term prison facility was neither cruel and unusual punishment nor unconstitutional per se. The court based its holding on the "totality of circumstances" associated with Chapman's and Jaworski's confinement. The "cruel and unusual" provisions of the Eighth Amendment must be construed in a "flexible and dynamic" manner. Thus, when all factors were considered, no evidence existed that Ohio authorities were wantonly inflicting pain on these or other inmates. These conditions, considered in their totality, did not constitute serious deprivation. Double-celling, made necessary by the unanticipated increase in prisoners in the facility, had not resulted in food deprivations, a decrease in the quality of medical care, or a decrease in sanitation standards.

Richardson v. Marsh, 481 U.S. 200, 107 S.Ct. 1702 (1987) **(Sixth Amendment; Confrontation Clause).** Clarissa Marsh was charged, with a companion, Benjamin Williams, and a third person, Martin, with assaulting Cynthia Knighton, and murdering Knighton's four-year-old son, and her aunt, Ollie Scott, at Scott's home. During Marsh's trial, Knighton testified as to Marsh's involvement in the murders. Furthermore, a confession, given by Williams, implicating Marsh, was read into the record shortly after his arrest. Williams did not take the stand to have his testimony rebutted by defense counsel. However, the judge instructed the jury to ignore references to Marsh in Williams's confession. Marsh was convicted of felony murder. She appealed by filing a writ of habeas corpus with the United States district court, alleging that her due-process right had been violated. Further, she alleged, her right to confront her accuser had been denied, when only Williams' confession was read without Williams actually testifying to authenticate it. The United States district court denied the writ, but the Sixth Circuit Court of Appeals granted it and reversed Marsh's conviction on grounds that she had been unable to confront and cross-examine her accuser. The state appealed to the SC, which reinstated Marsh's murder conviction. The SC held that the admission of a nontestifying codefendant's confession had not violated Marsh's rights under the confrontation clause because the judge had instructed the jury not to use the confession in any way against Marsh. Further, an inspection of the confession showed that it was not incriminating directly, but only indirectly, only when linked with other evidence introduced at Marsh's trial.

Richardson v. New York State Executive Department, 602 N.Y.S.2d 443 (1993) **(Corrections; Parole Boards).** In New York, Richardson committed a violent felony while on parole for an earlier one. The Parole Board revoked his parole and returned him to prison without further parole consideration, despite the fact that he had not, as yet, been tried and convicted on the new charge. The New York Supreme Court upheld the Parole Board action as constitutional.

Richmond v. Lewis, 506 U.S. 40, 113 S.Ct. 528 (1992) **(Death Penalty; Aggravating and Mitigating Circumstances Interpretation).** Richmond was convicted of first-degree murder and given the death penalty. He appealed, arguing that one of the aggravating factors used by the judge in sentencing was vague and constituted a violation of his Eighth Amendment rights. At the time, the aggravating circumstance in question in Arizona courts was "especially heinous, cruel, or depraved." The SC heard the case and reversed Richmond's conviction and sentence, holding that the aggravating circumstance was indeed unconstitutionally vague.

Richmond Newspapers, Inc., v. Virginia, 448 U.S. 555, 100 S.Ct. 2814 (1978) **(Fair Trials; Media Access).** A murder case was being tried in a Virginia court. The court closed the proceedings to the public, including newspaper coverage. The Richmond Newspapers, Inc., filed suit to gain access to the trial proceedings under the First Amendment. The SC ruled that the right of the public to criminal trials is fundamental, including a right of access by the media, such as newspaper reporters. The press cannot be prevented from publishing truthful information about trial proceedings as long as the information has been obtained lawfully.

Ricketts v. Adamson, 463 U.S. 1, 107 S.Ct. 2860 (1987) **(Courts; Plea Bargaining).** Adamson was charged with murder. He entered into a plea bargain whereby he would plead guilty to second-degree murder and testify against his co-defendants. The prosecutor indicated that if Adamson refused to cooperate, then the terms of his plea agreement would be null and void. Adamson was convicted of second-degree murder, but during the trial of co-defendants later, he refused to testify. The Arizona Supreme Court reversed his conviction on the grounds outlined by the prosecutor, and Adamson was tried again for first-degree murder. He was convicted and appealed, contending that this retrial was a violation of his double-jeopardy rights. The SC disagreed and upheld his first-degree murder conviction. The SC said that his prosecution for first-degree murder did not violate double-jeopardy principles, because his breach of the plea agreement removed the double-jeopardy bar that otherwise would have prevailed, assuming that under state law second-degree murder is a lesser included offense of first-degree murder.

Ristaino v. Ross, 424 U.S. 589, 96 S.Ct. 1017 (1976) **(Jury Trials; Jury Selection).** A black defendant was convicted of violent crimes against a white security guard. The defendant made a motion to question jurors about their racial prejudice during voir dire. An appeal was directed to the SC,

where it was argued that the defendant had a constitutional right to ask jurors about racial prejudice. The SC upheld his conviction, saying that defendants do not have a constitutional right to question jurors about their racial prejudice. Judges may ask jurors about their racial prejudice; defendants may not.

Robbins v. California, 453 U.S. 420, 101 S.Ct. 2841 (1981) **(Law Enforcement Officers or Agencies; Consent Searches).** Officers stopped Robbins in his automobile for driving "erratically." They smelled marijuana when Robbins got out of the vehicle, and they placed him under arrest and searched the vehicle incident to an arrest. This warrantless search yielded a container in the trunk of Robbins' vehicle. The officers opened this container and discovered marijuana. They used this evidence against Robbins to secure a conviction of possession of marijuana. He appealed, arguing that the search of the container in his trunk had required a valid search warrant. The SC agreed with Robbins and overturned his conviction, holding that a closed container may not be opened without a warrant, even if found during a lawful search of an automobile. This case was modified by a later case entitling officers to search containers in automobiles.

Roberts v. Lavallee, 389 U.S. 40, 88 S.Ct. 194 (1967) **(Corrections; Inmate Rights).** Roberts was an indigent who was convicted of various crimes incurring a 15-to 20-year prison sentence. Roberts appealed and demanded a free copy of the trial court transcript so that he could formulate an intelligent appeal of his sentence. His appeal was denied. The court declared that he was not entitled, as an indigent, to a free copy of the trial record for appeal purposes. The SC heard his petition and ruled in his favor, concluding that there was no doubt that the denial of a free transcript to the indigent Roberts was repugnant to his federal constitutional rights. Roberts had fully exhausted his state remedies and it was incumbent on the state to furnish Roberts with a free copy of the trial record because of his indigence.

Roberts v. Louisiana, 431 U.S. 633, 97 S.Ct. 1993 (1977) **(Mandatory Death Penalties).** Roberts was convicted of killing a police officer in Louisiana, where there was a mandatory death penalty for such an offense. The death penalty was imposed and Roberts appealed. The SC overturned the sentence, holding that mandatory death penalties are unconstitutional because they do not allow consideration of aggravating and mitigating circumstances.

Robinson v. California, 370 U.S. 660, 82 S.Ct. 1417 (1962) **(Corrections; Inmate Rights).** Robinson was convicted in Los Angeles of being addicted to narcotics. On appeal, the SC overturned his conviction, saying that the status of narcotic addition is not a crime and thus cannot be treated as a crime by a California trial court.

Robinson v. United States, ___U.S.___, 116 S.Ct. 501 (1995) **(Law Enforcement Officers or Agencies; Search and Seizure; Sentence Enhancements).** Robinson sold some crack cocaine to an undercover officer in a "controlled buy" set up in advance. The officer observed her obtain the crack cocaine from her bedroom of her one-bedroom apartment. A search warrant was obtained and her apartment was searched, disclosing more crack cocaine in a locked trunk in her bedroom closet together with an unloaded .22 caliber Derringer pistol. She was convicted of selling crack cocaine, and her sentence was enhanced because a weapon had been discovered in close proximity to the cocaine. The SC overturned the sentence enhancement, concluding that there was no evidence, other than mere proximity of the weapon near the cocaine itself, to indicate that Robinson intended actively to employ the weapon in the commission of the offense (*see Bailey v. United States* [1995] for a similar opinion). Offenders must *actively use* a weapon or have it readily available while committing their conviction offenses in order for sentence enhancements to be made.

Rochin v. California, 342 U.S. 165, 72 S.Ct. 205 (1952) **(Law Enforcement Officers or Agencies; Exclusionary Rule).** Rochin, a suspect allegedly trafficking in narcotics, was visited by sheriff's deputies one evening. Officers found him sitting on his bed partially dressed. Several white capsules were on a nearby nightstand in plain view. When officers attempted to seize them, Rochin grabbed the capsules and swallowed them. Officers immediately brought Rochin to a nearby hospital and ordered physicians to give him an emetic solution to cause him to vomit. The capsules were obtained through a stomach pump and turned out to be morphine. These capsules were used against him later in court and he was convicted. He appealed. His conviction was overturned because of the unreasonableness of the manner of the officer's search and seizure of the capsules. In a written opinion, the SC labeled the police tactics offensive and "conduct that shocks the conscience."

Rock v. Arkansas, 483 U.S. 44, 107 S.Ct. 2704 (1987) **(Sixth Amendment; Hypnotic Recollections of Events in Defendant Testimony; Evidentiary Rulings).** Rock was charged with shooting her husband. She underwent tape-recorded hypnosis sessions as a means of refreshing her memory. During her trial, she attempted to testify and provide details about the shooting that had been elicited under hypnosis, but the court prevented her from doing so. Instead, she was limited to testifying about the events as she recalled them before being subjected to hypnosis. Following her conviction, she appealed, alleging that her right to give testimony in her own behalf had been infringed by the judge's ruling limiting her testimony. The SC heard the case and reversed her conviction, holding that the Arkansas rule prohibiting hypnotically refreshed testimony was unconstitutional. Rock should have been permitted to give all relevant testimony, whether or not it had been induced hypnotically.

Roe v. Fauver, 43 CrL 2174 (1988) **(Corrections; Prisoners with AIDS).** Prisoners with AIDS in New Jersey prisons are barred from mingling with the general prison population. Roe, who had AIDS, was held in a form of solitary confinement. She objected that this constituted a degree of cruel and unusual punishment. However, the appellate court ruled that prison health considerations must take priority over individual comforts, and that although Roe was inconvenienced by the solitary confinement, the prison policy was designed to improve the safety of all prison inmates.

Rogers v. Richmond, 365 U.S. 534, 81 S.Ct. 735 (1961) **(Law Enforcement Officers or Agencies; Confessions).** Rogers was arrested on robbery charges. While jailed, he was subjected to a grueling intensive interrogation. Further, his lawyer was turned away when trying to reach him. There was considerable evidence that police used psychological tactics on Rogers and eventually secured a confession of murder from him. He was convicted. He appealed, contending that his confession had been coerced. His murder conviction was overturned, largely on procedural grounds, because the state trial court had misconstrued the applicable law relating to confessions, and it had erred in affirming a lower-court denial of Rogers' habeas corpus petition alleging the coercion.

Rosales-Lopez v. United States, 451 U.S. 182, 101 S.Ct. 1629 (1981) **(Corrections; Death Penalty).** Rosales-Lopez was suspected of conspiracy to admit illegal aliens into the United States. Prior to his trial, he asked the judge and prosecutor to conduct a voir dire to determine whether any prospective jurors were prejudiced against him and Mexicans generally. The judge refused to question jurors about potential racial or ethnic bias. Rosales-Lopez was convicted. He appealed, alleging that the failure of the judge to ask these questions had deprived him of significant due-process rights and a fair trial. The SC upheld his conviction, noting that the role of Rosales-Lopez in the smuggling operation had nothing to do with a racial or ethnic bias question, and thus the judge was not obligated to confront prospective jurors with this issue of prejudice.

Rose v. Clark, 478 U.S. 570, 106 S.Ct. 3101 (1986) **(Jury Instructions).** Charles Browning and Joy Faulk were shot to death while they sat in Browning's pickup truck in Rutherford County, Tennessee. Stanley Clark, Faulk's former boyfriend, became a suspect and was subsequently charged with murder. During his trial, Clark attempted to blame Faulk's ex-husband for the murders. Also, Clark claimed that at the time, he (Clark) was insane or incapable of forming the requisite criminal intent. The prosecution rejected both claims. During the issuance of instructions to the jury, the judge defined the elements of the crimes alleged, including malice, which involved a killing "upon sudden impulse" if committed with intent to harm another. Clark was convicted. He appealed. The Tennessee Supreme Court reversed Clark's conviction because the court believed that the jury instruction shifted the burden of proof to the defendant regarding the question of "malice." Thus, the court argued, the prosecution did not have to prove *all* criminal elements beyond a reasonable doubt. Eventually, the SC heard the case and reversed the lower court, reinstating Clark's conviction. In a carefully worded opinion, the SC said that the lower court would have to determine whether the error committed in this case (i.e., the jury instruction as to malice) was harmless beyond a reasonable doubt.

Rose v. Lundy, 455 U.S. 509, 102 S.Ct. 1198 (1982) **(Corrections; Habeas Corpus).** Lundy was a Tennessee prison inmate who had been convicted of rape and crimes against nature. He filed a writ of habeas corpus in federal court, seeking to overturn his conviction on various grounds, including the allegation that he had not been permitted to cross-examine his accusers adequately, that his fair trial chances had been impaired by the prosecutor's closing remarks, and that the trial judge had given improper jury instructions. The SC upheld Lundy's conviction, saying that Lundy had not exhausted all state remedies before bringing his action to federal courts. The significance of this case is that it obligates any state prisoner first to exhaust all state appeals before bringing a case to a federal court. Habeas corpus petitions challenge several things, including the fact, nature, and length of confinement. In Lundy's case, such a filing was tantamount to challenging his entire trial scenario, such that a new trial would have to be granted depending upon SC action. One intent of this ruling is to lessen the sheer numbers of prisoner petitions that are processed by federal courts.

Rose v. Mitchell, 443 U.S. 545, 99 S.Ct. 2993 (1979) **(Grand Juries).** James Mitchell, a black man, was accused of murder following an indictment from an all-white county grand jury in Tennessee. The trial itself was properly conducted and a jury determined Mitchell to be guilty. Later, as an inmate of the Tennessee State Prison, Mitchell filed a habeas corpus petition, alleging that the grand jury had been racially discriminatory since it excluded blacks. The SC overturned his conviction, noting that racial discrimination in the selection of a grand jury is a valid ground for setting aside a guilty verdict, even where a defendant has been found guilty beyond a reasonable doubt by a petit jury at a trial that was free of other constitutional error. Further, the SC declared that such claims of discrimination are rightly included as a part of a habeas corpus petition.

Rosenberg v. United States, 346 U.S. 273, 73 S.Ct. 1152 (1953) **(Corrections; Death Penalty).** Julius Rosenberg and his wife, Ethel, were convicted of violating the Espionage Act and sentenced to death. Rosenberg appealed, desiring a stay of execution: the appeal was rejected. The issue was whether a district judge had the power to impose the death sentence without a jury recommendation to that effect. The SC upheld the Rosenberg's death sentence, holding that judges do have the right to impose death sentences.

Ross v. Moffitt, 417 U.S. 600, 94 S.Ct. 243 (1974) **(Corrections; Inmate Rights).** This case involved a convicted indigent offender who desired to have court-appointed counsel in order to lodge an appeal with the North Carolina Supreme Court. The SC declared that indigent defendants are not entitled, as a matter of right, to court-appointed counsel for discretionary appeals to higher courts. Thus it is not a violation of due process to deny attorneys to convicted offenders when making such appeals.

Ross v. Oklahoma, 487 U.S. 85, 108 S.Ct. 2273 (1988) **(Corrections; Death Penalty).** Ross was accused of first-degree murder in Oklahoma. During the impaneling of a jury, a juror was not eliminated for cause, but should have been. Ross' lawyer had to use one of his peremptory challenges to excuse this particular juror. Ross' attorney regarded this as a "waste" of a perfectly good peremptory challenge, thus limiting the favorableness of the jury for Ross' benefit. Ross was convicted; he appealed, contesting this point. The SC upheld his conviction, holding that a failure to exclude a prospective juror for cause and causing the defense to use one of its peremptory challenges to do so does not deprive defendants of due process of law. Ross' right to an impartial jury was not violated when his lawyer was required to use a peremptory challenge to excuse a juror who should have been rejected for cause anyway.

Roth v. United States, 345 U.S. 476, 77 S.Ct. 1304 (1957) **(Obscenity).** Roth was convicted of violating a federal obscenity statute prohibiting the distribution of a periodical magazine containing nude photographs of persons through the United States mail. He appealed, contending that the statute under which he was convicted was a violation of his First Amendment right to free speech and free press. The SC disagreed, saying that the obscenity ordinance in question was not violative of any particular constitutional right. Thus, United States Post Office authorities may utilize the federal obscenity statute as the proper exercise of their power.

Roviaro v. United States, 353 U.S. 53, 77 S.Ct. 623 (1957) **(Informants).** Roviaro was convicted of illegally selling heroin and transporting it. His conviction was based in part upon information supplied by an unknown informant who remained unknown throughout Roviaro's trial. The government sought to keep the informant's identity confidential. Roviaro appealed, alleging that he had not had the Fifth Amendment right to cross-examine his accuser. Thus, it was conceivable that the informant might have had exculpatory evidence to give that might have been favorable to Roviaro. The SC reversed Roviaro's conviction, saying that where an informer's testimony may be relevant and helpful to the accused's defense, such informant identity should be disclosed and the informant should be compelled to testify through cross-examination. Thus the government had been wrong to withhold the identity of its undercover employee in the face of repeated demands by the accused for his disclosure.

Ruffin v. Commonwealth, 62 Va. (21 Gratt) 790 (1871) **(Corrections; Inmate Rights).** A Virginia judge declared that "prisoners have no more rights than slaves." This remark became infamous as the beginning of the hands-off era of the SC toward corrections. The SC declined to hear most corrections cases because of its belief that corrections personnel and administrators are in the best position to understand, and know what is best for, the prisoners they supervise.

Rufo v. Inmates of Suffolk County Jail, 502 U.S. 367, 112 S.Ct. 748 (1992) **(Corrections; Inmate Rights).** Suffolk County Jail was under a consent decree to improve jail conditions through new construction that would create several single-occupancy cells for pretrial detainees. Construction delays prevented the jail from being redesigned as planned, the jail inmate population escalated, and the sheriff made a motion to the court to modify the original consent decree temporarily to allow double-bunking because of overcrowding. The court denied the motion and the sheriff appealed. The SC overruled the lower-court decision, indicating that whenever factual conditions of original consent decrees change in ways that make it impossible to comply with such consent decree provisions, some relief of a temporary nature can be granted. Thus, consent decrees may be modified, provided there are circumstances that justify such modifications.

Rugendorf v. United States, 376 U.S. 528, 87 S.Ct. 408 (1966) **(Informants).** FBI agents obtained a search warrant for Rugendorf's residence, where they believed that a large quantity of stolen furs were stored. Information from reliable informants and from hearsay from other informants led to the issuance of the warrant. Furs were found matching descriptions of those that were stolen, and Rugendorf was convicted. He appealed, saying that "hearsay evidence" was an insufficient basis for probable cause to obtain a valid search warrant. The SC upheld his conviction, saying that reliable informant information had been supplemented with hearsay information, but that the hearsay information had merely corroborated the reliable-informant information. The search warrant, therefore, had been valid, and thus the evidence seized as the result of the warrant could be used against Rugendorf at his subsequent trial.

Rummel v. Estelle, 445 U.S. 263, 100 S.Ct. 1133 (1980) **(Eighth Amendment; Cruel and Unusual Punishment).** Rummel had previously been convicted of two nonviolent felonies. Under a Texas recidivist statute, he was convicted and given a life sentence. He appealed to the SC, which upheld the sentence. The SC said that life sentences for violating habitual-offender statutes are *not* cruel and unusual in violation of the Eighth Amendment (*see Solem v. Helm* [1983] for a comparative case.)

Rushen v. Spain, 464 U.S. 114, 104 S.Ct. 453 (1983) **(Eighth Amendment; Harmless Errors in Jury Instructions).** Spain was an inmate at San Quentin prison in California during a prison riot in 1971, where three prisoners and three corrections officers were killed. Spain was one of six prisoners tried on the murders of these persons, and he was convicted. During the voir dire, jurors were asked if they knew any members of the Black Panther Party, blacks who aggressively supported government reform on racial issues. No jurors indicated such knowledge. However, during the trial, one juror, Fagan, reported to the judge that she was familiar with someone involved in a murder case that was mentioned but was not one involving any of the specific defendants, including Spain. She went to the judge's chambers on several occasions to indicate her emotional concern over the mentioned case. The judge asked Fagan if her judgment would be impaired in deciding the guilt or innocence of the six defendants. She said that she could make an impartial judgment. Subsequently, they were convicted of murder, and Spain was sentenced to life imprisonment. Spain appealed and filed a habeas corpus petition with the federal district court, noting that he had not been permitted to be a party to the various exchanges between the juror, Fagan, and the judge, during the trial. Thus, he argued, he had been deprived of a fair trial. The United States district court as well as the Ninth Circuit Court of Appeals held that an unrecorded ex parte communication between the trial judge and a juror can never be

harmless error, and Spain's conviction was reversed. However, the government appealed. The SC heard the case and reinstated Spain's conviction and life sentence. The SC held that communications between the trial judge and the juror, as transpired in this particular case, were harmless. The judge had assured himself that the juror would maintain her impartiality throughout the trial, and the integrity of the proceeding had not been compromised.

Rutledge v. United States, ___U.S.___, 116 S.Ct. 1241 (1996) **(Double Jeopardy).** Rutledge was convicted in federal court of charges relating to conspiracy to distribute controlled substances and one count of conducting a continuing criminal enterprise in concert with others. Both convictions stemmed from the conspiracy to distribute cocaine. The court sentenced Rutledge to two concurrent life-without-parole terms and imposed special assessments of $50 for each count. Rutledge appealed on double-jeopardy grounds, and the SC heard his case. The SC held that Congress intended to authorize only one punishment. Thus, because Rutledge was convicted, based upon the same underlying conduct, of both the offense of conducting a continuing criminal enterprise and of conspiracy to distribute controlled substances, which was a lesser included offense of the "continuing criminal enterprise" offense, one of his convictions and concurrent sentences had to be vacated. Courts cannot impose multiple punishments for the same criminal activity, as that would violate the defendant's right against double jeopardy.

S

Sandin v. Conner, ___U.S. ___, 115 S.Ct. 2293 (1995) **(Corrections; Inmate Rights).** A Hawaiian prisoner, Conner, was placed in solitary confinement following a disciplinary hearing pertaining to a charge of misconduct. Conner wanted to call certain prisoners as witnesses on his behalf during the adjustment committee hearing, but the authorities denied his request. He appealed, arguing that his due-process rights had been violated because of this committee action. The SC heard Conner's case and determined that he did not have a liberty interest in committee proceedings. Further, it determined that the committee action had not affected his parole eligibility date or sentence length. The SC said that in Conner's case, discipline in segregated confinement did not present the type of atypical, significant deprivation in which a state might conceivably create a liberty interest. Additionally, his confinement did not present a case where the state's action would inevitably affect the duration of his sentence, because the chance that the misconduct finding would affect his parole status was simply too attenuated to invoke the due-process clause's procedural guarantee.

Santobello v. New York, 404 U.S. 257, 92 S.Ct. 495 (1971) **(Plea Bargaining; Prosecutorial Commitments).** Santobello was charged with two felony counts and pleaded guilty to a lesser included offense following a promise by the prosecutor not to make a sentence recommendation at the plea bargain hearing. Several months lapsed, and in the meantime, a new prosecutor was appointed and represented the government at Santobello's plea hearing. At this time, the prosecutor recommended the maximum sentence under the law, and Santobello moved to withdraw his guilty plea. The judge refused to allow the withdrawal of the guilty plea, and Santobello was sentenced to the maximum sentence. The SC heard Santobello's appeal. Santobello alleged that the prosecutor was honor bound to stand by his statement not to make a sentence recommendation, despite the fact that the judge said that he was "uninfluenced" by the prosecutor's recommendation. The SC overturned Santobello's conviction and allowed him to withdraw his guilty plea, saying that when a guilty plea rests to a significant degree on a promise or agreement by the prosecutor, then such a promise must be fulfilled. The significance of this case is that prosecutors cannot make promises to defendants to elicit guilty pleas unless they fulfill their promises.

Satterwhite v. Texas, 486 U.S. 249, 108 S.Ct. 1792 (1988) **(Death Penalty; Constitutional Errors in Jury Deliberations and Factual Considerations).** Satterwhite was charged in the murder of Mary Davis during a robbery in Texas. He was arrested and several psychiatric evaluations were made of him at the request of the court. A psychiatrist, Dr. Grigson, conducted some of these evaluations and delivered an opinion to the court that he regarded Satterwhite as having "a severe antisocial personality disorder" and that he was "extremely dangerous and will commit future acts of violence." Subsequently, Satterwhite was con-

victed by a jury. During the penalty phase of his trial, Dr. Grigson was called to testify about his "future dangerousness" over defense objections. It was also noted that Dr. Grigson's findings had not been delivered to defense counsel prior to the penalty phase of Satterwhite's trial. Following the imposition of the death sentence, Satterwhite appealed, alleging that his Sixth Amendment right to effective assistance of counsel had been violated. He further argued that Dr. Grigson's testimony about his "future dangerousness" should not have been allowed. The Texas Supreme Court heard the case and decided that although the testimony might be error, it was harmless. Satterwhite then appealed to the SC, which held that the finding of future dangerousness is critical in a sentence of death. Dr. Grigson was the only person to testify on this issue, and the prosecution had placed great weight on this testimony. The SC found it impossible to say beyond a reasonable doubt that Grigson's testimony about Satterwhite's future dangerousness had not influenced the jury in their sentence recommendation. Therefore, the SC reversed the Texas Supreme Court regarding the death sentence and remanded the case back to the trial court for further proceedings.

Saxbe v. Washington Post Co., 417 U.S. 843, 94 S.Ct. 2811 (1974) **(Corrections; Inmate Rights).** The *Washington Post* wished to conduct interviews with various federal prison inmates. At the time, the Federal Bureau of Prisons had a policy prohibiting such interviews. The *Post* filed a lawsuit challenging the constitutionality of this regulation. The SC upheld the right of the Federal Bureau of Prisons to forbid or prohibit interviews by the press or media generally with particular inmates. (*See the related case of Pell v. Procunier* [1974] for a similar decision affecting state prisons and their regulations).

Schad v. Arizona, 501 U.S. 624, 111 S.Ct. 2491 (1991) **(Death Penalty; Matter of Premeditation).** Schad was charged with the death of a 74-year-old motorist when he was apprehended by police in the victim's stolen vehicle in Prescott, Arizona. The prosecutor advanced various theories about first-degree murder and felony murder. Schad attempted to persuade the judge to instruct the jury on a lesser included offense of theft or robbery, because Schad believed that only circumstantial evidence linked him to the death of the victim. The judge denied Schad's request but did instruct the jury to consider first-degree and felony-murder charges and their elements in their deliberations. Schad appealed, alleging that his due-process rights had been violated when the judge failed to instruct the jury on the lesser included offense. The SC rejected Schad's appeal on the grounds that the failure of the judge to instruct the jury on the lesser included offense of robbery had not rendered the first-degree murder verdict the result of impermissible choice where sufficient evidence existed to support a second-degree murder conviction anyway.

Schall v. Martin, 467 U.S. 253, 104 S.Ct. 2403 (1984) **(Juvenile Law; Preventive Detention).** Martin, age 14, was arrested at 11:30 p.m. on December 13, 1977, in New York City. He was charged with first-degree robbery, second-degree assault, and criminal possession of a weapon. Martin lied to police at the time, giving a false name and address. Between the time of his arrest and December 29, when a fact-finding hearing was held, Martin was detained (a total of 15 days). His detention was based largely on the false information he had supplied to police and the seriousness of the charges pending against him. Subsequently, he was adjudicated a delinquent and placed on two years' probation. Later, his attorney filed an appeal, contesting his preventive detention as violative of the due-process clause of the Fourteenth Amendment. The SC eventually heard the case and upheld the detention as constitutional.

Scher v. United States, 305 U.S. 251, 59 S.Ct. 174 (1938) **(Law Enforcement Officers or Agencies; Vehicle Searches).** A reliable informant advised police of a particular liquor transaction that would occur on a certain evening, and police conducted surveillance. At one point, they saw Scher move his automobile from one location to another, and they followed him. When he parked in an open garage, police moved in and told Scher that he was suspected of carrying illegal liquor. Scher admitted that he was carrying "a little" for a party, and he told police that the liquor was in the trunk. Police arrested him and conducted a warrantless search of his trunk, where they discovered illegal whiskey. Scher was convicted. He appealed, contending that officers had needed a search warrant to search his trunk. The SC disagreed and upheld his conviction, holding that the officers had seen and heard suspicious activity. The officers properly could have stopped Scher's car and made a search when putting him under arrest. Passage of the car into the open garage had not destroyed this right. Thus, examination of an automobile accompanied by an arrest, without objection and upon admission of probable guilt was such that the officers had done nothing either unreasonable or oppressive.

Scheuer v. Rhodes, 416 U.S. 232, 94 S.Ct. 1683 (1974) **(Legal Liabilities of Police Officers).** Initial complaints filed by families or victims involved in the Kent State University shootings of students by national guardsmen in May 1970 were dismissed by lower courts, which accepted the good-faith argument that national guardsmen were acting consistently with statutes and governor orders to quell riots and campus disturbances. The SC reinstated the complaints, ordering consideration of further proceedings to determine the merits of the filings. The SC held that it was erroneous to accept the guardsmen's actions as good-faith behaviors. The courts had to determine whether those issues had merit.

Schick v. Reed, 419 U.S. 256, 95 S.Ct. 379 (1974) **(Death Penalty; Commutation to Life-Without-Parole Sentence).** Schick was a United States Army sergeant in Japan, where he was convicted of murdering an eight-year-old girl and sentenced to death in 1954. He alleged insanity when he was originally court-martialed, but the court rejected his defense. In March 1960, his case was sent to President Eisenhower, who commuted his death sentence to life imprisonment for the "term of his natural life." Subsequently, Schick learned that had he originally been given a simple sentence of life imprisonment, he would currently be eligible for parole. Thus, he petitioned the parole board for early release. His parole was denied. Schick appealed, alleging that it was "unfair" *not* to be eligible for parole, because many prisoners in the early 1970s were having their death sentences changed to simple life sentences and were becoming "parole eligible." The SC heard his case and determined that the fact of a presidential commutation order is not the equivalent of cases involving death penalties being changed to life sentences for prisoners when the case of *Furman v. Georgia* was decided in 1972. Thus, the "no-parole" decision of President Eisenhower was binding on Schick's case.

Schilb v. Kuebel, 404 U.S. 357, 92 S.Ct. 479 (1971) **(Bail).** In a case in Illinois where a defendant was ultimately acquitted, 1 percent of the bail amount was forfeited to the bail bond company, which by Illinois law is permitted to make a small amount of money as a commission for posting bail for criminal suspects. Schilb and others filed a class-action suit against the bail bond company as being discriminatory and unconstitutional in its procedures. They further challenged the release-on-own recognizance scheme as discriminatory. The SC upheld the Illinois bail law, saying that its fee of 1 percent of bail was not excessive and that there had been no discrimination between the poor and the rich; in short, the Illinois law did not violate any constitutional amendment.

Schmerber v. California, 384 U.S. 757, 86 S.Ct. 1826 (1966) **(Law Enforcement Officers or Agencies; Search and Seizure).** Schmerber was arrested in California for driving under the influence of alcohol following an accident. He was brought to a hospital, where a nurse drew a sample of his blood against his will, while he was being treated for injuries. The blood specimen became inculpatory evidence against him later in court, and he was convicted of DWI. He appealed, contending that the seizure of his blood had been unreasonable and had violated his Fourth Amendment rights. Furthermore, he argued that his own blood used against him was tantamount to self-incrimination and thus violated his Fifth Amendment rights. The SC disagreed on both counts, declaring that drawing blood without one's consent, when done by medical personnel, does not violate one's constitutional rights against unreasonable search and seizure. The SC rejected the Fifth Amendment violation argument by noting that this right pertained only to testimony, not blood evidence. The court added that exigent circumstances existed in that situation, because a delay would have prevented officers from obtaining a valid sample of Schmerber's blood to show its true alcohol content at or near the time of the accident.

Schneckloth v. Bustamonte, 412 U.S. 218, 93 S.Ct. 2041 (1973) **(Law Enforcement Officers or Agencies; Fourth Amendment; Search and Seizure; Consent).** One evening, police observed an automobile with a broken tail light and stopped it. The driver had no driver's license and was asked to step out of the car together with several other occupants. One passenger, Alcala, had a driver's license and told police that the automobile belonged to his brother. The officers asked if they could search the vehicle and Alcala consented. While conducting their search, the officers discovered stolen checks from a car wash and ar-

rested one of the passengers, Bustamonte. Bustamonte was later convicted of possessing checks with intent to defraud. He appealed, seeking to have the checks suppressed as evidence against him. The SC disagreed, saying that Alcala, who had constructive possession of the vehicle, was in a position to give police consent to conduct their search. Therefore, the evidence they later discovered as the result of that search was valid and had not violated Bustamonte's Fourth Amendment rights.

Schwartz v. Texas, 344 U.S. 199, 73 S.Ct. 232 (1952) **(Law Enforcement Officers or Agencies; Electronic Surveillance).** Schwartz was a pawnbroker who entered into a conspiracy with thieves Jarrett and Bennett to dispose of stolen property through the pawnshop. The thieves and Schwartz eventually had a falling out where one of the thieves informed on Schwartz. An agreement between Jarrett, Bennett, and the police set in motion a telephone call to Schwartz designed to implicate him. Jarrett called Schwartz and obtained various incriminating statements from him. Schwartz was later convicted based in part on incriminating evidence from those conversations. Schwartz appealed, contending that warrants were required for such telephonic interceptions of his conversations. The SC upheld his conviction, holding that one of the persons making the telephone call, Jarrett, had consented to the conversation being recorded. Thus, a participant who initiates a telephone call may record this conversation and this action does not violate the unreasonable-search-and-seizure provision of the Fourth Amendment. Police officers need a warrant as third parties, however, in order to intercept telephonic conversations between two or more other individuals. That was not the situation, here, as Jarrett had authorized the recording of the call to Schwartz, and Jarrett was one of the parties involved in the conversation. This type of recording is perfectly constitutional.

Scott v. Illinois, 440 U.S. 367, 99 S.Ct. 1158 (1979) **(Pretrial Detentions).** Scott, an indigent, was convicted of shoplifting and fined $50 following a bench trial. Scott appealed this conviction, contending that he had been deprived of court-appointed counsel. The SC rejected Scott's appeal outright, noting that only if a defendant faces a real term of incarceration of any duration can the court be obligated to furnish court-appointed counsel. In this case, the penalty was a simple fine of $50, and the fact that the offense included a statute with a fine of "up to $500" and an incarcerative term of "up to one year" was irrelevant, because the Sixth and Fourteenth Amendments require only that no indigent criminal defendant shall be sentenced to a term of imprisonment unless the state has afforded him the right to assistance of court-appointed counsel in his defense.

Scott v. United States, 436 U.S. 128, 98 S.Ct. 1717 (1978) **(Electronic Surveillance).** Under the Omnibus Crime Control and Safe Street Act of 1968, the government is required in wiretapping situations to conduct such electronic surveillance in a way that minimizes interception of extraneous or irrelevant communication. During an investigation of Frank Scott concerning allegations of narcotics distribution, considerable incriminating evidence was obtained against Scott as the result of government electronic surveillance. However, about 40 percent of the recorded telephonic information was irrelevant to the narcotics issue, and Scott's attorney moved to suppress all incriminating telephonic conversations, as their use did not comply with the act's provisions to minimize interceptions of irrelevant conversations. The SC heard Scott's appeal and decided against him. The intercepted conversations had been collected "in good faith" by federal agents, and the general conduct of the agents had complied with the spirit of the act and was reasonable and not violative of any Fourth Amendment provision.

See v. Seattle, 387 U.S. 541, 87 S.Ct. 1737 (1967) **(Law Enforcement Officers or Agencies; Searches).** A fire inspector wished to inspect See's residence in Seattle. See objected, saying that the inspector needed a properly executed search warrant. The inspector discovered the violation of a city ordinance. See was charged and convicted. He appealed and the SC overturned his conviction, holding that searches of the type authorized by the Seattle ordinance required warrants under the Fourth Amendment. Thus, administrative entry, without consent, upon portions of commercial premises not open to the public, may only be compelled through prosecution or physical force within the framework of a warrant procedure. This holding does not pertain to licensing requirements, such as firearms inspections of firearms dealers and the like.

Segura v. United States, 468 U.S. 796, 104 S.Ct. 3380 (1984) **(Law Enforcement Officers or Agencies; Exclusionary Rule).** A New York task force on drug-law enforcement suspected Segura of trafficking in cocaine. Other suspects were followed to their apartment, where Segura appeared and purchased cocaine. The agents obtained a search warrant for the apartment and entered it the following day. Then they went to Segura's apartment house, arrested Segura in the lobby, and took him to his apartment, where a man, Colon, opened the door. Standing in the doorway, officers could see in plain view drug paraphernalia and other incriminating items. They forced entry into the apartment and conducted a warrantless search of the premises. Later, at Segura's trial, all evidence was admitted, including that seized as the result of the warrantless search. He was convicted. He appealed, alleging his Fourth Amendment right against unreasonable searches and seizures had been violated. The SC upheld his conviction but held that the incriminating evidence seized without a warrant should have been suppressed. However, there was sufficient incriminating evidence without this other evidence to convict Segura. Thus the Fourth Amendment violation in his case was irrelevant and did not affect his lawful conviction.

Serfass v. United States, 420 U.S. 377, 95 S.Ct. 1055 (1975) **(Jeopardy Attaching).** Serfass was indicted for failing to register for the draft for the United States Armed Forces in Pennsylvania. Subsequently, he successfully had the indictment dismissed by a motion, but the government appealed and an appellate court reversed the dismissal. Serfass appealed this reversal, on the grounds that it constituted double jeopardy, because he believed that he was "being tried twice for the same offense." The SC upheld his indictment, holding that it is not double jeopardy to be first indicted without a trial to decide the case. The double-jeopardy clause does not bar an appeal by the government from dismissal of an indictment or information with respect to a criminal defendant who has not been put to trial. Persons must be placed on trial for an offense before they can claim double jeopardy, if they are subsequently charged again with that same offense.

Sgro v. United States, 287 U.S. 206, 53 S.Ct. 138 (1932) **(Law Enforcement Officers or Agencies; Electronic Surveillance).** A liquor search warrant was issued for searching Sgro's premises. However, the search warrant was not executed within 10 days following its issuance.

Thus, it became void. Officers then used the void warrant to search Sgro's premises. Evidence seized was used to convict Sgro of violating federal liquor laws, and he appealed. The SC overturned the conviction, holding that the expired and void warrant was an illegal device with which to initiate a new search of a constitutionally protected area. A new search warrant had to be obtained in order to conduct a reasonable search under the Fourth Amendment.

Shea v. Louisiana, 470 U.S. 51, 105 S.Ct. 1065 (1985) **(Self-Incrimination).** IRS agents interviewed Shea regarding an income tax liability. Subsequently, during the same interview, Shea made various incriminating statements that led to his indictment and conviction for income tax fraud. Shea appealed the conviction, alleging that he had not been told his Miranda rights during his interview, that he had not been advised that statements he made could be used against him later in court, and that therefore, his Fifth Amendment right against self-incrimination had been violated. The SC disagreed, holding that Shea was not in custody and was not being interrogated while in custody. If he had been arrested and taken into custody for interrogation purposes, then the Miranda warning would have had to be given him. Under other circumstances, however, the IRS had no obligation to tell Shea his rights. Thus his conviction was upheld.

Sheppard v. Maxwell, 384 U.S. 333, 86 S.Ct. 1507 (1966) **(Fair Trials).** Sheppard claimed that someone unknown to him entered his home in Bay Village, Ohio, and hit him on the head. When he awakened, he saw his wife had been injured and was sitting in a chair, bleeding and not moving. Early in the case, police suspected Sheppard of killing his wife and diverting attention from himself to so-called unknown assailants. The police made known their views to the media, which dramatized the event, as Sheppard was a well-respected physician in the community. Front-page headlines in the local newspapers created a media frenzy, with Sheppard at the center of it. During his subsequent trial, Sheppard was subjected to considerable media attention, and cameras and other media agents and apparatuses were admitted into the courtroom to witness the proceedings. This action by the court further intensified the media frenzy. In this milieu, Sheppard was convicted of murder. He appealed and the SC overturned his murder conviction, holding that the failure of the

state trial judge to protect Sheppard from inherently prejudicial publicity, which saturated the community, and to control disruptive influences in court had deprived Sheppard of a fair trial consistent with due process.

Sherman v. United States, 356 U.S. 369, 78 S.Ct. 819 (1958) **(Entrapment).** A paid government informant was instructed to meet Sherman, a drug addict, in a doctor's office and inquire about possible sources of drugs. Sherman repeatedly declined to provide the informant with drug information or sources of drugs. At some point, however, he eventually provided small quantities of drugs to the informant at his own cost plus expenses. Eventually, after several transactions, government agents arrested Sherman and he was convicted of drug offenses. Sherman appealed, alleging entrapment. The SC agreed and overturned his conviction. The SC stressed the significance of the phrase "entrapment occurs whenever the government induces persons to commit crimes they otherwise would never have committed." The persistence of the government informant in requesting drugs and Sherman's repeated avoidance and denials of involvement in drug trafficking were clear evidence to the SC that Sherman had never intended to traffic in drugs, without the substantial inducement and entrapment by the government and their paid informant.

Sibron v. New York, 392 U.S. 40, 88 S.Ct. 1889 (1968) **(Law Enforcement Officers or Agencies; Stop and Frisk).** Sibron, a convicted drug user and ex-convict, was observed by a police officer in a New York diner conversing with other persons, also known to be involved with drugs. Sibron was sitting at a table while as many as six or eight persons approached him and conversed over a period of a few hours. Nothing was observed exchanged between them, according to the observing officer. However, when Sibron left the diner, the officer approached and said, "Sibron, you know what I want." Sibron began to place his hand in his pocket, but the officer moved quickly and thrust his hand in it instead. The search yielded several glassine envelopes containing heroin. Sibron was subsequently convicted of heroin possession. However, he appealed to the SC, and his conviction was overturned. The court reasoned that officers should be able to protect themselves against possibly armed suspects. Thus, a "pat-down" and "frisk" are warranted under certain suspicious conditions. However, Sibron had not been observed doing anything illegal, and therefore his pocket search by the observing officer was unreasonable according to the Fourth Amendment. In short, the officer was entitled to pat down Sibron to detect a possible weapon; the officer would not have detected small glassine envelopes of heroin in such a pat-down, however, so the heroin evidence illegally obtained by the officer was excluded. This landmark case limited the scope of a police officer's search of suspicious persons to pat-downs and frisks, unless other special circumstances apply. Sibron's case did *not* involve special circumstances.

Silverman v. United States, 365 U.S. 505, 81 S.Ct. 679 (1961) **(Law Enforcement Officers or Agencies; Electronic Surveillance).** In the spring of 1958, Washington, D.C., police placed microphones throughout a house suspected as headquartering an illegal gambling operation. On the basis of information obtained by police from conversations overheard from such microphone placements, convictions were obtained against Silverman and others. Silverman appealed. The SC overturned his conviction, holding that the warrantless search and placement of microphones illegally throughout his residence had violated the unreasonable-search provisions of the Fourth Amendment. The SC held that these microphones represented a nonconsensual intrusion, without warrant, into a constitutionally protected area, a private home.

Silverthorne Lumber Co. v. United States, 251 U.S. 385, 40 S.Ct. 182 (1920) **(Law Enforcement Officers or Agencies; Exclusionary Rule).** Silverthorne Lumber Co. officials were arrested after being indicted on various charges. Following their arrest, federal agents without a search warrant went to the business premises and seized all records, effects, and personnel, directing that the personnel should present themselves at the Department of Justice as soon as possible. New indictments were secured against Silverthorne officials based upon the newly seized evidence. Silverthorne protested. The SC ruled that the evidence against Silverthorne Lumber Co. had been seized illegally and in violation of the Fourth Amendment and was therefore inadmissible. Also, it overturned contempt charges against the Silverthorne officials for not producing such materials. Corporations are protected just as are individuals, against illegal and/or unreasonable warrantless searches as specified in the Fourth Amendment.

Simmons v. United States, 390 U.S. 377, 88 S.Ct. 967 (1968) **(Law Enforcement Officers or Agencies; Lineups).** Simmons was suspected of armed robbery of a federally insured savings and loan association. Following the robbery, witnesses were shown photographs of various suspects, including Simmons. A description of the getaway car yielded information leading to Simmons' mother's residence, which FBI visited and entered. They found inculpatory evidence in the home, including a gun holster, a sack similar to the one used in the robbery, and several bill wrappers from the bank that had been robbed. Simmons was charged with and convicted of the armed robbery. He appealed, arguing that the search of his mother's home had not been by consent or warrant, and that the photograph lineup of him was suggestive. The SC rejected Simmons' contention that the lineup was suggestive and noted that at the trial, five of the witnesses had positively identified Simmons. Simmons' conviction was upheld as valid.

Simpson v. United States, 435 U.S. 6, 98 U.S. 909 (1978) **(Enhanced Sentences).** Simpson and his brother were charged in Kentucky in federal court with two separate bank robberies where dangerous weapons were used. They were convicted of a bank robbery charge (including the possession of a dangerous weapon) and also of the charge of using a dangerous weapon during the commission of a felony. Thus the district judge sentenced Simpson to two consecutive prison terms for each of the statute violations. He appealed. The SC reversed Simpson's conviction, declaring that sentence enhancements may not be permitted where different offenses are alleged and have stemmed from the same crime. In this case, there was a single transaction of "bank robbery with firearms." The prosecution added a second statute governing the use of weapons during the commission of felonies. The significance of the SC decision is that sentences may not be compounded or enhanced through the misapplication of two or more different statutes. Thus, where a prosecution grows out of a single transaction, such as bank robbery with firearms, defendants may not be sentenced according to two or more different statutes covering different dimensions of the offense.

Singer v. United States, 380 U.S. 24, 85 S.Ct. 783 (1965) **(Jury Trials).** Singer, charged with a federal crime, requested to have a bench trial instead of a jury trial. His request was denied, and he was subsequently convicted of the crime by a federal jury. He appealed, arguing that he should have been entitled to a bench trial. The SC disagreed and said that although Singer had a right to a jury trial under the circumstances, the constitutional requirement did not entitle a citizen to the opposite of that right, namely, a bench trial. Thus, defendants cannot elect to have a bench trial as a matter of right if jury trials are prescribed in federal proceedings (*see Duncan v. Louisiana* [1968]).

Skinner v. Oklahoma, 316 U.S. 535, 62 S.Ct. 1110 (1942) **(Sterilization of Criminals).** Skinner was a third-felony offender who had been convicted of stealing chickens in 1926, robbery with firearms in 1929, and robbery with firearms in 1934. An Oklahoma law proclaimed that persons who had committed such felonies should be sterilized, and, therefore, the court ordered Skinner sterilized. Skinner appealed, alleging that his equal-protection rights were being violated. Persons convicted on multiple occasions for embezzlement, for instance, would not be sterilized, whereas persons convicted on multiple occasions for larceny would be. Thus, Oklahoma was sterilizing convicted offenders selectively. The SC heard his case and ruled in Skinner's favor. It held that the Oklahoma law requiring sterilization of certain types of criminals was unconstitutional because the Oklahoma classification scheme determining who should or should not be sterilized denied equal protection under the law.

Skipper v. South Carolina, 476 U.S. 1, 106 S.Ct. 1669 (1986) **(Death Penalty).** Skipper was convicted of rape and murder following a jury trial. During the sentencing phase of the trial, the jury considered aggravating and mitigating circumstances. Skipper planned to introduce testimony from jailers and a "regular visitor" that he had exhibited good conduct and made a good adjustment while confined. The court refused to allow him to introduce such testimony during this phase of his trial. He was sentenced to death. He appealed. The SC overturned his conviction by noting that the sentencing jury must hear all relevant evidence in mitigation of punishment.

Smalis v. Pennsylvania, 476 U.S. 140, 106 S.Ct. 1745 (1986) **(Double Jeopardy).** Smalis and her husband were owners of a building housing a restaurant. The building caught fire and two tenants died as the result. The Smalises were charged with various crimes, including murder, voluntary manslaughter, and causing a catastrophe. They entered a demurrer, which acknowledged the facts of the fire but claimed that the state's case against them was insufficient to support a cause of action. The trial court sustained the demurrer and the state appealed. An appellate court quashed the government's appeal on the grounds that it was barred by the double-jeopardy clause. However, the Pennsylvania Supreme Court reversed that decision, saying that a demurrer is not the functional equivalent of an acquittal. The United States SC heard the Smalis' case and held that when the trial judge granted their demurrer, it was an "acquittal" under the double-jeopardy clause. Thus, the state would be barred from further criminal proceedings against the Smalises.

Smith v. Bennett, 365 U.S. 708, 81 S.Ct. 895 (1961) **(Corrections; Inmate Rights).** Smith, an indigent, was convicted of burglary and sentenced to 10 years in the Iowa State Penitentiary. He was paroled and violated one or more of his parole conditions. He was returned to prison and filed a motion to the Iowa Supreme Court. A $4 filing fee was required to accompany his motion. Because he didn't have $4, his petition was denied. He appealed. The SC heard Smith's case and overruled the Iowa Supreme Court, saying that indigents cannot be barred from access to the court because they cannot afford filing fees. To do so was a clear violation of Smith's Fourteenth Amendment rights.

Smith v. Daily Publishing Co., 443 U.S. 97, 99 S.Ct. 2667 (1979) **(Juvenile Law; Media Reports).** A 15-year-old Virginia student was killed at a junior high school. A 14-year-old classmate was charged with the crime. Reporters for local newspapers were monitoring police broadcasts and went to the arrest scene, where they learned the name of the juvenile suspect. The suspect's picture and name were published in the local newspaper following the murder. Suit was brought against the newspaper, the *Gazette*, for illegally publishing the name and photograph of the juvenile without permission of the juvenile court. The SC upheld the right of the juvenile to confidentiality and ruled against the newspaper. Juvenile court permission is required before any names or photographs of juveniles are published relative to crimes alleged. The newspaper's action was a violation of the First and Fourteenth Amendment.

Smith v. Hooey, 393 U.S. 374, 89 S.Ct. 575 (1969) **(Speedy Trials).** A federal prisoner sought a writ of mandamus to compel authorities to bring him to trial in a Texas court on state-related charges. The Texas Supreme Court said that it did not have the power to compel the presence of federal prisoners in Texas for a state trial. The SC disagreed and said that Texas must make a good-faith effort to bring the defendant to court for trial.

Smith v. Illinois, 390 U.S. 129, 88 S.Ct. 748 (1968) **(Courts; *Habeas Corpus* Petitions; Defendant Right of Cross-Examination and Scope of Cross-Examination).** Smith was accused in Cook County, Illinois, of the unlawful sale of narcotics. During Smith's trial, a confidential informant testified. On cross-examination, the informant gave his name as "James Jordan," acknowledged to be false. The defense counsel sought to determine "Jordan's" real name, but a prosecutor's objection was sustained. The defense also sought to determine where "Jordan" lived, but again, the court refused to allow an answer to this question. The prosecution gave as its reason, "witness safety and protection," but the process did not entitle Smith's attorney to cross-examine the adverse witness fully. Smith was convicted. He filed an appeal, alleging that he had been denied the privilege of cross-examining his accuser under the Sixth Amendment. The SC heard the case and reversed Smith's conviction, holding that the Sixth Amendment entitles defendants to cross-examine their accusers, and to elicit from them information that may discredit them. The SC noted, however, that cross-examination that is intended to annoy, harass, or humiliate informants is unwarranted. In any event, Smith's conviction was reversed because of the Sixth Amendment right violation.

Smith v. Illinois, 469 U.S. 91, 105 S.Ct. 490 (1984) **(Sixth Amendment; Right to Counsel).** Smith was suspected of armed robbery. Shortly after his arrest, he was taken to police headquarters for interrogation. He was told his Miranda rights but was ambivalent about whether he wanted an attorney to be present during questioning. Specifically, Smith said, "I wanna get a lawyer" prior to his questioning by police. However, he said "Yeah and no" when asked whether he wanted to talk with police at that time. In any event, Smith admitted to the crime. During his

trial, his attorney attempted to have the incriminating statements against him suppressed but was unsuccessful. Smith was convicted. He appealed to the SC, which overturned his conviction. The SC holding was a narrow one, not necessarily exploring the meticulous circumstances of Smith's confession or the conditions under which it was given. Rather, the SC reasoned that on several occasions during police questioning, Smith had indicated his intent to have an attorney present. Police were to *cease* their questioning at that point and obtain an attorney for Smith. They had failed to do so. Suspects who are in custody but invoke their right to counsel must be provided counsel before further interrogation is conducted.

Smith v. Maryland, 442 U.S. 735, 99 S.Ct. 2577 (1975) **(Wiretaps).** In this warrantless seizure case, police used a pen register to record telephone numbers dialed from a particular location. Subsequent incriminating information resulted from a knowledge of these other telephone numbers. Smith was convicted. He appealed, contending that police had had no right to "seize" these telephone numbers without a warrant. The SC declared that telephone numbers by themselves do not constitute conversation, incriminating or otherwise. Thus they are not protected by the Fourth Amendment. Furthermore, telephone numbers are freely available through the telephone company, and therefore persons have no reasonable expectation to privacy regarding interceptions of telephone numbers.

Smith v. Murray, 477 U.S. 527, 106 S.Ct. 2661 (1986) **(Corrections; Inmate Rights).** Smith was accused of murder in a Virginia court. At the defense counsel's request before Smith's trial, a psychiatrist examined Smith, and Smith told him about various events involving deviant sexual conduct. A jury trial followed. Neither side called the psychiatrist to testify. Smith was convicted. During the sentencing phase of the trial, the psychiatrist was called to testify and gave incriminating statements made to him by Smith. The defense objected without effect. Smith appealed to higher courts, alleging many issues. At no time during these state appeals, however, was the psychiatrist's testimony mentioned. Subsequently, after having exhausted his state remedies, Smith filed a habeas corpus petition where the psychiatric testimony issue was raised. The SC summarily rejected Smith's claim, inasmuch as he had failed to state such a claim during any of his state appeals. The SC ruled in Smith's case that when the alleged error was unrelated to Smith's innocence, and when Smith was represented by competent counsel and had a full and fair opportunity to press his claim in the state system but had failed to do so, Smith had failed to carry the burden of showing how the psychiatrist's testimony would have affected his sentence.

Smith v. Ohio, 494 U.S. 541, 110 S.Ct. 1288 (1990) **(Law Enforcement Officers or Agencies; Fourth Amendment; Searches Incident to an Arrest).** Smith was leaving a YMCA building with a companion in Ashland, Ohio, one evening, carrying a brown paper bag. Two police officers observed him and his friend. Neither Smith nor his companion was known to police. They approached the two men and said, "Come here a minute." Smith was standing by his car and threw the brown paper bag on the hood of the car and turned to face police. They immediately seized his bag, which he attempted to protect, and opened it, discovering drug paraphernalia. They placed Smith under arrest for possession of drug paraphernalia, and he was subsequently convicted. Smith appealed. The police and the state reasoned that the discovery of the drug paraphernalia had given them probable cause to arrest Smith. They contended that the search of the bag and seizure of its contents were made incident to an arrest and so were properly admissible against Smith during his subsequent trial. The state further argued that Smith had abandoned his property (the bag) when he tossed it on the hood of his car. Thus the abandoned property fell within the purview of police to investigate it and its contents. The SC rejected these arguments and overturned Smith's conviction, holding that justifying a search by an arrest and an arrest by the search "will not do" (at 1290). A citizen who attempts to protect his private property from inspection has clearly not abandoned that property. The police had lacked probable cause to search the bag, and thus the sheer fact that drug paraphernalia was discovered was irrelevant and did not justify the arrest. Searches of areas in the immediate vicinity of persons arrested on the basis of probable cause are legitimately within the scope of police authority, but no search can be justified without probable cause. This case is a good example of how the SC treats the matter of the ends justifying the means. Finding illegal contraband without first having probable cause to make an arrest does not justify the search of a person or

his personal effects, regardless of whatever is found.

Smith v. Phillips, 455 U.S. 209, 102 S.Ct. 940 (1982) **(Corrections; Death Penalty).** Phillips was convicted of murder in a New York court. During his trial, one of his jurors had submitted a job application to the District Attorney's Office for employment as an investigator. When prosecutors learned of it, they withheld the information from the defense. Later, Phillips' attorney found out about it and moved to vacate Phillips' conviction on grounds of prosecutorial misconduct. The judge denied the motion, and Phillips appealed to the SC. The SC held that a new trial is not required every time a juror has been placed in a potentially compromising situation. In the present case, it was determined that the juror's ability to make an impartial judgment had not been impaired. The critical question was whether Phillips had had a fair trial, not whether the conduct of the prosecutor in withholding the information about the juror was wrong. In this case, a fair trial had been conducted, and Phillips's conviction was affirmed.

Smith v. United States, 507 U.S.___, 113 S.Ct. 2050 (1993) **(Sentence Enhancements).** Smith was convicted in federal court of using a firearm during a drug sale. Essentially, he had traded a firearm for narcotics. The firearm was treated as a part of a drug transaction for purposes of sentence enhancement (e.g., if a person uses a gun, he does two years in prison). Smith appealed, alleging that he wasn't "using" the firearm but rather "trading" it. The SC heard his case and upheld his conviction with the enhancement for use of the firearm by declaring that "use" and "in relation to" are for all intents and purposes the same within the meaning of the statute.

Smith v. Wade, 461 U.S. 30, 103 S.Ct. 1625 (1983) **(Corrections; Damages).** Wade was a youthful first-offender in a prison. He had requested protective isolation because of previous violent incidents committed against him. He was initially placed in a cell with another inmate. Eventually, Smith, a corrections officer, placed a third inmate known for fighting in the cell with Wade and the other prisoner. Subsequently, Wade was sexually assaulted by one or both of the other cell occupants. He filed suit against Smith for disregarding his safety by placing these persons in the same cell with him. Damages were awarded to Wade, who had been placed in protective isolation at his request. Smith appealed, contending that the wrong instructions had been given to the jury by the judge about what damages should be imposed. The SC upheld the judge's decision and indicated that Smith had indeed acted in callous disregard for Wade's safety, and that his behavior could be interpreted as being actually malicious or having malicious intent. Thus, punitive damages can be awarded to inmates against corrections officers and other officials if they acted with callous disregard for the rights and safety of others.

Solem v. Helm, 463 U.S. 277, 103 S.Ct. 3001 (1983) **(Eighth Amendment; Cruel and Unusual Punishment).** A life sentence was imposed upon a convicted offender after he had been convicted of six prior nonviolent offenses. The offender appealed, contending that a life sentence was disproportionate punishment, given the offense, and was thus cruel and unusual. The SC upheld the sentence, saying that a life sentence for a habitual offender was not cruel and unusual in violation of the Eighth Amendment.

Solem v. Stumes, 465 U.S. 638, 104 S.Ct. 1338 (1984) **(Law Enforcement Officers or Agencies; Confessions).** Stumes was a suspect in a woman's death in Sioux Falls, South Dakota. Subsequently, he was arrested in Green Bay, Wisconsin, on unrelated charges (e.g., check forgery and perjury). While he was in jail awaiting trial, he talked to his attorney, who told him not to make any statements before returning to South Dakota. Sioux Falls police officers went to Wisconsin and brought Stumes back in an automobile. During the trip, Stumes was told his Miranda rights but talked with police. At one point, he admitted killing the woman. He was charged with and convicted of murder, based upon the confession he gave to police in the car and other incriminating evidence. He appealed. Without offering an opinion as to Stumes's guilt or innocence, the SC remanded the case to the trial court to determine whether police had acted properly when they initiated further conversation with Stumes on the auto trip back to South Dakota. Stumes' appeal alleged that the conduct of police who interrogated him ought to be evaluated in view of a decision in a contemporaneous case as yet unsettled. In this case, as was in *Edwards v. Arizona* (1981), it was held that once a suspect has invoked his silence privilege, police may not initiate new conversation with the suspect. The suspect, however, may initiate new conversation, and any incriminating statements uttered may be used against the suspect later in court. In the present case, the SC held that retroactive application of the *Edwards* case was not proper.

Solesbee v. Balkom, 339 U.S. 9, 70 S.Ct. 457 (1950) **(Corrections; Death Penalty).** Solesbee was convicted of murder. He filed a writ of habeas corpus, seeking to have a hearing on whether he was insane. Then he was sentenced to death. At the time, Georgia governors had the power of determining whether or not such a hearing should be convened, and determining on their own authority whether convicts were mentally competent. The SC rejected Solesbee's claim that he had a constitutional right to a postconviction proceeding to determine his sanity. The SC said that persons legally convicted and sentenced to death have no statutory or constitutional right to a judicially conducted or supervised trial or inquisition on the question of insanity subsequent to sentence.

Sorrells v. United States, 287 U.S. 435, 53 S.Ct. 138 (1932) **(Entrapment).** Sorrells was a resident of a North Carolina county. A revenue agent, undercover, approached him on numerous occasions, asking him repeatedly if he would supply the agent with illegal liquor. Sorrells was a war veteran, and the undercover agent used this information to become closer to Sorrells by stating that he, himself, was also a war veteran. After repeated requests to supply illegal liquor, Sorrells finally did so. He was arrested and convicted. He appealed on the grounds of entrapment. The SC heard his case and overturned his conviction. It said it was of the opinion that upon the evidence produced in this case, the defense of entrapment was available and that the trial court was in error by holding there was no entrapment and in refusing to submit this issue to the jury. Entrapment was generally defined as government enticement for persons to engage in criminal activities when such persons initially have no such inclinations for engaging in these criminal activities.

South Carolina v. Gathers, 490 U.S. 805, 109 S.Ct. 2207 (1989) **(Corrections; Death Penalty).** Gathers and some friends encountered a man, Haynes, in a public park and killed him. Specifically, Gathers beat Haynes with an umbrella, which Gathers subsequently shoved into Haynes' anus. During the trial, the prosecutor's closing remarks included reading various passages from a religious book Haynes had been carrying when he was killed. The prosecutor also engaged in extensive commentary about a voting card Haynes had carried, as well as commentary about his religious convictions and mental condition. Gathers was convicted of murder and first-degree sexual assault. He appealed, alleging prosecutorial misconduct and a violation of his due-process rights. The South Carolina Supreme Court heard Gathers's appeal and reversed his conviction. The state appealed. The United States SC affirmed the South Carolina Supreme Court, holding that the contents of Haynes' personal papers could not be said to relate directly to the circumstances of the crime. Thus the "contents" of whatever religious tracts victims are carrying are not directly relevant to the "circumstances of the crime."

South Dakota v. Neville, 499 U.S. 553, 103 S.Ct. 916 (1983) **(Confessions; Exceptions).** Neville was arrested and charged with driving while intoxicated. He was asked to take a blood-alcohol test and was advised that if he did not take such a test, his license would be revoked. Officers did not warn Neville, however, that his refusal could be used against him later in court, if the case went to trial. He refused to take the test and the case went to trial, where the prosecutor used Neville's refusal as evidence. Neville was convicted of DWI. He appealed, alleging that his refusal to take such a test ought to have been excluded because it was a violation of his right against self-incrimination under the Fifth Amendment. The SC upheld his conviction, saying that the blood-alcohol test is simple and not coercive; thus it does not violate the Fifth Amendment against self-incrimination.

South Dakota v. Opperman, 428 U.S. 364, 96 S.Ct. 3092 (1976) **(Law Enforcement Officers or Agencies; Searches Incident to Arrest).** Opperman's car had been impounded for various parking violations. Following customary procedures, police inventoried the car's contents and found marijuana in the glove compartment. Opperman was arrested, charged, and convicted of marijuana possession. He appealed, and his conviction was overturned by the South Dakota Supreme Court; then the prosecution appealed. The United States SC overturned the South Dakota SC, reinstating Opperman's conviction, saying that the police inventory of his vehicle had been a routine procedure followed by that particular police department. Thus, there had been no attempt to discover contraband known in advance to be in the vehicle.

Spaziano v. Florida, 468 U.S. 447, 104 S.Ct. 3154 (1984) **(Corrections; Death Penalty; Judicial Consideration of Jury Decision).** Judges in Florida are required to consider jury recommendations, whatever they may be, and to give them *great weight*. In Alabama, in contrast, judges are required to give jury recommendations *proper weight*.

Spevack v. Klein, 385 U.S. 511, 87 S.Ct. 625 (1967) **(Attorneys, Self-Incrimination).** Spevack, an attorney, was served with a subpoena *duces tecum* and refused to comply by not surrendering financial documents or testifying at a judicial inquiry. The grounds he cited were that the information would be incriminating, and thus he had exercised his Fifth Amendment right against self-incrimination. A New York higher court ordered Spevack disbarred, because, it said, the privilege against self-incrimination was not available to attorneys. He appealed. The SC reversed his disbarment, saying that the privilege against self-incrimination was not applicable to *records*, the basis upon which the New York court had disbarred him. The court could not disbar Spevack because of noncompliance with producing records.

Spinelli v. United States, 394 U.S. 410, 89 S.Ct. 584 (1972) **(Law Enforcement Officers or Agencies; Search and Seizure).** An informant alerted the FBI to Spinelli's allegedly illegal bookmaking activities in St. Louis. Spinelli was placed under FBI surveillance. During this surveillance, FBI agents observed Spinelli enter an apartment where a telephone was located, one supposedly used in this bookmaking activity. The FBI filed an affidavit with a United States magistrate, detailing its observations of Spinelli and its belief that he was engaged in illegal interstate bookmaking. Little information was relayed to the magistrate about the informant and the basis for the informant's reliability. FBI agents entered Spinelli's apartment, searched, and found materials implicating Spinelli in illegal bookmaking. He was convicted. He appealed and the SC overturned the conviction primarily because the FBI agents had not met the two-pronged test established by *Aguilar v. Texas* (1964). The two-pronged test is (1) How well is the informant known by the law-enforcement officer? and (2) How reliable has been previous information furnished by the informant? The SC also rejected a totality-of-circumstances test, concluding in part that it "paints too broad a brush," making an affidavit too vague to substantiate probable cause. Subsequently, in the case of *Illinois v. Gates* (1983), the SC modified the two-pronged test established in *Aguilar* and created an additional totality-of-circumstances test, making it currently unnecessary for law-enforcement officers to detail the nature of their relations with informants and informant reliability.

Springfield v. Kibbe, 480 U.S. 257, 107 S.Ct. 1114 (1987) **(Law Enforcement Officers or Agencies; Excessive Use of Force; Legal Liabilities of Public Officials).** In September 1981, Springfield, Massachusetts, police received a telephone call that Thurston was assaulting a woman with a knife in an apartment. Later, police discovered that Thurston had fled in an automobile. His automobile was seen on a highway and followed by police, who attempted to stop it. Thurston would not stop, even after police had erected roadblocks along the highway. At some point, an officer, Perry, gave chase and fired his weapon at Thurston, who was allegedly attempting to run Perry off the road. One bullet struck Thurston in the head, and he died shortly thereafter in a hospital. His relatives filed suit against Springfield police for negligent training, alleging that it had led an officer wrongfully to shoot and kill Thurston. The SC heard the case and decided the question of whether a city can be held liable for the inadequate training of its employees. The SC held that there was no evidence on the record of deliberate indifference or recklessness in the apprehension of Thurston's fleeing vehicle. Thus Thurston's relatives failed to prove essential elements of their claim, and therefore, the suit was dismissed as being improvidently granted.

Stack v. Boyle, 342 U.S. 1, 72 S.Ct. 1 (1951) **(Bail).** Stack was charged with conspiracy to commit a crime, and bail was set at $50,000. He protested, saying that the bail was excessive and that no hearing was ever held to determine how much bail should be set. The SC agreed with Stack and remanded the case back to the district court, where a hearing could be held on the bail issue. The Court held that bail had not been fixed by proper methods in this case. It did not try to determine or define "proper methods," however.

Stanford v. Kentucky, 492 U.S. 361, 109 S.Ct. 2969 (1989) **(Juvenile Law; Death Penalty).** Stanford was charged with murder committed when he was 17 years old. He was transferred to criminal court to stand trial for murder as an adult. He was convicted and sentenced to death.

He appealed, contending that he was too young to receive the death penalty and that the death penalty would be cruel and unusual punishment. The SC upheld his death penalty and ruled that it is not unconstitutional to apply the death penalty to persons who are convicted of murders they committed when they were 17 (*see Wilkins v. Missouri* [1989] for a comparative case).

Stanford v. Texas, 379 U.S. 476, 85 S.Ct. 506 (1965) **(Law Enforcement Officers or Agencies; Arrest; Searches Incident to Arrest).** Stanford was suspected of possessing and distributing Communist materials. A search warrant was issued ordering officers to go to Stanford's home and seize any materials relevant to Communism. He was convicted. He appealed, alleging that the statute under which the search warrant was issued was unconstitutionally vague about the place to be searched and the things to be seized. The SC agreed and reversed his conviction on those grounds.

State v. Bergman, 147 CrL 1475 (Ind. Ct. App., 2nd District) (1990) **(Corrections; Pardons).** The governor of Indiana pardoned a convict, Bergman, for a crime he had committed. Bergman sought to have his record expunged, in much the same way as in *Noonan*. The Indiana Court of Appeals declared that pardons "block out the very existence of the offender's guilt, so that, in the eye(s) of the law, he is thereafter as innocent as if he had never committed the offense." A pardon *does* expunge one's criminal record.

State v. Gervais, 608 A.2d 881 (R.I.Sup. May) (1992) **(Corrections; Pleas; Record Expungements).** In Rhode Island, Gervais, after entering a plea of nolo contendere, equivalent to a guilty plea, was convicted of a crime. The conviction was suspended pending the satisfactory completion of a term of probation. When the probation was completed, Gervais's conviction was dismissed. Gervais subsequently sought to expunge his record of the original charges. The Rhode Island Court of Appeals, seizing on a technicality, declared that "expungements of records can occur within forty-five days only when a person is acquitted or exonerated from the offense with which he or she is charged. A plea of nolo contendere and a successfully served term of probation, although not constituting a conviction, remain as a record and do not constitute exoneration of that charge." In effect, if Gervais had served a probationary term of less than 45 days, he could have had his criminal record expunged. However, his term of probation went well beyond 45 days. Therefore, his request for expungement was denied.

Steagald v. United States, 451 U.S. 204, 101 S.Ct. 1642 (1981) **(Law Enforcement Officers or Agencies; Searches).** Police agents had been advised by a confidential informant that a wanted fugitive would be at a particular house in Atlanta. They obtained an arrest warrant and proceeded to the house, which belonged to Gaultney. Police saw Gaultney and Steagald standing in front of the house, conversing. Mistaking one of them for the fugitive, the agents drew their weapons, approached Steagald and Gaultney, and frisked them, determining that neither was the fugitive they sought. Then they proceeded to the house, where Mrs. Gaultney met them. They ordered her to place her hands against the wall and they proceeded to search the premises thoroughly for their wanted fugitive, who was not there. Instead, they discovered a small quantity of cocaine. They obtained a search warrant for a subsequent search, which uncovered 43 pounds of cocaine. Steagald was charged with and convicted of possession of cocaine. He appealed, contending that a search warrant should have been obtained before officers entered the house initially, and that their subsequent search of the premises had been unreasonable and unlawful. The police contended that their arrest warrant had "entitled" them to search the premises to hunt for their fugitive, and that as the result of their search, the illegal contraband was discovered lawfully. The SC strongly disagreed, saying that neither exigent circumstances nor consent existed to entitle these officers to search the premises. Steagald's conviction was overturned, because a valid search warrant was required, based upon probable cause, and the officers conducting the search had possessed no such warrant. Thus all evidence subsequently seized was inadmissible in court against Steagald. The SC specifically noted that arrest warrants do not authorize searches of premises in any absolute sense. Search warrants are necessary for the types of searches conducted in this Atlanta residence. Otherwise, such searches are unlawful and violative of the Fourth Amendment provision against unreasonable searches and seizures.

Stinson v. United States, 507 U.S.___, 113 S.Ct. 1913 (1993) **(United States Sentencing Guidelines; Interpretations of Policy Statements).** Stinson pleaded guilty to a five-count in-

dictment resulting from a bank robbery. He was sentenced according to the United States Sentencing Guidelines and the statutory language that the instant offense of convict be a crime of violence. Later, the statutory language was changed to expressly exclude the felon-in-possession offense from the crime-of-violence definition. The sentencing court ignored this language change, however, and sentenced Stinson to the more serious penalty range. Stinson appealed and the SC overturned his sentence, saying that the lower court had erred when it ignored the Sentencing Commission language change. Such commentary by the Sentencing Commission is binding on federal court judges.

Stone v. Immigration and Naturalization Service, ___U.S.___, 115 S.Ct. 1537 (1995) **(Statute of Limitations on Deportation Decisions).** Stone was a Canadian who was convicted on January 3, 1983, of conspiracy and mail fraud. He served 18 months of a three-year term. In 1987, the INS issued a show-cause order as to why Stone should not be deported. In January 1988, a judge ordered his deportation. In July 1991, Stone appealed to the Board of Immigration (BIA) to reconsider his deportation. The motion was denied as frivolous. Stone then appealed to the SC, which upheld the deportation order. The reason given was that a 90-day period for hearing appeals to final deportation orders had expired. It probably wouldn't have mattered if Stone's motion had been timely within the 90-day period, because persons convicted of mail fraud are barred from establishing "good moral character" for legal immigrant status.

Stone v. Powell, 428 U.S. 465, 96 S.Ct. 3037 (1976) **(Corrections; Inmate Rights; Searches and Seizures).** An inmate filed a habeas corpus petition in a federal court seeking release from prison. The prisoner had already filed the same petition in a state court and the petition had been denied. The SC heard the appeal and rejected the argument of the inmate, concluding that a habeas corpus petition will not be heard in federal court after it has already been rejected in a state court. The SC stressed the fact that the inmate had a full and fair opportunity to argue the case in a state appellate court.

Stoner v. California, 376 U.S. 364, 84 S.Ct. 889 (1964) **(Law Enforcement Officers or Agencies; Consent Searches).** Stoner became a suspect in an armed-robbery investigation when police discovered a checkbook on the ground near the robbery scene. The checkbook had Stoner's name in it and checks made out to a hotel in another city. They went to the hotel and learned that Stoner was staying there. Although Stoner wasn't in his room, the hotel clerk admitted the officers into Stoner's room, without an arrest or search warrant. The police found evidence linking Stoner with the robbery, and he was arrested and convicted. Later, he appealed, arguing that the police officers had lacked a valid search warrant to enter and search his room. The SC agreed, overturning Stoner's conviction and suppressing the discovered evidence. Hotel clerks are not in the position of granting consent to police for warrantless searches of hotel guest rooms. There is a reasonable expectation of privacy, and thus Stoner's Fourth Amendment right against an unreasonable search of his premises and seizure of personal effects had been violated.

Stovall v. Denno, 388 U.S. 293, 87 S.Ct. 1967 (1967) **(Law Enforcement Officers or Agencies; Lineups).** Stovall was a murder suspect. The victim's wife was so severely injured that she was hospitalized in critical condition. Stovall was brought by police to the hospital, where the victim's wife identified him as the murderer. He was convicted. He appealed, alleging that he should have been subjected to a lineup with other black persons, and that he was the only black suspect shown to the victim's wife. The SC upheld Stovall's conviction, saying that under the circumstances, the victim's wife was the only person in the world who could actually exonerate Stovall, by simply saying, "He is not the man." In this case, and under these circumstances, police identification methods had been proper. The usual police lineup believed by Stovall to be appropriate was totally out of the question, given the victim's wife's condition in the hospital. Thus, traditional lineups may be circumvented depending upon the circumstances.

Strickland v. Washington, 466 U.S. 668, 104 S.Ct. 2052 (1984) **(Effective Assistance of Counsel).** Conduct in Strickland's case of whether ineffective assistance of counsel was rendered was measured according to the following standards: Was the counsel's conduct such that it undermined the functioning of the adversarial process so much that a trial could not be relied upon to render a just result? Did the counsel's behavior fall below the objective standard of reasonableness? There must

be a reasonable probability that, but for counsel's unprofessional errors, the result of the proceedings would have been different.

Stringer v. Black, 503 U.S. 222, 112 S.Ct. 1130 (1992) **(Eighth Amendment; Death Penalty; Aggravating Factors).** Stringer was convicted of capital murder in Mississippi. The penalty phase following conviction contained judicial instructions to the jury about the aggravating circumstance of finding the crime "especially heinous, atrocious, or cruel." He was sentenced to death. At the time of Stringer's conviction two important cases had not yet been decided that would ultimately declare the phrase "especially heinous, atrocious, or cruel" to be unconstitutionally vague. These cases were, respectively, *Clemons v. Mississippi* (1990) and *Maynard v. Cartwright* (1988). Thus Stringer, in a habeas corpus petition filed after these cases had been decided, sought to have his death sentence vacated because of the new rule established in these cases. Lower courts of appeals denied Stringer any relief, and he appealed to the SC. The SC vacated Stringer's death sentence, holding that it had became final prior to cases establishing that a statute making the "especially heinous, atrocious, or cruel" nature of the crime an aggravating circumstance violated the Eighth Amendment, and was not precluded from relying on cases on the ground that they represented a new rule.

Strunk v. United States, 412 U.S. 434, 93 S.Ct. 2260 (1973) **(Speedy Trial).** Strunk was arrested for a crime, tried 10 months later, and convicted. He appealed, arguing that the 10-month delay had been a violation of his speedy-trial rights. The SC heard the case and noted several considerations in determining whether speedy-trial rights of suspects have been violated: (1) whether there are overcrowded court dockets and understaffed prosecutor's offices; (2) whether defendants suffered substantial emotional distress because of long delays; and (3) whether an accused is released pending a trial and whether there is little or no immediate interest in having a trial.

Sullivan v. Louisiana, 507 U.S.___, 113 S.Ct. 2078 (1993) **(Death Penalty; Jury Instructions).** Sullivan was convicted of first-degree murder and given the death penalty. He appealed to the SC, alleging that his Sixth Amendment right to a trial by jury had been violated when the jury was given unconstitutional instructions about the meaning of reasonable doubt. The SC agreed and reversed Sullivan's conviction and death sentence. The basis for the reversal of conviction was the improper and unconstitutional phraseology used by the judge for the jury instructions about how to evaluate reasonable doubt. (*See Cage v. Louisiana* [1990] for a comparable case and the unconstitutional phraseology.)

Sumner v. Shuman, 483 U.S. 66, 107 S.Ct. 2716 (1987) **(Corrections; Death Penalty).** In Nevada, Shuman was convicted of first-degree murder and sentenced to life-without-parole. While in prison, he murdered another inmate and was convicted of this second murder. This time, he was sentenced to the death penalty. He appealed. Nevada had a statute imposing a mandatory death penalty on prisoners who commit murder while imprisoned and already serving life terms. The SC overturned Shuman's death sentence, indicating that mandatory death penalties are unconstitutional. The reason they are is because they do not consider aggravating and mitigating circumstances.

Superintendent, Massachusetts Correctional Institution, Walpole v. Hill, 472 U.S. 445, 105 S.Ct. 2768 (1985) **(Corrections; Inmate Rights).** Hill, an inmate at the Massachusetts State Prison at Walpole, received a disciplinary report charging that he had assaulted another inmate. Evidence consisted solely of an inmate's word that he saw three inmates moving away from an area where an inmate was subsequently found who had been beaten. An inference was made that Hill had assaulted the injured inmate, but no eyewitnesses had been present. The board decided in the absence of strong evidence that Hill was guilty and it placed him in isolation for 15 days with a loss of 100 days of good-time credit. Hill appealed. The SC upheld Hill's "sentence" imposed by the board because a lesser evidentiary standard exists in prison disciplinary hearings compared with evidentiary standards in court. From the limited factual evidence presented, a reasonable inference could have been drawn that Hill had been involved in the assault.

T

Tate v. Short, 401 U.S. 395, 91 S.Ct. 668 (1971) **(Corrections; Probation and Parole).** An indigent, Tate was unable to pay fines to a Houston traffic court. The court imposed cumulative fines of $425, which it ordered Tate to pay at the rate of $5 per day while incarcerated. He appealed. The SC overturned Tate's conviction and ruled such a method of fine repayment to be obviously unconstitutional. It was a violation of Tate's Fourteenth Amendment right to equal protection under the law to impose such a fine and incarceration repayment method. Fines cannot be converted to imprisonment in the event indigents cannot pay these fines. This would be tantamount to debtor's prisons, where debtors, unable to earn money, would be incarcerated until they could pay.

Taylor v. Alabama, 457 U.S. 687, 102 S.Ct. 2664 (1982) **(Law Enforcement Officers or Agencies; Exclusionary Rule).** Taylor was suspected of robbery. An uncorroborated tip from an informant led to his warrantless arrest without probable cause, where he was subjected to a grueling interrogation and lineup. Eventually, Taylor signed a confession, which was admitted into trial against him, and he was convicted. He appealed. The SC reversed Taylor's conviction, holding that the confession had been extracted illegally, through coercion, and could not be used against him. The confession should have been suppressed because it was the fruit of an illegal arrest.

Taylor v. Illinois, 484 U.S. 400, 108 S.Ct. 646 (1988) **(Eighth Amendment; Discovery and Cross-Examination).** In 1984, Taylor had a street fight with Bridges and Taylor attempted to kill him. Taylor had prepared for the fight by bringing a pipe and a gun. He beat Bridges with the pipe and shot him in the back. Taylor attempted to shoot Bridges in the head while Bridges was lying on the ground, but the gun misfired. All of this testimony and other incriminating evidence was presented at Taylor's trial. During the trial, Taylor's attorney attempted to introduce a late witness, Wormley, who allegedly had exculpatory information. The judge listened to Wormley's testimony outside the presence of the jury, and decided that Wormley should not be called as a defense witness because he lacked veracity and because the defense counsel had violated the rules of discovery by failing to notify the prosecution about Wormley in advance. Taylor was convicted. He appealed, alleging that his right to a fair trial had been violated when Wormley was not permitted to testify. The SC heard the case and rejected Taylor's arguments. It was not constitutional error to prohibit Wormley from testifying, said the SC.

Further, the voir dire examination of Wormley had probably protected the prosecution from undue prejudice resulting from *surprise*. Further, it was not unfair to hold Taylor responsible for his lawyer's misconduct. The defense has full authority to manage the conduct of the trial, and the client must accept the consequences of the lawyer's trial decisions.

Taylor v. Kentucky, 436 U.S. 478, 98 S.Ct. 1930 (1978) **(Jury Instructions)**. Taylor was accused of second-degree robbery. At the conclusion of his trial, the judge issued several jury instructions, but he failed to advise the jury about the "presumption of innocence" to which the defendant was entitled, which could be overcome by proof beyond a reasonable doubt. Taylor was convicted. He appealed to the SC, which overturned his conviction. The SC said that the judge's omission of the presumption-of-innocence statement had resulted in a violation of Taylor's right to a fair trial.

Taylor v. Louisiana, 419 U.S. 522, 95 S.Ct. 2664 (1975) **(Corrections; Death Penalty)**. Taylor was convicted of aggravated kidnapping by a jury consisting entirely of men, because Louisiana had a statute prohibiting females from jury service. He appealed. The SC overturned Taylor's conviction on the grounds that his due-process rights had been violated when women were systematically excluded from the jury. Thus, Louisiana's law excluding women from jury duty is unconstitutional.

Taylor v. United States, 286 U.S. 1, 52 S.Ct. 466 (1932) **(Law Enforcement Officers or Agencies; Arrests)**. Revenue agents received complaints over a period of one year about a residence where allegedly illegal whiskey was being manufactured. One evening, agents went to the address. Finding no one home, they went around the house to a garage, which was locked. They smelled what seemed to be whiskey coming from within the garage, and they shined their flashlights inside and saw cardboard boxes, which they assumed contained illegal whiskey. They broke into the garage and searched the boxes, retrieving illegal whiskey. They charged Taylor with having untaxed and illegal whiskey, and he was convicted. He appealed. The SC held the actions of the investigating agents to have been unreasonable. It declared that agents cannot base their reasons for search on odor of whiskey alone, without more supporting factual information. Their purpose was to secure evidence so that they could support some future arrest of Taylor. The conviction against Taylor was overturned.

Teague v. Lane, 489 U.S. 288, 109 S.Ct. 1060 (1989) **(Double Jeopardy)**. Teague, a black man, was accused of attempted murder. During jury selection, the prosecutor used all of his 10 peremptory challenges to exclude blacks from the jury. He was eventually convicted by an all-white jury. In the meantime, *Batson v. Kentucky* had recently been decided, in which blacks could not be excluded from jury duty by use of peremptory challenges. Teague sought to make this rule retroactive in his case, thus causing his conviction to be overturned and a new trial conducted. The SC rejected the retroactive principle relating to *Batson*, holding that convicted offenders are barred from making retroactive claims involving racial discrimination in jury selection. Further, Teague had failed to make a convincing case that the peremptory challenges had been used in a discriminatory fashion.

Tennessee v. Garner, 471 U.S. 1, 105 S.Ct. 1694 (1985) **(Law Enforcement Officers or Agencies; Deadly Force)**. A 15-year-old boy, Garner, and a friend were in an empty home in Memphis late at night when neighbors reported the "breaking and entering" to police. Police officers approached the home and saw someone fleeing. They shouted warnings to the fleeing suspects and finally shot at them. One bullet struck Garner in the back of the head, killing him instantly. The standard governing the use of deadly force was that *any* force could be employed, even deadly force, to prevent the escape of fleeing felons. Because burglary is a felony, those fleeing from the empty home were felony suspects and police believed they were entitled to shoot at them. Many years later, in 1985, the SC declared that deadly force had not been warranted in this case, as burglary is punishable with a few years in prison, not the death penalty. This landmark case was significant because it effectively nullified the fleeing-felon standard for using deadly force. Since then, deadly force may be applied to fleeing suspects only (1) if they pose a threat to the lives of officers or (2) if they pose a threat to the lives of others.

Terry v. Ohio, 392 U.S. 1, 88 S.Ct. 1868 (1968) **(Law Enforcement Officers or Agencies; Search and Seizure)**. A 35-year veteran police officer observed Terry and two companions standing on a Cleveland street corner. They moved up and down the street, looking in store windows, returning frequently to the corner and conversing. The officer was suspicious of this behavior and confronted them about their identities and business. He patted down Terry and discovered a revolver. Terry was charged with carrying a concealed weapon and convicted. Terry appealed and the SC eventually heard the case. The argument was whether police officers may "pat down and frisk" suspicious persons if they have reasonable suspicion that a crime is being contemplated. The SC upheld Terry's conviction, determining that police officers may pat down suspects as a means of protecting themselves and determining whether suspicious persons may be armed and pose a danger to them. (*See Sibron v. New York* [1968] as a limitation to the pat-down-and-frisk ruling in *Terry.*)

Texas v. Brown, 460 U.S. 730, 103 S.Ct. 1319 (1983) **(Law Enforcement Officers or Agencies; Search and Seizure).** Brown was a motorist stopped by police at a routine driver's license checkpoint. Brown was asked to show officers his driver's license, and while he was fumbling for it, a party balloon dropped out of his pocket. It appeared to be tied at one end. Officers knew or had strong reason to believe that such balloons were often receptacles for drugs, such as cocaine. Brown continued to search for his license, and he reached into his glove compartment. When he did so, the officer shined his flashlight into the glove box and saw in plain view other party balloons, including glassine envelopes containing a white substance. One balloon was retrieved by an officer and examined more closely. The balloon contained cocaine, and Brown was subsequently convicted of cocaine possession. He appealed, arguing that the search of his vehicle had violated his Fourth Amendment rights, because the cocaine had not been in plain view. In this case, the SC upheld the validity of the officer's search of these balloons, saying that the police do not have to be absolutely certain that an object contains contraband in order for it to be inspected and seized under the plain-view rule. The plain-view rule states that officers may seize any apparent illegal contraband if it is in plain view and if they are in a place they are entitled to be at the time they view it. Thus, police officers might accompany paramedics to a rescue of a heart attack victim and observe illegal drugs on the victim's nightstand. The contraband is subject to seizure, because the police are in a place they have a right to be when they see it in plain view.

Texas v. McCullough, 475 U.S. 134, 91 S.Ct. 547 (1971) **(Double Jeopardy; Plea Bargaining).** McCullough was convicted of murder in a Texas court and sentenced to 20 years by a jury. Because of prosecutorial misconduct, however, the judge declared that McCullough should receive a new trial. This time, a new trial also resulted in his conviction for murder, but McCullough elected to have the judge fix his sentence. The judge imposed a sentence of 50 years rather than the 20-year sentence imposed in the earlier trial. McCullough appealed, arguing that the increased sentence length was the result of judicial vindictiveness. The SC disagreed and upheld the judge's 50-year sentence, saying that the judge was the same one who had detected prosecutorial misconduct and ordered the new trial for McCullough. Thus, an interpretation of vindictiveness was overcome by the judge's behavior of fairness in supporting a new trial for McCullough.

Thigpen v. Roberts, 468 U.S. 27, 104 S.Ct. 2916 (1984) **(Sixth Amendment; Right to Appeal).** Roberts had been intoxicated while driving a pickup truck carrying a passenger, and the passenger was subsequently killed in an accident Roberts caused. He was convicted of several misdemeanors, including reckless driving, driving while his license was revoked, driving on the wrong side of the road, and driving while intoxicated. He appealed. A subsequent trial *de novo* was granted under Mississippi law. Before the trial could take place, an indictment was issued against Roberts for manslaughter, arising out of the same incident for which he had been convicted earlier. Roberts appealed the new indictment as unconstitutional, while his case was under appeal to a higher court. He was nevertheless tried on the manslaughter charge, convicted, and sentenced to a 20-year prison term. He filed a habeas corpus petition, alleging that it was unconstitutional for the state to try him on a manslaughter charge before his appeal could be heard on the previous misdemeanor charges. The SC heard his case and agreed with Roberts, because of the violation of his due-process rights. The SC declared that the prosecution of Roberts for manslaughter, following his invocation of his statutory right to appeal his misdemeanor convictions, had been unconstitutional. The resulting conviction could not stand.

Thompson v. Keohane, ___U.S.___, 116 S.Ct. 457 (1995) **(Law Enforcement Officers or Agencies; Custodial Interrogations; Confessions).** Two moose hunters in Alaska discovered the body of a woman who had been stabbed 29 times. A bulletin was issued by state troopers to the public at large for assistance in determining her identity. Thompson informed police that his missing wife, Dixie, seemed to fit the description of the victim. Thompson drove to the trooper's headquarters in his truck and identified certain of the victim's items as belonging to his wife. While at the headquarters, he was told by investigating officers that although he was free to leave at any time, they *knew* he had killed his wife and they suggested that he confess. Thompson was further advised during his presumed "noncustodial interrogation" that officers were preparing search warrants for his truck and home, and that they would probably discover something incriminating anyway. Thompson was being held in a small interview room with a tape recorder. He broke down and confessed. Following his confession, he was allowed to leave the troopers' headquarters. The police impounded his truck, but they gave him a ride home. Two hours later, after obtaining an arrest warrant, they arrived and arrested him for first-degree murder. Thompson was convicted of murder. He appealed. The SC was asked to determine whether Thompson had or had not been in custodial interrogation at the time his confession was made. If he had been in custody, then police would have had to tell him his Miranda rights first in order for his confession to be properly admissible later in court. In this instance, the SC used the following two-pronged standard: (1) What were the circumstances surrounding the interrogation? and (2) given those circumstances, would a reasonable person have felt he or she was not at liberty to terminate the interrogation and leave? Without providing a direct answer to this question, the SC vacated Thompson's murder conviction and remanded the case to a lower federal court for a habeas corpus action to determine the custody question. In essence, a subsequent court would determine whether Thompson had been in custody at the time he was interrogated; pending the outcome of this determination, his murder conviction was temporarily vacated.

Thompson v. Louisiana, 469 U.S. 17, 105 S.Ct. 409 (1984) **(Law Enforcement Officers or Agencies; Fourth Amendment; Warrantless Searches of Residences).** In May 1982, Jefferson Parish police officers responded to a report of a homicide by the daughter of Thompson. They went to the house and found Thompson's husband dead of a gunshot wound and Thompson lying unconscious nearby, apparently having recently ingested a drug overdose in a suicide attempt. The daughter reported that her mother had shot the father and then ingested a quantity of pills to attempt suicide. The officers transported Thompson to the hospital, where she was treated for a drug overdose, and they also secured the crime scene. Homicide investigators, without a warrant, arrived a few hours later and conducted a thorough search of every room in the house, discovering a pistol and other evidence. Because the search had been warrantless, Thompson sought to suppress the evidence (e.g., the gun and a suicide note, among other things) from the trial proceedings. Nevertheless, all evidence was subsequently admitted against her in a trial, and she was convicted of second-degree murder. She appealed. The SC said that a nonconsensual and warrantless search of the premises had been conducted by police who had had time to get a valid search warrant but had not done so. Therefore, the evidence against Thompson they had seized was inadmissible. The conviction was overturned.

Thompson v. Oklahoma, 487 U.S. 815, 108 S.Ct. 2687 (1988) **(Juveniles; Death Penalty).** Thompson was 15 years old when his brother-in-law was brutally murdered. Thompson was suspected. Under Oklahoma law, the district attorney filed a statutory petition to have him waived to criminal court, where he could be tried for murder as an adult. The waiver was granted and Thompson was tried, convicted, and sentenced to death. Thompson appealed, and his case was eventually reviewed by the SC. The SC concluded that "the Eighth and Fourteenth Amendments prohibit the execution of a person who was under 16 years of age at the time of his or her offense" (108 S.Ct. at 2700). Thompson's death sentence was overturned. Thompson's attorney had originally requested the Court to draw a line so that all those under age 18 would be exempt from the death penalty as a punishment, regardless of their crimes. The SC refused to do this. (*See also Stanford v. Kentucky* and *Wilkins v. Missouri*.)

Thornburgh v. Abbott, 490 U.S. 401, 109 S.Ct. 1874 (1989) **(Corrections; Inmate Rights).** Several federal prisoners filed suit against the Federal

Bureau of Prisons (FBP) to contest the regulations pertaining to the receipt of publications from different publishers. The FBP policy disallowed inmates to receive publications that were deemed detrimental to institutional order or discipline. The SC agreed with the FBP and its policy, saying that the government, in disallowing certain publications, must show (1) that there is a rational connection between the policy and the government interest put forward to justify it; (2) that there is a potential impact of the policy on correctional staff and inmates alike; (3) whether there are alternative means of asserting rights available to prisoners; and (4) the existence of available alternatives to the regulation (*see the case of Turner v. Safely* [1987] for a comparative ruling).

Tison v. Arizona, 481 U.S. 137, 107 S.Ct. 1676 (1987) **(Corrections; Death Penalty).** Tison was the son of a convicted murderer. He and his brother planned the escape of their father from prison by entering it with an ice chest filled with guns. They armed their father and another convicted murderer, who escaped with their father. Later, in Tison's presence, the father and the other convicted murderer abducted, robbed, and killed a family of four. Tison did nothing to prevent his father and the other man from killing the family. In fact, when apprehended later, Tison expressed surprise that the murders had occurred and denied any direct culpability. All four men were convicted. Under the felony-murder statute in Arizona, Tison and his brother were sentenced to death as the result of the felony-murder conviction. They appealed their death sentences, contending that they had not specifically killed anyone; therefore, they should receive a less serious sentence. The SC disagreed and upheld their death sentence, holding that their participation in the felony murder was major, and their mental state was one of reckless indifference to human life. Persons who do not actually kill others but participate in their killing may receive the death penalty.

Tower v. Glover, 467 U.S. 914, 104 S.Ct. 2820 (1984) **(Legal Liabilities).** Glover was charged with robbery. Tower represented Glover at his trial. Glover suspected that Tower had conspired with various state officials in negotiating his conviction. Glover appealed. Tower countered by alleging that he was immune from Title 42, U.S.C. Section 1983 suits. Also, a lower appellate court said that Glover had failed to make a valid argument concerning any conspiracy to convict him.

Glover appealed again. The SC heard the case and ruled in Glover's favor. The SC said that Glover's complaint adequately alleged conduct under "color of state law" for purposes of a Section 1983 action. Also, state public defenders are not immune from liability under this same section. The SC did not rule on the factual accuracy of the allegations; it merely said that Glover has a right to pursue his case in court.

Townsend v. Burke, 334 U.S. 736, 68 S.Ct. 1252 (1948) **(Corrections; Sixth Amendment Rights at Sentencing Hearings).** Townsend was a fugitive who had been indicted for burglary and armed robbery in 1945. Several of his accomplices had made confessions to police implicating him. He was arrested later in 1945, and he pleaded guilty to two charges of robbery and two charges of burglary. He was sentenced to a long prison term. He appealed on various grounds. First, he alleged that he had not been represented by counsel when he pleaded guilty in court. Second, he argued that his long detention by police without access to an attorney was unreasonable. He had also not been advised of the particularity of his crimes or the punishments associated with them. Thus he alleged that his due-process rights had been violated. The SC overturned his conviction and remanded the case for a new trial, holding that while counsel might not have changed the sentence, he could have taken steps to see that the conviction and sentence were not predicated on misinformation or misreading of court records, a requirement of fair play which absence of counsel withheld from this prisoner. Convicted offenders have the right to counsel at the time of their sentencing.

Townsend v. Sain, 372 U.S. 293, 83 S.Ct. 745 (1963) **(Law Enforcement Officers or Agencies; Confessions; Probation and Parole).** Townsend was suspected of murder in Cook County, Illinois. Following his arrest, he was subjected to intensive questioning by police. A doctor from the police department administered Townsend an injection of phenobarbital, known as "truth serum." Under this drug, Townsend gave a confession. He was convicted. He appealed, recanting his confession and saying it had been given involuntarily. He asked to have his confession testimony excluded. His request was rejected, and the doctor who administered the truth serum was not required to testify, although Townsend's attorney had made such a request. Townsend appealed to the SC, which overturned his conviction, and remanded the case for retrial, not intending to question the factual evidence but rather, to allow the originating trial court the opportunity of hearing the evidence concerning the concealment of testimony by the doctor about the phenobarbital and other matters. Factual discrepancies would be resolved through further court action.

Trammel v. United States, 445 U.S. 40, 100 S.Ct. 906 (1980) **(Spousal Incrimination).** Otis Trammel was charged with importing and conspiring to import heroin in the United States district court of Colorado. Before the trial, government prosecutors indicated their intention to call Trammel's wife to testify against him. Trammel objected on the grounds that people cannot be compelled to make incriminating statements to others about their spouses. Trammel's wife was granted immunity and testified against Trammel voluntarily. He was convicted. Trammel appealed, moving to suppress her testimony. The SC upheld Trammel's conviction, holding that people may voluntarily act as witnesses against their spouses. Trammel's wife had been granted immunity from prosecution and thus had testified freely. The fact that she was the defendant's wife was immaterial to whether she testified voluntarily. She could have refused to testify. Thus Trammel's claim of spousal privilege was rejected.

Trop v. Dulles, 356 U.S. 86, 78 S.Ct. 590 (1958) **(Corrections; Inmate Rights).** Trop was an American citizen stationed in French Morocco during World War II. One day he escaped from a stockade where he had been confined briefly for a breach of discipline. Later in the day, he was picked up by military authorities as he was walking back to the military compound. He was charged with desertion and given a general court-martial. His sentence was three years hard labor and a dishonorable discharge, among other things. In 1952, Trop applied for a passport but was denied one because he had lost his citizenship as the result of the conviction and dishonorable discharge. Trop appealed. He contended that the loss of citizenship was cruel and unusual punishment. The SC agreed and reinstated Trop's citizenship. Loss of citizenship may constitute cruel and unusual punishment in view of the offense.

Tuggle v. Netherland, ___U.S.___, 116 S.Ct. 283 (1995) **(Death Penalty; Jury Instructions; Consideration of Aggravating and Mitigating Circumstances).** Tuggle was accused of first-degree murder in a Virginia court. During the trial,

unrebutted testimony was given by a psychiatrist indicating Tuggle's future dangerousness and "vileness" as an aggravating circumstance. He was convicted. He appealed, alleging that the state had not afforded him, as an indigent, the opportunity of rebutting the "dangerousness" prediction made by the state psychiatrist. The SC remanded the case (*Tuggle v. Virginia*, 471 U.S. 1096, 105 S.Ct. 2315 [1985]) to the Virginia Supreme Court, which invalidated the "future dangerousness" aggravating circumstance but nevertheless upheld Tuggle's death sentence. Then Tuggle sought to invalidate the death sentence on grounds that a constitutional error had been committed and that a new trial should be granted. The SC heard Tuggle's appeal and remanded the case to the Fourth Circuit Court of Appeals. The SC concluded by saying that invalidation of one aggravator does not necessarily require that the death sentence should be set aside, but existence of a valid aggravator does not always excuse constitutional error in admission or exclusion of evidence. Essentially, the Fourth Circuit Court was to determine whether such error was "harmless" or "reversible."

Turner v. Louisiana, 379 U.S. 466, 85 S.Ct. 546 (1965) **(Fair Trials; Court Officer Involvement with Jurors).** In a three-day murder trial, deputy sheriffs were in continuous contact with jurors, eating meals with them and chatting with them informally about the trial. Later, the deputies testified against Turner, and he was convicted. Turner appealed, arguing that substantial prejudice against him had been created by the deputy sheriff-juror relation. The SC agreed and reversed his conviction, holding that the credibility attached to the deputy sheriff's testimony by the jury was such that the jury could not have been impartial in their deliberations.

Turner v. Murray, 476 U.S. 28, 106 S.Ct. 1683 (1986) **(Jury Trials; Jury Selection).** Turner was accused of an interracial crime. During voir dire, he asked the judge to insist that prospective jurors be advised of the victim's race and questioned about their possible racial bias. The judge denied this request. Turner was convicted. He appealed to the SC, which overturned the conviction, saying that defendants under the Sixth and Fourteenth Amendments are entitled to insist that prospective jurors be advised of the victim's race as well as whether the jurors have racial bias (*see Ristaino v. Ross* [1986] and *Ham v. South Carolina* [1976).

Turner v. Safley, 482 U.S. 78, 107 S.Ct. 2254 (1987) **(Corrections; Inmate Rights)**. Prison inmates filed a class-action suit against the Missouri Division of Corrections, alleging that prison regulations forbidding or restricting mail between family members who are inmates at other institutions are unconstitutional. Further, the inmates alleged that a rule was unconstitutional that permitted inmates to marry only when there were compelling circumstances, such as pregnancy or the birth of an illegitimate child. The SC declared that regulations prohibiting inmate marriages are unconstitutional. However, regulations regarding mail exchanges between related inmates in different prisons, as well as other inmate rights, should be determined as follows: such regulations are valid as long as they are related reasonably to legitimate penological interests, such as prison security, rehabilitation, security, and the orderly running of the institution. Thus this case sets specific standards that declare the difference between inmate and institutional rights. Institutional regulations will prevail under the conditions specified above. One example of why prisons would *not* want to permit certain types of mail exchanges between prisoners in different institutions is the potential for institutional disruption and the perpetuation of inmate gang activities. Gang members of different institutions would be in a better position to establish regular mail networks between other gang members elsewhere. This is a legitimate concern and penological interest that would suffice to prohibit such prisoner information exchanges.

U

United States v. A Parcel of Land in Rumson, N.J., 507 U.S. 111, 113 S.Ct. 1126 (1993) **(Asset Forfeiture)**. The SC declared that in asset-forfeiture cases, innocent parties cannot have their property seized by the government as the result of criminal activities committed by others. Thus, if assets associated with drug transactions are later acquired by a new and innocent owner, the government cannot seize this property from the new and innocent owner.

United States v. Aguilar, ___U.S.___, 115 S.Ct. 2357 (1995) **(Judicial Misconduct; Crimes Committed by Judges)**. A grand jury had convened to investigate a crime. A wiretap had been placed on a suspect's telephone. Following the expiration of the wiretap, Aguilar, a federal judge, advised certain persons outside the United States Department of Justice that such a wiretap had been placed, thus potentially obstructing justice. The FBI interviewed Judge Aguilar, in order to report back to the grand jury, and he gave false statements to it. Aguilar was charged with and convicted of (1) obstructing justice by disclosing the fact that a wiretap had been placed on a suspect's telephone; and (2) of giving false statements to the FBI during a grand jury investigation. Aguilar appealed, contending that the fact that the wiretap order had expired had removed any obligation on his part to remain quiet about it. Further, he contended that he had had no idea that the FBI would report his false statements to the grand jury. The SC heard Aguilar's appeal. The SC upheld the obstruction-of-justice charge, holding that the expiration of the wiretap order did not relieve Aguilar of the obligation to refrain from telling anyone about it. However, it overturned his conviction for making false statements to the FBI, because, they reasoned, the judge did not know such false statements were intended for grand jury purposes.

United States v. Agurs, 427 U.S. 97, 96 S.Ct. 2392 (1976) **(Discovery)**. Agurs was charged with first-degree murder in the killing of her boyfriend, Sewell. Sewell was known to carry knives. Agurs took one away from him and stabbed him repeatedly. During her trial, information about Sewell's prior criminal record of assault and carrying a deadly weapon and his bad character were excluded from the prosecution's case against Agurs. Agurs was convicted. She appealed, arguing that this information about the victim would have helped her own case. The SC upheld Agurs's conviction, holding that the prosecutor was under no constitutional duty to disclose or volunteer any exculpatory information in the case against Agurs. The SC adopted a standard for evaluating the materiality of evidence. If such evidence would have been persuasive and produced reasonable doubt about the guilt of the defendant, then it would have been material. Under the circumstances, however, such disclosures would have been irrelevant.

United States v. Alvarez-Machain, 504 U.S. 655, 112 S.Ct. 2188 (1992) **(Law Enforcement Officers or Agencies; Arrest)**. A Mexican citizen, Alvarez-Machain, was indicted in the United States by federal authorities for his role in the murder of a DEA agent. Alvarez-Machain was abducted by federal agents in Mexico and taken back to the United States by force to face trial. He was convicted. He appealed, contending that his abduction by federal agents had violated the Extradition Treaty between Mexico and the United States, which therefore lacked the authority to try him. The SC disagreed and upheld his conviction. The SC said that no violation of the treaty existed, and that simple abduction of a criminal suspect by force from another country did not deprive the United States of jurisdiction over that criminal case.

United States v. Apfelbaum, 445 U.S. 115, 100 S.Ct. 948 (1980) **(Self-Incrimination).** Apfelbaum was granted immunity by the government in exchange for his testimony before a grand jury. He testified falsely at the grand jury proceeding and was later indicted and convicted of a crime, where his grand jury testimony was used against him. He appealed, contending that his Fifth Amendment right against self-incrimination had been violated when the government used his "immune" grand jury testimony. The SC upheld Apfelbaum's conviction, saying that the Fifth Amendment right against self-incrimination does not protect false testimony given before grand juries. Thus, any false testimony before a grand jury may be used as evidence against someone, regardless of whether immunity had previously been granted in exchange for that testimony.

United States v. Ash, 413 U.S. 300, 93 S.Ct. 1568 (1973) **(Lineups; Right to Counsel).** Ash, a black man, was suspected of intent to rob a federally insured bank. A government informant, McFarland, brought Ash's name to the attention of the FBI, and color photographs of Ash and other blacks were shown to witnesses at the bank. They made uncertain identifications of Ash. Subsequently, Ash was indicted for the robbery and arrested. Color photographs were again shown to witnesses, but a black-and-white photograph of Ash was included. Again, witnesses were uncertain about Ash's identity. Trial was held almost three years following the robbery. Most witnesses could not positively identify Ash, but testimony was presented against him by McFarland. Ash was convicted and sentenced to concurrent sentences of 80 months to 12 years. Ash appealed. He contended that his attorney should have been present at the photo ID sessions. The SC did not specifically rule on the merits of Ash's conviction, but it

did remand the case to the trial court for further proceedings on other issues. The SC said, however, that the Sixth Amendment does not grant the right to counsel in photographic displays conducted by the government for the purpose of allowing the witness to attempt to identify offenders.

United States v. Bachsian, 4 F.3rd 288 (1993) **(Corrections; Restitution).** Bachsian was convicted of theft. He was required to pay restitution for the merchandise still in his possession under the Victim Witness Protection Act. Bachsian claimed, however that he was indigent and unable to make restitution. The ninth Circuit Court of Appeals declared in Bachsian's case that it was *not* improper to impose restitution orders on an offender at the time of sentencing, even if the offender was unable to pay restitution then. In this instance, records indicated that Bachsian was considered by the court as having a future ability to pay, based on a presentence investigation report. Eventually, Bachsian would become financially able and in a position to make restitution to his victim. His restitution orders were upheld. Also, bankruptcy does not discharge an offender's obligation to make restitution, although the *amount* and *rate* of restitution payments may be affected (*see Baker v. State* [1993]; *State v. Hayes* [1993]).

United States v. Bagley, 473 U.S. 667, 105 S.Ct. 3375 (1985) **(Discovery).** As a result of an undercover investigation by the Bureau of Alcohol, Tobacco, and Firearms (BATF), Bagley was indicted in the United States District Court in Washington for breaking various narcotics and firearms statutes. His attorney filed a motion for discovery, obligating the government to disclose evidentiary materials it planned to use in court against Bagley, specifically, any documents that might be interpreted as "inducements, deals, or promises" made to government informants. The government supplied his attorney with various documents, including writings from various government witnesses. A trial was held and Bagley was convicted. Later, he filed for additional government documentation under the Freedom of Information Act. New materials he received indicated that some of the government witnesses had received payment for their services and informant work. Bagley sought to overturn his conviction with this new information, alleging that the government had not complied with the discovery requirement. The SC heard Bagley's appeal and upheld his conviction, ruling that the "newly discovered" information would be materially relevant only if the introduction of this new evidence would have resulted in a different trial outcome. Other evidence was more than sufficient to establish Bagley's guilt beyond any reasonable doubt. The SC acknowledged that the defense's case had been hampered to an extent by the nondisclosure of this information. Nevertheless, the SC said that the new information would not have affected the conviction significantly.

United States v. Benchimol, 471 U.S. 453, 105 S.Ct. 2103 (1985) **(Plea Bargaining).** Following a plea-bargaining conviction, the offender appealed, saying that the prosecutor did not make a recommendation enthusiastically. The SC upheld the conviction, saying that prosecutors are under no obligation to make recommendations or to make them enthusiastically.

United States v. Biswell, 408 U.S. 311, 92 S.Ct. 1593 (1972) **(Corrections; Probation and Parole).** Biswell was a firearms dealer. Under the Gun Control Act of 1968, a police officer and a Treasury agent visited Biswell at his place of business. They asked to inspect his books and a locked gun locker. When Biswell asked if they had a search warrant, they replied that they didn't need one. A subsequent search yielded illegal weapons, including sawed-off shotguns that Biswell was not licensed to possess. He was convicted of violating firearms laws. He appealed and the SC heard his case, in which he alleged that the agents had needed a search warrant to search his premises. The SC upheld his conviction, holding that regulatory inspections of businesses may proceed without warrants where specifically authorized by statute. Thus they held the search of Biswell's business by these officers and agents to be reasonable and not violative of his Fourth Amendment rights.

United States v. Brignoni-Ponce, 422 U.S. 873, 95 S.Ct. 2574 (1975) **(Law Enforcement Officers or Agencies; Vehicle Searches).** The Border Patrol stopped a vehicle containing persons apparently of Mexican descent. Officers asked about their illegal-alien status and other concerns and searched the vehicle, which yielded contraband. The result was a conviction. An appeal to the SC resulted in a declaration that the Border Patrol may not stop automobiles simply because of the apparent Mexican ancestry of the occupants. Border Patrol stops are justified only by consent, probable cause, or an awareness of specifically articulable facts, together with rational inferences therefrom.

United States v. Broce, 488 U.S. 563, 109 S.Ct. 757 (1989) **(Plea Bargaining).** Broce and another person entered guilty pleas in United States District Court to two separate charges of conspiracy, specifically to rig bids on certain state highway projects. Following their conviction on the two charges, Broce attempted to have their two conspiracies treated as one conspiracy and thus to have the earlier convictions set aside. He claimed, among other things, that the "two" conspiracies resulted from a common deal or incident and that there was truly only one conspiracy. Thus the second conspiracy conviction was double jeopardy under the law. The SC heard Broce's case and determined that their plea bargains had been voluntarily entered into and their pleas of guilty to the two charges had been accepted by the court. The guilty pleas and convictions foreclosed the double-jeopardy challenge and the convictions stood.

United States v. Calandra, 414 U.S. 338, 94 S.Ct. 613 (1974) **(Unlawful Searches and Seizures).** Calandra became a suspect in a loan-shark operation when his name was found on a card possessed by others involved in this activity. When he was summoned to appear before a grand jury investigating the matter, he refused to testify, saying that this was an "illegal search and seizure" in violation of his Fourth Amendment rights. The SC disagreed, saying that this privilege may not be invoked for purposes of testifying to the grand jury.

United States v. Chadwick, 433 U.S. 1, 97 S.Ct. 2476 (1977) **(Law Enforcement Officers or Agencies; Search and Seizure).** The DEA established a "courier profile" of persons in the 1970s who trafficked in narcotics. Such profiles were used to stop and search suspicious persons at ports of entry into the United States, in airports, bus terminals, and rail stations. Chadwick was a train passenger in San Diego traveling to Boston. San Diego DEA officials observed that he was carrying a large footlocker, which appeared to be leaking talcum powder, a substance often used to disguise the odor of marijuana. DEA agents in Boston intercepted Chadwick, in the company of two others, just as he was about to place the footlocker in the trunk of an automobile. The agents arrested Chadwick and his companions and took them and the footlocker to a nearby federal building, where the footlocker was subsequently opened without warrant or permission from Chadwick, yielding a large quantity of marijuana. The DEA agents justified their warrantless search of the footlocker by citing "exigent circumstances"; they had had to act quickly to prevent Chadwick and his friends from disposing of the illegal contraband. Chadwick was subsequently convicted on drug-related charges. He appealed, moving to suppress the footlocker evidence by contending that police had lacked a valid search warrant. The SC overturned Chadwick's conviction, noting that the footlocker was "luggage" and thus a warrantless search of it was unjustified. The SC stressed the fact that the footlocker was only "incidentally" about to be loaded into a vehicle; although police officers were ordinarily entitled to search a vehicle and its contents in a "search incident to an arrest," a warrant must be obtained to search any luggage found. This holding was modified in *United States v. Ross* (1982), where officers needed no warrant to search paper bags, leather pouches, and glove compartments of cars when arresting suspects because of the lesser standard applying to them pertaining to an expectation of privacy. *California v. Acevedo* (1991) greatly modified the Chadwick holding.

United States v. Chavez, 416 U.S. 562, 94 S.Ct. 1849 (1974) **(Electronic Surveillance).** Chavez was indicted for conspiracy to distribute cocaine. As a part of the RICO statute, wiretaps may be ordered on requests from the United States Attorney General or the Assistant Attorney General. Wiretaps were ordered for Chavez's telephone line by the executive assistant to the United States Attorney General. They disclosed considerable incriminating information. Chavez's attorneys moved to suppress this information on the grounds that procedurally, the person who ordered the wiretaps was not authorized to do so. The trial court granted the motion to suppress and the government appealed. The SC reversed the motion to suppress. It held, however, that when it is clearly established that authorization for a wiretap has been given by the Attorney General, but the application and interception order incorrectly states that approval has instead been given by a specially designated executive assistant to the Attorney General, the misidentification, by itself, will not render telephonic interceptions "unlawful." Thus the granted motion to suppress was in error. However, it is appropriate to recommend in the future that "strict adherence" by the government to the

provisions for authorizing wiretaps be more in keeping with congressional intent of the RICO statute whenever wiretaps are ordered. (*See United States v. Giordano* [1974] for a comparative case.)

United States v. Cortez, 449 U.S. 411, 101 S.Ct. 690 (1981) **(Law Enforcement Officers or Agencies; Search and Seizure).** Border Patrol officers were investigating trafficking in illegal aliens between the Mexican-United States border. They discovered a path which appeared to be one used by illegal aliens entering the United States. There were some distinctive shoe prints and tire tracks, indicative of a particular kind of truck. Watching officers saw an approaching truck similar to the one they suspected had left the tire tracks. They stopped the truck and questioned Cortez, the truck driver, and his passenger, who happened to be wearing shoes matching prints made at the illegal border crossing. The officers opened the truck and discovered six illegal aliens. Cortez was convicted of transporting illegal aliens. He appealed, protesting unlawful search. The SC upheld the conviction, saying that the totality-of-circumstances test applied in this case. Objective facts and particular circumstances may lead police to make investigatory stops and subsequent arrests, if the totality of circumstances suggests that a crime has been committed.

United States v. Crews, 445 U.S. 463, 100 S.Ct. 1244 (1980) **(Law Enforcement Officers or Agencies; Exclusionary Rule).** A woman was assaulted and robbed at gunpoint. She notified police and described the assailant. Crews was seen later in the vicinity by police, who stopped him, took him to the police station briefly, photographed him, and released him. Later, the woman was shown Crews's photograph and she identified him as the man who had attacked her. Crews was later arrested and placed in a lineup. The victim again identified him as her attacker. Crews was later charged and tried for armed robbery. During the trial, the victim again identified Crews. He was convicted. He appealed, contending that his initial detention by police and photographing had been unwarranted and not supported by probable cause. Further, he argued that the lineup identification evidence should have been considered inadmissible for the same reason. The SC ruled that the actions by police officers in detaining and arresting Crews constituted police misconduct. This misconduct also applied to the photograph and lineup identification of Crews by the victim. However, his conviction was upheld, because the victim also made an in-court identification of Crews independent of the police photograph and lineup, under an exception to the exclusionary rule called the independent-untainted-source doctrine. The SC said that the illegality of Crews' detention could not deprive the government of the opportunity to prove his guilt through the introduction of evidence wholly untainted by the police misconduct.

United States v. Dionisio, 410 U.S. 1, 93 S.Ct. 764 (1973) **(Law Enforcement Officers or Agencies; Lineups; Pretrial Identification).** Dionisio and about 20 others were advised that they were suspects in an illegal-gambling investigation. They were subpoenaed before a grand jury and ordered to submit vocal recordings of themselves for comparison with various messages police had intercepted through telephonic wiretapping. Dionisio refused and was held in contempt of court. He was ordered to jail for 18 months. He appealed, arguing that no one could compel him to give evidence against himself in violation of his Fifth Amendment rights and that the "seizure" of his voice pattern through a vocal recording was unreasonable in violation of his Fourth Amendment rights. The SC disagreed with Dionisio, saying that grand juries may compel a person to give vocal recordings and that such an intrusion is not an unreasonable seizure under Fourth Amendment protection (*see Schmerber v. California* [1966] and *Winston v. Lee* [1985] as comparative cases).

United States v. Di Re, 332 U.S. 581, 68 S.Ct. 222 (1948) **(Law Enforcement Officers or Agencies; Stop and Frisk).** During World War II, it was illegal to have counterfeit gasoline ration coupons. Buffalo, New York, police received information from an informant, Reed, that someone named Buttitta was selling counterfeit coupons. A detective with the Buffalo police department followed Buttitta's car. When it finally came to an appointed place, the police went to the car and found the informer, Reed. They asked Reed if he had illegal coupons, and he said yes and that he had obtained them from the driver, Buttitta. Di Re was sitting next to Buttitta. All persons were taken to the police station, where Di Re was ordered to turn out his pockets and place the contents on the table. Gasoline coupons fell out, and he was thoroughly searched, which yielded another 100 concealed in his underwear. These coupons were counterfeit,

and Di Re was convicted of possession of counterfeit gasoline coupons. He appealed, contesting that his unreasonable search and seizure had violated his Fourth Amendment rights. The SC held that Di Re's mere presence with Buttitta had not entitled police to presume that he, too, was guilty of possessing fraudulent coupons. Nothing had been said or done by Buttitta to incriminate Di Re. Therefore, the police had had no justification to search Di Re. Thus, the warrantless search of Di Re was not based upon any reasonable suspicion or probable cause, so his conviction was overturned.

United States v. Dixon, 507 U.S.___, 113 S.Ct. 2849 (1993) **(Fifth Amendment; Self-Incrimination).** Dixon was arrested for second-degree murder and released on bond. While on bond, he was "forbidden [to] commit any criminal offense." During this period Dixon was arrested again and charged with cocaine possession. He was convicted shortly thereafter of contempt, and of the cocaine possession, and was sentenced to 180 days in jail. Later, he moved to dismiss the cocaine indictment, because his "contempt" conviction involved the identical drug charges. The trial court granted his motion and dismissed the indictment. The government appealed to the SC. The SC upheld the indictment dismissal, holding that where a criminal contempt sanction was imposed upon Dixon for violating an order of conditional release by violating a drug offense which was incorporated into his release conditions, the later attempt to prosecute him for the drug offense itself was barred as an instance of double jeopardy.

United States v. Doe, 465 U.S. 553, 104 S.Ct. 1237 (1983) **(Fifth Amendment; Self-Incrimination).** John Doe was owner of several sole proprietorships. In late 1980, a grand jury investigation of corruption in awarding county and municipal contracts resulted in subpoenas served on Doe and his proprietorships. The subpoenas sought various financial and business records. Doe filed a motion to have these records suppressed under the theory that his right against self-incrimination would be violated by disclosing those records to government prosecutors. The SC heard the appeal and said that the records sought in the subpoenas were not privileged communications of the Fifth Amendment variety, and thus their production before a grand jury would not violate Doe's Fifth Amendment rights. However, the "act" of compelling the submission of incriminating records by court order requires a statutory grant-of-use immunity. Thus, Doe's records were subject to subpoena, but a grant of immunity had to be made to him so that the incriminating information disclosed by the records could not be used against him later in a criminal prosecution.

United States v. Donavan, 429 U.S. 413, 97 S.Ct. 658 (1977) **(Law Enforcement Officers or Agencies; Electronic Surveillance)**. Donavan was one of several defendants indicted for illegal gambling on the basis of information gleaned from an authorized wiretap by the FBI. Because the identities of many of the persons involved in this conspiracy were unknown, and thus could not be inventoried in the wiretap authorization, the defendants moved to suppress these indictments. A lower court granted the motion, but the SC overturned this decision and reinstated the indictments, holding that it is not necessary to identify each and every person subject to a wiretap.

United States v. Dunn, 480 U.S. 294, 107 S.Ct. 1134 (1987) **(Law Enforcement Officers or Agencies; Plain View Rule; Open Field Searches)**. Drug agents investigated Dunn, who was suspected of manufacturing drugs in large quantities in a private laboratory located on his property. With a properly executed warrant, police placed a beeper in a container used by Dunn to transport drugs. Eventually, the officers located Dunn's farm. Passing through several gates, fences, and other perimeter guards, they shined their flashlights into a large barn about 50 yards from Dunn's house. They could hear a motor running, and they saw drug equipment through the side boards. They secured a search warrant and entered the barn, where they seized a quantity of illegal drugs. Dunn was convicted of drug manufacturing. He appealed, seeking to suppress the barn evidence because he believed that police had had no legal authority to observe his barn in the middle of a heavily protected area. The SC upheld Dunn's conviction, saying that because the barn itself was not part of the curtilage of Dunn's home but rather was separately fenced, police were not required to obtain a search warrant to look at it or through its side boards. The SC stressed how close the barn was to Dunn's house; whether it was in a separate enclosure; the nature and uses of the area; and any evident concealment attempts. These guidelines gave greater parameters for police when conducting searches of open fields or yards (*see Oliver v. United States* [1984] for comparison).

United States v. Dunnigan, 507 U.S. 87, 113 S.Ct. 1111 (1993) **(Perjury; Sentence Enhancements)**. Dunnigan was accused of conspiracy to distribute cocaine. She testified in her own behalf, but it was subsequently determined that she had committed perjury during her testimony. She was convicted, and the judge enhanced her sentence because of her perjury. Dunnigan appealed, arguing that her testimony was self-incriminating and that she should not be further punished because of her perjury statements. The SC disagreed and upheld her sentence enhancement. Under the United States Sentencing Commission Guidelines, if the court finds the defendant committed perjury at the trial, then the sentence can be enhanced.

United States v. Edwards, 415 U.S. 800, 94 S.Ct. 1234 (1974) **(Law Enforcement Officers or Agencies; Searches Incident to Arrest)**. Edwards was arrested for attempting to break into a United States post office and was taken to jail. Jail officials exchanged Edwards' clothes for jail garments and searched his clothes for evidence of the break-in. Paint chips matching those from the United States post office window were found in Edwards' clothing and this, as well as other incriminating evidence, led to his conviction. Edwards appealed, moving to suppress the paint chips and other evidence from his clothing, contending that the search had been a violation of his Fourth Amendment right against unreasonable searches and seizures. The SC disagreed, saying that whenever a suspect is arrested, it is not violative of his Fourth Amendment rights for police to conduct a more thorough search of his clothes and seize what is believed to be evidence of a crime (*see United States v. Robinson* [1973]).

United States v. Felix, 503 U.S. 378, 112 S.Ct. 1377 (1992) **(Double Jeopardy)**. Felix was charged with various drug offenses in 1987, including attempt to manufacture an illegal drug, methamphetamine, in Oklahoma. He was convicted. Subsequently, he was indicted on charges of conspiracy to manufacture, possess, and distribute methamphetamines. He claimed that this charge was a case of double jeopardy, because he had already been convicted on other charges stemming from the same offense. The SC upheld his conviction and held that the double-jeopardy clause did not bar the government's prosecution of Felix because essentially different conduct was being alleged in different indictments. Double jeopardy *would* have attached if two prosecutions had stemmed from the same conduct.

United States v. Gaudin, ___U.S.___, 115 S.Ct. 2310 (1995) **(Jury Trial; Judge's Instructions to Juries).** Gaudin was convicted in a United States district court on charges of making false statements on federally insured mortgages. He appealed to the SC, arguing, in part, that certain statements he made had been considered by the *judge*, not the *jury*, as materially relevant to his case. He believed that the jury should decide the materiality of these statements rather than the judge. Thus the judge's jury instructions and conduct were at issue. The SC declared that the jury must decide whether every element of a crime has been proved beyond a reasonable doubt. In Gaudin's case, the judge had preempted the jury's right by determining the materiality of one of the crime elements. The SC overturned Gaudin's conviction, holding that the judge's refusal to submit the question of "materiality" to the jury was unconstitutional. The significance of the case is that juries, not presiding judges, must be given the right to determine the materiality of each and every crime element.

United States v. Giordano, 416 U.S. 505, 94 S.Ct. 1820 (1974) **(Electronic Surveillance).** According to a RICO statute, federal judges were authorized to approve wiretaps of telephones of those suspected of violating federal laws. An application for a wiretap was authorized by a specially designated executive assistant to the Attorney General for the purpose of investigating Dominic Giordano. Once Giordano was arrested and charged with various narcotics violations, the wiretap was removed. Nevertheless, the wiretap revealed considerable incriminating information, which was intended to be used against Giordano at his later federal trial. He was convicted. His attorney moved successfully to suppress this incriminating information. The government appealed, and the SC heard the case. The SC upheld the suppression decision, holding that primary or derivative evidence secured by wiretaps pursuant to court order issued in response to an application that was not in fact authorized by the Attorney General or Assistant Attorney General specifically designated by him must be suppressed upon proper motion. In Giordano's case, it developed that the executive assistant to the Attorney General was not empowered by statute to authorize applications for wiretap orders.

United States v. Goodwin, 457 U.S. 368, 102 S.Ct. 2485 (1982) **(Sixth Amendment; Prosecutorial Misconduct).** Goodwin was stopped by a United States park policeman on the Baltimore-Washington Parkway for speeding. When Goodwin stepped from his car, the officer observed a clear plastic bag underneath the armrest next to the driver's seat. The officer asked Goodwin to return to his car and retrieve the bag. When Goodwin got into his car, he placed the car in gear and accelerated rapidly. Goodwin's car struck the officer but did not seriously injure him. He got into his own car and pursued Goodwin, but Goodwin eluded him in a high-speed chase. Because of license information, Goodwin's identity was known and a warrant was issued for his arrest. Goodwin was arrested and arraigned before a United States magistrate, where a trial date was set. Before trial, Goodwin fled to Virginia. Three years later, he was found in custody in Virginia and returned to Maryland to stand trial on the earlier charges. Through a plea agreement, he entered a guilty plea but later changed his mind, insisting on a jury trial instead. About six weeks later, the prosecutor obtained a four-count indictment including one felony count of assaulting a federal officer. A jury trial resulted in Goodwin's conviction on these charges. Goodwin appealed, alleging that raising the original misdemeanor charge of assaulting an officer to the higher level of a felony assault charge was vindictiveness on the prosecutor's part and thus had violated Goodwin's due-process rights. The SC found no evidence of vindictiveness on the prosecutor's part and therefore no due-process violation.

United States v. Gouveia, 467 U.S. 180, 104 S.Ct. 2292 (1984) **(Corrections; Inmate Rights).** At the federal prison in Lompoc, California, Gouveia and four other inmates were suspected of murdering a fellow inmate. These prisoners were placed temporarily in the Administrative Detention Unit at Lompoc, where they were isolated from one another. In the meantime, prison authorities conducted a hearing and determined that these prisoners were involved in the murder. Later, a grand jury indicted them and at their arraignments, they were provided court-appointed counsel, as they were indigent. They were convicted of the murder. Gouveia appealed, alleging that he should have been permitted access to a court-appointed attorney while he was in administrative detention. The SC upheld his conviction, saying that inmates under investigation for a crime and held in administrative detention are not automatically entitled to court-appointed counsel before any judicial proceedings have been launched against them. The rights of prisoners do not include court-appointed counsel until they are indicted.

United States v. Granderson, ___U.S.___, 114 S.Ct. 1259 (1994) **(Probation and Parole; Sentencing; United States Sentencing Guidelines).** Granderson, a letter carrier for the United States Post Office, was convicted of destruction of mail and sentenced to five years' probation, although the United States Sentencing Guidelines provided for a 0-to-6-month incarcerative term. Subsequently, Granderson's probation was revoked when it was discovered that he possessed a controlled substance. U.S.C. Section 3565(a) of Title 18, the criminal code, provides that one-third of the original sentence should be imposed as a punishment when revoking a federal probation. Thus, relying on the five-year (60-month) probationary term, the judge sentenced Granderson to 20 months of imprisonment. Granderson appealed, contending that the United States Sentencing Guidelines govern incarcerative terms, not probationary sentences. A circuit court of appeals reversed this sentence and ordered Granderson released. Its logic was that the original sentence was the United States Sentencing Guidelines of 0-6 months, not the original probationary sentence. Because Granderson had already served 11 months of imprisonment at the time of the appellate decision, his immediate release was ordered. The government appealed, and the SC heard the case. The SC upheld the circuit court of appeals, concluding that indeed, the United States Sentencing Guidelines governed this situation, not the probationary sentence imposed by the federal judge.

United States v. Hale, 422 U.S. 71, 95 S.Ct. 2133 (1975) **(Self-Incrimination).** Hale was accused of a crime. During his trial, the prosecutor commented about the fact that Hale had remained silent after being given the Miranda warning at the time of his arrest. The fact of silence was interpreted as incriminating by the prosecutor, and Hale was convicted. He appealed. The SC declared that prosecutors are forbidden to comment about whether a defendant's invocation of his right to silence is potentially incriminating. Prosecutors are barred from inferring something nefarious or

incriminating from a defendant's refusal to answer police questions following a Miranda warning.

United States v. Halper, 490 U.S. 435, 109 S.Ct. 1892 (1989) **(Double Jeopardy).** Halper was a medical service manager convicted of filing 65 inflated Medicare claims. He was sentenced to prison and given a fine of $5,000. Subsequently in a civil action, the United States government filed a civil suit against him, asking the court for a summary judgment under the False Claims Act. Halper appealed. The monetary punishment associated with false claims is $2,000 per claim, or a total of $130,000. In view of the actual amount of money involved in the fraudulent claims for which Halper had already been convicted and the government's expenses of $16,000, the difference between $16,000 and $130,000 was so dramatic as to be violative of Halper's right against double jeopardy. The SC vacated the judgment against Halper and sent the case back to a lower court where the government could determine more reasonable monetary sanctions against Halper without violating his double-jeopardy rights.

United States v. Harris, 403 U.S. 573, 91 S.Ct. 2075 (1971) **(Informants; Searches and Seizures).** An informant provided incriminating information about Harris to a government tax collector. Harris was later arrested and charged with possession of untaxed liquor. He moved to suppress the evidence on the ground that the search warrant had been insufficient in establishing adequate facts to search for and seize the untaxed liquor. The SC upheld Harris' conviction, concluding that the affidavit supporting the warrant had been sufficient. The informant was deemed credible, in part because the information he provided the federal tax collector implicated the informant himself. There was also sufficient factual basis for believing the informant.

United States v. Havens, 446 U.S. 620, 100 S.Ct. 1912 (1980) **(Law Enforcement Officers or Agencies; Fourth Amendment; Illegally Seized Evidence Used for Impeachment).** Havens was suspected of importing and conspiring to import cocaine. During his trial and under direct examination, he denied various facts pertaining to the cocaine allegations. While cross-examining him, the prosecutor used illegally obtained evidence to contradict Havens, who was subsequently convicted. He appealed to the SC, alleging that because the evidence used against him had been illegally seized and was otherwise inadmissible, it should have been excluded. The SC disagreed and upheld his conviction, holding that evidence that is otherwise inadmissible as the result of a Fourth Amendment violation may be used to impeach the credibility of the defendant when the defendant gives testimony that is contradicted by such illegally seized evidence. Thus, when defendants testify, they must testify truthfully "or suffer the consequences" (at 1912).

United States v. Henry, 447 U.S. 264, 100 S.Ct. 2183 (1980) **(Right to Counsel)**. Henry was accused of armed robbery and indicted by a grand jury. While in jail awaiting trial, he acquired a new cellmate, who was a paid informant of the government. Acting on the government's instructions, the informant was supposed to elicit incriminating statements from Henry so that the government could have better evidence against him. Henry made such statements and was convicted. He appealed. The SC overturned Henry's conviction on the grounds that the conversations he had with the informant constituted an interrogation because the informant was acting as an extension of the government, which had paid him to conduct an interrogation of Henry, although the government didn't interpret the situation in that context. Nevertheless, the significance of this case is that whenever defendants are in custody and are questioned by police or their agents (e.g., paid informants), that situation simulates an interrogation and requires the presence of the defendant's attorney. (*See Massiah v. United States* (1964) for a similar case and SC holding.)

United States v. Hensley, 469 U.S. 221, 105 S.Ct. 675 (1985) **(Law Enforcement Officers or Agencies; Stop and Frisk)**. A motorist, Hensley, was a convicted felon from St. Bernard, Ohio, traveling through Kentucky. A recent robbery in Kentucky led police officers to suspect Hensley, although there was no evidence linking him to the crime. A "wanted" poster of Hensley was circulated among contiguous states, and a Covington, Kentucky police officer observed Hensley on a highway. He stopped and questioned Hensley and then arrested him, largely because of the "wanted" poster he had seen. In a search incident to the arrest, the officer found weapons in Hensley's automobile. Hensley was never charged with the robbery, but he was charged with, and convicted of, being a felon in possession of firearms, a prohibited act. He appealed, arguing that the police had lacked probable cause to stop him initially and

therefore the weapons subsequently found in his car should have been excluded as evidence. The SC upheld the conviction of Hensley, contending that the "wanted" poster had provided police with sufficient grounds to stop and question Hensley. The SC stressed the increasing mobility of United States citizens and the greater importance of information exchanges about felons and crimes among the states.

United States v. Inadi, 475 U.S. 387, 106 S.Ct. 1121 (1986) **(Sixth Amendment Right to Cross-Examine One's Accusers)**. Inadi was convicted of a crime, partly on the basis of the evidence of co-conspirators who gave statements to the prosecutor implicating Inadi. At no time did the prosecutor actually call the co-conspirators to testify; rather, he introduced their inculpatory statements into the record. Inadi appealed, saying that his Sixth Amendment right to cross-examine his accusers had been violated, and that the prosecutor had not shown that these witnesses were unavailable. The SC upheld Inadi's conviction, saying that it did not intend for its ruling in *Ohio v. Roberts* (1980) to be interpreted to mean that no out-of-court statements could ever be read into trial records. The SC said that prosecutors are not required to show the unavailability of co-conspirators. Thus, prior testimony may be introduced without actually calling co-conspirators to testify against a defendant. The confrontation clause of the Sixth Amendment allows for the introduction of such out-of-court statements as a part of its mission in the truth-determining process.

United States v. Jackson, 428 U.S. 153, 88 S.Ct. 1209 (1976) **(Death Penalty)**. Jackson was indicted by a federal district court bench trial on charges of kidnapping a person in violation of the Federal Kidnapping Act. He sought to dismiss the indictment, arguing that the capital-punishment clause of this act is unconstitutional. The SC held that the capital-punishment clause violates the Fifth and Sixth Amendments, but its elimination does not jeopardize the act in other respects. Thus the indictment against Jackson was valid despite the capital-punishment clause being declared unconstitutional.

United States v. Jakobetz, 747 F.Supp. 250, 113 S.Ct. 104 (cert. denied) (1992) **(DNA Profiling)**. The SC held that DNA profiling is admissible as evidence in criminal trials.

United States v. Janis, 428 U.S. 433, 96 S.Ct. 3021 (1976) **(Search and Seizure; Admissibility** of Illegally Seized Evidence). Janis was suspected by Los Angeles police of illegal betting. They obtained a search warrant and searched two of his apartments. The searches yielded betting slips, wagering records, and nearly $5,000 in cash. Janis was arrested and charged with bookmaking. He moved to have the evidence seized suppressed, because there were defects in the warrant. A judge agreed and ordered all materials returned to Janis with the exception of the currency. In the meantime, IRS agents with the Criminal Investigation Division commenced an investigation of Janis's records seized by Los Angeles police and calculated that he owed the government considerable money on his illegal betting activity. The judge ordered Janis' money held until a civil court determination could be made, because IRS levies were in effect concerning the money. Janis's attorney argued that the money ought to be returned as well, because the original IRS investigation was prompted by illegally seized evidence; if the evidence were suppressed, then the IRS would have no foundation to continue their action against Janis. The Ninth Circuit Court of Appeals ordered the return of Janis's money. The government appealed. The SC overturned the decision of the circuit court, holding that while the warrant may have been defective, the IRS had not participated in its issuance. The Los Angeles police officers had been acting in good faith when they advised the IRS of Janis's bookmaking documents. Thus, the IRS, an independent agency, came by this information properly, despite the warrant's defects. Therefore, the SC said, the IRS had not violated Janis's Fourth Amendment rights. The significance of this case is that although warrants may be defective and officers proceed in good faith, independent agencies, such as the IRS, are entitled to use illegally seized evidence against suspects for their own agency purposes in federal civil tax proceedings.

United States v. Jeffers, 342 U.S. 48, 72 S.Ct. 93 (1951) (Law Enforcement Officers or Agencies; Consent Searches). In September 1949, Roberts came to the Dunbar Hotel in Washington, D.C., and requested that the house detective, Scott, let him into Jeffers' room, where, Roberts said, some "stuff was stashed." Scott told Roberts to check back later. In the meantime, Scott called the police, who came to the hotel. With the assistance of a house key, the officers and Scott opened the room door and searched for narcotics. They

discovered cocaine. Jeffers was subsequently charged with and convicted of cocaine possession. He appealed, arguing that his Fourth Amendment right against unreasonable searches and seizures had been violated. He claimed that the officers had needed a warrant to search his locked premises. The government said that it had not invaded Jeffers' privacy, because he wasn't in the room when the police searched it. The SC heard the case and overturned Jeffers' conviction, holding that police were required to obtain a search warrant in order to search his premises; therefore, the illegal cocaine was suppressed as evidence against him. In a related matter, Jeffers filed a motion to get his illegal cocaine back. The SC said that illegal contraband, no matter how it is seized, legally or otherwise, is not subject to return to those from whom it was taken.

United States v. Johns, 469 U.S. 478, 105 S.Ct. 881 (1985) (Law Enforcement Officers or Agencies; Warrantless Searches and Inventories of Vehicles). Johns and others were believed by federal authorities to be involved in drug smuggling. United States customs officers conducted surveillance of Johns's movements, tracking him and his associates to an airfield about 50 miles from the Mexican border. Johns and a companion off-loaded cargo and left in their aircraft. Customs officers conducted surveillance of the aircraft in their own aircraft, following it to its final destination, which was Tucson, Arizona. Customs officers approached trucks on the airfield and smelled marijuana. They also observed several large packages wrapped in dark green plastic. Their prior experience led them to believe that the packages contained marijuana, so they arrested all suspects and seized the packages. Johns was indicted and convicted of smuggling marijuana, after the trucks were searched, without warrant, at a customs headquarters three days later. Johns sought to suppress the evidence, arguing that the three-day delay in searching the trucks for marijuana should have required officers to obtain a search warrant first. The SC heard the appeal and upheld Johns's conviction, holding that although the officers could have searched the packages in the trucks lawfully incident to an arrest at the airfield, there is no requirement that the warrantless search of the vehicles should occur contemporaneously with the seizure of the unlawful contraband.

United States v. Jorn, 400 U.S. 70, 91 S.Ct. 547 (1971) (Double Jeopardy). Jorn was tried in federal district court for income tax fraud. After the trial, the judge dismissed the jury, aborted the trial so that witnesses could consult with their attorneys, and ordered a new trial. Jorn contended on appeal that another trial on the same charges would constitute double jeopardy. A circuit court of appeals dismissed the case, but the government appealed. The SC agreed with Jorn and upheld the case dismissal, contending that this was a clear instance of double jeopardy.

United States v. Kahn, 415 U.S. 143, 94 S.Ct. 977 (1974) **(Law Enforcement Officers or Agencies; Searches).** As the result of government-authorized wiretaps in Kahn's home, incriminating information was obtained not only against Kahn, but also against Kahn's wife. Both were convicted. They appealed, alleging that the purpose of the wiretaps had been to intercept Kahn's calls, not those of Mrs. Kahn. The SC said that the search warrant authorizing the wiretaps was constitutional. Further, the phraseology of the wiretap order, "others as yet unknown," covered persons such as Mrs. Kahn. The ruling applied that legally intercepted conversations not necessarily involving Mr. Kahn did not have to be suppressed as evidence. Therefore, the convictions were upheld.

United States v. Karo, 468 U.S. 705, 104 S.Ct. 3296 (1984) **(Law Enforcement Officers or Agencies; Electronic Surveillance).** Karo was suspected of being a co-conspirator in an enterprise to distribute cocaine. A court order was obtained by DEA agents to install a beeper in a clothing container used by Karo and others to smuggle cocaine. The agents tracked the container by monitoring the beeper, and they discovered various addresses of homes and businesses that appeared to be involved in the cocaine distribution conspiracy. The beeper monitoring had been done without a specific search warrant. DEA agents eventually obtained a search warrant based upon probable cause and entered several of the homes and businesses previously monitored through the concealed beeper. Karo and others were eventually convicted of this conspiracy. They appealed. The SC overturned Karo's conviction on other grounds but declared that in order for beepers to be installed and monitored, especially in private dwellings, a valid search warrant based upon probable cause must be obtained first (*see United States v. Knotts* [1983] for a comparative case).

United States v. Knotts, 460 U.S. 276, 103 S.Ct. 1081 (1983) **(Law Enforcement Officers or Agencies; Seizures; Electronic Surveillance).** Knotts was suspected of trafficking in a narcotic ingredient. He was under surveillance at a cabin. Also, police installed a beeper inside a container of the drug ingredient sold to Armstrong, a friend of Knotts's. The beeper was used to track Armstrong's movements, as well as the container. Knotts and Armstrong unloaded the container into Knotts's cabin in plain view of watching officers. The officers obtained a search warrant and searched his premises for the illegal drug ingredient. Knotts was convicted. He appealed, contending that the beeper was an illegal intrusion into his privacy and in violation of his Fourth Amendment right against illegal searches and seizures. The SC disagreed, saying that beepers used as surveillance enhancements are neither "searches" nor "seizures" and therefore do not violate a person's right to privacy or Fourth Amendment rights.

United States v. Lanza, 260 U.S. 377 43, S.Ct. 141 (1922) **(Double Jeopardy).** Lanza was convicted of violating a Prohibition law of the State of Washington. The federal government moved to charge him with the same offense, but the SC said that to do so would be a case of double jeopardy and threw out the federal case.

United States v. Lee, 274 U.S. 559, 47 S.Ct. 746 (1927) **(Law Enforcement Officers or Agencies; Searches Incident to an Arrest).** On February 16, 1925, a United States Coast Guard cutter spotted a 30-foot motorboat in Gloucester Harbor in Massachusetts. The cutter lost sight of the boat, but later spotted it again, making furtive movements, about 20 miles off the Massachusetts coast near Boston. Coast Guardsmen boarded the vessel and found Lee and two associates with 71 cases of pure grain alcohol. Lee and his associates were later prosecuted for violating Prohibition statutes and were convicted. Their boat was seized as an instrument of the crime. Lee, the registered owner of the boat, appealed both the search and the seizure, claiming that they were illegal, because they had taken place beyond the 12-mile limit of the territorial waters of the United States. Thus, Lee claimed, his Fourth Amendment right against unreasonable searches and seizures had been violated. The SC heard the case and upheld Lee's conviction and boat seizure, saying that the search and seizure of the boat were incident to an arrest. That the arrest was made on the high seas did not violate the United States Constitution, inasmuch as the persons violating the law were United States citizens and had been observed earlier within the 12-mile limit. The theory of "hot pursuit" might be applicable here, although the SC did not articulate it. However, the SC did indicate that probable cause existed for the search undertaken.

United States v. Leon, 468 U.S. 897, 104 S.Ct. 3405 (1984) **(Law Enforcement Officers or Agencies; Exclusionary Rule).** Leon, a suspected drug trafficker, was placed under surveillance by Burbank, California, police. Subsequently, police obtained search warrants for three residences and several automobiles under Leon's control. Acting on the search warrants, they seized large quantities of inculpatory drug evidence, which was used against Leon at a trial later, where he was convicted. He appealed to the SC, which upheld his conviction. Although the SC declared the search warrants invalid; they noted in a rambling and extensive opinion that the officers who abided by the directives outlined by the invalid warrants had been acting in good faith, presuming that the issued warrants were valid. The SC also noted that this decision was not to be interpreted as a blanket generalization authorizing officers to act in all instances where defective warrants are issued. The SC simply weighed the benefits of suppressing the evidence obtained in Leon's case against the costs of exclusion. The significance of this case is that it creates a good-faith exception to the exclusionary rule. The SC's message is that evidence may be admissible if the fault for defective warrants rests with judges, not police officers. The target of the exclusionary rule is police misconduct, not judicial misconduct.

United States v. Levi, 2 F.2d 842 (1993) **(Corrections; Probation Revocation).** During his first 11 months of supervised release, Levi committed one or more probation violations. The judge revoked his probation and declared that he must spend the remaining 13 months incarcerated. The Eighth Circuit Court of Appeals upheld the judge's action, because the 13-month imprisonment was within the two-year sentence of probation originally imposed by the same judge.

United States v. Lombardi, 5 F.3rd 568 (1993) **(Corrections; Sentencing; Fines and Restitution).** In a federal case, Lombardi was convicted of mail fraud involving more than $190,000 of unaccounted for funds. He was fined $60,000 as a part of his sentence and obligated to make restitution in the sum of $190,000. Lombardi protested, claiming that he was unable to pay these amounts. The First Circuit Court of Appeals disagreed, indicating that Lombardi had never accounted for the whereabouts of these illegally obtained funds. His restitution order remained effective. Failure to make restitution, in Lombardi's case, would result in incarceration.

United States v. Loud Hawk, 474 U.S. 302, 106 S.Ct. 648 (1986) **(Speedy Trials).** Loud Hawk was indicted for possession of firearms and dynamite. For various reasons, the indictment was dismissed. During a 46-month period during which Loud Hawk was free, various appeals by the government were dismissed or affirmed by higher appellate courts. Subsequently, a circuit court of appeals upheld a dismissal of an indictment against Loud Hawk, but the government appealed. The SC reinstated Loud Hawk's indictment, holding that his right to a speedy trial had not been violated because he was not under indictment and had remained free during the period when it was being appealed. Thus, with no indictment, there was no urgency to bring about his trial. The SC concluded that based on the facts, the delays in question were not sufficiently long to justify dismissal of the case against Loud Hawk on speedy-trial grounds.

United States v. Lovasco, 431 U.S. 783, 97 S.Ct. 1444 (1977) **(Speedy Trials).** Lovasco was indicted for various federal offenses. During the next 17 months, the government prepared an investigative report. Lovasco appealed to the circuit court of appeals, where his indictment was dismissed. The government appealed to the SC, who reversed the lower court, reinstating Lovasco's indictment. The SC held that there is no constitutional requirement for the prosecution to file charges promptly once it has assembled sufficient evidence to prove guilt beyond a reasonable doubt, even if the investigation of Lovasco was incomplete. Such a requirement might impair prosecutors by preventing them from filing additional indictments against suspects for other crimes, and it might pressure prosecutors into resolving doubtful cases in favor of early and possibly unwarranted prosecution. Thus prosecutors are not under a duty to file charges as soon as probable cause exists but before they are satisfied that they will be able to establish guilt of a suspect beyond a reasonable doubt.

United States v. Mara, 410 U.S. 19, 93 S.Ct. 774 (1973) **(Fifth Amendment; Right Against Self-Incrimination; Handwriting Samples).** Mara was compelled to give a handwriting sample to compare with words written on paper during a commission of a crime. He was convicted partially on the basis of this handwriting comparison. He appealed. The SC upheld the conviction, saying that handwriting specimens are not violations of the right against self-incrimination in the Fifth Amendment.

United States v. Marion, 404 U.S. 307, 92 S.Ct. 455 (1971) **(Speedy Trial).** In April 1970, indictments were issued against Marion and Cratch on 19 counts of operating a business engaged in fraudulent activity. The acts covered by the indictment were alleged to have been committed between March 1965 and February 1967. Marion alleged that because there was a three-year delay between the overt acts alleged and the indictment, his speedy-trial rights under the Sixth Amendment had been violated. The SC heard the case and disagreed. The speedy-trial provision of the Sixth Amendment begins when an indictment is delivered, not when overt acts are alleged. Furthermore, the allegations were within the proper statute of limitations for prosecuting such offenses. Thus Marion's rights had not been violated.

United States v. Martinez-Fuerte, 428 U.S. 543, 96 S.Ct. 3074 (1976) **(Border Stops and Searches; Fourth Amendment).** The Border Patrol established checkpoints for illegal Mexican aliens at various places along a major interstate highway. Martinez-Fuerte was apprehended in one of these roving checkpoints and was convicted of transporting illegal aliens. He appealed to the SC, which upheld the convictions. The SC said that such checkpoint stops, particularly in view of their location and notoriety for illegal alien trafficking, are not in violation of any Fourth Amendment right. Such checkpoints are permissible and need not be prefaced by a judicial warrant. Even if stops are conducted because persons appear to have Mexican ancestry, that does not make such checkpoints and searches unconstitutional.

United States v. Matlock, 415 U.S. 164, 94 S.Ct. 988 (1974) **(Law Enforcement Officers or Agencies; Consent Searches).** Matlock was a robbery suspect. Based upon probable cause, of-ficers went to Matlock's residence, where they arrested Matlock in his front yard. A Mrs. Graff also lived in the home and admitted officers at their request, although they did not have a search warrant. They asked Mrs. Graff if they could look in various rooms, and she agreed. Eventually, money from the robbery was recovered from a closet in Matlock's bedroom. Police did not know that the bedroom they were searching was Matlock's. On the basis of the evidence, Matlock was indicted for robbery and convicted later at trial. He moved to suppress the evidence obtained because he claimed that the search had been invalid without a proper search warrant. An appeals court granted his motion and the evidence was excluded. The government appealed, and the SC heard the case. The SC upheld Matlock's conviction, concluding that consensual searches of premises by persons sharing the premises with a suspect are valid. Thus Mrs. Graff was in a position to grant officers permission to conduct a warrantless search of the premises, because she shared them with Matlock.

United States v. McDonald, 456 U.S. 1, 102 S.Ct. 1497 (1982) **(Speedy Trial).** McDonald was charged with several murders under military law in May 1970. Later that year, charges were dismissed. In 1974, the United States Justice Department renewed the case against McDonald and a federal grand jury indicted him. McDonald appealed, alleging that the government had violated his speedy-trial rights by waiting four years to bring an indictment against him. The SC disagreed, saying that the speedy-trial provision has no application after the government drops charges and decides to reopen a case several years later.

United States v. Mendenhall, 446 U.S. 544, 100 S.Ct. 1870 (1980) **(Law Enforcement Officers or Agencies; Seizures).** Mendenhall was approached by DEA agents at a Detroit airport and asked to accompany them to a room where she could be searched. Mendenhall did not refuse but said that she had a plane to catch. The agents advised her that if she were carrying no narcotics, then she would be free to leave. Her original detention was based on a profile of drug couriers that the DEA had devised. She consented to a strip search, which yielded incriminating heroin, and she was convicted. She appealed, arguing that her Fourth Amendment right against unreasonable search and seizure had been violated. The SC upheld Mendenhall's conviction, holding that she had freely consented to the search of her person, and that expressing the need to "catch a plane" did not obligate officers to secure an arrest warrant or a search warrant to search her further. The SC stressed the "totality of circumstances" surrounding her investigative detention and subsequent search. She had also been advised that she did not have to consent to the search. The SC said that "nothing in the record suggests that [Mendenhall] had any objective reason to believe that she was not free to end the conversation in the concourse and proceed on her way." Perhaps this case suggests that citizens ought to be aware of their rights when approached by police officers or DEA agents in airports and other public transportation facilities, and of the citizen's right simply to "walk away" when no grounds exist otherwise for a search of one's person.

United States v. Miller, 425 U.S. 435, 96 S.Ct. 1619 (1976) **(Law Enforcement Officers or Agencies; Search Warrants for Bank Records).** Miller was convicted in Georgia of violating various liquor laws (e.g., operating an unregistered still) and of intent to defraud the government. During his trial, Miller's bank records were used as evidence against him. He was convicted. He appealed, moving to suppress the incriminating bank records. A circuit court of appeals reversed his conviction. The government appealed the case to the SC, where Miller's conviction was reinstated. The SC held that Miller had no Fourth Amendment interest in the bank records, which were business records, not private papers.

United States v. Monsanto, 491 U.S. 600, 100 S.Ct. 2657 (1989) **(Asset Forfeiture; Right to Counsel; Sixth Amendment).** Peter Monsanto was indicted by a federal grand jury for RICO violations, including large-scale heroin dealing and distribution. Following the indictment, a government motion to freeze Monsanto's assets was granted. Monsanto objected, claiming that there should have been an exemption freeing his assets so that he could retain counsel. The SC heard Monsanto's appeal and declared that the federal drug forfeiture statute authorizes the federal district court to enter pretrial orders that freeze assets of indicted persons, even when they seek to use these assets to pay attorney fees.

United States v. Montoya de Hernandez, 473 U.S. 531, 105 S.Ct. 3304 (1985) **(Unreasonable Searches and Seizures).** Montoya de Hernandez, was a woman drug smuggler who operated as a "mule." Mules are persons who swallow large quantities of heroin or cocaine in glassine envelopes or rubber containers. Later, after they have entered into the United States, they can defecate the containers and recover the smuggled drug. Based upon a reliable informant's tip, DEA agents established surveillance and intercepted Montoya de Hernandez at the airport when she exited a flight from Columbia. They detained her for 16 hours, until eventually, she defecated. The United States customs officials and DEA agents recovered the drugs, which were used as evidence to convict her of drug smuggling. She appealed, alleging that the lengthy airport detention had been unreasonable and violative of her Fourth Amendment search-and-seizure rights. The SC disagreed, concluding that at border crossings, drug couriers who are profiled based upon compelling information from reliable informants may be intercepted and held, considering the reasonable suspicion existing that they might be using their alimentary canal as a repository for smuggled drugs. This case illustrates the fact that different search-and-seizure standards exist in different locations throughout the United States. Thus at international borders, especially at ports of entry known for illegal drug trafficking, such searches and seizures are not unreasonable, whereas they might be considered unreasonable if attempted in cities such as Kansas City, Missouri; Lima, Ohio; Wheeling, West Virginia; or Oklahoma City, Oklahoma.

United States v. Muniz, 374 U.S. 150, 83 S.Ct. 1850 (1963) **(Corrections; Federal Tort Claims Act).** A federal prison inmate got in a fight with another inmate. A prison guard viewing the fight chose not to intercede and locked the door to the area where the fight was occurring, thus confining it to a limited space. Serious injuries were incurred by the first inmate, including a fractured skull and a partial loss of vision in one eye. Lower courts denied the prisoner relief when he filed suit. However, the SC declared that the prisoner could file a suit under the Federal Tort Claims Act of 1946 to recover damages from the federal government and from the negligence of the prison guard, who was also a government employee.

United States v. Nachtigal, 507 U.S. 1, 113 S.Ct. 1072 (1993) **(Petty Offenses and Jury Trials).** Nachtigal was convicted of DUI in a national park while driving a motor vehicle under the influence of alcohol. When he appeared before the United States magistrate, Nachtigal asked for a jury trial but was denied one. His offense carried a penalty of six months in prison; thus, the offense was a petty one for which jury trials are not available. He appealed the conviction on the grounds that he had been denied a jury trial. The SC upheld his conviction, saying that jury trials may not be granted in petty-offense cases (*see Blanton v. North Las Vegas* [1989] for a comparative case).

United States v. New York Telephone Co., 434 U.S. 159, 98 S.Ct. 364 (1977) **(Law Enforcement Officers or Agencies; Electronic Surveillance).** The FBI suspected that illegal gambling was occurring at a specified New York City address. It requested the assistance of the telephone company in order to install listening devices on telephones at the location. The telephone company refused to comply with the FBI request, and a court opinion was delivered in favor of the telephone company. The SC reversed this order, however, and declared that it is proper to direct that a communication common carrier should furnish the applicant forthwith all information, facilities, and technical assistance as are necessary to accomplish the interception unobtrusively. Thus, telephone companies are subject to such orders and requests from official government agencies, such as the FBI.

United States v. Nobles, 422 U.S. 225, 95 S.Ct. 2160 (1975) **(Fifth Amendment; Self-Incrimination).** Nobles was accused in a United States district court in California of bank robbery. During his trial, the defense attempted to introduce an investigator's statements and interviews with prosecution witnesses for impeachment purposes. The judge ruled such statements would be admissible to the extent that the entire copy of the investigator's report should also be introduced. The defense declared that portions of the report were confidential and their introduction thus might violate the Fifth Amendment rights of Nobles. The judge declared that none of the report could be introduced if only selected portions of it were to be used for impeachment purposes. In view of this all-or-nothing declaration, the investigator was not called to testify. Following Nobles' conviction, Nobles appealed, arguing that his right to a fair trial had been denied. The SC upheld his conviction, saying that the Fifth Amendment privilege against self-incrimination applies *only* to defendants, and not to third parties, such as investigators, who may or may not present incriminating information in their court testimony. Thus

it was basically a defense choice to include the potentially incriminating testimony of the investigator, part of which may have helped to impeach a government witness, or to exclude the entirety of such testimony under court discovery provisions.

United States v. Noonan 47 CrL 1287 (3rd Cir.) (1990) **(Corrections; Pardons and Record Expungements).** Noonan was convicted and sentenced in 1969 for "failing to submit to induction into the armed forces." President Jimmy Carter granted him a pardon on January 21, 1977, wherein Carter declared a "full, complete, and unconditional pardon" to persons convicted during the Viet Nam War for refusing induction. Noonan sought to have his record of the original conviction expunged. An expungement order has the effect of wiping one's slate clean, as though the crime and the conviction had never occurred. Noonan believed that his conviction, which remained on his record, adversely affected his employment chances. Thus he sought to expunge it from his record because of the pardon he had received from Carter. However, the Third Circuit Court of Appeals, a federal appellate court, refused to grant his request. The court declared that "a pardon does not blot out guilt nor does it restore the offender to a state of innocence in the eye of the law." In short, at least in Noonan's case, the presidential pardon was effective in removing the punishment but not the criminal record.

United States v. Ojeda Rios, 495 U.S. 257, 110 S.Ct. 1845 (1990) **(Wiretaps; Electronic Surveillance).** Ojeda Rios was under electronic surveillance for alleged illegal activity. Tape recordings were made telephonically from his residence. The government secured the tapes but did not "seal" them. Ojeda Rios sought to suppress these tapes, because they had not been sealed in a timely manner and the government gave no satisfactory explanation for why they had not been sealed. Under the Omnibus Crime Control and Safe Streets Act, recordings of intercepted communications must be sealed immediately upon expiration of the period of order authorizing such interceptions. The SC held that the sealing rule had, indeed, been violated and ruled the tape recordings inadmissible against Ojeda Rios. The case was returned to the trial court for a determination to be made as to whether or not the government's explanation for the sealing delay of 82 days was reasonable.

United States v. Ortiz, 422 U.S. 891, 95 S.Ct. 2585 (1975) **(Law Enforcement Officers or Agencies; Searches and Seizures).** Ortiz was stopped at a Border Patrol checkpoint about 66 miles north of the Mexican border. Officers requested to search Ortiz's vehicle, but Ortiz refused. The officers searched it anyway, discovering illegal aliens. Ortiz was convicted of transporting them. He appealed. His conviction was overturned, however, when the SC ruled that a checkpoint so far removed from the Mexican border was unreasonable. Further, the Border Patrol agents had had no probable cause or even reasonable suspicion to arrest Ortiz or search his vehicle without warrant or permission. Thus checkpoints are like "roving patrols" of Border Patrol officers—there must be probable cause, consent, or warrant before an automobile is searched (*see Almeida-Sanchez* [1973] for a comparative case).

United States v. Owens, 484 U.S. 554, 108 S.Ct. 838 (1988) **(Sixth Amendment; Cross-Examination of Witnesses).** In a federal prison, a correctional counselor was severely assaulted by an inmate. An FBI investigation followed, in which Foster, the counselor, disclosed that his memory was not too good. Nevertheless, he was able to describe his attack, name his attacker, Owens, and identify Owens from Owens' photograph. During the subsequent trial, however, defense counsel cross-examined Foster and determined that he could not remember seeing his assailant or other details of the assault. Nevertheless, Foster's prior out-of-court statements became a part of the court record against Owens, who was convicted. He appealed to the SC, alleging that his Sixth Amendment right to cross-examine his accuser had been infringed because only out-of-court statements had been used against him, and that Foster, his accuser, could not recall details of the assault during the trial. Owens further alleged that Foster's prior out-of-court statements to FBI agents were nothing more than hearsay. The SC disagreed and upheld Owens' conviction. The SC said that Owens' confrontation rights had not been violated by the introduction of out-of-court statements from Foster, even though Foster admitted he could not recall specific details of the assault. Also, the SC said that Foster's out-of-court identification of Owens as his assailant was admissible against Owens, where Foster was present in court to be cross-examined about those statements.

United States v. Paradise, 480 U.S. 149, 107 S.Ct. 1053 (1987) **(Discrimination; Law Enforcement Agencies Employment).** The NAACP filed a class-action suit against the Alabama Department of Public Safety, alleging that although the department hired blacks as troopers, no blacks held officer ranks. The suit was initiated in 1972 and continued until 1981, when it was shown that the department had not complied with federal court orders to obtain a certain proportion of black highway patrol officers. The SC said that out of 232 state troopers at the rank of corporal or above, there were no black ones as of November 1978. It ordered Alabama officials to fill at least 50 percent of their promotions with black officers until such time that at least 25 percent of black proportionate representation in officer ranks was achieved. The SC said that this measure would fulfill the equal-protection clause of the Fourteenth Amendment.

United States v. Pattman, 535 F.2d. 1062 (8th Cir.) (1976) **(Probation Revocation; Hearsay Evidence at Proceedings).** Hearsay evidence that is "demonstrably reliable" need not be subject to confrontation and cross-examination in revocation proceedings.

United States v. Perez, 9 Wheat. 579 (1824) **(Double Jeopardy; Juries).** Whenever juries do not agree on a verdict and a case is retried, retrial does not constitute double jeopardy for defendants.

United States v. Place, 462 U.S. 696, 103 S.Ct. 2637 (1983) **(Law Enforcement Officers or Agencies; Stop and Frisk).** Place was suspected of narcotics possession. His luggage was the subject of a 90-minute detention while a trained narcotics-detection dog sniffed it. Place was convicted. He appealed. A circuit court of appeals reversed Place's conviction because the 90-minute investigative detention of his luggage was unreasonable in violation of his Fourth Amendment rights. The government appealed. The SC affirmed the reversal of Place's conviction.

United States v. Ramsey, 431 U.S. 606, 97 S.Ct. 1972 (1977) **(Law Enforcement Officers or Agencies; Vehicle Searches).** Ramsey had been receiving large envelopes from Thailand. A warrantless search of these envelopes by customs officials yielded large quantities of narcotics. Ramsey was convicted of various narcotics offenses. An appeal to the SC was of no avail, where the SC held that border-search exceptions to searches of letters and other items are within the guidelines of customs statutes. Thus customs officials do not require a search warrant to conduct inspections of suspicious mail in international commerce.

United States v. Reed, 573 F.2d. 1020 ((8th Cir.) (1978) **(Probation Revocation).** An appellate court ruled that accumulation of several technical program violations does not justify revoking a probation program, given the rehabilitative nature of such a program.

United States v. Robinson, 414 U.S. 218, 94 S.Ct. 467 (1973) **(Law Enforcement Officers or Agencies; Searches Incident to Arrest).** Robinson was stopped for operating a motor vehicle without a valid operator's license. It was known that Robinson's license had previously been revoked. Robinson was formally arrested on the basis of probable cause. While arrested, Robinson was searched extensively by police, who found heroin capsules in a crumpled cigarette package. These capsules became evidence against Robinson later when he was subsequently convicted of possession of heroin. Robinson appealed, contending that the scope of an officer's search was limited to "pat-downs and frisks" in view of the *Terry v. Ohio* (1968) and *Sibron v. New York* (1968) rulings. The SC heard the case and upheld Robinson's conviction, noting that the difference between *Terry* and the Robinson case was that Terry was not in custody when a police officer conducted a pat-down and frisk of Terry's outer clothing. Further, the *Sibron* case, which suppressed heroin found in Sibron's pocket when he was not under arrest, also differed from the Robinson case because Robinson had been placed under arrest, with probable cause, and then searched. Police have a right to search suspects extensively whenever suspects have been arrested, based upon probable cause. A custodial arrest of a suspect based on probable cause is a reasonable intrusion under the Fourth Amendment.

United States v. Robinson, 485 U.S. 25, 108 S.Ct. 864 (1988) **(Fifth Amendment; Right Against Self-Incrimination).** Robinson had been investigated by insurance agents on arson-related insurance claims using the United States mails. He was indicted for mail fraud. At his trial in a United States district court in Tennessee, Robinson chose *not* to testify in his own behalf. In summation, defense counsel claimed that the government had not allowed Robinson to testify in his own behalf. Upon hearing this, the prosecutor demanded a sidebar conference out of the jury's presence to raise the issue of improper statements from the defense counsel. During this hearing, the judge agreed that the defense had "opened the door" by commenting about Robinson's failure to testify. Thus, when the jury reconvened, the prosecutor advised them that Robinson could have taken the stand and told his side of the story. Because he didn't, the jury was urged to make an adverse inference about Robinson's guilt. The judge gave the jury instructions at the trial's conclusion, instructing them *not* to make inferences about the fact that Robinson had not testified. Despite these admonitions, the jury found Robinson guilty. He appealed, alleging that the prosecutorial conduct was prejudicial and that his right against compulsory self-incrimination had been violated. The SC rejected Robinson's arguments, basically concluding that Robinson could have taken the stand and given testimony in his own behalf. Furthermore, it was *his* counsel, *not* the prosection, who mentioned first the fact that he didn't testify. Thus the prosecution's reference to the defendant's opportunity to testify, ordinarily prohibited, was acceptable as a response to the defense assertion that Robinson was barred from testifying. There were no constitutional-rights violations in this process.

United States v. Ross, 456 U.S. 798, 102 S.Ct. 2157 (1982) **(Law Enforcement Officers or Agencies; Consent Searches).** A reliable informant advised police that Ross was dealing drugs out of his car in a designated location. Police went to the location, observed Ross as described by the informant, and made a warrantless arrest. Then they searched his vehicle, where they found heroin and other illegal substances in containers in the trunk. He was convicted, but he appealed, arguing that police had violated his Fourth Amendment rights against unreasonable searches and seizures. The SC upheld Ross' conviction, saying that following a lawful arrest based upon probable cause, a person's car may be searched without warrant, as well as bags and other containers found within it. (*See United States v. Chadwick* [1977]), which prohibits warrantless searches of large footlockers, even if found in vehicles being searched incident to an arrest and the police have time to get a warrant.

United States v. Russell, 411 U.S. 423, 93 1637 (1973) **(Entrapment).** Russell and several other persons were suspected of selling methamphetamine, an illegal drug. Government drug agents met with Russell and his friends and offered to manufacture and market the drug and share the profits with them. One agent, Shapiro, offered to provide an essential, hard-to-get chemical component necessary for the manufacturing process. Russell and his partners agreed to participate. They were convicted. Russell appealed, contending that he had been the victim of entrapment, as the government supplied the essential chemical in the furtherance of the illegal activity. The SC disagreed and upheld Russell's conviction. The SC said that entrapment was not proved merely because a government agent supplied an essential chemical leading to the production of an illegal drug that Russell would have manufactured anyway. Russell was already predisposed to commit the illegal act of manufacturing these drugs. Predisposition, stressed by the SC, is one significant determinant of whether entrapment exists.

United States v. Salerno, 481 U.S. 739, 107 S.Ct. 2095 (1987) **(Pretrial Detention).** Salerno and others were arrested for several serious crimes and held without bail under the Bail Reform Act of 1984 as dangerous. He was convicted and sentenced to 100 years in prison. He appealed, being among the first to challenge the constitutionality of the new Bail Reform Act and its provision that specifies that dangerous persons may be detained prior to trial until such time as their case may be decided. He objected that the new act violated the Eighth Amendment provision against "cruel and unusual" punishment. The SC upheld the constitutionality of pretrial detention and declared that it did not violate the defandant's rights under the Eighth Amendment if a specific defendant was found to be dangerous.

United States v. Santana, 427 U.S. 38, 96 S.Ct. 2406 (1976) **(Law Enforcement Officers or Agencies; Arrest).** An undercover police officer offered a woman, McCafferty, money to buy heroin. She accepted the money, drove to the home of Santana, went inside, and came back out with heroin, which she delivered to the officer. When asked about the money given to her, McCafferty said that Santana had it. McCafferty was placed under arrest, while other officers placed Santana's house under surveillance. Later, they observed Santana in the front doorway holding a brown paper bag. Officers approached and Santana attempted to flee back into her home. In hot pursuit, officers caught her, and two bags of heroin fell from her hands. The undercover "buy" money was found in her purse. She was arrested and subsequently convicted of possessing heroin

with intent to distribute. Santana appealed and the case was heard by the SC. She claimed the warrantless arrest and search of her belongings was a violation of her Fourth Amendment rights. The SC disagreed, contending that she was in a public place when she was standing in her doorway. The totality-of-circumstances rule also governed here, because her appearance and identification followed closely a situation where drugs were purchased by undercover officers. Further, the police had engaged in "hot pursuit" when they followed her into her own home and therefore had not violated her privacy. Thus a retreating suspect from a public place into a private one precludes pursuing police officers from having to first obtain an arrest or search warrant (*see especially Warden v. Hayden* [1967]).

United States v. Scott, 437 U.S. 82, 98 S.Ct. 2187 (1978) **(Double Jeopardy).** Scott was indicted on three narcotics counts. Two of the counts were dismissed on a motion by the defense. After a federal trial was held and Scott was convicted of the one remaining narcotics count, federal prosecutors sought to reindict him on the two narcotics counts that had been dismissed. They alleged that the indictments had been sound but had been prejudiced by a preindictment delay. Scott objected to these new indictments and claimed that he could not be tried on charges stemming from dismissed indictments. The SC heard Scott's appeal and ruled against him, saying that because he had initiated the motions to dismiss the indictments against him, that act did not preclude the government from seeking new indictments on the same charges. Scott's right against double jeopardy had not been violated.

United States v. Sharpe, 470 U.S. 675, 105 S.Ct. 1568 (1985) **(Law Enforcement Officers or Agencies; Stop and Frisk).** Sharpe was following an overloaded truck in his own automobile when DEA agents, suspicious of possible drug trafficking, stopped him. They called for highway patrol officers to watch Sharpe while they investigated the overloaded truck. An initial encounter with the truck driver, Savage, led to an uninvited search of the truck's contents after DEA agents "smelled marijuana." Considerable quantities of marijuana were discovered in the truck, and both Savage and Sharpe were arrested and subsequently convicted of possessing a controlled substance. An appeal eventually reached the SC, arguing that the DEA agents had had no right to detain Sharpe for more than 20 minutes while other agents pursued and stopped Savage's truck. The SC avoided setting a specific time limit regarding how long criminal suspects may be stopped and detained under these circumstances. It held that because of the purpose of the stop, the reasonableness of it, and the reasonableness of the means of investigation by the DEA officers, such warrantless intrusion into Savage's truck and the length of Sharpe's detention had not violated the Fourth Amendment. The significance of this case is that no set time limit is placed upon officers to stop and detain suspicious persons while others connected with them are also being investigated. However, the SC also said that police officers must be able to justify the length of particular stops and detentions if the case reaches court.

United States v. Sheffield, 161 F.Supp. 387 (Md.) (1958) **(Criminal Intent)**. Sheffield stole an automobile in one state and drove it through several other states. He reversed direction and began driving back to his originating state. He was stopped, arrested, and convicted of auto theft. He appealed, saying that he had intended to return the car to the rightful owner. The court of appeals rejected his argument, saying that it is sufficient feloniously to deprive the lawful owner of a vehicle for an indefinite period, and that it is inadequate to claim return of that vehicle to the originating state and leaving it somewhere in the city from which it was taken. The conviction was upheld.

United States v. Sokolow, 490 U.S. 1, 109 S.Ct. 1581 (1989) **(Law Enforcement Officers or Agencies; Search and Seizure)**. The Drug Enforcement Administration has developed a drug courier profile for use at ports of entry, airports, and bus and train depots. On the basis of this profile, Sokolow and a companion were observed at an airport purchasing with cash two roundtrip tickets to Hawaii. Both men appeared nervous and possessed only carry-on luggage. They were stopped by DEA agents and taken to a private airport office, where their luggage was examined by narcotics-detecting dogs. The dogs reacted as though the luggage contained drugs. Officers obtained a search warrant, and the bags were searched. The search yielded more than 1,000 grams of cocaine. Sokolow was subsequently convicted. He appealed, arguing that DEA agents had lacked probable cause to stop initially and search his personal effects. Essentially, he was contesting use of the drug courier profile. The SC down-

played the significance of profiling, favoring the totality-of-circumstances justification for stopping, questioning, and subsequently searching persons who fit profiles as drug couriers.

United States v. Staples, ___U.S.___, 114 S.Ct. 1793 **(Ignorance of the Law, Knowledge of Criminal Act)**. Staples was convicted in federal court for possessing a machine gun. He appealed, arguing that he did not know that the semi-automatic rifle he had purchased had been modified so that it was capable of firing multiple rounds from one trigger pull, thus making it function as a machine gun. He argued that the government was required to prove, beyond a reasonable doubt, that he had known such a weapon was in fact a machine gun. The SC overturned Staples' conviction, saying that the government had not proved beyond a reasonable doubt that Staples had known the weapon had been modified. The statute prohibiting possession of a machine gun did not have a statement of mens rea or intent to commit a crime. Therefore, the SC relied upon common law to resolve such a question and directed the case back to the originating trial court to retry, this time using the mens rea condition as an important crime element. The prosecution was required to prove that Staples had known the firearm was automatic rather than semi-automatic as he claimed.

United States v. Valenzuela-Bernal, 458 U.S. 858, 102 S.Ct. 3440 (1982) **(Sixth Amendment; Confrontation Clause)**. Valenzuela-Bernal was charged with transporting illegal aliens. During his trial, he attempted to compel several prior passengers and illegal aliens to appear in court as witnesses in his behalf. It was concluded that these other witnesses would have nothing relevant to contribute. He appealed, alleging that his Fifth and Sixth Amendment rights had been violated because of the government "failure" to produce these other witnesses in his behalf. The SC ruled otherwise and held that there were no Fifth and Sixth Amendment rights violations. The SC stressed the materiality requirement in its decision, noting that sanctions against the government can be sustained only if there is a reasonable likelihood that the testimony of the illegal aliens could have affected the jury decision. The SC declared that in this case such testimony would have no perceptible effect.

United States v. Van Leeuwen, 397 U.S. 249, 90 S.Ct. 1029 (1970) **(Law Enforcement Officers or Agencies; Searches)**. Van Leeuwen arranged to send coins from different addresses in Seattle, Washington, and Van Nuys, California, to Nashville, Tennessee. A postal clerk became suspicious of the mailed packages, partly because they appeared to be mailed from a fictitious address (the postal worker knew that the address was a vacant lot) and alerted police. A search warrant was obtained, but police were unable to search the packages immediately because of various delays. The next day, the packages were searched and yielded illegal gold coins from Canada. The packages were resealed and forwarded. Van Leeuwen was arrested when he picked them up in Nashville. He was convicted. He appealed, alleging that his Fourth Amendment rights had been violated because of the lengthy delay between the police obtaining search warrants and actually searching the packages. The SC upheld his conviction, saying that no interest protected by the Fourth Amendment had been violated by forwarding the packages the following day rather than the day they were deposited. There had also been sufficient probable cause upon which to obtain a search warrant, because Van Leeuwen had given a fictitious address and had a car with Canadian license plates.

United States v. Ventresca, 380 U.S. 102, 85 S.Ct. 741 (1965) **(Law Enforcement Officers or Agencies; Search and Seizure).** Ventresca was suspected of operating an illegal distillery. Police conducting surveillance of Ventresca's property discovered deliveries of large amounts of sugar and numerous empty tin containers. Subsequently, they saw numerous filled tin containers being loaded into automobile trunks and driven off. They detected the odor of fermenting mash when they walked along the sidewalk in front of Ventresca's home. On the basis of these observations and impressions, officers obtained a search warrant and raided Ventresca's premises, finding an illegal still and a large quantity of illegal alcohol. Ventresca was convicted. He appealed, seeking to suppress the incriminating evidence seized, on the grounds that the officers had lacked probable cause when obtaining their search warrant. The SC heard the case and upheld Ventresca's conviction, holding that the officers had acted properly by first securing a search warrant based upon probable cause, supported by oath or affirmation, describing the place to be searched and the things to be seized.

United States v. Verdugo-Urquidez, 494 U.S. 259, 110 S.Ct. 1056, (1990) **(Law Enforcement Officers or Agencies; Arrests).** Verdugo-Urquidez was arrested by Mexican police, who delivered him to United States authorities. Subsequently, United States authorities conducted a warrantless search of Verdugo-Urquidez's residence in Mexico and obtained incriminating information against him, which was used to convict him in a United States court. He appealed. A lower appellate court ruled to suppress the evidence seized in Mexico, because the Fourth Amendment right against unreasonable search and seizure had been violated. The SC upheld Verdugo-Urquidez's conviction, saying that the Fourth Amendment does not apply in Mexico against persons who are Mexican residents, who are not United States citizens, and who have no voluntary attachment to the United States.

United States v. Villamonte-Marquez, 462 U.S. 579, 103 S.Ct. 2573 (1983) **(Law Enforcement Officers or Agencies; Searches and Seizures).** United States customs officials were patrolling a water channel connecting Lake Charles, Louisiana, with the Gulf of Mexico, when they observed an anchored boat caused to be upset by a passing sailboat. The boat rocked violently, and when customs officers went aboard to see if the occupants of the boat were all right, they smelled marijuana and saw through an open hatch a large quantity of marijuana wrapped in burlap. Further searching produced more marijuana, and Villamonte-Marquez, captain of the boat, was charged and convicted of conspiring to import, possess, and distribute marijuana. He appealed, saying that the search and seizure had been unreasonable, in violation of his Fourth Amendment rights. The case went through various levels of appeals, eventually reaching the SC, where it was decided that United States customs officials are authorized to board any vessel located in waters providing easy access to the open sea, in order to examine the ship's manifest and other documents, even without suspecting any wrongdoing. The SC reinstated Villamonte-Marquez's original conviction.

United States v. Wade, 388 U.S. 218, 87 S.Ct. 1926 (1967) **(Law Enforcement Officers or Agencies; Lineups).** Wade was a participant in a bank robbery. He drove away from the bank with an accomplice. Eyewitnesses saw them in the bank and gave descriptions to police. Subsequently, Wade was arrested and indicted for robbery. A lawyer was appointed for him. Later at the jail, police placed Wade in a lineup with other men for two bank workers to view. Both bank workers identified Wade as the robber. Wade's attorney was not notified of the lineup. Later, at Wade's trial, the same bank employees reidentified Wade as the robber and he was convicted, in some part, upon the testimony of these eyewitnesses. Wade appealed, moving to suppress the testimony of the eyewitnesses, because he had been subjected to a lineup without his attorney present. The SC agreed and overturned Wade's conviction, saying that lineups are critical stages, and whenever indicted offenders have counsel appointed for them, those attorneys should be present at these critical stages. In Wade's case, because he was represented by counsel and his counsel was not present at his lineup, his right to counsel had been violated.

United States v. Washington, 431 U.S. 181, 97 S.Ct. 1814 (1977) **(Grand Juries).** Washington was indicted for receiving stolen property on the basis of his self-incriminating testimony before a grand jury in a related matter. Washington sought to dismiss the indictment, contending that he had not waived his right against self-incrimination when he appeared before the grand jury. The SC upheld his indictment, holding that when a witness suspected of wrongdoing gives self-incriminating testimony before a grand jury, this information may be used against him in later criminal prosecution even though the witness is not informed in advance of his testimony that he is a potential defendant in danger in indictment.

United States v. Watson, 423 U.S. 411, 96 S.Ct. 820 (1976) **(Law Enforcement Officers or Agencies; Arrests).** A postal inspector was advised by a reliable informant that Watson possessed stolen credit cards, had given the informant some cards, and planned to give him more cards in the future. The inspector arranged for the informant to meet with Watson later where the credit-card exchange could be observed by police. The informant was supposed to give police a signal whenever Watson gave him stolen credit cards. A signal was given by the informant and Watson was stopped, arrested, told his Miranda rights, and searched by police, who found no stolen credit cards. They asked Watson if they could search his vehicle, which was nearby. Watson agreed, and an envelope with stolen credit cards was found. Wat-

son was charged with and convicted of possession of stolen credit cards. He appealed, arguing that police had had no business arresting him in a public place without first obtaining a valid arrest warrant. The SC upheld Watson's conviction, saying that sufficient probable cause had existed that a crime had been committed (on the basis of the reliable informant's information) for police officers to investigate and make an arrest. The significance of this case is that it permits officers to make warrantless arrests of suspects in a public place and with probable cause.

United States v. Wheeler, 435 U.S. 313, 98 S.Ct. 1079 (1978) **(Double Jeopardy).** Wheeler was a Navajo tribe member who was convicted in tribal court of contributing to the delinquency of a minor. Later, a federal grand jury indicted Wheeler on statutory rape charges arising from the same incident. Wheeler sought to dismiss the indictment on the grounds of double jeopardy. The SC refused to dismiss the indictment, holding that the Navajo tribal court was not an arm of the federal government but rather an independent sovereign. Thus a federal prosecution arising from the same incident where Wheeler was convicted by a tribal court did not violate his right against double jeopardy.

United States v. White, 401 U.S. 745, 97 S.Ct. 1122 (1971) **(Law Enforcement Officers or Agencies; Electronic Surveillance).** A criminal suspect, White, was under police surveillance. An informant, a friend of White's, wore an electronic transmitter and engaged White in incriminating conversations at his restaurant, home, and automobile. No warrant had been issued for such electronic surveillance. The informant was never called to testify, but the incriminating recorded conversations were admitted later at White's trial, where he was convicted. White appealed, alleging that a warrant should have been issued for such recordings, and that his Fourth Amendment rights had been violated as a result. The SC disagreed and said that voluntary statements made by a criminal suspect to a paid government informant are admissible as evidence against the suspect, even if the informant does not testify and if the information is introduced at trial through the testimony of FBI agents who did the original recording of the conversation. Compare this case with the same situation in *Massiah v. United States* (1964). Massiah was previously indicted and represented by counsel but in Massiah's case, the incriminating information provided through an informant was inadmissible because Massiah's attorney was not present during the "interrogation." The "interrogation" was considered such because the informant was acting on behalf of the FBI investigating Massiah. The crucial element was whether Massiah was represented by counsel. If White had been previously indicted and represented by counsel, then the *Massiah* ruling would have governed his case and the incriminating evidence could have been suppressed effectively.

United States v. Williams, 504 U.S. 36, 112 S.Ct. 1735 (1992) **(Grand Jury Indictments; Exculpatory Evidence).** Williams was indicted by a federal grand jury for various crimes, including making false statements for the purpose of influencing the action of a federally insured financial institution. During the presentation of the case, federal prosecutors omitted various exculpatory statements to the grand jury. Williams later saw the entire grand jury record and moved to have the indictment dismissed because of the government failure to introduce these exculpatory statements. His motion was granted and the indictment was dismissed. The government appealed. The SC heard the case and ruled in the government's favor, holding that prosecutors are not under any particular duty to present exculpatory evidence during grand-jury proceedings. The indictment was reinstated.

United States v. Wilson, 420 U.S. 332, 95 S.Ct. 1013 (1975) **(Self-Incrimination).** Wilson was indicted on charges of embezzling money from a labor organization. He was convicted. He filed several motions, including one to dismiss the indictment. The motion to dismiss the indictment was granted. Then he sought to have his embezzlement conviction set aside because of the lack of a valid indictment. The government appealed to have the original indictment upheld. The SC upheld the original indictment and Wilson's conviction.

United States v. Wong, 431 U.S. 174, 97 S.Ct. 1823 (1977) **(Grand Juries).** Wong testified before a grand jury in a criminal matter. She was indicted for perjury. She moved to have the indictment suppressed, alleging that she had not understood the warning of her right not to answer self-incriminating questions before the grand jury. The United States district court granted the suppression motion. The government appealed. The SC thought otherwise and reinstated her indictment on perjury charges. The SC held that a witness

who is called to testify before a grand jury while under investigation for criminal activity, and who is later indicted for perjury relating to that grand jury testimony, is not entitled to have false testimony suppressed on the ground that no effective warning of the Fifth Amendment privilege to remain silent was given.

United States Department of Justice v. Landano, 507 U.S.___, 113 S.Ct. 2014 (1993) **(Freedom of Information Act; Corrections; Inmate Rights).** Landano, convicted of murder, sought to obtain investigative files from the FBI under the Freedom of Information Act (FOIA). The FBI gave Landano only partial files and withheld other files. Landano appealed to the SC, where the case was heard. The government claimed that it had denied certain files to Landano because of confidential sources. The SC declared that the FBI is not entitled to the presumption that all sources supplying information to the FBI in the course of a criminal investigation are confidential and thus exempted from FOIA requests. Thus Landano was entitled to those files. The SC declared, however, that if it can be shown, through in camera affidavits, that some of the confidential informants might be jeopardized by such disclosures, then some of this information may be exempted from FOIA requests.

Uveges v. Pennsylvania, 335 U.S. 437, 69 S.Ct. 184 (1948) **(Sixth Amendment Right to Counsel)** In October 1938, Elmer Uveges, a 17-year-old, was charged in four separate indictments for different burglaries. He entered guilty pleas to all four charges and was sentenced to four consecutive terms totaling 80 years in prison. Later, he filed a habeas corpus petition, alleging that his due-process rights had been violated when he was not informed of his right to counsel and had not been offered counsel during the period between his arrest and conviction. Uveges also alleged that he had been intimidated by prosecutors who threatened him and coerced a guilty plea from him on the promise that he would be sentenced for a short term to a nearby reformatory. The SC heard Uveges' case and reversed his convictions. Indigents are entitled to counsel whether they elect to stand trial or plead guilty, where the seriousness of the proceedings would otherwise render the proceedings fundamentally unfair. The SC held that under the requirements of due process, Uveges' case required the presence of counsel at his trial. He should not have pleaded guilty without having an offer of the advice of counsel. The fact that he was young and inexperienced was clearly advantageous to prosecutors. Thus Uveges had been denied a fair hearing, and his sentences had to be vacated in this light and a new trial granted with counsel provided.

V

Vale v. Louisiana, 399 U.S. 30, 90 S.Ct. 1969 (1970) **(Law Enforcement Officers or Agencies; Search and Seizure; Arrest).** Vale, a suspected drug user, was under police surveillance. One evening while police were observing his home, a known drug addict spoke with Vale on his front porch and some object was exchanged between them. The police intercepted the drug addict as he left Vale, and arrested Vale outside his front door. Without a warrant, police proceeded to enter Vale's home and search it incident to the arrest. While searching, they discovered heroin and other narcotics in Vale's bedroom. Vale was convicted. He appealed, contending that police had needed a valid search warrant to search his premises and that a search incident to his arrest had violated his Fourth Amendment right against an unreasonable search and seizure. The SC agreed with Vale and overturned his conviction. No exigent circumstances existed in this case, because Vale didn't know that his activities were being observed or that he would have time to dispose of his illegal drugs. Arrests of suspects must occur *in* their homes, not outside of them, and even in this instance, police should have limited their search to areas immediately under the suspect's control, such as the room he was arrested in, not other rooms, such as bedrooms, kitchens, garages, and attics. (*See Chimel v. California* (1969) for a specific SC statement on the scope of searches incident to arrests.)

Vasquez v. Hillery, 474 U.S. 254, 106 S.Ct. 6167 (1986) **(Equal Protection Clause; Fourteenth Amendment; Grand Juries and Racial Composition).** Hillery, a black man, was indicted in 1962 for murder in a California court. He sought to dismiss the indictment on the grounds that black persons had been deliberately excluded from the grand jury that issued it. He was unsuccessful and was ultimately convicted of first-degree murder. Sixteen years later, Hillery filed a habeas corpus suit alleging that the racial composition of the grand jury had adversely affected his conviction in violation of the equal-protection clause of the Fourteenth Amendment. The state countered that the fair trial Hillery was ultimately given had removed any taint of the racially biased grand jury that had issued the original indictment. The SC granted Hillery's petition, thus reversing his conviction, rejecting the idea that the biased racial composition of the grand jury had been a "harmless error." Rather, the SC declared, discrimination in grand jury selections undermines the structural integrity of criminal tribunals, and fair trials cannot correct such problems. The SC ruled that convictions of any defendants indicted by grand juries from which members of their race have been systematically excluded must be reversed.

Victor v. Nebraska, ___U.S.___, 114 S.Ct. 1239 (1994) **(Jury Instructions from Judges on "Beyond a Reasonable Doubt" Standard).** Victor was convicted in a Nebraska court of first-degree murder and sentenced to death. In the judge's instructions to the jury, he said that *reasonable* doubt can be equated with a *substantial* doubt. Victor sought to have his conviction reversed on the grounds that "substantial doubt" was an overstatement of the amount of doubt jury members would need to deliver an acquittal. The SC heard the case and declared that the matter of "substantial doubt" compared with "beyond a reasonable doubt" was unexceptional proposition. In fact, the SC had upheld the constitutionality of the phrase "substantial doubt" in the case of *Cage v. Louisiana* (1990). Victor's murder conviction and death sentence were upheld.

Vitek v. Jones, 445 U.S. 480, 100 S.Ct. 1254 (1980) **(Corrections; Inmate Rights).** Jones was a Nebraska inmate transferred from a prison cell to the penitentiary hospital for mental illness. This transfer was made without a hearing. Jones later was placed in solitary confinement and set his mattress on fire, suffering burns. Subsequently, he was transferred, again without a hearing, to a state mental hospital for commitment for an indefinite period. Jones sued under Title 42, U.S.C. Section 1983, alleging that his due-process rights had been violated when he was transferred to a mental hospital without a hearing. The SC agreed with Jones and held that before prisoners may be transferred to a mental institution from a prison, they are entitled to a hearing on the transfer. This is to insure that their due-process rights are observed. (See *Morrissey v. Brewer* [1972] for a comparative case in due-process rights of probationers and parolees).

W

Wainwright v. Greenfield, 474 U.S. 284, 106 S.Ct. 634 (1986) **(Self-Incrimination).** Greenfield was suspected of sexual battery. At the time of his arrest, he was told his Miranda rights, and he refused to answer questions about the alleged crime. He pled not guilty by reason of insanity. During his trial, the prosecutor commented about the fact that Greenfield refused to answer police questions, and that this was evidence of his "sanity." Greenfield was subsequently convicted. He appealed. The SC overturned Greenfield's conviction, saying that it is fundamentally unfair for prosecutors to comment upon a defendant's silence invoked as the result of a Miranda warning. This is a violation of the due-process clause of the Fourteenth Amendment (*see Doyle v. Ohio* [1976] for a comparative case).

Wainwright v. Goode, 464 U.S. 78, 104 S.Ct. 378 (1983) **(Death Penalty; Aggravating Circumstances).** Goode kidnapped a 10-year-old boy in Florida, sexually assaulted him, and then strangled him with a belt. Goode fled to Maryland and later to Virginia, where he committed another murder. He was convicted of murder in Virginia and then returned to Florida, where he was again convicted of murder and given the death penalty. The judge cited three aggravating factors and two mitigating ones and imposed the death penalty. Later, Goode appealed, alleging ineffective assistance of counsel, because his counsel had failed to challenge the judge's remarks, especially some that made reference to nonstatutory aggravating factors, such as predicting Goode's future dangerousness. A lower court reversed the Florida decision by concluding that the judge's reliance on such a nonstatutory factor had been arbitrary and capricious. Goode then appealed to the SC, which reinstated the penalty of death, stating that no sound basis had been provided by Goode to show that the procedures followed by the Florida judge necessarily produced an arbitrary and freakish sentence forbidden by the Eighth Amendment.

Wainwright v. Witt, 469 U.S. 412, 105 S.Ct. 844 (1985) **(Death-Qualified Juries).** Witt was convicted of first-degree murder by a Florida jury and sentenced to death. He appealed, arguing that it was wrong of the trial judge to exclude a prospective juror because of her views on the death penalty. A lower court set aside the conviction, remanding the case to the lower court for a new trial. The government appealed and the SC reinstated the original conviction and death penalty, saying that the finding of juror bias by the trial judge had been made under the proper standard. The proper standard is whether a juror's attitudes about the death penalty would substantially impair his or her ability to determine the proper penalty in the punishment phase of a two-phase trial. Potential jurors in capital murder cases may be excluded if their views would prevent or substantially impair the performance of their duties in accordance with their instructions and oath (*see Witherspoon v. Illinois* [1968]).

Walder v. United States, 347 U.S. 62, 74 S.Ct. 354 (1954) **(Corrections; Searches and Seizures).** In May 1950 Walder was indicted for possessing cocaine. He moved to have the evidence suppressed, because the search and seizure tactics used by police were questionable. His motion was granted and his case was dismissed. Later, he was indicted in January 1952 for four additional narcotics transactions. During his trial, he was asked whether he had ever dealt in narcotics, and he said no. An officer who arrested him in 1950 gave impeaching testimony, which Walder sought to suppress. He was convicted. He appealed, contending that the original cocaine seized from him was the result of an illegal search and seizure. The SC upheld his conviction, saying that impeachment evidence may come from formerly illegal searches and seizures from those involved in the seizures of cocaine. Thus it was not improper to introduce testimony that Walder had engaged formerly in cocaine sales, even though the evidence was subsequently excluded and the charges against him were dismissed.

Walrath v. United States, 830 F.Supp. 444 (1993) **(Corrections; Parole Requirements).** Penile plethysmography is a test administered to convicted sex offenders. The test involves attaching devices to a prospective parolee's penis in order to determine his subsequent reaction to various forms of sexual stimuli. An erection is incriminating in this instance, and the offender may be denied parole. The test is also used to determine whether a sex offender continues to pose a threat to society. In an Illinois federal action, a convicted sex offender, Walrath, was required to submit to a penile plethysmograph test as one condition preceding his parole by the Illinois Parole Board. Walrath claimed that such a test would violate his Fifth Amendment right against self-incrimination. The United States district court in Illinois upheld the United States Parole Commission's administration of the test to Walrath, holding that "there is no indication that any results from Walrath's plethysmograph could be used to criminally prosecute him for other acts. Instead, the results, like the treatment, might legitimately be used to assess the threat Walrath poses to society."

Walton v. Arizona, 497 U.S. 639, 110 S.Ct. 3047 (1990) **(Eighth Amendment; Death Penalty).** Walton and two friends, while at a bar in Arizona, determined they would steal someone's car at random. They encountered Thomas Powell, an off-duty Marine, kidnapped him, stole his car, and shot him to death, execution-style, in the desert. Following their arrest, they all made inculpatory statements suggesting that the killing was especially cruel and heinous. Walton told his friends, for instance, that after he shot Powell in the back of the head, he saw Powell "pee in his pants" and that he had never seen someone do that before. Walton was convicted of first-degree murder, armed robbery, kidnapping, and theft. At his sentencing hearing, the jury was given instructions by the judge, including one that two aggravating circumstances were present if the jury found the murder was committed (1) in "an especially heinous, cruel, or depraved manner" and (2) for pecuniary gain. The jury found that such circumstances existed and recommended the death penalty for Walton. Walton appealed, alleging that these instructions and the nature of weighing aggravating circumstances in relation to mitigating ones were "facially vague." Therefore, he alleged his Sixth and Eighth Amendment rights had been violated. The SC heard his case and upheld his murder conviction and death penalty, holding that Arizona was not required to call aggravating circumstances "elements" of offense or permit only the jury to determine the existence of such circumstances; "especially heinous, cruel, or depraved" aggravating circumstance as construed by the Arizona Supreme Court furnished suffi-

cient guidance to jurors to satisfy Eighth and Fourteenth Amendments.

Warden v. Hayden, 387 U.S. 294, 87 S.Ct. 1647 (1967) **(Law Enforcement Officers or Agencies; Arrest; Search and Seizure).** A cab company robbery was reported to police, and a description of the man was provided by eyewitnesses. A pedestrian followed the man to his home and reported immediately to police. They went to the house and a woman answered the door. They asked if they could come in and look around. She consented. They found Hayden "pretending to be asleep." Further, they found a shotgun and pistol in a toilet water tank, clothes fitting the robber's description in a washing machine, and a bag containing money with the cab company name imprinted on it. Hayden was arrested and convicted. He appealed, alleging that the police had had no right to enter his home without a valid warrant based upon probable cause. The SC disagreed and said that police in hot pursuit of a criminal suspect do not need a search warrant to enter his home. Even more important was the fact that Mrs. Hayden had given police permission to enter the home and conduct a search of it. Thus consent provides an additional exception to the exclusionary rule that would ordinarily require a search warrant before incriminating evidence can be searched for and seized.

Washington v. Chrisman, 455 U.S. 1, 102 S.Ct. 812 (1982) **(Law Enforcement Officers or Agencies; Fourth Amendment; Searches Incident to An Arrest).** In late January 1978, the Washington State University campus police observed a student, Overdahl, carrying a half-gallon bottle of gin as he was leaving his dormitory. Campus regulations forbade alcoholic beverages in possession of students, so the campus police stopped Overdahl and asked for ID. He told police that his ID was in his dorm room and they accompanied him back to his room to obtain it. When they entered the room, another student, Chrisman, was placing a small box in a medicine cabinet. Officers observed in plain view several seeds and a pipe lying on a nearby table. One of the officers, based upon his experience, believed the seeds to be marijuana and that the pipe was used for smoking marijuana. He entered the room, inspected the seeds, and smelled the pipe, confirming his suspicions. Both students were told their Miranda rights and questioned. They admitted to smoking marijuana and possessing it. Also, they voluntarily consented to permit the officers to search their room. The officers found more marijuana, LSD, and other controlled substances. Chrisman was charged with and convicted of marijuana possession. He appealed, alleging that the officers had had no right to enter his room and seize anything without first obtaining a warrant. The Washington Supreme Court reversed Chrisman's conviction on various grounds, particularly because it believed the officers had not been entitled to accompany Overdahl into the room while he secured his ID. Therefore, the Washington SC reasoned, the evidence seized ought to have been suppressed, and it overturned Chrisman's conviction. The government appealed. The United States SC disagreed and reinstated Chrisman's conviction. The SC argued that from the first officer's vantage point in the doorway of the dorm room, the seeds and suspicious pipe were in plain view, which created probable cause to investigate further by entering the room. The officers were in a place where they had a right to be, and therefore their seizure of the drugs and drug paraphernalia was lawful. Furthermore, after being told their Miranda rights, the students had consented to further search of their room. Thus the seizure of controlled substances was justified, the evidence admissible, and the convictions upheld.

Washington v. Harper, 494 U.S. 210, 110 S.Ct. 1028 (1990) **(Confessions; Inmate Rights).** Harper was a psychologically disturbed inmate in prison for robbery. He was eventually paroled but on condition that he participate in psychiatric treatment at a hospital. About a year later, Harper assaulted two nurses in a Seattle hospital, and his parole was revoked. When he returned to prison, prison psychiatrists determined that he should be administered antipsychotic medication. Harper agreed for a time to take this medication, but a while later, he refused to continue. The medicine was forcibly administered thereafter. Harper filed a Title 42, U.S.C. Section 1983 claim, alleging that he had not been given a hearing to determine whether due process was violated by having to take such medication forcibly. The SC disagreed with Harper, saying that it is proper whenever inmates have serious mental illnesses for treatment to be administered with antipsychotic drugs against their will and without a judicial hearing.

Washington v. Texas, 388 U.S. 14, 87 S.Ct. 1920 (1967) **(Fair Trials).** Washington was charged with a crime in a Texas court. He demanded that the prosecutors obtain witnesses in his favor who were available to testify. The prosecution refused to serve these witnesses with subpoenas because defendants had a right to such witnesses only in federal proceedings, not in state proceedings. Washington was convicted. He appealed, arguing that he had not received a fair trial, since exculpatory witnesses had not been called by the prosecution at the defendant's request. The SC overturned Washington's conviction, saying that under the Sixth Amendment, compulsory process for obtaining witnesses in one's favor is so fundamental and essential to a fair trial that it should be incorporated into the due-process clause of the Fourteenth Amendment and thus would be applicable to both federal and state courts. The significance of this case is that compulsory process is guaranteed in state as well as federal trials, so that witnesses favorable to the defense must be called by the prosecution.

Watts v. Indiana, 338 U.S. 49, 69 S.Ct. 1347 (1949) **(Confessions; Exceptions).** Watts was suspected of murder while attempting to commit rape. He was arrested and subjected to lengthy and grueling interrogation, which several witnesses characterized as inquisitional. Subsequently he confessed, but he recanted the confession in court later. He was convicted. He appealed, alleging that his confession had been coerced. Rejecting his confession, the SC scolded the trial court by saying that it was naive to think that this protective custody had been less than an inquisition. Coerced confessions are inadmissible in court; therefore, the SC overturned his conviction.

Wayte v. United States, 470 U.S. 598, 105 S.Ct. 1524 (1985) **(Corrections; Death Penalty).** Wayte was charged with willfully failing to register for the Selective Service System ("draft"). The government subsequently invoked a passive enforcement policy, where the rules governing such prosecutions of draftdodgers were relaxed. However, Wayte sent letters and other forms of communication to the government, declaring that he never intended to register for the draft. Wayte was prosecuted. He appealed, arguing that the government was discriminating against him by such a prosecution. The SC rejected Wayte's arguments, saying that the government regulation was within its constitutional power, that such regulation furthered an important or substantial government interest, that the government interest was unrelated to the suppression of free speech, and that the incidental restriction on alleged First Amendment freedoms was no greater than was essential to the furtherance of that interest.

Weatherford v. Bursey, 429 U.S. 545, 97 S.Ct. 837 (1977) **(Law Enforcement Officers or Agencies; Sixth Amendment; Right to Effective Assistance of Counsel).** Weatherford was an undercover officer in Columbia, South Carolina, "playing along" with Brett Bursey and other associates to learn what they intended to do in connection with vandalizing Selective Services offices. When all were arrested for vandalism of Selective Service offices, Weatherford was taken into custody with the others. Bursey retained counsel. Weatherford did so as well, to maintain the pretense of conspiring with Bursey. Before the trial was held, Weatherford, continuing his undercover role, met frequently with Bursey and his counsel and discussed with them Bursey's plans for defense. At no time did Weatherford ask Bursey for information; rather, Bursey volunteered information about his defense plans. Weatherford also advised Bursey and his attorney that Weatherford planned to sever his case from Bursey's. Even under these changed circumstances and anticipated severance, however, Bursey continued to disclose details of his defense to Weatherford. Later at Bursey's trial, Weatherford gave incriminating testimony, which led to Bursey's conviction. Bursey filed a Title 42, U.S.C. Section 1983 civil-rights suit against Weatherford. Bursey alleged that his Sixth Amendment rights had been violated when he was deprived of effective assistance of counsel in his meetings with undercover agent Weatherford. Thus Bursey claimed that he had had a fundamentally unfair trial although Weatherford denied that he had given any of Bursey's plans or defense strategy to the prosecution. The SC upheld Bursey's conviction and rejected his civil-rights claim against Weatherford, holding that Bursey had not been deprived of his right to effective assistance of counsel or been denied a fair trial, and that the Sixth Amendment does not establish a rule per se forbidding an undercover agent from meeting with a defendant's counsel. In short, incriminating statements given voluntarily to an undercover officer who does nothing to elicit such statements are admissible against criminal defendants, despite the fact that these defendants are represented by counsel at the time.

Weeks v. United States, 232 U.S. 383, 34 S.Ct. 351 (1914) **(Law Enforcement Officers or Agencies; Searches and Seizures; Exclusionary Rule).** Weeks was suspected of using the mails to send lottery tickets, a form of prohibited gambling. United States marshals entered Weeks' home without a warrant, conducted a search, and discovered lottery tickets, which were used as evidence against Weeks in his later trial. Weeks was convicted of unlawful use of the mail. He appealed, arguing that law-enforcement officers should have obtained a search warrant before entering his home and seizing materials later used in his conviction. The SC agreed with Weeks and overturned his conviction. Weeks had been gainfully employed at the time and was an unlikely flight risk, and the United States marshals had had plenty of time to obtain a valid search warrant. They simply failed to do so. This case set a precedent, at least for *federal* law-enforcement officers. It established the *exclusionary rule*, which says that evidence seized illegally is inadmissible in court. Subsequently, some states chose to abide by the exclusionary rule, while other states chose not to abide by it, citing various exceptions or special circumstances. These became known as *exclusionary* and *nonexclusionary* states. An unusual situation developed following *Weeks,* whereby states would obtain evidence against criminal suspects illegally and turn over this information to federal authorities for their own prosecutions of these same suspects. The reasoning behind the practice became known as the *silver-platter doctrine*, since state officers were delivering illegally obtained evidence to federal prosecutors on a "silver platter," so to say. Ultimately, in *Elkins v. United States* (1960) and *Mapp v. Ohio* (1961), the silver-platter doctrine was eliminated, and both state and federal laws were harmonized relative to protocol to be followed in searches and seizures conducted against criminal suspects.

Weems v. United States, 217 U.S. 349, 30 S.Ct. 544 (1910) **(Corrections; Probation and Parole).** Weems was a government officer stationed in the Philippine Islands convicted of falsifying a public and official document. He was sentenced to fifteen years hard labor. Weems appealed, contending that his sentence was excessive and disproportionate to the offense committed. Thus, he argued, the sentence violated his Eighth Amendment right against cruel and unusual punishment. The SC agreed with Weems and said that any sentence that is disproportionate to the offense committed violates the Eighth Amendment prohibition against cruel and unusual punishment.

Welsh v. Wisconsin, 466 U.S. 740, 104 S.Ct. 2091 (1984) **(Seizures).** Welsh was a motorist whom a witness observed driving erratically. He swerved off a road and stopped in a field, later abandoning his vehicle and going into his home nearby. Welsh had damaged no property, and thus, from all outward appearances, he had not committed a jailable offense. The witness advised police that Welsh appeared to be either "drunk" or "very sick." Police discovered Welsh's address from the automobile registration, went to his home, and arrested him for driving while intoxicated. He was convicted. Welsh appealed and the SC heard his case. The SC reversed Welsh's DWI conviction, noting that police were in violation of Welsh's Fourth Amendment rights by intruding into his home at night to arrest him for a nonjailable offense. The SC stressed the minor nature of the infraction leading to Welsh's arrest and said that this minor event was insufficient to establish probable cause to justify such an intrusion into his home.

West v. Atkins, 487 U.S. 42, 108 S.Ct. 2250 (1988) **(Corrections; Inmate Rights).** West was an inmate in a North Carolina prison. He injured his leg and was transported outside the prison to a hospital in Raleigh, where he could be treated by a private physician under contract with the prison system. The doctor placed West's leg in a cast and repeated this procedure over several months. Eventually West was released but still evidenced some leg swelling. He filed suit against the doctor and others, under a Title 42, U.S.C. Section 1983 civil rights action, alleging that he was subject to cruel and unusual punishment because of continuing leg pain. The doctor claimed that he was not a state employee and thus could not be sued under a Section 1983 action. The SC disagreed, saying that when doctors are treating prison inmates, even though they are not actually corrections employees, they are acting on behalf of the system under the authority of state law. Thus they are conceivably liable for their actions when sued by prisoners.

Wheat v. United States, 486 U.S. 153, 108 S.Ct. 1692 (1988) **(Sixth Amendment; Right to Counsel).** Wheat was suspected of conspiracy to possess and distribute 1,000 pounds of marijuana. In a United States District Court in California, he

and several other persons were indicted in a far-flung interstate conspiracy. Several defendants wished to enter guilty pleas, others wished to go to trial. Wheat was represented by counsel, but he wished to change his counsel to another lawyer who was also representing one of the co-conspirators. The judge denied his request to change counsel, holding that the proposed substitution would create conflict-of-interest problems, since the co-defendants may have to give adverse testimony against other co-defendants. Wheat was convicted. He appealed, alleging that the federal trial judge's refusal to allow him to change attorneys had violated his Sixth Amendment right to counsel of his choice. The SC rejected Wheat's argument, saying that it was not a violation of Wheat's Sixth Amendment rights to refuse the counsel substitution, in view of the irreconcilable and unwaivable conflicts that would have arisen had counsel been switched. In multiple-defendant actions, judges must take appropriate actions and measures, including the issuance of separate representation orders, that protect criminal defendants against counsel's conflicts of interest.

White v. Illinois, 502 U.S. 346, 112 S.Ct. 736 (1992) **(Confrontation Clause; Trials).** White was charged with molesting a four-year-old girl, S.G. S.G. gave statements incriminating White to the police and to her mother and babysitter. S.G. was not required to testify against White, but her statements to the others were permitted under an exception to a hearsay rule. White was convicted. He appealed, contending that because he had been unable to confront his accuser, his due-process rights to a fair trial had been violated. The SC upheld White's conviction, holding that spontaneous statements made under medical circumstances at hospitals are exceptions to the hearsay rule and may be used against White in the absence of any testimony from a four-year-old witness-accuser.

White v. Maryland, 373 U.S. 59, 83 S.Ct. 1050 (1963) **(Corrections, Probation and Parole; Appointment of Counsel).** White, an indigent, was suspected of murder. At his arraignment, he entered a not guilty plea, but later at a preliminary hearing, he pleaded guilty. He was not represented by counsel at the preliminary hearing, and his guilty plea was introduced later in the trial as evidence against him. He was convicted. White appealed, contending that the preliminary hearing was a critical stage requiring appointment of counsel to represent him. Thus the guilty plea he entered should have been inadmissible in court later. The SC agreed with White and overturned his conviction, saying that preliminary hearings are critical stages in which indigent defendants must be represented by counsel.

White v. Texas, 310 U.S. 530, 60 S.Ct. 1032 (1939) **(Confessions).** White was accused of rape in Texas. Prior to his trial, Texas Rangers allegedly took White from the county jail into the nearby woods and beat him, attempting to get a confession from him. Subsequently, he signed a confession but recanted it during his trial. He was convicted and sentenced to death. He appealed. The SC overturned his conviction, holding that the confession had indeed been coerced by the Texas Rangers. Coerced confessions are inadmissible in court.

Whitley v. Albers, 475 U.S. 312, 106 S.Ct. 1078 (1986) **(Corrections; Inmate Rights).** During a riot in the Oregon penitentiary, a corrections officer was taken hostage. After officials conferred about what to do in the situation, it was agreed that force should be used to effect the rescue of the officer; therefore, other correctional officers were armed and entered the riot area. They were instructed to "shoot low" in the event that they saw any prisoner who might pose a risk to them. As they entered the riot area, they saw a prisoner on a stairwell, and they fired, wounding the prisoner in the knee. The correctional officer was rescued and the riot was quelled. Afterwards, the wounded prisoner filed a Title 42, U.S.C. Section 1983 civil-rights action against the prison staff participating in the shooting. The SC decided in favor of the prison staff and their forceful methods, indicating that the infliction of pain in the course of prison security measures does not violate the Eighth Amendment protecting persons from cruel and unusual punishment. Thus prison officials may use forceful means to quell prison riots, and any resultant injuries to prisoners are neither "cruel and unusual" nor unconstitutional.

Whiteley v. Warden, Wyoming State Penitentiary, 401 U.S. 560, 91 S.Ct. 1031 (1971) **(Law Enforcement Officers or Agencies; Warrantless Searches Incident to an Arrest).** In November 1964, various business establishments in Saratoga, Wyoming, were burglarized, and two suspects were identified. Information was transmitted to law-enforcement agencies around the state to be on the lookout for persons of a particular de-

scription driving a particular type of car. Officers in Casper, Wyoming, spotted a car one evening that seemed like the one described in the radio bulletin and stopped it. They immediately arrested the suspects without a warrant and proceeded to search the vehicle without a warrant, not knowing whether the persons in the vehicle were the actual perpetrators of the burglary. They discovered some stolen rare coins, and an arrest warrant was issued after the fact of the arrest. It eventually was revealed that the basis for the complaint leading to the radio announcement was a tip by an unknown informant to a sheriff, and that that fact and other supporting factual evidence were omitted from the original complaint. Thus the justice of the peace issuing the original complaint had no basis for properly doing so. Whitely, the suspect, moved to have such evidence removed from the record but was denied. He was convicted of breaking and entering and of being a habitual criminal. He appealed to the SC through a habeas corpus petition, claiming that his right agains unreasonable searches and seizures had been violated and thus, his conviction should be vacated. The SC heard Whiteley's appeal and reversed his conviction, holding that the complaint upon which the arrest warrant was issued could not be supported by a finding of probable cause or of any factual data tending to corroborate an informant's tip about Whiteley. Thus Whiteley's arrest had violated his constitutional rights under the Fourth and Fourteenth Amendments, and the evidence obtained as the result of the illegal arrest had to be excluded as incriminating evidence against Whiteley. (See good-faith exception for a comparison of subsequent SC policy in this regard.)

Whitmore v. Arkansas, 495 U.S. 149, 110 S.Ct. 1717 (1990) **(Corrections; Death Penalty).** Simmons was convicted of capital murder and sentenced to death. He made statements under oath that he wanted no action taken on his behalf and no appeals of the death sentence. Nevertheless, another death-row inmate, Whitmore, interceded and appealed Simmons' death sentence. The SC rejected this appeal, since the person bringing the appeal lacked standing. This decision makes it extremely difficult for those organizations that oppose the death penalty to file appeals for prisoners sentenced to death.

Whitus v. Georgia, 385 U.S. 598, 87 S.Ct. 643 (1967) **(Corrections; Death Penalty).** Whitus and another person were convicted of murder in 1960. Several appeals later, Whitus alleged that the jury composition was unconstitutionally discriminatory because a disproportionately lower number of blacks were on the jury compared with the list of candidates. The SC overturned Whitus' conviction, holding that sufficient evidence existed to show that Georgia had indeed engaged in questionable jury-selection practices. Nevertheless, the SC held that a prisoner whose conviction is reversed by the SC need not go free if he is in fact guilty, for Georgia may indict and try him again by a procedure that conforms to constitutional requirements.

Wilkerson v. Utah, 99 U.S. 130 (1878) **(Death Penalty; Firing Squads).** The SC decided that public execution by firing squads is not cruel and unusual punishment under the Eighth Amendment.

Wilkins v. Missouri, 492 U.S. 361, 109 S.Ct. 2969 (1989) **(Juvenile Law; Death Penalty).** Wilkins was 16 when he stabbed to death a woman who was managing a convenience store. There was evidence of aggravating circumstances and torture of the woman. Wilkins was transferred to criminal court and prosecuted as an adult. He was convicted of the murder. He was sentenced to death. He appealed, arguing that 16 is too young an age for execution, which is therefore cruel and unusual punishment. This landmark case set a minimum age at which juveniles can be executed. The SC ruled that if juveniles are 16 or older at the time they commit a capital crime, they can suffer execution in those jurisdictions with death penalties. The year before, in *Thompson v. Oklahoma*, the SC had said that persons who were 15 at the time they committed murder could not be executed. The *Wilkins* case effectively drew this line at age 16 (*see Stanford v. Kentucky* [1989] for a similar ruling).

Will v. Michigan Department of State Police, 491 U.S. 58, 109 S.Ct. 2304 (1989) **(Legal Liabilities of Public Officials).** Wills, a Michigan police officer, was denied a promotion. He sued the State of Michigan under Title 42, U.S.C., Section 1983, alleging that authorities were holding against him a record of his brother who had a prior history as a student activist. The SC declared that state law-enforcement officials, acting in their official capacity, have absolute immunity. However, they may be sued in their personal capacity. The SC also distinguished between state officials and municipal officials, such as local police, who do not enjoy the same type and degree of immunity enjoyed by state officials.

Williams v. Florida, 399 U.S. 78, 90 S.Ct. 1893 (1970) **(Juries; Jury Sizes).** Williams was arrested and charged with robbery. At his subsequent trial, a 6-member jury found him guilty. Williams appealed, alleging among other things that he should have had a jury of 12 members, rather than 6 members. Florida law proclaimed that 12-member juries would be convened in capital cases, but only 6-member juries would hear all other types of cases. The SC heard Williams' appeal and affirmed the Florida provision, saying that the "jury . . . composed of 12 is a historical accident, unnecessary to effect the purposes of the jury system and wholly without significance except to mystics."

Williams v. Illinois, 399 U.S. 235, 90 S.Ct. 2018 (1970) **(Corrections; Inmate Rights; Probation and Parole).** Williams was convicted of petty theft and sentenced to one year in jail, a $500 fine, and $5 court costs. State law provided that at the end of one year of imprisonment, if offenders could not pay their fines and court costs, they must "work off" these payments at the rate of $5 per day. Thus Williams would be required to be incarcerated an additional 101 days before he could pay the fine and court costs. He appealed. The SC ruled that this additional time served behind bars to "work off" such fines is unconstitutional, because it violates the equal-protection clause of the Fourteenth Amendment.

Williams v. Oklahoma, 358 U.S. 576, 79 S.Ct. 521 (1958) **(Presentence Procedures).** Williams was accused of robbing a gas station and kidnapping and murdering a motorist. He was convicted of the murder and sentenced to life imprisonment. He was also tried on the kidnapping charge, as these were separate and distinct crimes in Oklahoma. At the time, the prosecutor read into the record aggravating factual information about Williams and his crime spree involving the murdered motorist. A second conviction resulted, and Williams appealed, seeking to suppress the additional evidence admitted at his second trial. The SC said that the consideration of one crime in the sentencing of another crime does not constitute double jeopardy for the same offense. The convictions were upheld, with the SC declaring that Williams had raised no objections at either trial concerning the admissibility of the negative factual information.

Williams v. Puckett, 624 So.2d 496 (1993) **(Corrections; Parole Eligibility; Mandatory Sentences).** A Mississippi man convicted of armed robbery and forgery was given a mandatory sentence of 10 years for robbery plus a 5-year term for forgery. In Mississippi, inmates become eligible for parole by statute after serving 10 years of longer terms imposed. However, since the armed-robbery conviction involved a mandatory prison term of 10 years, this meant that the entire 10-year sentence had to be served. Then, according to Mississippi law, the inmate had to serve at least one-fourth of the 5-year term for the forgery conviction before he would actually be eligible for parole. Even then, the Mississippi Parole Board would not be obligated automatically to grant his early release.

Wilson v. Ellis, 859 P.2d 744 (1993) **(Corrections; Indigent Probationers and Probation Revocation).** An indigent defendant had his probation revoked after admitting to a probation violation. When he asked for a transcript of his revocation proceedings, he was refused. The Arizona Court of Appeals rejected this lower-court denial and declared that the offender *did* have a right to pursue a challenge of the revocation proceeding itself, despite his waiver of appeal rights, in the context of a post-conviction remedy.

Wilson v. Seiter, 501 U.S. 294, 111 S.Ct. 2321 (1991) **(Corrections; Official Conduct; Inmate Rights).** Wilson was a felon incarcerated in the Hocking, Ohio, Correctional Facility. Filing a Title 42, U.S.C. Section 1983 civil-rights claim against prison officials, he alleged that the conditions of his confinement violated his constitutional rights under the Eighth and Fourteenth Amendments. These conditions were improper ventilation, inadequate heating and cooling, excessive noise, unclean and inadequate restrooms, unsanitary dining facilities and food preparation, and housing with mentally and physically abusive inmates. The suit was rejected by the SC, which declared that prison officials must exhibit deliberate indifference to prisoner needs and living conditions before inmates will successfully prevail in their suits. Further, a culpable state of mind must be demonstrated on the part of prison officials. These difficult criteria mean that suits by prisoners alleging poor prison conditions will be difficult to sustain.

Winston v. Lee, 470 U.S. 753, 105 S.Ct. 1611 (1985) **(Seizures).** Lee claimed to have been shot in the left side of his chest and robbed by someone fleeing down the street. Police officers were simultaneously investigating a robbery and shooting where a store owner had been shot but had wounded the assailant in return. The store owner advised police that he thought that he had shot his assailant in the chest. While both men were being treated at the same hospital in town, the store owner recognized Lee as the robber. The officers obtained a court order for doctors to remove a bullet from Lee's chest, but the doctors advised police that the surgery might be dangerous. Lee sought to bar doctors from removing the bullet because the act would be an unwarranted bodily intrusion. The SC agreed with Lee, saying that such surgery was unwarranted, as it would violate his Fourth Amendment right. The SC said that states cannot compel surgical intrusions into one's body, even if that intrusion would produce evidence of a crime.

Wisconsin v. Mitchell, 507 U.S.___, 113 S.Ct. 2194 (1993) **(Sentence Enhancements; First Amendment Rights).** Mitchell was convicted of aggravated battery and theft, and his sentence was enhanced under a Wisconsin statute because he targeted his victim by reason of the victim's race. Mitchell appealed, arguing that he should not be punished more because he had selected a person of a particular race to attack. Thus, Mitchell declared, the Wisconsin statute was unconstitutional because it violated his free-speech rights. The SC heard Mitchell's case and upheld the constitutionality of the Wisconsin statute, whereby offenders may have their sentences enhanced if it is proved that they attacked their victim because of the victim's race.

Witherspoon v. Illinois, 391 U.S. 510, 88 S.Ct. 1770 (1968) **(Corrections; Death Penalty).** Witherspoon was charged and convicted of capital murder in Arkansas. During the voir dire, the judge asked prospective jurors their views on the death penalty and whether they could vote for it if it were the prescribed punishment. Witherspoon appealed, saying that persons who said that they could not vote for the death penalty had been excluded as jurors and thus prosecutors had deprived Witherspoon of a fair trial by generating a death-qualified jury. The SC upheld Witherspoon's conviction, saying that the Constitution does not prevent the exclusion for cause of prospective jurors whose opposition to the death penalty is so strong as to prevent or substantially impair their performance of duties relative to delivering a death penalty sentence. These types of jurors became known as Witherspoon-excludables.

Withrow v. Williams, 507 U.S. 680, 113 S.Ct. 1745 (1993) **(Corrections; Self-Incrimination).** Williams, an inmate in a Michigan prison, was suspected of a double murder. During the investigation, he was interrogated by police, who did not immediately tell him his Miranda rights. He made several pre-Miranda warning statements that were inculpatory and several more after the warning by police. Williams admitted to providing a weapon to the man who actually did the killing. A bench trial resulted in Williams' conviction and he was given two concurrent life sentences for the two felony-murder convictions. Williams appealed, alleging that his Miranda rights had been violated by police. Williams alleged that police had told him throughout all pre- and post-Miranda questioning that if he confessed, he would be given lenient treatment, and that that inducement was sufficient to overcome his will against giving incriminating information to them. Williams claimed that his admissions had been involuntarily made throughout the entire interrogation, and thus, the admissions should have been suppressed. The SC heard his case and ruled that Williams' statements to police were involuntary and thus excludable as evidence against him, in view of the violation of the Miranda warning.

Witte v. United States, ___U.S.___, 115 S.Ct. 2199 (1995) **(Double Jeopardy).** Witte was a drug trafficker who was charged with and convicted of marijuana in a federal district court. Simultaneously, Witte, together with several other co-conspirators, was also named as trafficking in cocaine, although no charges had been brought against him before his conviction for the marijuana offense. When the presentence investigation report of Witte had been completed by the federal probation officer, the uncharged criminal conduct of cocaine distribution was added to Witte's base offense to yield a score higher than that yielded by using only the marijuana charge. Consequently, Witte was sentenced to a longer term. Subsequently, he was indicted for conspiring to distribute cocaine, and he moved to quash this indictment on the grounds of double jeopardy. The federal district court dismissed the indictment following a motion by Witte's attorney. The government appealed and the circuit court of appeals reinstated the indictment. Witte appealed. The SC

heard Witte's case and upheld the circuit court of appeals decision to reinstate the indictment. The SC argued that because consideration of relevant conduct in determining a defendant's sentence within the legislatively authorized punishment range does not constitute punishment for that conduct within the meaning of double-jeopardy clause, Witte's prosecution on cocaine charges did not violate the prohibition against multiple punishments. In other words, current indictable conduct (conspiracy to distribute cocaine) may serve to enhance present sentences in federal criminal convictions, and subsequent charges may be brought against these same persons citing the same indictable conduct.

Wolf v. Colorado, 338 U.S. 25, 69 S.Ct. 1359 (1949) **(Law Enforcement Officers or Agencies; Searches and Seizures; Exclusionary Rule).** Wolf was a physician in Colorado, a non-exclusionary state (*see Weeks v. United States*, 1914). He was suspected of performing illegal abortions. State officers entered his office illegally and seized numerous papers and documents implicating him in such activity. Despite the fact that this evidence was obtained in an unreasonable manner, with several procedural errors and warrant defects, he was convicted. Because the governing case at the time was *Weeks*, forbidding the admissibility of evidence seized by federal law-enforcement officers without a valid search warrant, Wolf sought to apply the same standard to the officers who seized his property and papers from his Colorado office. He sought to declare the evidence inadmissible by citing the Fourteenth Amendment equal-protection clause, suggesting that the states should follow the federal precedent set in *Weeks*. The SC decided to uphold Wolf's conviction and avoid obligating states to adhere to an exclusionary rule applicable only to federal officers and those states that chose to adopt it.

Wolff v. McDonnell, 418 U.S. 539, 94 S.Ct. 2963 (1974) **(Corrections; Inmate Rights).** Basic elements of a procedural due process must be present when decisions are made concerning the discipline of a prison inmate. In this Nebraska case, the SC ruled that in procedures resulting in loss of good-time or in solitary confinement, due process requires the following: advance written notice of the violation, written statement of fact findings, the prisoner's right to call witnesses and present evidence where it will not be hazardous to the operation of the institution, mail from attorneys to be opened and inspected in the presence of inmates, and prison records to be expunged if not in accord with required procedures. This case also dealt with the question of whether letters determined to be from attorneys may be opened by prison authorities in the presence of the inmate or whether such mail must be delivered unopened if normal detection techniques fail to indicate contraband. The SC did not add a great deal of clarity to this issue in their decision. It indicated that attorneys must clearly identify themselves by placing their names and addresses in plain view on envelopes and that the letters should show that they came from lawyers. In any event, prison authorities may inspect and read any document leaving and entering the institution in an effort to determine whether inmates are abusing their rights by communicating about "restricted matters."

Wong Sun v. United States, 371 U.S. 471, 83 S.Ct. 407 (1961) **(Law Enforcement Officers or Agencies; Exclusionary Rule).** Wong Sun was a suspected drug dealer. Federal narcotics agents learned from various informants the identity of a drug dealer named Sea Dog, who was Wong Sun. The agents went to where Wong Sun lived, arrested him, and searched his premises, discovering no narcotics. He was released. Several days later Wong Sun and another suspect, an associate, gave statements to federal officers but did not sign these statements. Subsequently, Wong Sun returned to the federal offices and admitted to the accuracy of his statement given a few days earlier. He and the associate were subsequently convicted of transportation and concealment of heroin. Wong Sun appealed, alleging that his statements were inadmissible as evidence against him, because several illegal acts had been perpetrated by federal officers earlier against him and his associate. The SC agreed to the extent that, indeed, illegal acts by federal officers had nullified certain evidence against Wong Sun and his associate. However, when Wong Sun revisited the federal offices and admitted to the accuracy of his previous statements, this admission removed the taint overshadowing the illegally obtained evidence. The significance of this complex case is that it articulated the fruits-of-the-poisonous-tree doctrine, which says that if the tree (a police search, for instance) is poisoned (an illegal search), the fruit from the tree (the evidence obtained from the illegal search) is poisoned also (made inadmissible). Thus Wong Sun's original statements were

inadmissible because they were fruits of the poisonous tree; however, his later admission about the accuracy of his previous statements had removed the "taint" from the poisonous tree and rendered his statements admissible against him.

Wood v. Bartholomew, ___U.S.___, 116 S.Ct. 7 (1995) **(Death Penalty; Fair Trial Test; Admissibility of Material Evidence).** Bartholomew was charged with murdering a laundromat attendant during a robbery in August 1981. Bartholomew's brother, Randy, and his girlfriend, Dormady, testified against him during his trial. Randy testified that while sitting with Dwayne in a car outside the laundromat, Dwayne told him that he intended to rob it and "leave no witnesses." Subsequently, Bartholomew perpetrated the robbery, firing two shots into the head of the laundromat operator. Dormady testified that Bartholomew told her that he had "put two bullets in the kid's head." Bartholomew testified in his own behalf; he declared that the murder was *not* premeditated, since his pistol accidentally discharged twice (the pistol was a single-action revolver and could only be fired by pulling back the hammer for each shot). Dormady and Randy Bartholomew both took lie detector tests, with Dormady's having questionable results. Although her testimony in court was incriminating against Bartholomew, her lie detector results were not admitted into evidence. Bartholomew was convicted. He appealed because the prosecutor had failed to produce these polygraph results. The SC rejected Bartholomew's appeal, holding that evidence is "material" to the extent that its admission at trial would have a reasonable probability of affecting the trial outcome. In this case, the SC said it would not have affected the outcome because of other evidence. To acquit Bartholomew of aggravated murder, the jury would have had to believe that Bartholomew's single-action revolver discharged accidentally, not once but twice, by tragic coincidence depositing a bullet to the back of the victim's head, execution-style, as the victim lay face down on the floor.

Woodson v. North Carolina, 428 U.S. 280, 96 S.Ct. 2978 (1980) **(Corrections; Death Penalty).** Woodson and others were convicted of first-degree murder. Woodson was a lookout and did not participate in the actual murder. However, the death penalty for such an offense was mandatory in North Carolina. He appealed to the SC, which overturned his death penalty sentence, declaring that mandatory death-penalty statutes are unconstitutional. The major reason they are unconstitutional is that aggravating and mitigating circumstances cannot be considered.

Wyrick v. Fields, 459 U.S. 42, 103 S.Ct. 394 (1982) **(Law Enforcement Officers or Agencies; Waiver of Right to Counsel; Miranda Warnings).** Fields was a soldier stationed at Fort Leonard Wood, Missouri. He was charged with raping an 81-year-old woman. Following his arrest in September 1974, Fields requested a polygraph examination. This request was granted and Fields signed a written consent document containing his Miranda rights. Further, an officer read those rights aloud to Fields and asked him if he wished to have his attorney present. Fields said no. Following the polygraph test, the examiner indicated to Fields that there had been some deceit. At that time, Fields admitted to having intercourse with the woman but claimed it was consensual. He also made similar admissions to Missouri police, who also had told him his Miranda rights before questioning. Fields was convicted. He filed a habeas corpus petition, alleging that his confessions had been "coerced." The SC rejected Fields' claim and upheld his conviction, noting that Fields had been repeatedly and amply advised of his rights and had voluntarily, knowingly, and intelligently had those rights. Thus there was no rights violation as a reason for overturning his conviction.

— Y —

Ybarra v. Illinois, 444 U.S. 85, 100 S.Ct. 338 (1979) **(Law Enforcement Officers or Agencies; Searches Incident to Arrest).** A reliable informant advised police officers that a bartender in a certain bar was selling heroin in small tinfoil packets to customers. Further, the informant said that the bartender had told him that heroin would be available for purchase on a given date. With this information, police obtained a search warrant authorizing a "search of the tavern for evidence of the offense of possession of a controlled substance." They entered the bar and advised all present, including customers, that they would be searched. A pat-down of Ybarra, a customer, disclosed a cigarette package, which the searching officer said contained "objects." He retrieved the cigarette package and found heroin in six tinfoil

packets. Ybarra was convicted. He appealed, contending that the search had been unreasonable and violative of the Fourth Amendment and the equal-protection clause of the Fourteenth Amendment. The SC agreed with Ybarra and overturned his conviction, noting that police officers had had no reason to suspect him individually as a person in possession of controlled substances. Their warrant was confined to a tavern search, not specific persons in the tavern who were unknown to the police and their informant.

Youngberg v. Romeo, 457 U.S. 307, 102 S.Ct. 2452 (1982) **(Corrections; Inmate Rights).** Romeo was a mentally retarded man with a history of violence. He was involuntarily committed to a state mental hospital, where he sustained numerous physical injuries at the hands of others. His mother filed a suit on his behalf, alleging that her son was entitled to safe conditions of confinement, freedom from bodily restraints, and training or rehabilitation. The SC heard the case and declared that Romeo was entitled to conditions of reasonable care and safety, reasonably nonrestrictive confinement conditions, and such training as might be required by these interests. The judge had given an improper jury instruction in Romeo's commitment proceeding when he advised the jury to consider the standard of cruel and unusual punishment as set forth in the Eighth Amendment.

Younger v. Gilmore, 404 U.S. 15, 92 S.Ct. 250 (1971) **(Corrections; Inmate Rights; Court Access).** Gilmore and other inmates filed suit against the California Department of Corrections, alleging that the law library in the prison contained rules that were unconstitutionally restrictive and limited Gilmore's access to the courts. Almost every book was a single issue and many pages were either lost or stolen. The rules governing inmate access to books were also greatly restrictive. The SC declared that in this particular case, California had indeed violated prisoner rights of access to the courts by the greatly restrictive library rules and also their right to equal protection under the Fourteenth Amendment. The SC required the California system (and any other similar system through the United States) to beef up the law library selections and develop law library guidelines that would not violate prisoner rights and deny them access to courts or effective legal assistance (*see Bounds v. Smith* [1977] and *Lynch v. Gilmore* [1969] for a comparative case).

Z

Zafiro v. United States, 506 U.S. 534, 113 S.Ct. 933 (1993) **(Joint Trials for Defendants).** Various defendants, including Zafiro, opposed being tried together in federal court on various drug charges, alleging that such a joinder would violate Rule 14 of the Federal Rules of Criminal Procedure, and that the defenses to be offered by these defendants would be mutually antagonistic. The SC rejected their appeal, saying that joinders do not make mutually exclusive defenses unconstitutional per se, and that defendants are required to show where prejudice might occur. There was no prejudice in this particular case.

Zant v. Stephens, 462 U.S. 862, 103 S.Ct. 2733 (1983) **(Corrections; Death Penalty; Cruel and Unusual Punishment; Eighth Amendment).** Stephens was convicted of murder. The jury considered three aggravating circumstances and sentenced him to death. Stephens appealed, arguing that the third aggravating circumstance was so vague that it should have nullified the imposition of the death penalty. The SC said that the third aggravating circumstance was immaterial and irrelevant, since there were two other clear aggravating circumstances that sufficed to warrant imposition of the death penalty.

Zap v. United States, 328 U.S. 624, 66 S.Ct. 1277 (1946) **(Law Enforcement Officers or Agencies; Consent Searches).** Zap was a government contractor who did experimental work on government airplane wings. He was convicted of making false claims against the United States on the basis of information obtained in a search of his offices by FBI agents. This inspection was done as a part of the Department of Navy agreement authorizing such records inspections. Zap appealed, alleging that the search of his offices had violated his Fourth Amendment rights, and that evidence obtained against him resulting from this search should have been suppressed. The SC upheld Zap's conviction, holding that inspections of one's offices pursuant to government contractual agreements do not violate the Fourth Amendment search-and-seizure provision.

Zicarelli v. New Jersey State Commission of Investigation, 406 U.S. 472, 92 S.Ct. 1670 (1972) **(Self-Incrimination).** Zicarelli was subpoenaed to testify in a case involving organized crime. New Jersey prosecutors extended to him immunity from prosecution in exchange for his testimony. Despite this immunity, Zicarelli refused to answer some of the questions. He was cited for contempt and jailed. He appealed. The SC heard his case and affirmed the contempt citation, concluding that there is no legal reason justifying nonresponse if immunity has been granted.

Zurcher v. Stanford Daily, 436 U.S. 547, 98 S.Ct. 1970 (1978) **(Law Enforcement Officers or Agencies; Searches).** In the aftermath of a college campus disturbance, police searched for those who were demonstrating and who had attacked and injured several police officers. Photographs of the incident had been taken by the student newspaper staff on the scene, and some of them were subsequently published in the *Stanford Daily*. The district attorney's office obtained a search warrant for the newspaper's premises to locate photos and other materials that might help to identify those who had injured the police officers. Over the objections of newspaper staffers, police searched the offices and seized various photographs of the incident. The student newspaper filed suit, alleging that the search warrant was unconstitutional and that their photographs had been unlawfully seized. The SC disagreed, concluding that it is constitutional under the Fourth Amendment to issue search warrants for premises of nonsuspects if it is believed on the basis of probable cause that fruits, instrumentalities, or evidence of a crime might be found there.

INDEX
of
UNITED STATES
SUPREME COURT
CASES

Index

Confessions

Confrontation Clause

Cruel and Unusual Punishment

Custodial Interrogations

Deadly Force

Death-Qualified Juries

Death Penalty

Discovery

Double Jeopardy

Eighth Amendment

Electric Chair

Electronic Surveillance, Wiretapping

Exclusionary Rule

Executions

Federal Tort Claims

Firing Squads

First Amendment

Fifth Amemendment

Fines

Fourteenth Amendment

Fourth Amendment

Gas Chamber

Good-Faith Exception

Grand Juries

Habeas Corpus Petitions

Hearsay

Immigration Checkpoints

Indictments

Indigent Clients

Informants

Inmate Rights

Insanity Pleas

Liabilities of Public Officials

Searches and Seizures

Searches Incident to an Arrest

Sobriety Checkpoints

Solitary Confinement

Speedy Trials

Stop and Frisk

Victim Impact Statements